GUIDE TO

THE HOUSE

OF

COMMONS

2017

THE TIMES

GUIDE TO

THE HOUSE

OF

COMMONS

2017

TIMES BOOKS
LONDON

First published in 2017 by Times Books

An imprint of HarperCollins Publishers
Westerhill Road
Bishopbriggs
Glasgow G64 2QT
www.harpercollins.co.uk

A catalogue record for this book is available from the
British Library

ISBN 978-0-00-826333-1

10 9 8 7 6 5 4 3 2 1

Printed and bound by CPI Group (UK) Ltd.,
Croydon, CR0 4YY

Editor: Ian Brunskill
Deputy Editor: Matthew Lyons
Assistant Editor: Max Young
Researchers: Nasim Asl, Jack Dyson, Anna Gross,
Liam Hill, Liam Kelly, Ailsa McNeil, Emily Riddell

Additional research: Christiana Bishop, Ellen Daniel,
Martha Elwell, Charlotte Irwin, Mimi Launder,
Harriet Pavey, Bridie Pearson-Jones, Susanna Smith
Design: Mark Grayson, Andrew Keys, Stephen Petch
Copy-editing: Sarah Willcox
Picture research: Olivia Harris, Laura Lean

Thanks to: Rachel Allegro, Ian Amis, Alan Ashton,
Gerry Breslin, George Brock, Rebecca Callanan,
Jessica Carsen, David Charter, Anthony Coates,
Sam Coates, Magnus Cohen, Michael Derringer,
Paul Dunn, Josie Eve, Hannah Fletcher, Helen Glancy,
Fiona Gorman, Rana Greig, Jeremy Griffin,
Tim Hames, Dylan Hamilton, Robert Hands,
Jonathan Hewett, Raphael Hogarth, Jennifer Hudson,
Cerys Hughes, Jack Kingham, Jethro Lennox,
Robbie Millen, Claire Overman, Pia Sarma,
Fay Schlesinger, Tim Shearring, Mike Smith,
Sam Stewart, Matthew Swift and the *Times* graphics
team, Craig Tregurtha, Emma Tucker, Pauline Watson,
Liesl Wickins, Danny Wilkins, John Witherow,
Sarah Woods

Contents

General election 2017

POLL TO CLEAR THE AIR HAS ADDED TO THE FOG

by Francis Elliott

Few begrudged Theresa May a break. Since entering No 10 as the unopposed successor to David Cameron the previous July, Britain's new prime minister had steadied a nation shocked at its decision to leave the European Union. She had balanced cabinet and party promising to make a success of Brexit. Mrs May had sketched, in outline at least, a more interventionist domestic agenda, being prepared to put the state at the service of those "just about managing" to prove that she was not just a Brexit prime minister.

She had even negotiated Donald Trump's arrival in the White House without mishap and had won from him a promise of support as Britain left the EU. On March 29 she triggered the start of the formal exit by invoking Article 50 of the Lisbon treaty. There was no going back. But how was she going to go forward?

"Walking in Wales is an opportunity to get out and about and see scenery and clear your mind and your thinking," she said on April 10 at the start of a five-day holiday with her husband, Philip. It was a typically anodyne remark but one that concealed a startling truth. She needed to clear her mind and thinking because she was about to take the biggest, and perhaps worst, decision of her life.

Mrs May's official spokesman had squashed speculation the previous month of an early election. "There is no change in our position on an early general election: there isn't going to be one. It's not going to happen."

It was a denial to add to those from her own lips. "I think it's right that the next general election is in 2020," she had said in October. "This isn't about political games, it's about what is right for the country. I think an early general election would introduce a note of instability for people."

David Davis and Philip Hammond had wanted her to change her mind for months. The Brexit secretary argued that the electoral and negotiating timetables were misaligned. The chancellor agreed that since it was clear that a transitional period after formal exit in March 2019 was needed to avoid damaging disruption Britain would not have actually "taken back control" in 2020. Further, an economy that had confounded expectations of an immediate plunge after Brexit was starting to show signs of weakening as consumer and business confidence declined. No government ever wants to fight an election in a recession: better to fight an election under a cloud than in the midst of a downpour.

Not everyone was so sure that a snap election was a good idea. Sir Patrick McLoughlin, the party chairman, worried about whether there was sufficient time to prepare an effective election machine and about the poor historical record, which suggested that voters punished those who called them to the polls unexpectedly.

Under the cover of a "strategy session" she summoned Sir Lynton Crosby, the election consultant who oversaw Mr Cameron's 2015 triumph, to Chequers in February to discuss her options. Chris Wilkins, director of strategy at No 10, opened by sketching the sort of positive offer that Mrs May could make building on the speech she delivered on entering Downing Street in which she had promised to address the "burning injustices" like racism and classism that still bedevilled Britain. Sir Lynton was dismissive, according to one witness, insisting that voters did not want more change. She could win, he said, only on a campaign based on her reputation for sober stability. It was agreed that he would work up a fuller document, known as a "values study", using polling and focus group data to find her most effective messages. This became the basis of a confidential memo on the election given to Mrs May in late March.

The Australian consultant has denied that he warned her against the snap poll. He has said that Mrs May was "absolutely right in her judgment that she needed the strongest possible position in order that she could negotiate the democratic will of the British people."

Perhaps to cover tracks in case the Chequers summit was uncovered, a version of the Australian's advice found its way into the *New Statesman* on April 5 when it was reported that Sir Lynton had told Mrs May that the Tories would lose seats to the Lib Dems in the South West and London in an early election. This turned out to be a rare case in which the spin turned out to be closer to the substance.

On April 18, a Tuesday following a bank holiday Monday, lobby journalists arriving at Westminster were told to be in Downing Street at 11am. Shortly before then Mrs May strode out and dropped her bombshell. She said she had "recently and reluctantly come to this conclusion ... the only way to guarantee certainty and stability for the years ahead is to hold this election and seek your support for the decisions I must take.

"It will be a choice between strong and stable leadership in the national interest, with me as your prime minister, or weak and unstable coalition government, led by Jeremy Corbyn, propped up by the Liberal Democrats, who want to reopen the divisions of the referendum, and Nicola Sturgeon and the SNP. Every vote for the Conservatives will make it harder for opposition politicians who want to stop me from getting the job done. Every vote for the Conservatives will make me stronger when I negotiate for Britain with the prime ministers, presidents and chancellors of the European Union."

Mr Corbyn and his close team watched the announcement without surprise. Seumas Milne, the former *Guardian* journalist now the Labour leader's media chief, had told journalists before Christmas that the party was on a war footing. *Plus ça change*, most thought: Mr Corbyn had been in conflict for his entire leadership with the bulk of his own MPs. A vote of no confidence and a second leadership election a year after he won in September 2015 had failed to dislodge the man many thought was piloting the party to an electoral wipeout.

Mr Corbyn and his closest ally, John McDonnell, the shadow chancellor; his political secretary, Karie Murphy; Mr Milne and James Schneider, a young Momentum organiser — the core leadership team — had only an uncertain grip over the party machinery. Relations with Labour's HQ were mistrustful at best. For all the talk of readying for battle Labour's preparations for the election were said to be no more than rudimentary as Mr Corbyn's team moved into the headquarters building on Victoria Street after Mrs May's announcement.

More significantly Labour's electoral coalition, which had been unwinding for decades, appeared close to total collapse after the Brexit vote. Voters in former industrial heartlands had responded to the Leave campaign message, particularly on immigration. Its more prosperous, better-educated voters had, in the main, voted to Remain. Labour's position through the referendum campaign and its aftermath had been at best studied ambiguity, and at worst incoherent muddle. Mr Corbyn refused to say that he thought immigration was too high. It was wrong for workers to be undercut, he said, but always added that immigrants kept the health service working and that immigration had contributed to national life more than it had taken from it. Together with his opposition to the use of nuclear weapons, Mr Corbyn's stance on an issue that was consistently identified as among the most important to voters appeared to be at odds with most of those whose support Labour would need to form the next government, or indeed simply to avoid losing more ground to the Tories.

In the weeks leading up to April 18 Mrs May had been shown polling that indicated that a softening Labour vote made about 60 seats much more marginal than they appeared. Across the northeast of England, the Midlands and into Wales, constituencies where a majority had voted for Brexit were in play, she was told. Seats with an older-than-average demographic and with lower-than-average numbers of non-white voters were particularly attractive to Conservative strategists looking to exploit what they thought was Labour's inability to respond to the Brexit vote. To drive home the point that Mrs May was attacking Labour's supposedly soft underbelly she flew by helicopter to Bolton North East, a seat held by Labour with a majority of about 5,000 after her Downing Street statement.

In a visit lasting less than 15 minutes she said that the government had already achieved record levels of growth since the EU referendum, and provided a "clear vision" for the future: "That's what leadership looks like."

In his campaign launch, hurriedly arranged the next day in Westminster, Mr Corbyn insisted that despite the polls the result was not a foregone conclusion. He said that the election was a question of the establishment versus the people. He turned his fire on big business and the rich and pledged to break up the "cosy cartels" that ran Britain.

Coverage was dominated by the Labour leader's continuing difficulty to frame a position on Europe. Senior Labour figures had floated the prospect that the party could campaign on a call for a second referendum and Mr Corbyn was slow enough to close down the suggestion to allow hostile newspapers to lambast his "dithering" over the issue.

The mood in Tim Farron's office was upbeat. The Liberal Democrats' victory in a by-election in Richmond Park caused by Zac Goldsmith's resignation over Heathrow had swelled hopes of a renaissance following the loss of 49 seats in the 2015 election. As the only UK-wide party committed to remaining in the single market and to a second referendum on EU membership the Lib Dems believed they had a strong offer to put before an electorate 48 per cent of which had voted to Remain.

In Bute House the prospect of another general election was less appealing. Nicola Sturgeon, Scotland's first minister and SNP leader, had been forced to call for a second independence referendum despite clear evidence that most Scots opposed another vote. Enmeshed by her own rhetoric over Brexit, that a decision to take Scotland out of the EU despite its decision to Remain was sufficient cause for another independence referendum, Ms Sturgeon had been forced to follow through on her threat. After seven years in power the SNP administration was starting to suffer from incumbency dogged in particular by awkward questions over Scotland's relative failure to close an attainment gap between children from richer and poorer households. No one doubted that the 2015 triumph, in which it won all but three of the nation's 58 seats at Westminster, was a high-water mark but the only question was how low the tide would ebb.

Under the terms of the Fixed-term Parliaments Act a two-thirds majority is needed in the Commons for an election to be called at an earlier date than the statutory five years allows. Most Labour MPs and the Lib Dems voted for an early dissolution; the SNP abstained. Thirteen voted against, including ten Labour MPs.

The first test of whether Mrs May was on course for the landslide predicted by most opinion polls was a set of council and mayoral elections in England, Wales and Scotland on May 4. The results were encouraging for the Conservatives but not overwhelmingly so. Indeed the projected national vote share calculated by Professor John Curtice pointed to only a modest increase in the Tory majority if replicated at a general election.

Despite the polling industry's failure to accurately predict the outcome of the 2015 general election most of the media continued to put more trust in it than in the evidence of actual votes cast and Mrs May entered the first week of the general election's formal "short campaign" reportedly on course for a three-figure majority. Even on the polling figures this was overdone: Professor Curtice had been cautioning against a landslide from the moment the snap election was called.

The start of the ground campaign revealed the type of Labour seats she was targeting: Bolton, Bury, Halifax, Stoke, Newport. Campaign literature and branding accentuated the prime minister over her party, reflecting her advisers' belief that wavering Labour voters were attracted to her as a unifying national figure above politics.

An analysis of Mr Corbyn's first visits suggested that he was selecting constituencies to defend rather than attack. Commentators noted a preference for metropolitan seats in London, Manchester, Liverpool and Birmingham. The Labour leader was also more comfortable with a traditional campaign style, including walkabouts and rallies. The contrast can be overstated: neither campaign team allowed regular close access.

Mrs May took more questions from lobby journalists than Mr Corbyn (but arguably answered fewer). The Labour leader gave fewer interviews and only to a very select band of approved journalists.

At about 2pm on May 11 Mr Schneider took a call from Jack Blanchard, political editor at the *Daily Mirror*, who told him that an entire copy of the manifesto had been leaked. By 10pm at least two newspapers had put most of the document online. The main points picked up from the draft were commitments to take the railways back into public ownership, reverse the privatisation of Royal Mail and create at least one publicly owned energy company in each region. Other policies highlighted included a commitment to levy income tax at 45p on incomes over £80,000 and at 50p on earnings over £125,000. Tuition fees would be abolished.

Under the terms of Labour's constitution the manifesto had to be cleared by a so-called Clause V meeting that 80 Labour MPs, union officials and activists' representatives were entitled to attend. Most of the text was cleared without dispute. Tensions over the Labour leader's unilateralist stance were parked with a text that committed to the deterrent but also to efforts to disarm. Mr Corbyn's car ran over a BBC cameraman's foot on the way in to the meeting in Savoy Place. Len McCluskey, the Unite general secretary, fell down the stairs on the way out. The headline in the next day's *Sun* newspaper read: "Crash, Bang, Wallies".

The formal launch of the manifesto, entitled *For the Many, Not the Few*, took place in Barnsley. Its introduction framed the election as a choice between "more of the same" or action to correct a "rigged system". A spending package of about £48 billion to fund the abolition of tuition fees, extra cash for the NHS and schools and sundry other pledges would be met from the proceeds of income tax rises, the cancellation of planned cuts to corporation tax and more aggressive enforcement against evasion. The Institute for Fiscal Studies queried the amount Labour said it would raise, suggesting that it was underestimating the extent to which individuals and companies would act to avoid higher levies.

There was little reaction from the Conservatives. Mr Hammond had not been on the national stage since before the local elections. On May 12 *The Times* revealed that a serious rift had developed between Mr Hammond and Mrs May's aides. Some speculated that the chancellor would be sacked in a post-election reshuffle.

Tensions had come to a head over the preparation of the Conservative manifesto under the direction of Nick Timothy, one of Mrs May's two chiefs of staff. (The other, Fiona Hill, had become the campaign's communications director). Mr Hammond had clashed with Mr Timothy in the fallout over the March budget. Now the pair were at odds over policies including a cap on energy bills.

The real surprise was saved for the day itself. To its architects the social care floor, which exposed all but the last £100,000 of an individual's wealth to the full costs of their residential or domiciliary care, addressed a shortfall in funding while correcting some of the unfair consequences of the global financial crash and positioning the Tories on the side of the young. It was, of course, also an act of monumental electoral self-harm.

Had it been prepared in less secrecy someone might have raised the alarm. As it was the manifesto was handed to cabinet ministers for the first time as they arrived in Halifax on May 18 for its launch. Long on ambitious rhetoric — it proposed solutions to "five great challenges" — but short on details (with no costings whatsoever) it would later be called the worst in history. The launch would be seen as Mrs May's zenith but the decline was at first gradual. The *Daily Mail*, her most reliable supporter hailed her bravery. As the tide of opinion swept against the social care policy even that newspaper began to report the backlash.

It took until the weekend for the dam to burst. By the Sunday Mrs May faced a truly awful choice: either she could stick with the social care policy, face down the critics and spend the rest of the campaign making the case or she could U-turn and surrender her image as a strong and stable leader. Fatally, she sought a third way, suggesting that she had intended to introduce a cap as well as a floor on social care costs all along. "Nothing has changed," she insisted. To watching voters, who saw her mocked as "weak and wobbly" by journalists, doubts over her honesty began to take hold.

At 10.31pm fans, many of them young girls, were streaming out of the Manchester Arena at the end of an Ariana Grande concert towards a foyer filled with waiting parents. In among them a 22-year-old Manchester-born man, Salman Abedi, detonated a suicide vest killing himself and 22 others around him. It was the deadliest attack since the July 7, 2005 attacks on London. Campaigning was paused to the frustration of some on the left who believed that Mrs May had been handed a reprieve.

Within three days full campaigning resumed, more or less at the point at which it had broken off with questions over Mrs May's credibility. With doubts over her character emerging she was about to be punished for another campaign miscalculation. Mr Cameron's decision to take part in head-to-head TV debates in the 2010 election when he was the clear frontrunner is held to have cost him an outright majority by opening the field to Nick Clegg and the Lib Dems. There was no way Mrs May was going to make that mistake, aides said. Instead she made a different one. Mr Corbyn had said that he would not take part in a debate featuring seven leaders unless Mrs May did so. Then at the last moment he changed tack and said that he would, after all, show up at the Cambridge event on May 30. Instead of sensing the danger the Tories pressed ahead, fielding Amber Rudd instead and ensuring that Mrs May's non-appearance dominated the debate and its coverage. Now voters had a new epithet to add to weak, wobbly and dishonest as they considered the woman demanding a landslide majority with which to crush saboteurs at home and abroad. Evasive.

Part of the calculation for Mrs May not participating was that she had agreed to two events in which she and Mr Corbyn appeared separately but sequentially. Mr Corbyn had outperformed low expectations in the first of these, hosted jointly by Sky and Channel 4 News on May 29. He had bested Jeremy Paxman, dealing easily with his attempts to draw out a more radical personal agenda than that offered by Labour's manifesto.

The impact of the programme had been limited, however, because of the Manchester attack the following day. The second, a BBC *Question Time Special*, took place on June 2. This time both leaders fared less well. A nurse challenged the prime minister to explain why she was in effect being paid the same today as she had been in 2009. "How can that be fair in the light of the job that we do?"

Mrs May's answer that "hard choices" had been necessary and there was no "magic money tree" for the NHS went down badly in the studio audience and, polling later showed, among voters as a whole. What was the Tories' offer to Britain's five million public sector workers? More austerity.

For his part Mr Corbyn became tetchy when pressed by the audience on whether he would authorise a retaliatory nuclear strike. "I don't want to be responsible for millions of deaths and neither do you," he snapped.

Tory strategists had been growing frustrated that their attempts to remind voters of the Labour leader's record and associations including with the IRA were failing to get traction outside their own media partisans. At last, it seemed to CCHQ, it was winning control of the media narrative just before the crucial last set of Sunday papers dropped helping to shape the final days of the campaign. Just as the first editions were going "off-stone" on June 3 a white Renault van drove into pedestrians on London Bridge, the start of Britain's third terrorist attack in three months. Eight people were killed and 48 were injured, including four unarmed police officers who attempted to stop the assailants. The three attackers, who wore fake explosive vests, were all shot dead by the police.

After Manchester both main parties had refrained from seeking to exploit terrorism for political capital. With just four days of the campaign remaining, however, Mrs May decided that she had no choice but to respond with a promise of tough action. There had been "far too much tolerance of extremism", she said in a statement on the steps of Downing Street on June 4. "Enough is enough." She said that legal changes might be necessary to check what she said threatened to become a self-perpetuating wave of copycat, unsophisticated attacks that had rendered unsafe previous assumptions about who posed a risk and when.

Labour, however, was quick to counter her effort to frame the response to the attack in terms of the proper balance of security and liberty. This was a vulnerable area given Mr Corbyn's record but especially so because Diane Abbott, the party's shadow home secretary, had become a liability after a disastrous radio interview on May 2. Her efforts to cost Labour's policy on providing an extra 10,000 police officers were so excruciating that the interview was one of the few moments of the campaign that ordinary people could recall unprompted. The Tories gleefully hammered away at Ms Abbott's apparent innumeracy at every opportunity.

After London Bridge, however, no one was in much mood for laughing. Mr Milne and Mr McDonnell took the decision to remove Ms Abbot from the frontline, insisting that she was unwell. Although she subsequently disclosed that she had diabetes, the timing of her leave of absence was entirely political and not of her own choosing. It was left to Emily Thornberry, the shadow foreign secreaty, to lead efforts to frame the terrorism debate in austerity. Had the government not cut police numbers, she argued, the country would be better defended against this emerging threat. Mrs May's record as home secretary, once her strongest suit, no longer looked quite so impressive.

She was, nevertheless, sufficiently confident of a big win in the final days of the campaign that she signed off a closing tour that included a number of Labour seats with majorities of more than 5,000. On the eve of polling day Jim Messina, the US political consultant brought in to help the Tory campaign, told senior figures that the Tories would win a majority of 68. Senior Labour people were no less gloomy about their chances. Asked for their prediction a senior member of Mr Corbyn's team said: "We'll lose 40 seats."

When at 10pm on June 8 Professor Curtice's exit poll predicted instead that the Tories would win 314 to Labour's 266 there was a stunned silence in CCHQ. The final results were only slightly less awful for Mrs May. The final Tory tally of 318 seats was a net loss of 13; Labour had gained 30 seats on 262. The SNP had a poor night losing 21 seats and reduced to 35. The Liberal Democrats had largely stood still, adding just 4 seats to take their tally to 12.

When she came to give her speech at her own Maidenhead count it was a drawn prime minister who appeared on stage to lay claim to No 10. Her voice cracking, she said: "At this time more than anything else, this country needs a period of stability. And if ... the Conservative Party has won the most seats and probably the most votes, then it will be incumbent on us to ensure we have that period of stability, and that is exactly what we will do."

Mr Corbyn had watched the exit poll at his house in Islington. One senior figure who spoke to the Labour leader minutes later said that he had been as shocked as anyone else: "None of us expected it, that's the truth." Some pollsters came closer than others. Labour's team claim to have picked up key factors, the trend away from Tories among better educated voters and greater youth engagement, that helped to determine the result. No one anticipated the scale of those effects.

An election called to deliver a personal mandate for a Brexit strategy that included the threat of walking away from the EU without agreement had instead delivered Britain's second hung parliament in seven years. It was as if voters had subverted Mrs May's negotiating slogan and decided that no government was better than a bad government. It fell to her, clinging to power but at the mercy of her internal opponents in and out of the cabinet, and needing the support of the DUP to command a majority, to prove that she was not about to deliver both.

Francis Elliott is political editor of The Times

HOW THE POLLSTERS RIGHTED 2015 WRONGS

by Anthony Wells

Most polling companies began the 2017 campaign having got the previous general election wrong and with a variety of different changes all aimed at correcting the problem of understating Conservative support. Ultimately many of these changes ended up backfiring and getting the election wrong in the other direction. This time a few companies did get things right, however, perhaps providing a way forward for the industry.

The story the polls told during the 2017 campaign was a straightforward one. A regular bit of election "lore" is that campaigns and manifestos do not usually make much difference: in 2017 they clearly did. At the beginning of the election campaign the polls showed a collapse in Ukip support and an extremely large lead for the Conservative party, in many cases more than 20 points. As the campaign progressed Labour gradually whittled away the Tory lead. All the polls showed the same trend, the difference was the degree. Depending on the different methodologies polling companies were using some still ended the campaign with double-digit Conservative leads; others saw the Conservative lead cut to single figures. The contrast was largely down to the way different polling companies had tried to address the failure of 2015.

After the 2015 result the polling industry held an internal inquiry to try to work out what had gone wrong, concluding that the reason the polls were wrong was because the samples (the people interviewed for polls) were not properly representative: 2015's polls contained too many people who were engaged and interested in politics. The result was to distort the turnout. The polls in 2015 contained lots of enthusiastic young Labour voters when in reality most young people were not that interested in politics at all and stayed at home.

Polling companies took two main approaches to solving this problem. The first was to treat the cause: to spend more time and money improving how representative polling samples were. Some internet polling companies spent time recruiting people who were less engaged with politics; some changed sample quotas and weights to try to ensure that their samples were less overly "political", such as weighting by level of interest or attention paid to politics, or highest educational qualification. The second approach was to treat the symptom, to accept that there was a problem with polling samples that meant that younger respondents were too likely to say they would vote, and instead model turnout based on past elections. Where polls have traditionally asked respondents to estimate their own likelihood to vote, this approach meant that companies instead estimated respondents' likelihood to vote based on their age, class or housing tenure. The effect of this was to weight down groups that normally voted Labour and increase the Tory share in the polls.

The second approach would have produced more accurate results at the 2015 election and would probably have resulted in more accurate polling at other past elections too. It did, however, rely on an assumption that the pattern of turnout at one election is a useful predictor of the pattern of turnout at the next election. Were turnout patterns to change and young people to suddenly become more likely to vote there was a risk that it could go horribly wrong. This, of course, was what happened.

Polling company	C	Lab	LD	Ukip	C lead
	%	%	%	%	
Survation	41	40	8	2	+1
Surveymonkey	42	38	6	4	+4
Kantar Public	43	38	7	4	+5
Opinium	43	36	8	5	+7
YouGov	42	35	10	5	+7
Ipsos MORI	44	36	7	4	+8
Panelbase	44	36	7	5	+8
ComRes	44	34	9	5	+10
ICM	46	34	7	5	+12
BMG	43	33	8	5	+13
Final GB Result	43.5	41.0	7.6	1.9	+2.5

Source: British Polling Council & Surveymonkey

These different approaches set the pattern of the polls at the 2017 general election. Some polling companies concentrated on improving their samples, some used new ways of modelling turnout, many used a bit of both. This resulted in a broad spread of results. Companies such as ICM and ComRes, who relied heavily on a demographic turnout model, showed the Conservatives retaining a double-digit lead throughout the campaign. Companies that still relied largely upon asking people how likely they were to vote, like Survation, Opinium or YouGov, ended up showing smaller Conservative leads. Ultimately the smaller leads turned out to be correct, with Kantar, Surveymonkey and Survation producing the final polls that were closest to the actual Conservative lead.

As well as the different approaches to traditional polling there were some more radical departures. YouGov and Lord Ashcroft both produced seat projections based on multilevel regression and poststratification (MRP). This is a method taken from academia, a way of projecting national figures on to sub-national units, in this case using large national surveys of voting intention to project support levels in all 632 British parliamentary constituencies. In the case of YouGov the figures were based on about 7,000 surveys a day, with each projection using a week of data. Clearly even a sample of 50,000 people is not enough to get a decent sample size in each individual seat, so instead MRP works by modelling voting intention based on past vote, age, gender, education and other demographics and then applying that model to each individual constituency.

When first released in mid-May the YouGov model predicted a hung parliament, causing raised eyebrows and some degree of mockery (not least from Jim Messina, the US consultant brought in to help the Conservative party campaign, who tweeted that he had spent the day "laughing at yet another stupid poll from YouGov"). By the end of the campaign the model was showing a Conservative lead of four points and correctly predicting a hung parliament. The model's more striking predictions included showing Canterbury leaning to Labour and Kensington being too close to call, findings that looked highly unusual but would eventually turn out to correctly foresee two of Labour's more surprising gains.

The election ends up a mixed bag for the polling companies. It has gone down as another polling error but some of the traditional pollsters, notably Survation and Kantar, did well (as did Surveymonkey, a US company better known in this country for its survey platform). The YouGov MRP model also performed admirably and managed not only to get the result right but also to call some of the more difficult-to-foresee constituency results. Other companies did less well, with three companies showing double-digit Tory leads in their final polls and the Lord Ashcroft MRP model predicting a solid Tory majority.

After the mistakes of 2015 the next general election was always going to be an experimental one, where polling companies used different approaches and then learnt from those that were a success. Only time will tell how polling companies respond to the experience of 2017, what successful methods are retained and which failed attempts are discarded. Certainly it looks as if polling companies will be wary of relying too much on demographic turnout models (although it would be wrong to discard it completely: Kantar's polling and the YouGov MRP model included 2015 turnout patterns as one factor among many). After the performance of the YouGov MRP model we might also expect to see MRP become a regular feature at future elections, albeit one that is probably too expensive for regular monthly voting intention figures.

Anthony Wells is research director for YouGov

SNAP ELECTION, HIGH TURNOUT? HOW QUAINT

by Colin Rallings and Michael Thrasher

There was a retro feel to the general election of June 8, 2017. First, Theresa May showed that the Fixed Term Parliaments Act of 2011 was little practical impediment to a prime minister exercising their age-old prerogative to call an election at a time of their own choosing. This contest was little more than two years since its 2015 predecessor and eleven months after Mrs May became leader of the Conservative Party, as the last remaining candidate, and was asked to form a government.

Second, more people participated in the election than in any other this century. Nonetheless the UK-wide turnout of nearly 69 per cent still fell short of the 72 per cent recorded at the 2016 EU referendum.

Third, when the results were announced it became clear that those who did vote had flocked to the Conservative and Labour parties in numbers and proportions not seen for a generation. The two parties together polled 84.5 per cent of the British vote, the biggest concentration of support since 1970, and have 91.6 per cent of all MPs elected in Britain, the greatest proportion since 1992. The Conservatives won more votes than at any election since 1992 and a share of the vote equivalent to that achieved by Margaret Thatcher in her decisive victories of 1983 and 1987. Labour, scarcely to be outdone, registered its highest vote share since 2001 and more votes than at all but four other elections since the Second World War.

Such comparative success had an adverse impact on the other parties. The Liberal Democrats made very modest seat gains but their vote share slipped to levels last seen in 1970. There was some comfort, though, in that they re-established their position as the (albeit distant) third party of British politics. Ukip, which had assumed that mantle in 2015, lost more than 3 million votes and had a share less than that achieved in 2005. The nationalist parties in Wales and Scotland also fell back. Plaid Cymru had the compensation of gaining an extra seat despite polling fewer votes. The SNP was unable to maintain its hegemony in Scotland, but remains the largest party there and provides the third biggest bloc of MPs in the new House of Commons.

The return to two-party politics is reflected in the pattern of party competition after the election. All bar 14 of the 573 seats across England and Wales are now held by either Labour or the Conservatives, with one in second place to the other in 519 of them. The Liberal Democrats were runners up in only 37 constituencies (55 in 2015) and Ukip plummeted from 120 second places (and one victory) last time to none at all.

The actual election result, on the other hand, had a more modern feel. For the second time in three contests, but for only the third occasion in almost 90 years, no party was returned with an overall majority.

The Conservatives' vote share increased for an unprecedented fifth consecutive time for an established party but they lost a net 13 seats and, crucially, their narrow parliamentary advantage. Labour benefited from a 2.0 percentage point swing from the Conservatives since 2015: although both parties gained vote share for the second election running, the rise in Labour support was higher. Labour won an additional 30 seats to better its 2010 losing performance but still has 55 fewer MPs than do the Conservatives and is 64 seats away from a Commons majority.

Distribution of first and second places

	C	Lab	LD	SNP	PC	Green	ICHC	Ind	DUP	SF	APNI	SDLP	UUP	Total 1st
C		273	29	13			1	1						317
Lab	246		7	7	2									262
LD	8			4										12
SNP	9	25	1											35
PC	1	2	1											4
Green		1												1
Speaker						1								1
Ind								1						1
DUP										4	3	1	2	10
SF									4			2	1	7
Total 2nd	264	301	38	24	2	1	1	1	5	4	3	3	3	650

THE BATTLE FOR VOTES

Across the UK more than 32.2 million votes were cast from a record eligible electorate of 46.8 million. With turnout rising as well, a million and a half more votes were cast than in 2015.

The Conservative share of the UK vote was 42.3 per cent and that for Labour 40.0 per cent, a combined share of 83.3 per cent. With all the other big British parties suffering a decline in vote share, both were positively supported by a larger proportion of the electorate than has been the case for some time. Almost three in ten of all electors voted Conservative, the party's best result since 1992; and 28.3 per cent voted Labour, ironically, a stronger endorsement than Tony Blair received at his second landslide victory in 2001.

The Liberal Democrat share was down by half a percentage point to 7.4 per cent and the SNP moved to fourth place in the UK despite its relative decline. It polled a greater share of the total votes from Scotland alone (3.0 per cent) than did either Ukip (1.8 per cent) or the Greens (1.6 per cent) across the UK. In Northern Ireland the Democratic Unionists increased their lead over Sinn Fein with the two parties together winning all but one of the province's 18 seats.

The analysis that follows concentrates on the situation in Great Britain with Northern Ireland discussed separately alongside country-specific analyses for the other nations of the UK.

Conservative candidates won 43.4 per cent of the British popular vote, a rise of 5.8 points compared with 2015. Despite the total being the largest for a quarter of a century and the increase bigger than at any election since 1979, however, the party made a net loss of 13 seats: 20 gains — 12 from the SNP, 6 from Labour, and 1 each from the Liberal Democrats and Ukip — were more than wiped out by losses to Labour (28) and the Liberal Democrats (5). In Scotland the party won a greater share of the vote than at any election since 1979; in Wales they reached levels of support not seen since the introduction of the universal franchise, but still lost three seats.

Outside Scotland the Conservatives registered double-figure increases in support in both Conservative and Labour-held constituencies that had voted by two to one or more to leave the EU and/or had voted heavily for Ukip in 2015. Unfortunately for the party, however, most Labour seats had big enough majorities to withstand such an impressive advance. Conversely, the Conservatives actually lost ground in pro-Remain London and were becalmed in constituencies with a high ethnic minority population.

Labour lost the election but arguably developed a momentum not seen since 1997. The party gained seats (30) for the first time since that election and registered its largest one-off increase in vote share (9.8 points) since its first widely fought election in 1918. Yet it remains 55 seats behind the Conservatives in the House of Commons, has only 4 more MPs than it did when losing to David Cameron in 2010 and is still far adrift of the SNP in Scotland.

Labour's fortunes were often the mirror image of those of the Conservatives. Most areas outside Scotland that had voted heavily for Remain swung decisively in Labour's direction, an average rise in vote share of 11.6 points compared to a loss of 1.6 for the Conservatives. The Liberal Democrats, whose campaign was predicated on their perceived ability to become the party of ardent Remain voters, saw their share rise by only 0.8 points in the same seats. Across London and in ethnically diverse constituencies there was a double-digit advance for Labour; in seats with a large student population the party's share was up by more than 14 points compared to a paltry 1.4 points for the Conservatives. Crucially, the party made more headway than the Conservatives in every country and English region except the North East. It is still relatively weak in the south of England but is now the Conservatives' closest challenger even there.

The Liberal Democrats entered the election with hopes of regaining several of the 49 seats they lost in 2015. In the event they did make five gains in England and three in Scotland but this was tempered by four losses, one to each of the Conservatives and Plaid Cymru and two to Labour. They also lost votes and vote share in each country to record their lowest share in England since 1959, in Scotland since 1970 and in Wales since the party was founded in the mid-19th century. There was a small uptick in their vote in seats lost to the Conservatives in 2015, in London and the South East and in constituencies with a high proportion of graduates. On the other hand they were victims of a further surge in Labour support in most of the mainly urban seats they lost to Jeremy Corbyn's party in 2015. As has been the case in the past, the explanation for Liberal Democrat victories now needs to be sought in the circumstances of particular constituencies rather than in the broad sweep of changing patterns of voting behaviour.

The nationalist parties in Scotland and Wales were also squeezed by the two-party revival and both suffered a loss of vote share. Plaid Cymru did become the third party in Wales in both votes and seats for only the second time but it is a long way behind the winner almost everywhere. The SNP slump was more marked after a greater than 13 per cent swing to the Conservatives. It remains by far the largest party in Scotland but all except 5 of its remaining 35 seats are now held by margins of less than 10 per cent. The Conservatives are in second place in 7 of them, Labour in 22, and the Liberal Democrats in 1.

Ukip's fall from grace was dramatic. It contested nearly 250 fewer seats than in 2015. Its sole elected MP had left the party in March to sit as an Independent and his putative successor in Clacton finished about 24,000 votes behind the Conservative winner. In not a single constituency did Ukip increase its share of the vote and in only two (Thurrock and Hartlepool) did that share reach double figures. Overall fewer than one in fifty voters chose Ukip in 2017 compared with the more than one in eight that supported it in 2015. The party that had threatened to break the mould of British politics just two years ago became the biggest electoral victim of the 2016 referendum result.

The Greens also failed to build on their encouraging 2015 performance. They fielded 100 or so fewer candidates but their vote share was down disproportionately from 3.8 per cent to 1.6 per cent. Their joint leader, Caroline Lucas, did retain Brighton Pavilion with an absolute majority of all votes cast, benefiting from having no Liberal Democrat opponent and probably also from some symbolic support by usual Labour voters. The seat was one of only seven in England and Wales where Labour's share declined; on the other hand in the two constituencies abutting it — Brighton Kemptown and Hove — the party's share was up by an average of 20 percentage points. Putting the Speaker's seat aside, there were only two other constituencies, Bristol West and the Isle of Wight, where the Greens topped 10 per cent of the vote, compared with 16 such cases in 2015.

Excluding the Speaker, the 375 Independent and small party candidates polled fewer than 250,000 votes in total and all but 18 of them lost their deposits. Lady Sylvia Hermon retained Down North but otherwise the most successful individual candidate was again Claire Wright in Devon East, who polled more than 21,000 votes (35 per cent of the total). In all 55 registered small parties contested the election with 5 of them fielding 10 or more candidates, including the Christian Peoples Alliance with 31 and the Yorkshire Party with 21.

ENGLAND

More than 80 per cent of the UK electorate lives in England and it returns a similar proportion of members of parliament. About 29.2 million votes were cast for a total of 2,716 candidates but all bar 10 of the 533 successful MPs were drawn from the Conservative and Labour parties.

The Conservative vote share exceeded 45 per cent for the first time since 1992 but despite this the party made a net loss of 22 seats. Labour's share was its best since 1997 but (thanks in large measure to a higher turnout and an increased electorate) it secured more actual votes than at any election since 1951. On that dimension at least Mr Corbyn did outperform Mr Blair.

The overall swing from the Conservatives to Labour in England was 3 per cent, enabling Labour to make a net gain of 21 seats. The party now controls 36 more English constituencies than it did when losing power in 2010 and has 69 fewer English MPs than the Conservatives compared with 106 fewer then. There was a swing to Labour in every English region except the North East and it is the regions that provide vital clues to the election outcome.

Increasingly a case can be made for treating London as another country in electoral terms. In 2010 it was the region that registered by far the smallest drop in Labour support; in 2015 it swung to Labour by 3.4 points compared to an English average of only 1.1 points. In 2017 the Conservative vote share in London actually dropped and Labour won more than half of all votes cast in the capital for the first time since the Attlee landslide of 1945. This had two important consequences: first, it contributed to Labour making four gains in London; second, it enabled the party to successfully defend some very marginal seats. The demographic and political characteristics of London (it was the only English region to vote Remain) make it very hard for the Conservatives to bounce back there in the near future.

Labour also performed above average in the South East and South West, regions where the party previously held only 8 of the 139 seats. It gained 7 seats, almost all of them in large urban areas with big student populations. In Canterbury and Portsmouth South its vote share jumped by more than 20 points; in Brighton Kemptown, Bristol North West, Plymouth Sutton & Devonport and Reading East it was up by more than 15 points.

For their part the Conservatives tended to do better in the English regions where Ukip had been strongest in 2015. Although they lost their one marginal seat in the North East, elsewhere in that region their vote share increased by more than Labour's. Although the gap was not usually sufficient to threaten Labour, they did gain Middlesbrough South & East Cleveland where it appears that the Ukip vote fell to the Conservatives by a margin of two to one. The Conservative-to-Labour swing in both the East Midlands and Yorkshire & The Humber was in the order of one percentage point, and there were glimpses of what might have been as the party swept up the Ukip vote in both Derbyshire North East (Labour since 1935) and Mansfield (Labour since 1923). There were isolated similar outcomes on the other side of the Midlands in Stoke-on-Trent South (Labour since its creation in 1950) and Walsall North (Labour bar a short by-election interlude since 1955).

Such cases were few and far between, though. The Conservatives had appeared to enter the election assuming that most Ukip voters would naturally gravitate towards them as a governing party committed to leaving the EU. In the event too many Labour majorities were beyond the reach of even the most ardent Leave voters; too many target constituencies like Birmingham Northfield, Chorley and Dewsbury reacted to Ukip standing aside by swinging left rather than right. Such a pattern was more devastating for the party where it led to seat losses. London and other metropolitan Remain areas might be understandable but in Bury North, High Peak and Peterborough the absence of Ukip led to a disproportionate increase in Labour rather than Conservative support and the defeat of Eurosceptic sitting MPs.

For the Liberal Democrats in England this was, to be polite, a patchy election. They polled fractionally more votes and won two more seats than in 2015 but their share was down in every region except two. They lost Southport (Liberal Democrat since 1997) to the Conservatives and the two student seats of Leeds North West and Sheffield Hallam to Labour. In the latter the former leader Nick Clegg was unable to persuade Conservative voters again to lend him their votes to keep Labour out as they had done in 2015. On the other hand they made five gains from the Conservatives – four in constituencies that had voted clearly to Remain in the EU and where Labour started a long way off the pace (Bath, Kingston & Surbiton, Twickenham, and Oxford West & Abingdon). They also failed by only 45 votes to win the similar Richmond Park constituency which they had taken in a rather unusual by-election in 2016. In essence, though, this was poor recompense for a campaign promising a second referendum after the Brexit negotiations.

Ukip had performed well for little tangible reward across England in 2015. Now, however, they became victims of the cliché the further they rise, the harder they fall as their vote share dropped from 14.1 per cent to 2.1 per cent. The party lost ground in every seat it contested but its sharpest decline came in three symbolic seats. In Clacton, which had elected the party's first MP in a 2014 by-election and again at the following general election, Ukip lost more than 16,000 votes and dropped to a humiliating third place. A distant third was also their fate in Thanet South, where Nigel Farage had come quite close to winning in 2015, and in Boston & Skegness, which Paul Nuttall, the party leader, chose to contest. The best that can be said of these results is that at least the party retained its deposit, which it did not in 295 of the 333 other cases in England.

SCOTLAND

It was always unlikely that the SNP would be able to replicate its spectacular performance of 2015. Then it won half the vote and 56 of the 59 seats in Scotland. That outcome gave the unionist opposition parties a clearer picture of the tactical situation in each constituency and highlighted which might be best placed to defeat the SNP. In the 2016 Scottish parliament elections Nicola Sturgeon's party also failed to retain its overall majority at Holyrood, losing 6 seats and polling 400,000 fewer votes than at the general election.

This time the SNP fell back by more than 13 percentage points to 36.9 per cent and lost no fewer than 21 of its 56 seats. On both counts, though, this was still its second best result. It lost ground in every constituency and suffered some notable individual losses. The former first minister Alex Salmond in Gordon and Westminster leader Angus Robertson in Moray were both defeated by Conservatives. In Banff and Buchan Eilidh Whiteford, who had inherited that seat from Mr Salmond in 2010, had a 10 per cent swing from the Conservatives in 2015 converted into a 20 per cent swing in the opposite direction. The SNP is now in the potentially threatening position of holding 30 of its 35 seats by a margin of less than 10 percentage points.

Thanks to the Conservative revival the election had an old-fashioned feel in Scotland, too. The party's share nearly doubled to 28.6 per cent as it leapt over Labour into second place with 12 gains and 13 seats overall. This marked the first time it had beaten its traditional rival in both votes and seats since 1955. As recently as 2010 the party had languished in fourth place in Scotland. There was a Conservative clean sweep in the south of Scotland and the Borders and a series of solid gains in the more affluent areas of the northeast. One of the Conservatives' more surprising victories was in Renfrewshire East. Although one of the country's most prosperous constituencies, this had been Labour since 1997 and the Conservatives were reduced to a distant third last time. It is possible that a backlash against Labour among the constituency's relatively large Jewish population (the party suffered its second largest fall in share of the vote anywhere in Britain) was one factor helping the Conservatives across the line.

Labour retained Edinburgh South and took back six other seats across the central belt, including Gordon Brown's former stronghold of Kirkcaldy & Cowdenbeath and Glasgow North East, where it had suffered a 39 per cent swing to the SNP in 2015. The party's overall share of the vote at 27.1 per cent, however, was less than three points better than then and its second lowest since 1918. There is a long way to go before Scotland once again makes a significant contribution towards Labour success nationally.

The Liberal Democrat share of the vote in Scotland declined by almost 1 point to 6.8 per cent. On the other hand the party did manage to regain three of its four most marginal target seats and failed by just two votes to win the fourth (Fife North East). In none of these cases was there a dramatic increase in the Liberal Democrat vote; rather the party came through the middle as the SNP vote dropped sharply.

WALES

As in 2015 the election in Wales more closely resembled that in England rather than Scotland. The vote share for each of the two largest parties increased and the combined Conservative-Labour total exceeded 80 per cent for the first time since 1979.

The Labour share rose by almost twice as much as that of the Conservatives resulting in a swing to Labour of 2.9 per cent, virtually the same as in England. The Conservative share, 36.6 per cent, was the party's highest for a hundred years, but they lost three seats to Labour – Cardiff North, Gower, and Vale of Clwyd – to emerge with a relatively poor return of 8 out of 40 MPs.

For its part Labour polled more votes and a greater share (48.9 per cent) than at any election since 1997. The swing to Labour in Cardiff North was more than double the Welsh average, perhaps reflecting the strong Remain vote in one of the nation's most middle-class constituencies. It now has 28 MPs in Wales, nearly three-quarters of the total.

Every other party saw its vote share decline. Plaid Cymru was down by almost two percentage points to record its lowest figure since 1997. It did have the consolation of winning Ceredigion from the Liberal Democrats to add to its existing three seats. The Liberal Democrats also dropped by two points and now have no MPs in Wales for the first time since the Liberal Party was founded in 1859. All 32 Ukip candidates lost their deposits (none of the party's 40 candidates had done so in 2015), as did all ten Greens. A similar fate befell the 11 Independent and smaller party candidates.

NORTHERN IRELAND

There was a hardening of two-party politics here, albeit featuring a different cast from the rest of the UK. The 18 constituencies attracted 109 candidates (29 fewer than in 2015) with turnout increasing by more than 7 percentage points to 65.4 per cent. This was the highest level in the province since 2001 and noteworthy in that the general election was held just three months after a similar turnout at the March 2017 assembly contest following the collapse of the power-sharing agreement.

With no pact with the Ulster Unionists in place this time the Democratic Unionist Party contested every constituency except Fermanagh & South Tyrone and again topped the poll. Its share was ten points up on 2015 and it gained two seats for a total of ten, a record return for the party on each count. In Antrim South the sitting UUP MP Danny Kinahan was deposed; in Belfast South the Social Democratic and Labour Party's Alasdair McDonnell saw the unionist vote coalesce around Emma Little-Pengelly, who became the sole female within the DUP's Westminster ranks.

The UUP had a wretched election. It now has no representatives in the Commons and its 10.3 per cent vote share is an all-time low. Until 1997 it was the largest party in Northern Ireland and regularly returned a majority of its MPs.

Sinn Fein was rather further behind the DUP this time than either in 2015 or at the 2017 assembly election, but it gained three seats with a 5-point increase in vote share. It took Down South on an almost 9 per cent direct swing from the SDLP, with a similar swing being sufficient to narrowly win Foyle, an SDLP stronghold for more than 30 years. This was the fifth election running that the SDLP has lost vote share and now it, like the UUP, has no MPs.

Fermanagh & South Tyrone maintained its reputation as a constituency with fierce party competition. A Sinn Fein majority of 4 in 2010 and a UUP one of 530 in 2015 turned into a victory for the former Sinn Fein incumbent Michelle Gildernew by the relatively generous 875 votes.

Sylvia Hermon won Down North as an Independent for the third time and was the only candidate to break the DUP/SF duopoly. The UUP again did not contest the seat against its former colleague but a surge in DUP support made it a marginal. Other smaller groups did not fare well. The Alliance's Naomi Long failed to win back Belfast East and saw her vote share drop again, as it did for her party as a whole. The Northern Ireland branch of the UK Conservative Party fielded 7 candidates compared with 16 in 2015 and polled fewer than 4,000 votes in total. The Greens made no progress and the Traditional Unionist Voice party had a single representative.

TURNOUT

At more than 46.8 million the registered electorate in the United Kingdom was the largest ever but although turnout rose by more than 2 percentage points to 68.8 per cent the number of votes cast, 32.2 million, remained some way below the record 33.6 million at the 1992 general election.

Turnout was up by about 3 points in England and Wales, and by more than 7 in Northern Ireland. In Scotland, on the other hand, it fell from 71.1 per cent in 2015 to 66.4 per cent. This re-established the pattern common since devolution in which turnout at general elections north of the border has been less than that in England and Wales, and marked the unwinding of the legacy of the extraordinarily high turnout at the 2014 independence referendum.

Across the UK a total of 274 constituencies had turnouts in excess of 70 per cent (181 in 2015) and it fell below 60 per cent in only 33 (96 in 2015). The highest turnouts in England were in Twickenham (79.5 per cent) and Oxford West & Abingdon (79.4 per cent), both gained by the Liberal Democrats. The highest in Wales, as it had been in 2015, was Cardiff North (77.4 per cent), a Labour gain. The lowest turnout in England was Leeds Central (53.2 per cent); in Wales it was Swansea East (60.1 per cent).

Once again the highest turnouts in Scotland were in Dunbartonshire East (78.1 per cent) and Renfrewshire East (76.7 per cent). In four of the seven Glasgow constituencies turnout slipped below 57 per cent.

In Northern Ireland turnout in the tightly fought Fermanagh & South Tyrone (72.6 per cent) was more than seven points higher than in any other constituency. The lowest was in the DUP stronghold of Strangford (60.2 per cent).

Of arguably more interest in the context of this election are the changes in turnout. It increased by 6 or more percentage points in 44 constituencies in Great Britain including 14 in London alone. Indeed across London turnout was up by nearly 5 points, more than in any other region, and exceeded that in the capital at the 2016 referendum. Outside Scotland participation fell in only 28 seats. The biggest drops were in the Speaker's Buckingham seat (-3.2 per cent) and in Rochester & Strood (-2.8 per cent) where there had been a sitting Ukip MP in 2015.

It is striking that across England and Wales the longstanding correlation between a constituency's marginality and its level of turnout was weakened further. For the second election running there was no statistically significant relationship between a party's majority going into the election and the turnout in that seat. Although average turnout rose by most in those constituencies where a party was defending a majority of less than 5 per cent (+3.6 points), it increased to almost the same extent in places where the margin was 20 per cent or more (+3.2 points). In seats between those two extremes the average increase in turnout was lower.

In fact increases in turnout appeared this time to be more strongly associated with a constituency's demographic characteristics. It was up by five percentage points in constituencies with the highest Black, Muslim, and Asian populations, as well as in those with a highly educated population. On the other hand, it rose by less than average in places with the largest proportions of pensioners and by less than one point in Conservative-held constituencies that had either decisively voted Leave in the 2016 referendum and/or showed substantial support for Ukip in the 2015 general election.

BENCHMARKING THE NEXT ELECTION

Although the 2017 general election appeared to herald the return of two-party politics, nothing can be taken for granted. Evidence from the British Election Study shows not only that many fewer voters are "very strong" supporters of a political party than in the Conservative/Labour heyday of the 1960s, but also that four in ten of them are likely to switch parties between elections.

Nonetheless the result on June 8 sets the baseline for the next election. The Conservatives need a swing of less than 0.5 per cent to gain the nine seats required for an overall majority in the House of Commons. A majority of 50, the barest minimum that Mrs May was hoping for this time, would require them to win Stoke-on-Trent North and everything easier on a swing from Labour of just over 2.8 per cent. That equates to a lead over Labour in the popular vote of about 8 percentage points.

Labour's task is rather tougher despite the prevailing optimism in the party about the 2017 result. A swing of more than 1.5 per cent is needed for it to overtake the Conservatives to become the largest single party in parliament; one of 4.8 per cent (or a poll lead of more than 7 points) to achieve an overall majority of seats. That is nearly twice as much as the party has managed at any election other than in 1997 since the Second World War. A comfortable majority of 50 can be reached only by threatening seats such as Rushcliffe, currently held by more than 8,000 votes by the Father of the House, Kenneth Clarke.

The key marginal constituencies that each party must target are relatively evenly spread across the country with one notable exception. Labour's future fortunes disproportionately rest on its ability to recover in Scotland. Six of the 30 seats it must gain to become the largest party, and 14 of the 78 required for a majority of 30, are currently held by the SNP. For every one of those it fails to take, another more difficult constituency in England or Wales must be captured.

The Conservative cause may also be assisted by the likely outcome of the parliamentary boundary reviews, which were resurrected in 2016. The evening out of electorates and a reduction in the size of the House of Commons from 650 to 600 members could allow the party to contest the next election as if it had already secured an overall majority.

Although all four UK commissions are due to report to the relevant secretary of state by September 2018, it may not be plain sailing from then on. An election called earlier than say the autumn of 2019 could well be fought on the current boundaries in any event. And receiving legislative consent for the changes, even by statutory instrument, could be scuppered by opposition across the House. For example the provisional proposals for Northern Ireland suggest that the DUP could lose ground to Sinn Fein. It is hard to see Arlene Foster's party going into the lobbies to sanction that.

Colin Rallings and Michael Thrasher are emeritus professors at the University of Plymouth and associate members of Nuffield College, Oxford

Concise summary results by country

	VOTES	VOTES %	% CHANGE	CANDIDATES	ELECTED	LOST DEP
ENGLAND						
C	12,346,007	45.4	4.6	532	296	0
Lab	11,389,508	41.9	10.3	532	227	0
LD	2,121,760	7.8	-0.4	530	8	293
Ukip	557,390	2.1	-12.1	336	0	295
Green	507,199	1.9	-2.3	447	1	439
Others	244,585	0.9	0.2	339	1	323
Total Vote	27,166,449			2,716	533	1,350
Electorate	39,297,181					
Turnout	69.1%					
SCOTLAND						
C	757,949	28.6	13.7	59	13	0
Lab	717,007	27.1	2.8	59	7	0
LD	179,062	6.8	-0.8	59	4	46
SNP	977,568	36.9	-13.1	59	35	0
Ukip	5,302	0.2	-1.4	10	0	10
Green	5,886	0.2	-1.1	3	0	2
Others	6,921	0.3	0.1	17	0	16
Total Vote	2,649,695			266	59	74
Electorate	3,988,441					
Turnout	66.4%					
WALES						
C	528,839	33.6	6.3	40	8	0
Lab	771,354	48.9	12.1	40	28	0
LD	71,039	4.5	-2.0	40	0	36
PC	164,466	10.4	-1.7	40	4	16
Ukip	31,376	2.0	-11.6	32	0	32
Green	5,128	0.3	-2.2	10	0	10
Others	3,612	0.2	-0.1	11	0	11
Total Vote	1,575,814			213	40	105
Electorate	2,298,161					
Turnout	68.6%					

	VOTES	VOTES %	% CHANGE	CANDIDATES	ELECTED	LOST DEP
NORTHERN IRELAND						
DUP	292,316	36.0	10.3	17	10	0
SF	238,915	29.4	4.9	18	7	4
SDLP	95,419	11.7	-2.2	18	0	5
UUP	83,280	10.3	-5.8	14	0	3
APNI	64,553	7.9	-0.6	18	0	8
Green	7,452	0.9	0.0	7	0	5
C	3,895	0.5	-0.8	7	0	7
TUV	3,282	0.4	-1.9	1	0	0
Others	23,071	2.8	-0.9	9	1	7
Total Vote	812,183			109	18	39
Electorate	1,242,698					
Turnout	65.4%					
GREAT BRITAIN						
C	13,632,795	43.4	5.8	631	317	0
Lab	12,877,869	41.0	9.8	631	262	0
LD	2,415,862	2,371,861	7.6	-0.5	629 12	375
SNP	977,568	3.1	-1.7	59	35	0
Ukip	594,068	1.9	-11.0	378	0	337
Green	518,213	1.7	-2.2	460	1	451
PC	164,466	0.5	-0.1	40	4	16
Others	255,118	0.8	0.4	367	1	350
Total Vote	31,391,958			3,195	632	1,529
Electorate	45,583,783					
Turnout	68.9%					
UNITED KINGDOM						
C	13,636,690	42.3	5.5	638	317	7
Lab	12,877,869	40.0	9.5	631	262	0
LD	2,371,861	7.4	-0.5	629	12	375
SNP	977,568	3.0	-1.7	59	35	0
Ukip	594,068	1.8	-10.7	378	0	337
Green	525,665	1.6	-2.1	467	1	456
DUP	292,316	0.9	0.3	17	10	0
SF	238,915	0.7	0.2	18	7	4
PC	164,466	0.5	-0.1	40	4	16
SDLP	95,419	0.3	0.0	18	0	5
UUP	83,280	0.3	-0.1	14	0	3
APNI	64,553	0.2	0.0	18	0	8
TUV	3,282	0.0	0.0	1	0	0
Others	278,189	0.9	0.4	376	2	357
Total Vote	32,204,141			3,304	650	1,568
Electorate	46,826,481					
Turnout	68.8%					

Voting in the English regions

	C	LAB	LD	GREEN	UKIP	OTHERS	TOTAL
EAST MIDLANDS							
votes	1,195,982	954,635	101,612	34,355	56,358	14,516	2,357,458
votes %	50.7	40.5	4.3	1.5	2.4	0.6	100.0
2015 votes %	43.5	31.6	5.6	3.0	15.8	0.6	100.0
change	7.3	8.9	-1.3	-1.5	-13.4	0.0	0.0
seats	31	15	0	0	0	0	46
2015 seats	32	14	0	0	0	0	46
electorate							3,415,899
turnout %							69.0
2015 turnout %							66.5
change							2.5
EASTERN							
votes	1,690,819	1,012,368	244,054	58,704	77,793	10,588	3,094,326
votes %	54.6	32.7	7.9	1.9	2.5	0.3	100.0
2015 votes %	49.0	22.0	8.2	3.9	16.2	0.5	100.0
change	5.6	10.7	-0.3	-2.0	-13.7	-0.2	0.0
seats	50	7	1	0	0	0	58
2015 seats	52	4	1	0	1	0	58
electorate							4,432,644
turnout %							69.8
2015 turnout %							67.5
change							2.3
LONDON							
votes	1,268,800	2,086,595	336,725	67,561	49,369	19,448	3,828,498
votes %	33.1	54.5	8.8	1.8	1.3	0.5	100.0
2015 votes %	34.9	43.7	7.7	4.9	8.1	0.8	100.0
change	-1.8	10.8	1.1	-3.1	-6.8	-0.3	0.0
seats	21	49	3	0	0	0	73
2015 seats	27	45	1	0	0	0	73
electorate							5,459,427
turnout %							70.1
2015 turnout %							65.4
change							4.7
NORTH EAST							
votes	440,613	709,738	58,409	16,080	49,348	5,878	1,280,066
votes %	34.4	55.4	4.6	1.3	3.9	0.5	100.0
2015 votes %	25.3	46.9	6.5	3.6	16.7	0.9	100.0
change	9.1	8.5	-1.9	-2.3	-12.8	-0.4	0.0
seats	3	26	0	0	0	0	29
2015 seats	3	26	0	0	0	0	29
electorate							1,938,346
turnout %							66.0
2015 turnout %							61.8
change							4.2

	C	LAB	LD	GREEN	UKIP	OTHERS	TOTAL
NORTH WEST							
votes	1,301,562	1,972,632	193,053	39,608	68,946	19,705	3,595,506
votes %	36.2	54.9	5.4	1.1	1.9	0.5	100.0
2015 votes %	31.2	44.6	6.5	3.2	13.6	0.7	100.0
change	5.0	10.3	-1.1	-2.1	-11.7	-0.2	0.0
seats	20	54	1	0	0	0	75
2015 seats	22	51	2	0	0	0	75
electorate							5,302,587
turnout %							67.8
2015 turnout %							64.3
change							3.5
SOUTH EAST							
votes	2,495,350	1,326,320	487,203	143,873	104,509	78,572	4,635,827
votes %	53.8	28.6	10.5	3.1	2.3	1.7	100.0
2015 votes %	50.8	18.3	9.4	5.2	14.7	1.5	100.0
change	3.0	10.3	1.1	-2.1	-12.4	0.2	0.0
seats	72	8	2	1	0	1	84
2015 seats	78	4	0	1	0	1	84
electorate							6,507,917
turnout %							71.2
2015 turnout %							68.6
change							2.6
SOUTH WEST							
votes	1,542,296	875,213	448,730	68,010	33,160	35,250	3,002,659
votes %	51.4	29.1	14.9	2.3	1.1	1.2	100.0
2015 votes %	46.5	17.7	15.1	5.9	13.6	1.2	100.0
change	4.9	11.4	-0.2	-3.6	-12.5	0	0
seats	47	7	1	0	0	0	55
2015 seats	51	4	0	0	0	0	55
electorate							4,181,098
turnout %							71.8
2015 turnout %							69.5
change							2.3
WEST MIDLANDS							
votes	1,356,486	1,175,095	122,287	46,347	50,106	15,901	2,766,222
votes %	49.0	42.5	4.4	1.7	1.8	0.6	100.0
2015 votes %	41.8	32.9	5.5	3.3	15.7	0.8	100.0
change	7.2	9.6	-1.1	-1.6	-13.9	-0.2	0
seats	35	24	0	0	0	0	59
2015 seats	34	25	0	0	0	0	59
electorate							4,132,560
turnout %							66.9
2015 turnout %							64.1
change							2.8

	C	LAB	LD	GREEN	UKIP	OTHERS	TOTAL
YORKSHIRE AND THE HUMBER							
votes	1,054,099	1,276,912	129,687	32,661	67,801	44,727	2,605,887
votes %	40.5	49.0	5.0	1.3	2.6	1.7	100.0
2015 votes %	32.6	39.1	7.1	3.5	16.0	1.6	100.0
change	7.9	9.9	-2.1	-2.2	-13.4	0.1	0
seats	17	37	0	0	0	0	54
2015 seats	19	33	2	0	0	0	54
electorate							3,926,703
turnout %							66.4
2015 turnout %							63.3
change							3.1

Seats that changed hands 2015–17

CONSERVATIVE GAINS

From Labour
Copeland
Derbyshire NE
Mansfield
Middlesbrough S &
    Cleveland E
Stoke-On-Trent S
Walsall N

From Liberal Democrats
Southport

From SNP
Aberdeen S
Aberdeenshire West &
    Kincardine
Angus
Ayr, Carrick & Cumnock
Banff & Buchan
Berwickshire, Roxburgh
    & Selkirk
Dumfries & Galloway
Gordon
Moray
Ochil & Perthshire S
Renfrewshire E
Stirling

From Ukip
Clacton

LABOUR GAINS

From Conservatives
Battersea
Bedford
Brighton Kemptown
Bristol NW
Bury N
Canterbury
Cardiff N
Colne Valley
Crewe & Nantwich
Croydon Central
Derby N
Enfield Southgate
Gower
High Peak
Ipswich
Keighley
Kensington
Lincoln
Peterborough
Plymouth Sutton &
    Devonport
Portsmouth S
Reading E
Stockton S
Stroud
Vale Of Clwyd
Warrington S
Warwick & Leamington
Weaver Vale

From Liberal Democrats
Leeds NW
Sheffield Hallam

From SNP
Coatbridge, Chryston &
    Bellshill
East Lothian
Glasgow NE
Kirkcaldy &
    Cowdenbeath
Midlothian
Rutherglen &
    Hamilton W

LIB DEM GAINS

From Conservative
Bath
Eastbourne
Kingston & Surbiton
Oxford W & Abingdon
Twickenham

From SNP
Caithness, Sutherland &
    Easter Ross
Dunbartonshire E
Edinburgh W

PLAID CYMRU GAINS

From Liberal Democrats
Ceredigion

DUP GAINS

From SDLP
Belfast S

From UUP
Antrim S

SINN FEIN GAINS

From SDLP
Down South
Foyle

From UUP
Fermanagh & Tyrone S

Three-way marginal seats

CONSTITUENCY	1ST	% MAJ 1ST OVER 2ND	2ND	% MAJ 1ST OVER 3RD	3RD
Lanark & Hamilton East	SNP	0.5	C	0.7	Lab
East Lothian	Lab	5.5	SNP	6.5	C
Edinburgh North & Leith	SNP	2.9	Lab	6.8	C
Linlithgow & Falkirk East	SNP	5.2	Lab	7.3	C
Fife North East	SNP	0.0	LD	8.7	C
Edinburgh South West	SNP	2.2	C	8.8	Lab
Ceredigion	PC	0.3	LD	9.1	Lab
Paisley & Renfrewshire North	SNP	5.6	Lab	9.9	C
Dunfermline & Fife West	SNP	1.7	Lab	10.8	C
Midlothian	Lab	2.0	SNP	10.9	C
Ayrshire Central	SNP	2.8	C	11.1	Lab
Ayrshire North & Arran	SNP	7.7	C	11.4	Lab
Belfast South	DUP	4.6	SDLP	12.2	APNI
Southport	C	6.1	Lab	12.3	LD
Edinburgh West	LD	5.7	SNP	12.4	C
Falkirk	SNP	9.1	Lab	12.8	C
Carmarthen East & Dinefwr	PC	9.5	Lab	13.0	C
Caithness, Sutherland & Easter Ross	LD	6.6	SNP	13.2	C
Renfrewshire East	C	8.8	SNP	13.3	Lab
East Kilbride, Strathaven & Lesmahagow	SNP	7.1	Lab	13.5	C
Kirkcaldy & Cowdenbeath	Lab	0.6	SNP	13.5	C
Airdrie & Shotts	SNP	0.5	Lab	14.4	C
Ynys Mon	Lab	14.1	C	14.5	PC
Sheffield Hallam	Lab	3.7	LD	14.6	C
Stirling	C	0.3	SNP	15.0	Lab
Kilmarnock & Loudoun	SNP	13.5	Lab	15.7	C
Livingston	SNP	7.4	Lab	15.7	C
Ayr, Carrick & Cumnock	C	6.0	SNP	16.3	Lab
Dundee East	SNP	15.5	C	16.8	Lab
Inverclyde	SNP	1.0	Lab	17.0	C
Argyll & Bute	SNP	2.8	C	17.8	LD
Rutherglen & Hamilton West	Lab	0.5	SNP	18.0	C
Motherwell & Wishaw	SNP	0.8	Lab	18.3	C
Aberdeen North	SNP	11.3	Lab	18.6	C
Ross, Skye & Lochaber	SNP	15.4	C	19.3	LD
Thurrock	C	0.7	Lab	19.4	UKIP
Glasgow East	SNP	0.2	Lab	19.9	C

Seats in rank order of % majority

CONSTITUENCY	% MAJ	MAJ	2ND	CONSTITUENCY	% MAJ	MAJ	2ND
Conservative seats				**Conservative seats**			
1 Southampton Itchen	0.07	31	Lab	45 Carlisle	6.04	2,599	Lab
2 Richmond Park	0.07	45	LD	46 Southport	6.08	2,914	Lab
3 Stirling	0.30	148	SNP	47 Ochil & Perthshire South	6.20	3,359	SNP
4 St Ives	0.61	312	LD	48 Rossendale & Darwen	6.41	3,216	Lab
5 Pudsey	0.61	331	Lab	49 Angus	6.58	2,645	SNP
6 Hastings & Rye	0.63	346	Lab	50 Truro & Falmouth	6.69	3,792	Lab
7 Chipping Barnet	0.64	353	Lab	51 Scarborough & Whitby	6.81	3,435	Lab
8 Thurrock	0.69	345	Lab	52 Walsall North	6.82	2,601	Lab
9 Preseli Pembrokeshire	0.74	314	Lab	53 Stevenage	6.86	3,386	Lab
10 Calder Valley	1.05	609	Lab	54 Carmarthen West & Pembrokeshire South	7.37	3,110	Lab
11 Norwich North	1.10	507	Lab	55 Devon North	7.78	4,332	LD
12 Broxtowe	1.55	863	Lab	56 Loughborough	7.88	4,269	Lab
13 Stoke-On-Trent South	1.59	663	Lab	57 Cities Of London & Westminster	8.14	3,148	Lab
14 Telford	1.61	720	Lab	58 Cheadle	8.26	4,507	LD
15 Bolton West	1.83	936	Lab	59 Filton & Bradley Stoke	8.26	4,190	Lab
16 Aberconwy	1.98	635	Lab	60 Clwyd West	8.45	3,437	Lab
17 Northampton North	2.00	807	Lab	61 Moray	8.74	4,159	SNP
18 Hendon	2.05	1,072	Lab	62 Shipley	8.77	4,681	Lab
19 Mansfield	2.11	1,057	Lab	63 Renfrewshire East	8.77	4,712	SNP
20 Middlesbrough South & Cleveland East	2.14	1,020	Lab	64 Banff & Buchan	8.87	3,693	SNP
21 Milton Keynes South	2.67	1,725	Lab	65 Erewash	9.11	4,534	Lab
22 Northampton South	2.82	1,159	Lab	66 Worthing East & Shoreham	9.61	5,106	Lab
23 Pendle	2.85	1,279	Lab	67 Sherwood	9.74	5,198	Lab
24 Morecambe & Lunesdale	3.06	1,399	Lab	68 Lewes	10.16	5,508	LD
25 Milton Keynes North	3.09	1,975	Lab	69 Gloucester	10.21	5,520	Lab
26 Finchley & Golders Green	3.16	1,657	Lab	70 Nuneaton	10.29	4,739	Lab
27 Camborne & Redruth	3.25	1,577	Lab	71 Colchester	10.60	5,677	Lab
28 Putney	3.31	1,554	Lab	72 Aberdeen South	10.68	4,752	SNP
29 Harrow East	3.46	1,757	Lab	73 St Albans	10.72	6,109	LD
30 Watford	3.57	2,092	Lab	74 Uxbridge & Ruislip South	10.78	5,034	Lab
31 Copeland	3.95	1,695	Lab	75 Wimbledon	10.91	5,622	Lab
32 Morley & Outwood	4.02	2,104	Lab	76 Dumfries & Galloway	10.94	5,643	SNP
33 Vale Of Glamorgan	4.08	2,190	Lab	77 Plymouth Moor View	11.05	5,019	Lab
34 Corby	4.48	2,690	Lab	78 Shrewsbury & Atcham	11.39	6,627	Lab
35 Cheltenham	4.51	2,569	LD	79 Rochford & Southend East	11.74	5,548	Lab
36 Swindon South	4.81	2,464	Lab	80 Halesowen & Rowley Regis	11.84	5,253	Lab
37 Gordon	4.86	2,607	SNP	81 Altrincham & Sale West	12.17	6,426	Lab
38 Worcester	4.88	2,508	Lab	82 Wycombe	12.30	6,578	Lab
39 Crawley	4.89	2,457	Lab	83 Dover	12.39	6,437	Lab
40 Blackpool North & Cleveleys	4.93	2,023	Lab	84 Wells	12.46	7,582	LD
41 Chingford & Woodford Green	5.19	2,438	Lab	85 Hazel Grove	12.49	5,514	LD
42 Reading West	5.56	2,876	Lab	86 Thanet South	12.84	6,387	Lab
43 Derbyshire North East	5.68	2,860	Lab	87 Devon East	13.31	8,036	Ind
44 Ayr, Carrick & Cumnock	6.00	2,774	SNP	88 South Ribble	13.53	7,421	Lab

CONSTITUENCY	% MAJ	MAJ	2ND

Conservative seats

CONSTITUENCY	% MAJ	MAJ	2ND
89 Rushcliffe	13.74	8,010	Lab
90 Cornwall North	14.13	7,200	LD
91 Welwyn Hatfield	14.26	7,369	Lab
92 York Outer	14.43	8,289	Lab
93 Stafford	14.89	7,729	Lab
94 Swindon North	15.18	8,335	Lab
95 Kingswood	15.39	7,500	Lab
96 Aberdeenshire West & Kincardine	15.40	7,950	SNP
97 Harlow	15.68	7,031	Lab
98 Macclesfield	15.85	8,608	Lab
99 Rugby	16.00	8,212	Lab
100 Stourbridge	16.24	7,654	Lab
101 Redditch	16.29	7,363	Lab
102 Bournemouth East	16.33	7,937	Lab
103 Elmet & Rothwell	16.47	9,805	Lab
104 Monmouth	16.50	8,206	Lab
105 Basingstoke	16.92	9,466	Lab
106 Bournemouth West	17.33	7,711	Lab
107 Winchester	17.49	9,999	LD
108 Waveney	17.49	9,215	Lab
109 Cannock Chase	17.53	8,391	Lab
110 Warwickshire North	18.04	8,510	Lab
111 Great Yarmouth	18.06	7,973	Lab
112 Hemel Hempstead	18.07	9,445	Lab
113 Amber Valley	18.12	8,300	Lab
114 Rochester & Strood	18.32	9,850	Lab
115 Forest Of Dean	18.36	9,502	Lab
116 Croydon South	18.62	11,406	Lab
117 Somerset North East	18.94	10,235	Lab
118 Gravesham	19.08	9,347	Lab
119 Dumfriesshire, Clydesdale & Tweeddale	19.28	9,441	SNP
120 Gillingham & Rainham	19.30	9,430	Lab
121 Wrekin, The	19.31	9,564	Lab
122 Chelsea & Fulham	19.44	8,188	Lab
123 Brecon & Radnorshire	19.45	8,038	LD
124 Hexham	19.98	9,236	Lab
125 Bexleyheath & Crayford	20.08	9,073	Lab
126 Burton	20.13	10,047	Lab
127 Banbury	20.14	12,399	Lab
128 Dudley South	20.21	7,730	Lab
129 Weston-Super-Mare	20.46	11,544	Lab
130 Hitchin & Harpenden	20.47	12,031	Lab
131 Bromley & Chislehurst	20.55	9,590	Lab
132 St Austell & Newquay	20.55	11,142	Lab
133 Portsmouth North	21.11	9,965	Lab
134 Berwickshire, Roxburgh & Selkirk	21.12	11,060	SNP

Conservative seats

CONSTITUENCY	% MAJ	MAJ	2ND
135 Southend West	21.19	10,000	Lab
136 Kettering	21.38	10,562	Lab
137 Harborough	21.58	12,429	Lab
138 Cleethorpes	21.74	10,400	Lab
139 Worthing West	22.18	12,090	Lab
140 Thanet North	22.22	10,738	Lab
141 Congleton	22.44	12,619	Lab
142 Dorset South	22.53	11,695	Lab
143 Derbyshire South	22.74	11,970	Lab
144 Derbyshire Mid	23.06	11,616	Lab
145 Wyre & Preston North	23.26	12,246	Lab
146 Eddisbury	23.27	11,942	Lab
147 Chatham & Aylesford	23.30	10,458	Lab
148 Wellingborough	23.40	12,460	Lab
149 Aldershot	23.44	11,473	Lab
150 Thornbury & Yate	23.81	12,071	LD
151 Chelmsford	23.87	13,572	Lab
152 Ribble Valley	23.91	13,199	Lab
153 Huntingdon	24.24	14,475	Lab
154 Staffordshire Moorlands	24.25	10,830	Lab
155 Dartford	24.32	13,186	Lab
156 Basildon South & Thurrock East	24.38	11,490	Lab
157 Sutton & Cheam	24.43	12,698	LD
158 Selby & Ainsty	24.56	13,772	Lab
159 Cambridgeshire South	24.57	15,952	Lab
160 Eastleigh	24.75	14,179	LD
161 Yeovil	24.78	14,723	LD
162 Leicestershire North West	24.81	13,286	Lab
163 Aylesbury	24.93	14,656	Lab
164 Taunton Deane	25.20	15,887	LD
165 Beverley & Holderness	25.24	14,042	Lab
166 Fylde	25.41	11,805	Lab
167 Bedfordshire South West	25.47	14,168	Lab
168 Cambridgeshire South East	25.65	16,158	Lab
169 Wyre Forest	26.08	13,334	Lab
170 Folkestone & Hythe	26.18	15,411	Lab
171 Ruislip, Northwood & Pinner	26.19	13,980	Lab
172 Tamworth	26.21	12,347	Lab
173 Bridgwater & Somerset West	26.51	15,448	Lab
174 Montgomeryshire	26.61	9,285	LD
175 Spelthorne	26.79	13,425	Lab
176 Totnes	26.81	13,477	Lab
177 Devon Central	27.11	15,680	Lab
178 Norfolk South	27.29	16,678	Lab
179 Wantage	27.33	17,380	Lab
180 Brigg & Goole	27.44	12,363	Lab
181 Suffolk Coastal	27.57	16,012	Lab
182 Romford	27.59	13,778	Lab

CONSTITUENCY	% MAJ	MAJ	2ND	CONSTITUENCY	% MAJ	MAJ	2ND
Conservative seats				**Conservative seats**			
183 Somerset North	27.59	17,103	Lab	230 Cornwall South East	32.77	17,443	Lab
184 Yorkshire East	27.81	15,006	Lab	231 Leicestershire South	32.87	18,631	Lab
185 Berwick-Upon-Tweed	27.91	11,781	Lab	232 Newark	32.97	18,149	Lab
186 Torbay	27.91	14,283	LD	233 Suffolk West	32.97	17,063	Lab
187 Harwich & Essex North	28.07	14,356	Lab	234 Gainsborough	33.10	17,023	Lab
188 Cambridgeshire North West	28.14	18,008	Lab	235 Newton Abbot	33.23	17,160	Lab
189 Norfolk North West	28.25	13,788	Lab	236 Bedfordshire Mid	33.23	20,983	Lab
190 Broadland	28.26	15,816	Lab	237 Broxbourne	33.26	15,792	Lab
191 Isle Of Wight	28.29	21,069	Lab	238 Wiltshire South West	33.47	18,326	Lab
192 Poole	28.50	14,209	Lab	239 Thirsk & Malton	33.97	19,001	Lab
193 Bracknell	28.66	16,016	Lab	240 Bognor Regis & Littlehampton	34.07	17,494	Lab
194 Norfolk Mid	28.90	16,086	Lab	241 Penrith & The Border	34.24	15,910	Lab
195 Derbyshire Dales	28.90	14,327	Lab	242 Tiverton & Honiton	34.25	19,801	Lab
196 Sutton Coldfield	29.02	15,339	Lab	243 Maidstone & The Weald	34.27	17,723	Lab
197 Chippenham	29.10	16,630	LD	244 Skipton & Ripon	34.38	19,985	Lab
198 Ashford	29.19	17,478	Lab	245 Havant	34.45	15,956	Lab
199 Beckenham	29.22	15,087	Lab	246 Epsom & Ewell	34.55	20,475	Lab
200 Shropshire North	29.42	16,355	Lab	247 Lichfield	34.72	18,581	Lab
201 Sittingbourne & Sheppey	29.60	15,211	Lab	248 Devon West & Torridge	34.78	20,686	Lab
202 Charnwood	29.62	16,341	Lab	249 Gosport	34.78	17,211	Lab
203 Bury St Edmunds	29.67	18,441	Lab	250 Witney	34.86	21,241	Lab
204 Hereford & Herefordshire South	29.74	15,013	Lab	251 Norfolk South West	34.94	18,312	Lab
205 Basildon & Billericay	29.83	13,400	Lab	252 Stone	34.97	17,495	Lab
206 Devon South West	29.92	15,816	Lab	253 Runnymede & Weybridge	34.97	18,050	Lab
207 Haltemprice & Howden	29.95	15,405	Lab	254 Faversham & Kent Mid	35.00	17,413	Lab
208 Tatton	30.11	14,787	Lab	255 Meriden	35.13	19,198	Lab
209 Woking	30.27	16,724	Lab	256 Northamptonshire South	35.14	22,840	Lab
210 Hertfordshire North East	30.29	16,835	Lab	257 Braintree	35.21	18,422	Lab
211 Tunbridge Wells	30.37	16,465	Lab	258 Kenilworth & Southam	35.22	18,076	Lab
212 Suffolk Central & Ipswich North	30.40	17,185	Lab	259 Grantham & Stamford	35.51	20,094	Lab
213 Bromsgrove	30.67	16,573	Lab	260 Aldridge-Brownhills	35.56	14,307	Lab
214 Guildford	30.70	17,040	LD	261 Surrey South West	35.73	21,590	ICHC
215 Wokingham	31.49	18,798	Lab	262 Somerton & Frome	35.85	22,906	LD
216 Hornchurch & Upminster	31.62	17,723	Lab	263 Clacton	35.85	15,828	Lab
217 Hertford & Stortford	31.73	19,035	Lab	264 Epping Forest	35.93	18,243	Lab
218 Dorset Mid & Poole North	31.79	15,339	LD	265 Romsey & Southampton North	36.00	18,046	LD
219 Sussex Mid	31.92	19,673	Lab	266 Solihull	36.25	20,571	Lab
220 Harrogate & Knaresborough	32.02	18,168	LD	267 Louth & Horncastle	37.22	19,641	Lab
221 Dorset West	32.03	19,091	LD	268 Bexhill & Battle	37.27	22,165	Lab
222 Old Bexley & Sidcup	32.19	15,466	Lab	269 Chichester	37.75	22,621	Lab
223 Hertfordshire South West	32.23	19,550	Lab	270 Worcestershire West	37.77	21,328	Lab
224 Hertsmere	32.44	16,951	Lab	271 Fareham	37.81	21,555	Lab
225 Bedfordshire North East	32.49	20,862	Lab	272 Witham	37.87	18,646	Lab
226 Salisbury	32.51	17,333	Lab	273 Horsham	37.89	23,484	Lab
227 Bosworth	32.67	18,351	Lab	274 Tewkesbury	38.21	22,574	Lab
228 Reigate	32.73	17,614	Lab	275 Sleaford & North Hykeham	38.36	25,237	Lab
229 Suffolk South	32.73	17,749	Lab	276 Orpington	38.57	19,461	Lab

CONSTITUENCY	% MAJ	MAJ	2ND	CONSTITUENCY	% MAJ	MAJ	2ND
Conservative seats				**Labour seats**			
277 Hampshire North West	38.59	22,679	Lab	6 Barrow & Furness	0.44	209	Con
278 Ludlow	38.60	19,286	Lab	7 Keighley	0.46	239	Con
279 Boston & Skegness	38.65	16,572	Lab	8 Rutherglen & Hamilton West	0.52	265	SNP
280 Esher & Walton	38.93	23,298	Lab	9 Kirkcaldy & Cowdenbeath	0.56	259	SNP
281 Henley	39.04	22,294	Lab	10 Glasgow North East	0.76	242	SNP
282 Daventry	39.05	21,734	Lab	11 Ashfield	0.88	441	Con
283 Wealden	39.08	23,628	Lab	12 Stroud	1.08	687	Con
284 Arundel & South Downs	39.64	23,883	Lab	13 Bishop Auckland	1.16	502	Con
285 Cambridgeshire North East	39.92	21,270	Lab	14 Peterborough	1.27	607	Con
286 Newbury	40.07	24,380	LD	15 Colne Valley	1.51	915	Con
287 Chesham & Amersham	40.07	22,140	Lab	16 Bedford	1.63	789	Con
288 Rutland & Melton	40.13	23,104	Lab	17 Ipswich	1.63	836	Con
289 Surrey East	40.39	23,914	Lab	18 Stockton South	1.65	888	Con
290 Richmond (Yorks)	40.53	23,108	Lab	19 Midlothian	1.95	885	SNP
291 Saffron Walden	40.99	24,966	Lab	20 Warwick & Leamington	2.23	1,206	Con
292 Stratford-On-Avon	41.02	21,958	Lab	21 Penistone & Stocksbridge	2.66	1,322	Con
293 Tonbridge & Malling	41.31	23,508	Lab	22 Lincoln	3.16	1,538	Con
294 Windsor	41.51	22,384	Lab	23 Portsmouth South	3.49	1,554	Con
295 Devizes	41.78	21,136	Lab	24 Coatbridge, Chryston & Bellshill	3.52	1,586	SNP
296 Castle Point	42.21	18,872	Lab	25 Sheffield Hallam	3.73	2,125	LD
297 Worcestershire Mid	42.34	23,326	Lab	26 Warrington South	4.11	2,549	Con
298 Rayleigh & Wickford	42.39	23,450	Lab	27 Derby North	4.14	2,015	Con
299 Mole Valley	42.55	24,137	LD	28 High Peak	4.31	2,322	Con
300 Wiltshire North	42.60	22,877	LD	29 Battersea	4.39	2,416	Con
301 Cotswolds, The	42.71	25,499	Lab	30 Wakefield	4.70	2,176	Con
302 Sevenoaks	42.79	21,917	Lab	31 Wolverhampton South West	5.16	2,185	Con
303 New Forest East	42.82	21,995	Lab	32 Wrexham	5.22	1,832	Con
304 Herefordshire North	43.05	21,602	Lab	33 East Lothian	5.52	3,083	SNP
305 Surrey Heath	43.14	24,943	Lab	34 Stoke-On-Trent North	5.65	2,359	Con
306 Beaconsfield	43.80	24,543	Lab	35 Dewsbury	5.87	3,321	Con
307 Staffordshire South	44.48	22,733	Lab	36 Vale Of Clwyd	6.15	2,379	Con
308 Brentwood & Ongar	45.36	24,002	Lab	37 Reading East	6.79	3,749	Con
309 Maidenhead	45.43	26,457	Lab	38 Gower	7.17	3,269	Con
310 Dorset North	46.26	25,777	Lab	39 Blackpool South	7.22	2,523	Con
311 Hampshire East	46.66	25,852	Lab	40 Great Grimsby	7.22	2,565	Con
312 Maldon	46.67	23,430	Lab	41 Darlington	7.32	3,280	Con
313 New Forest West	47.21	23,431	Lab	42 Weaver Vale	7.76	3,928	Con
314 Meon Valley	47.41	25,692	Lab	43 Rother Valley	7.84	3,882	Con
315 Hampshire North East	48.19	27,772	Lab	44 Cardiff North	8.02	4,174	Con
316 South Holland & The Deepings	49.48	24,897	Lab	45 Bolton North East	8.40	3,797	Con
317 Christchurch	49.71	25,171	Lab	46 Scunthorpe	8.53	3,431	Con
Labour seats				47 Bristol North West	8.80	4,761	Con
				48 Enfield Southgate	9.01	4,355	Con
1 Kensington	0.05	20	Con	49 Gedling	9.08	4,694	Con
2 Dudley North	0.06	22	Con	50 Leeds North West	9.13	4,224	LD
3 Newcastle-Under-Lyme	0.07	30	Con	51 Bury North	9.13	4,375	Con
4 Crewe & Nantwich	0.09	48	Con	52 Bassetlaw	9.29	4,852	Con
5 Canterbury	0.33	187	Con	53 Workington	9.42	3,925	Con

CONSTITUENCY	% MAJ	MAJ	2ND	CONSTITUENCY	% MAJ	MAJ	2ND
Labour seats				**Labour seats**			
54 Croydon Central	9.90	5,652	Con	102 Tynemouth	20.52	11,666	Con
55 Dagenham & Rainham	10.15	4,652	Con	103 Enfield North	21.10	10,247	Con
56 Birmingham Northfield	10.52	4,667	Con	104 Newcastle Upon Tyne North	21.43	10,349	Con
57 Delyn	10.76	4,240	Con	105 Lancashire West	21.49	11,689	Con
58 Bridgend	10.87	4,700	Con	106 Newport East	21.74	8,003	Con
59 Halifax	11.14	5,376	Con	107 Hemsworth	22.14	10,174	Con
60 Don Valley	11.24	5,169	Con	108 Sunderland Central	22.16	9,997	Con
61 Bolsover	11.37	5,288	Con	109 Bermondsey & Old	22.17	12,972	LD
62 Clwyd South	11.62	4,356	Con	Southwark			
63 Alyn & Deeside	11.70	5,235	Con	110 Redcar	22.29	9,485	Con
64 Bury South	11.70	5,965	Con	111 Ellesmere Port & Neston	22.36	11,390	Con
65 Stoke-On-Trent Central	11.76	3,897	Con	112 Erith & Thamesmead	22.52	10,014	Con
66 Wirral West	12.21	5,365	Con	113 Cambridge	22.64	12,661	LD
67 West Bromwich West	12.36	4,460	Con	114 Hull West & Hessle	23.22	8,025	Con
68 Wolverhampton North East	12.56	4,587	Con	115 Wolverhampton South East	23.45	8,514	Con
69 Hyndburn	12.86	5,815	Con	116 Doncaster Central	23.55	10,131	Con
70 Newport West	13.03	5,658	Con	117 Southampton Test	24.53	11,503	Con
71 Plymouth Sutton &	13.29	6,807	Con	118 Wansbeck	24.58	10,435	Con
Devonport				119 Derby South	24.83	11,248	Con
72 Chorley	13.50	7,512	Con	120 Ealing Central & Acton	24.95	13,807	Con
73 Eltham	13.64	6,296	Con	121 Durham, City Of	25.59	12,364	Con
74 Ynys Mon	14.07	5,259	Con	122 Bristol East	26.37	13,394	Con
75 Lancaster & Fleetwood	14.48	6,661	Con	123 Harrow West	26.44	13,314	Con
76 Sedgefield	14.57	6,059	Con	124 Tooting	26.57	15,458	Con
77 Heywood & Middleton	15.28	7,617	Con	125 Westminster North	26.59	11,512	Con
78 Burnley	15.77	6,353	Con	126 Hampstead & Kilburn	26.64	15,560	Con
79 Birmingham Edgbaston	15.86	6,917	Con	127 Torfaen	26.65	10,240	Con
80 Chester, City Of	16.26	9,176	Con	128 Cardiff West	26.92	12,551	Con
81 Bradford South	16.32	6,700	Con	129 Sheffield South East	27.06	11,798	Con
82 Batley & Spen	16.66	8,961	Con	130 Huddersfield	27.39	12,005	Con
83 Coventry South	16.91	7,947	Con	131 Blaydon	28.03	13,477	Con
84 Coventry North West	17.21	8,580	Con	132 Hull East	28.37	10,396	Con
85 Oldham East & Saddleworth	17.39	8,182	Con	133 Ashton Under Lyne	28.40	11,295	Con
86 Ilford North	18.21	9,639	Con	134 Swansea West	28.43	10,598	Con
87 Hartlepool	18.29	7,650	Con	135 Pontypridd	28.70	11,448	Con
88 Durham North West	18.35	8,792	Con	136 Makerfield	28.85	13,542	Con
89 Worsley & Eccles South	18.36	8,379	Con	137 Exeter	29.08	16,117	Con
90 Wirral South	18.42	8,323	Con	138 Nottingham North	29.12	11,160	Con
91 Blyth Valley	18.63	7,915	Con	139 Caerphilly	29.25	12,078	Con
92 Stalybridge & Hyde	19.04	8,084	Con	140 Cardiff South & Penarth	29.30	14,864	Con
93 Birmingham Erdington	19.57	7,285	Con	141 Bristol South	29.40	15,987	Con
94 West Bromwich East	19.73	7,713	Con	142 Feltham & Heston	29.42	15,603	Con
95 Warrington North	19.75	9,582	Con	143 Normanton, Pontefract	29.47	14,499	Con
96 Brentford & Isleworth	19.77	12,182	Con	& Castleford			
97 Chesterfield	20.04	9,605	Con	144 Leicester West	29.48	11,060	Con
98 Brighton Kemptown	20.05	9,868	Con	145 Rochdale	29.61	14,819	Con
99 Walsall South	20.18	8,892	Con	146 Houghton & Sunderland	29.75	12,341	Con
100 Leigh	20.38	9,554	Con	South			
101 Stockton North	20.40	8,715	Con	147 Llanelli	29.81	12,024	Con

CONSTITUENCY	% MAJ	MAJ	2ND
Labour seats			
148 Durham North	29.89	12,939	Con
149 Sefton Central	29.99	15,618	Con
150 Rotherham	30.03	11,387	Con
151 Luton South	30.18	13,925	Con
152 Brent North	30.23	17,061	Con
153 Norwich South	30.37	15,596	Con
154 Leeds East	30.77	12,752	Con
155 Luton North	30.81	14,364	Con
156 Bolton South East	31.01	13,126	Con
157 Birmingham Selly Oak	31.04	15,207	Con
158 Sheffield Heeley	31.27	13,828	Con
159 Slough	31.31	16,998	Con
160 Nottingham South	31.50	15,162	Con
161 Islwyn	31.62	11,412	Con
162 Washington & Sunderland West	31.89	12,940	Con
163 Leeds North East	32.06	16,991	Con
164 Edinburgh South	32.43	15,514	SNP
165 Hove	32.57	18,757	Con
166 Barnsley East	32.58	13,283	Con
167 Wythenshawe & Sale East	32.60	14,944	Con
168 Neath	32.99	12,631	Con
169 Doncaster North	33.14	14,024	Con
170 Coventry North East	33.50	15,580	Con
171 Wentworth & Dearne	33.68	14,803	Con
172 Wigan	33.71	16,027	Con
173 Stockport	34.85	14,477	Con
174 York Central	34.99	18,575	Con
175 Denton & Reddish	35.55	14,077	Con
176 South Shields	35.58	14,508	Con
177 Hammersmith	35.69	18,651	Con
178 St Helens North	36.65	18,406	Con
179 Blaenau Gwent	36.77	11,907	PC
180 Vauxhall	36.79	20,250	LD
181 Tyneside North	37.16	19,284	Con
182 Birmingham Yardley	37.24	16,574	Con
183 Ogmore	37.28	13,871	Con
184 Swansea East	37.45	13,168	Con
185 Ealing North	37.50	19,693	Con
186 Oldham West & Royton	37.56	17,198	Con
187 Leeds West	37.81	15,965	Con
188 Hayes & Harlington	37.90	18,115	Con
189 Hull North	38.58	14,322	Con
190 Middlesbrough	38.93	13,873	Con
191 Greenwich & Woolwich	39.01	20,714	Con
192 Stretford & Urmston	39.26	19,705	Con
193 Barnsley Central	39.77	15,546	Con
194 Jarrow	40.13	17,263	Con
195 Salford & Eccles	40.18	19,132	Con

CONSTITUENCY	% MAJ	MAJ	2ND
Labour seats			
196 Newcastle Upon Tyne Central	40.27	14,937	Con
197 Easington	40.95	14,892	Con
198 Warley	41.00	16,483	Con
199 Gateshead	41.21	17,350	Con
200 Birmingham Perry Barr	41.59	18,383	Con
201 Cynon Valley	41.63	13,238	Con
202 Rhondda	41.74	13,746	PC
203 Islington South & Finsbury	42.17	20,263	Con
204 Cardiff Central	42.60	17,196	Con
205 Leicester East	42.78	22,428	Con
206 Blackburn	42.87	20,368	Con
207 Oxford East	43.20	23,284	Con
208 Lewisham West & Penge	43.54	23,162	Con
209 Preston	44.17	15,723	Con
210 Mitcham & Morden	44.42	21,375	Con
211 Lewisham East	44.94	21,213	Con
212 Bradford East	45.02	20,540	Con
213 Barking	45.32	21,608	Con
214 Sheffield Brightside & Hillsborough	45.72	19,143	Con
215 St Helens South & Whiston	46.03	24,343	Con
216 Newcastle Upon Tyne East	46.26	19,261	Con
217 Streatham	47.11	26,285	Con
218 Poplar & Limehouse	47.12	27,712	Con
219 Bradford West	48.11	21,902	Con
220 Wallasey	48.23	23,320	Con
221 Edmonton	48.34	21,115	Con
222 Merthyr Tydfil & Rhymney	48.69	16,334	Con
223 Blackley & Broughton	48.86	19,601	Con
224 Ealing Southall	48.93	22,090	Con
225 Leyton & Wanstead	48.96	22,607	Con
226 Hornsey & Wood Green	49.34	30,738	LD
227 Leeds Central	49.71	23,698	Con
228 Nottingham East	49.81	19,590	Con
229 Dulwich & West Norwood	50.15	28,156	Con
230 Aberavon	50.38	16,761	Con
231 Halton	51.30	25,405	Con
232 Holborn & St Pancras	51.71	30,509	Con
233 Leicester South	51.98	26,261	Con
234 Bristol West	52.14	37,336	Con
235 Brent Central	53.54	27,997	Con
236 Croydon North	54.28	32,365	Con
237 Ilford South	54.89	31,647	Con
238 Manchester Withington	55.73	29,875	LD
239 Sheffield Central	57.96	27,748	Con
240 Birkenhead	58.43	25,514	Con
241 Bethnal Green & Bow	59.16	35,393	Con
242 Garston & Halewood	60.07	32,149	Con

CONSTITUENCY	% MAJ	MAJ	2ND
Labour seats			
243 Islington North	60.47	33,215	Con
244 West Ham	60.54	36,754	Con
245 Hackney North & Stoke Newington	62.42	35,139	Con
246 Birmingham Hall Green	62.50	33,944	Con
247 Manchester Central	63.24	31,445	Con
248 Lewisham Deptford	63.32	34,899	Con
249 Camberwell & Peckham	65.00	37,316	Con
250 Walthamstow	66.50	32,017	Con
251 Birmingham Hodge Hill	66.88	31,026	Con
252 Liverpool Wavertree	67.52	29,466	Con
253 Hackney South & Shoreditch	68.52	37,931	Con
254 Manchester Gorton	69.05	31,730	Con
255 Birmingham Ladywood	69.51	28,714	Con
256 Tottenham	70.09	34,584	Con
257 East Ham	70.42	39,883	Con
258 Bootle	71.99	36,200	Con
259 Liverpool West Derby	72.86	32,908	Con
260 Liverpool Riverside	74.86	35,947	Con
261 Knowsley	76.08	42,214	Con
262 Liverpool Walton	77.14	32,551	Con
Liberal Democrat seats			
1 Oxford West & Abingdon	1.36	816	Con
2 Westmorland & Lonsdale	1.50	777	Con
3 Carshalton & Wallington	2.70	1,369	Con
4 Eastbourne	2.80	1,609	Con
5 Edinburgh West	5.66	2,988	SNP
6 Caithness, Sutherland & Easter Ross	6.61	2,044	SNP
7 Kingston & Surbiton	6.63	4,124	Con
8 Norfolk North	6.73	3,512	Con
9 Dunbartonshire East	10.31	5,339	SNP
10 Bath	11.48	5,694	Con
11 Twickenham	14.73	9,762	Con
12 Orkney & Shetland	19.60	4,563	SNP
Scottish National seats			
1 Fife North East	0.00	2	LD
2 Perth & Perthshire North	0.04	21	Con
3 Glasgow South West	0.17	60	Lab
4 Glasgow East	0.21	75	Lab
5 Airdrie & Shotts	0.51	195	Lab
6 Lanark & Hamilton East	0.53	266	Con
7 Motherwell & Wishaw	0.76	318	Lab
8 Inverclyde	0.98	384	Lab
9 Dunfermline & Fife West	1.65	844	Lab
10 Edinburgh South West	2.22	1,097	Con
11 Argyll & Bute	2.76	1,328	Con

CONSTITUENCY	% MAJ	MAJ	2ND
Scottish National seats			
12 Ayrshire Central	2.81	1,267	Con
13 Edinburgh North & Leith	2.87	1,625	Lab
14 Glasgow North	3.17	1,060	Lab
15 Glasgow South	4.55	2,027	Lab
16 Dunbartonshire West	5.19	2,288	Lab
17 Linlithgow & Falkirk East	5.20	2,919	Lab
18 Paisley & Renfrewshire North	5.61	2,613	Lab
19 Paisley & Renfrewshire South	6.09	2,541	Lab
20 Glasgow Central	6.30	2,267	Lab
21 Glasgow North West	6.59	2,561	Lab
22 Na H-Eileanan An Iar	6.80	1,007	Lab
23 East Kilbride, Strathaven & Lesmahagow	7.15	3,866	Lab
24 Livingston	7.39	3,878	Lab
25 Ayrshire North & Arran	7.66	3,633	Con
26 Edinburgh East	7.87	3,425	Lab
27 Glenrothes	8.09	3,267	Lab
28 Falkirk	9.15	4,923	Lab
29 Inverness, Nairn, Badenoch & Strathspey	9.33	4,924	Con
30 Cumbernauld, Kilsyth & Kirkintilloch East	9.73	4,264	Lab
31 Aberdeen North	11.26	4,139	Lab
32 Kilmarnock & Loudoun	13.48	6,269	Lab
33 Dundee West	13.60	5,262	Lab
34 Ross, Skye & Lochaber	15.39	5,919	Con
35 Dundee East	15.48	6,645	Con
Plaid Cymru seats			
1 Ceredigion	0.26	104	LD
2 Arfon	0.33	92	Lab
3 Carmarthen East & Dinefwr	9.52	3,908	Lab
4 Dwyfor Meirionnydd	15.98	4,850	Con
Green seat			
1 Brighton Pavilion	25.48	14,699	Lab
Speaker			
1 Buckingham	48.83	25,725	Green
Independent seat			
1 Down North	3.08	1,208	DUP
Sinn Fein seats			
1 Foyle	0.37	169	SDLP
2 Fermanagh & South Tyrone	1.64	875	UUP
3 Down South	4.81	2,446	SDLP

CONSTITUENCY	% MAJ	MAJ	2ND
Sinn Fein seats			
4 Newry & Armagh	23.31	12,489	DUP
5 Tyrone West	23.78	10,342	DUP
6 Ulster Mid	27.61	12,890	DUP
7 Belfast West	53.29	21,652	DUP

CONSTITUENCY	% MAJ	MAJ	2ND
Democratic Unionist seats			
1 Belfast North	4.53	2,081	SF
2 Belfast South	4.57	1,996	SDLP
3 Antrim South	7.43	3,208	UUP
4 Upper Bann	15.59	7,992	SF
5 Belfast East	19.76	8,474	APNI
6 Londonderry East	21.55	8,842	SF
7 Antrim East	41.75	15,923	APNI
8 Antrim North	42.60	20,643	SF
9 Lagan Valley	42.80	19,229	UUP
10 Strangford	47.34	18,343	APNI

Seats in rank order of percentage turnout

CONSTITUENCY	% TURNOUT	1ST
1 Twickenham	79.5	LD
2 Oxford West & Abingdon	79.4	LD
3 Richmond Park	79.1	Con
4 Winchester	78.8	Con
5 Wirral West	78.5	Lab
6 Wirral South	78.4	Lab
7 St Albans	78.3	Con
8 Dunbartonshire East	78.1	LD
9 Rushcliffe	78.0	Con
10 Hornsey & Wood Green	77.9	Lab
11 Westmorland & Lonsdale	77.9	LD
12 Devon Central	77.8	Con
13 Sheffield Hallam	77.6	Lab
14 Hove	77.6	Lab
15 Chester, City Of	77.4	Lab
16 Surrey South West	77.4	Con
17 Hitchin & Harpenden	77.4	Con
18 Cardiff North	77.4	Lab
19 Kenilworth & Southam	77.4	Con
20 Hampshire North East	77.3	Con

CONSTITUENCY	% TURNOUT	1ST
631 Stoke-On-Trent North	58.4	Lab
632 Middlesbrough	58.4	Lab
633 Easington	58.3	Lab
634 Stoke-On-Trent Central	58.2	Lab
635 Leicester West	57.9	Lab
636 Great Grimsby	57.5	Lab
637 Hull West & Hessle	57.4	Lab
638 Hull North	57.4	Lab
639 Nottingham North	57.3	Lab
640 Birmingham Erdington	57.2	Lab
641 Walsall North	56.6	Con
642 Glasgow South West	56.2	SNP
643 Blackley & Broughton	56.0	Lab
644 Glasgow Central	55.9	SNP
645 Hull East	55.5	Lab
646 Manchester Central	55.1	Lab
647 West Bromwich West	54.7	Lab
648 Glasgow East	54.6	SNP
649 Leeds Central	53.2	Lab
650 Glasgow North East	53.0	Lab

Vote share change since 2015 by party

CONSTITUENCY	% CHANGE	1ST
Top and bottom 20 constituencies only, where 2015 and 2017 can be compared		
Conservative		
1 Gordon	29.0	Con
2 Inverness, Nairn, Badenoch & Strathspey	24.6	SNP
3 Clacton	24.6	Con
4 Ochil & Perthshire South	20.8	Con
5 Ayr, Carrick & Cumnock	20.3	Con
6 Boston & Skegness	19.8	Con
7 Aberdeen South	19.3	Con
8 Ashfield	19.3	Lab
9 Banff & Buchan	19.2	Con
10 Aberdeenshire West & Kincardine	19.0	Con
11 Heywood & Middleton	18.9	Lab
12 Ross, Skye & Lochaber	18.6	SNP
13 Mansfield	18.5	Con
14 Argyll & Bute	18.3	SNP
15 Renfrewshire East	18.0	Con
16 Berwickshire, Roxburgh & Selkirk	17.9	Con
17 Stoke-On-Trent North	17.9	Lab
18 Burnley	17.5	Lab
19 Stoke-On-Trent Central	17.2	Lab
20 Linlithgow & Falkirk East	17.1	SNP
619 Ilford South	-5.0	Lab
620 Strangford	-5.1	DUP
621 Poplar & Limehouse	-5.3	Lab
622 Brentford & Isleworth	-5.3	Lab
623 Wimbledon	-5.6	Con
624 Enfield Southgate	-6.7	Lab
625 Cities Of London & Westminster	-7.5	Con
626 Harrow West	-7.8	Lab
627 Ealing Central & Acton	-7.9	Lab
628 Hammersmith	-8.2	Lab
629 Hove	-8.4	Lab
630 Westminster North	-8.5	Lab
631 Vauxhall	-8.6	Lab
632 Tooting	-8.8	Lab
633 Putney	-9.7	Con
634 Hampstead & Kilburn	-10.0	Lab
635 Kensington	-10.1	Lab
636 Chelsea & Fulham	-10.3	Con
637 Battersea	-10.8	Lab
638 Richmond Park	-13.1	Con

CONSTITUENCY	% CHANGE	1ST
Labour		
1 Bristol West	23.3	Lab
2 York Central	22.8	Lab
3 Truro & Falmouth	22.5	Con
4 Cardiff Central	22.4	Lab
5 Hove	21.8	Lab
6 Bristol South	21.7	Lab
7 Norwich South	21.7	Lab
8 Portsmouth South	21.5	Lab
9 Bristol East	21.5	Lab
10 Canterbury	20.5	Lab
11 Worthing East & Shoreham	19.8	Con
12 Camborne & Redruth	19.3	Con
13 Aberavon	19.2	Lab
14 Brighton Kemptown	19.2	Lab
15 Colchester	19.1	Con
16 Bournemouth East	18.9	Con
17 St Austell & Newquay	18.8	Con
18 Bradford East	18.7	Lab
19 Bournemouth West	18.5	Con
20 Luton South	18.2	Lab
612 Oxford West & Abingdon	-0.1	LD
613 Edinburgh North & Leith	-0.1	SNP
614 St Albans	-0.2	Con
615 Norfolk North	-0.3	LD
616 Ayrshire Central	-0.3	SNP
617 Edinburgh South West	-0.4	SNP
618 Brighton Pavilion	-0.5	Green
619 Ayrshire North & Arran	-0.5	SNP
620 Waveney	-0.9	Con
621 Paisley & Renfrewshire North	-0.9	SNP
622 Kilmarnock & Loudoun	-1.5	SNP
623 Twickenham	-2.3	LD
624 Richmond Park	-3.2	Con
625 Ayr, Carrick & Cumnock	-3.4	Con
626 Stirling	-3.4	Con
627 Dumfries & Galloway	-3.8	Con
628 Paisley & Renfrewshire South	-4.1	SNP
629 Aberdeen South	-6.2	Con
630 Renfrewshire East	-7.3	Con
631 Ochil & Perthshire South	-8.4	Con
Liberal Democrat		
1 Richmond Park	25.8	Con
2 Bath	17.6	LD
3 Oxford West & Abingdon	14.8	LD
4 Twickenham	14.7	LD

CONSTITUENCY	% CHANGE	1ST
5 St Albans	13.9	Con
6 Witney	13.7	Con
7 Vauxhall	13.7	Lab
8 Kingston & Surbiton	10.3	LD
9 Winchester	10.1	Con
10 St Ives	9.4	Con
11 Norfolk North	9.3	LD
12 Eastbourne	8.7	LD
13 Devon North	8.6	Con
14 Guildford	8.4	Con
15 Cheltenham	8.2	Con
16 Esher & Walton	7.9	Con
17 Orkney & Shetland	7.2	LD
18 Hazel Grove	6.7	Con
19 Kensington	6.6	Lab
20 Newbury	6.4	Con
610 Norwich South	-8.1	Lab
611 Chesterfield	-8.4	Lab
612 Torbay	-8.7	Con
613 Watford	-9.0	Con
614 Oldham East & Saddleworth	-9.3	Lab
615 Argyll & Bute	-9.7	SNP
616 Solihull	-10.0	Con
617 Colchester	-10.5	Con
618 Bristol West	-11.6	Lab
619 Redcar	-11.8	Lab
620 Aberdeenshire West & Kincardine	-12.8	Con
621 Ashfield	-12.9	Lab
622 Cardiff Central	-13.7	Lab
623 Berwickshire, Roxburgh & Selkirk	-14.0	Con
624 Burnley	-14.4	Lab
625 Ross, Skye & Lochaber	-15.0	SNP
626 Hornsey & Wood Green	-15.7	Lab
627 Inverness, Nairn, Badenoch & Strathspey	-19.0	SNP
628 Gordon	-21.1	Con
629 Bradford East	-27.7	Lab

Green

1 Brighton Pavilion	10.4	Green
2 Isle Of Wight	4.0	Con
3 Glasgow North	3.5	SNP
4 Buckingham	2.5	Speaker
5 Down North	1.1	Ind
6 Skipton & Ripon	0.7	Con
7 Warwickshire North	0.1	Con
8 Hertfordshire North East	0.0	Con
9 Harrow East	-0.2	Con
10 Gainsborough	-0.2	Con
11 Leicestershire North West	-0.2	Con

CONSTITUENCY	% CHANGE	1ST
12 Cannock Chase	-0.2	Con
13 Wyre Forest	-0.3	Con
14 Telford	-0.3	Con
15 Dorset South	-0.3	Con
16 Staffordshire South	-0.3	Con
17 Tonbridge & Malling	-0.3	Con
18 West Bromwich East	-0.3	Lab
19 Stafford	-0.4	Con
20 Sutton & Cheam	-0.4	Con
431 Tottenham	-6.7	Lab
432 Bethnal Green & Bow	-6.7	Lab
433 Manchester Central	-6.8	Lab
434 Newcastle Upon Tyne East	-6.9	Lab
435 Dulwich & West Norwood	-6.9	Lab
436 Camberwell & Peckham	-7.2	Lab
437 Truro & Falmouth	-7.2	Con
438 Manchester Gorton	-7.5	Lab
439 Sheffield Central	-7.8	Lab
440 Nottingham East	-8.1	Lab
441 Oxford East	-8.3	Lab
442 Liverpool Riverside	-8.8	Lab
443 Hackney South & Shoreditch	-8.8	Lab
444 Bristol South	-8.9	Lab
445 Holborn & St Pancras	-9.4	Lab
446 Lewisham Deptford	-9.5	Lab
447 Bath	-9.7	LD
448 Hackney North & Stoke Newington	-10.0	Lab
449 Norwich South	-11.0	Lab
450 Bristol West	-14.0	Lab

Ukip

1 E Kilbride, Strathaven & Lesmahagow	-0.9	SNP
2 Glasgow South West	-1.0	SNP
3 Kirkcaldy & Cowdenbeath	-1.2	Lab
4 Glasgow East	-1.2	SNP
5 Rutherglen & Hamilton West	-1.3	Lab
6 Motherwell & Wishaw	-1.4	SNP
7 Lanark & Hamilton East	-1.5	SNP
8 Hornsey & Wood Green	-1.5	Lab
9 Falkirk	-1.7	SNP
10 Tooting	-2.3	Lab
11 Battersea	-2.5	Lab
12 Finchley & Golders Green	-2.5	Con
13 Streatham	-2.6	Lab
14 Tottenham	-2.6	Lab
15 Brent Central	-2.9	Lab
16 Ealing Southall	-3.0	Lab
17 Islington North	-3.3	Lab
18 Hammersmith	-3.4	Lab
19 Harrow West	-3.5	Lab

CONSTITUENCY	% CHANGE	1ST
20 Richmond Park	-3.5	Con
358 Folkestone & Hythe	-18.4	Con
359 Cambridgeshire North East	-18.4	Con
360 Dudley North	-18.5	Lab
361 Isle Of Wight	-18.6	Con
362 West Bromwich West	-18.8	Lab
363 Hornchurch & Upminster	-19.1	Con
364 Basildon South & Thurrock East	-19.8	Con
365 Bradford South	-19.8	Lab
366 Mansfield	-19.8	Con
367 Great Grimsby	-20.3	Lab
368 Rother Valley	-20.6	Lab
369 Thanet North	-21.2	Con
370 Rotherham	-21.4	Lab
371 Dagenham & Rainham	-22.8	Lab
372 Rochester & Strood	-25.1	Con
373 Heywood & Middleton	-25.7	Lab
374 Castle Point	-25.9	Con
375 Boston & Skegness	-26.1	Con
376 Thanet South	-26.4	Con
377 Clacton	-36.8	Con

Scottish National

1 Berwickshire, Roxburgh & Selkirk	-3.8	Con
2 Edinburgh East	-6.7	SNP
3 Edinburgh North & Leith	-6.9	SNP
4 Edinburgh South West	-7.4	SNP
5 Glasgow Central	-7.8	SNP
6 Ross, Skye & Lochaber	-7.9	SNP
7 Fife North East	-8.1	SNP
8 Dumfriesshire, Clydesdale & Tweeddale	-8.2	Con
9 Perth & Perthshire North	-8.2	SNP
10 Argyll & Bute	-8.3	SNP
11 Orkney & Shetland	-8.8	LD
12 Stirling	-8.9	Con
13 Dumfries & Galloway	-9.0	Con
14 Aberdeenshire West & Kincardine	-9.1	Con
15 Renfrewshire East	-9.3	Con
16 Dunbartonshire East	-10.0	LD
17 Aberdeen South	-10.2	Con
18 Inverness, Nairn, Badenoch & Strathspey	-10.2	SNP
19 Paisley & Renfrewshire South	-10.3	SNP
20 Edinburgh West	-10.3	LD
40 Glasgow North East	-15.9	Lab
41 Kirkcaldy & Cowdenbeath	-16.0	Lab
42 Ayrshire Central	-16.0	SNP
43 Midlothian	-16.2	Lab
44 Dunbartonshire West	-16.2	SNP

CONSTITUENCY	% CHANGE	1ST
45 Lanark & Hamilton East	-16.2	SNP
46 Cumbernauld, Kilsyth & Kirkintilloch E	-16.3	SNP
47 Airdrie & Shotts	-16.3	SNP
48 Glasgow South West	-16.5	SNP
49 Inverclyde	-16.6	SNP
50 E Kilbride, Strathaven & Lesmahagow	-16.8	SNP
51 Livingston	-16.8	SNP
52 Dundee East	-16.9	SNP
53 Glenrothes	-17.0	SNP
54 Caithness, Sutherland & Easter Ross	-17.1	LD
55 Coatbridge, Chryston & Bellshill	-17.5	Lab
56 Motherwell & Wishaw	-18.0	SNP
57 Glasgow East	-18.1	SNP
58 Falkirk	-18.8	SNP
59 Banff & Buchan	-21.1	Con

Plaid Cymru

1 Blaenau Gwent	12.3	Lab
2 Dwyfor Meirionnydd	4.3	PC
3 Ceredigion	1.6	PC
4 Carmarthen East & Dinefwr	0.9	PC
5 Montgomeryshire	0.4	Con
6 Preseli Pembrokeshire	0.2	Con
7 Caerphilly	-0.2	Lab
8 Torfaen	-0.4	Lab
9 Delyn	-1.1	Lab
10 Carmarthen W & Pembrokeshire S	-1.1	Con
11 Newport East	-1.1	Lab
12 Cardiff North	-1.2	Lab
13 Pontypridd	-1.2	Lab
14 Monmouth	-1.3	Con
15 Brecon & Radnorshire	-1.3	Con
16 Alyn & Deeside	-1.3	Lab
17 Merthyr Tydfil & Rhymney	-1.3	Lab
18 Vale Of Glamorgan	-1.3	Con
19 Newport West	-1.5	Lab
20 Aberconwy	-1.9	Con
21 Swansea West	-2.3	Lab
22 Cardiff Central	-2.5	Lab
23 Ogmore	-2.6	Lab
24 Clwyd West	-2.6	Con
25 Wrexham	-2.6	Lab
26 Bridgend	-2.9	Lab
27 Vale Of Clwyd	-3.0	Lab
28 Cynon Valley	-3.1	Lab
29 Ynys Mon	-3.1	Lab
30 Arfon	-3.1	PC
31 Cardiff South & Penarth	-3.1	Lab
32 Islwyn	-3.1	Lab
33 Aberavon	-3.3	Lab

CONSTITUENCY	% CHANGE	1ST	CONSTITUENCY	% CHANGE	1ST
34 Gower	-3.5	Lab	4 Strangford	-2.9	DUP
35 Neath	-4.2	Lab	5 Antrim North	-4.9	DUP
36 Clwyd South	-4.2	Lab	6 Down South	-5.4	SF
37 Cardiff West	-4.4	Lab	7 Belfast South	-5.6	DUP
38 Rhondda	-4.7	Lab	8 Antrim East	-7.0	DUP
39 Llanelli	-4.7	Lab	9 Londonderry East	-7.7	DUP
40 Swansea East	-5.6	Lab	10 Ulster Mid	-9.0	SF
			11 Tyrone West	-10.7	SF
Democratic Unionist			12 Upper Bann	-12.5	DUP
			13 Newry & Armagh	-24.4	SF
1 Antrim East	21.2	DUP			
2 Strangford	17.7	DUP	**APNI**		
3 Antrim North	15.6	DUP			
4 Down North	14.5	Ind	1 Belfast South	1.0	DUP
5 Ulster Mid	13.6	SF	2 Strangford	0.9	DUP
6 Lagan Valley	11.7	DUP	3 Upper Bann	0.8	DUP
7 Upper Bann	10.9	DUP	4 Down North	0.7	Ind
8 Tyrone West	9.5	SF	5 Newry & Armagh	0.7	SF
9 Down South	9.3	SF	6 Antrim East	0.6	DUP
10 Belfast South	8.2	DUP	7 Ulster Mid	0.4	SF
11 Antrim South	8.1	DUP	8 Fermanagh & South Tyrone	0.4	SF
12 Belfast East	6.4	DUP	9 Tyrone West	0.1	SF
13 Londonderry East	5.8	DUP	10 Antrim North	0.0	DUP
14 Belfast West	5.6	SF	11 Belfast West	0.0	SF
15 Foyle	3.7	SF	12 Down South	-0.2	SF
16 Belfast North	-0.8	DUP	13 Foyle	-0.4	SF
			14 Londonderry East	-1.4	DUP
Sinn Fein			15 Belfast North	-1.9	DUP
			16 Antrim South	-2.4	DUP
1 Belfast West	12.5	SF	17 Lagan Valley	-2.8	DUP
2 Down South	11.4	SF	18 Belfast East	-6.8	DUP
3 Foyle	8.2	SF			
4 Belfast North	7.8	DUP	**SDLP**		
5 Tyrone West	7.2	SF			
6 Newry & Armagh	6.8	SF	1 Belfast South	1.3	DUP
7 Londonderry East	6.8	DUP	2 Lagan Valley	1.3	DUP
8 Ulster Mid	5.8	SF	3 Belfast East	0.1	DUP
9 Antrim South	5.2	DUP	4 Down North	0.0	Ind
10 Antrim North	4.0	DUP	5 Upper Bann	-0.4	DUP
11 Upper Bann	3.4	DUP	6 Fermanagh & South Tyrone	-0.5	SF
12 Belfast South	2.5	DUP	7 Strangford	-0.7	DUP
13 Antrim East	2.4	DUP	8 Londonderry East	-1.5	DUP
14 Fermanagh & South Tyrone	1.8	SF	9 Antrim East	-1.5	DUP
15 Lagan Valley	0.6	DUP	10 Antrim North	-1.7	DUP
16 Down North	0.6	Ind	11 Ulster Mid	-2.6	SF
17 Strangford	0.2	DUP	12 Antrim South	-2.7	DUP
18 Belfast East	0.0	DUP	13 Belfast West	-2.8	SF
			14 Tyrone West	-3.7	SF
Ulster Unionist			15 Belfast North	-3.7	DUP
			16 Down South	-7.2	SF
1 Lagan Valley	1.6	DUP	17 Newry & Armagh	-7.2	SF
2 Fermanagh & South Tyrone	-0.9	SF	18 Foyle	-8.6	SF
3 Antrim South	-1.9	DUP			

MPs who stood down before the election

CONSERVATIVE
Burns, Simon Chelmsford
Garnier, Edward Harborough
Haselhurst, Alan Saffron Walden
Howarth, Gerald Aldershot
Lilley, Peter Hitchin & Harpenden
Lumley, Karen Redditch
Mackintosh, David Northampton S
Osborne, George Tatton
Pickles, Eric Brentwood & Ongar
Turner, Andrew Isle of Wight
Tyrie, Andrew Chichester
Watkinson, Angela Hornchurch
& Upminster

INDEPENDENT
Carswell, Douglas Clacton
McGarry, Natalie Glasgow E
Thomson, Michelle Edinburgh W

LABOUR
Allen, Graham Nottingham N
Anderson, Dave Blaydon
Blenkinsop, Tom Middlesborough
S & Cleveland E
Burnham, Andy Leigh
Dowd, Jim Lewisham W & Penge
Dugher, Michael Barnsley E
Glass, Pat Durham NW

Johnson, Alan Hull W & Hessle
Mactaggart, Fiona Slough
Marris, Rob Wolverhampton SW
Rotheram, Steve Liverpool Walton
Smith, Andrew Oxford E
Stuart, Gisela Birmingham
Edgbaston
Wright, Iain Hartlepool

LIBERAL DEMOCRAT
Pugh, John Southport

SINN FEIN
Doherty, Pat Tyrone W

Defeated MPs

CONSERVATIVE
Ansell, Caroline Eastbourne
Barwell, Gavin Croydon Central
Berry, James Kingston & Surbiton
Bingham, Andrew High Peak
Blackwood, Nicola Oxford W
& Abingdon
Borwick, Victoria Kensington
Brazier, Julian Canterbury
Burrowes, David Enfield Southgate
Carmichael, Neil Stroud
Colvile, Oliver Plymouth Sutton
& Devonport
Davies, Byron Gower
Davies, James Vale Of Clwyd
Drummond, Flick Portsmouth S
Ellison, Jane Battersea
Evans, Graham Weaver Vale
Fuller, Richard Bedford
Gummer, Ben Ipswich
Hopkins, Kris Keighley
Howlett, Ben Bath
Jackson, Stewart Peterborough
Kirby, Simon Brighton Kemptown
Leslie, Charlotte Bristol NW
Mathias, Tania Twickenham
McCartney, Jason Colne Valley
McCartney, Karl Lincoln
Mowat, David Warrington S
Nuttall, David Bury N
Solloway, Amanda Derby N

Timpson, Edward Crewe
& Nantwich
Wharton, James Stockton S
White, Chris Warwick
& Leamington
Williams, Craig Cardiff N
Wilson, Rob Reading E

LABOUR
Danczuk, Simon Rochdale
Engel, Natascha Derbyshire NE
Flello, Robert Stoke-On-Trent S
Meale, Alan Mansfield
Winnick, David Walsall N

LIBERAL DEMOCRAT
Clegg, Nick Sheffield Hallam
Mulholland, Greg Leeds NW
Olney, Sarah Richmond Park
Williams, Mark Ceredigion

SCOTTISH NATIONAL
Ahmed-Sheikh, Tasmina
Ochil & Perthshire S
Arkless, Richard Dumfries
& Galloway
Boswell, Philip Coatbridge,
Chryston & Bellshill
Donaldson, Stuart Aberdeenshire
W & Kincardine
Ferrier, Margaret Rutherglen

& Hamilton W
Kerevan, George East Lothian
Kerr, Calum Berwickshire,
Roxburgh & Selkirk
McCaig, Callum Aberdeen S
McLaughlin, Anne Glasgow NE
Monaghan, Paul Caithness,
Sutherland & Easter Ross
Mullin, Roger Kirkcaldy &
Cowdenbeath
Nicolson, John Dunbartonshire E
Oswald, Kirsten Renfrewshire E
Paterson, Steven Stirling
Robertson, Angus Moray
Salmond, Alex Gordon
Thompson, Owen Midlothian
Weir, Mike Angus
Whiteford, Eilidh Banff & Buchan
Wilson, Corri Ayr, Carrick
& Cumnock

SOCIAL DEMOCRATIC AND
LABOUR
Durkan, Mark Foyle
McDonnell, Alasdair Belfast S
Ritchie, Margaret Down South

ULSTER UNIONIST
Elliott, Tom Fermanagh
& South Tyrone
Kinahan, Danny Antrim S

By-elections 2015-17

Oldham West & Royton

Held on December 3, 2015. Caused by death of Rt Hon Michael Meacher.

		Electorate	Turnout %	Change from 2015 %
		69,033	40.1	
Jim McMahon	Lab	17,209	62.1	7.3
John Bickley	Ukip	6,487	23.4	2.8
James Daly	C	2,596	9.4	-9.6
Jane Brophy	LD	1,024	3.7	0.0
Simeon Hart	Green	249	0.9	-1.0
Sir Oink A-Lot	Loony	141	0.5	–
Majority		10,722		

Tooting

Held on June 16, 2016. Caused by resignation of Sadiq Khan.

		74,701	42.8	
Rosena Allin-Khan	Lab	17,894	55.9	8.7
Dan Watkins	C	11,537	36.1	-5.8
Esther Obiri-Darko	Green	830	2.6	-1.5
Alexander Glassbrook	LD	820	2.6	-1.4
Elizabeth Jones	Ukip	507	1.6	-1.3
Des Coke	CPP	164	0.5	–
Majority		6,357		

Richmond Park

Held on December 1, 2016. Caused by resignation of Zac Goldsmith.

		77,243	53.4	
Sarah Olney	LD	20,510	49.7	30.4
Zac Goldsmith	Ind*	18,638	45.1	-13.1
Christian Wolmar	Lab	1,515	3.7	-8.7
Howling Laud Hope	Loony	184	0.4	–
Fiona Syms	Ind	173	0.4	–
Dominic Stockford	CPA	164	0.4	–
Majority		1,872		

*Zac Goldsmith stood as the Conservative candidate in 2015

Stoke-on-Trent Central

Held on February 23, 2017. Caused by resignation of Tristram Hunt.

		55,572	38.1	
Gareth Snell	Lab	7,853	37.1	-2.2
Paul Nuttall	Ukip	5,233	24.7	2.1
Jack Brereton	C	5,154	24.3	1.8
Zulfiqar Ali	LD	2,083	9.8	5.7
Adam Colclough	Green	294	1.4	-2.2
Barbara Fielding	Ind	137	0.6	–
Incredible Flying Brick	Loony	127	0.6	–
David Furness	BNP	124	0.6	–
Godfrey Davies	CPA	109	0.5	–
Majority		2,620		

Sheffield, Brightside & Hillsborough

Held on 5 May 2016. Caused by death of Harry Harpham.

		Electorate	Turnout %	Change from 2015 %
		68,439	33.0	
Gill Furniss	Lab	14,087	62.4	5.8
Steve Winstone	Ukip	4,497	19.9	-2.2
Mohammed Shaffaq	LD	1,385	6.1	1.6
Spencer Pitfield	C	1,267	5.6	-5.4
Christine Gilligan Kubo	Green	938	4.2	-0.1
Stevie Manion	Yorkshire	349	1.5	–
Majority		9,590		

Batley & Spen

Held on October 20, 2016. Caused by death of Jo Cox.

		79,781	25.6	
Tracy Brabin	Lab	17,506	85.8	42.6
Therese Hirst	ED	969	4.8	–
David Furness	BNP	548	2.7	–
Gary Kitchin	Ind	517	2.5	–
Anti Corbyn	By-election	241	1.2	–
Jack Buckby	No/Yes	220	1.1	–
Henry Mayhew	Ind	153	0.8	–
Ali-Waqas Khan	Ind	118	0.6	–
Majority		16,537		

Sleaford & North Hykeham

Held on December 8, 2016. Caused by resignation of Stephen Phillips.

		88,712	37.0	
Caroline Johnson	C	17,570	46.9	-2.7
Victoria Ayling	Ukip	4,426	13.5	-2.2
Ross Pepper	LD	3,606	11.0	5.3
Jim Clarke	Lab	3,363	10.2	-7.0
Marianne Overton	Lincs Ind	2,892	8.8	3.6
Sarah Stock	Ind	462	1.4	–
The Iconic Arty-Pole	Loony	200	0.6	–
Paul Coyne	ND	186	0.6	–
Majority		13,144		

Source: House of Commons Library

Ogmore

Held on 5 May 2016. Caused by resignation of Huw Irranca-Davies.

		Electorate	Turnout %	Change from 2015 %
		55,027	42.4	
Christopher Elmore	Lab	12,166	52.2	-0.8
Glenda Davies	Ukip	3,808	16.3	1.0
Abi Thomas	PC	3,683	15.8	5.7
Alex Williams	C	2,956	12.7	-3.3
Janet Ellard	LD	702	3.0	0.0
Majority		8,358		

Witney

Held on October 20, 2016. Caused by resignation of David Cameron.

		82,277	46.7	
Robert Courts	C	17,313	45.0	-12.3
Elizabeth Leffman	LD	11,611	30.2	23.8
Duncan Enright	Lab	5,765	15.0	-1.4
Larry Sanders	Green	1,363	3.5	-1.3
Dickie Bird	Ukip	1,354	3.5	-5.2
Helen Salisbury	NHAP	433	1.1	-3.7
Daniel Skidmore	Ind	151	0.4	–
Alasdair De Voil	Loony	129	0.3	–
Majority		5,702		

Copeland

Held on February 23, 2017. Caused by resignation of Jamieson Reed.

		60,602	51.3	
Trudy Harrison	C	13,748	44.3	8.5
Gillian Troughton	Lab	11,601	37.3	-4.9
Rebecca Hanson	LD	2,252	7.2	3.8
Fiona Mills	Ukip	2,025	6.5	-9.0
Michael Guest	Ind	811	2.6	-1.3
Jack Lenox	Green	515	1.7	–
Roy Ivinson	Ind	116	0.4	–
Majority		2,147		

- Results omit candidates who polled fewer than 100 votes
- Key to abbreviations is on page 60

The new parliament

THE SKY WON'T FALL IN IF PARLIAMENT IS HUNG

by Dennis Kavanagh

There is a well-established British belief that one-party majority government is normal and beneficial. Its supporters praise it for its ability to provide strong and stable government. Coalition government is regarded as a poor second and a minority one as worst of all. Some Conservatives already wish that the post-election deal with the Democratic Unionist Party, with its sectarian and illiberal views on social issues, had not taken place.

Yet the idea that single-party majority government in the UK is the norm is open to challenge. The Constitution Unit at University College London has noted that only half the 20 governments in the 20th century were one-party majority. Five were coalitions, including the wartime governments of Lloyd George and Churchill, and another five were minority governments. Two of the last three general elections have resulted in hung parliaments and that in 2015 produced a Conservative majority of 12.

Perhaps it is time to accept that the odds on hung parliaments have shortened and we need to look more seriously at making them work. Hung parliaments have become more likely because of two related developments. One has been the decline in support for the Conservative and Labour parties. Their 90 per cent plus vote share in the 1950s fell to an average of less than 70 per cent between 1983 and 2015. Their share of seats in the Commons also fell because of the rise of third parties, notably the Liberal Democrats until 2010 and the SNP in 2015. These trends made it less likely for a general election to produce a Commons with a clear majority for one party. Hence the irony of 2017: it saw the return of two-party politics (more than 82 per cent of the vote) but no one-party majority.

Whitehall has not been idle in the face of these developments. In 2010 the Cabinet Manual included a section on the procedures for a hung parliament and officials facilitated the smooth formation of the coalition. In 2014 a committee report on coalition government recommended the provision of official support to the parties involved in negotiations and a 12-day gap between an election and the first meeting of the new parliament.

The traditional response to a hung parliament has been for the government to call another election and hope to get a clear majority. The Liberal prime minister HH Asquith tried this twice in 1910 and failed on both occasions. Harold Wilson in 1966 (defending a majority of three) called an election and did better but when he tried it again in 1974 he ended with a majority of three. The Fixed-term Parliaments Act, however, now severely limits the scope for a prime minister to call an election. Requiring a two-thirds majority (435 MPs) to vote in favour of an early election it in effect needs both Labour and Conservative parties to vote for one. It is difficult to envisage circumstances in which both will think it advantageous.

Another option is to form a coalition, as David Cameron did in 2010, the first in peacetime since 1931. But even if the numbers add up, as they just about do for the Conservatives and the DUP, the abrupt collapse in support and longer-term damage to the Liberal Democrats after their entry into coalition in 2010 is likely to put off other small parties.

We may now have to look to minority rule backed by a "confidence and supply" agreement as the more likely response in a hung parliament. Under this arrangement the minor party agrees to support the government on no confidence votes, the Budget and supply motions. This operated in the Lib-Lab pact between March 1977 and May 1978.

For lessons in coping we should look to Europe, where single-party majority rule is unusual because of the plurality of parties and the proportional electoral systems. Forming a government can sometimes be so complex that it can take several months for one to be constructed, as in Spain last year. The parties have developed their own practices and conventions to cope with the lack of a single-party majority. In Denmark, Norway and the Netherlands, for example, a principle of negative parliamentarianism allows the formation of a minority government. Instead of requiring a positive vote of confidence from the legislature the government can remain in office until a vote of censure is carried against it.

Nearer to home, Scotland and Wales have experimented with coalition and minority rule without the sky falling in. One party often prefers to rule in a minority rather than share power with another party.

There are four conditions that may improve the durability of a minority government. One is the goodwill it gains if it is a first-time government. Second, a government will be well placed if new MPs believe they owe their election to the leader's popularity: a "coat-tails effect". Third, it helps if the ruling party is united in voting on key issues. A final condition is if the prime minister can credibly threaten opposition parties with an election in which they are likely to lose ground.

Mrs May's government meets none of these conditions. It is a second-time government and has just lost its majority in an election that it chose to call. Far from there being a coat-tails effect, 13 Tory seats were lost and others made more marginal. The party and Cabinet are divided on Brexit, the issue that will dominate the parliament, and disloyalty and cussedness now seems to be part of Conservative DNA. Finally, after the June debacle, ministers want to avoid another election at all costs.

The downsides of the minority option are well known. The pressure on the government means that key players are the chief whip, struggling to assemble a majority, and the chancellor, who is expected to open the purse strings. Harold Wilson, in March 1974, opportunistically avoided necessary tough decisions on the economy to prepare the ground for an election in October. It also creates uncertainty for business and markets because the government's life span is so unpredictable. The same faults were apparent when governments had small or uncertain majorities, like Attlee's in 1950, Wilson's in 1964 and 1974, and Major's from 1995 as a result of by-election losses and defections.

What to do in these unpropitious circumstances? Far from being strong and stable a minority government must learn to accept defeats. The 1974-79 Labour governments of Wilson and Callaghan lost more than 50 bills but survived; it helped that none were on a vote of no confidence. The Westminster systems in Canada, Australia and New Zealand are also familiar with minority governments that survive defeats. It can be done. Second, shrewd party managers will reduce the need for deals and stitch-ups with minor parties and bloody-minded MPs by avoiding as much legislation as possible. There is much that government can do without passing more laws.

The main hurdle here is the unavoidable Brexit legislation, but the Labour opposition is perhaps as divided as the government.

Above all, a minority government is more likely to endure the more it does not behave like a majority. If the government survives until 2022 then Westminster and Whitehall will have probably adapted with new rules and practices and perhaps more consensual patterns of behaviour. Such pressure will only increase if it is followed by another hung parliament.

Dennis Kavanagh is emeritus professor of politics at Liverpool University

Her Majesty's Government

Prime Minister, First Lord of the Treasury and Minister for the Civil Service	**Theresa May**
Chancellor of the Exchequer and First Secretary of State	**Philip Hammond**
First Secretary of State and Minister for the Cabinet Office	**Damian Green**
Secretary of State for the Home Department	**Amber Rudd**
Secretary of State for Foreign and Commonwealth Affairs	**Boris Johnson**
Secretary of State for Defence	**Michael Fallon**
Lord Chancellor and Secretary of State for Justice	**David Lidington**
Secretary of State for Education	**Justine Greening**
Secretary of State for Exiting the European Union	**David Davis**
Secretary of State for International Trade and President of the Board of Trade	**Dr Liam Fox**
Secretary of State for Business, Energy and Industrial Strategy	**Greg Clark**
Secretary of State for Health	**Jeremy Hunt**
Secretary of State for Work and Pensions	**David Gauke**
Secretary of State for Transport	**Chris Grayling**
Secretary of State for Communities and Local Government	**Sajid Javid**
Lord President of the Council and Leader of the House of Commons	**Andrea Leadsom**
Leader of the House of Lords and Lord Privy Seal	**Baroness Evans of Bowes Park**
Secretary of State for Scotland	**David Mundell**
Secretary of State for Wales	**Alun Cairns**
Secretary of State for Northern Ireland	**James Brokenshire**
Secretary of State for Environment, Food and Rural Affairs	**Michael Gove**
Secretary of State for International Development	**Priti Patel**
Secretary of State for Digital, Culture, Media and Sport	**Karen Bradley**
Chancellor of the Duchy of Lancaster	**Sir Patrick McLoughlin**

General election 2017: results by constituency

ABBREVIATIONS OF PARTIES WITH MPS AFTER THE GENERAL ELECTION IN 2017
C Conservative; **Lab** Labour; **Lab Co-op** Labour and Co-operative; **LD** Liberal Democrat;
PC Plaid Cymru; **SNP** Scottish National Party; **Green** Green; **DUP** Democratic Unionist Party;
SF Sinn Fein; **Ind** Independent; **Speaker** The Speaker

MINOR PARTIES
Active Dem Movement for Active Democracy; **AD** Apolitical Democrats; **Alliance** Alliance; **AWP** Animal Welfare Party; **Blue** Blue Revolution; **BNP** British National Party; **Bradford** Better For Bradford; **Citizens** Citizens Independent Social Thought Alliance; **Comm Lge** Communist League; **Compass** Compass Party; **Concordia** Concordia; **CPA** Christian Peoples Alliance; **DDI** Demos Direct Initiative; **Elvis** Church of the Militant Elvis; **Eng Dem** English Democrats; **Friends** Friends Party; **GM Homeless** Greater Manchester Homeless Voice; **Good** The Common Good; **Green Soc** Alliance for Green Socialism; **Humanity** Humanity; **Ind** Independent; **JACP** Justice and Anti-Corruption Party; **Just** The Just Political Party; **Lib** Liberal; **Libertarian** Libertarian Party; **Loony** Monster Raving Loony Party; **Money** Money Free Party; **ND** No description; **NE Party** The North East Party; **NHAP** National Health Action Party; **North** North of England Community Alliance; **Open** Open Borders Party; **Patria** Patria; **PBP** People Before Profit; **Peace** The Peace Party; **Pirate** Pirate Party UK; **Populist** Populist Party; **Radical** The Radical Party; **Realist** The Realists' Party; **Rebooting** Rebooting Democracy; **Referendum** Scotland's Independence Referendum Party; **SCP** Scottish Christian Party; **S New** Something New; **Soc Dem** Social Democratic Party; **Soc Lab** Socialist Labour Party; **Southampton** Southampton Independents; **Southend** Southend Independent Association; **Sovereign** Independent Sovereign Democratic Britain; **Space** Space Navies Party; **SPGB** Socialist Party of Great Britain; **TUV** Traditional Unionist Voice; **Ukip** UK Independence; **Wessex Reg** Wessex Regionalist; **Women** Women's Equality Party; **Worth** The New Society of Worth; **WP** Workers' Party; **WRP** Workers' Revolutionary Party; **WVPTFP** War Veteran's Pro-Traditional Family Party; **Yorkshire** Yorkshire First/The Yorkshire Party; **Young** Young People's Party UK

Abbreviations of additional parties that stood in by-elections 2015-17:
BP Elvis Bus-Pass Elvis Party; **By-election** By-election Protest; **CPP** Christian Peoples Party; **Eccentric** Eccentric Party of Great Britain; **Eng Ind** English Independence; **GMBE** Give Me Back Elmo; **Immigrants** Immigrants Political Party; **Lincs Ind** Lincolnshire Independent; **Love** One Love Party; **No/Yes** No to Terrorism, Yes to Britain

EU REFERENDUM RESULT
The estimates of how each constituency in England, Scotland and Wales voted in the EU referendum were provided by Chris Hanretty, professor of politics at Royal Holloway, University of London. The referendum was counted at local authority level, rather than at constituency level, except in Northern Ireland. Although some local authorities have released more detailed information, not all have done so. For full details of the estimates see "A real interpolation and the UK's referendum on EU membership" by Chris Hanretty, in the *Journal Of Elections, Public Opinion And Parties.*

Aberavon

LABOUR HOLD MAJORITY 16,761 (50.4%)

STEPHEN KINNOCK
BORN Jan 1, 1970
MP 2015-

Son of former Labour leader Neil Kinnock and husband of former Danish prime minister Helle Thorning-Schmidt. Became Labour member aged 15. Dir, WEF 2009-12. Dir, British Council 2005-08. Champions local steel-making; member: APPG, steel and metal-related industries; chairman, steel 2020 sub-cttee. Campaigned for Remain, voted to trigger Article 50. Yet to rebel. Corbyn sceptic. Member, Consensus. Honorary associate, National Secular Society. Married, two daughters. Ed: Drayton Manor HS; Queens' Coll, Cambridge (BA modern languages); Coll of Europe.

Electorate	Turnout %	from 2015 %	Change
49,891	66.68		
*S Kinnock Lab	22,662	68.12	+19.22
S Vidal C	5,901	17.74	+5.87
A Bennison PC	2,761	8.30	-3.32
C Jones Ukip	1,345	4.04	-11.73
C Phillips LD	599	1.80	-2.63

CHALLENGERS
Sadie Vidal (C) Marketing manager, UK Digital Solutions. Deputy chairwoman, Conservative Future Wales. Cllr, Bridgend County BC 2017-. Contested Welsh Assembly 2016. **Andrew Bennison** (PC) Former Tata Steel worker, now at BAE Systems. **Caroline Jones** (Ukip) Former teacher. Contested: Bridgend 2015; European election 2014. Elected to Welsh Assembly 2016. Ukip Wales health spokesperson.

Former Tory, defected to Ukip 2013. **Cen Phillips** (LD) Left school at 16. Spent 20 years working in support role, Swansea University. Contested: Aberavon local election 2017; Llanelli 2015. Europhile.

CONSTITUENCY PROFILE
A working-class area in industrial South Wales where manufacturing makes up more than a quarter of employment. The seat also contains the huge Tata steelworks in Port Talbot. This constituency has been represented by Labour since 1922, including by Ramsay MacDonald during his first term as prime minister.

EU REFERENDUM RESULT
60.1% Leave   Remain 39.9%

Aberconwy

CONSERVATIVE HOLD MAJORITY 635 (2.0%)

GUTO BEBB
BORN Oct 9, 1968
MP 2010-

Business consultant, founded an economic consultancy. Business development dir, Innovas Wales 2006-10. Co-founded a bookshop that he ran with his wife. Former party chairman, Caernarfon Plaid Cymru; defected to Tories over Europe. EU reformer who helped to drive I Want a Referendum Campaign after Lisbon treaty signed. Eventually campaigned for Remain but voted to trigger Article 50. Contested: Conwy 2005; Welsh Assembly 2003; Ogmore by-election 2002. Parly under-sec, Wales 2016-; Treasury whip 2016-17. Handful of minor rebellions during coalition years.

Electorate	Turnout %	from 2015 %	Change
45,251	71.05		
*G Bebb C	14,337	44.59	+3.09
E Owen Lab	13,702	42.62	+14.38
W Jones PC	3,170	9.86	-1.87
S Lesiter-Burgess LD	941	2.93	-1.69

Member: Conservative Friends of Israel; Open Europe. Member, 1922 exec cttee 2011-14. Fluent Welsh speaker. Married, five children. Ed: Ysgol Syr Hugh Owen; University of Wales, Aberystwyth (BA history).

CHALLENGERS
Emily Owen (Lab) Cllr, Conwy County BC 2016-17; youngest council member. Volunteer, the Refugee Crisis Foundation, Calais. Jeremy Corbyn supporter. **Wyn Jones** (PC) Photography entrepreneur who founded his

own firm. Cllr, Conwy County BC 2001-. **Sarah Lesiter-Burgess** (LD) Employment law adviser. Established human resources consultancy 2004. Cllr, Glan Conwy Comm C. Contested: Welsh Assembly 2016; Aberconwy 2015.

CONSTITUENCY PROFILE
This Welsh seat contains coastal as well as rural Welsh-speaking areas. It has been held by the Conservatives since 2010 when Labour-voting Bagnor was removed from the seat. Nearly a quarter of its constituents are retired. This is a relatively poor constituency, where tourism is a significant employer.

EU REFERENDUM RESULT
52.2% Leave   Remain 47.8%

Aberdeen North

SNP HOLD MAJORITY 4,139 (11.3%)

KIRSTY BLACKMAN
BORN Mar 20, 1986
MP 2015-

Career politician. Cllr, Aberdeen CC 2007-15. SNP spokeswoman, House of Lords 2015-17. Previously parly asst to: Mark McDonald MSP, Brian Adam MSP, Brian Don MSP. Censured by Commons clerks for bringing children to select cttee meeting 2016. Champions gender equality and working mothers. Europhile, voted against Article 50. Yet to rebel against party whip. Married, one son, one daughter. Ed: Robert Gordon's Coll.

CHALLENGERS
Orr Vinegold (Lab) Brand management, L'Oréal 2012-15. Head of marketing, Savsé

	Electorate	Turnout %	from 2015 %	Change
	62,130	59.16		
*K Blackman SNP	15,170	41.27	-15.16	
O Vinegold Lab	11,031	30.01	+4.07	
G O'Keeffe C	8,341	22.69	+10.62	
I Davidson LD	1,693	4.61	-0.06	
R Durkin Ind	522	1.42		

2016-17. **Grace O'Keeffe** (C) Office manager to Alexander Burnett MSP 2016-. Conservative campaign manager: Aberdeenshire West 2015-16; Aberdeenshire West & Kincardine 2014-15. Helped to co-ordinate Better Together campaign in northeast Scotland. **Isobel Davidson** (LD) Wildlife consultant. Dir, Museum of Scottish Lighthouses. Cllr, Aberdeenshire CC 2007-. Contested Scottish parliament 2016. **Richard Durkin** (Ind)

Offshore surveyor. Spent 18 years fighting a legal battle over his credit rating with HFC bank.

CONSTITUENCY PROFILE
Returned Labour MPs from 1935 to 2015. Aberdeen University makes for a substantial student vote. Aberdeen Harbour within the seat provides employment through servicing the North Sea oil industry. More than 35 per cent of households are in social housing and homeownership rates are low. The seat is relatively diverse compared with most other Scottish seats, having a large number of EU residents.

EU REFERENDUM RESULT
43.1% Leave   Remain 56.9%

Aberdeen South

CONSERVATIVE GAIN MAJORITY 4,752 (10.7%)

ROSS THOMSON
BORN Sep 21, 1987
MP 2017-

Former retail sector customer adviser. Dir, Friends of Hazlehead Park. MSP, NE Scotland 2016-17; Conservative spokesman, higher education. Spearheaded Vote Leave Scotland. Contested: Aberdeen S 2015; Gordon 2010. Serial Holyrood candidate: Aberdeen South & North Kincardine 2016; Aberdeen Donside 2013, 2011; Dyce, Bucksburn & Danestone 2011; Coatbridge & Chryston 2007. Cllr, Aberdeen CC 2012-17. Chairman, Aberdeen City Con Assoc 2013-14. Trustee: Aberdeen international youth festival; Chris Anderson Trust. Volunteer, Aberdeen Arts Centre. Civil

	Electorate	Turnout %	from 2015 %	Change
	64,964	68.47		
R Thomson C	18,746	42.14	+19.31	
*C McCaig SNP	13,994	31.46	-10.19	
C O'Dwyer Lab	9,143	20.55	-6.20	
J Wilson LD	2,600	5.84	+1.21	

partnership. Ed: University of Aberdeen (MA politics & international relations).

CHALLENGERS
Callum McCaig (SNP) MP, for Aberdeen S 2015-17. Cllr, Aberdeen CC 2007-15; leader 2011-12. Campaigned to Remain, voted against Article 50. SNP group leader, energy & climate change. APPG vice-chairman: offshore oil and gas; oil refining sector; renewable and sustainable energy. **Callum O'Dwyer** (Lab) Mechanical

engineer, oil and gas. Poet and writer. Aberdeen West CLP vice-chairman. **Jenny Wilson** (LD) Higher education administrator and trainee registry officer. Member, Scottish Lib Dem Conference Cttee.

CONSTITUENCY PROFILE
Labour from 1997 to 2010, having flipped with the Conservatives until 1992 and switched to the SNP in 2015. A mixed constituency with urban northern and rural western areas, along with a high proportion of university-educated voters. Energy is a significant employer, with the North Sea oil industry.

EU REFERENDUM RESULT
32.1% Leave   Remain 67.9%

Aberdeenshire West & Kincardine

CONSERVATIVE GAIN MAJORITY 7,949 (15.4%)

ANDREW BOWIE
BORN May 28, 1987
MP 2017-

Royal Navy junior warfare officer 2007-10. Head of office to Liam Kerr MSP 2016-17; parly asst and rural affairs adviser to Ian Duncan MEP 2015-16. Tory northeast Scotland campaign manager, general election 2015. Married. Ed: Inverurie Academy; Britannia Royal Naval Coll; University of Aberdeen (MA history and politics; vice-president, Conservative and Unionist Association).

CHALLENGERS
Stuart Donaldson (SNP) MP, Aberdeenshire W & Kincardine 2015-17. Became MP aged just 23, older only than Mhairi

	Electorate	Turnout %	from 2015 %	Change
	72,477	71.23		
A Bowie C	24,704	47.85	+19.02	
*S Donaldson SNP	16,754	32.45	-9.12	
B Black Lab	5,706	11.05	+6.55	
J Waddell LD	4,461	8.64	-12.76	

Black, and was the youngest MP to lose his seat in 2017. APPG vice-chairman: Austria; better Brexit for young people; body image; digital economy; Lyme disease. His grandfather and mother were both SNP MPs. **Barry Black** (Lab) Customer services adviser and undergraduate student, Robert Gordon University. Contested Aberdeenshire W & Kincardine 2015. **John Waddell** (LD) Contested: Holyrood 2016; local elections 2017. Caseworker for Mike Rumbles MSP.

CONSTITUENCY PROFILE
This rural area is located to the southwest of the city of Aberdeen, and has one of the lowest population densities in the UK. It possesses little social housing relative to the more urban seats in Aberdeen. There is little diversity in the population, which is 98 per cent white. As with all Aberdeen constituencies, there's considerable employment in servicing the oil and gas industry. It was held by Lib Dem Sir Robert Smith from 1997 until the SNP briefly claimed it between 2015 and 2017. The Lib Dems have since been pushed into fourth position.

EU REFERENDUM RESULT

38.5% Leave	Remain 61.5%

Airdrie & Shotts

SNP HOLD MAJORITY 195 (0.5%)

NEIL GRAY
BORN Mar 16, 1986
MP 2015-

Former athlete who represented Scotland in 400m. Worked as journalist on local newspapers and BBC Radio Orkney. Aide to Alex Neil MSP: campaign manager 2011; constituency office manager 2008-15. Campaigned to Remain, voted against triggering Article 50. SNP spokesman, fair work & employment 2015-. Yet to rebel. APPG vice-chairman: children who need palliative care; poverty; Scottish sport; sport; women & work; youth employment. Married, one daughter. Ed: Kirkwall GS; University of Stirling (BA politics & journalism).

	Electorate	Turnout %	from 2015 %	Change
	64,146	59.24		
*N Gray SNP	14,291	37.61	-16.33	
H McFarlane Lab	14,096	37.09	+2.98	
J Donnellan C	8,813	23.19	+15.54	
E McRobert LD	802	2.11	+0.58	

CHALLENGERS
Helen McFarlane (Lab) Programme director, NHS Education for Scotland 2006-: seconded to Scottish Health Council. Women's rights and equality campaigner. **Jennifer Donnellan** (C) Westminster stalwart: former aide to Matthew Hancock MP; appointed to Treasury council of economic advisers 2014; special adviser to Greg Hands MP; special adviser to David Mundell MP. **Ewan McRobert** (LD) IT system

developer. Contested South Lanarkshire C 2017.

CONSTITUENCY PROFILE
Held by the Labour Party until 2015, this working-class part of Scotland has struggled to recover from the decline of the steel industry. Only 16 per cent of the constituents hold a university degree and 28 per cent of the population live in social housing. Fewer than two per cent of residents are from EU member states. The constituency is distinctively religious, with 70 per cent claiming to be Christian. This has contributed to historical accusations of sectarianism.

EU REFERENDUM RESULT

39.8% Leave	Remain 60.2%

Aldershot

CONSERVATIVE HOLD MAJORITY 11,478 (23.4%)

LEO DOCHERTY
BORN Oct 4, 1976
MP 2017-

British army veteran; served in Iraq and Afghanistan 2001-07. Wrote a book about his time in the armed forces called *Desert of Death* 2007. Cllr, South Oxfordshire DC 2011-15. Selected to defend Aldershot after local activists lobbied for prominent Eurosceptic Daniel Hannan to be considered. Contested Caerphilly 2015. Dir, Conservative Middle East Council 2010-. Voted Leave. Contributor to conservativehome.com. Keen traveller. Took part in a seven-week bike ride to Jerusalem. Ed: School of Oriental and African Studies, University of London; RMA, Sandhurst.

	Electorate	*Turnout %*	*from 2015 %*	*Change*
	76,205	64.24		
L Docherty C	26,955	55.06	+4.47	
G Puffett Lab	15,477	31.61	+13.28	
A Hilliar LD	3,637	7.43	-1.39	
R Swales Ukip	1,796	3.67	-14.20	
D Wallace Green	1,090	2.23	-2.16	

CHALLENGERS
Gary Puffett (Lab) Fire safety adviser, Magnox. Spent 26 years as a firefighter. Member, Unite; workplace rep. Cllr, Greenham PC. Chairman, Newbury Labour Party. Contested Aldershot 2015. **Alan Hilliar** (LD) Business technology consultant. Contested: Chichester 2005; Surrey Heath 2010; Aldershot 2015. Cllr, Guildford BC 1985-95. **Roy Swales** (Ukip) Former police officer. Contested: New Forest East 2015; Hampshire PCC

2016. Served in Lebanon, Sudan and Northern Ireland in the army. **Donna Wallace** (Green) Supply teacher. Contested local elections 2015, 2017.

CONSTITUENCY PROFILE
This constituency is deprived compared with its surrounding area. It is a military town and contains the Aldershot barracks, home to 4,000 troops. The area has the largest proportion of Buddhists in the UK, explained by the settling of former Ghurkhas. Aldershot has returned Conservative MPs since its creation in 1918. Leo Docherty succeeds the retired Sir Gerald Howarth.

EU REFERENDUM RESULT

57.9% Leave	Remain 42.1%

Aldridge-Brownhills

CONSERVATIVE HOLD MAJORITY 14,307 (35.6%)

WENDY MORTON
BORN Nov 9, 1967
MP 2015-

Ran small manufacturing and electronics business 1992-2015. Lobbied for William Hague's Keep the Pound campaign. Successfully steered private members' bill that guarantees Great Ormond Street retains Peter Pan royalties, 2016. Cllr, Richmondshire DC 2001-06, resigned over bullying accusations. Former chairwoman, Richmond Cons. Contested: Tynemouth 2010; Newcastle Central 2005. Campaigned to Remain, voted for Article 50. Never rebelled. PPS to Jo Johnson 2016. Member international development select cttee 2015-. Chairwoman, APPG

	Electorate	*Turnout %*	*from 2015 %*	*Change*
	60,363	66.66		
*W Morton C	26,317	65.41	+13.36	
J Fisher Lab	12,010	29.85	+7.48	
I Garrett LD	1,343	3.34	-0.03	
M Beech Loony	565	1.40	+0.91	

on sustainable development goals. Married. Ed: Wensleydale Sch; Open University (MBA).

CHALLENGERS
John Fisher (Lab) IT system implementation manager. Cllr, Redditch BC 2012-. **Ian Garrett** (LD) History teacher. Cllr, Sandwell MBC 1994-2002. Contested: Aldridge-Brownhills 2015; West Bromwich East 2010, 2005, 2001; Birmingham Erdington 1997. **Mark Beech** (Loony) Ran as the Good Knight Sir Nosdar. Student teacher.

Contested Aldridge-Brownhills, winning 197 votes, 2015.

CONSTITUENCY PROFILE
A mixed area, with the affluent Aldridge forming a Conservative-supporting suburbia coexisting with Brownhills, a former mining community. The Tories have held this seat since 1979. Only 0.8 per cent of residents come from other EU countries. There is a Sikh community and many pensioners; 70 per cent of the population describe themselves as Christians. A quarter of the workforce is in construction or manufacturing and 75 per cent of homes are owner-occupied.

EU REFERENDUM RESULT

67.8% Leave	Remain 32.2%

Altrincham & Sale West

CONSERVATIVE HOLD MAJORITY 6,426 (12.2%)

GRAHAM BRADY
BORN May 20, 1967
MP 1997-

	Electorate	Turnout %	from 2015 % Change
	73,220	72.10	
*G Brady C	26,933	51.02	-1.97
A Western Lab	20,507	38.85	+12.16
J Brophy LD	4,051	7.67	-0.71
G Coggins Green	1,000	1.89	-2.03
N Taylor Lib	299	0.57	

Charming rightwinger with a striking resemblance to the Duke of York. Previously worked in PR. Dep chairman, Centre for Policy Studies 2016-. Joined party at 16 to save grammar schools. Eurosceptic, successfully lobbied to ensure Conservative Party had neutral stance during referendum campaign. Yet to rebel against Theresa May; previous rebellions on Europe, HS2 and constitutional issues. Shadow min and PPS roles 1999-2007, resigned from front bench over grammar schools. Chairman, 1922 cttee 2010-. Youngest Conservative MP in 1997. Married, one daughter, one son. Ed: Altrincham GS; Durham University (LLB law).

CHALLENGERS
Andrew Western (Lab) Civil engineering consultant. Cllr, Trafford MBC 2006-; leader Lab group 2014-. **Jane Brophy** (LD) NHS dietitian. Cllr, Trafford MBC 1994-. Contested: Greater Manchester mayoralty 2017; Oldham West & Royton by-election 2015; Altrincham & Sale West 2015, 2010. **Geraldine Coggins** (Green)

Counsellor. Contested Stretford & Urmston 2015. **Neil Taylor** (Lib) Entrepreneur. Cllr, Trafford MBC 2006-14.

CONSTITUENCY PROFILE
A producer of Conservative MPs since 1945. Between 2001 and 2010 it was the only Tory seat in Manchester. Altrincham is a market town; Sale is affluent; the east of the constituency has a mix of commuter towns; the west is made up of rural villages. More than 40 per cent of residents have a degree. Property is a disproportionate employer. There is a significant Jewish community and a surviving grammar-school system.

EU REFERENDUM RESULT
38.5% Leave   Remain 61.5%

Alyn & Deeside

LABOUR HOLD MAJORITY 5,235 (11.7%)

MARK TAMI
BORN Oct 3, 1962
MP 2001-

	Electorate	Turnout %	from 2015 % Change
	63,041	71.00	
*M Tami Lab	23,315	52.09	+12.05
L Knightly C	18,080	40.39	+8.45
J Hurst PC	1,171	2.62	-1.28
D Griffiths Ukip	1,117	2.50	-15.08
P Williams LD	1,077	2.41	-1.79

Long-serving union man who was later elected to parliament. Formerly head of policy, AEEU Amicus. Member, TUC general council. Anti-proportional representation and supporter of compulsory voting. Leaked Labour papers listed him as hostile to Jeremy Corbyn in 2016; made no leadership nominations in 2015 or 2016. Campaigned to Remain in the EU, voted to trigger Article 50. Opposition pairing whip 2011-; Treasury whip 2007-10. Chairman, APPG on stem-cell transplantation. Lives in Llanfynydd. Called for support for children with leukaemia after son's battle with the illness. Married, two sons. Ed: Enfield GS; University of Wales, Swansea (BA history).

CHALLENGERS
Laura Knightly (C) Legal secretary studying law. Previously worked for manufacturing and financial multinationals in London. Contested Alyn & Deeside 2015. Cllr, Conwy CBC 2014-17. **Jacqueline Hurst** (PC) Independent social worker. Contested Alyn & Deeside 2015.

David Griffiths (Ukip) Defected to Ukip from the Conservatives in Feb 2017. Former Colwyn Bay cllr. Contested local elections 2017. **Peter Williams** (LD) General manager of a retailer. Contested Alyn & Deeside Welsh Assembly 2016, 2011.

CONSTITUENCY PROFILE
Returned Labour MPs since 1983 but not always with large majorities. The southern part of the area is rural and creates a roughly equal number of middle- and working-class voters. A fifth of those employed work in manufacturing, with Tata Steel, Toyota and BAE Systems in the constituency.

EU REFERENDUM RESULT
58.1% Leave   Remain 41.9%

Amber Valley

CONSERVATIVE HOLD MAJORITY 8,300 (18.1%)

NIGEL MILLS
BORN Apr 21, 1974
MP 2010-

Former chartered accountant who later worked as a tax adviser. Endured two recounts before winning the seat in 2010. Brexiteer. Apologised for playing Candy Crush during a cttee meeting on pension reforms 2014. Regular rebel during coalition years, including over Syrian chemical weapons, launching airstrikes on Isis in Iraq and plain cigarette packaging. Chairman, APPG on unconventional oil & gas. Cllr: Amber Valley BC 2004-11; Heanor & Loscoe TC 2007-11. Married. Ed: Loughborough GS; Newcastle University (BA classics).

	Electorate	Turnout %	from 2015 %	Change
	68,065	67.30		
*N Mills C	25,905	56.55	+12.57	
J Dawson Lab	17,605	38.43	+3.65	
K Smith LD	1,100	2.40	-0.57	
M McGuinness Green	650	1.42	-0.96	
D Bamford Ind	551	1.20		

CHALLENGERS
James Dawson (Lab) Worked in social services for Nottinghamshire CC. Cllr, Erewash BC 2011-. **Kate Smith** (LD) Gift shop asst. Previously worked across Europe and Japan. Cllr, Crich PC 2003-08. Contested Amber Valley 2015, 2005. Has lived in Amber Valley for more than 30 years. **Matt McGuinness** (Green) Musician. Founding dir, community arts organisation. Amber Valley BC candidate 2016 and 2015.

Daniel Bamford (Ind) Brexiteer who wants to leave the EU immediately. Against first past the post. Wants an Australian-style points-based immigration system.

CONSTITUENCY PROFILE
This working-class constituency was lost by the Conservatives to Labour in 1997, but won back again in 2010. The former coalmining towns in Alfreton and Oakerthorpe have recovered, with light industry that employs a fifth of employees in plastics, textiles and concrete. These towns are balanced by rural areas in the constituency.

EU REFERENDUM RESULT

65.3% Leave   Remain 34.7%

Angus

CONSERVATIVE GAIN MAJORITY 2,645 (6.6%)

KIRSTENE HAIR
BORN Aug 12, 1989
MP 2017-

Overturned an 11,000 SNP majority to win Angus. Ruth Davidson hailed the victory on Twitter. Vowed to be a public servant, not a party servant. Activist, Better Together. Exec assistant, DC Thomson 2016-. Event manager, Wilde Thyme 2012-2013. Party conference organiser, Scottish Conservatives 2012-13. Born and brought up in Angus. Ed: University of Aberdeen (MA politics).

CHALLENGERS
Mike Weir (SNP) MP for Angus 2001-17. Called on the government to force energy companies to lower charges for

	Electorate	Turnout %	from 2015 %	Change
	63,840	62.96		
K Hair C	18,148	45.15	+16.15	
*M Weir SNP	15,503	38.57	-15.67	
W Campbell Lab	5,233	13.02	+4.21	
C Sneddon LD	1,308	3.25	+0.52	

poorer families and pensioners in 2007. SNP chief whip 2015-17. Shadow SNP spokesman: business 2010-15; energy and climate change 2010-15. Select cttees: panel of chairs 2010-15; energy and climate change 2009-10; business and enterprise 2008-09. Solicitor and partner, J&DG Shiell. **William Campbell** (Lab) Former school head. MSP candidate, Angus S 2011. Cllr, Fife C 2012-17. Church organist. **Clive Sneddon** (LD) Cllr, NE Fife DC 1980-96; leader 1988-96. Contested: Dundee E 2010, 2005;

Angus S Scottish parliament 2016, 2011.

CONSTITUENCY PROFILE
This homogeneous constituency — 95 per cent of residents are British — had been held by the SNP since 1987. It was a Conservative seat before then, but has subsequently been an SNP marginal for 30 years. There is a substantial agricultural industry, with a pharmaceutical sector in Montrose, and a high proportion of employees who work from home. The constituency contains Arbroath, site of the 1320 declaration of Scottish independence.

EU REFERENDUM RESULT

48.2% Leave   Remain 51.8%

Antrim East

DUP HOLD MAJORITY 15,923 (41.7%)

SAMMY WILSON
BORN Apr 4, 1953
MP 2005-

Former teacher and asst chief examiner, A-level economics. Cllr, Belfast CC 1981-2010. MLA 1998-2015. Outspoken: dismissed environmental campaigns as green guff; called Irish "the leprechaun language". Brexiteer. Rebelled to vote against plain cigarette packaging and increasing alcohol duty. Stormont min, finance 2009-13. DUP Westminster spokesman, Treasury, W&P, educ, 2010-. Former member, NI policing board. Divorced. Ed: Queen's University, Belfast (BA economics and politics); Stranmillis Teaching Coll (DipEd).

	Electorate	Turnout %	from 2015 %	Change
	62,908	60.63		
*S Wilson DUP	21,873	57.34	+21.21	
S Dickson Alliance	5,950	15.60	+0.61	
J Stewart UUP	4,524	11.86	-6.97	
O McMullan SF	3,555	9.32	+2.41	
M McKillop SDLP	1,278	3.35	-1.54	
M Logan C	963	2.52	+0.89	

CHALLENGERS
Stewart Dickson (Alliance) Former arbitration secretary, NI Labour Relations Agency. Cllr, Carrickfergus BC 1985-2012. MLA, Antrim East 2011-. Contested Antrim East 2015. **John Stewart** (UUP) Sales director. MLA, Antrim East 2017-. Cllr, Mid and East Antrim BC 2014-; Carrickfergus BC 2011-14. **Oliver McMullan** (SF) Pub owner. Cllr, Larne BC 2011; Moyle DC 1993-2011. MLA,

Antrim E 2011-17. Contested Antrim E 2010, 2015. **Margaret Anne McKillop** (SDLP) Cllr, Causeway Coast and Glens BC 2011-. Contested Antrim E 2015. **Mark Logan** (C) Chief spokesman, British consulate, Shanghai 2012-16.

CONSTITUENCY PROFILE
Strongly Unionist constituency, with the Roman Catholic population concentrated in particular areas. There are pockets of deprivation but it is otherwise middle class: nearly three quarters of residents are property owners. Home to the University of Ulster campus at Jordanstown.

EU REFERENDUM RESULT
55.2% Leave   Remain 44.8%

Antrim North

DUP HOLD MAJORITY 20,643 (42.6%)

IAN PAISLEY JR
BORN Dec 12, 1966
MP 2010-

Career politician nicknamed Baby Doc after his father Papa Doc, the late DUP founder. Campaigned for Brexit, and thinks that the Republic of Ireland will follow Britain out of the European Union. DUP Westminster spokesman: energy 2015-; CLG 2015-; CMS 2015-; W&P 2010-15. Select cttees: Panel of chairs 2016-; Northern Ireland 2010-. MLA, Antrim N 1998-2010. Member, Northern Ireland policing board. Married, two daughters, two sons. Ed: Methodist Coll Belfast, Queen's University Belfast (BA history; MSSc Irish politics).

	Electorate	Turnout %	from 2015 %	Change
	75,657	64.05		
*I Paisley DUP	28,521	58.85	+15.65	
C McShane SF	7,878	16.26	+3.98	
J Minford UUP	3,482	7.19	-4.87	
T Gaston TUV	3,282	6.77	-8.88	
P O'Lynn Alliance	2,723	5.62	+0.01	
D O'Loan SDLP	2,574	5.31	-1.67	

CHALLENGERS
Cara McShane (SF) Lawyer. Cllr, Causeway Coast and Glens BC 2005-. **Jackson Minford** (UUP) Traffic engineer. Son of Nat Minford, member of Northern Ireland parliament 1951-72. **Timothy Gaston** (TUV) Fire, health and safety officer. Cllr, Mid & East Antrim BC 2014-; deputy mayor 2015-. **Patricia O'Lynn** (Alliance) PhD student. Interested in education and crime. **Declan O'Loan** (SDLP)

Maths teacher. Honorary consul for Romania in Northern Ireland. MLA 2007-11. Cllr, Mid & East Antrim BC 2014-; Ballymena BC 1993-2014.

CONSTITUENCY PROFILE
This solidly Unionist seat contains a mixture of rural villages and manufacturing towns. Held by the late Rev Ian Paisley from 1970 until his retirement 40 years later, this is a prosperous area that includes the Bushmills whiskey distillery. Almost a quarter of Northern Ireland's manufacturing industry is concentrated in the constituency, centred on Ballymena.

EU REFERENDUM RESULT
62.2% Leave   Remain 37.8%

Antrim South

DUP GAIN MAJORITY 3,208 (7.4%)

PAUL GIRVAN
BORN Jul 6, 1963
MP 2017-

	Electorate	Turnout %	Change from 2015 %
	68,244	63.26	
P Girvan DUP	16,508	38.24	+8.14
*D Kinahan UUP	13,300	30.81	-1.89
D Kearney SF	7,797	18.06	+5.20
N Kelly Alliance	3,203	7.42	-2.37
R Lynch SDLP	2,362	5.47	-2.72

Deselected by local party in 2007 but later returned to the fold. Previously electronics engineer and parliamentary assistant. Cllr, Newtownabbey BC 1997-2013; mayor 2002-04. MLA, Antrim S 2010-; 2003-07. Criticised for saying during a radio interview in 2013 that he had "no problem about burning a tricolour on top of a bonfire". Subsequently issued statement saying he wanted to see a reduction in flag burning but suggested that perceived attacks on "eleventh night" bonfires, an annual Ulster Protestant celebration, could provoke "an increase of incidents".

CHALLENGERS
Danny Kinahan (UUP) MP for Antrim S 2015-17. Fine arts and antiques expert. Spent eight years in the army; served in the Falklands, Cyprus and Northern Ireland. High Sheriff of Antrim, 1996-97. Cllr, Antrim BC 2005-10. MLA, Antrim S 2009-15. Backed Remain, voted to trigger Article 50. Never rebelled. Cousin of singer Chris de Burgh. **Declan Kearney** (SF) National chairman, Sinn Fein; apologised "for all of the lives lost during the Troubles", 2015. MLA, Antrim S 2016-. Contested Antrim S 2015. **Neil Kelly** (Alliance) Learning disability nurse and nursing manager. Cllr, Antrim and Newtownabbey BC 2010-. Contested Antrim S 2015.

CONSTITUENCY PROFILE
Situated just to the east of Belfast, this seat is a commuter haven. It is homogeneous: nearly 90 per cent of residents are white and two thirds are Protestant. The constituency is a Unionist marginal. Since 2000 it has oscillated between the DUP and UUP in each election except 2010, when William McCrea was re-elected for the DUP.

EU REFERENDUM RESULT
50.6% Leave   Remain 49.4%

Arfon

PLAID CYMRU HOLD MAJORITY 92 (0.3%)

HYWEL WILLIAMS
BORN May 14, 1953
MP 2001-

	Electorate	Turnout %	Change from 2015 %
	41,367	68.19	
*H Williams PC	11,519	40.84	-3.10
M Griffiths Clarke Lab	11,427	40.51	+10.25
P Parry C	4,614	16.36	+3.24
C Davies LD	648	2.30	-0.38

Advocate of a "radical alliance" with the SNP and the Green Party to oppose the Conservatives. Leader, PC Westminster 2015-. Remainer, voted against Article 50. Welsh speaker; often champions the language. Lecturer, Centre for Social Work Practice. Former social policy consultant and commentator. Project manager, Gofal Cymru. Kurdish activist; has spoken in a number of rallies and events supporting Kurdistan. Interested in the Kurdish language. Born in Pwllheli. Divorced, three daughters. Ed: Glan y Môr Sch; University of Wales, Cardiff (BSc psychology).

CHALLENGERS
Mary Griffiths Clarke (Lab) Has alleged Theresa May called the general election 2017 to take attention away from investigations into Tory electoral fraud. Socialist who writes for the *Morning Star*. Contested Dwyfor Meirionnydd 2015. Photographer and video producer. Dir, Lambeth Law Centre. Dyslexic and has ME. Former co-chairwoman, Disability Labour. From a farming family. **Philippa Parry** (C) Believes tax increases targeted only at high earners is an ineffective way of raising revenue and that tuition fees should not be abolished. **Calum Davies** (LD) First language Welsh speaker. Retail worker from Bethesda.

CONSTITUENCY PROFILE
This seat has been held by Plaid Cymru since its creation in 2010. There is a large student population and considerable employment in education in Bangor, a university city. There is significant employment in hill farming and tourism. Snowdonia National Park is in the south of the constituency. Religious observance is low.

EU REFERENDUM RESULT
35.8% Leave   Remain 64.2%

Argyll & Bute

SNP HOLD MAJORITY 1,328 (2.8%)

BRENDAN O'HARA
BORN Apr 27, 1963
MP 2015-

One of the beneficiaries of the Liberal Democrat wipeout of 2015. Independent television producer. Contested Glasgow Central 1992; Springburn 1987. Supported Remain in the referendum; voted against the triggering of Article 50. Shadow SNP Westminster group leader of defence 2015-. Married, two daughters. Ed: St Andrew's, Carntyne; University of Strathclyde (MA in economic & modern history).

CHALLENGERS
Gary Mulvaney (C) Chartered accountant. Dir, Helensburgh Toyota. Contested Argyll & Bute

	Electorate	Turnout %	Change from 2015 %
	67,230	71.50	
*B O'Hara SNP	17,304	36.00	-8.25
G Mulvaney C	15,976	33.24	+18.33
A Reid LD	8,745	18.19	-9.73
M Kelly Lab	6,044	12.57	+2.18

2010. Cllr, Argyll & Bute, 2003-. **Alan Reid** (LD) Spent 14 years as MP for Argyll and Bute 2001-15. Opposition LD whip 2010, 2002-05. Shadow LD min: Scotland 2007-10; NI 2006-10; trade & industry 2005-06. Former computer project manager. Contested: Argyll and Bute 2015; Dumbarton 1997; Paisley South 1992, 1990 by-election. **Michael Kelly** (Lab) Co-op worker. Gained attention from the local press after what was described as a shambolic performance at a hustings event in Oban.

CONSTITUENCY PROFILE
Covers a swathe of sparsely populated countryside and 26 islands, including Mull, Tiree and Iona. Its main towns are Oban, a ferry port, and Helensburgh, which is within commuting distance of Glasgow. It is also home to HM Naval Base Clyde, commonly known as Faslane Trident submarine base. Residents are relatively elderly and 59 per cent describe themselves as Christian. Employment is largely in tourism, forestry, fishing and wind farms. Among the employed, 18 per cent work mainly at or from home, which is three times the UK average.

EU REFERENDUM RESULT

39.4% Leave   Remain 60.6%

Arundel & South Downs

CONSERVATIVE HOLD MAJORITY 23,883 (39.6%)

NICK HERBERT
BORN Apr 7, 1963
MP 2005-

Dir of public affairs, British Field Sports Society. Contested Northumberland 1997. Backbencher. Campaigned to remain in the EU. Co-founder, Reform think tank 2002. Led No campaign against adopting the Euro. Launched Freedom to Marry campaign 2012. APPG chairman: tuberculosis; LGBT rights. Min, policing and criminial justice 2010-12. Shadow SoS: Defra 2009-10; justice 2007-09. Shadow min, home affairs 2005-07. Select cttee: home affairs 2005-06. Ed: Haileybury Sch; Magdalene College, Cambridge (BA law and land economy).

	Electorate	Turnout %	Change from 2015 %
	80,766	74.61	
*N Herbert C	37,573	62.36	+1.57
C Fife Lab	13,690	22.72	+11.52
S Kapadia LD	4,783	7.94	+0.75
J Prior Green	2,542	4.22	-2.17
J Wallace Ukip	1,668	2.77	-11.67

CHALLENGERS
Caroline Fife (Lab) Regional organiser, Unison. Contested Storrington division in West Sussex CC elections. Chairwoman, Arundel & South Downs CLP. **Shweta Kapadia** (LD) Qualified architect. Cllr, Elmbridge BC 2000-; chairwoman, planning committee. Historic environment and design champion. Council-nominated director of a housing trust. Former member, Arts Council England.

CONSTITUENCY PROFILE
This rural West Sussex seat is demographically imbalanced, with large numbers of retired constituents and people over 45, and few between the ages of 16 and 44. There is a 76 per cent home ownership rate, 50 per cent of households have at least two cars or vans and 16 per cent of working adults are self-employed. Some work in agriculture; others are professionals. This middle-class seat, made up of picturesque villages, has been Conservative since 1997, when it was created. Arundel, and the castle of the same name, is the historic seat of the dukes of Norfolk.

EU REFERENDUM RESULT

49.7% Leave   Remain 50.3%

Ashfield

LABOUR HOLD MAJORITY 441 (0.9%)

GLORIA DE PIERO
BORN Dec 21, 1972
MP 2010-

Former broadcast journalist and political editor, *GMTV*. Jeremy Corbyn sceptic who resigned from shadow cabinet after EU referendum result. Labour leadership nominations: Liz Kendall 2015; Owen Smith 2016. Remainer, voted to trigger Article 50. Shad min: justice 2017-; young people and voter registration 2015-16; women and equalities 2013-15. Born in Bradford to Italian immigrants. Married. Ed: University of Central England; University of Westminster (BA social science); Birkbeck, University of London (MSc social and political theory).

	Electorate	Turnout %	from 2015 %	Change
	78,099	64.01		
*G De Piero Lab	21,285	42.58	+1.55	
T Harper C	20,844	41.69	+19.28	
G Turner Ind	4,612	9.23		
R Young Ukip	1,885	3.77	-17.64	
B Charlesworth LD	969	1.94	-12.89	
A Rangi Green	398	0.80		

CHALLENGERS
Tony Harper (C) Retired senior police officer, served for 36 years. Cllr, Broxtowe BC 2015-. Contested Nottingham PCC 2016. **Gail Turner** (Ind) Worked at Inland Revenue. Cllr, Nottinghamshire CC 2009-15; Ashfield DC 2003-15; Selston PC 2003-15. **Ray Young** (Ukip) From a family of miners. Chairman, Ashfield & Sherwood Ukip branch. **Bob Charlesworth** (LD) Worked as an engineer at Rolls-

Royce. Contested Derby North 2001, 1997, 1992. Cllr, Broxtowe BC 2007-15.

CONSTITUENCY PROFILE
This working-class constituency in west Nottinghamshire used to have mining and textile industries. After their decline it has had to reinvent itself as part of the Nottingham commuter belt. Ashfield is relatively deprived and fairly homogeneous, compared with the English average; only 1.5 per cent of residents are from EU countries. It has been held by Labour since 1955, apart from two years of Tory representation after the 1977 by-election.

EU REFERENDUM RESULT

70.5% Leave   Remain 29.5%

Ashford

CONSERVATIVE HOLD MAJORITY 17,478 (29.2%)

DAMIAN GREEN
BORN Jan 17, 1956
MP 1997-

First secretary of state, in effect Theresa May's deputy, 2017-. Financial journalist: BBC Radio, Channel 4, *The Times*. Contested Brent East 1992. Opposed Brexit. Chairman, Parliamentary Mainstream. Vice-president, Tory Reform Group. Appointed to the front bench 1998. Shad SoS, transport 2003-04; education and skills 2001-03. Shad min, home affairs 2005-10. SoS, work and pensions 2016-17. Min of state, home office 2010-12. Select cttees include: national security strategy 2015-16; European scrutiny 2015-16. Arrested in 2008 on suspicion of aiding and abetting misconduct

	Electorate	Turnout %	from 2015 %	Change
	87,396	68.51		
*D Green C	35,318	58.98	+6.53	
S Gathern Lab	17,840	29.79	+11.35	
A Gee-Turner LD	3,101	5.18	-0.80	
G O'Brien Ukip	2,218	3.70	-15.12	
M Rossi Green	1,402	2.34	-1.96	

in public office; no case was brought. Married, two daughters. Ed: Reading Sch; Balliol Coll, Oxford (BA PPE; pres, Oxford Union).

CHALLENGERS
Sally Gathern (Lab) Former teacher. Parish councillor. Contested Kent CC 2017. **Adrian Gee-Turner** (LD) Contested Croydon N 2005; Dagenham 2001. Former cllr, Hackney BC. **Gerald O'Brien** (Ukip) Former dir of communications

for an international Christian missionary charity.

CONSTITUENCY PROFILE
Held by the Conservatives since the 1930s, including by the cabinet minister and former *Daily Telegraph* editor Bill Deedes between 1950 and 1975, this Kent seat covers a large rural base, with mild urban deprivation. A railway hub since the 19th century, Ashford has excellent commuter links, with a Eurostar stop and high-speed rail to London. This makes for an interesting socio-economic mix, with managers commuting into work and skilled traders working locally.

EU REFERENDUM RESULT

59.9% Leave   Remain 40.1%

Ashton-Under-Lyne

LABOUR HOLD MAJORITY 11,295 (28.4%)

ANGELA RAYNER
BORN Mar 28, 1980
MP 2015-

	Electorate	Turnout %	from 2015 %	Change
	67,674	58.77		
*A Rayner Lab	24,005	60.36	+10.59	
J Rankin C	12,710	31.96	+9.83	
M Jackson Ukip	1,878	4.72	-17.04	
C Hicks LD	646	1.62	-0.80	
A Hunter-Rossall Green	534	1.34	-2.59	

Rising star. Youngest ever shadow education secretary tipped for party leadership. A rare breed: loyal to Jeremy Corbyn but also sang praises of Tony Blair and New Labour legacy. Previously a trade union official. Northwest regional convener, Unison; branch secretary, Stockport council. Former care assistant. Nominated Andy Burnham for leadership 2015; Corbyn 2016. Rebelled once, against renewing Trident. Remainer; voted to trigger Article 50. Shadow SoS education 2016-. Shadow min: women and equalities 2016; work and pensions 2016. Opposition

whip 2015-16. Married, three children, two with disabilities. Eldest son born when she was 16. Ed: Avondale HS.

CHALLENGERS
Jack Rankin (C) Graduate financial analyst, business development, Centrica, 2014-. Cllr, RB Windsor & Maidenhead 2015-. **Maurice Jackson** (Ukip) Semi-retired and self-employed electrician. Former Labour member. **Carly Hicks** (LD) Trainee solicitor,

Addleshaw Goddard 2016-. Senior parliamentary adviser, Chris Davies MEP 2012-14. **Andy Hunter-Rossall** (Green) Mathematics teacher. Organises Canal Clean Up events.

CONSTITUENCY PROFILE
The seat has returned a Labour MP since 1935. Structural unemployment emerged with the decline of the textile industry, but a growing retail trade has helped to ameliorate this. The town of Ashton, in the east of the constituency, is working class; Droylsden, in the west, is affluent. Ashton has a small number of Indian and Pakistani communities.

EU REFERENDUM RESULT
61.8% Leave   Remain 38.2%

Aylesbury

CONSERVATIVE HOLD MAJORITY 14,696 (24.9%)

DAVID LIDINGTON
BORN Jun 30, 1956
MP 1992-

	Electorate	Turnout %	from 2015 %	Change
	82,546	71.16		
*D Lidington C	32,313	55.01	+4.33	
M Bateman Lab	17,617	29.99	+14.85	
S Lambert LD	5,660	9.64	-0.98	
V Srao Ukip	1,296	2.21	-17.51	
C Simpson Green	1,237	2.11	-1.75	
K Michael Ind	620	1.06		

Worked for BP and Rio Tinto before entering politics. Formerly special adviser to Douglas Hurd at Home Office and FCO. Contested Vauxhall 1987. Justice sec and lord chancellor 2017-; lord president of the council and commons leader 2016-17; foreign office min 2010-16. PPS to: William Hague 1997-99; Michael Howard 1994-97. Captained winning *University Challenge* team twice: once while a student in 1979, again in "champion of champions" tournament in 2002. Criticised for claiming £1,300 for toiletries and dry cleaning, which he subsequently repaid. Anglican. Married, four sons. Ed:

Sidney Sussex Coll, Cambridge (BA history; PhD Elizabethan history; president CUCA).

CHALLENGERS
Mark Bateman (Lab) Retired primary school head. Cllr, Aylesbury Vale DC and Aylesbury TC 2015-. Serial local elections candidate. **Steven Lambert** (LD) Contested Aylesbury 2015, 2010. Lib Dem leader, Aylesbury Vale DC and Buckinghamshire CC. Board

member, Vale of Aylesbury Housing Trust. **Vijay Srao** (Ukip) Farmer. Cllr, Downley PC 2015-.

CONSTITUENCY PROFILE
This affluent seat has returned a Conservative MP at every election since 1924. It is a middle-class area that includes semi-rural commuter towns and villages in the south. The number of Asian residents — about 10,000 — is greater than the UK average. Ukip campaigned in 2015 against HS2 and came second. At 70 per cent, the employment rate is high. There is considerable employment in the public sector.

EU REFERENDUM RESULT
51.8% Leave   Remain 48.2%

Ayr, Carrick & Cumnock

CONSERVATIVE GAIN MAJORITY 2,774 (6.0%)

BILL GRANT
BORN Aug 26, 1951
MP 2017-

	Electorate	Turnout %	from 2015 % Change
	71,241	64.88	
B Grant C	18,550	40.13	+20.30
*C Wilson SNP	15,776	34.13	-14.70
C Mochan Lab	11,024	23.85	-3.40
C Leslie LD	872	1.89	+0.25

Surprise Tory victory for son of a miner. Spent more than 30 years serving in Strathclyde fire & rescue, reaching deputy commander before retiring. Magistrate for ten years. Cllr, South Ayrshire 2007-17. Known locally as "the nicest wee cooncillor in Ayr"; due to retire from politics before snap election was called. Second attempt at winning the seat after coming second in 2010 election. Active Rotarian. Vintage-motorcycle enthusiast. Married, two daughters. Ed: Glaisnock Secondary Sch, Cumnock; Fire Service Coll/Lancaster University (HND).

CHALLENGERS
Corri Wilson (SNP) MP for Ayr, Carrick and Cumnock 2015-17. Worked in the civil service for two decades as well as the voluntary sector. Former member, local NHS partnership forum. Cllr, South Ayrshire C 2012-15. **Carol Mochan** (Lab) Runs a kennel business in Mauchline. Contested Carrick, Cumnock and Doon Valley for the Scottish parliament 2016. **Callum Leslie** (LD) Freelance esports broadcaster and producer. Contested

Westminster seat of Kirkcaldy & Cowdenbeath 2015.

CONSTITUENCY PROFILE
Divided between the coastal town of Ayr, the rural, prosperous Carrick and the working-class Cumnock. It also encompasses several former mining villages. The legacy of decline is still felt in the area and there is a high proportion of households without adults in employment. The population has a considerable number of elderly people. A quarter of residents occupy socially rented housing. The seat was strongly Labour supporting until the SNP won it in 2015.

EU REFERENDUM RESULT

44.1% Leave   Remain 55.9%

Ayrshire Central

SNP HOLD MAJORITY 1,267 (2.8%)

PHILIPPA WHITFORD
BORN Dec 24, 1958
MP 2015-

	Electorate	Turnout %	from 2015 % Change
	68,997	65.35	
*P Whitford SNP	16,771	37.20	-15.98
C Hollins Martin C	15,504	34.39	+17.05
N McDonald Lab	11,762	26.09	-0.32
T Inglis LD	1,050	2.33	+0.52

Consultant breast surgeon until the 2015 election. Helped to develop Scottish breast cancer care guidelines. Medical volunteer at UN hospital, Gaza, 1991-92. Spent parliamentary recess in West Bank and Gaza operating on Palestinian women with breast cancer, 2016. Left Labour in protest of Iraq war policies and joined the SNP in 2011. Active in Women for Independence campaign. Youtube video of her warning of NHS privatisation if Scotland remained part of the Union went viral. Feminist blogger. Born in Belfast, moved to Scotland aged ten. Voted against triggering

Article 50. SNP Westminster spokeswoman, health. Member, health select cttee 2015-17. Married to a German GP. One son. Ed: University of Glasgow (MBChB).

CHALLENGERS
Caroline Hollins Martin (C) Maternal health professor, Edinburgh Napier University. Spent 11 years as a midwife. **Nairn McDonald** (Lab) 21 years old. Social sciences student, community activist. Secretary, Kilwinning Community Council.

Member, Scottish youth parliament 2011-15. **Tom Inglis** (LD) Cybersecurity consultant and software designer.

CONSTITUENCY PROFILE
A coastal seat containing the working-class towns of Irvine and its more middle-class counterpart, Troon. Ayrshire Central is fairly ethnically homogeneous, at nearly 99 per cent white. It was held by Labour from 1959 before being lost to the SNP in 2015. Contains a fairly large proportion of retirees, and while median income is below the Scottish average, home ownership is above average, at roughly two thirds.

EU REFERENDUM RESULT

41.6% Leave   Remain 58.4%

Ayrshire North & Arran

SNP HOLD MAJORITY 3,633 (7.7%)

PATRICIA GIBSON
BORN May 12, 1968
MP 2015-

	Electorate	Turnout %	from 2015 % Change
	73,174	64.82	
*P Gibson SNP	18,451	38.90	-14.27
D Rocks C	14,818	31.24	+16.45
C Rimicans Lab	13,040	27.49	-0.48
M Dickson LD	1,124	2.37	+0.71

Former teacher. Campaigns against medical negligence after stillbirth of son in 2009. Voted against Article 50. Conducted the SNP MPs singing *Ode to Joy* in House of Commons as members voted to trigger Article 50. Cllr, Glasgow CC 2007-12. SNP spokeswoman, education 2007-11. Contested Ayrshire North & Arran 2010. Successfully lobbied for law change to tackle nuisance telephone callers. Never rebelled. Married to the SNP MSP Kenneth Gibson. Ed: St Gerald's Secondary Sch; University of Glasgow (BA English and politics); Open University (modular courses: child development; approaches to literature).

CHALLENGERS
David Rocks (C) Music teacher. Chairman, Irvine branch 2010-. **Christopher Rimicans** (Lab) 18-year-old anti-Trident activist. Student. Hit the headlines with a speech against nuclear deterrent at the Scottish Labour conference 2015. **Mark Dickson** (LD) Humanitarian aid worker, worked in Afghanistan with charities 2007-11. Manages projects for the Mentor Initiative humanitarian organisation in Iraq and Syria 2015-.

CONSTITUENCY PROFILE
Returned a Conservative MP until the 1987 boundary changes brought southern industrial areas into coexistence with the northern commuting towns of Skelmorlie and Largs. The constituency includes the mining village of Garnock Valley. Represented by Labour from 1987-2015. The SNP held the area's Holyrood seats from 2005, foreshadowing their 2015 victory in the constituency. The population is homogeneous, at 99 per cent white, and elderly.

EU REFERENDUM RESULT
42.4% Leave   Remain 57.6%

Banbury

CONSERVATIVE HOLD MAJORITY 12,399 (20.1%)

VICTORIA PRENTIS
BORN Mar 24, 1971
MP 2015-

	Electorate	Turnout %	from 2015 % Change
	83,818	73.45	
*V Prentis C	33,388	54.23	+1.23
S Woodcock Lab	20,989	34.09	+12.80
J Howson LD	3,452	5.61	-0.32
D Bird Ukip	1,581	2.57	-11.31
I Middleton Green	1,225	1.99	-2.64
R Edwards Ind	927	1.51	

Barrister; spent 17 years in civil service and has defended government in key cases such as 7/7 inquiry. Founder and former chairwoman, benefactors' board of the Oxford Hospital Trust. Former dir anti-HS2 group Transport Sense; rebelled on HS2 vote, March 2016. Campaigns for bereaved mothers after losing three babies; vice-chairwoman, APPG on baby loss 2016-. Backed Remain, voted for Article 50. PPS to John Hayes 2016-. Select cttees: justice 2015-; statutory instruments 2015-. Father, Tim Boswell, was MP for Daventry 1987-2010. Married, two daughters. Ed: London (BA Eng lit); Downing Coll, Cambridge (LLB law).

CHALLENGERS
Sean Woodcock (Lab) Neighbourhood officer. Cllr, Cherwell DC 2012-; leader Labour group 2013-. Contested Banbury 2015. **John Howson** (LD) Visiting prof, Oxford Brookes University. Cllr, Oxfordshire CC 2013-. Contested Banbury 2015. **Dickie Bird** (Ukip) Former head porter, Oriel Coll, Oxford. Contested Banbury 2015; Witney 2016 by-election. **Ian Middleton** (Green) Runs jewellery business. Contested Banbury 2015. **Roseanne Edwards** (Ind) Reporter, *Banbury Guardian*. Contested Banbury 2015, 2010.

CONSTITUENCY PROFILE
Affluent, has returned a Conservative MP since 1992. The M40 and rail link to Marylebone makes it popular with commuters to London and Birmingham. Has a high rate of full-time employment and a large working-age population. Agriculture remains an important part of the economy.

EU REFERENDUM RESULT
50.3% Leave   Remain 49.7%

Banff & Buchan

CONSERVATIVE GAIN MAJORITY 3,693 (8.9%)

DAVID DUGUID
BORN Oct 8, 1970
MP 2017-

Career in oil and gas industry; first as production chemist, later moved into planning and management. Spent most of career at BP, went freelance in 2016. Has worked in Azerbaijan, North Sea, Asia and Americas. Formerly project manager, Hitachi Consulting. First time contesting any election. Grew up on a farm on the banks of the River Deveron. Married, one son, one daughter. Ed: Banff Academy; Robert Gordon University (MSc chemistry).

CHALLENGERS
Eilidh Whiteford (SNP) MP 2010-17. Former literature

	Electorate	Turnout %	from 2015 % Change
	67,601	61.60	
D Duguid C	19,976	47.97	+19.15
*E Whiteford SNP	16,283	39.10	-21.14
C Stott Lab	3,936	9.45	+3.65
G Milne LD	1,448	3.48	-1.67

lecturer, Glasgow University. Co-ordinator, Scottish Carers' Alliance 2001-03. Policy adviser, Oxfam 2003-09. Long-term SNP activist, first got involved in politics during Alex Salmond's successful election in this seat, 1987. Successfully steered private members' bill on ratifying Istanbul convention preventing violence against women, 2017. Voted against Article 50. **Caitlin Stott** (Lab) Researcher, Scottish Labour. Formerly policy officer, homeless charity Shelter. Stepdaughter of Iain Gray MSP.

Galen Milne (LD) MD, Thistle Scientific research firm. Former Highland League referee. Contested Falkirk 2015; Banff & Buchan 2010.

CONSTITUENCY PROFILE
Historically an SNP-Conservative marginal. The seat was vacated by Alex Salmond in 2010, who had been MP for 23 years, so he could focus on his role as first minister. The constituency finds considerable employment in energy with the St Fergus gas terminal, and in fishing with its ports of Fraserburgh and Peterhead. Farming is significant in Turriff. One of the most northerly seats.

EU REFERENDUM RESULT
61.4% Leave   Remain 38.6%

Barking

LABOUR HOLD MAJORITY 21,608 (45.3%)

DAME MARGARET HODGE
BORN Sep 8, 1944
MP 1994-

Public sector consultant, Price Waterhouse 1992-94. Originally member of left-wing Islington council, later nominated Tony Blair for Labour leadership 1994. Supported Liz Kendall 2015; Owen Smith 2016. Triggered vote of no confidence, with Ann Coffey, in Jeremy Corbyn after EU referendum. Remainer, voted for Article 50. Rarely rebels. Vice-president, Fabian Society. Minister: CMS 2009-10; 2007-08; T&I 2006-07. Select cttee chairwoman: public accounts 2010-15; liaison cttee 2010-15. Cllr, Islington 1973-94; leader 1982-92. Divorced, one daughter, one son. Remarried, widowed,

	Electorate	Turnout %	from 2015 % Change
	77,020	61.90	
*M Hodge Lab	32,319	67.78	+10.08
M Talati C	10,711	22.46	+6.15
R Gravett Ukip	3,031	6.36	-15.85
S Butterfield Green	724	1.52	-0.52
P Pearce LD	599	1.26	-0.05
N Falvey Ind	295	0.62	

two daughters. Ed: Bromley HS; Oxford HS; LSE (BSc government studies).

CHALLENGERS
Minesh Talati (C) Implant dentist. **Roger Gravett** (Ukip) Site manager. Contested Barking 2015. **Shannon Butterfield** (Green) Risk manager, Bank of America, M&S Money. Global stress-testing manager, HSBC. **Pauline Pearce** (LD) Co-founder, Caribbean food

business. Contested Hitchin & Harpenden 2015.

CONSTITUENCY PROFILE
Held by Labour since 1945, this area has a history of racial tension. There are significant Indian, Pakistani and Bangladeshi communities, and more than a fifth of residents are black. The BNP came third in 2005 and 2010, playing on fears over housing in a constituency where 30 per cent of residents rent from the local authority. Ukip replaced the Conservatives as the second party in 2015. Main sources of employment are transport, construction and the public sector.

EU REFERENDUM RESULT
60.0% Leave   Remain 40.0%

Barnsley Central

LABOUR HOLD MAJORITY 15,546 (39.8%)

DAN JARVIS
BORN Nov 30, 1972
MP 2011-

Former army officer. In March 2011 became first person to resign military commission to contest parliamentary by-election since Second World War. Tipped for leadership bid in 2015 but ruled himself out to put family first. Nominated Andy Burnham for Labour leadership 2015; supported Owen Smith 2016. Rebelled to vote for Syrian airstrikes 2015. Remainer, voted for Article 50. Shadow min: foreign affairs 2015; justice 2013-15; CMS 2011-13. Widowed, remarried, three children. Ed: Rushcliffe CS; Aberystwyth University (BA international politics and strategic studies);

	Electorate	Turnout %	from 2015 % Change
	64,204	60.88	
*D Jarvis Lab	24,982	63.91	+8.18
A Ford C	9,436	24.14	+9.14
G Felton Ukip	3,339	8.54	-13.18
R Trotman Green	572	1.46	-1.10
D Ridgway LD	549	1.40	-0.70
S Morris Eng Dem	211	0.54	-0.76

RMA Sandhurst.

CHALLENGERS
Amanda Ford (C) NHS midwife. Cllr, Teignbridge DC 2015-. **Gavin Felton** (Ukip) Spent 24 years in army seeing action in Kuwait, Kosovo and Iraq. Regional constituency manager. Contested South Yorkshire PCC 2016. **Richard Trotman** (Green) Owner, IT consultancy. **David Ridgway** (LD) Former personal finance consultant. Cllr, Kirklees

DC 2008-16. Contested Barnsley Central 2015. **Stephen Morris** (Eng Dem) General secretary, Workers of England Union. Contested Greater Manchester mayoralty 2016; Monmouth parliamentary seat 2015.

CONSTITUENCY PROFILE
Held by Labour since its creation in 1983. Its predecessor, Barnsley, was held by Labour from 1935. This is a relatively poor area; it is north of Sheffield and makes an effective commuter area between Sheffield and Leeds. There are few EU residents. In the early 1980s a fifth of the workforce was in coalmining and pit closures hit the area hard.

EU REFERENDUM RESULT

68.2% Leave   Remain 31.8%

Barnsley East

LABOUR HOLD MAJORITY 13,283 (32.6%)

STEPHANIE PEACOCK
BORN Dec 19, 1986
MP 2017-

Former secondary school teacher, specialising in history and politics. Regional political officer, GMB 2013-17. Parly asst to John Cryer 2010; Sylvia Heal 2005-10. Contested Halesowen and Rowley Regis, 2015. Former partner of Labour's deputy leader, Tom Watson. Ed: Queen Mary, UOL (BA modern and contemporary history); Canterbury Christ Church University (PGCE); UCL Institute of Education (MA educational leadership).

CHALLENGERS
Andrew Lloyd (C) Spent 23 years as an army chaplain

	Electorate	Turnout %	from 2015 % Change
	69,204	58.92	
S Peacock Lab	24,280	59.54	+4.82
A Lloyd C	10,997	26.97	+12.37
J Dalton Ukip	3,247	7.96	-15.52
T Devoy Yorkshire	1,215	2.98	
N Turner LD	750	1.84	-1.32
K Riddiough Eng Dem	287	0.70	-0.44

stationed across the world. Has since worked in charity sector. Sought fairer education funding for Barnsley. **James Dalton** (Ukip) Contested local elections 2016, 2014. Criticised for controversial "keep Islam out" tweet. Writes for *Ukip Daily*. **Tony Devoy** (Yorkshire) Previously a Labour cllr. Career in mining, building and distribution industries. **Nicola Turner** (LD) Runs company that makes CCTV equipment.

Contested Selby and Ainsty 2015, 2012. Cllr, Kirklees MBC 2006-; leader, Liberal Democrat group 2014-.

CONSTITUENCY PROFILE
This working-class consistency has been a safe Labour seat since its creation in 1983. The wider area has been represented by Labour since at least the Second World War. The area is homogeneous: over 98 per cent of residents are white. The BNP won 3,000 votes in 2010. The area is an ex-mining community and, typical of former pit areas, there is relatively high unemployment. A fifth of residents live in council housing.

EU REFERENDUM RESULT

71.0% Leave   Remain 29.0%

Barrow & Furness

LAB CO-OP HOLD MAJORITY 209 (0.4%)

JOHN WOODCOCK
BORN Oct 14, 1978
MP 2010-

Former journalist, *North West Evening Mail*. Aide to John Hutton 2005-08; special adviser to Gordon Brown in No 10. Said he could not "countenance ever voting to make Jeremy Corbyn Britain's prime minister" before election. Announced he was suffering from depression in 2013. Was reported to the standards commissioner for breaking the rules on the use of prepaid House of Commons envelopes. Chairman, Labour Friends of Israel 2011-13. Shadow transport min 2010-13. Divorced, two daughters. Ed: Tapton Comprehensive Sch; University of Edinburgh.

	Electorate	Turnout %	from 2015 %	Change
	69,474	68.50		
*J Woodcock Lab Co-op	22,592	47.47	+5.14	
S Fell C	22,383	47.03	+6.54	
L Birchall LD	1,278	2.69	-0.02	
A Piper Ukip	962	2.02	-9.69	
R O'Hara Green	375	0.79	-1.66	

CHALLENGERS
Simon Fell (C) Career in crime prevention. Stood in 2015 general election. Member, British Council TN2020 network of future leaders. Patron, Fair Votes for All campaign. **Loraine Birchall** (LD) Consultant, West Cumbria development agency. Ran for Cumbria PCC 2016. **Alan Piper** (Ukip) Criticised for making a joke about female genital mutilation on *Newsnight*. **Robert O'Hara** (Green) Business owner and manager; former

secondary school teacher. Has lived in Ulverston for more than 14 years.

CONSTITUENCY PROFILE
Normally represented by a Labour MP although the Conservatives held it from 1983 to 1992. Barrow is an industrial, working-class area. There is a deep-water port, and BAE Systems provides 5,000 jobs in ship-building. Twenty per cent of employees work in manufacturing; 8.5 per cent of over-16s have an apprenticeship qualification, the highest proportion in any UK constituency; 1 per cent of residents are from EU countries.

EU REFERENDUM RESULT
57.3% Leave   Remain 42.7%

Basildon & Billericay

CONSERVATIVE HOLD MAJORITY 13,400 (29.8%)

JOHN BARON
BORN Jun 21, 1959
MP 2001-

Captain, Fusiliers, served in Northern Ireland, Cyprus and Germany. Formerly investment fund manager; dir, Hendersons then Rothschild. Contested Basildon 1997. Long-time Brexiteer. Tabled amendment to Queen's Speech with Peter Bone, expressing regret that government had not announced an EU referendum, helping to persuade David Cameron to promise one 2013. Has opposed military interventions since being elected, except for initial deployment in Afghanistan. Resigned as shadow min to vote against Iraq war 2003. Regularly rebels on Europe and HS2.

	Electorate	Turnout %	from 2015 %	Change
	69,149	64.96		
*J Baron C	27,381	60.96	+8.28	
K Block Lab	13,981	31.13	+7.45	
T Hughes Ukip	2,008	4.47	-15.37	
A Harrison LD	1,548	3.45	-0.36	

Chairman, APPG on cancer. Shadow health min 2003-07, 2002-03. Opposition whip 2007-10. Foreign affairs select cttee 2010-. Married, two daughters. Ed: Queen's Coll, Taunton; Jesus Coll, Cambridge (BA history and politics); RMA Sandhurst.

CHALLENGERS
Kayte Block (Lab) Solicitor advocate. Cllr, Basildon BC 2016-; vice-chairwoman, infrastructure, growth and development cttee. **Tina Hughes** (Ukip) Cllr, Rochford

DC 2016-. **Antonia Harrison** (LD) Hypnotherapist. Vice-chairwoman, Portsmouth Lib Dems.

CONSTITUENCY PROFILE
Socio-economically mixed: the constituency contains affluent Billericay and Basildon, which is the commercial centre of south Essex, although it does contain pockets of severe deprivation. Labour historically performs well in council elections. Construction and financial services industries each make up 10 per cent of employment in this constituency, which was created in 2010, and 1.6 per cent of residents are from the EU.

EU REFERENDUM RESULT
67.1% Leave   Remain 32.9%

Basildon South & Thurrock East

CONSERVATIVE HOLD MAJORITY 11,490 (24.4%)

STEPHEN METCALFE
BORN Jan 9, 1966
MP 2010-

Worked in family's printing business. Brexiteer. Campaigns to protect green spaces. PPS to Chris Grayling. Select cttees: science and technology 2010-15, 2016-17; liaison 2016-17. Chairman, APPG on artificial intelligence. Former dep chairman, Essex Conservative Party. Member: Conservative Friends of Israel; Conservative Christian Fellowship. Trustee, Age Concern Basildon. President, Northlands Park community association. Actively involved with local church. Married, two children. Ed: Loughton Sch; Buckhurst Hill County HS Sixth Form.

	Electorate	Turnout %	from 2015 % Change
	73,541	64.07	
*S Metcalfe C	26,811	56.90	+13.50
B Taylor Lab	15,321	32.51	+7.31
P Whittle Ukip	3,193	6.78	-19.76
R Banerji LD	732	1.55	-1.42
S Harman Green	680	1.44	
P Borg BNP	383	0.81	

CHALLENGERS
Byron Taylor (Lab) Works in IT. Cllr, Basildon BC 2012-16. Leader, Basildon BC's Labour group 2014-15. **Peter Whittle** (Ukip) Deputy leader, Ukip. Urged LGBT Britons to join after he was made Ukip's first gay dep leader. Member, GLA 2016-. Contested: Eltham 2015; London mayoral election 2016. **Reetendra Banerji** (LD) Management consultant. Former assistant head, Westminster

Academy. **Paul Borg** (BNP) Former builder. Secretary, Essex BNP. Contested Hornchurch & Upminster 2015.

CONSTITUENCY PROFILE
A combination of rural communities and deprivation in Langdon Hills makes this a socio-economically mixed constituency. Strongly supports Brexit and the Ukip candidate came second in 2015. EU residents make up 1.4 per cent of the population. There is a small Indian community. The seat comprises few managers and professionals and has a significant working-class population.

EU REFERENDUM RESULT

73.0% Leave   Remain 27.0%

Basingstoke

CONSERVATIVE HOLD MAJORITY 9,466 (16.9%)

MARIA MILLER
BORN Mar 26, 1964
MP 2005-

Background in advertising and PR. Early believer in Cameron project, made shadow min six months after being elected. Remainer, voted for Article 50. Infrequently rebels. Campaigns on women, family and equality issues. Led calls for revenge pornography law and compulsory sex and relationship education in schools. SoS, CMS 2012-14. Min women & equalities 2012-14; forced to resign and apologise to the House over expenses scandal. Chairwoman, women & equalities select cttee 2015-; member, liaison cttee 2015-. Min disabled people 2010-12. Married, two sons, one

	Electorate	Turnout %	from 2015 % Change
	81,873	68.35	
*M Miller C	29,510	52.73	+4.18
T Bridgeman Lab	20,044	35.82	+8.11
J Shaw LD	3,406	6.09	-1.30
A Stone Ukip	1,681	3.00	-12.62
R Winter Green	1,106	1.98	
S Neville Libertarian	213	0.38	

daughter. Ed: Brynteg CS; LSE (BSc economics).

CHALLENGERS
Terry Bridgeman (Lab) Retired maintenance engineer. Cllr, Rushmore BC 2012-, 2007-08, 1990-2002, 1979-86; mayor 2013-14. **John Shaw** (LD) Charity worker. Cllr, Basingstoke and Deane BC 1998-2014. **Alan Stone** (Ukip) Antiques dealer. Contested Basingstoke 2015. **Richard Winter** (Green)

Accountant. Chairman, Basingstoke Green Party. **Scott Neville** (Libertarian) Works in IT and retail.

CONSTITUENCY PROFILE
Reliably Conservative with a young age profile, Basingstoke is relatively affluent and has a high number of ABC1s. It has the second-highest rate of economically active residents in the UK and the second-highest rate of full-time employment at 78.4 per cent and 50.4 per cent, respectively. A fifth of residents live in social renting, but little is provided by local councils. The proportion of residents from the EU is 4 per cent.

EU REFERENDUM RESULT

53.6% Leave   Remain 46.4%

Bassetlaw

LABOUR HOLD MAJORITY 4,852 (9.3%)

JOHN MANN
BORN Jan 10, 1960
MP 2001-

Career as union official: head of research and education, AEEU; national training officer, TUC. Previously ran family's conference-organising company. Outspoken Blue Labour. Frequent Corbyn critic, admitted he was wrong after election. Called for new whistle-blowing service for victims of sexual harassment in parliament. Brexiteer, voted to trigger Article 50. Rarely rebels. Publicly confronted Ken Livingstone and called him a "Nazi apologist" over controversial comments 2016. Chairman, APPG against antisemitism. PPS to: Tessa Jowell 2007-10; Richard Carbon

	Electorate	Turnout %	from 2015 % Change
	78,535	66.53	
*J Mann Lab	27,467	52.57	+3.95
A Simpson C	22,615	43.28	+12.60
L Duveen LD	1,154	2.21	-0.49
N Turner Ind	1,014	1.94	

2005-07. Cllr, Lambeth BC 1986-90. Married, three children. Ed: Bradford GS; University of Manchester (BA economics).

CHALLENGERS
Annette Simpson (C) Formerly trade printing company manager and Jobcentre adviser. School governor. Cllr, Bassetlaw DC 2006-. **Leon Duveen** (LD) Self-employed IT contractor. Served 18 months compulsory military service, Israeli army. Contested Bassetlaw 2015. **Nigel Turner** (Ind) Dir, North Notts

Community Leisure charity. Leave campaigner.

CONSTITUENCY PROFILE
As a former mining area still with a sizeable working-class population, it is a safe Labour seat and has been held by the party since 1929. There is a growing Conservative representation on Bassetlaw council, however. The population is elderly and suffers from high rates of poor health, as is often seen in former mining areas that have suffered decline. There is some employment in manufacturing and wholesale trade. The part-time working rates are high.

EU REFERENDUM RESULT

68.3% Leave   Remain 31.7%

Bath

LIBERAL DEMOCRAT GAIN MAJORITY 5,694 (11.5%)

WERA HOBHOUSE
BORN Feb 8, 1960
MP 2017-

Former radio journalist, professional artist and modern languages teacher.
Pro-European. Born in Hanover, Germany and came to Britain in 1990. Fluent in English, German and French. Contested: Somerset NE 2015; Heywood & Middleton 2010. Cllr, Rochdale BC 2004-14; leader, Lib Dem group 2011-14. Originally elected as a Conservative. During her time there she fought a proposal to build 600 homes and a children's nursery on land contaminated with asbestos. Married, two daughters, two sons. Ed: University of Manchester (BA history).

	Electorate	Turnout %	from 2015 % Change
	66,769	74.26	
W Hobhouse LD	23,436	47.27	+17.59
*B Howlett C	17,742	35.78	-2.03
J Rayment Lab	7,279	14.68	+1.50
E Field Green	1,125	2.27	-9.68

CHALLENGERS
Ben Howlett (C) MP, Bath 2015-17. Remainer. Select cttees: pensions 2015-17; women and equalities 2015-17. Cllr, Harwich TC 2007-11. Chairman, Conservative Future 2010-13. Leader, Conservative group, Harwich TC. **Joe Rayment** (Lab) Works for a homelessness, alcohol and substance misuse charity. Cllr, Bath & NE Somerset C 2015-. **Eleanor Field** (Green) Project manager. Contested Bath & NE Somerset C 2015.

CONSTITUENCY PROFILE
This is a small Somerset seat comprising the ancient Roman town of Bath, surrounded by the constituency of North East Somerset. It was a Liberal Democrat seat between 1992 and 2015, held by Don Foster, and was formerly the seat of the Conservative cabinet minister Chris Patten. With the University of Bath and Bath Spa University on its outskirts, it is home to more than 15,000 undergraduate and postgraduate students, and 15 per cent of the constituency's residents work in the education sector. It has strong tourism, software and service industries.

EU REFERENDUM RESULT

31.7% Leave   Remain 68.3%

Batley & Spen

LAB CO-OP HOLD MAJORITY 8,961 (16.7%)

TRACY BRABIN
BORN May 9, 1961
MP 2016-

Elected in 2016 to replace the murdered MP and close friend Jo Cox. Former *Coronation Street*, *EastEnders* and *Emmerdale* actress. Juggled a 30-year acting and writing career with being a Labour Party and trade union activist. Senior campaigner, Friends of the Earth. Member, Amnesty International. Contested Keighley 2010. Shadow education min 2017-. Select cttee, women and equalities 2016-17. Born in Batley. Married, three children. Ed: Heckmondwike GS; Loughborough University (BA drama); London Coll of Printing (MA screenwriting).

	Electorate	Turnout %	from 2015 %	Change
	80,153	67.10		
*T Brabin Lab Co-op	29,844	55.49	+12.25	
A Myatt C	20,883	38.83	+7.59	
J Lawson LD	1,224	2.28	-2.47	
A Lukic Ind	1,076	2.00		
A Freeman Green	695	1.29	-1.15	
M Hanif Ind	58	0.11		

CHALLENGERS
Ann Myatt (C) Consultant NHS dermatologist. Contested: Westmorland & Lonsdale 2015; Hemsworth 2010. **John Lawson** (LD) Cllr, Kirklees C 2010-; dep leader, LD group. Contested Batley & Spen 2015. **Aleks Lukic** (Ind) IT teacher. Ukip candidate Batley & Spen 2015. **Alan Freeman** (Green) Ex-RAF engineer who later became a psychologist. Now works in technical sales.

CONSTITUENCY PROFILE
This is the seat of the murdered Labour MP Jo Cox, who was elected in 2015 but killed outside her Birstall constituency surgery by an extreme-right terrorist one week before the EU referendum. Located between Bradford, Leeds, Huddersfield and Wakefield, its major settlements include Batley, Birstall and Heckmondwike. The seat had been represented by the Conservatives between 1983 and 1997, and by Labour MPs ever since. It has a large Asian population. A significant proportion of the constituency's residents work in manufacturing and construction.

EU REFERENDUM RESULT
59.6% Leave	Remain 40.4%

Battersea

LABOUR GAIN MAJORITY 2,416 (4.4%)

MARSHA DE CORDOVA
BORN Jan 23, 1976
MP 2017-

Registered blind after being born with eye condition nystagmus. Tireless disability rights campaigner: engagement and advocacy dir, Thomas Pocklington Trust 2016-; chief exec, South East London, Vision 2015-16; spoke about disabled rights in her maiden speech. Previously worked as officer and policy manager, Action for Blind People. Cllr, Lambeth BC 2014-. Ed: Hanham HS; London South Bank University (LLB law).

CHALLENGERS
Jane Ellison (C) MP 2010-17. Appointed Treasury special adviser after election defeat.

	Electorate	Turnout %	from 2015 %	Change
	77,572	70.98		
M de Cordova Lab	25,292	45.94	+9.11	
*J Ellison C	22,876	41.55	-10.83	
R Davis LD	4,401	7.99	+3.60	
C Coghlan Ind	1,234	2.24		
L Davis Green	866	1.57	-1.72	
E Power Ukip	357	0.65	-2.46	
D Lambert SPGB	32	0.06		

Comes from Tory left. Previously worked in marketing for John Lewis. Cllr, Barnet BC 2006-08, 1991-94. Remainer, voted for Article 50. Led govt crusade for plain cigarette packaging. Treasury financial sec 2016-17; parly under-sec public health 2013-16. Contested by-elections: Pendle 2005; Tottenham 2000; Barnsley East and Mexborough 1997; Barnsley East 1996. **Richard Davis** (LD) Group head

of analytics, Lloyds 2011-. Former research scientist. Contested European elections 2012. School governor.

CONSTITUENCY PROFILE
Located in south London, this constituency has been a bellwether since 1987. Iconic Battersea Power Station in the north of the constituency. It has the greatest proportion of university-educated residents and residents in employment in the UK in 2011 census. Among the most expensive constituencies for average house prices. Contains Clapham Junction, reputedly one of the busiest train stations in Europe.

EU REFERENDUM RESULT
22.0% Leave	Remain 78.0%

Beaconsfield

CONSERVATIVE HOLD MAJORITY 24,543 (43.8%)

DOMINIC GRIEVE
BORN May 24, 1956
MP 1997-

	Electorate	Turnout %	from 2015 % Change
	77,534	72.26	
*D Grieve C	36,559	65.25	+2.01
J English Lab	12,016	21.45	+10.02
P Chapman LD	4,448	7.94	+0.55
J Conway Ukip	1,609	2.87	-10.88
R Secker Green	1,396	2.49	-1.70

Barrister and QC. Served in Territorial Army 1981-83. President, Franco-British Society; awarded légion d'honneur for work in Franco-British relations 2016. Contested Norwood 1987. Cllr, Hammersmith and Fulham 1982-86. Abstained on same-sex marriage and HS2. Passionately pro-European but voted for Article 50. Withdrew support from Open Britain group after the launch of tactical voting campaign targeted Tory seats. Attorney-general 2010-14. Reshuffled amid reports he was at odds with Cameron over European Convention on Human Rights. Chairman, joint intelligence and security cttee 2015-17. Son of Percy Grieve, MP for Solihull 1964-83. Practising Anglican, formerly dep church warden. Married, two sons. Ed: Westminster Sch; Magdalen Coll, Oxford (BA, MA modern history; president OUCA 1977); London Polytechnic (PgDip law).

CHALLENGERS
James English (Lab) Public affairs consultant, Gplus Europe. **Peter Chapman** (LD) Former local magistrate. Cllr, Gerrards Cross PC 2003-11. Contested Beaconsfield 2005, 2015. **Jon Conway** (Ukip) Owner, theatre and pantomime production company. **Russell Secker** (Green) Retired computer programmer. Volunteers at local hospitals and foodbanks.

CONSTITUENCY PROFILE
Beaconsfield and its previous incarnations have only ever returned Conservative MPs since 1950. Significant proportion of residents are employed in higher managerial occupations. Tony Blair, aged 29, was an unsuccessful candidate in Beaconsfield's 1982 by-election.

EU REFERENDUM RESULT
49.0% Leave   Remain 51.0%

Beckenham

CONSERVATIVE HOLD MAJORITY 15,087 (29.2%)

BOB STEWART
BORN Jul 7, 1949
MP 2010-

	Electorate	Turnout %	from 2015 % Change
	67,928	76.01	
*B Stewart C	30,632	59.33	+2.05
M Ahmad Lab	15,545	30.11	+10.68
J Ireland LD	4,073	7.89	+0.97
R Fabricant Green	1,380	2.67	-1.18

Decorated army colonel who completed seven tours in Northern Ireland. Interested in defence and Northern Ireland affairs. Select cttees: NI affairs 2016-17; defence sub-cttee 2015-17; defence 2010-17; arms export controls 2010-14. Has spoken about resigning as an MP because of his anger about squeezes to military spending. Freelance writer, broadcaster, lecturer. Political consultant. Allegedly referred to a *Spectator* magazine journalist as "totty". Brexiteer. Publications: *Broken Lives* 1993; *Leadership Under Pressure* 2009. Raised in RAF family. Divorced, remarried, six children. Ed: RMA Sandhurst; Wales (international politics), Army Staff Coll; Joint Services Staff Coll.

CHALLENGERS
Marina Ahmad (Lab) Helps to set up projects on housing estates. Qualified barrister. Contested: London assembly 2016; Beckenham 2015. **Julie Ireland** (LD) Set up IT consultancy. Contested London assembly 2016. Secretary, Bromley Lib Dems. **Ruth Fabricant** (Green) Retired infant teacher. Contested: Beckenham 2015; Bromley BC 2014.

CONSTITUENCY PROFILE
This is a southeast London seat in the borough of Bromley with Lewisham to the north and Orpington to the south. It is an affluent area, with high house prices and high levels of homeownership and self-employment. Many residents work in finance and insurance, with administrative and secretarial roles among the most common occupations. The seat has been held by the Tories since 1950. Beckenham workers earn nearly 50 per cent more than the average UK employee.

EU REFERENDUM RESULT
48.4% Leave   Remain 51.6%

Bedford

LABOUR GAIN MAJORITY 789 (1.6%)

MOHAMMAD YASIN
BORN Oct 1, 1971
MP 2017-

Works as a private hire driver in Milton Keynes. Admitted to not having read the Labour Party's manifesto in full during campaign. Cllr, Bedford BC 2006-; served as adult services portfolio holder 2015-17. Taunted Theresa May in his election victory speech by saying: "I would like to thank Theresa May for calling this strong and stable election. It's not strong and stable any more, is it?" Vowed to save Bedford Hospital, build more homes and increase police funding. Has lived in Bedford for 25 years. Muslim. Married, four children. Ed: Mirpur Degree Coll, Kashmir.

	Electorate	Turnout %	from 2015 %	Change
	71,829	67.49		
M Yasin Lab	22,712	46.85	+6.65	
*R Fuller C	21,923	45.22	+2.64	
H Vann LD	2,837	5.85	+1.60	
L Bywater Green	1,008	2.08	-0.98	

CHALLENGERS
Richard Fuller (C) MP, Bedford 2010-17. Brexiteer. International business career before returning to politics. National chairman, Young Conservatives 1985-87. Small business ambassador. Patron, Tory Reform Group. Select cttees: business, energy and industrial strategy 2016-17; regulatory reform 2015-17; business, innovation and skills 2015-16; regulatory reform 2012-15. Christian. **Henry Vann** (LD) Cllr, Bedford BC 2011-; portfolio holder for education. Contested

Bedford 2010 when, at the age of 23, he was the youngest candidate. Member, Co-operative Society; Fawcett Society. **Lucy Bywater** (Green) Works in publishing. Contested Bedford BC 2015, 2011, 2009, 2007.

CONSTITUENCY PROFILE
Consisting of Bedford and its smaller neighbour, Kempston, it was won marginally by Labour in the landslide victories of 1945 and 1966, and held under Tony Blair and Gordon Brown. It is a diverse seat with a large south Asian community, significant numbers of EU citizens and higher than average levels of unemployment.

EU REFERENDUM RESULT

51.9% Leave   Remain 48.1%

Bedfordshire Mid

CONSERVATIVE HOLD MAJORITY 20,983 (33.2%)

NADINE DORRIES
BORN May 21, 1957
MP 2005-

Former nurse, brought up on council estate. Businesswoman who sold company to Bupa, then served as director for them. Taught in Africa. Author of novels drawing on Liverpool Catholic upbringing. Outspoken, socially conservative blogger. Long-time backbencher, whip withdrawn in 2012 for appearing on *I'm a Celebrity . . . Get Me Out of Here!*. Reinstated 2013. Dogged by expenses rows. Christian. Advocates lowering abortion limit. Recent campaigns against local bank branch closures. Occasional rebel. Brexiteer. Wrote letter to 1922 cttee calling for David Cameron's

	Electorate	Turnout %	from 2015 %	Change
	83,800	75.36		
*N Dorries C	38,936	61.66	+5.61	
R Meades Lab	17,953	28.43	+12.56	
L French LD	3,798	6.01	-1.21	
G Ellis Green	1,794	2.84	-1.40	
A Kelly Loony	667	1.06	+0.55	

resignation before referendum. Sobbed in press conference where Boris Johnson pulled out of Tory leadership contest. Divorced, three children. Ed: Halewood Grange; Warrington District Sch of Nursing.

CHALLENGERS
Rhiannon Meades (Lab) Actor and musician. Women's officer, Mid Beds CLP. **Lisa French** (LD) Community manager. Council member, Electoral Reform Society. **Gareth Ellis**

(Green) Green energy engineer. Contested Bedfordshire Mid, 2015. **Ann Kelly** (Loony) Historian and author. Cllr, Flitwick TC 2005-13; mayor 2010-12. Contested Bedfordshire Mid 2015.

CONSTITUENCY PROFILE
This seat has been held by the Conservatives since their 1931 landslide victory. It is mostly rural, with the largest town, Flitwick, home to about 12,000 people. The area is predominantly populated with ABC1s. Construction and education are among the most likely sources of employment for residents.

EU REFERENDUM RESULT

52.9% Leave   Remain 47.1%

Bedfordshire North East

CONSERVATIVE HOLD MAJORITY 20,862 (32.5%)

ALISTAIR BURT
BORN May 25, 1955
MP 2001-; 1983-97

Former solicitor turned headhunter, Whitehead Mann GKR. Lost marginal Bury North in Blair's landslide 1997. Remain campaigner, settled in Tory Left. Thought lack of UK intervention in Syria 2013 was a mistake. PPS Michael Howard 2003-05; Ian Duncan Smith 2002-03; Kenneth Baker 1985-90. Min: Middle East (FCO and international development) 2017-; community and social care 2015-16. Opp whip 2008-10. Shadow SoS, communities and local govt 2005-08. Dep chairman Conservative Party 2007-10. Cllr, Hackney BC 1982-83. Select cttee: exiting the EU 2016-17.

	Electorate	Turnout %	from 2010 %	Change
	86,988	73.83		
*A Burt C	39,139	60.95	+1.48	
J Vaughan Lab	18,277	28.46	+12.70	
S Rutherford LD	3,693	5.75	-0.08	
D Strachan Ukip	1,896	2.95	-11.67	
P Fleming Green	1,215	1.89	-2.43	

Patron, Habitat for Humanity GB; Bishop Simeon Trust. Member, Conservative Friends of Israel. Has completed ten London marathons. Practising Christian. Married, two children. Ed: Bury GS; St John's Coll, Oxford (jurisprudence).

CHALLENGERS
Julian Vaughan (Lab)
Underground train driver. Aslef Union rep, 2007-. Voted Remain.
Stephen Rutherford (LD)
Aerospace engineer. Contested

2005. **Duncan Strachan** (Ukip) Practising solicitor. Biggleswade town cllr and former mayor.
Philippa Fleming (Green) Nursery nurse who has worked in admin and customer service. Suffers from Ehlers-Danlos syndrome.

CONSTITUENCY PROFILE
A mostly rural constituency, its biggest towns are Biggleswade, with about 17,000 people, and Sandy, which is home to more than 11,000. Three quarters of households are owner occupied. Along with its predecessor seat, Bedfordshire North, it has returned Conservative MPs since 1983.

EU REFERENDUM RESULT
53.4% Leave   Remain 46.6%

Bedfordshire South West

CONSERVATIVE HOLD MAJORITY 14,168 (25.5%)

ANDREW SELOUS
BORN Apr 27, 1962
MP 2001-

Director, CNS Electronics 1988-94. Underwriter for Great Lakes Reinsurance. Territorial Army officer, Hon Artillery Co, Royal Regiment of Fusiliers 1981-94. Contested Sunderland N 1997. Bow Group 1982-. Chairman, Conservative Christian Fellowship 2001-. Rarely rebels. Campaigned to Remain. In the executive or shadow from 2006 to 2016 and was asked to step down from the government when Theresa May became prime minister. Married, three daughters. Ed: Eton Coll; London School of Economics (BSc economic industry & trade).

	Electorate	Turnout %	from 2010 %	Change
	79,670	69.83		
*A Selous C	32,961	59.25	+4.26	
D Scott Lab	18,793	33.78	+13.51	
D Norton LD	2,630	4.73	-0.43	
M Rennie Green	950	1.71	-2.40	
M Mafoh CPA	301	0.54		

CHALLENGERS
Daniel Scott (Lab) Small business owner. Treasurer, local triathlon club. Former school governor. **Daniel Norton** (LD) Energy industry career. Inspired to take a more active role in politics during the referendum; led Bedford campaign to Remain. **Morvern Rennie** (Green) Worked in hospital and events industry until 2013. Volunteered with the Scottish Green Party until 2014. Brought up in rural Aberdeenshire. **Morenike Mafoh**

(Christian People's Alliance) Pastor, counsellor, Sunday school teacher and youth mentor. Registered General Nurse.

CONSTITUENCY PROFILE
Conservative stronghold since its creation in 1983. Its predecessor seat included some of Luton, however, and returned Labour MPs in 1950 and 1966. The Labour challenge in 1997 reduced the majority from 21,273 to a mere 132 votes. There are high rates of economic activity in this seat, with local employment found in retail, education and manufacturing. Education rates are poor after GCSE level.

EU REFERENDUM RESULT
58.1% Leave   Remain 41.9%

Belfast East

DUP HOLD MAJORITY 8,474 (19.8%)

GAVIN ROBINSON
BORN Nov 22, 1984
MP 2015-

Barrister. Campaigned to Leave. DUP spokesman on justice, home affairs and human rights 2015-. Select cttees: defence 2016-17; NI affairs 2015-16. APPG vice-chairman: democratic participation (co-chairman); financial technology; funerals and bereavement; health. Cllr, Belfast CC 2010-15. Lord mayor, Belfast 2012-13. Married. Ed: Queen's University Belfast (LLB law; MA Irish politics).

CHALLENGERS
Naomi Long (Alliance) Former consultant engineer. Cllr, Belfast CC 2001-10. MLA, Belfast East 2003-10; 2016-. Lord mayor,

	Electorate	Turnout %	Change from 2010 %
	63,495	67.55	
*G Robinson DUP	23,917	55.76	+6.43
N Long Alliance	15,443	36.01	-6.78
H Legge UUP	1,408	3.28	
M O'Donnell SF	894	2.08	+0.01
G Milne Green	561	1.31	-1.36
S Bodel C	446	1.04	-1.79
S de Faoite SDLP	167	0.39	+0.07
B Beck Ind	54	0.13	

Belfast 2009-10. Alliance Party dep leader 2006-16; leader 2016-. MP, Belfast East 2010-15. Cttees: NI affairs 2010-15; Electoral commission 2010-15. **Hazel Legge** (UUP) PA to UUP party sec. Cllr, Lisburn & Castlereagh CC. **Mairead O'Donnell** (SF) Long-time community activist and charity worker. Cllr, Belfast CC 2016-. **Georgina Milne**

(Green) Research statistician and PhD student. Cllr, Belfast CC 2016-. Candidate, NI Assembly 2017. **Sheila Bodel** (C) Employment support officer. Candidate, NI assembly 2017.

CONSTITUENCY PROFILE
Held by Naomi Long of the Alliance Party in 2010-15, the seat had been held by the former first minister Peter Robinson between 1979 and 2010. The constituency has never returned a nationalist in its 132-year history. Stormont, the home of the Northern Ireland assembly, is in the north. It also contains parts of the boroughs of Belfast and Castlereagh.

EU REFERENDUM RESULT
51.4% Leave   Remain 48.6%

Belfast North

DUP HOLD MAJORITY 2,081 (4.5%)

NIGEL DODDS
BORN Aug 20, 1958
MP 2001-

Set to play kingmaker in this parliament. Trained barrister, later worked at European parliament secretariat. Survived an IRA assassination attempt while visiting son in hospital 1996. Cllr, Belfast CC 1985-97; youngest-ever lord mayor 1988-89; 1991-92. Formerly vice-pres, NI association of local authorities. MLA, Belfast North 1998-2010. Brexiteer. Tends not to rebel. DUP dep leader 2008-; Westminster leader 2010-. Stormont min: soc dev 1999-2000, 2000-01; enterprise 2007-08; finance 2008-09. OBE 1992. Privy cllr. Married, two children. Ed: Portora Royal

	Electorate	Turnout %	Change from 2010 %
	68,249	67.31	
*N Dodds DUP	21,240	46.24	-0.80
J Finucane SF	19,159	41.71	+7.79
S Nelson Alliance	2,475	5.39	-1.86
M McAuley SDLP	2,058	4.48	-3.74
M O'Hara Green	644	1.40	
G Weir WP	360	0.78	-1.48

Sch, Enniskillen; St John's Coll, Cambridge (LLB law); Queen's University Belfast (cert PLS).

CHALLENGERS
John Finucane (SF) Solicitor. Youngest son of Pat Finucane, who was shot dead in front of his wife and children by loyalist paramilitaries 1989. **Sam Nelson** (Alliance) Alliance party elections director. Partner Nuala McAllister is Alliance cllr and lord mayor, Belfast.

Martin McAuley (SDLP) Party press officer. Was constituency adviser to Conall McDevitt MLA. **Malachai O'Hara** (Green) Health and wellbeing officer. Contested Stormont 2017. **Gemma Weir** (WP) Contested Belfast N 2015.

CONSTITUENCY PROFILE
With a staunchly Unionist electoral history, the Roman Catholic population of Belfast North overtook the Protestant population in the 2011 census. About 30,000 residents have no qualifications, significantly higher than the UK average, and in 2016 its unemployment rate was nearly 8 per cent.

EU REFERENDUM RESULT
49.6% Leave   Remain 50.4%

Belfast South

DUP GAIN MAJORITY 1,996 (4.6%)

EMMA LITTLE PENGELLY
BORN Dec 31, 1979
MP 2017-

Barrister; previously law lecturer, University of Ulster. Adviser to Ian Paisley and Peter Robinson at Stormont. MLA, Belfast South 2015-17. Junior Stormont minister 2015-17. Elected dep pres, Queen's University Belfast students' union 1998. Daughter of convicted loyalist gunrunner, Noel Little. Married. Ed: Markethill HS; Queen's University Belfast (LLB law, cert PLS); Harvard (Kennedy Sch).

CHALLENGERS
Alasdair McDonnell (SDLP) MP 2005-17. Spent 30 years as doctor. MLA, Belfast South 1998-

	Electorate	Turnout %	from 2010 %	Change
	66,105	66.11		
E Little Pengelly DUP	13,299	30.43	+8.21	
*A McDonnell SDLP	11,303	25.86	+1.32	
P Bradshaw Alliance	7,946	18.18	+0.95	
M Ó Muilleoir SF	7,143	16.34	+2.48	
C Bailey Green	2,241	5.13	-0.62	
M Henderson UUP	1,527	3.49	-5.62	
C Salier C	246	0.56	-0.93	

2011. Contested: Belfast South 2001, 1997, 1992, 1987, 1983, 1982 by-election 1979. Voted against Article 50. SDLP big beast. Party leader 2011-15. **Paula Bradshaw** (Alliance) Ran an urban regeneration charity. Cllr, Belfast CC 2014-16. MLA, Belfast South 2016-. **Máirtín Ó Muilleoir** (SF) Founder, Belfast Media Group. Cllr: Belfast CC 1987-97; 2011-14. MLA, Belfast South 2014-.

Stormont fin min 2016-17. **Clare Bailey** (Green) Community development worker. MLA, Belfast South 2016-. **Michael Henderson** (UUP) Sales manager. Cllr, Castlereagh BC 1998-. **Clare Salier** (C) Management consultant. Cllr, Wandsworth BC 2014-.

CONSTITUENCY PROFILE
Electing Unionists at every election between 1985 and 2005, Belfast South has since elected an SDLP candidate. It contains the campus of Queen's University Belfast and is, on average, better qualified and enjoys lower unemployment than the other seats in Belfast.

EU REFERENDUM RESULT

30.5% Leave   Remain 69.5%

Belfast West

SINN FEIN HOLD MAJORITY 21,652 (53.3%)

PAUL MASKEY
BORN Jun 10, 1967
MP 2011-

Former apprentice glazier. Development co-ordinator, Failte Feirste Thair (Welcome to west Belfast) tourism organisation. Life-long republican activist. Cllr, Belfast CC 2001-09; SF group leader 2005-07. MLA, Belfast West 2007-12. Two brothers interned for dissident republican activities during the Troubles. Married, two children. Ed: Edmund Rice Coll.

CHALLENGERS
Frank McCoubrey (DUP) Former member, Ulster Democratic Party; then leading member, Ulster Political

	Electorate	Turnout %	from 2010 %	Change
	62,423	65.09		
*P Maskey SF	27,107	66.71	+12.47	
F McCoubrey DUP	5,455	13.43	+5.58	
G Carroll PBP	4,132	10.17	-9.07	
T Attwood SDLP	2,860	7.04	-2.80	
S Eastwood Alliance	731	1.80	-0.00	
C Campbell WP	348	0.86	-0.83	

Research Group. Joined DUP 2012. High sheriff, Belfast 2009. **Gerry Carroll** (PBP) Long-time activist previously banned from Belfast city centre for taking part in student protests. MLA, Belfast West 2016-. Cllr, Belfast CC 2014-16. Contested Belfast West 2015. Atheist and revolutionary socialist. **Tim Attwood** (SDLP) Former dir Citizens Advice Belfast. Cllr, Belfast CC 1995-; SDLP group leader. **Sorcha Eastwood** (Alliance) Was

married on polling day, voted in wedding dress. **Conor Campbell** (WP) Contested Stormont elections 2016.

CONSTITUENCY PROFILE
Belfast West has a large Sinn Fein majority held by Gerry Adams 1983-92 and 1997-2011. With nearly five times as many Roman Catholic residents as Protestant ones, this seat last elected a Unionist to the Westminster parliament in 1964. Like Belfast North, it ranks among the seats with the greatest number of residents with no qualifications, and its unemployment rate was nearly 9 per cent in 2016.

EU REFERENDUM RESULT

25.9% Leave   Remain 74.1%

Bermondsey & Old Southwark

LABOUR HOLD MAJORITY 12,972 (22.2%)

NEIL COYLE
BORN Dec 30, 1978
MP 2015-

Disability rights campaigner. Former director of policy and campaigns at Disability Rights UK and head of policy National Centre for Independent Living 2007-09. Accused Corbyn aides of censoring critics after being the target of a formal complaint when he questioned Labour's communications strategy. Pro-Remain, voted against Article 50. Cllr, Southwark BC 2010-16; dep mayor 2014-15; dep cabinet member 2011-13. Member, work and pensions select cttee 2016-17. Vice-chairman, Walworth Community C 2010-11. Previously PA to Ben Bradshaw MP. Married, one child. Ed:

	Electorate	Turnout %	from 2010 %	Change
	87,227	67.09		
*N Coyle Lab	31,161	53.25	+10.18	
S Hughes LD	18,189	31.08	-3.25	
S Baillie C	7,581	12.95	+1.19	
E Jones Ukip	838	1.43	-4.90	
J Tyson Green	639	1.09	-2.84	
J Clarke Ind	113	0.19	+0.05	

Bedford Sch; University of Hull (BA British politics and legislative studies).

CHALLENGERS
Sir Simon Hughes (LD) MP, 1983-2015. Justice minister, 2013-15. Won Bermondsey in a bitter by-election, issuing "straight choice" leaflets against gay Labour candidate Peter Tatchell. Later came out as bisexual. LD deputy leader 2010-14. **Siobhan Baillie** (C)

Solicitor. Cllr, Camden BC 2014-. **Elizabeth Jones** (Ukip) Deputy chairwoman, Ukip Lambeth. **John Tyson** (Green) Joined Greens after EU referendum.

CONSTITUENCY PROFILE
Once a Labour stronghold, then a Liberal/Lib Dem seat from the infamously homophobic 1983 Bermondsey by-election, until Coyle won it back in 2015. Contains King's College London campuses and South Bank University. Also has one of the biggest South American populations in any UK consituency and a significant proportion of its residents work in financial services.

EU REFERENDUM RESULT

26.1% Leave — Remain 73.9%

Berwick-Upon-Tweed

CONSERVATIVE HOLD MAJORITY 11,781 (27.9%)

ANNE-MARIE TREVELYAN
BORN Apr 6, 1969
MP 2015-

Chartered accountant, previously worked at PwC. Campaigner for increased investment in north Northumberland: founder, Dual the A1 campaign; chairwoman of the iNorthumberland advisory group. Governor on the Northumbria healthcare trust. School governor. Campaigned to Leave the European Union in the 2016 referendum, member of the Conservatives for Britain group. Member, public accounts select cttee 2015-. Contested Berwick-upon-Tweed 2010. Married, two children. Ed: St Paul's Girls' School; Oxford Polytechnic (BA mathematics).

	Electorate	Turnout %	from 2010 %	Change
	58,774	71.82		
*A Trevelyan C	22,145	52.46	+11.39	
S Dickinson Lab	10,364	24.55	+9.61	
J Pörksen LD	8,916	21.12	-7.79	
T Stewart Green	787	1.86	-1.82	

CHALLENGERS
Scott Dickinson (Lab) Cllr, Northumberland CC 2013-. Project director of an organisation that provides local employment advice and training. Business chairman, Northumberland CC. Chairman, health and wellbeing scrutiny board. Chairman, East Chevington PC. **Julie Pörksen** (LD) Agricultural economist. Has worked in business as well as charities. Lived in Peru for two years working to support fair trade and agricultural

workers' rights. Trustee, Ashray charity.

CONSTITUENCY PROFILE
The northernmost English constituency. It was represented by Sir Alan Beith, Liberal and then Liberal Democrat, from 1971 until his retirement from parliament in 2015. The town of Berwick-upon-Tweed itself, in the far north of the seat, is home to about 12,000 people, with Morpeth in the south of the constituency contributing a further 14,000. It shares Northumberland national park with its neighbouring seat, Hexham. The seat was once held by William Beveridge.

EU REFERENDUM RESULT

55.3% Leave — Remain 44.7%

Berwickshire, Roxburgh & Selkirk

CONSERVATIVE GAIN MAJORITY 11,060 (21.1%)

JOHN LAMONT
BORN Apr 15, 1976
MP 2017-

	Electorate	Turnout %	from 2010 %	Change
	73,191	71.55		
J Lamont C	28,213	53.88	+17.87	
*C Kerr SNP	17,153	32.76	-3.85	
I Davidson Lab Co-op	4,519	8.63	+3.72	
C Burgess LD	2,482	4.74	-13.96	

Solicitor: Freshfields; Brodies. Contested Berwickshire Roxburgh & Selkirk 2005, 2010, 2015. MSP for Ettrick, Roxburgh & Berwickshire 2007-17. Scottish Conservative: chief whip 2011-16; parliamentary business manager 2011-16; spokesman, justice 2010-11. Chairman, local Conservative association. Member, 1922 exec cttee 2017-. First UK politician to complete Ironman triathlon. Ed: University of Glasgow (MA law).

CHALLENGERS
Calum Kerr (SNP) MP for Berwickshire Roxburgh & Selkirk 2015-17. Worked in sales for IT companies. Shad

SNP Westminster spokesman, digital 2016-17. SNP spokesman environment and rural affairs 2015-17. Select cttee: European scrutiny 2015-16. **Ian Davidson** (Lab) Former community service manager. MP for Glasgow Pollok (formerly Glasgow Govan) 1992-2005; Glasgow South West 2005-15. Campaigned to Leave the EU. Against Scottish independence. Sec, trade union group of Labour MPs. Select cttees: liaison 2010-15; Scottish affairs 2005-15. **Caroline Burgess** (LD) Worked

for NHS Scotland. Campaigned to increase space on buses for parents and the disabled.

CONSTITUENCY PROFILE
Held by the former Scottish secretary Michael Moore from 2005 to 2015, when it was won by the SNP. This Scottish borders seat is mostly rural and the cumulative population of its largest two towns, Galashiels and Hawick, is about 30,000. The predecessor seats had been represented by the former Liberal Party leader David Steel. The constituency has a high proportion of agricultural workers compared with the rest of Britain.

EU REFERENDUM RESULT
43.3% Leave   Remain 56.7%

Bethnal Green & Bow

LABOUR HOLD MAJORITY 35,393 (59.2%)

RUSHANARA ALI
BORN Mar 14, 1975
MP 2010-

	Electorate	Turnout %	from 2010 %	Change
	86,071	69.51		
*R Ali Lab	42,969	71.82	+10.63	
C Chirico C	7,576	12.66	-2.58	
A Masroor Ind	3,888	6.50		
W Dyer LD	2,982	4.98	+0.46	
A Polson Green	1,516	2.53	-6.74	
I de Wulverton Ukip	894	1.49	-4.59	

Spotted at university by the Labour luminary Michael Young; later became associate director, Young Foundation. Parly asst to Oona King. Worked on human rights at FCO. Co-founder: Tower Hamlets Summer University; UpRising employability charity; One Million Mentors. First MP of Bangladeshi origin, appointed trade envoy to that country in 2016. Nominated Jeremy Corbyn for leadership but backed Yvette Cooper 2015. Ran for the deputy leadership but pulled out. Voted no confidence in Corbyn 2016. Remainer, voted against Article 50. Resigned from front bench

after refusing to support military intervention in Iraq 2014. Shadow min: intl dev 2010-13; education 2013-14. Ed: Mulberry Sch; Tower Hamlets Coll; St John's Coll, Oxford (BA PPE).

CHALLENGERS
Charlotte Chirico (C) District prosecutor CPS. Cllr, Merton BC 2014-. **Ajmal Masroor** (Ind) Chairman, Islamic Society of Britain. Contested Bethnal Green

& Bow 2010. **William Dyer** (LD) Politics student. **Alistair Polson** (Green) Barrister. Contested Bethnal Green & Bow 2015. **Ian de Wulverton** (Ukip) Psychiatric nurse. Contested Ealing North 2010.

CONSTITUENCY PROFILE
Has been Labour in all but one parliament since 1974. Comprising the northern half of Tower Hamlets in the East End of London, it is one of the most ethnically diverse seats in the country, with a large community of Bangladeshi origin. About three tenths of residents at the 2011 census were born outside the EU.

EU REFERENDUM RESULT
30.9% Leave   Remain 69.1%

Beverley & Holderness

CONSERVATIVE HOLD MAJORITY 14,042 (25.2%)

GRAHAM STUART
BORN Mar 12, 1962
MP 2005-

Entrepreneur. Started *What's on in Cambridge* guide while at university and failed exams. Later sole proprietor, Go Enterprises; director, Marine Publishing Co. Self-described deficit hawk. Founder, Community Hospitals Acting Nationally Together 2005. Voted to repeal Human Rights Act 2012. Rarely rebels. Campaigned to Remain, voted for Article 50. Backed Theresa May for leadership 2016. Assistant govt whip 2016-. Chairman, education select cttee 2010-15; criticised Michael Gove for rushed changes to policy. Married, two daughters. Ed: Glenalmond Coll;

	Electorate	Turnout %	from 2010 % Change
	80,657	69.03	
*G Stuart C	32,499	58.37	+10.22
J Boal Lab	18,457	33.15	+8.17
D Healy LD	2,808	5.04	-0.46
L Walton Yorkshire	1,158	2.08	
R Howarth Green	756	1.36	-2.06

Selwyn Coll, Cambridge (BA law and philosophy).

CHALLENGERS
Johanna Boal (Lab) Prison service librarian. Poet and novelist. School governor. Corbynista. **Denis Healy** (LD) Business development manager, Institute of Mechanical Engineers. Contested Beverley & Holderness 2015. Cllr, East Riding 2016-; dep leader, Lib Dem group. **Lee Walton** (Yorkshire) IT entrepreneur.

Contested Beverley & Holderness 2015, had a heart attack the week before polling day. Cllr, Hornsea TC 2013-; mayor 2016-.
Richard Howarth (Green) Biodiesel engineer. Contested Beverley & Holderness 2015.

CONSTITUENCY PROFILE
Mostly rural seat in East Riding. Its biggest town, Beverley, is home to about 30,000 people. Labour came within 1,000 votes of winning in 2001, but the Conservative majority has grown at every subsequent election. High rates of homeownership and a large number of retired residents.

EU REFERENDUM RESULT

58.7% Leave   Remain 41.3%

Bexhill & Battle

CONSERVATIVE HOLD MAJORITY 22,165 (37.3%)

HUW MERRIMAN
BORN Jul 13, 1973
MP 2015-

Barrister, moved from criminal to commercial law. Led team of lawyers unwinding Lehman Brothers insolvency in London. Former trustee, youth charity set up in aftermath of Brixton riots. Worked in hobby farming venture with his neighbour, a butcher. Enjoys growing fruit and vegetables and beekeeping. Cllr, Wealden DC 2007-15. Contested Derbyshire NE 2010. Champion of foreign-aid spending. One rebellion, voted to legalise assisted dying. Did not declare EU stance before referendum; later said he voted Remain, voted for Article 50. Member, Council of Europe.

	Electorate	Turnout %	from 2010 % Change
	78,512	75.75	
*H Merriman C	36,854	61.97	+7.19
C Bayliss Lab	14,689	24.70	+10.58
J Kemp LD	4,485	7.54	-0.06
G Bastin Ukip	2,006	3.37	-15.04
J Kent Green	1,438	2.42	-2.67

APPG chairman: bees, BBC. Married, three daughters. Ed: Buckingham Co Sec Mod; Aylesbury Coll; Durham University (LLB law).

CHALLENGERS
Christine Bayliss (Lab) Spent nine years as police officer, then civil servant; Treasury, Manchester CC, DfE. Founder and owner, education consultancy business. **Joel Kemp** (LD) Insurance worker. Lib Dem activist since he was 16.

Geoffrey Bastin (Ukip) Worked in local government, retail and construction. Contested Bexhill & Battle 2015. **Jonathan Kent** (Green) Former journalist. Contested Bexhill & Battle 2015.

CONSTITUENCY PROFILE
An affluent seat consisting of the seaside retirement area of Bexhill and wide rural spaces. The seat has been represented by the Conservatives since its creation in 1983. This is a retirement hotspot in the UK, with a significant gender gap that comes with the higher life expectancy of women. Home ownership rates are high, as is self-employment.

EU REFERENDUM RESULT

57.7% Leave   Remain 42.3%

Bexleyheath & Crayford

CONSERVATIVE HOLD MAJORITY 9,073 (20.1%)

DAVID EVENNETT
BORN Jun 3, 1949
MP 2005-; 1983-97

Worked as an insurance broker, City director and lecturer. MP for Erith & Crayford 1983-97, won back revised seat in 2005 at the second attempt. PPS: Michael Gove 2010-12; Gillian Shepherd 1996-97; John Redwood 1993-95; Baroness Blatch 1992-93. Government whip 2012-; shadow min, BIS 2009-10. Opposition whip 2005-09. In favour of an elected House of Lords. Cllr, Redbridge BC 1974-78. Married, two sons. Ed: Buckhurst Hill County HS for Boys, Ilford; London School of Economics (BSc, analytical and descriptive economics; MSc government).

	Electorate	Turnout %	from 2010 % Change
	65,315	69.19	
*D Evennett C	25,113	55.57	+8.32
S Borella Lab	16,040	35.50	+9.28
M Ferro Ukip	1,944	4.30	-16.72
S Reynolds LD	1,201	2.66	-0.34
I Lobo Green	601	1.33	-0.84
P Finch BNP	290	0.64	

CHALLENGERS
Stefano Borella (Lab) Pastry chef. Teaches at La Cucina Caldesi. Cllr, Bexley BC 2010-; shadow cabinet member for education. **Mike Ferro** (Ukip) Retired sailing instructor. Became disillusioned with Conservative Party's stance on the European Union in 2012. Unsuccessfully ran for councillor on Bexley BC in 2014. Climate change denier. **Simone Reynolds** (LD) Community mental health

advocate, Mind in Bexley. Vice-chairwoman, Bexley Liberal Democrats.

CONSTITUENCY PROFILE
In southeast London, on the border with Kent. It was represented by a Labour MP from 1997 to 2005, but has been Conservative since. One of the most pro-Brexit seats in Greater London. A predecessor constituency, Bexley, was once held by the former prime minister Edward Heath. This is a middle-class commuter area with high levels of home ownership and its residents are more likely than average to work in finance or construction.

EU REFERENDUM RESULT
65.3% Leave   Remain 34.7%

Birkenhead

LABOUR HOLD MAJORITY 25,514 (58.4%)

FRANK FIELD
BORN Jul 16, 1942
MP 1979-

Campaigner on poverty and welfare. Member, Reform think tank advisory board. Teacher. Tormentor of Sir Philip Green over collapse of BHS. Campaigns for full employee rights for gig economy workers. Tabled motion to delay what he called "terrifying" tax credit cuts, supported by 20 Tory MPs, 2015. Blue Labour. Campaigned for Leave in the EU referendum. Loaned Jeremy Corbyn nomination for party leadership, 2015. Subsequently outspoken Corbyn critic. Chairman, W&P select cttee 2015-. Chairman, independent review on poverty and life chances as Cameron's

	Electorate	Turnout %	from 2010 % Change
	64,484	67.71	
*F Field Lab	33,558	76.86	+6.61
S Gardiner C	8,044	18.42	+2.99
A Brame LD	1,118	2.56	-1.14
J Clough Green	943	2.16	+1.73

poverty tsar 2010. Co-chairman, cross-party group on balanced migration. Occasionally rebels: Europe, HS2. Anglican; previously chairman: King James Bible Trust, Churches Conservation Trust. Unmarried, no children. Ed: St Clement Danes GS; University of Hull (BSc economics and politics).

CHALLENGERS
Stewart Gardiner (C) Town planner. Cllr: Knutsford TC 2008-; mayor 2011-12; cllr, Cheshire East C 2011-. **Allan**

Brame (LD) Retired teacher. Contested Birkenhead 2015. **Jayne Clough** (Green) Lecturer, University of Liverpool medical school.

CONSTITUENCY PROFILE
This Wirral seat and its predecessors have elected Labour MPs at every election since the Second World War. The incumbent MP Frank Field has not received fewer than three fifths of the vote since 1987. The area is characterised by relatively high levels of unemployment after the decline in ship-building, with care and social work among the overrepresented occupations.

EU REFERENDUM RESULT
51.7% Leave   Remain 48.3%

Birmingham Edgbaston

LAB CO-OP HOLD MAJORITY 6,917 (15.9%)

PREET KAUR GILL
BORN Nov 21, 1972
MP 2017-

First female Sikh MP. Career in social care and children's services. Carried out research on street children in India with Unicef. Campaigns for black and minority ethnic representation; board member, The Sikh Network group of activists and professionals. Member, West Midlands police and crime panel. Cllr, Sandwell BC 2012-; formerly cabinet member for public health and protection. Father was bus driver who moved from India to Birmingham in 1950s. Married, two children. Ed: Lordswood Girls' Sch; University of East London (BA sociology & social work).

	Electorate	Turnout %	from 2010 %	Change %
	68,091	64.05		
P Gill Lab Co-op	24,124	55.32	+10.47	
C Squire C	17,207	39.45	+1.16	
C Green LD	1,564	3.59	+0.72	
A Kiff Green	562	1.29	-2.03	
D Rodgers Good	155	0.36		

CHALLENGERS
Caroline Squire (C) Self-employed public affairs and communications consultant. Previously adviser at the lobbying firm Finsbury and at Sainsbury's. Worked for Conservative whips' office in House of Lords. Serves in First Aid Nursing Yeomanry. Great-great-granddaughter of Victorian industrialist Joseph Chamberlain. **Colin Green** (LD) Software engineer. Contested Birmingham Selly Oak 2015. Chairman, SW

Birmingham Liberal Democrats. **Alice Kiff** (Green) Student at the University of Birmingham (BA philosophy). Formerly press officer, Young Greens of England and Wales.

CONSTITUENCY PROFILE
Gained by Labour for the first time in 1997, and only narrowly won in 2010. Contains the University of Birmingham and houses some of its student population. It is also home to large Muslim and Sikh communities. The seat has been represented by successive women MPs continuously since 1953 and Neville Chamberlain was elected here in the 1930s.

EU REFERENDUM RESULT
47.3% Leave   Remain 52.7%

Birmingham Erdington

LABOUR HOLD MAJORITY 7,285 (19.6%)

JACK DROMEY
BORN Sep 21, 1948
MP 2010-

Worked his way up TGWU, elected dep gen sec in 2003. Former sec, Brent Trades Council. Machine minder, Alperton Carton Company. Founder member, Greater London Enterprise Board. Distanced himself from Tony Blair in cash for honours, secret loans row in 2006, at which time he was Labour Party treasurer (2004-10). Resigned as shadow min policing in 2016 in opposition to Jeremy Corbyn's leadership and supported Owen Smith's challenge in the Labour leadership ballot. Shadow min: labour 2016-; home affairs 2013-16; CLG 2010-13. A

	Electorate	Turnout %	from 2010 %	Change %
	65,067	57.20		
*J Dromey Lab	21,571	57.96	+12.34	
R Alden C	14,286	38.39	+7.55	
A Holtom LD	750	2.02	-0.77	
J Lovatt Green	610	1.64	-1.09	

Remainer, but is dedicated to campaigning for best Brexit for Britain. Married to Harriet Harman MP, one daughter, two sons. Ed: Cardinal Vaughan GS, London.

CHALLENGERS
Robert Alden (C) Cllr Birmingham CC 2006- leader, Conservative group 2014-. Contested Birmingham Erdington 2010. School governor. Director, Erdington Town Centre Business Improvement District. **Ann Holtom** (LD) Local

campaigner, including road safety issues. Cllr, Birmingham CC 2002-12. **James Lovatt** (Green) Studying MA media, campaigning & social change at University of Westminster. Contested Birmingham Perry Barr 2015.

CONSTITUENCY PROFILE
The Birmingham seat that voted for Brexit by the largest margin, Erdington has been represented by Labour MPs since 1974. Significant areas of deprivation are found in this seat. Its unemployment rate was 7 per cent at the beginning of 2017, within the top ten of all constituencies.

EU REFERENDUM RESULT
63.0% Leave   Remain 37.0%

Birmingham Hall Green

LABOUR HOLD MAJORITY 33,944 (62.5%)

ROGER GODSIFF
BORN Jun 28, 1946
MP 1992-

Former bank clerk and political officer for trade union Association of Professional, Executive, Clerical and Computer Staff (APEX) and its successor, GMB. Sat on the St Ermins Group, caucus of moderate trade unionists. Contested Birmingham Yardley 1983, came third. MP: Birmingham Sparkbrook & Small Heath 1997-2010; Small Heath 1992-97. Position on Jeremy Corbyn unclear. Did not nominate a leader in 2015. Pro-Brexit but abstained from Article 50 vote. Rebelled in 2005 against legislation allowing for 90-day detention without trial.

Electorate	Turnout %	from 2010 %	Change
	78,271	69.39	
*R Godsiff Lab	42,143	77.60	+17.77
R Ranger C	8,199	15.10	-2.61
J Evans LD	3,137	5.78	-5.83
P Cox Green	831	1.53	-3.15

Controversy in expenses scandal after being accused of claiming for gardening equipment and household items. Cllr, London Borough of Lewisham 1971-90; mayor 1977-90. Married, one son, one daughter. Born in London. Ed: Catford Comprehensive School.

CHALLENGERS
Reena Ranger (C) Founder and chairwoman of Women Empowered. Dir of a shipping company. Cllr, Three Rivers DC 2015-. **Jerry Evans** (LD)

Archaeologist. Cllr, Birmingham CC 2003-16. Contested Birmingham Hall Green 2015. **Patrick Cox** (Green) Teacher. Former policy officer for Greens.

CONSTITUENCY PROFILE
A densely populated and young constituency, more than a quarter of its residents were 15 or under in the 2011 census. Nearly half the residents are Asian or British Asian, with about two thirds of Pakistani origin. A Conservative seat from 1950 until 1997, but it has been Labour ever since. Salma Yaqoob of the Respect Party came within 3,800 votes of winning in 2010.

EU REFERENDUM RESULT

33.6% Leave   Remain 66.4%

Birmingham Hodge Hill

LABOUR HOLD MAJORITY 31,026 (66.9%)

LIAM BYRNE
BORN Oct 2, 1970
MP 2004-

Author of infamous "there's no money left" note after 2010 election. Technology entrepreneur. Former employee of NM Rothschild and Accenture. Author. Advised Labour Party on its national business campaign and reorganisation of Millbank 1996-97. Dubbed as hostile to Jeremy Corbyn in leaked papers. Remainer, but voted for Article 50. Frontbencher in various roles from 2005 to 2015. Shadow digital min 2017-. Created the new UK Border Agency, designed an immigration points system and legislated for ID cards for foreign nationals.

Electorate	Turnout %	from 2010 %	Change
	75,698	61.29	
*L Byrne Lab	37,606	81.06	+12.66
A Reza C	6,580	14.18	+2.71
M Khan Ukip	1,016	2.19	-9.14
P Bennion LD	805	1.74	-4.66
C Thomas Green	387	0.83	-1.20

Married, three children. Ed: University of Manchester (BA politics and history); Harvard Business School (MBA, Fulbright Scholar).

CHALLENGERS
Ahmereen Reza (C) Dir, British Pakistan Foundation. **Mohammed Khan** (Ukip) Cllr, Tendring DC 2015-. **Phil Bennion** (LD) Arable farmer. MEP for W Midlands since 2012. Cllr, Lichfield DC 1999-2011. LD employment and transport

spokesman 2012-. **Clare Thomas** (Green) Wants to introduce a new Clean Air Act.

CONSTITUENCY PROFILE
More than a quarter of residents were aged 15 or under in the 2011 census. Large Asian community, mainly Pakistani origin. Had the highest proportion of Muslim residents of any constituency in 2011 census, as well as one of the lowest rates of residents having academic qualifications. At 8.6 per cent in January 2017, it had the third-highest unemployment rate of all constituencies. Labour since its creation in 1983, but Lib Dems came close second in 2004.

EU REFERENDUM RESULT

51.5% Leave   Remain 48.5%

Birmingham Ladywood

LABOUR HOLD MAJORITY 28,714 (69.5%)

SHABANA MAHMOOD
BORN Sep 17, 1980
MP 2010-

Former barrister specialising in professional indemnity litigation. First elected Muslim woman to hold cabinet-level role. Controversially took part in a demonstration calling for the boycott of goods from Israeli settlements. Shadow chief secretary to Treasury, 2015; resigned after Jeremy Corbyn's 2015 leadership victory. Identified as "hostile" to Corbyn in leaked papers. Remainer, but voted for Article 50. Born in Birmingham. Father was Birmingham Labour Party chairman. Lived in Saudi Arabia between 1981 and 1986 after father moved there to work

	Electorate	Turnout %	from 2010 % Change
	70,023	58.99	
*S Mahmood Lab	34,166	82.71	+9.09
A Browning C	5,452	13.20	+0.46
L Dargue LD	1,156	2.80	-1.03
K Dennis Green	533	1.29	-2.89

as civil engineer. Ed: Oxford University (BA jurisprudence); Inns of Court School of Law.

CHALLENGERS
Andrew Browning (C) Founder of Greater Thought. Seconded to Cabinet Office implementation unit during the coalition. **Lee Dargue** (LD) Teacher and health campaigner. Lib Dems' West Midlands health spokesman; vice-chairman educ assoc. **Kefentse Dennis** (Green) Campaigned to improve Birmingham City Hospital.

CONSTITUENCY PROFILE
Densely populated. More than a quarter of the population of Indian or Pakistani descent, and a fifth of residents are black/Afro-Caribbean. It has the highest rate in Birmingham of households in which no person speaks English as a main language, at nearly 20 per cent, and the highest jobseekers' claimant rate, at 9.3 per cent, of any constituency at the beginning of 2017. Ladywood was Labour's eighth safest seat in 2017. It has elected Labour MPs at every general election since 1945, although the Liberals held it for a year after a by-election in 1969.

EU REFERENDUM RESULT
35.6% Leave   Remain 64.4%

Birmingham Northfield

LABOUR HOLD MAJORITY 4,667 (10.5%)

RICHARD BURDEN
BORN Sep 1, 1954
MP 1992-

Former trade union district officer, TGWU. Outspoken supporter of Palestinians: chairman, Britain-Palestine APPG; campaigned for motion calling on the government to recognise Palestine. Shadow transport min 2013-15, resigned in opposition to Jeremy Corbyn's leadership. Keen motor enthusiast: former amateur racing driver; motor sports adviser to Richard Caborn, 2002-07; chairman, APPG motor. Campaigned for regeneration in the Midlands, set up Climb project to attract investment to southwest Birmingham. Chairman, Labour Campaign

	Electorate	Turnout %	from 2010 % Change
	72,322	61.32	
*R Burden Lab	23,596	53.21	+11.58
M Powell-Chandler C	18,929	42.68	+6.97
R Harmer LD	959	2.16	-1.01
E Masters Green	864	1.95	-0.80

for Electoral Reform 1996-98. Founded Joint Action for Water Services to oppose water privatisation. Married, three stepchildren. Ed: Wallasey Tech GS; Bramhall Comp; St John's FE Coll, Manchester; University of York (BA politics); University of Warwick (MA industrial relations).

CHALLENGERS
Meg Powell-Chandler (C) Adviser to BEIS, DCLG and No 10. Head of briefing for Conservative Party. Public affairs

and policy consultant for Crisis. **Roger Harmer** (LD) Consultant in business development, fundraising and sustainability. Cllr, Birmingham CC 2014-, 2008-12, 1995-2001. **Eleanor Masters** (Green) Mental health nurse.

CONSTITUENCY PROFILE
A somewhat marginal seat, it has been won by Labour at every general election since 1950 except for the three in which Margaret Thatcher was Conservative leader. One of the least diverse seats in Birmingham, it has a higher-than-average rate of residents lacking education qualifications.

EU REFERENDUM RESULT
61.8% Leave   Remain 38.2%

Birmingham Perry Barr

LABOUR HOLD MAJORITY 18,383 (41.6%)

KHALID MAHMOOD
BORN Jul 13, 1961
MP 2001-

	Electorate	Turnout %	from 2010 %	Change
	70,106	63.04		
*K Mahmood Lab	30,109	68.12	+10.69	
C Hodivala C	11,726	26.53	+5.04	
H Singh LD	1,080	2.44	-2.41	
S Bhatoe Soc Lab	592	1.34		
V Rana Green	591	1.34	-1.89	
H Singh Open	99	0.22		

Former engineer and trade unionist. Initially backed Brexit but left the Vote Leave campaign, citing the group's emphasis on immigration. Subsequently joined Remain but voted to trigger Article 50. A Muslim who condemned 2017 Westminster attacker, saying he was "not of my religion". Nominated Yvette Cooper for leadership 2015, but now supports Jeremy Corbyn. Had lifesaving kidney transplant from live donor 2014. Controversy after claiming £1,350 to stay at five-star London hotel with girlfriend. Shadow min, FCO 2016-. Cllr, Birmingham CC 1990-93. Twice divorced, one child from each marriage. Ed: University of Central England.

CHALLENGERS
Charlotte Hodivala (C) Sales manager for healthcare manufacturer. Cllr, Sutton Coldfield TC; mayor 2016-. **Shangara Bhatoe** (Soc Lab) Charity worker. Contested Newport East 2015. **Vijay Rana** (Green) Called for empty homes to be brought into use. **Harjinder Singh** (Open) Contested seat for Ukip 2015; known as Ukip's "waving man" for waving at hundreds of cars a day.

CONSTITUENCY PROFILE
A young and ethnically diverse community, where more than 40,000 residents were under 25 at the 2011 census and more than a third are of south Asian descent. The biggest sectors of employment are retail, manufacturing and health and social care. Perry Barr has elected Labour MPs at every general election since 1950, except 1964 and 1970. The Labour vote share has been above 50 per cent since 2010.

EU REFERENDUM RESULT
51.2% Leave | Remain 48.8%

Birmingham Selly Oak

LABOUR HOLD MAJORITY 15,207 (31.0%)

STEVE MCCABE
BORN Aug 4, 1955
MP 1997-

	Electorate	Turnout %	from 2010 %	Change
	74,370	65.87		
*S McCabe Lab	30,836	62.95	+15.30	
S Shrubsole C	15,629	31.91	+2.90	
D Radcliffe LD	1,644	3.36	-2.20	
J Pritchard Green	876	1.79	-3.29	

Former social worker and adviser to the Central Council of Education and Training in Social Work. Cllr, Birmingham CC 1990-98. Campaigned to Remain, voted for Article 50. Vocal critic of Jeremy Corbyn critic: nominated Yvette Cooper in 2015 leadership race; voted no confidence in Corbyn. PPS to Charles Clarke 2002-04. Shad home min 2013-15. Opposition whip 2010; govt whip 2007-10; asst govt whip 2006-07. Cttees: work & pensions 2015-17; panel of chairs 2015-17; home affairs 2010-13, 2005-06; NI affairs 1998-03; deregulation 1997-99. APPGs: chairman, looked after children & care leavers; vice-chairman boys' brigade; libraries; sec, Japan. Married. Ed: Port Glasgow HS; University of Edinburgh (Cert Qual social work); University of Bradford (MA social work).

CHALLENGERS
Sophie Shrubsole (C) Operations dir, Westminster Business Council. Cllr, Tonbridge & Malling BC 2012-. **David Radcliffe** (LD) Head of resource planning, University of Birmingham. Cllr, Birmingham CC 2004-14. Contested Birmingham Selly Oak 2010. **Julian Pritchard** (Green) Community campaigner. Candidate, Birmingham CC 2016.

CONSTITUENCY PROFILE
The seat had more than 7,000 education sector employees in 2011, and is one of the less ethnically diverse seats in Birmingham. Originally a consistently Conservative seat, Selly Oak first elected a Labour MP at the October 1974 general election, and has done so since 1992, after the Conservatives under Margaret Thatcher won it back in 1979.

EU REFERENDUM RESULT
46.9% Leave | Remain 53.1%

Birmingham Yardley

LABOUR HOLD MAJORITY 16,574 (37.2%)

JESS PHILLIPS
BORN Oct 9, 1981
MP 2015-

Outspoken backbencher and feminist. Former business development manager, Women's Aid. Cllr, Birmingham CC 2012-16. Socialist: relinquished Labour Party membership 1997-2010. Critic of Jeremy Corbyn and nominated Yvette Cooper for leadership 2015; Owen Smith 2016. Women's rights advocate; publicly clashed with Corbyn over number of women in shadow cabinet. Campaigned for Remain but voted for Article 50. PPS to Lucy Powell 2015-16. APPG chairwoman: domestic violence; sex equality; women & work (co-chairwoman). Women's PLP

	Electorate	Turnout %	from 2010 % Change
	72,581	61.31	
*J Phillips Lab	25,398	57.07	+15.45
M Afzal C	8,824	19.83	+5.83
J Hemming LD	7,984	17.94	-7.66
P Clayton Ukip	1,916	4.31	-11.82
C Garghan Green	280	0.63	-1.07
A Nowshed Ind	100	0.22	

chairwoman 2016-. Married, two children. Ed: University of Leeds (BA history & social policy); University of Birmingham (PgDip public sector management).

CHALLENGERS
Mohammed Afzal (C) Dir, Conservative Friends of Pakistan. Contested Manchester Gorton 2015. **John Hemming** (LD) Founder, John Hemming Trading. MP, Birmingham

Yardley 2005-15. **Paul Clayton** (Ukip) Community tutor. Birmingham CC candidate 2016. Contested Birmingham Yardley 2015. **Christopher Garghan** (Green) Birmingham CC candidate 2016.

CONSTITUENCY PROFILE
About a quarter of the seat's residents are of south Asian descent and it has a large Irish community. Yardley changed hands between Labour and the Conservatives nine times between 1918 and 2005, before being won by the Liberal Democrat John Hemming, who lost the seat to Labour ten years later.

EU REFERENDUM RESULT

60.1% Leave   Remain 39.9%

Bishop Auckland

LABOUR HOLD MAJORITY 502 (1.2%)

HELEN GOODMAN
BORN Jan 2, 1958
MP 2005-

Formerly: senior civil servant, Treasury; executive of two children's charities; dir, Commission on the Future of Multi-ethnic Britain. Jeremy Corbyn critic; nominated Yvette Cooper for leadership in 2015. Campaigned to Remain, voted for Article 50. Shad min: work and pensions 2014-15; CMS 2011-14; justice 2010-11. Shad SoS work and pensions 2010. Select cttees: procedure 2016-17, 2011-14; treasury 2015-17. Member of APPGs: Denmark; Ukraine; body image; cultural heritage; fair business banking; rural services; wellbeing economics. Patron, North East Call to Action on

	Electorate	Turnout %	from 2010 % Change
	67,661	63.97	
*H Goodman Lab	20,808	48.08	+6.68
C Adams C	20,306	46.92	+14.42
C Morrissey LD	1,176	2.72	-1.66
A Walker BNP	991	2.29	

Global Poverty and Climate Change. Married, two children. Ed: Lady Manners Sch, Bakewell; Somerville Coll, Oxford (BA PPE).

CHALLENGERS
Christopher Adams (C) Entrepreneur and independent strategy consultant. Contested Bishop Auckland 2015. **Ciaran Morrissey** (LD) Policy officer, Young Liberals. Newcastle CC by-election candidate: Sep 2016; Nov 2016. **Adam Walker** (BNP) Former school

teacher. Chairman, BNP 2015-. Contested: Rotherham 2015, Bishop Auckland 2010.

CONSTITUENCY PROFILE
The largest seat in Co Durham, covering an area in the county's southwest. Bishop Auckland itself is a former mining town with a population of 16,000. Manufacturing makes up one of the largest sources of employment, including many of the 1,000 employees at the pharmaceutical company Glaxosmithkline at Barnard Castle. It has been a Labour seat for all but four years since 1918 and was once the seat of the former chancellor Hugh Dalton.

EU REFERENDUM RESULT

60.9% Leave   Remain 39.1%

Blackburn

LABOUR HOLD MAJORITY 20,368 (42.9%)

KATE HOLLERN
BORN Apr 12, 1955
MP 2015-

	Electorate	Turnout %	from 2010 %	Change
	70,657	67.24		
*K Hollern Lab	33,148	69.77	+13.49	
B Eastwood C	12,780	26.90	-0.38	
D Miller Ind	875	1.84		
I Ahmed LD	709	1.49	-0.68	

Selected to succeed Jack Straw as Blackburn's Labour candidate in 2014. Accused MoD of cost-cutting after an incident involving six Gurkhas at a training range in Kent 2016. Cllr, Blackburn & Darwen BC 1995-2015; council leader 2010-15, 2004-07. Former manager, Newman's Footwear and contracts manager, Blackburn College. Nominated Andy Burnham in the 2015 Labour leadership race, but no animosity towards Jeremy Corbyn. Campaigned to Remain but voted in favour of Article 50. Shadow min: communities & local govt 2016-; defence 2016. Select cttees: education 2015-16; Armed Forces Bill 2015; education, skills & economy sub 2015-16. Lived in Lancashire for 40 years. Two children, two grandchildren.

CHALLENGERS
Bob Eastwood (C) Operations and security adviser, English Football League. Retired chief superintendent, Lancashire Constabulary. Contested Blackburn 2015. **Duncan Miller** (Ind) Learning and development manager, Express Gifts.

Campaigned on a single policy: to oust Venky's, the owners of Blackburn Rovers. **Ifran Ahmed** (LD) IT consultant. Nelson Liberal Democrats spokesman. Member, Liberal Youth.

CONSTITUENCY PROFILE
Blackburn is an old industrial town that once had a thriving textiles industry. Manufacturing remains one of the largest sectors in terms of employment in the area alongside retailing. More than a third of its population is south Asian, mostly of Indian and Pakistani descent. The seat has been consistently Labour since 1945 and was held by Barbara Castle.

EU REFERENDUM RESULT

53.7% Leave	Remain 46.3%

Blackley & Broughton

LABOUR HOLD MAJORITY 19,601 (48.9%)

GRAHAM STRINGER
BORN Feb 17, 1950
MP 1997-

	Electorate	Turnout %	from 2010 %	Change
	71,648	55.99		
*G Stringer Lab	28,258	70.45	+8.52	
D Goss C	8,657	21.58	+6.54	
M Power Ukip	1,825	4.55	-11.91	
C Gadsden LD	737	1.84	-0.52	
D Jones Green	462	1.15	-3.07	
A Ajoku CPA	174	0.43		

Former board chairman, Manchester Airport; analytical chemist; branch officer, MSF. Cllr, Manchester CC 1979-96; leader 1984-96. Backbencher since 2001, currently sits on panel of chairs select cttee 2017-. Prominent eurosceptic, campaigned to Leave EU. First MP to call for Gordon Brown to resign as MP and a vocal critic of Ed Miliband as leader. Did not nominate a leader 2015. Position on Jeremy Corbyn is unclear. Manchester United fan. Plays squash. Married, one son, one stepdaughter, one stepson. Ed: Moston Brook HS; University of Sheffield (BSc chemistry).

CHALLENGERS
David Goss (C) Chief of staff to Liam Fox 2014-. Weekend duty press officer 2011-14. **Martin Power** (Ukip) Social worker. Former member of Irish government statutory board to oversee £120 million fund to support survivors of Irish institutional abuse. **Charles Gadsden** (LD) Contested Worsley and Eccles South 2010. **David Jones** (Green) Environmental scientist and academic. Green Party energy working group member.

CONSTITUENCY PROFILE
Comprising an area of north Manchester and some of eastern Salford, Blackley & Broughton is home to a large number of Muslim and Jewish residents, about 19,000 and 8,000, respectively. Counting its predecessor seat of Manchester Blackley, it has elected Labour MPs since 1964. Blackley & Broughton also contains Strangeways Prison, and it had the second lowest turnout of any constituency in 2015. Very narrowly voted to Leave the EU in the 2016 referendum.

EU REFERENDUM RESULT

50.0% Leave	Remain 50.0%

Blackpool North & Cleveles

CONSERVATIVE HOLD MAJORITY 2,023 (4.9%)

PAUL MAYNARD
BORN Dec 16, 1975
MP 2010-

Proud northerner. Supporter of Brexit. Advocate for disabilities; has mild cerebral palsy and epilepsy. Allegedly received mocking in parliament for his disability. Parly under sec, transport 2016. Longstanding special adviser to Liam Fox 1999-2007. Speechwriter to William Hague. PPS to Oliver Letwin 2012-15. Contested Twickenham at 2005 general election. Worked at Reform think tank. Management consultant. Lay reader at local Roman Catholic church. Member, Twentieth Century Society. Ed: St Ambrose Coll; University Coll, Oxford (BA modern history).

	Electorate	Turnout %	from 2010 %	Change %
	63,967	64.11		
*P Maynard C	20,255	49.39	+4.95	
C Webb Lab	18,232	44.46	+8.49	
P White Ukip	1,392	3.39	-11.39	
S Close LD	747	1.82	-0.58	
D Royle Green	381	0.93	-1.33	

CHALLENGERS
Chris Webb (Lab) Cllr, Manchester CC 2015-. Parly assistant to Afzal Khan MEP 2015-16. Political organiser, North West Labour Party. **Paul White** (Ukip) Contested Fylde 2015. Hotel manager. Ed: Barr Beacon Sch. **Sue Close** (LD) Treasurer, Blackpool Lib Dems. **Duncan Royle** (Green) Environmental consultant and qualified accountant. Worked in finance roles for BAE Systems Warton.

CONSTITUENCY PROFILE
A bellwether constituency, this has been Conservative-held since 2010 and before, although Labour won it in the landslide of 1997. Nearly 20,000 of its residents are aged 65 or over. The public sector and tourism are significant employers and there is high unemployment during the off season. The Park and Claremont wards are severely deprived. Lying on the west Lancashire coast, this seat comprises about half of Blackpool's unitary authority area, along with Cleveleys, whose twin town Thornton is in the neighbouring seat of Wyre and Preston North.

EU REFERENDUM RESULT
66.9% Leave   Remain 33.1%

Blackpool South

LABOUR HOLD MAJORITY 2,523 (7.2%)

GORDON MARSDEN
BORN Nov 28, 1953
MP 1997-

Historian and public relations consultant. Previously editor of *History Today* and *New Socialist* and former lecturer at the Open University. Public affairs adviser, English Heritage. Contested Blackpool S 1992. Nominated Jeremy Corbyn in the 2015 leadership contest but voted for Yvette Cooper. Shadow min: education 2015-; BIS 2015-16, 2010-13; transport 2013-15. PPS to: John Denham 2009-10; Tessa Jowell 2003-05; Lord Irvine of Lairg 2001-03. Chairman, APPG for Veterans. Pres, British Resorts Assoc. Chairman, Fabian Society 2000-01. Ed: Stockport GS; New Coll, Oxford (BA

	Electorate	Turnout %	from 2010 %	Change %
	58,450	59.80		
*G Marsden Lab	17,581	50.30	+8.53	
P Anthony C	15,058	43.08	+9.28	
N Matthews Ukip	1,339	3.83	-13.47	
B Greene LD	634	1.81	-0.48	
J Warnock Green	341	0.98	-1.62	

history); Warburg Inst, London (PhD); Harvard (intl relations, Kennedy scholar).

CHALLENGERS
Peter Anthony (C) Entertainer for 30 years. Runs a café bar in St Annes. Contested Blackpool S 2015. Chairman, Queendeans Association charity. **Noel Matthews** (Ukip) Worked in IT. Former registered nurse. Cllr, Wesham TC. Ukip regional organiser, NW England. Was senior aide to the former Ukip

leader Paul Nuttall. **Bill Greene** (LD) Studying at The Open University. Cllr, Fylde C. **John Warnock** (Green) Works in property maintenance. Co-ordinator, Blackpool & Fylde Green Party 2014-.

CONSTITUENCY PROFILE
Blackpool South is a compact seat, home to Blackpool's three piers and pleasure beach. Its tourist attractions mean that it is the UK seat whose residents are most likely to be employed in accommodation and food services. The seat was Conservative for 52 years after the 1945 general election, but has remained Labour since 1997.

EU REFERENDUM RESULT
67.8% Leave   Remain 32.2%

Blaenau Gwent

LABOUR HOLD MAJORITY 11,907 (36.8%)

NICK SMITH
BORN Jan 14, 1960
MP 2010-

Former director of policy and partnerships at the Royal College of Speech and Language Therapists. Shadow min Defra 2015-16; resigned from role and voiced fear for Labour's future before 2016 leadership election. Opposition whip 2016-17. Campaigned to Remain, but voted for Article 50. Found to have claimed £1,326.61 in expenses for energy bills in 2013 *Mirror* investigation. Member, public accounts cttee 2010-15. Divorced, two daughters. Ed: Tredegar Comp Sch; Coventry Uni (BA history, politics & intl rel); Birkbeck Coll, London (MSc economic & social change).

	Electorate	Turnout %	from 2010 %	Change
	51,227	63.22		
*N Smith Lab	18,787	58.01	+0.00	
N Copner PC	6,880	21.25	+12.25	
T West C	4,783	14.77	+3.98	
D May Ukip	973	3.00	-14.91	
V Browning Ind	666	2.06		
C Sullivan LD	295	0.91	-1.05	

CHALLENGERS
Nigel Copner (PC) Head and chairman of a research centre at the University of South Wales. School gov. Wants to improve standard of education. **Tracey West** (C) Former air cabin stewardess. Contested Blaenau Gwent 2015, finished third; contested Welsh assembly 2016. **Dennis May** (Ukip) Ran for seat in Torfaen County BC. Brexiteer. **Vicki Browning** (Ind) Established Orion's Reusables,

sells eco-friendly baby products. Lived in Tredegar entire life. **Cameron Sullivan** (LD) Failed run in 2017 Merthyr Tydfil County BC elections. Born in South Wales.

CONSTITUENCY PROFILE
This south Wales seat consists of the towns of Tredegar, Ebbw Vale, Brynmawr and Abertilley, formerly mining and steel towns. The biggest sector is manufacturing. The seat has always been Labour except during the 2005 parliament when it was represented by an Independent MP. Its predecessor, Ebbw Vale, was the seat of Nye Bevan and Michael Foot.

EU REFERENDUM RESULT

62.0% Leave	Remain 38.0%

Blaydon

LABOUR HOLD MAJORITY 13,477 (28.0%)

LIZ TWIST
BORN Jul 10, 1956
MP 2017-

Retired regional head of health, Unison. Samaritans listener. Cllr, Gateshead BC 2012-; cabinet member for housing. Selected ahead of a Unison official and a member of Labour's national policy forum after Dave Anderson decided not to seek re-election; previously worked in Anderson's constituency office. Volunteer, the Samaritans. Widowed. Ed: Notre Dame HS; University Coll of Wales, Aberystwyth (BA history; PgDip archive administration).

CHALLENGERS
Thomas Smith (C) EU public policy director, UBS. Formerly

	Electorate	Turnout %	from 2010 %	Change
	68,459	70.24		
L Twist Lab	26,979	56.11	+6.95	
T Smith C	13,502	28.08	+10.64	
J Wallace LD	4,366	9.08	-3.15	
R Tolley Ukip	2,459	5.11	-12.38	
P McNally Green	583	1.21	-2.45	
M Marchetti Libertarian	114	0.24		
L Marschild Space	81	0.17		

government relations manager, Prudential Assurance and worked on public policy at HSBC. Honorary secretary, LGBT+ Conservatives. Contested Gateshead 2015. School governor. Lives in Barnet. **Jonathan Wallace** (LD) Self-employed horticulturalist and communications businessman. Produces own food. Blogger. Cllr, Gateshead BC 1987-; deputy opposition leader 2011-. **Ray**

Tolley (Ukip) Retired IT teacher turned education consultant.

CONSTITUENCY PROFILE
An old coalmining seat southwest of Newcastle-upon-Tyne, consisting of a small area of western Gateshead, several towns and the rural area between them. The town of Blaydon has a population of about 16,000. The demographic is overwhelmingly white. Blaydon has lower levels of unemployment and is more affluent than the North East average. There is a high number of apprentices. Labour has won the seat at every election since 1935.

EU REFERENDUM RESULT

56.1% Leave	Remain 43.9%

Blyth Valley

LABOUR HOLD MAJORITY 7,915 (18.6%)

RONNIE CAMPBELL
BORN Aug 14, 1943
MP 1987-

Brexit campaigner, argued that the North East would benefit from leaving the EU. From old Labour left, supporter of Jeremy Corbyn. Rowed with Andrew Griffiths in chamber after Esther McVey was targeted by Labour over welfare cuts 2015. Select cttees: health 2005-07; catering 2001-10; public administration 1997-2001. Former chairman, Lab MPs' northern regional group. Cllr: Blyth Valley BC 1974-88; Blyth BC 1969-74. NUM-sponsored, former lodge chairman, Bates Colliery, Blyth. Miner for 28 years. Married, one daughter, five sons. Ed: Blyth Ridley County HS.

	Electorate	Turnout %	from 2010 Change %
	63,371	67.05	
*R Campbell Lab	23,770	55.94	+9.63
I Levy C	15,855	37.31	+15.61
J Reid LD	1,947	4.58	-1.31
D Furness Green	918	2.16	-1.62

CHALLENGERS
Ian Levy (C) Works for NHS. **Jeff Reid** (LD) Owns stationery company. Previously sales director. Cllr: Northumberland CC 2008-, leader of LD 2008-, leader of council 2009-13; Blyth Valley BC 1999-2008, 1987-91, council leader 2008-13, leader of LD 2000-08. Awarded Freedom of Borough, 2008. Contested Blyth Valley 2010, 2005, 2001. **Dawn Furness** (Green) Opera singer, burlesque dancer, music teacher, film-maker. Contested Blyth Valley 2015.

CONSTITUENCY PROFILE
This southern Northumberland seat consists of the towns of Blyth and Cramlington. Blyth was once home to the coalmining and shipbuilding industries. Cramlington was a new town built in the 1950s and 1960s and is nine miles north of Newcastle upon Tyne. Blyth Valley has elected Labour MPs at every election since its inception in 1950, with the exception of February 1974 when the incumbent Eddie Milne was deselected by his local party before going on to win as an independent. His successor, Ronnie Campbell, has been the MP ever since.

EU REFERENDUM RESULT

60.5% Leave   Remain 39.5%

Bognor Regis & Littlehampton

CONSERVATIVE HOLD MAJORITY 17,494 (34.1%)

NICK GIBB
BORN Sep 3, 1960
MP 1997-

Former KPMG accountant 1984-97. Worked on a kibbutz in 1983. Min schools 2014-16, 2010-12; standards 2016. Frontbench spokesman: trade and industry 1997-98, 1999-2001; Treasury 1998-99. Select cttees: draft voting eligibility (prisoners) bill 2013; educ & skills 2003-2005; public accounts 2001-03; Treasury sub-cttee 1998; Treasury 1998; soc sec 1997-98. Campaigned Remain. Born in Amersham, Buckinghamshire. Ed: Maidstone GS, Kent; Roundhay School, Leeds; Thornes House School, Wakefield; Durham University (BA law)

	Electorate	Turnout %	from 2010 Change %
	75,827	67.72	
*N Gibb C	30,276	58.96	+7.63
A Butcher Lab	12,782	24.89	+11.08
F Oppler LD	3,352	6.53	-2.47
P Sanderson Ind	2,088	4.07	
P Lowe Ukip	1,861	3.62	-18.11
A Bishop Green	993	1.93	-2.19

CHALLENGERS
Alan Butcher (Lab) Works for an air ambulance company. Contested Bognor Regis & Littlehampton 2015. **Francis Oppler** (LD) Previously stated the Conservatives do not listen to local people. Contested Bognor Regis & Littlehampton 2015. **Paul Sanderson** (Ind) Awarded MBE in 2006 for services to young people. Former community and pastoral leader at Littlehampton Academy.

Patrick Lowe (Ukip) Was escorted out of a local election team meeting by two PCSOs in 2015. Contested Sussex PCC 2016. **Andrew Bishop** (Green) Worked in further education for a decade. Advocates soft Brexit.

CONSTITUENCY PROFILE
On the West Sussex coast, the seat consists primarily of the two towns in its name. It has pockets of deprivation typical of seaside resorts with seasonal tourism. A large retired population at about 14,000 and high levels of home ownership. A safe seat in which the Conservative majority has grown at every election since 2001.

EU REFERENDUM RESULT

64.8 Leave   Remain 35.2%

Bolsover

LABOUR HOLD MAJORITY 5,288 (11.4%)

DENNIS SKINNER
BORN Feb 11, 1932
MP 1970-

The Beast of Bolsover. A coalminer for 21 years who joined Labour in 1956. Famously thrown out of the Commons chamber for twice branding then-PM David Cameron "dodgy Dave" and expelled in 1992 for likening John Gummer, then agriculture secretary, to a "slimy wart" on Margaret Thatcher's nose. Brexit supporter; believes leaving the EU will aid British socialism. Member, Socialist Campaign Group. Corbyn supporter. Flicked the V-sign towards rebellious backbenchers in 2016. Chairman, Labour Party 1988-89. Member, Labour Party NEC 1979-92, 1994-98, 1999-

	Electorate	Turnout %	from 2010 % Change
	73,429	63.35	
*D Skinner Lab	24,153	51.92	+0.69
H Harrison C	18,865	40.55	+16.09
P Rose Ukip	2,129	4.58	-16.40
R Shipman LD	1,372	2.95	-0.38

2010. Divorced, three children, four grandchildren. Born in Clay Cross. Ed: Tupton Grammar School; Ruskin Coll, Oxford.

CHALLENGERS
Helen Harrison (C) Runs a physiotherapy business. Governor, Kettering General Hospital Foundation Trust 2013-15. Campaigned to keep open and improve Bolsover Hospital. Cllr, East Northants Council. **Philip Rose** (Ukip) Unsuccessfully contested Ashfield 2015. Stood for Amber

Valley BC 2016. **Ross Shipman** (LD) Chairman, North East Derbyshire & Bolsover District Liberal Democrats.

CONSTITUENCY PROFILE
One of 17 constituencies to vote Leave by a margin of more than 40 per cent, this mostly rural east Derbyshire seat once had a thriving coalmining industry. Among the largest employers is Sports Direct, whose headquarters at Shirebrook employs about 3,000 people. A tourism industry has emerged in recent years, including tours of Bolsover Castle. Constituents have elected a Labour MP at every election since 1950.

EU REFERENDUM RESULT

70.4% Leave   Remain 29.6%

Bolton North East

LABOUR HOLD MAJORITY 3,797 (8.4%)

SIR DAVID
CRAUSBY
BORN Jun 17, 1946
MP 1997-

Former lathe turner and steward works convenor at AEEU. Cllr, Bury DC 1979-92. Contested: Bolton NE 1992; Bury North 1987. In minority of Labour MPs who voted to oppose equal marriage and same-sex adoption. Supported challenge to Corbyn's leadership. Knighted in 2017 new year honours. Voted against Iraq War 2003. Won Commons Speech of the Year, *House* magazine awards 2011. Member, cttees: panel of chairs 2010-17; defence 2001-10. Chairman, Amicus trade union parly group. Sec, Unite 2010-. Member, UK delegation to Nato parly assembly 2014-. Married, two

	Electorate	Turnout %	from 2010 % Change
	67,233	67.20	
*D Crausby Lab	22,870	50.62	+7.66
J Daly C	19,073	42.21	+9.40
H Lamb Ukip	1,567	3.47	-15.34
W Fox LD	1,316	2.91	+0.05
L Spencer Green	357	0.79	-1.77

sons. Ed: Derby GS, Bury; Bury Tech College.

CHALLENGERS
James Daly (C) Legal aid solicitor. Contested Bolton NE 2015. Cllr, Bury North 2012-. Leader, Bury Conservative Group 2017-. Board member, Bury CAB. **Harry Lamb** (Ukip) Industrial chemist. Managing director, HiCharms, which imports chemicals from China to Europe. Contested Bolton NE 2015. **Warren Fox** (LD) Sales

and marketing manager. Worked as support worker for adults with mental health and learning difficulties. Charity trustee and director, All Souls Bolton. **Liz Spencer** (Green) Retired mental health worker.

CONSTITUENCY PROFILE
A young and diverse constituency, with nearly 20,000 residents aged under 16, and more than 16,000 ethnic minority residents at the 2011 census. On average, higher rates of pay and lower rates of unemployment than Bolton South East. Elected Tories from 1983 until 1997 and has been Labour ever since.

EU REFERENDUM RESULT

58.1% Leave   Remain 41.9%

Bolton South East

LABOUR HOLD MAJORITY 13,126 (31.0%)

YASMIN QURESHI
BORN Jul 5, 1963
MP 2010-

Criminal law barrister. Previously a CPS prosecutor, and CPS policy adviser. Head, criminal legal section of the UN mission in Kosovo. Human rights adviser to Ken Livingstone as mayor of London. Volunteer legal adviser South Law Centre 1993-2000. USDAW, GMB. Largely supportive of Jeremy Corbyn. Remainer, but supported Article 50. Opposed Iraq war, vocal about Muslim women's rights. Accused President Trump of inciting hatred. Criticised for drawing parallels between Israeli treatment of Palestinians to the Holocaust. Shadow min justice 2016-17. Pakistani-born. Married.

	Electorate	Turnout %	from 2010 %	Change
	68,886	61.44		
*Y Qureshi Lab	25,676	60.67	+10.22	
S Pochin C	12,550	29.65	+9.31	
J Armstrong Ukip	2,779	6.57	-17.06	
F Harasiwka LD	781	1.85	-0.79	
A Johnson Green	537	1.27	-1.68	

Ed: Westfield Comp, Watford; South Bank (BA law); Council of Legal Ed; UCL (LLM).

CHALLENGERS
Sarah Pochin (C) Magistrate. Governor, Berkeley Primary School. Volunteered at Leighton Hospital. Cllr, Cheshire EC 2015. **Jeff Armstrong** (Ukip) Magistrate. Came second in Bolton SE 2015, one of the best performances from a Ukip candidate in the northwest. **Frank Harasiwka** (LD) School

governor. Contested Bolton SE 1987, 1997, 2001, 2005. **Alan Johnson** (Green) Works in social care. Green Party member for 14 years. Contested Bolton SE 2010 and 2015. Local election candidate since 2004. Contested Bolton C. Unison delegate.

CONSTITUENCY PROFILE
A diverse community, with about a fifth of residents of Asian descent. Very low proportion of university-educated residents, with a significant number of jobs coming from the wholesale and retail sector. A relatively poor constituency, Bolton SE has elected a Labour MP at every election since 1983.

EU REFERENDUM RESULT

63.0% Leave   Remain 37.0%

Bolton West

CONSERVATIVE HOLD MAJORITY 936 (1.8%)

CHRIS GREEN
BORN Aug 12, 1973
MP 2015-

Scientific instrumentation engineer and engineering ambassador in schools. Has worked in the pharmaceutical and manufacturing industries. Member, science and technology select cttee 2015-. Taught English in Rwanda. Former member, Territorial Army. Contested Manchester Withington 2010. Brexit supporter. Does not want fracking in his constituency but has welcomed it elsewhere. Supports regional devolution. APPGs: health; manufacturing, vice-chairman. Born in Northern Ireland and grew up in a deprived part of Liverpool. Fitness enthusiast.

	Electorate	Turnout %	from 2010 %	Change
	72,797	70.13		
*C Green C	24,459	47.91	+7.28	
J Hilling Lab	23,523	46.07	+7.09	
M Tighe Ukip	1,587	3.11	-12.18	
R Forrest LD	1,485	2.91	-1.10	

CHALLENGERS
Julie Hilling (Lab) Youth worker turned union official: senior regional organiser, TSSA; NW learning organiser, NASUWT. MP Bolton West 2010-15. Opposition whip 2013-15. National president, CYWU. Chairwoman: Socialist Education Assoc. Amnesty; Howard League for Penal Reform; Labour Friends of Palestine; Unite. **Martin Tighe** (Ukip) Financial analyst. Previously worked at international banking organisation and as factory

worker. **Rebecca Forrest** (LD) Science teacher. Environmental campaigner. Volunteers at local Rainbows group. Joined the Lib Dems in 2016.

CONSTITUENCY PROFILE
This is the largest and most rural seat of the three Bolton constituencies, incorporating the towns of Horwich and Westhoughton. Its residents tend to be older, whiter and more likely to own their homes than their neighbours to the east. A marginal seat, which stayed Labour in 2010 but switched to the Conservatives in 2015: each time the winning candidate was fewer than 1,000 votes ahead.

EU REFERENDUM RESULT

55.6% Leave   Remain 44.4%

Bootle

LABOUR HOLD MAJORITY 36,200 (72.0%)

PETER DOWD
BORN Jun 20, 1957
MP 2015-

Family has history of Labour activism. Worked in health and social care for 35 years in Merseyside. Qualified social worker with interest in education and mental health. Nominated Andy Burnham for 2015 leadership. Now supports Jeremy Corbyn. Campaigned in favour of remaining in the EU, but voted to trigger Article 50. Shadow chief sec to the Treasury 2017. Shadow fin sec to the Treasury 2016-17. Cllr, Sefton C 1991-2015; leader 2013-15. Cllr, Merseyside CC 1981-86. Board member, Liverpool City Region Combined Authority. Chairman, Merseyside Fire Authority

	Electorate	Turnout %	from 2010 % Change
	72,872	69.01	
*P Dowd Lab	42,259	84.03	+9.58
C Fifield C	6,059	12.05	+3.99
D Newman LD	837	1.66	-0.50
A Gibbon Green	709	1.41	-1.91
K Bryan Soc Lab	424	0.84	

1990s. Chairman, Merseyside Fire and Rescue Service; South Sefton Primary Care Trust. Ed: University of Liverpool; Lancaster University.

CHALLENGERS
Charles Fifield (C) Chartered surveyor. Contested Vale Royal BC 2007. Cllr, Cheshire West and Chester 2011-. **David Newman** (LD) Career in financial services and call-centre management. **Alison Gibbon** (Green) Worked in citizens' advice and legal

services. Contested Sefton C 2015. **Kim Bryan** (Soc Lab) Contested Sefton C 2016.

CONSTITUENCY PROFILE
An old docking town to Liverpool's north, Bootle has been consistently Labour since the Second World War. Prominent sectors of employment for Bootle's residents include retail, social care and transport. Two by-elections were held in the seat in 1990, the second after the death of Michael Carr, Bootle's MP for just 57 days. The former Ukip leader Paul Nuttall stood in this seat in 2005, 2010 and 2015.

EU REFERENDUM RESULT

54.8% Leave	Remain 45.2%

Boston & Skegness

CONSERVATIVE HOLD MAJORITY 16,572 (38.6%)

MATT WARMAN
BORN Sep 1, 1981
MP 2015-

Supporter of Remain despite Boston having the largest majority of Brexit voters in the UK. Wrote a public defence of his constituency after *The New European* published an article that mocked Skegness. Technology editor for 16 years, *Daily Telegraph*. Co-chairman, APPG on broadband and digital communication. Used to campaign for better broadband. Member, science & technology select cttee, 2015-17. Member, Conservative Rural Action Group, NUJ. Married, one daughter. Ed: Haberdashers' Aske's Boys Sch; Durham University (BA English).

	Electorate	Turnout %	from 2010 % Change
	68,391	62.70	
*M Warman C	27,271	63.60	+19.80
P Kenny Lab	10,699	24.95	+8.47
P Nuttall Ukip	3,308	7.71	-26.08
P Smith LD	771	1.80	-0.54
V Percival Green	547	1.28	-0.57
M Gilbert Blue	283	0.66	

CHALLENGERS
Paul Kenny (Lab) Community worker. Contested Boston & Skegness 2015. GMB. **Paul Nuttall** (Ukip) Former lecturer. MEP for North West England 2009-. Ukip leader 2016-17; dep leader 2010-16; chairman 2008-10. Ukip spokesman for education, life skills and training 2014-16. Contested: Stoke-on-Trent Central 2017 by-election; Bootle 2015, 2010, 2005. **Philip Smith** (Lib Dem). Owns florist

shop. Career in IT. Former cllr and cabinet member, Mansfield DC; dep exec mayor. **Victoria Percival** (Green) Runs small business.

CONSTITUENCY PROFILE
A coastal Lincolnshire seat with higher than average levels of employment in agriculture and fishing. In 2011 it had one of the highest rates of EU migration, with nearly 8,000 residents from the post-2001 accession states. Has elected Conservative MPs since 1997. The only seat to vote Leave with a majority of 50 per cent, it was the most pro-Brexit constituency in the referendum.

EU REFERENDUM RESULT

75.6% Leave	Remain 24.4%

Bosworth

CONSERVATIVE HOLD MAJORITY 18,351 (32.7%)

DAVID TREDINNICK
BORN Jan 19, 1950
MP 1987-

Executive career came to an end after being forced to resign as a PPS in wake of cash for questions scandal, 1994. Has since thrown himself into backbench parliamentary work. Interested in health. Advocates homeopathy and consistently voted against same-sex marriage. Chairman of APPG for integrated healthcare 2002-. Member of select cttee: health 2010-15; science and technology 2013-15. Lieutenant Grenadier Guards 1968-71. Remainer, but voted for Article 50. Divorced, one daughter, one son. Ed: Eton Coll; Cape Town (MBA); St John's Coll, Oxford (MLitt).

	Electorate	Turnout %	from 2010 Change %
	80,633	69.66	
*D Tredinnick C	31,864	56.73	+13.92
C Kealey Lab	13,513	24.06	+6.60
M Mullaney LD	9,744	17.35	4.96
M Gregg Green	1,047	1.86	

CHALLENGERS
Chris Kealey (Lab) Worked at FCO. Signed 2016 letter urging Jeremy Corbyn to quit. Appointed MBE in 2010 for his work in Afghanistan. **Michael Mullaney** (LD) Worked as carer for elderly and disabled people. Cllr, Hinckley & Bosworth 2011-. Contested Bosworth 2010 and 2015. Former chairman, East Midlands Lib Dems. **Mick Gregg** (Green) Social worker for child asylum seekers. Formerly social worker for NHS mental health services and council child

protection services. Lived near Hinckley for the past 12 years.

CONSTITUENCY PROFILE
A rural west Leicestershire seat spread out around the town of Market Bosworth, the constituency has high levels of homeownership and a low claimant rate. The larger town, Hinckley, lies in the south of the seat. The most significant local employment sectors are retail and manufacturing. Although Labour held this seat for the first 25 years after the Second World War, it has been Conservative ever since, with Labour coming within 2 per cent of victory in 1997.

EU REFERENDUM RESULT

60.8% Leave   Remain 39.2%

Bournemouth East

CONSERVATIVE HOLD MAJORITY 7,937 (16.3%)

TOBIAS ELLWOOD
BORN Aug 12, 1966
MP 2005-

Former soldier Royal Green Jackets. Later worked in business development: London Stock Exchange, Allen and Overy. Researcher, Tom King MP. Hailed a hero and appointed to Privy Council after attempting mouth-to-mouth resuscitation on PC Keith Palmer during Westminster terror attack 2017. Active Army reservist. Rarely rebels. Remainer, voted for Article 50. Min: FCO 2014-17; defence 2017-. PPS: Liam Fox, 2010-11; David Liddington, 2011-13; Jeremy Hunt, 2013-14. Married, two sons. Ed: Vienna Int Sch; Loughborough University (BA design and

	Electorate	Turnout %	from 2010 Change %
	74,591	65.18	
*T Ellwood C	25,221	51.88	+2.66
M Semple Lab	17,284	35.55	+18.94
J Nicholas LD	3,168	6.52	-1.85
D Hughes Ukip	1,405	2.89	-13.62
A Keddie Green	1,236	2.54	4.74
K Wilson Ind	304	0.63	

technology); City, University of London (MBA); Kennedy School of Government (senior exec course nat/internat studies).

CHALLENGERS
Mel Semple (Lab) Sociology and social policy academic, University of Bath. **Jon Nicholas** (LD) Conflict management consultant who has worked in former Yugoslavia, Caucasus and Indonesia. **David Hughes** (Ukip) Ran an electrical retailing

business. Served in police service until 1970. Chairman, Ukip Bournemouth East. **Alasdair Keddie** (Green) IT engineer. **Kieron Wilson** (Ind) 22-year-old final-year politics student at time of election.

CONSTITUENCY PROFILE
This half of the Dorset town stretches farther along Poole Bay and contains more of the town's beaches. As such, it is overrepresented with industries such as tourism and real estate. High levels of EU migration, with about 7,000 residents in 2011. No Bournemouth seat has failed to elect a Conservative since the 1920s.

EU REFERENDUM RESULT

53.7% Leave   Remain 46.3%

Bournemouth West

CONSERVATIVE HOLD MAJORITY 7,711 (17.3&)

CONOR BURNS
BORN Sep 24, 1972
MP 2010-

Background in communications and financial services. Eurosceptic. Admirer of Margaret Thatcher. Claimed to have felt unable to take Holy Communion at church after his bishop voiced displeasure for politicians who voted for same-sex marriage. Pro-life. Contested Eastleigh 2005, 2001. Claimed he was so poor after 2005 that he had to choose between paying mortgage or council tax. PPS to: Owen Paterson 2012; Hugo Swire 2010-12; Greg Clark 2016-. Board member, Spitfire Tribute Foundation. Ed: St Columba's Coll, St Albans; University of Southampton (BA modern

	Electorate	Turnout %	from 2010 % Change
	73,195	60.81	
*C Burns C	23,812	53.50	+5.25
D Stokes Lab	16,101	36.18	+18.50
P Dunn LD	2,929	6.58	-1.27
S Bull Green	1,247	2.80	-4.64
J Halsey Pirate	418	0.94	

history & politics, Chairman, Conservative association).

CHALLENGERS
David Stokes (Lab) Works in construction. Campaign organiser, Bournemouth Labour Party. Voiced support for Jeremy Corbyn. **Phil Dunn** (LD) Qualified teacher. Supporter of free school meals and extended childcare provision for very young children. **Simon Bull** (Green) Cllr, Bournemouth BC 2015-; first Green Party cllr on

Bournemouth BC. Humanist funeral celebrant. **Jason Halsey** (Pirate Party) Background in technology. Deputy secretary of Pirate Party.

CONSTITUENCY PROFILE
Containing the University of Bournemouth, the seat is younger than Bournemouth East and its residents are significantly more likely to be students. The seat is marginally better off than its neighbour in terms of average earnings and lower unemployment. A safe seat, Bournemouth West has been represented by Conservative MPs since it was created in 1950.

EU REFERENDUM RESULT

57.7% Leave   Remain 42.3%

Bracknell

CONSERVATIVE HOLD MAJORITY 16,016 (28.7%)

PHILLIP LEE
BORN Sep 28, 1970
MP 2010-

Junior doctor at various hospitals, then GP for a decade. Continues to practise as a GP. Joined the Conservative Party in 1992. Parly under-sec, justice 2016-. Select cttees: administration 2010-12; energy & climate change 2010-15. Executive vice-chairman: parliamentary space committee 2010-15; Conservative Middle East Council. Remainer, voted for Article 50, critical of £350 million Brexit bus promise. Born in Buckinghamshire. Married, one daughter. Ed: Sir William Borlase's GS, Marlow; King's Coll London; Keble Coll, Oxford (MSc human biology

	Electorate	Turnout %	from 2010 % Change
	79,199	70.57	
*P Lee C	32,882	58.83	+3.06
P Bidwell Lab	16,866	30.18	+13.31
P Smith LD	4,186	7.49	-0.01
L Amos Ukip	1,521	2.72	-12.99
O Barreto Ind	437	0.78	

& biological anthropology); St Mary's Hospital Med Sch at Imperial Coll London (MBBS).

CHALLENGERS
Paul Bidwell (Lab) Passionate about the provision of quality services for over-65s. Trustee, elderly day centre. Cllr, Bracknell Forest C 2015-. **Patrick Smith** (LD) Senior project manager of an audio-visual company. Contested Bracknell 2015. **Len Amos** (Ukip) Contested Hampshire CC 2017. **Olivio**

Barreto (Ind) Financial and management consultant. Ukip candidate for Bracknell BC 2015 and Bracknell TC 2015 elections.

CONSTITUENCY PROFILE
A compact and affluent Berkshire seat with a significant proportion of residents in managerial jobs. The most overrepresented sector is information and communication. Nearly two thirds of homeowners have mortgages, which is much higher than the national average. Bracknell is a safe Conservative seat where their majority was more than 10,000 even after Labour's high national watermark in 1997.

EU REFERENDUM RESULT

53.2% Leave   Remain 46.8%

Bradford East

LABOUR HOLD MAJORITY 20,540 (45.0%)

IMRAN HUSSAIN
BORN Jun 7, 1978
MP 2015-

Barrister, Altaf Solicitors. Cllr, Bradford MDC 2002-; deputy leader 2010-15. Member: Unite; Unison; GMB. Member, West Yorkshire police and crime panel. Contested Bradford West by-election 2012. Married, two children. Jeremy Corbyn supporter who nominated him in 2015 Labour leadership election. Shad min: international development 2016-17; justice 2017-. Infrequent rebel; voted against replacing Trident nuclear submarines and 2015 welfare bill, which he described as "cruel and unfair". Campaigned to Remain in the EU, voted to trigger Article 50. Ed: Lincoln's Inn.

	Electorate	Turnout %	from 2010 %	Change
	70,389	64.81		
*I Hussain Lab	29,831	65.39	+18.75	
M Trafford C	9,291	20.37	+9.06	
D Ward Ind	3,576	7.84		
J Barras Ukip	1,372	3.01	-6.90	
M Jewell LD	843	1.85	-27.68	
P Parkins Bradford	420	0.92		
A Stanford Green	289	0.63	-1.47	

CHALLENGERS
Mark Trafford (C) Barrister, specialises in common and criminal law. Associate lecturer, Oxford Institute of Legal Practice. **David Ward** (Ind) Suspended from Liberal Democrats after making anti-Israel comments that he denies were antisemitic. Lib Dem MP Bradford East 2010-15. **Jonathan Barras** (Ukip) Bartender. **Mark Jewell** (LD) Works in aerospace industry. Cllr, Lancashire CC 2009-13.

CONSTITUENCY PROFILE
Densely populated area in west Yorkshire – about two fifths of residents are of Asian descent, mostly Pakistani. A young seat, it has more than 30,000 residents under the age of 16. The largest industry is retail, with routine and manual jobs more common than managerial jobs. Incomes are well below average for the region. Bradford East's predecessor, Bradford North, was Labour from 1987 to 2010, but the East was Lib Dem from 2010 before switching back to Labour in 2015.

EU REFERENDUM RESULT
55.2% Leave   Remain 44.8%

Bradford South

LABOUR HOLD MAJORITY 6,700 (16.3%)

JUDITH CUMMINS
BORN Jun 26, 1967
MP 2015-

Labour Party organiser, was agent for Chris Leslie when he won Nottingham East 2010. Cllr, Leeds CC 2012-16; Bradford MDC 2004-07. Member: GMB; Unison; Tribune Group. Nominated Yvette Cooper for leadership 2015; Owen Smith 2016. Member: West Yorkshire Fire and Rescue Authority; Aire Valley Regeneration Board; Halton Moor and Osmondthorpe project for the elderly. Opposition whip 2015-. Member, Armed Forces Bill select cttee 2015. Married, two children. Ed: University of Leeds (BA politics & parliamentary studies); Ruskin Coll, Oxford.

	Electorate	Turnout %	from 2010 %	Change
	67,752	60.59		
*J Cummins Lab	22,364	54.48	+11.06	
T Graham C	15,664	38.16	+11.89	
S Place Ukip	1,758	4.28	-19.81	
S Thomas LD	516	1.26	-1.65	
T Hirst Eng Dem	377	0.92		
D Parkinson Green	370	0.90	-2.40	

CHALLENGERS
Tanya Graham (C) Has worked in the public and private sector. Contested Bradford South 2015. Comms officer for Kris Hopkins MP. Cllr, Craven DC 2016-. Governor, Bradford District Care Trust. Campaigned to Remain in the EU. **Stephen Place** (Ukip) Owned company delivering apprenticeships in animal care and first aid. Former mounted officer, West Yorkshire Police. Chairman, Ukip Richmond, North Yorkshire. **Stuart Thomas** (LD) Chairman, Wigan, Leigh & Makerfield Liberal Democrats. **Therese Hirst** (English Democrats) Previously teacher and law lecturer. Campaigner for Veritas and member, Campaign for an Independent Britain.

CONSTITUENCY PROFILE
Of the three Bradford seats, Bradford South is the least diverse – with the population about three quarters white – with the lowest unemployment and the highest proportion of managerial jobs. Homeownership is higher than the other Bradford seats, but still lower than the national average.

EU REFERENDUM RESULT
63.6% Leave   Remain 36.4%

Bradford West

LABOUR HOLD MAJORITY 21,902 (48.1%)

NASEEM SHAH
BORN Nov 13, 1973
MP 2015-

Suspended from Labour Party in 2016 for having posted "problem solved" when she suggested on Facebook that Israel's population be moved to America. After the controversy, resigned as PPS to John McDonnell. Readmitted to Labour in July 2016. Select cttee, home affairs 2015-17. Had a turbulent childhood, including her mother's imprisonment for the murder of an abusive partner and an arranged marriage at 15. Became politically active after campaigning with women's groups for her mother's release. Former chairwoman, Sharing Voices mental health charity. Mother of three. Known as Naz.

	Electorate	Turnout %	from 2010 % Change
	67,568	67.38	
*N Shah Lab	29,444	64.67	+15.09
G Grant C	7,542	16.57	+1.28
S Yaqoob IND	6,345	13.94	
D Hodgson Ukip	885	1.94	-5.85
A Griffiths LD	712	1.56	-1.35
C Hickson Green	481	1.06	-1.64
H Khadim IND	65	0.14	
M Hijazi Ind	54	0.12	-0.13

CHALLENGERS
George Grant (C) Director of a financial inclusion company. Contested Bradford W 2015. **Salma Yaqoob** (Ind) Former Respect Party leader but left party in 2014. Cllr, Birmingham CC, 2006-14. **Derrick Hodgson** (Ukip) Aims to integrate all faiths into British culture. **Alun Griffiths** (LD) GP. Cllr, Bradford MDC 2016-.

CONSTITUENCY PROFILE
One of the UK's youngest and most ethnically diverse constituencies. Bradford West has a population of about 50,000 under-25s and a similar number of residents of Pakistani descent. In 2011 it was the constituency with the second largest proportion of Muslim residents. It also has one of the highest levels of economic inactivity of any seat in the UK and one of the lowest average incomes. Although it has elected Labour MPs at every election for more than 40 years, it is one of two seats to elect George Galloway as a Respect MP, which it did in a 2012 by-election.

EU REFERENDUM RESULT

46.7% Leave   Remain 53.3%

Braintree

CONSERVATIVE HOLD MAJORITY 18,422 (35.2%)

JAMES CLEVERLY
BORN Sep 4, 1969
MP 2015-

TA officer; had army aspirations dashed by injury. Former magazine and digital publisher. Rose to prominence after paying an emotional tribute in the HoC to his friend PC Keith Palmer, who was killed during the 2017 Westminster terror attack. Active on Twitter, mocked Jeremy Corbyn's slogan that only Labour could "unlock the talent of black, Asian and minority ethnic people" by posting a series of photographs of black and Asian Conservative politicians. Tweeted a series of unusual re-election pledges in April 2017, including: "to continue to surprise old ladies";

	Electorate	Turnout %	from 2010 % Change
	75,316	69.48	
*J Cleverly C	32,873	62.82	+8.99
M Fincken Lab	14,451	27.62	+9.13
P Turner LD	2,251	4.30	-0.65
R Bingley Ukip	1,835	3.51	-15.31
T Pashby Green	916	1.75	-1.36

"to continue to take the mickey out of Labour". Select cttees: international trade 2016-17; consolidation bills 2015-17. President, Ulysses Trust. Married, two sons. Ed: Colfe's Sch; Thames Valley University (BA hospital management).

CHALLENGERS
Malcolm Fincken (Lab) Retired teacher. Contested: Braintree 2015; Saffron Walden 1997. Former cllr: Braintree DC; Halstead TC. **Peter Turner** (LD)

Dir of a North Essex fostering agency. Contested Braintree 2005, 2001.

CONSTITUENCY PROFILE
Neighbouring the Essex-Suffolk border, this Essex seat largely contains skilled working-class people. The area is sparsely populated, with most of its residents based in the towns of Braintree and Halstead. House prices are extremely low and home ownership is high. The seat lacks diversity and has a large proportion of residents who do not observe a religion. The Conservatives have grown their vote share since winning the seat from Labour in 2005.

EU REFERENDUM RESULT

61.5% Leave   Remain 38.5%

Brecon & Radnorshire

CONSERVATIVE HOLD MAJORITY 8,038 (19.4%)

CHRISTOPHER DAVIES
BORN Aug 18, 1967
MP 2015-

Rural auctioneer and estate agent. Managed a veterinary practice in Hay-on-Wye. Brexit supporter focused on getting a good deal for Wales. Member, select cttees: EFRA 2015-17; Welsh affairs 2015-17. Cllr, Powys CC 2012-15. Contested 2011 Welsh assembly election for Brecon & Radnorshire. Member, Brecon Beacons National Park Authority. Commentator at Royal Welsh Show. Married, two daughters. Ed: Moriston Comp Sch & Sixth Form.

CHALLENGERS
James Gibson-Watt (LD) Local businessman, owns two shops.

	Electorate	Turnout %	from 2010 %	Change
	56,010	73.80		
*C Davies C	20,081	48.58	+7.53	
J Gibson-Watt LD	12,043	29.14	+0.81	
D Lodge Lab	7,335	17.75	+3.01	
K Heneghan PC	1,299	3.14	-1.27	
P Gilbert Ukip	576	1.39	-6.94	

Instrumental in campaign to save local secondary school from closing. Cllr, Powys CC 2015-; leader of LD group. Member, NFU. **Dan Lodge** (Lab) Barrister for Thompson's solicitors. Contested Welsh assembly Preseli Pembrokeshire 2016. Adviser to Peter Hain when he was SoS for Wales. Press officer to the MPs Nick Ainger and Nia Griffith. Former leader, Fabians Cymru. **Kate Heneghan** (PC) Works for NHS Wales. Trained as a nurse and

midwife. Parent governor at local school.

CONSTITUENCY PROFILE
A huge constituency in the county of Powys, its biggest towns have populations of about 8,000. More than half of the residents are 45 or older; 98 per cent are white, and nearly half own their home. About a quarter of workers are self-employed, one of the highest rates in the UK. This constituency elected Labour MPs between 1939 and 1979, and has since swung back and forth between Conservatives and Liberal Democrats. The seat is home to the Royal Welsh Show.

EU REFERENDUM RESULT
51.9% Leave   Remain 48.1%

Brent Central

LABOUR HOLD MAJORITY 27,997 (53.5%)

DAWN BUTLER
BORN Nov 3, 1969
MP 2015-; 2005-10

First person to use sign language in the House of Commons when she called on the government to give British Sign Language legal status. Falsely accused Costa Coffee of not paying its tax in a 2017 radio interview. Resigned from shadow cabinet after Jeremy Corbyn's decision to impose a three-line whip for the Article 50 vote. Shadow min for diverse communities 2016-17. MP for Brent South from 2005 until its abolition in 2010. Contested Brent Central 2010. Named MP of the Year at the Women in Public life Awards 2009. Born to Jamaican immigrants. Ed: Waltham Forest Coll of FE (Dip).

	Electorate	Turnout %	from 2010 %	Change
	80,845	64.69		
*D Butler Lab	38,208	73.06	+10.94	
R Bhansali C	10,211	19.53	-0.82	
A Georgiou LD	2,519	4.82	-3.55	
S Lish Green	802	1.53	-2.53	
J North Ukip	556	1.06	-2.87	

CHALLENGERS
Rahoul Bhansali (C) Extensive business experience. Has advised companies on the use of technology. Contested Streatham 2010. Backs Theresa May's stance on Brexit. **Anton Georgiou** (LD) Helped to set up BrentRefugeeAction Group. Remainer. Contested: Brent C 2014; London Assembly 2014. **Shaka Lish** (Green) Singer, songwriter, vocal producer and DJ. Passionate about community, the environment, equality, the

NHS, animals and education. **Janice North** (Ukip) Believes foreign aid should be cut to pay for NHS.

CONSTITUENCY PROFILE
A constituency with one of the largest black populations in the UK, with more than 40,000 residents of mixed race or Afro-Caribbean descent at the 2011 census. Also has one of the largest Irish populations, and a significant Hindu population. Brent Central's predecessor, Brent East, was Ken Livingstone's seat from 1974 to 2001, but the Lib Dems won it at a by-election in 2003 before losing Brent Central in 2015.

EU REFERENDUM RESULT
42.9% Leave   Remain 57.1%

Brent North

LABOUR HOLD MAJORITY 17,061 (30.2%)

BARRY GARDINER
BORN Mar 10, 1957
MP 1997-

Frequently appeared on TV and radio to support Labour's 2017 general election campaign. Was listed as "neutral but not hostile" to Corbyn in 2016 leaked documents. Mayor, City of Cambridge 1992-94. Shadow min: climate change 2015; Defra 2013-15. Shadow SoS: international trade 2016-; energy and climate change 2016. Select cttees: environment, food and rural affairs 2010-13; energy and climate change 2010-13. Married, four children. Ed: University of St Andrews (BA philosophy; MA moral philosophy); Harvard University (John Kennedy scholarship political philosophy),

	Electorate	Turnout %	from 2010 %	Change
	82,556	68.37		
*B Gardiner Lab	35,496	62.89	+8.61	
A Jogia C	18,435	32.66	-0.87	
P Lorber LD	1,614	2.86	-2.13	
M Lichten Green	660	1.17	-1.78	
E Jeffers Ind	239	0.42	+0.05	

where he worked under the tutelage of renowned political theorist John Rawls; University of Cambridge (PhD moral philosophy).

CHALLENGERS

Ameet Jogia (C) Victim of racist abuse scrawled in voting booth during 2017 election campaign. Cllr, Harrow C 2014-. **Paul Lorber** (LD) Czechoslovakian refugee. Cllr, Brent C 1982-2014. Contested Brent N 2015. **Michaela Lichten** (Green) Carer for husband. **Elcena Jeffers** (Ind) Disabled pensioner. Contested Brent N 2015.

CONSTITUENCY PROFILE

Brent North is a diverse London constituency. It has a large Asian community of about 70,000, mostly of Indian descent, and a sizeable black and Arab community. In 2011 this constituency had the highest proportion of residents born outside the EU. Large working-age population. It has been won by Labour since 1997, having been held by Sir Rhodes Boyson, a rightwing junior minister under Thatcher well known for his mutton-chop sideburns.

EU REFERENDUM RESULT

42.6% Leave   Remain 57.4%

Brentford & Isleworth

LABOUR HOLD MAJORITY 12,182 (19.8%)

RUTH CADBURY
BORN May 14, 1959
MP 2015-

Former consultant. Ancestors founded chocolate firm, Cadbury. Lifelong Quaker, opposed military action in Syria. Backed no confidence vote against Jeremy Corbyn in 2016. Remain campaigner, who rebelled on the vote for Article 50. Dep leader Houslow C 2010-12. Shadow min housing 2016-. Co-chairwoman APPG on cycling. Member, women and equalities select cttee 2015-17. Married, two sons. Ed: University of Salford (BSc social sciences).

CHALLENGERS

Mary Macleod (C) London-born, Scotland-raised consultant,

	Electorate	Turnout %	from 2010 %	Change
	85,151	72.38		
*R Cadbury Lab	35,364	57.38	+13.63	
M Macleod C	23,182	37.62	-5.33	
J Bourke LD	3,083	5.00	+0.98	

and ambassador for London Women's Forum helping female board members in financial services. Former MP and member of 'Team Theresa' for Brentford & Isleworth 2010-15. Adviser to secretary of state for Scotland, 2015-16. PPS to: Theresa Villiers 2014-15; Maria Miller 2012-14; Nick Herbert 2010-12. Member, home affairs select cttee 2010. **Joe Bourke** (LD) Self-employed chartered accountant and part-time lecturer at University of West London. Firmly against Heathrow's third runway.

CONSTITUENCY PROFILE

A west London seat stretching from Chiswick to Hounslow, this is a diverse constituency with a significant Indian community. It has one of the largest Buddhist, Hindu and Sikh communities in the UK, and is significantly larger than the London average. A significant proportion of its residents commute into London and have managerial and administrative jobs. Brentford & Isleworth tracked the national picture between 1997 and 2010, but was one of four London seats that Labour won from the Tories in 2015. The Green candidate stood down to endorse the Labour candidate in 2017.

EU REFERENDUM RESULT

43.3% Leave   Remain 56.7%

Brentwood & Ongar

CONSERVATIVE HOLD MAJORITY 24,002 (45.4%)

ALEX BURGHART
BORN Sep 7, 1977
MP 2017-

	Electorate	Turnout %	from 2010 % Change
	74,911	70.63	
A Burghart C	34,811	65.79	+6.96
G Barrett Lab	10,809	20.43	+7.92
K Chilvers LD	4,426	8.37	-0.45
M McGough Ukip	1,845	3.49	-13.32
P Jeater Green	915	1.73	-0.96
L Kousoulou Ind	104	0.20	

Former adviser to Theresa May, focusing on social justice during first year of her premiership. Previously policy dir, Centre for Social Justice, where he worked with PM's former chief of staff Fiona Hill on modern slavery. Began career as history teacher and tutor at King's Coll London. Contested Islington North 2015. Married, two children. Ed: Millfield Sch; Christ Church Coll, Oxford (BA history); King's Coll London (PhD, modern history).

CHALLENGERS
Gareth Barrett (Lab) Worked in public affairs for the food and drink industry. Policy manager, British Soft Drinks Association. Cllr, Brentwood BC 2014-; Labour group leader 2015-. Contested Epping Forest 2015. **Karen Chilvers** (LD) Marketing consultant specialising in healthcare and retail. Owns marketing strategy business. Children's author. Cllr, Brentwood BC 2012-; 2007-11. Contested Hornchurch & Upminster 2010. **Mick McGough** (Ukip) Chartered accountant. National cttee member,

Campaign for an Independent Britain. Former member, Ukip NEC. Contested Brentwood & Ongar 2015, 2010.

CONSTITUENCY PROFILE
This Essex seat, perched on Greater London's northeast border, is characterised by high levels of home ownership and self-employment. Its residents are overrepresented in the finance and construction sectors. Brentwood & Ongar has elected Conservatives since its creation in 1974 and, until this election, was the seat of former Tory party chairman and communities secretary Sir Eric Pickles.

EU REFERENDUM RESULT

61.2% Leave   Remain 38.8%

Bridgend

LABOUR HOLD MAJORITY 4,700 (10.9%)

MADELEINE MOON
BORN Mar 27, 1950
MP 2005-

	Electorate	Turnout %	from 2010 % Change
	62,185	69.56	
*M Moon Lab	21,913	50.66	+13.59
K Robson C	17,213	39.79	+7.61
R Watkins PC	1,783	4.12	-2.93
J Pratt LD	919	2.12	-2.05
A Williams Ukip	781	1.81	-13.18
I Robson Ind	646	1.49	-0.44

Background in health and social care. Can be unpredictable; received backlash in her marginally Leave-majority constituency after voting against Article 50. APPG chairwoman: suicide and self-harm prevention group; kidney group; RAF section of armed forces group. Select cttees: defence 2009-17; Welsh affairs 2005-06; environment, food and rural affairs 2005-07. Widowed, one son. Ed: Whinney Hill Sch; Durham GS; Madeley Coll, Staffordshire (CertEd); Keele University (BEd); Cardiff University (CQSW DipSW social work).

CHALLENGERS
Karen Robson (C) Former *Western Mail's* Welsh Woman of the Year for her disability rights campaigning. Established Cardiff Metropolitan University's disability service. Contested Cardiff Central 2010; Welsh Assembly Cardiff South and Penarth candidate 2007. **Rhys Watkins** (PC) Construction site manager and charity campaigner. **Jonathan Pratt** (LD) Former Royal Fleet

Auxiliary member. Now works for family business, selling Welsh and Celtic giftware. Volunteer HM Coastguard Search and Rescue, Porthcrawl.

CONSTITUENCY PROFILE
A small part of South Wales stretching east from the town of Bridgend, population about 50,000, towards the Glamorgan coast and the smaller towns of Porthcawl and Pyle. Among the sectors in which many of its residents are employed are manufacturing, retail, health and social care. Represented by Labour MPs since 1987 and its AM is Welsh First Minister Carwyn Jones.

EU REFERENDUM RESULT

50.3% Leave   Remain 49.7%

Bridgwater & Somerset West

CONSERVATIVE HOLD MAJORITY 15,448 (26.5%)

IAN LIDDELL-GRAINGER

BORN Feb 23, 1959
MP 2001-

	Electorate	Turnout %	from 2010 %	Change
	89,294	65.25		
*I Liddell-Grainger C	32,111	55.11	+9.16	
W Hinckes Lab	16,663	28.60	+10.99	
M Kravis LD	6,332	10.87	-1.56	
S Smedley Ukip	2,102	3.61	-15.56	
K Powell Green	1,059	1.82	-3.02	

Ran a 250-acre arable farm. Rose to Major in the TA and still on the reserve list. Became a consultant to Army Land Command HQ and the MoD. Severed business ties upon entering Parliament. Contested Torridge and West Devon 1997. Select cttees: statutory instruments 2010-17; Speaker's advisory cttee on works of art 2010-16; environmental audit 2007-10; Crossrail bill 2005-07. APPG chairman: energy studies & nuclear energy; patient access to medical technology; pharmaceutical industry; taxation; dyslexia. Brexiteer. Lives in Williton.

Born in Scotland. Married, three children. Ed: Millfield Sch.

CHALLENGERS

Wes Hinckes (Lab) IT specialist. Passionate about disability and social care after seeing many of the difficulties his autistic sister has had to overcome. Cllr, Sedgemoor DC 2015-. **Marcus Kravis** (LD) Dir, renewable energy company. Contested: Somerset CC 2017; Somerset N 2015. **Simon Smedley** (Ukip) Chartered surveyor. Contested

Somerset CC 2013. **Kay Powell** (Green) Contested: Devon CC 2017; Exeter CC 2016. Supporter of an open-border policy.

CONSTITUENCY PROFILE

A large area stretching from Exmoor National Park to the Somerset Levels. Older, whiter and more sparsely populated than most other constituencies. It has a prominent tourist industry, especially on Exmoor, the Quantocks and in the coastal town of Minehead. The seat has been Conservative since its creation in 2010, but its predecessor, Bridgwater, had been held by the Conservatives since 1950.

EU REFERENDUM RESULT

62.1% Leave   Remain 37.9%

Brigg & Goole

CONSERVATIVE HOLD MAJORITY 12,363 (27.4%)

ANDREW PERCY

BORN Sep 18, 1977
MP 2010-

	Electorate	Turnout %	from 2010 %	Change
	66,069	68.20		
*A Percy C	27,219	60.41	+7.38	
T Smith Lab	14,856	32.97	+5.77	
D Jeffreys Ukip	1,596	3.54	-11.93	
J Lonsdale LD	836	1.86	+0.09	
I Pires Green	550	1.22	-0.89	

Brexiteer. Former secondary school teacher. Claims to have taught in "some of the toughest schools in Hull". School governor. Member of the teachers' union Voice (Professional Association of Teachers). Closed Twitter account in 2016 after being targeted by online trolls. Junior min, communities and local government 2016-17. Select cttees: regulatory reform 2015-17; health 2015-16; panel of chairs 2015-16; NI affairs 2012-15; health 2012-15; regulatory reform 2010-15; procedure 2010-11. Vice-chairman, Hull and Goole Port health authority. Supporter:

Countryside Alliance; National Trust; Campaign Against Political Correctness. Born in East Yorkshire. Son of school secretary and foundry worker. Ed: Wyke Sixth Form College; University of York; University of Leeds.

CHALLENGERS

Terence Smith (Lab) Undergraduate. Became Britain's youngest mayor in 2016, aged just 19. Mayor, Goole C 2016-. **David Jeffreys** (Ukip)

Tesco maintenance engineer. Contested Brigg & Goole 2015. **Jerry Lonsdale** (LD) Business owner. **Isabel Pires** (Green) Lecturer in biomedical science.

CONSTITUENCY PROFILE

A large and sparsely populated constituency to the south of the Humber, with residents that are older and whiter than the UK average. It also has higher than average levels of homeownership and median income. The towns of Brigg and Goole are either side of Scunthorpe. Created in 1997, Brigg & Goole was Labour under Tony Blair and Gordon Brown but its MP has been Conservative since 2010.

EU REFERENDUM RESULT

66.2% Leave   Remain 33.8%

Brighton Kemptown

LAB CO-OP GAIN MAJORITY 9,868 (20.1%)

LLOYD RUSSELL-MOYLE
BORN Sep 14, 1986
MP 2017-

Youth worker. Vice-chairman, British Youth Council. Formerly: young trainer at National Youth Agency; consultant to UN on children and youth; chairman, Woodcraft Folk progressive education movement, 2011-13; vice-president, European Youth Forum in Brussels; youth participation officer, East Sussex CC. Socialist who served as treasurer for Education Not for Sale, an anti-capitalist student campaign group. Cllr, Brighton and Hove CC 2016-. Contested Lewes 2015. Chairman, Brighton and Hove Labour 2016-. PPS to Richard Burgon 2017-. Fellow, RSA. Ed: Priory Sch, Lewes;

	Electorate	Turnout %	from 2010 % Change
	67,893	72.48	
L Russell-Moyle Lab Co-op	28,703	58.33	+19.18
*S Kirby C	18,835	38.28	-2.40
E Tester LD	1,457	2.96	-0.05
D Haze ND	212	0.43	

Sussex Downs Coll; University of Bradford (BA peace studies); University of Sussex (LLM international law).

CHALLENGERS
Simon Kirby (C) MP 2010-17. Successful businessman in Brighton: co-founder, Webb Kirby chain of restaurants and nightclubs. Remain supporter. Economic sec to Treasury 2016-17, responsibility for Brexit's effect on financial services was taken away owing to concerns that he lacked business

experience. Asst whip 2015-16. PPS to: Jeremy Hunt 2014-15; Hugh Robertson 2012-14. **Emily Tester** (LD) Second-year government student at LSE. Cllr, West Sussex TC.

CONSTITUENCY PROFILE
Kemptown stretches beyond the east of Brighton into more rural Sussex. Kemptown is the heart of Brighton's LGBT community. A bellwether from 1979 until 2017, Labour having gained the seat despite the Conservative plurality in the Commons. The Greens won 7 per cent of the vote here in 2015, but didn't stand this time, bolstering Labour's chances.

EU REFERENDUM RESULT

43.6% Leave　　　　　Remain 56.54

Brighton Pavilion

GREEN HOLD MAJORITY 14,689 (25.5%)

CAROLINE LUCAS
BORN Dec 9, 1960
MP 2010-

Dynamic environmentalist who has been awarded several titles for her contributions to parliament. Worked in charity sector before entering politics. MEP for South East England 1999-2010. First Green Party MP. Green Party leader 2008-12, co-leader 2016-. Contested Oxford East 1992. Member, environment audit cttee 2010-. Author of *Honourable Friends?*, describing her environmental input to parliament. Cllr, Oxfordshire CC 1993-97. Married, two sons. Ed: Malvern Girls' Coll; University of Exeter (BA English literature; PhD English); University of Kansas (Dip journalism).

	Electorate	Turnout %	from 2010 % Change
	75,486	76.41	
*C Lucas Green	30,139	52.25	+10.42
S Curtis Lab	15,450	26.79	-0.47
E Warman C	11,082	19.21	-3.55
I Buchanan Ukip	630	1.09	-3.89
N Yeomans Ind	376	0.65	+0.44

CHALLENGERS
Solomon Curtis (Lab) politics student at the University of Sussex aged 20. Contested Wealden 2015. Former vice-chairman, British Youth Council. Former MYP. **Emma Warman** (C) Qualified barrister. Deputy chairwoman of LGBT+ Conservatives. Contested Cardiff South and Penarth 2015. Grew up in Wales. **Ian Buchanan** (Ukip) Contested Brighton Kemptown 2015. Cllr, East Sussex CC 2013-17.

CONSTITUENCY PROFILE
Sandwiched between Hove and Brighton Kemptown. The University of Sussex is in the north of the seat, and more of Brighton's students live in Pavillion than in Kemptown or Hove. The seat also has the highest average income of Brighton's three constituencies and in the 2011 census had the highest proportion of people claiming to have no religion of any seat in the entire country. Pavilion elected Conservative MPs from 1950 to 1997, a Labour MP in the following three elections and its current MP, Caroline Lucas of the Green Party since 2010.

EU REFERENDUM RESULT

25.9% Leave　　　　　Remain 74.1%

Bristol East

LABOUR HOLD MAJORITY 13,394 (26.4%)

KERRY MCCARTHY
BORN Mar 26, 1965
MP 2005-

Former solicitor and director of Luton airport. First vegan MP, dedicated to reducing food waste and food poverty; patron of FoodCycle; set up APPG on food waste. Resigned as shadow environment secretary, 2015-16, in opposition to Corbyn's leadership. Roles in the shadow cabinet included shadow min FCO, 2011-15. PPS to: Douglas Alexander 2007-09; Rosie Winterton 2007. Cllr, Luton BC 1999-2003. Member, Labour National Policy Forum 1998-2005. Ed: Denbigh HS; University of Liverpool (BA Russian & politics); City of London Polytechnic (law).

	Electorate	Turnout %	Change from 2010 %
	72,414	70.15	
*K McCarthy Lab	30,847	60.72	+21.45
T Clarke C	17,453	34.36	+3.70
C Lucas LD	1,389	2.73	-3.08
L Francis Green	1,110	2.19	-6.10

CHALLENGERS
Theodora Clarke (C) Art historian, lecturer and critic. Founder and editor, *Russian Art & Culture* magazine. Contested Bristol East 2015. Dir, Conservative Friends of International Development 2016-. Vice-chairwoman, Cities of London & Westminster Conservatives 2013-14. Dir of communications, Conservative Women's Organisation 2011-13. **Chris Lucas** (LD) Runs media and consultancy business. Background in sales

management. Contested Ealing North 2010. Cllr, Three Rivers DC 2010-14. **Lorraine Francis** (Green) Social worker. Contested Bristol East 2015.

CONSTITUENCY PROFILE
This mostly suburban seat has the highest rate of homeownership in the Bristol seats, but the lowest average income. The reconfigured Bristol East seat elected a Conservative MP in 1983, the election in which Tony Benn lost his seat, although the constituency has been Labour since 1992. Sir Stafford Cripps, one of Attlee's chancellors, once held this seat.

EU REFERENDUM RESULT
46.8% Leave   Remain 53.2%

Bristol North West

LABOUR GAIN MAJORITY 4,761 (8.8%)

DARREN JONES
BORN Nov 13, 1986
MP 2017-

Consumer-rights lawyer: Bond Dickinson, BT. Allowed time off work to contest election on the understanding he would lose. Sceptical of Corbyn, backed Andy Burnham and Owen Smith for leadership. Self-described working-class boy, grew up on Lawrence Weston council estate. Hailed himself as "the first ever Darren" to be elected to Commons in maiden speech. Contested: Bristol NW 2015; Torridge & Devon West 2010. Married. Ed: Plymouth University (BSc human bioscience; president student union); UWE (PgDip law); University of Law (LPC).

	Electorate	Turnout %	Change from 2010 %
	75,431	71.72	
D Jones Lab	27,400	50.65	+16.25
*C Leslie C	22,639	41.85	-2.10
C Downie LD	2,814	5.20	-1.00
S Bousa Green	1,243	2.30	-3.40

CHALLENGERS
Charlotte Leslie (C) MP 2010-17. Dir, Conservative Middle East Council. Previously worked as lifeguard and swimming teacher. Researcher: BBC; Policy Exchange. Former editor Bow Group's *Crossbow* magazine. Supported Leaving the EU. **Celia Downie** (LD) Garden historian and consultant. Contested Leominster 2001. **Sharmila Bousa** (Green) Runs wellbeing and "eco styling" businesses. Worked for 15 years in communications and

development in arts and charity sectors. Gave up campaigning in the constituency as part of a "progressive alliance".

CONSTITUENCY PROFILE
Stretching from the Bristol's northwest suburbs up to the port of Avonmouth, Bristol North West is the second most affluent of the Bristol constituencies and the only Conservative/Labour marginal in the city. Bristol North East has changed hands from Labour to the Conservatives ten times since 1950, mostly, although not in 2017, corresponding with whichever the party in government.

EU REFERENDUM RESULT
38.9% Leave   Remain 61.1%

Bristol South

LABOUR HOLD MAJORITY 15,987 (29.4%)

KARIN SMYTH
BORN Sep 8, 1964
MP 2015-

Former manager, NHS Bristol Clinical Commissioning Group. Non-exec dir, Bristol North Primary Care Trust 2002-06. Political asst to Valerie Davey MP 1997-2001. Corbyn sceptic: nominated Yvette Cooper 2015; supported Owen Smith 2016. Campaigned to Remain, voted to trigger Article 50. Shadow leader of the Commons 2017-. PPS to Sir Keir Starmer 2016-17. APPG vice-chairwoman: clinical leadership and management. Member, Unison. Married, three children. Ed: Uxbridge Technical Coll; UEA (BA economic & social studies); University of Bath (MBA).

	Elec.	Turn. %	Change from 2010 %
	83,009	65.51	
*K Smyth Lab	32,666	60.07	+21.70
M Weston C	16,679	30.67	+6.33
B Nutland LD	1,821	3.35	-5.34
I Kealey Ukip	1,672	3.07	-13.41
T Dyer Green	1,428	2.63	-8.90
J Langley Ind	116	0.21	

CHALLENGERS
Mark Weston (C) Chief of staff to Ashley Fox MEP. Cllr, Bristol CC 2006-; leader Conservative group. Former political agent, Gloucestershire Conservatives. **Benjamin Nutland** (LD) MD, export company. Unicef children's champion. Member of Young Leaders UK initiative, US embassy in London. **Ian Kealey** (Ukip) Runs a guest house. Ran for PCC 2012. **Tony**

Dyer (Green) Worked in the construction industry, later reskilled to join the IT training industry. PCC for Bristol South. Ran for Bristol mayor 2016. **John Langley** (Ind) Former porn film producer and star. Previously vice-chairman of Ukip. Keen interest in housing and homelessness.

CONSTITUENCY PROFILE
Bristol South is the whitest and most working class of the city's four seats. It has elected Labour MPs since 1935, with the Conservatives coming within 1,500 votes in 1987 after the deselection of the former Labour chief whip Michael Cocks.

EU REFERENDUM RESULT

48.0% Leave   Remain 52.0%

Bristol West

LABOUR HOLD MAJORITY 37,336 (52.1%)

THANGAM DEBBONAIRE
BORN Aug 3, 1966
MP 2015-

Campaigner against domestic violence. Moved to Bristol to be first national children's officer of Women's Aid. Research manager, Respect UK. Dir & lead independent practitioner, Domestic Violence Responses. Former professional cellist. Shadow min, CMS 2016; resigned from position in opposition to Corbyn's leadership, but rejoined front bench as opp whip 2016-. Remain campaigner, voted against Article 50 despite being Labour whip. Diagnosed with breast cancer after becoming MP, called for parliament to allow MPs to vote remotely.

	Electorate	Turnout %	Change from 2010 %
	92,986	77.01	
*T Debbonaire Lab	47,213	65.93	+30.27
A Tall C	9,877	13.79	-1.39
M Scott Cato Green	9,216	12.87	-13.96
S Williams LD	5,201	7.26	-11.58
J Rodgers Money	101	0.14	

Chairwoman, APPG on refugees. Ed: Bradford Girls' GS; Chetham's Sch of Music; St John's City Coll of Technology; Royal Coll of Music; Oxford University (maths, did not complete); University of Bristol (MSc management).

CHALLENGERS
Annabel Tall (C) Chartered engineer. Cllr, North Somerset DC 2011-15. **Molly Scott Cato** (Green) Professor of strategy and sustainability at the University of

Roehampton 2012-14. MEP for SW England 2014-; Cllr, Stroud DC 2011-14; leader Green group 2012-14. **Stephen Williams** (LD) Chartered tax adviser. MP for Bristol W 2005-15. Parly under-sec for CLG 2013-15.

CONSTITUENCY PROFILE
Densest, most diverse and most affluent Bristol seat, with 20,000 black and mixed-race residents and Bristol's largest student population. It is also the second most Remain seat in the UK. It was Conservative for more than 100 years before turning Labour in 1997. The Lib Dems won it in 2005 and 2010, but it now has Bristol's biggest Labour majority.

EU REFERENDUM RESULT

20.7% Leave   Remain 79.3%

Broadland

CONSERVATIVE HOLD MAJORITY 15,816 (28.3%)

KEITH SIMPSON
BORN Mar 29, 1949
MP 1997-

Military historian. Dir, Cranfield Security Studies Institute, Cranfield University. Senior lecturer in war studies and international affairs at the Royal Military Academy, Sandhurst. Author of five books. Political adviser to secretaries of state 1988-90: George Younger; Tom King. MP, Mid Norfolk 1997-2010. Shadow min: foreign and commonwealth affairs 2005-10. Shadow spokesman: environment, food and rural affairs 2001-02; defence 1998-99. Opposition whip 1999-2001. Select cttees: intelligence and security 2015-17. PPS to William Hague. Privy cllr

	Electorate	Turnout %	from 2010 %	Change
	77,334	72.38		
*K Simpson C	32,406	57.90	+7.40	
I Simpson Lab	16,590	29.64	+10.86	
S Riley LD	4,449	7.95	-1.80	
D Moreland Ukip	1,594	2.85	-13.88	
A Boswell Green	932	1.67	-2.58	

2015-. Remainer. Urged Theresa May to be flexible in Brexit negotiations. Married, one child. Ed: Thorpe GS, Norfolk; University of Norfolk; King's College London.

CHALLENGERS
Iain Simpson (Lab) Democratic socialist. Against proportional representation. Backed Liz Kendall for Labour leadership 2015. Cllr, London Borough of Lambeth 2014-. **Steve Riley** (LD) Self-employed. Contested

Broadland 2015. **David Moreland** (Ukip) Former Met Police CID officer. Contested Norfolk PCC 2016. **Andrew Boswell** (Green) Worked in computing research. Contested Broadland 2015.

CONSTITUENCY PROFILE
A large and sparsely populated seat in rural Norfolk, the largest town in Broadland is Fakenham, with a population of about 8,000. More than half of Broadland's residents are aged 45 or over, 98 per cent are white and it has high rates of homeownership and self-employment. It has been a Conservative safe seat since its creation in 2010.

EU REFERENDUM RESULT
54.1% Leave   Remain 45.9%

Bromley & Chislehurst

CONSERVATIVE HOLD MAJORITY 9,590 (20.6%)

BOB NEILL
BORN Jun 24, 1952
MP 2006-

Elected MP for Bromley & Chislehurst after the sudden death of Eric Forth in 2006. Contested Dagenham 1987, 1983. Parly under sec DCLG 2010-12. Select cttees: national security strategy 2015-17; liaison 2015-17; justice 2015-17, 2012-13, 2007-10; political and constitutional reform 2013-15; constitutional affairs 2006-07. Vice-chairman, Conservative Party 2012-15. Remainer. Rarely rebels, but did vote in favour of an amendment on parliamentary resolution of a new relationship with the EU. Married. Ed: Abbs Cross GS, Hornchurch; LSE (law).

	Electorate	Turnout %	from 2010 %	Change
	65,113	71.66		
*B Neill C	25,175	53.95	+0.98	
S Hyde Lab	15,585	33.40	+11.21	
S Webber LD	3,369	7.22	+0.78	
E Jenner Ukip	1,383	2.96	-11.30	
R Robertson Green	1,150	2.46	-1.67	

CHALLENGERS
Sara Hyde (Lab) Works for a criminal justice charity which helps female convicts to get jobs after leaving prison. Vice-chairwoman, Fabian Women's Network. Deputy chairwoman, Electoral Reform Society. Contested London Assembly 2016. **Sam Webber** (LD) Senior comms consultant for PoliticsHome. Contested: Bromley & Chislehurst 2015, 2010; Bromley London BC 2012. **Emmett Jenner** (Ukip)

Labelled Corbyn "a weapon of mass destruction for Labour". Contested Bromley & Chislehurst 2015, 2010. **Roisin Robertson** (Green) Former journalist. Contested Bromley & Chislehurst 2015, 2010; London Assembly 2016.

CONSTITUENCY PROFILE
A suburban, affluent seat southeast of Lewisham, it is whiter than most in London, with about a sixth of residents in an ethnic minority and a high rate of self-employment. A Conservative safe seat, although the Lib Dems came within 634 votes of winning it at a by-election in 2006.

EU REFERENDUM RESULT
49.8% Leave   Remain 50.2%

Bromsgrove

CONSERVATIVE HOLD MAJORITY 16,573 (30.7%)

SAJID JAVID
BORN Dec 5, 1969
MP 2010-

Free-market Thatcherite.
Worked in business and
finance. Vice-president,
Chase Manhattan Bank. Also
worked for Deutsche Bank.
SoS: communities and local
government 2016-; business,
innovation and skills 2015-16;
CMS 2014-15. Min for equality
2014. Financial sec to the
Treasury 2013-14. Ministerial
champion for the Midlands
Engine. Economic sec to the
Treasury 2012-13. Select cttees:
public accounts 2012-13; work
and pensions 2010. Publicly
supported Remain, but said he
was a Eurosceptic and Brussels
basher. Son of immigrants.

	Electorate	Turnout %	from 2010 % Change
	73,571	73.45	
*S Javid C	33,493	61.98	+8.13
M Thompson Lab	16,920	31.31	+9.10
N Lewis LD	2,488	4.60	-0.40
S Esposito Green	1,139	2.11	-1.20

Father arrived in Britain from
Punjab with £1 in his pocket.
Married, four children. Ed:
University of Exeter (economics
and politics).

CHALLENGERS
Dr Michael Thompson
(Lab) Physics teacher. Cllr,
Bromsgrove DC 2015-.
Chairman, Bromsgrove Labour
Party. Dep leader, Labour group
on Bromsgrove DC. Helped
to pass a motion banning
circuses that use wild animals
on council-owned land. Vegan.

Neil Lewis (LD) Entrepreneur.
Worked at the Economist Group.
Determined to stay in the single
market. Giovanni Esposito
(Green). Known as Spoz. Former
chassis design engineer and
Birmingham poet laureate.

CONSTITUENCY PROFILE
This affluent, mostly rural,
Worcestershire seat is
characterised by a high level of
homeownership. About half of
its residents are aged 45 or older
and employment is high in the
education sector. Bromsgrove
has returned a Conservative
MP at every election since 1950,
although Labour won a by-
election here in 1971.

EU REFERENDUM RESULT

55.4% Leave   Remain 44.6%

Broxbourne

CONSERVATIVE HOLD MAJORITY 15,792 (33.3%)

CHARLES WALKER
BORN Sep 11, 1967
MP 2005-

Worked in communication and
marketing positions in the IT
sector. Perennial backbencher.
Made headlines for opening
up to the House of Commons
about his mental-health issues
in 2012. Received an OBE in
2015. Started delivering political
leaflets at the age of six. Select
cttees: Speaker's committee
for IPSA 2010-17; liaison
2012-17; procedure 2012-17;
panel of chairs 2010-17; public
administration 2007-11; Scottish
affairs 2005-10. Brexit supporter.
Former board director, Blue
Arrow. Teetotal. Married, three
children. Ed: University of
Oregon.

	Electorate	Turnout %	from 2010 % Change
	73,502	64.60	
*C Walker C	29,515	62.16	+6.11
S Norgrove Lab	13,723	28.90	+10.50
T Faulkner Ukip	1,918	4.04	-15.68
A Graham LD	1,481	3.12	-0.07
T Evans Green	848	1.79	-0.86

CHALLENGERS
Selina Norgrove (Lab)
Contested Hertfordshire CC
2017. **Tony Faulkner** (Ukip)
Contested Hertfordshire CC
2017, 2013. **Andy Graham (LD)**
Owns Snap Theatre Company.
Set up a charity to develop
teacher training support in
Rwanda, Romania, Bangladesh,
the Gambia and the UK. Cllr,
West Oxfordshire DC 2015-.
Contested: Witney 2015; Clacton
by-election 2014. **Tabitha Evans**
(Green) Scientist. Prioritises

environmental and social justice
issues.

CONSTITUENCY PROFILE
This Hertfordshire seat
consists mainly of the towns
of Cheshunt, Hoddeson and
Broxbourne. It enjoys higher
than average median income
and homeownership levels.
There is significant social
renting, but not from councils.
Workers in the constituency are
twice as likely to commute by
train, relative to the UK average.
A significant proportion of
residents work in construction.
No Conservative candidate in
Broxbourne has received less
than half the vote since 1997.

EU REFERENDUM RESULT

65.5% Leave   Remain 34.5%

Broxtowe

CONSERVATIVE HOLD MAJORITY 863 (1.6%)

ANNA SOUBRY
BORN Dec 7, 1956
MP 2010-

	Electorate	Turnout %	from 2010 % Change
	74,017	74.99	
*A Soubry C	25,983	46.81	+1.59
G Marshall Lab	25,120	45.25	+8.06
T Hallam LD	2,247	4.05	+0.08
F Loi Ukip	1,477	2.66	-7.96
P Morton Green	681	1.23	-1.66

Emerging leader of Tory left. Said after snap election that Theresa May should "consider her position" after "dreadful campaign". Waxes lyrical about benefits of immigration. Former regional TV journalist and shop steward, NUJ. Criminal barrister, called to Bar in 1995. First female Conservative elected to National Union of Students executive. Elected rector, University of Stirling. Outspoken Europhile; voted for Article 50. Founding member of Open Britain group. Infrequent rebel; voted to give Commons final say over Brexit deal. Min: defence, 2014-15; business, 2015-16. Divorced,

two daughters. Ed: Hartland GS, Worksop; University of Birmingham (LLB law).

CHALLENGERS
Greg Marshall (Lab) Water resource adviser, Environment Agency. Cllr, Broxtowe BC 2011-. Amateur sportsman. **Tim Hallam** (LD) Former RAF aircraft technician; now owns engineering business. Contested Nottinghamshire CC 2017. **Fran Loi** (Ukip) British-Italian

business consultant. Contested Nottingham East 2015; Nottinghamshire PCC 2016. Ukip Nottinghamshire county chairman. **Pat Morton** (Green) Former lecturer, Sheffield Hallam University. Fellow, RICS.

CONSTITUENCY PROFILE
This seat, to the west of Nottingham, has high levels of homeownership and a significant proportion of its residents work in education. Something of a bellwether marginal, since 1983 Broxtowe has been won by the party in government. Just 389 votes separated the Conservatives from Labour in 2010, and 863 in 2017.

EU REFERENDUM RESULT
52.5% Leave   Remain 47.5%

Buckingham

SPEAKER HOLD MAJORITY 25,725 (48.8%)

JOHN BERCOW
BORN Jan 19, 1963
MP 1997-

	Electorate	Turnout %	from 2010 % Change
	79,616	66.17	
*J Bercow Speaker	34,299	65.11	+0.64
M Sheppard Green	8,574	16.28	+2.49
S Raven Ind	5,638	10.70	
B Mapletoft Ukip	4,168	7.91	-13.83

157th Speaker of the House of Commons 2009-. A controversial choice, predominantly supported by Labour MPs rather than his own party. He has travelled from the right of the Conservative Party to its left. Appointed by Norman Tebbit as vice-chairman of Conservative Collegiate Forum. Controversially told the Commons he was "opposed to an address by President Trump in Westminster Hall". Special adviser: chief secretary to the Treasury; SoS for National Heritage. Shadow SofS intl devt 2003-04. Shadow spokesman: work and pensions 2002; home affairs 2000-01. Shadow chief sec

Treasury 2001-02. Shadow educ min 1999-2000. Select cttees: Speaker's cttee IPSA 2010-17, 2009-10; Speaker's cttee electoral commission 2010-17, 2009-10; House of Commons commission 2009-17. Contentiously admitted to voting Remain. Once a promising tennis player. Married, three children. Ed: Finchley Manorhill School; University of Essex (BA government).

CHALLENGERS
Michael Sheppard (Green) Environmental campaigner.

Scott Raven (Ind) Crowdfunded money for the campaign. Politics teacher. **Brian Mapletoft** (Ukip) Accountant. Cllr, Haslemere PC 2011-15. Contested Wycombe DC 2015.

CONSTITUENCY PROFILE
A large, rural constituency in which nearly half the population is aged 45 or older. About a fifth of workers in the seat are self-employed, and many work in managerial and administrative-level jobs. The weekly wage is around a fifth greater than the average UK wage. Before becoming the Speaker's seat, Buckingham was a safe Conservative seat.

EU REFERENDUM RESULT
48.9% Leave   Remain 51.1%

Burnley

LABOUR HOLD MAJORITY 6,353 (15.8%)

JULIE COOPER
BORN Jun 20, 1960
MP 2015-

Former high school English teacher who then joined her husband running their community pharmacy. Cllr, Burnley BC 2005-15; council leader 2012-14. Contested Burnley 2010. Sponsored by Unite union. Introduced private member's bill proposing hospital car parking charge exemption for carers that was filibustered by Conservative MPs. Nominated Andy Burnham for Labour leadership 2015; Owen Smith 2016. Campaigned to Remain, voted to trigger Article 50. Yet to rebel. Shadow health min 2016-. PPS to Seema Malhotra 2015-16. Married, two children.

Electorate	Turnout %	from 2010 % Change
64,714	62.26	
*J Cooper Lab	18,832	46.74 +9.12
P White C	12,479	30.97 +17.45
G Birtwistle LD	6,046	15.01 -14.45
T Commis Ukip	2,472	6.14 -11.13
L Fisk Green	461	1.14 -0.99

CHALLENGERS
Paul White (C) Works in marketing and PR. Brexiteer. Northwest dir, Vote Leave. Cllr: Lancashire CC 2013-17; Pendle BC 2011-. Went on holiday the day after being selected as Tory candidate. **Gordon Birtwistle** (LD) MP for Burnley 2010-15. Former textile manufacturer apprentice who later ran his own firm. Cllr, Burnley BC. Contested Burnley 1997, 1992; 1982 for SDP. **Tom Commis** (Ukip) IT support worker, BT. Chairman,

Ukip Pendle. Contested Burnley 2015. **Laura Fisk** (Green) NHS healthcare worker.

CONSTITUENCY PROFILE
This east Lancashire constituency, containing the former cotton town of Burnley, has an Asian community of about 10,000. A large proportion of constituents work in manufacturing, with more than 20,000 residents in routine and manual jobs, and it suffers from higher than average unemployment. This seat in Labour's heartlands had been held by the party for 65 years until the Lib Dems won it in 2010.

EU REFERENDUM RESULT

66.6% Leave   Remain 33.4%

Burton

CONSERVATIVE HOLD MAJORITY 10,047 (20.1%)

ANDREW GRIFFITHS
BORN Oct 19, 1970
MP 2010-

Former high-street banker. Worked for his family's engineering business in the West Midlands. Supporter: Burton Addiction Centre; East Staffordshire CAB. School governor. Contested: W Midlands euro election 2004; Dudley North 2001. Lord Commissioner 2016-17. Political and constitutional reform select cttee 2010-13. Chief of staff to: Eric Pickles 2007-10; Hugo Swire 2006-07; Theresa May 2004-06. Former adviser to European agricultural spokesman Neil Parish MEP. Adviser to W Midlands MEP team in Brussels 1999-2004. Remainer. APPG

Electorate	Turnout %	from 2010 % Change
73,954	67.49	
*A Griffiths C	28,936	57.98 +7.84
J McKiernan Lab	18,889	37.85 +10.51
D Hardwick LD	1,262	2.53 +0.03
S Hales Green	824	1.65 -0.83

chairman: beer; Kashmir. APPG sec, misuse of drugs and alcohol. Born in Staffordshire. Married. Ed: High Arcal Sch, Sedgley.

CHALLENGERS
John McKiernan (Lab) Anti-austerity. Wants to reverse Tory cuts. Unsuccessfully contested: Staffordshire CC 2017; East Staffordshire BC by-election 2008. **Dominic Hardwick** (LD) Runs clothing business. Worked in office of the Liberal Democrat local government minister Andrew Stunell. Contested five

local elections. **Simon Hales** (Green) Life-long socialist. Believes action to tackle climate change is urgently needed. Inspired by Black Lives Matter and Disabled People Against Cuts.

CONSTITUENCY PROFILE
This slim north Staffordshire seat has Burton upon Trent in its south and stretches west to Uttoxeter. Other than these towns, the seat is mostly rural. The biggest sources of employment here are manufacturing and retail. This is typically a Conservative seat, with the exceptions of 1945 and the New Labour period.

EU REFERENDUM RESULT

64.8% Leave   Remain 35.3%

Bury North

LABOUR GAIN MAJORITY 4,375 (9.1%)

JAMES FRITH
BORN Apr 23, 1977
MP 2017-

Founder and director of youth unemployment social enterprise, All Together. Board member, Whatuni.com. Occasional columnist, *New Statesman*. Cllr, Bury MBC 2011-15. Bolton West Labour campaigns & comms manager, general election 2005. Contested Bury North 2015; defeated by 378 votes. Married, three children. Ed: Taunton Sch; Manchester Metropolitan University (BA politics & economics).

CHALLENGERS
David Nuttall (C) Solicitor and notary public. Former legal practice owner. Cllr, Rotherham

	Electorate	Turnout %	from 2010 % Change
	67,587	70.88	
J Frith Lab	25,683	53.61	+12.51
*D Nuttall C	21,308	44.48	+2.54
R Baum LD	912	1.90	-0.16

MBC 1992-96; 2004-06. MEP candidate, Yorkshire & the Humber 1999. Contested: Sheffield Hillsborough 1997; Morecambe & Lunesdale 2001; Bury North 2005. MP, Bury North 2010-17. Cttees: procedure 2010-15, 2015-17; panel of chairs 2015-17; backbench business 2015-16, 2016-17. Introduced EDM to overturn smoking ban. **Richard Baum** (LD) Magistrate and NHS auditor. Contested Bury North 2010; 2015. During the 2017 campaign, he encouraged supporters to vote Labour.

CONSTITUENCY PROFILE
A bellwether marginal covering most of the old mill town of Bury itself, as well as the market town of Ramsbottom to its north. Although levels of unemployment exceed the national average, Bury North enjoys higher than average earnings and a greater proportion of residents are homeowners than the UK average. The constituency has a sizeable Asian and Asian British population, with many residents of Pakistani heritage. Won by Labour under Tony Blair, it swang back to the Conservatives under Cameron, and returned to Labour in 2017.

EU REFERENDUM RESULT

53.7% Leave   Remain 46.3%

Bury South

LABOUR HOLD MAJORITY 5,965 (11.7%)

IVAN LEWIS
BORN Mar 4, 1967
MP 1997-

Former chief exec: charity Contact Community Care Group; Manchester Jewish Federation. Campaigned to Remain but voted in favour of triggering Article 50. Corbyn critic; nominated Liz Kendall 2015; called on Corbyn to resign after Brexit vote. Front bench incl: economic sec to the Treasury 2005-06; min of state, FCO 2009-10; shadow min foreign & commonwealth affairs 2010; shadow SofS for NI 2013-15, intnl dev 2011-13, CMS 2010-11. Cttees: deregulation 1997-99; health 1999; intnl dev 2017. Sought Labour candidacy, Greater Manchester mayoral

	Electorate	Turnout %	from 2010 % Change
	73,723	69.16	
*I Lewis Lab	27,165	53.28	+8.22
R Largan C	21,200	41.58	+6.95
I Henderson Ukip	1,316	2.58	-10.76
A Page LD	1,065	2.09	-1.49
P Wright Ind	244	0.48	

race 2017. Two children. Ed: William Hulme GS, Manchester; Stand Sixth Form Coll; Bury Coll.

CHALLENGERS
Robert Largan (C) Chartered accountant. Cllr, Hammersmith & Fulham BC 2014-17. Worked for Greg Hands MP. **Ian Henderson** (Ukip) Dep northwest chairman, Ukip. Contested Bury North, 2015. **Andrew Page** (LD) Photographer. Mental health and

LGBT rights campaigner. Former union rep, Unison.

CONSTITUENCY PROFILE
Bury South covers a little of the town's southern edge, but consists mainly of the former mill towns of Radcliffe, Whitefield and Prestwich. At about 10,000, Bury South has one of the largest Jewish populations of any seat in Britain. Although earnings are less than the UK average, home ownership levels are greater than typically seen across the country. The constituency elected a Conservative MP from 1983 to 1997, but has been Labour ever since.

EU REFERENDUM RESULT

54.5% Leave   Remain 45.5%

Bury St Edmunds

CONSERVATIVE HOLD MAJORITY 18,441 (29.7%)

JO CHURCHILL
BORN Mar 18, 1964
MP 2015-

Cancer survivor. Diagnosed with illness at the age of 31 and again in her mid-40s. Second bout truncated PhD in small and medium-sized enterprise and social responsibility at the University of Nottingham. Campaigns for Breakthrough Breast Cancer. Cllr, Lincolnshire CC 2013-15. First female representative for Bury St Edmunds. Select cttees: environmental audit 2015-16; women and equalities 2015-17. PPS to Mike Penning 2016-. Member, exec cttee of CPA 2016-. Remainer, but against second referendum. Petition launched against her for decision

	Electorate	Turnout %	from 2010 % Change
	87,758	70.83	
*J Churchill C	36,794	59.19	+5.58
B Edwards Lab	18,353	29.53	+11.81
H Korfanty LD	3,565	5.74	-0.30
H Geake Green	2,596	4.18	-3.73
L Byrne Ind	852	1.37	

to vote for disability cuts and yet fundraise for a head-injury charity. Runs two contracting companies. Brought up in East Anglia. Married, four daughters. Ed: Dame Alice Harper Sch, Bedford (BSc business; MSc occupational psychology).

CHALLENGERS
Bill Edwards (Lab) Principal, food consultants. Contested: Bury St Edmunds 2015; Braintree 2010. **Helen Korfanty** (LD) Solicitor. Contested Suffolk PCC

2016. **Helen Geake** (Green) Archaeologist. Contested Bury St Edmunds 2015. **Liam Byrne** (Ind) Supermarket worker. Recipient of organ transplant.

CONSTITUENCY PROFILE
With Bury St Edmunds in the west, and the smaller town of Stowmarket in the southeast, this constituency also consists of rural north Suffolk villages. It is characterised by low levels of economic inactivity among its residents, a disproportionate number of whom work in higher managerial jobs. The seat has elected Conservative MPs since it became a single-member constituency in 1885.

EU REFERENDUM RESULT

54.0% Leave   Remain 46.0%

Caerphilly

LABOUR HOLD MAJORITY 12,078 (29.2%)

WAYNE DAVID
BORN Jul 1, 1957
MP 2001-

Stepped down from the bench in 2016 because he believed under Jeremy Corbyn's "leadership the prospects for Labour . . . [at a general election were] not good". Rejoined shadow cabinet later that year. Accused of racism in 2016 after saying in an interview with BBC Radio Wales: "The only people who have coloured skin . . . are people who run takeaways." Shadow min: armed forces 2016-; political reform in cabinet office 2015-16; Scotland 2015-16; justice 2015-16; constitutional reform 2011-13; foreign affairs 2010-11; Wales 2010. Select cttees: Welsh affairs 2007; conventions

	Electorate	Turnout %	from 2010 % Change
	64,381	64.14	
*W David Lab	22,491	54.46	+10.12
J Pratt C	10,413	25.21	+8.62
L Whittle PC	5,962	14.44	-0.20
L Wilks Ukip	1,259	3.05	-16.29
K David LD	725	1.76	-0.57
A Creak Green	447	1.08	-1.24

2006. Remarried. Ed: Cardiff University (BA history and Welsh history; PGCE); Swansea University (economic history).

CHALLENGERS
Jane Pratt (C) Cllr, Monmouthshire CC 2017-. **Lindsay Whittle** (PC) Former housing manager. Leader, Caerphilly Co BC 1976-, leader 1999-2004, 2008-11. AM, National Assembly 2011-16. **Liz Wilks** (Ukip) Contested Welsh

Assembly 2016. **Kay David** (LD) Part-time lecturer. Contested Caerphilly 2010. **Andrew Creak** (Green) Passionate about LGBTIQA+ issues. Contested Welsh Assembly 2016.

CONSTITUENCY PROFILE
This constituency is a former industrial area north of Cardiff and has an elderly population, 98 per cent of which is white. About a fifth of its residents live in social housing. The seat has returned Labour MPs for the best part of a century. This election is the first since the end of the Second World War in which the Conservatives have won even a quarter of the vote.

EU REFERENDUM RESULT

55.1% Leave   Remain 44.9%

Caithness, Sutherland & Easter Ross

LIBERAL DEMOCRAT GAIN MAJORITY 2,044 (6.6%)

JAMIE STONE
BORN June 16, 1954
MP 2017-

Worked in the oil industry. Cllr, Highland C 1986-2011, 2012-. MSP, Caithness, Sutherland & Ross 1999-2011; candidate 2016. Lib Dem Holyrood spokesman, housing; dep spokesman, health. Campaigned against Scottish independence. Champion of local issues. Captain, Scottish parliament's *University Challenge* team 2004. Married, three children. Ed: Tain Royal Academy; University of St Andrews (MA history and geology).

CHALLENGERS
Paul Monaghan (SNP)
MP 2015-17. Campaigned to

	Electorate	Turnout %	from 2010 %	Change
	46,868	65.93		
J Stone LD	11,061	35.79	+0.73	
*P Monaghan SNP	9,017	29.18	-17.13	
S Mackie C	6,990	22.62	+15.82	
O Bell Lab	3,833	12.40	+3.45	

Remain; voted against Article 50. Former head of planning and development, Northern Constabulary. Director, Highland Homeless Trust; Inverness MS Therapy Centre. Board member, UHI North Highland College. **Struan Mackie** (C) Consultant, PwC. Cllr, Highland C 2017-. Vice-chairman, Caithness, Sunderland & Easter Ross Conservatives. MSP candidate, Caithness, Sutherland & Ross 2016. **Olivia Bell** (Lab) Former *Inverness Courier* reporter. Parliamentary assistant to MSPs

David Stewart and Rhoda Grant 2015.

CONSTITUENCY PROFILE
This seat is in the rural northernmost tip of the mainland. Much of the electorate, which is 99.2 per cent white, is concentrated in Easter Ross in the south, where there is a strong oil industry. About a fifth of its constituents work in skilled trade occupations. Industries include fishing, farming, construction and tourism – with a particular focus on John O'Groats. In the 2015 election the previously Lib Dem stronghold turned SNP, with 46.3 per cent of the vote.

EU REFERENDUM RESULT
51.3% Leave   Remain 48.7%

Calder Valley

CONSERVATIVE HOLD MAJORITY 609 (1.0%)

CRAIG WHITTAKER
BORN Aug 30, 1962
MP 2010-

Founder of a local Calderdale charity, Together Looked after Children. Former retail manager at Wilkinsons and PC World. Cllr, Heptonstall PC 1998-2003; Calderdale MBC 2003-11. Election agent to Elizabeth Truss 2005. Former chairman of the Calder Valley Conservatives. Campaigned to Remain in the European Union; voted to trigger Article 50. PPS to: James Brokenshire 2015-16; Karen Bradley 2016-. Education cttee 2010-15. APPG: libraries (vice-chairman); sexual violence in conflict (co-chairman); street children. Three children. Ed: Tighes Hill Coll.

	Electorate	Turnout %	from 2010 %	Change
	79,045	73.44		
*C Whittaker C	26,790	46.15	+2.53	
J Fenton Glynn Lab	26,181	45.10	+9.75	
J Battye LD	1,952	3.36	-1.62	
P Rogan Ukip	1,466	2.53	-8.59	
R Holden Ind	1,034	1.78		
K Turner Green	631	1.09	-2.82	

CHALLENGERS
Josh Fenton Glynn (Lab) Third-sector worker at: Oxfam 2008-09; Child Poverty Action Group 2009-10; End Hunger UK 2017-. North West Field director, Britain Stronger in Europe. Former research consultant, USDAW. Cllr, Calderdale MBC 2016-. **Janet Battye** (LD) Social worker. Cllr, Calderdale MBC 2002-16; Lib Dem leader 2010-12. Spearheaded Calderdale campaign to Save Our Pubs.

Paul Rogan (Ukip) Semi-retired carpet salesman. Chairman, Ukip Calder Valley. **Rob Holden** (Ind) Works in IT. **Keiran Turner** (Green) Aid worker. Dir, Aid Convoy. Democracy and campaigns asst, Bradford University students union.

CONSTITUENCY PROFILE
This is a relatively affluent constituency, where incomes tend to be higher than the Yorkshire and Humber average, and more people are employed in managerial-level jobs than average. Home ownership is relatively high. The seat has been a bellwether since its creation in 1983.

EU REFERENDUM RESULT
53.2% Leave   Remain 46.8%

Camberwell & Peckham

LABOUR HOLD MAJORITY 37,316 (65.0%)

HARRIET HARMAN
BORN Jul 30, 1950
MP 1982-

One of Labour's most successful female MPs. Prominent feminist. Criticised for using a pink battle bus to appeal to women in the 2015 GE. Masterminded Equality Act. Qualified solicitor. Former legal officer for the National Council for Civil Liberties (now Liberty) where she took the first cases for women under the Equal Pay and Sex Discrimination Acts. Formed first PLP women's group. Acting leader 2010 and 2015. Dep leader 2007-15. Shadow sec: CMS 2010-15; international development 2010-11. Select cttees: liaison 2015-17; human rights 2015-17. Admitted to underestimating

	Electorate	Turnout %	from 2010 % Change
	85,586	67.08	
*H Harman Lab	44,665	77.80	+14.54
B Spencer C	7,349	12.80	-0.37
M Bukola LD	3,413	5.94	+0.94
E Margolies Green	1,627	2.83	-7.23
R Towey CPA	227	0.40	
S Aminata WRP	131	0.23	+0.02

Corbyn after GE 2017 results. Remainer – called the vote for the Brexit bill the "unhappiest night of voting in the House of Commons I've ever been in". Voted for Article 50. Married, three children. Ed: University of York (BA politics).

CHALLENGERS
Ben Spencer (C) Mental health NHS doctor. Governor, NHS Foundation Trust. **Michael Bukola** (LD) Nurse. Contested

London Assembly 2016. **Eleanor Margolies** (Green) Air-pollution campaigner. **Ray Towey** (CPA) NHS doctor for 20 years. Contested London Assembly 2016.

CONSTITUENCY PROFILE
Dense south London seat. Fewer than one in twelve residents are aged 65 or above, less than half the UK figure, while over a third are under 25. It is a diverse seat, with the highest black, African and Carribean demographic of any seat in the country. Very high levels of council renting with low incomes, for London. The seat has elected a Labour MP at every opportunity.

EU REFERENDUM RESULT

31.5% Leave   Remain 68.5%

Camborne & Redruth

CONSERVATIVE HOLD MAJORITY 1,577 (3.3%)

GEORGE EUSTICE
BORN Sep 28, 1971
MP 2010-

Comes from farming background and worked in family fruit business before entering politics. Campaign dir, anti-EU "No" campaign 1999-2003; head of press, Conservative Party 2003-05; press secretary, David Cameron 2005-07. Ukip MEP candidate 1999. Staunch Brexiteer. Parly under-sec, Defra 2013-15; min of state, Defra 2015-. Rural affairs cttee 2010-13. Energy & climate change adviser to Cameron 2013-15. Cleared after being subject to police investigation for 2015 general election expenses. Married. Ed: Truro Cathedral Sch; Truro Sch; Cornwall Coll.

	Electorate	Turnout %	from 2010 % Change
	67,462	71.83	
*G Eustice C	23,001	47.47	+7.24
G Winter Lab	21,424	44.21	+19.25
G Williams LD	2,979	6.15	-6.25
G Garbett Green	1,052	2.17	-3.51

CHALLENGERS
Graham Winter (Lab) Senior adviser, waste management, Environment Agency. Cllr, Camborne Town C 2015-. Former trustee: Donald Thomas Centre; Camborne Community Centre. Amateur actor. **Geoff Williams** (LD) Former further education lecturer. Cllr, Basildon BC 1981-85, 1986-2016. National Trust volunteer. Awarded MBE in 2013 for services to local govt. Contested Basildon South & Thurrock East 2010, 2015. **Geoff Garbett** (Green) Associate

lecturer, Open University. Cllr, Carharrack PC 2013-. Founder member, South West Greens. Contested: Taunton 1979; Camborne & Redruth 2015.

CONSTITUENCY PROFILE
This has been a Conservative seat since 2010. The constituency forms a five-mile urban corridor parallel to Cornwall's west coast. Once prosperous from copper and tin mining, the area declined so much in 2000-06 that it received a development fund from the EU. A high proportion of constituents are aged over 65, and more than a fifth of constituents do not own a passport.

EU REFERENDUM RESULT

58.4% Leave   Remain 41.6%

Cambridge

LABOUR HOLD MAJORITY 12,661 (22.6%)

DANIEL ZEICHNER
BORN Nov 9, 1956
MP 2015-

Former national officer, Unison. Cllr, South Norfolk DC 1995-2003. Parly researcher to John Garrett MP 1992-97 and Charles Clarke MP 1997-99. Corbyn sceptic: nominated Yvette Cooper 2015 and Owen Smith 2016. Voted Remain and against Article 50. Environmentalist. House of Lords reform advocate. Shadow min, transport 2015-. Science & technology cttee 2015. APPG chairman: bullying; data analytics; future of work; London Stansted to Cambridge corridor (co-chairman). Leading member: Labour campaign for electoral reform. Patron: Cambridge e-Luminate Festival. Married.

	Electorate	Turnout %	from 2010 %	Change
	78,003	71.71		
*D Zeichner Lab	29,032	51.90	+15.89	
J Huppert LD	16,371	29.27	-5.59	
J Hayward C	9,133	16.33	+0.65	
S Tuckwood Green	1,265	2.26	-5.67	
K Garrett Rebooting	133	0.24		

Ed: Trinity Sch; King's Coll, Cambridge (BA history).

CHALLENGERS
Julian Huppert (LD) Fellow, Clare Coll Cambridge. Former lecturer, physics and public policy, Cambridge. Cllr, Cambridgeshire CC 2001-09. MP, Cambridge 2010-15. Cttees: home affairs 2010-15; human rights 2010-11; draft Defamation Bill 2011. **John Hayward** (C) Conservative Party policy forum manager, CCHQ. Former exec

dir, social reform charity: Jubilee Centre. **Stuart Tuckwood** (Green) Staff nurse, NHS. Steward, Unison.

CONSTITUENCY PROFILE
Home not just to Cambridge University and Anglia Ruskin, but also hi-tech industry and a regional commercial centre. More than one in every six adults is in full-time education, and Cambridge has the highest proportion of residents in professional occupations of any seat. Around a third use a bicycle as means of travel. The 2015 election returned a Labour MP after 10 years of Lib Dem representation.

EU REFERENDUM RESULT

26.2% Leave   Remain 73.8%

Cambridgeshire North East

CONSERVATIVE HOLD MAJORITY 21,270 (39.9%)

STEVE BARCLAY
BORN May 3, 1972
MP 2010-

Comes from a working-class background. Solicitor by trade, specialising in financial crime prevention. Previously head of anti-money laundering and sanctions for Barclays Bank, FSA, Guardian Royal Exchange, Axa Insurance. Served briefly in army, sponsored through university. Campaigned for Brexit, opposed further outsourcing of government to Brussels. Econ sec Treasury 2017-; govt whip 2016-. Asst whip 2015-16. Member, public accounts select cttee 2010-14. Contested Lancaster & Wyre 2001, lost by 481 votes; Manchester Blackley 1997. Adviser to Liam Fox as

	Electorate	Turnout %	from 2010 %	Change
	84,404	63.13		
*S Barclay C	34,340	64.45	+9.36	
K Rustidge Lab	13,070	24.53	+10.09	
D Fower LD	2,383	4.47	+0.00	
R Talbot Ukip	2,174	4.08	-18.42	
R Johnson Green	1,024	1.92	-1.59	
S Goldspink Eng Dem	293	0.55		

Conservative Party chairman 2005. Selected by open primary. Rugby player and keen skydiver. Married, two children. Ed: Peterhouse, Cambridge (BA history); Coll of Law, Chester.

CHALLENGERS
Ken Rustidge (Lab) Iraq veteran. NUT official. **Darren Fower** (LD) Previously media development officer and business analyst. Cllr 2004-; group leader and deputy leader of council

group. Contested Peterborough 2015. **Robin Talbot** (Ukip) Tanker driver from Wittering. Military background. **Ruth Johnson** (Green) Career in financial services. Former teacher. **Stephen Goldspink** (Eng Dem) Former Peterborough councillor.

CONSTITUENCY PROFILE
This is a rural and agricultural constituency, with an economy built on farming, packaging, distribution, construction and education. There are small Indian and Chinese communities within the constituency. Car and homeownership levels are high. Tory territory since 1987.

EU REFERENDUM RESULT

69.4% Leave   Remain 30.6%

Cambridgeshire North West

CONSERVATIVE HOLD MAJORITY 18,008 (28.1%)

SHAILESH VARA
BORN Sep 4, 1960
MP 2005-

Claims to have invited more than 25,000 local residents to coffee mornings to hear their opinions on local and international issues. Has presented three local petitions to the PM. Denied claims that he had tried to claim for council tax, cleaning and mortgage payments incurred before he became an MP. Remainer, but voted for Brexit bill. Parly under-sec: work & pensions 2015-16; MoJ, 2013-16. Assistant whip 2010-12. Shadow dep leader of House 2006-10. Select cttees: finance and services 2011-13; administration 2010-11. Vice-chairman Conservative

	Electorate	Turnout %	from 2010 %	Change
	93,223	68.64		
*S Vara C	37,529	58.65	+6.16	
I Ramsbottom Lab	19,521	30.51	+12.62	
B Smith LD	3,168	4.95	-0.74	
J Whitby Ukip	2,518	3.93	-16.16	
G Guthrie Green	1,255	1.96	-1.57	

Party 2001-05. Legal adviser and business consultant, London First. Solicitor: Richards Butler; CMS Cameron McKenna. Vice-pres, Small Business Bureau. Married, two sons. Ed: Aylesbury GS; Brunel University (LLB law).

CHALLENGERS
Iain Ramsbottom (Lab) Market trader. Anti-austerity. Chairman, NW Cambridgeshire CLP. **Bridget Smith** (LD) Former primary school teacher. Author. Cllr, S Cambridgeshire

DC 2008-. **John Whitby** (Ukip) Dir, Skyline Corporate Communications 2007-. Cllr, Peterborough CC 2015. **Greg Guthrie** (Green) Civil engineer.

CONSTITUENCY PROFILE
Contains a mix of suburban and rural land. Economically active, the seat has high employment, despite one in four constituents being aged over 65. Strongly Tory since its creation in 1997, there are still pockets of deprivation in Peterborough residential developments. Includes affluent rural village in Huntingdonshire and parts of Peterborough to the south of the River Nene.

EU REFERENDUM RESULT

56.9% Leave   Remain 43.1%

Cambridgeshire South

CONSERVATIVE HOLD MAJORITY 15,952 (24.6%)

HEIDI ALLEN
BORN Jan 18, 1975
MP 2015-

Former businesswoman. Worked for ExxonMobil and Royal Mail. Selected to replace Andrew Lansley on all-woman shortlist prior to GE 2015. Awarded Conservative Newcomer MP of the Year 2015. Supported government's efforts to take in more child refugees from Syria. Cllr, St Albans DC 2012-14, some controversy over not declaring parliamentary ambitions earlier. Remainer, but voted for Article 50. Work and pensions select cttee 2015-17. Failed to progress to the final round of voting to become the Conservative candidate for the 2017 Cambridgeshire

	Electorate	Turnout %	from 2010 %	Change
	85,257	76.15		
*H Allen C	33,631	51.80	+0.69	
D Greef Lab	17,679	27.23	+9.58	
S van de Ven LD	12,102	18.64	+3.42	
S Saggers Green	1,512	2.33	-3.92	

and Peterborough mayoral election. MD of family business, RS Bike Paint, launched by parents in 1978. Lives in Steeple Morden. Married. Ed: UCL (BSc astrophysics).

CHALLENGERS
Dan Greef (Lab) Former teacher. Believes grammar schools are a direct attack on social mobility. Contested Cambridge S 2015. **Susan van de Ven** (LD) Cllr, Cambridgeshire CC 2004-06, 2006-10, 2017-. Founder: the Meldreth, Shepreth and Foxton

Community Rail Partnership; A10 Corridor Cycling Campaign. Authored *One Family's Response to Terrorism*. Joined party in 2003 because of its stance on Iraq war. **Simon Saggers** (Green) Charity worker. Contested: Cambridge S 2015, 2010, 2005, 2001; Cambridgeshire CC 2016.

CONSTITUENCY PROFILE
A safe Tory seat. Economically active with high employment in professional occupations. Mostly rural with much of the electorate scattered across small prosperous villages and one ward of Cambridge. Duxford is home to the Imperial War Museum's aviation branch.

EU REFERENDUM RESULT

38.5% Leave   Remain 61.5%

Cambridgeshire South East

CONSERVATIVE HOLD MAJORITY 16,158 (25.6%)

LUCY FRAZER
BORN May 17, 1972
MP 2015-

	Electorate	Turnout %	from 2010 % Change
	86,121	73.16	
*L Frazer C	33,601	53.33	+4.86
H Jones Lab	17,443	27.69	+12.54
L Nethsingha LD	11,958	18.98	-1.20

Barrister; appointed to the Queen's Counsel in 2013. Labelled by Michael Gove as one of the future stars of the Conservative Party. Encountered controversy after using maiden speech in the House of Commons to describe how Oliver Cromwell incorporated Scotland into his Protectorate and transported the Scots as slaves to the colonies. Campaigned to Remain, but voted for Article 50. PPS to Ben Gummer 2016-17. Born in Yorkshire. Married. Ed: Newham College, University of Cambridge (BA law; president of the Cambridge Union).

CHALLENGERS
Huw Jones (Lab) Crop scientist. Contested Cambridgeshire SE 2015. Focused campaign on the issue of education, pointing to the falling quality of Cambridgeshire's schools. Governor, Impington Village College. Member, Morris Educational Trust. Collected food donations for a local Trussell Trust food bank. Helped to deliver aid to Calais refugees in 2016. Lives in southeast Cambridgeshire.
Lucy Nethsingha (LD) Primary school teacher. Remainer,

campaigns against a hard Brexit. Cllr: Cambridge CC 2016-; Cambridgeshire CC 2009-. Dep leader, Cambridgeshire CC Lib Dem Group. Born in Cornwall.

CONSTITUENCY PROFILE
Conservative since its creation in 1983. Covers rural areas between Cambridge and Newmarket. Economically active, with about two thirds of constituents in employment. A high proportion work in professional, scientific or technical industries. Population centres in Ely and Soham. The west of the seat includes Cambridge airport and Cambridge Science Village.

EU REFERENDUM RESULT
45.3% Leave   Remain 54.7%

Cannock Chase

CONSERVATIVE HOLD MAJORITY 8,391 (17.5%)

AMANDA MILLING
BORN Mar 12, 1975
MP 2015-

	Electorate	Turnout %	from 2010 % Change
	74,540	64.22	
*A Milling C	26,318	54.98	+10.79
P Dadge Lab	17,927	37.45	+3.71
P Allen Ukip	2,018	4.22	-13.25
P Woodhead Green	815	1.70	-0.22
N Green LD	794	1.66	-1.04

Background in market research specialising in financial services, including as director and head of clients at Optimisa Research, and director of Quaestor. Opposed to Brexit, but not a Remain campaigner. Investigated the collapse of BHS and working practices at Sports Direct as member of BIS select cttee. PPS to Baroness Anelay 2016-17. Cllr, Rossendale BC 2009-14; dep Conservative leader. Ed: Moreton Hall Sch; UCL (BSc economics & statistics).

CHALLENGERS
Paul Dadge (Lab) Owns IT business. Formerly part-time

firefighter. Called a hero after photographs were circulated in the international press of him helping casualties after the 7/7 attack in London. A book, *The Man and the Mask*, was published about his actions. Community first responder.
Paul Allen (Ukip) Director of a property business.
Paul Woodhead (Green) Environmental consultant and waste management expert. Proprietor at PEW Consultancy. Cllr, Cannock Chase DC 2011-.

School governor. Presenter of a show on local radio. Chairman of the Cannock Chase Green Party.

CONSTITUENCY PROFILE
Previously a relatively safe Labour seat, with a majority in excess of 20 per cent in the 2001 and 2005 elections, the constituency was a surprise gain for the Conservatives in 2010. Aidan Burley won the seat with a swing of 14 per cent, one of the largest from Labour to the Tories in any contest in 2010. The Staffordshire constituency is homogeneous, almost 98 per cent white, and economically active, with about two thirds of constituents employed.

EU REFERENDUM RESULT
68.9% Leave   Remain 31.1%

Canterbury

LABOUR GAIN MAJORITY 187 (0.3%)

ROSIE DUFFIELD
BORN Jul 1, 1971
MP 2017-

Canterbury's first-ever
Labour MP, overturning 176
years of Tory representation.
Canterbury Action Network
co-founder. Former teaching
assistant turned political satirist.
Animal rights campaigner; has
attended anti-fox hunt and Peta
protests. Supports proportional
representation. Ambassador,
50:50 Parliament. Participant,
Jo Cox Women in Leadership
scheme. Chairwoman,
Canterbury CLP 2013-.
Contested local elections 2015.
Member: Canterbury Amnesty
International; Unison; Co-op,
Open Labour. Single mother,
two sons.

	Electorate	Turnout %	from 2010 Change %
	78,137	72.69	
R Duffield Lab	25,572	45.02	+20.48
*J Brazier C	25,385	44.69	+1.83
J Flanagan LD	4,561	8.03	-3.62
H Stanton Green	1,282	2.26	-4.75

CHALLENGERS
Julian Brazier (C) MP
Canterbury 1987-2017. Former
chartered consolidated and
HB Maynard management
consultant. Territorial Army
officer. Interested in defence.
Avid Brexiteer. Knighted in
2016. **James Flanagan** (LD)
Local heritage and pro-Remain
campaigner. Government affairs
adviser, International power
energy firm. Contested 2015. Cllr,
Canterbury CC 2007-15. **Henry
Stanton** (Green) Local teacher.
Calls for progressive alliance

between Lab, LD and Green to
beat Brazier were rejected.

CONSTITUENCY PROFILE
Historically a solid Conservative
seat, having been represented
by the party continuously
from the 19th century until
the 2017 election and a shock
victory for Labour. Before
this election the nadir of Tory
dominance had been when
the majorities were less than
10,000 in 1997 and 2001. An
economically active cathedral
town, with surrounding villages
and seaside towns including
Whitstable. Only 2.8 per cent
unemployment and one fifth in
professional occupations.

EU REFERENDUM RESULT

45.3% Leave   Remain 54.7%

Cardiff Central

LABOUR HOLD MAJORITY 17,196 (42.6%)

JO STEVENS
BORN Sep 6, 1966
MP 2015-

Human rights lawyer; former dir,
Thompsons Solicitors. Long-time
Labour Party activist. Nominated
Andy Burnham 2015. Voted to
express confidence in Corbyn,
but then backed Owen Smith,
2016. Campaigned to Remain;
resigned from shadow cabinet
to vote against invoking Article
50. Shadow justice min 2016;
shadow solicitor-general 2016;
shadow SofS for Wales 2016-17.
Cttees: business, innovation &
skills 2015-16; standards 2015-16;
privileges 2015-16; justice 2017.
Two children. Ed: Elfred HS;
University of Manchester (LLB
law); Manchester Metropolitan
University (Law Society finals).

	Electorate	Turnout %	from 2010 Change %
	59,288	68.09	
*J Stevens Lab	-	25,193	62.41	+22.40
G Stafford C	7,997	19.81	+5.13
E Parrott LD	5,415	13.41	-13.71
M Hooper PC	999	2.47	-2.51
B Smith Green	420	1.04	-5.33
S Mohammed Ukip	343	0.85	-5.62

CHALLENGERS
Gregory Stafford (C) Dir,
Federation of Specialist
Hospitals. Cllr, Ealing BC
2007-; leader of the opposition
2014-. **Eluned Parrott** (LD)
Former community engagement
manager. Member, Welsh
National Assembly 2011-16.
Mark Hooper (PC) Lib Dem
Welsh Assembly candidate, 2005;
2007. **Benjamin Smith** (Green)
University student. Young
Greens press officer. **Sarul-Islam**

Mohammed (Ukip) President,
commonwealth business and
investment council for Wales.
Plaid Cymru cllr, Cardiff CC
2004-12. Ukip candidate, Welsh
Assembly 2014.

CONSTITUENCY PROFILE
The smallest and most densely-
populated seat in Cardiff. About
24,000 full-time students, well
over a quarter of the population,
live in Cardiff Central. It is one
of the more diverse Welsh seats:
about 80 per cent of residents
are white and 10 per cent are
Asian or of Asian descent. Fewer
than half of households are
owner-occupied, with well over a
third in the private rented sector.

EU REFERENDUM RESULT

32.0% Leave   Remain 68.0%

Cardiff North

LABOUR GAIN MAJORITY 4,174 (8.0%)

ANNA MCMORRIN
BORN Sep 23, 1971
MP 2017-

Welsh govt adviser, environment and sustainability 2008-14. Previously: campaigns and communications officer, Friends of the Earth; climate change negotiator, the UN. Supported Owen Smith's leadership campaign 2016. Remainer. Member, Co-op Party. Married, two children. Ed: University of Southampton (BA French & politics); Cardiff University (PGDip journalism).

CHALLENGERS
Craig Williams (C) Cllr, Cardiff CC 2008-15. Welsh Assembly candidate: 2007; 2011. Contested Cardiff South and Penarth 2012.

	Electorate	Turnout %	from 2010 %	Change
	67,221	77.39		
A McMorrin Lab	26,081	50.13	+11.87	
*C Williams C	21,907	42.11	-0.33	
S Webb PC	1,738	3.34	-1.16	
M Hemsley LD	1,714	3.29	-0.52	
G Oldfield Ukip	582	1.12	-6.61	

MP for Cardiff North 2015-17. Campaigned to Remain; voted for Article 50. PPS to David Gauke. Cttees: work & pensions 2015-16; Welsh affairs 2015-17; Scottish affairs 2017. Married, two children. **Steffan Webb** (PC) Former further education teacher. Contested Cardiff CC 2017. **Matthew Hemsley** (LD) Campaigns and advocacy manager, Oxfam Cymru. Former press officer & policy and media adviser, Sustrans. Campaign officer & research assistant,

Don Foster 2010. **Gary Oldfield** (Ukip) Self-employed electrician.

CONSTITUENCY PROFILE
More than 8,000 students live in this seat. About three quarters of homes in Cardiff North are owner-occupied, while social renting is well below average. With Wales's largest hospital and not far from Cardiff University, health and education are significant sources of employment. It also has the lowest unemployment and highest average income of the four Cardiff seats. This is the first time Labour has held the seat without winning a parliamentary majority.

EU REFERENDUM RESULT
39.1% Leave   Remain 60.9%

Cardiff South & Penarth

LAB CO-OP HOLD MAJORITY 14,864 (29.3%)

STEPHEN DOUGHTY
BORN Apr 15, 1980
MP 2012-

Former head of Oxfam Cymru. SofS for international development 2009-10. Corbyn critic: nominated Liz Kendall 2015; resigned from front bench live on the *Daily Politics Show* 2016; supported Owen Smith's leadership campaign 2016. Campaigned to Remain; voted against Article 50. Opp whip 2013-15; shadow min: business, innovation & skills 2015; foreign & commonwealth affairs 2015-16. Cttees: Welsh affairs 2012-15; international devt 2016-17; arms export controls 2016-17; international devt sub 2016-17. Ed: Llantwit Major Comp Sch;

	Electorate	Turnout %	from 2010 %	Change
	76,499	66.32		
*S Doughty Lab Co-op	30,182	59.49	+16.70	
B Rees C	15,318	30.19	+3.38	
I Titherington PC	2,162	4.26	-3.12	
E Sands LD	1,430	2.82	-2.15	
A Bevan Ukip	942	1.86	-11.91	
A Slaughter Green	532	1.05	-2.69	
J Hedges Pirate	170	0.34		

Corpus Christi Coll, Oxford (BA PPE); St Andrews University.

CHALLENGERS
Bill Rees (C) Business executive, Centrica. Contested Merthyr Tydfil & Rhymney 2015. **Ian Titherington** (PC) Drainage engineer. **Emma Sands** (LD) Public affairs manager. Former policy adviser, Welsh National Assembly. **Andrew Bevan** (Ukip) Factory worker. **Anthony**

Slaughter (Green) Garden designer. Deputy leader, Wales Green Party 2014-15.

CONSTITUENCY PROFILE
This coastal area is the least affluent Cardiff seat by income. Home ownership is well below average, while more than a fifth of households are privately rented. Compared with much of Wales, it is a fairly diverse seat, with a small but substantial Asian and black population. Including its predecessor Cardiff South East, the seat has elected only Labour MPs since 1950, and was for many years represented by James Callaghan, prime minister from 1976 to 1979.

EU REFERENDUM RESULT
42.8% Leave   Remain 57.2%

Cardiff West

LABOUR HOLD MAJORITY 12,551 (26.9%)

KEVIN BRENNAN
BORN Oct 16, 1959
MP 2001-

Researcher to predecessor
Rhodri Morgan 1995-2001. Cllr,
Cardiff CC 1991-2001. Ran "Yes
for Wales" devolution campaign.
Corbyn sceptic: nominated Andy
Burnham 2015; resigned from
shadow cabinet 2016; supported
Owen Smith's leadership
challenge 2016. Campaigned to
Remain; voted against Article
50. Min: children, schools and
families 2009-10; BIS 2010.
Shad min: BIS 2010, 2015-16;
education 2010; culture, media
& sport 2016-. APPGs: brain
tumours (vice-chairman); folk
arts (chairman). Married, one
child. Ed: St Alban's RC Comp
Sch, Pontypool; Pembroke

	Electorate	Turnout %	from 2010 Change %
	67,221	69.37	
*K Brennan Lab	26,425	56.67	+16.02
M Smith C	13,874	29.75	+4.60
M Deem PC	4,418	9.47	-4.45
A Meredith LD	1,214	2.60	-2.12
R Lewis Ukip	698	1.50	-9.74

Coll, Oxford (BA PPE); Cardiff
University (PGCE); University of
Glamorgan (MSc education and
management).

CHALLENGERS
Matt Smith (C) Personal injury
lawyer. Former chairman,
Bethnal Green & Bow Con
Assoc. Candidate: Tower
Hamlets BC 2011; Welsh
Assembly 2011. **Michael Deem**
(PC) Senior caseworker, Welsh
AM Neil McEvoy. Candidate:
Welsh Assembly 2016; Cardiff

CC 2017. **Alex Meredith** (LD)
Solicitor. Cllr, Faringdon TC
2014-. Contested Wantage,
2015. **Richard Lewis** (Ukip)
Policy adviser, Ukip AM Gareth
Bennett. Candidate: Welsh
Assembly 2003; Cardiff CC 2016.

CONSTITUENCY PROFILE
Cardiff West has the smallest
population of full-time students
of any Cardiff seat. Home to
a 7 per cent Asian and Asian
British population, significantly
above average for Wales. Home
ownership, while higher than
in Cardiff Central or South, is
slightly lower than the Welsh
average. Labour dominance was
broken in the 1979-83 elections.

EU REFERENDUM RESULT
43.8% Leave   Remain 56.2%

Carlisle

CONSERVATIVE HOLD MAJORITY 2,599 (6.0%)

JOHN STEVENSON
BORN Jul 4, 1963
MP 2010-

Qualified solicitor; partner,
Bendles. Cllr, Carlisle CC 1999-
2010. Interested in business and
local govt reform. Campaigned
to Remain in the EU; voted to
trigger Article 50. Member, 1922
exec cttee 2017-. Occasional
rebel during coalition years, but
has not defied whip since 2015.
Voted against gay marriage.
APPG chairman: family business;
food and drink manufacturing;
West Coast main line.
Investigated and cleared over
2015 election battle bus expenses
probe. Married. Ed: Aberdeen
GS; Dundee University (MA
history and politics); Chester
Coll of Law (LLB law).

	Electorate	Turnout %	from 2010 Change %
	62,294	69.12	
*J Stevenson C	21,472	49.87	+5.55
R Alcroft Lab	18,873	43.83	+6.03
F Mills Ukip	1,455	3.38	-9.01
P Thornton LD	1,256	2.92	+0.36

CHALLENGERS
Ruth Alcroft (Lab) Supply
teacher. Education officer and
dir, Susan's Farm Community
Interest Company, Houghton.
Cllr, Carlisle CC 2016-. Former
cllr, Rossendale BC. **Fiona
Mills** (Ukip) NHS accountant.
Chairwoman, Ukip Cumbria.
Criticised for tweet comparing
Adolf Hitler to the modern
left. Contested: Carlisle 2015;
Copeland by-election 2017;
local elections 2015, 2016.
Peter Thornton (LD) Retired
businessman and photographer.

Cllr: South Lakeland DC 2003-;
Cumbria CC 2016-.

CONSTITUENCY PROFILE
Only a few miles from the
Scottish border, this is a highly
homogeneous region, with only
5 per cent of residents born
outside the UK. The workforce
is characterised by high levels of
part-time work and low levels
of self-employment. Routine
and semi-routine work is more
common, and average incomes
are significantly below the
national average. First won by
Labour in 1922, Carlisle had
been held by Labour MPs for 88
years until Stevenson gained the
constituency in 2010.

EU REFERENDUM RESULT
60.6% Leave   Remain 39.4%

Carmarthen East & Dinefwr

PLAID CYMRU HOLD MAJORITY 3,908 (9.5%)

JONATHAN EDWARDS
BORN Apr 26, 1976
MP 2010-

Worked as chief of staff for Adam Price MP. Outspoken, dubbed "the Member for Wales" for his strong criticism of Westminster and for being one of the party's main strategic thinkers. Pro-EU, and voted against Article 50 bill. Interested in social justice and foreign affairs. Shadow spokesman for transport 2010-; BIS 2010-; Treasury 2010-; foreign intervention 2015-. Married, three children. Ed: Ysgol Gymraeg Rhydaman; Ysgol Gyfun Maes yr Yrfa; University of Wales Aberystwyth (BA history and politics; MA international history).

	Electorate	Turnout %	from 2010 %	Change
	55,976	73.30		
*J Edwards PC	16,127	39.31	+0.88	
D Darkin Lab	12,219	29.78	+5.57	
H Hughes C	10,778	26.27	+5.11	
N Hamilton Ukip	985	2.40	-8.67	
L Prosser LD	920	2.24	-0.11	

CHALLENGERS
David Darkin (Lab) Architect who runs his own practice in Llanelli. Vice-chairman and treasurer, Royal Society of Architects; vice-president Llanelli Chamber of Trade & Commerce; chairman, Friends of Llanelli Train Station.
Havard Hughes (C) City worker, specialising in financial regulation. Defected from Lib Dems to Conservatives in 2007. Welsh speaker from Rhydargaeau. **Neil Hamilton**

(Ukip) Former disgraced Conservative MP for Tatton 1983-97 after his involvement in cash-for-questions affair.

CONSTITUENCY PROFILE
More than a fifth of residents are aged 65 or above. Home ownership is well above average, at nearly three quarters of households. More than a third of households in the constituency have no adult in employment. The predecessor seat of Carmarthen elected only Labour MPs from 1979, but this seat was gained by Plaid Cymru in 2001, and Labour's support has receded at every successive election until 2017.

EU REFERENDUM RESULT

53.2% Leave   Remain 46.8%

Carmarthen West & Pembrokeshire South

CONSERVATIVE HOLD MAJORITY 3,110 (7.4%)

SIMON HART
BORN Aug 15, 1963
MP 2010-

Former chief executive of lobby group Countryside Alliance, now chairman. Came under fire for his continued work with CA while serving on environment cttee. Worked as a chartered surveyor in Carmarthen, and served with TA for seven years. Leading voice against abuse faced by politicians, 2017. Vocal supporter of fox hunting. Select cttees: political and constitutional reform 2010-14; Welsh affairs 2012-15; environment, food and rural affairs 2015-17. Married, two children. Ed: Radley College; Royal Agricultural College, Cirencester.

	Electorate	Turnout %	from 2010 %	Change
	58,548	72.12		
*S Hart C	19,771	46.82	+3.14	
M Tierney Lab	16,661	39.46	+10.78	
A Thomas PC	3,933	9.31	-1.10	
A Cameron LD	956	2.26	-0.12	
P Edwards Ukip	905	2.14	-9.50	

CHALLENGERS
Marc Tierney (Lab) Former broadcaster and manager at Radio Pembrokeshire. Chairman, Friends of Narberth Library, Cleddau Community Media.
Abi Thomas (PC) Community cllr, Laugharne Township 2017-. Contested Ogmore by-election 2016. Member, Pembrokeshire Community Health Council.
Alistair Cameron (LD) English teacher. Cllr, Cheltenham BC 1986-98; Gloucestershire CC 2000-05. Contested Tewkesbury

2005; 2010; 2015. **Phil Edwards** (Ukip) Support worker, local counselling charity.

CONSTITUENCY PROFILE
A historically marginal seat, fought closely by Labour and the Conservatives, that was held by Labour during the New Labour period and has been Conservative ever since. More than a third of households have no adults in employment. More than a fifth of residents are aged 65 or more. Incomes are low on average for the region. The constituency was created in 1997 from parts of the former marginal seats of Pembroke and Carmarthen.

EU REFERENDUM RESULT

55.2% Leave   Remain 44.8%

Carshalton & Wallington

LIBERAL DEMOCRAT HOLD MAJORITY 1,369 (2.7%)

TOM BRAKE
BORN May 6, 1962
MP 1997-

Former computer software consultant, Hoskyns. Human rights and environmental activist while a university student. Cllr: Sutton BC 1994-97; Hackney BC 1988-90. Contested Carshalton & Wallington 1992. One of the first male MPs to not wear a tie in Commons chamber after 2017 general election. Parliamentary Secretary and deputy Commons leader 2012-15. Treasury whip 2014-15. Lib Dem chief whip, shadow Commons leader and foreign affairs spokesman 2015-. Married, two children. Ed: Lycée International, St. Germain-en-Laye; Imperial Coll, London (BSc physics).

	Electorate	Turnout %	from 2010 %	Change
	70,849	71.64		
*T Brake LD	20,819	41.02	+6.15	
M Maxwell Scott C	19,450	38.32	+6.62	
E Ibrahim Lab	9,360	18.44	+3.43	
S Khan Green	501	0.99	-2.15	
N Mattey Ind	434	0.86		
A Dickenson CPA	189	0.37	+0.00	

CHALLENGERS
Matthew Maxwell Scott (C) Communications director and former speech writer to BBC director-general Lord Hall of Birkenhead. Dir, Access to Justice, a campaigning group for injured people, since 2016. Chairman, Sutton Conservative Federation 2016-. Contested Carshalton & Wallington 2015. Cllr, Wandsworth BC 2010-14. **Emina Ibrahim** (Lab) Cllr, Haringey BC 2014-.

CONSTITUENCY PROFILE
Carshalton and Wallington is one of two south London seats in the borough of Sutton. Bordering Surrey, the constituency is characterised by levels of home ownership that are more in line with the UK average than with London's much lower average. It is somewhat less diverse than many more central London seats, with seven out of ten residents identifying themselves as white British. Carshalton and Wallington was the only seat to elect a Lib Dem MP in all of London and the southeast in 2015, and was a Conservative seat prior to Tom Brake winning it in 1997.

EU REFERENDUM RESULT
56.3% Leave   Remain 43.7%

Castle Point

CONSERVATIVE HOLD MAJORITY 18,872 (42.2%)

REBECCA HARRIS
BORN Dec 22, 1967
MP 2010-

Former marketing executive at Phillimore & Co, publishers of British local history, 1997-2007. In 2001 took a sabbatical to work in Conservative research dept, looking at foot & mouth epidemic and campaigned against green-belt development. Campaigned to Leave the EU. Voted against investigations into the Iraq war. Former cllr, Chichester DC 1999-2003. Worked as adviser to Tim Yeo MP. Asst whip 2017-. Select cttees: regulatory reform, 2012-17; business, Innovation and Skills, 2010-15; Married, one son. Ed: Bedales School; LSE (BSc government).

	Electorate	Turnout %	from 2010 %	Change
	69,470	64.36		
*R Harris C	30,076	67.27	+16.42	
J Cooke Lab	11,204	25.06	+11.24	
D Kurten Ukip	2,381	5.33	-25.87	
T Holder LD	1,049	2.35	+0.58	

CHALLENGERS
Joe Cooke (Lab) Diversity and press officer, Castle Point constituency Labour Party. Carer and former systems analyst. Contested Castle Point 2015. Trustee, Castle Point Citizens Advice Bureau. **David Kurten** (Ukip) Former chemistry teacher. Ukip's education and apprenticeships spokesman 2016-. **Tom Holder** (LD) Head of campaigns at Understanding Animal Research. Contested Greenwich & Woolwich 2015.

CONSTITUENCY PROFILE
Castle Point is a coastal Essex seat between Basildon and Southend-on-Sea. It has one of the highest levels of home ownership in the country, a high rate of UK-born residents, and incomes are above the national average. Labour first held this seat during the 1997 parliament, but hasn't won it since. The former MP, Bob Spink, was technically the first Ukip MP after his defection from the Conservatives in 2008. Rebecca Harris's 2017 majority is the largest any candidate has won in Castle Point since 1987, partly because of Ukip's collapse in the seat.

EU REFERENDUM RESULT
72.7% Leave   Remain 27.3%

Ceredigion

PLAID CYMRU GAIN MAJORITY 104 (0.3%)

BEN LAKE
BORN Jan 22, 1993
MP 2017-

Plaid Cymru's youngest ever MP. Former press officer to AM Elin Jones before working in the National Assembly. Particularly concerned by the potential impact of Brexit on rural areas. Ed: Lampeter Comprehensive Sch; Trinity Coll, Oxford (BA history).

CHALLENGERS
Mark Williams (LD) MP for Ceredigion 2005-17. Former teacher and deputy head. Leader of the Welsh Liberal Democrats and Lib Dem Wales spokesman 2016-17. Shadow minister: innovation, universities and skills 2007-10; Wales 2006-10;

	Electorate	Turnout %	from 2010 %	Change
	52,889	75.19		
B Lake PC	11,623	29.23	+1.57	
*M Williams LD	11,519	28.97	-6.88	
D Mulholland Lab	8,017	20.16	+10.50	
R Davis C	7,307	18.37	+7.36	
T Harrison Ukip	602	1.51	-8.72	
G Ham Green	542	1.36	-4.22	
Sir Dudley Loony	157	0.39		

education 2005-6. Select cttees: Welsh affairs 2005-17. Married, four children. **Dinah Mulholland** (Lab) London-born, moved to Wales nearly 20 years ago. Works on a zero-hours contract in support services at University of Wales Trinity St David. One daughter. **Ruth Davis** (C) Head of public policy at BT security. Adviser to Crispin Blunt MP, when he was a shadow minister for counterterrorism.

CONSTITUENCY PROFILE
This seat, formerly known as Cardigan, is on the west of Wales and its biggest settlement is the coastal town of Aberystwyth. Although Aberystwyth has a university, only about 3,000 students live in the seat. More than four in five households are owner-occupied, one of the highest proportions in the UK. Before Mark Williams was first elected in 2005, Plaid Cymru had held the seat since 1992. The Lib Dems losing this seat means it is the first time no Welsh commons seat has been held by a Liberal for the first time since the Liberal Party was founded in 1859.

EU REFERENDUM RESULT

45.4% Leave   Remain 54.6%

Charnwood

CONSERVATIVE HOLD MAJORITY 16,341 (29.6%)

EDWARD ARGAR
BORN Dec 9, 1977
MP 2015-

Former management consultant and head of public affairs, Serco. Parents were both teachers. Contested Oxford East 2010. Supported Remain. PPS to Nick Gibb 2015-. Procedure cttee 2015-16. Co-chairman, dementia APPG. Cllr Westminster CC 2006-15; unsuccessful leadership candidate 2012. Former trustee of regeneration and employment charity, Groundwork London. Non-executive board member of local NHS trust. Ed: Harvey GS; Oriel Coll, Oxford (BA history; MSt historical research).

CHALLENGERS
Sean Kelly-Walsh (Lab) Local

	Electorate	Turnout %	from 2010 %	Change
	78,071	70.67		
*E Argar C	33,318	60.38	+6.07	
S Kelly-Walsh Lab	16,977	30.77	+8.85	
S Sansome LD	2,052	3.72	-3.18	
V Connor Ukip	1,471	2.67	-13.27	
N Cox Green	1,036	1.88		
S Denham BNP	322	0.58	-0.35	

organiser for Unison 2015-. Former East Midlands LGBT Labour Party rep. Exec student union officer 2013-15. Contested 2015. **Simon Sansome** (LD) Writer and local campaigner. Adult social services worker. Cllr, Charnwood BC 2014-. Contested Birstall, 2010; Charnwood 2015. **Victoria Connor** (Ukip) Contested Leicester CC 2015. **Nick Cox** (Green) Retired police officer. Treasurer, local Green Party branch.

CONSTITUENCY PROFILE
Charnwood is located between Leicester and Loughborough, made up mainly of satellite towns around Leicester. The seat's population is skewed in terms of age, with a greater proportion of older residents than is typical, and it also has a significant Asian population, comprising about one in ten residents. Incomes tend to be above average and more than four fifths of households are owner-occupied. Charnwood is a safe Conservative seat, and has elected only Conservative MPs since its creation in 1997, when Stephen Dorrell held the seat until 2015.

EU REFERENDUM RESULT

57.9% Leave   Remain 42.1%

128 | THE NEW PARLIAMENT

Chatham & Aylesford

CONSERVATIVE HOLD MAJORITY 10,458 (23.3%)

TRACEY CROUCH
BORN July 24, 1975
MP 2010-

Moderniser and self-confessed One Nation Tory. Would-be lawyer who shunned being a solicitor for political career. Head of public affairs, Aviva, 2005-10. One of two Tories to abstain in tuition fees vote; opposed press regulations. Anti-fox hunting. Called badger-culling barbaric and indiscriminate. Did not openly declare for EU referendum. Select cttees: CMS 2012-15; political and constitutional reform 2013-15. Parliamentary under-secretary DCMS 2015-. Football enthusiast: FA qualified coach and manager of local girls' team. First Tory min to take maternity

	Electorate	Turnout %	from 2010 Change %
	70,419	63.75	
*T Crouch C	25,587	57.00	+6.82
V Maple Lab	15,129	33.70	+10.12
N Bushill Ukip	2,225	4.96	-14.97
T Quinton LD	1,116	2.49	-0.67
B Hyde Green	573	1.28	-1.28
J Gibson CPA	260	0.58	+0.27

leave 2016. Partner, one child. Ed: University of Hull (LLB law and politics).

CHALLENGERS
Vince Maple (Lab) Cllr, Medway 2007-; Labour group leader 2012-. Previously GMB trade union regional organiser 2008-11. **Nicole Bushill** (Ukip) Named for spreading hate material online by Hope Not Hate. Shared anti-Halal posts on personal social media.

CONSTITUENCY PROFILE
Chatham and Aylesford is a compact Kent seat, containing most of Chatham and several smaller towns and villages, such as Snodland, Ditton and Aylesford, further south. About a third of the seat's residents are under 25, and while incomes are well below the southeast average, they are roughly in line with the national average. Construction and retail are among the most overrepresented industries in which residents work. Labour held the seat from its creation in 1997 until 2010, and Tracey Crouch almost doubled her majority in 2015 and increased her vote again in 2017.

EU REFERENDUM RESULT

63.9% Leave   Remain 36.1%

Cheadle

CONSERVATIVE HOLD MAJORITY 4,507 (8.3%)

MARY ROBINSON
BORN Aug 23, 1955
MP 2015-

Owned accountancy practice with husband. Cllr, South Ribble BC. Chairwoman, local conservative association. Supported Remain. Select cttees: administration 2017-; communities and local gov 2015-. Married, four children. Ed: Leyton Hill Convent Sch; Preston Poly (accountancy foundation); Lancashire polytechnic (LLB law).

CHALLENGERS
Mark Hunter (LD) Former marketing executive, Guardian Media Group. MP for Cheadle 2005-15. Lib Dem chief whip 2010-14. PPS to Nick Clegg

	Electorate	Turnout %	from 2010 Change %
	72,780	74.98	
*M Robinson C	24,331	44.59	+1.48
M Hunter LD	19,824	36.33	+5.37
M Miller Lab	10,417	19.09	+2.75

2007-10. Leader, Stockport MBC 2002-05. North West regional authority. Cllr, Stockport MBC, 1996-2005. Contested: Stockport 2001; Ashton-under-Lyne 1987. **Martin Miller** (Lab) Chief exec, Diocese of Manchester, the Church of England. Contested Cheadle 2015. Cllr, Stockport Metropolitan BC 2008-. Greater Manchester Poverty Commission.

CONSTITUENCY PROFILE
Cheadle is on the southern edge of Greater Manchester, bordering the Cheshire seats of

Macclesfield and Tatton. More than a fifth of residents are aged 65 or above, and the seat is predominantly white, with an Asian population of about 7,000. About five sixths of households are owner-occupied, one of the highest proportions of any seat in the country, and incomes tend to be above the national average. The seat has been mostly Conservative since its creation in 1950, but was held by the Liberal Democrats from 1966 to 1970, and again from 2001 until their nationwide collapse in 2015, with Mark Hunter holding the seat from 2005 after a by-election caused by the death of his predecessor, Patsy Calton.

EU REFERENDUM RESULT

42.7% Leave   Remain 57.3%

Chelmsford

CONSERVATIVE HOLD MAJORITY 13,572 (23.9%)

VICKY FORD
BORN Sep 21, 1967
MP 2017-

Vice-president in loan syndication, JP Morgan 1988-2000. Contested Birmingham Northfield 2005. Cllr, South Cambridgeshire DC 2006-09. MEP, east of England 2009-17; chairwoman, internal market and consumer affairs cttee 2014-17. Bureau of the European Conservative and Reformist Group. Lead negotiator, ECR group, inter-group political discussions. Contributor, The Tax Reform Commission. Succeeds Sir Simon Burns. Born and raised in Northern Ireland. Married, three children. Ed: Trinity Coll, Cambridge (BSc maths and economics).

	Electorate	Turnout %	from 2010 Change %
	81,045	70.16	
V Ford C	30,525	53.68	+2.15
C Vince Lab	16,953	29.82	+12.20
S Robinson LD	6,916	12.16	+0.28
N Carter Ukip	1,645	2.89	-11.33
H Reza Green	821	1.44	-2.07

CHALLENGERS
Chris Vince (Lab) Maths teacher. Cllr, Springfield PC 2012-. Contested Chelmsford 2015, first Lab runner-up since 1970; Essex PCC 2016.
Stephen Robinson (LD) Comms consultant. Cllr: Essex CC 2012-; Chelmsford CC 2011; Epping Forest DC 1990-98. Chairman, North Chelmsford Community Trust. Campaigned to Remain in the EU. Founder, Don't Choke Chelmsford. Contested Chelmsford 2015, 2010.

CONSTITUENCY PROFILE
This constituency is centered on the city in Essex from which it takes its name, and the county's only city. Incomes in the seat are well above the national average and while home ownership exceeds national levels, the figure is typical for the region. More than twice the UK-wide proportion of Chelmsford's residents work in the finance and insurance sector. The constituency has not elected a non-Conservative representative since the Second World War, and its MP for many years was Norman St. John-Stevas, a minister in Margaret Thatcher's government.

EU REFERENDUM RESULT
50.7% Leave   Remain 49.3%

Chelsea & Fulham

CONSERVAITVE HOLD MAJORITY 8,188 (19.4%)

GREG HANDS
BORN Nov 14, 1965
MP 2005-

Interested in eastern Bloc; spent his gap year working there in 1984. Former city banker who speaks five languages. British and American dual national. Supported Remain. PPS to George Osborne 2010-11. Assistant whip 2011-13. Deputy chief whip 2013-15. Chief sec to Treasury 2015-16. Minister of state, dept of int trade 2016-. Member: Conservative Way Forward; Conservative Friends of Israel. Former president, Conservative Friends of Poland. Patron, Fulham Boys School. Married, two children. Ed: Dr Challoner's GS, Bucks; Robinson Coll, Cambridge (BA history).

	Electorate	Turnout %	from 2010 Change %
	63,728	66.11	
*G Hands C	22,179	52.65	-10.30
A De'Ath Lab	13,991	33.21	+10.09
L Rowntree LD	4,627	10.98	+5.79
B Cashmore Green	807	1.92	-1.75
A Seton-Marsden Ukip	524	1.24	-3.83

CHALLENGERS
Alan De'Ath (Lab) Pastoral and academic leader. Cllr, Hammersmith & Fulham 2014-. Secretary, Hammersmith & Fulham CLP. **Louise Rowntree** (LD) Lawyer. Public affairs and communications consultant. **Bill Cashmore** (Green) Actor and playwright. Co-founder, Actors in Industry.

CONSTITUENCY PROFILE
The seat, made up of wards from the Hammersmith, Fulham and Kensington London boroughs, lies along the north of the Thames. It is a very wealthy constituency: mean income is higher only in two other seats in the country: the neighbouring constituencies of Kensington and Chelsea and Cities of London and Westminster. About a third of accomodation is in the private rented sector, more than double the national average. It also has among the highest concentration of European and North American passport holders of any constituency. No party other than the Conservatives has represented any incarnations of the Chelsea constituency since 1910.

EU REFERENDUM RESULT
29.1% Leave   Remain 70.9%

Cheltenham

CONSERVATIVE HOLD MAJORITY 2,569 (4.5%)

ALEX CHALK
BORN Aug 8, 1976
MP 2015-

Barrister: experienced in prosecuting terrorism offences, also represented journalists during phone-hacking scandal. First Conservative MP for Cheltenham in 23 years. Remainer, voted to trigger Article 50. Campaigned to change minimum sentence for stalking from five to ten years. Member, Criminal Bar Association; Serious Fraud Office Panel of Counsel. Pro bono APPG chairman. Member, justice select cttee 2015-. Cllr, Hammersmith and Fulham BC, 2006-14. Ed: Magdalen Coll, Oxford (BA modern history); City University of London

	Electorate	Turnout %	from 2010 %	Change
	78,875	72.28		
*A Chalk C	26,615	46.68	+0.55	
M Horwood LD	24,046	42.18	+8.17	
K White Lab	5,408	9.49	+2.22	
A Van Coevorden Green	943	1.65	-3.35	

(GDL); Inns of Court School of Law.

CHALLENGERS
Martin Horwood (LD) MP for Cheltenham 2005-15. Works in advertising and voluntary sector. Contested: Cities of London and Westminster 2001; Oxford East 1992. Founder, tribal peoples APPG. Ed: The Queen's Coll, Oxford (BA modern history). **Keith White** (Lab) Maths and computer studies teacher; communications and scientific officer, GCHQ 1987-2010. Vice-

chairman, Cheltenham CLP 2014-.

CONSTITUENCY PROFILE
This constituency covers almost the entire urban area of Cheltenham which gives the seat its name, along with a little land to the east. It is home to several Gloucestershire University campuses and halls, housing about 9,000 students. Although it is a fairly affluent constituency, the level of home ownership is in line with the UK average and the rate of private renting is well above average. Cheltenham has a strong Conservative history, although the Lib Dems held the seat between 1992 and 2015.

EU REFERENDUM RESULT
42.9% Leave   Remain 57.1%

Chesham & Amersham

CONSERVATIVE HOLD MAJORITY 22,140 (40.1%)

CHERYL GILLAN
BORN Apr 21, 1952
MP 1992-

Formerly a senior marketing consultant at Ernst & Young. Marketing director, Kidsons Impey 1991-93; dir, the BFI's British Film Year 1984-86. Supported Leaving the EU. Opponent of HS2, which will run through this constituency. She has admitted frustration at toeing the party line. SoS for Wales 2010-12. Shadow min: home 2003-05; foreign and commonwealth affairs 1998-01; trade and industry 1997-98. Opposition whip 2001-03. Embroiled in expenses scandal for claiming dog food and for employing her husband as constituency office manager.

	Electorate	Turnout %	from 2010 %	Change
	71,645	77.12		
*C Gillan C	33,514	60.66	+1.61	
N Dluzewska Lab	11,374	20.59	+7.86	
P Jones LD	7,179	12.99	+3.96	
A Booth Green	1,660	3.00	-2.50	
D Meacock Ukip	1,525	2.76	-10.93	

Married. Ed: Cheltenham Ladies Coll; Coll of Law.

CHALLENGERS
Nina Dluzewska (Lab) Stay-at-home parent. Ran the local Remain campaign during 2016 referendum. **Peter Jones** (LD) Cllr, Chiltern DC 1991-; Lib Dem group leader. Contested: Milton Keynes South 2010; Aylesbury 2005. **Alan Booth** (Green) Local cllr, set up local residents' association and co-runs a village cafe each week.

CONSTITUENCY PROFILE
This mainly rural south Buckinghamshire seat on the outskirts of Greater London is characterised by very high levels of self-employment and incomes that tend to be well above the UK average. More than three in four households are owner-occupied; residents are unlikely to live in private rented accommodation. The seat has elected Conservatives at every election since its creation in 1974. The Conservative candidate has never won fewer than half of the votes cast in this constituency, and it and its predecessor seats have all been Conservative since 1924.

EU REFERENDUM RESULT
45.0% Leave   Remain 55.0%

Chester, City of

LABOUR HOLD MAJORITY 9,176 (16.3%)

CHRIS MATHESON
BORN Jan 2, 1968
MP 2015-

	Electorate	Turnout %	from 2010 % Change
	72,859	77.44	
*C Matheson Lab	32,023	56.76	+13.53
W Gallagher C	22,847	40.49	-2.56
L Jewkes LD	1,551	2.75	-2.86

Formerly a manager in the electricity industry, Unite HR manager and officer. Won seat with the third smallest majority in 2015. Remain campaigner who resigned as justice PPS in response to the result of the EU referendum. Backed Owen Smith in 2016 Labour leadership contest. Re-joined shadow cabinet when Smith lost. PPS to John Healey 2016-17. Member, CMS select cttee 2015-17. Criticised in 2013 when it was revealed that he was Tom Blenkinsop's landlord for a property he rented on expenses. Married, two daughters. Ed: Manchester Grammar School;

LSE (BSc economics and politics).

CHALLENGERS
Will Gallagher (C) Strategic dir, East West Rail. Former operations dir of young people's programme the National Citizen Service. Special adviser to Chris Grayling 2012-15. Contested Alyn and Deeside 2010. **Elizabeth Jewkes** (LD) Runs management consultancy business and is the dir of a local social enterprise. Author of policy to raise income tax threshold in Liberal Democrat 2010 manifesto.

CONSTITUENCY PROFILE
Chester is the second largest settlement and the only city in Cheshire. The seat contains the University of Chester and there are about 8,000 students living in the constituency. Home ownership levels are about average, but the levels of private renting are higher than typical. It is a relatively affluent seat in terms of income. Chester has elected Conservatives for almost the entirety of the 20th century, with Labour winning the seat for the first time in 1997. Although the Conservatives gained the constituency in 2010, Labour won it back by just 93 votes in 2015.

EU REFERENDUM RESULT

42.3% Leave   Remain 57.7%

Chesterfield

LABOUR HOLD MAJORITY 9,605 (20.0%)

TOBY PERKINS
BORN Aug 12, 1970
MP 2010-

	Electorate	Turnout %	from 2010 % Change
	72,063	66.51	
*T Perkins Lab	26,266	54.80	+6.90
S Pitfield C	16,661	34.76	+16.70
T Snowdon LD	2,612	5.45	-8.38
S Bent Ukip	1,611	3.36	-13.15
D Wadsworth Green	777	1.62	-1.35

Sports enthusiast. Founder of rugby clothing company, Club Rugby, and goalkeeper for parly football team. Campaigned for Remain. Son of film critic VF Perkins. Resigned from front bench in 2016, calling on Jeremy Corbyn to quit. Ran Liz Kendall's unsuccessful leadership campaign in 2015. Shadow min: armed forces 2015-16; small businesses 2011-15; children & families 2010-11. Qualified rugby coach and ex-Sheffield Tigers Rugby Union player. Cllr, Chesterfield BC 2003-10. Married, two children. Ed: Trinity Sch, Leamington; Silverdale Sch, Sheffield.

CHALLENGERS
Spencer Pitfield (C) Head of instrumental studies, Birkdale Sch, Sheffield. Leave supporter. Contested: Sheffield Brightside and Hillsborough by-election 2016; Penfistone and Stocksbridge 2010; Sheffield Hallam 2005. Dir, Conservative trade unionists. Stepped down as national director, Conservative Policy Forum in 2015. Awarded OBE for his work on the 2015 manifesto. **Tom Snowdon** (LD) Chartered engineer;

procurement manager in renewable energy sector.

CONSTITUENCY PROFILE
A compact town seat in northern Derbyshire which is closer to Sheffield than Derby. It is homogeneous: 96 per cent of residents are white. A fifth of residents live in social housing, over a quarter have no qualifications, health is generally poor, and incomes are low. Historically this is a Labour seat; the Liberals built up strength here during the 1980s when the seat was represented by Tony Benn, eventually winning it in 2001, but the seat swung back to Labour in 2010.

EU REFERENDUM RESULT

59.3% Leave   Remain 40.7%

Chichester

CONSERVATIVE HOLD MAJORITY 22,621 (37.8%)

GILLIAN KEEGAN
BORN May 13, 1968
MP 2017-

Worked as an apprentice at Delco Electronics in Merseyside, Liverpool, aged 16. Lived and worked abroad in manufacturing, banking and IT for 25 years. Technology start-up investor. Voted Remain in 2016 EU referendum. Entered politics in 2013. Cllr, Chichester DC 2014-. Contested St Helens South and Whiston 2015. Married, two stepsons. Ed: John Moores University (BA business studies); London Business School (Sloan Fellowship, MSc leadership and strategy).

CHALLENGERS
Mark Farwell (Lab) Teaches

	Electorate	Turnout %	from 2010 %	Change
	84,996	70.50		
G Keegan C	36,032	60.14	+2.46	
M Farwell Lab	13,411	22.38	+10.25	
J Brown LD	6,749	11.26	+2.75	
H Barrie Green	1,992	3.32	-3.22	
A Moncreiff Ukip	1,650	2.75	-12.19	
A Emerson Patria	84	0.14	-0.05	

public policy at Southampton Solent University. Trade union activist. **Jonathan Brown** (LD) Works locally as risk manager. Cllr, Southbourne DC 2016-. Chairman: Chichester Lib Dems; Liberal Democrats for Free Syria. **Heather Barrie** (Green) Local businesswoman supplying Fairtrade coffee. Campaigns for publicly owned rail network. **Andrew Moncrieff** (Ukip) Worked in engineering and lectured MBA. District cllr.

CONSTITUENCY PROFILE
This coastal West Sussex seat, located between Portsmouth and Bognor Regis, also stretches north into the South Downs. The constituency is characterised by an ageing population, of which about a quarter are aged 65 or over. There are high levels of self-employment. Home ownership and incomes are roughly in line with the regional average. Chichester has elected Conservatives at every election since 1924. The election of a Liberal MP in 1923 was the only time the Conservatives lost here since Chichester became a one-member constituency in 1868.

EU REFERENDUM RESULT

50.7% Leave   Remain 49.3%

Chingford & Woodford Green

CONSERVATIVE HOLD MAJORITY 2,438 (5.2%)

IAIN DUNCAN SMITH
BORN April 9, 1954
MP 1992-

Conservative leader 2001-03; the "quiet man" who was ousted as leader by his own MPs. Right-wing former Scots Guard lieutenant who saw active service in Northern Ireland and Rhodesia. Later worked for defence contractor and property company. Contested Bradford West, 1987. SoS work and pensions 2010-16: architect of Universal Credit welfare system; resigned from position in protest at proposed disability cuts 2016. Founder, Centre for Social Justice. Eurosceptic. Married, two sons, two daughters. Ed: HMS Conway Cadet Sch; RMA Sandhurst.

	Electorate	Turnout %	from 2010 %	Change
	66,078	71.07		
*I Duncan Smith C	23,076	49.14	+1.20	
B Mahmood Lab	20,638	43.95	+15.15	
D Unger LD	2,043	4.35	-1.13	
S King Green	1,204	2.56	-1.67	

CHALLENGERS
Bilal Mahmood (Lab) Corporate finance solicitor, China Construction Bank. Treasurer, Walthamstow CLP. Former trustee, English Speaking Union. Member: Co-operative Party, GMB and Community Union. Contested Chingford & Wood Green, 2015. **Deborah Unger** (LD) Works as an anti-corruption activist for non-profit organisation, Transparency International. Novelist. Formerly *Guardian* and *The Economist* journalist.

CONSTITUENCY PROFILE
Chingford and Woodford Green is situated on London's northern edge. It is hardly the most diverse seat in the city, but over a quarter of the population belongs to an ethnic minority. Home ownership is above the national average, a rarity among London seats, and although incomes tend to be lower than the Greater London average, they are higher than the UK average. Although the constituency has always elected Conservatives, the majority at the 2017 election is the smallest margin Duncan Smith has achieved since the seat was created in 1997.

EU REFERENDUM RESULT

49.9% Leave   Remain 50.1%

Chippenham

CONSERVATIVE HOLD MAJORITY 16,638 (29.1%)

MICHELLE DONELAN
BORN Apr 8, 1984
MP 2015-

Worked as a marketing professional at AETN UK. Previously employed in various international managerial roles. Made first speech at Conservative party conference aged 15. Soft Eurosceptic who ultimately voted Remain. Member: education, skills and the economy sub-cttee 2015-17; education cttee 2015-17. Diagnosed with Lyme disease by constituent during a surgery in 2016. Trustee of local Help Victims of Domestic Violence charity. Contested Wentworth and Dearne 2010. Ed: County HS, Leftwich; University of York (BA history and politics).

	Electorate	Turnout %	from 2010 %	Change
	76,432	74.76		
*M Donelan C	31,267	54.72	+7.16	
H Belcher LD	14,637	25.62	-3.76	
A Newman Lab	11,236	19.66	+11.43	

CHALLENGERS
Helen Belcher (LD) Trans businesswoman and campaigner for LGBT equality and press regulation. Named by *The Independent on Sunday* as one of the most influential LGBT people in the UK for three years running. Provided evidence to Leveson Inquiry. Founded her own software company in 2004. Qualified teacher. **Andrew Newman** (Lab) Telecoms engineer, Colston Engineering. Branch secretary, GMB. Chairman of Swindon Local Campaign Forum.

CONSTITUENCY PROFILE
There are other towns in this western Wiltshire constituency just east of Bath, including Melksham, Corsham and Bradford-upon-Avon, although Chippenham, with its population of more than 45,000, dominates the area. Home ownership and typical incomes are both slightly above the regional average. The seat has a fairly low level of unemployment, although the levels of part-time employment are above average. The constituency was re-created in 2010 from two Conservative seats, but was won by a Lib Dem in 2010, who subsequently lost the seat in 2015.

EU REFERENDUM RESULT
51.6% Leave   Remain 48.4%

Chipping Barnet

CONSERVATIVE HOLD MAJORITY 353 (0.6%)

THERESA VILLIERS
BORN Mar 5, 1968
MP 2005-

Barrister, Lincoln's Inn. Former law lecturer, King's College London. London MEP 1999-2005. Opponent of expanding southeast airport capacity. Supports hunting ban. Brexiteer who backed Andrea Leadsom for party leadership. Left front bench after refusing a demotion in Theresa May's first reshuffle 2016. SoS for Northern Ireland 2012-16. Transport min, 2010-12. Shadow: SoS transport 2007-10; Treasury chief secretary, 2005-07. Member of aristocratic Villiers family. Divorced. Ed: Francis Holland Sch; University of Bristol (LLB law); Jesus Coll, Oxford (BCL).

	Electorate	Turnout %	from 2010 %	Change
	77,020	71.96		
*T Villiers C	25,679	46.33	-2.26	
E Whysall Lab	25,326	45.70	+11.55	
M Ray LD	3,012	5.43	+0.94	
P Fletcher Green	1,406	2.54	-2.18	

CHALLENGERS
Emma Whysall (Lab) Personal injury lawyer, Lyons Davidson Solicitors. Member: Unite and Co-operative Party. Remain campaigner. Contested local elections 2016. **Marisha Ray** (LD) Former industrial researcher and academic. Later board member, Whittington Hospital NHS Trust. Cllr, Islington BC 2002-10. Contested: GLA 2016; Chipping Barnet 2015; Croydon North 2012. Born to Bangladeshi immigrant parents.

CONSTITUENCY PROFILE
Chipping Barnet is a north London seat, with Hertfordshire situated on its northern border. Proportionally it has large Jewish and Hindu populations, at about 8,000 and 6,000 respectively, as well as a Muslim population of more than 8,000 people. Home ownership is well above the London average, and even slightly above the national average, and self-employment and typical incomes are also above average. This constituency has elected Conservative MPs at every election since 1974. Labour came within just over 1,000 votes in 1997, but 2017 is the tightest result it has had.

EU REFERENDUM RESULT
41.1% Leave   Remain 58.9%

Chorley

LABOUR HOLD MAJORITY 7,512 (13.5%)

LINDSAY HOYLE
BORN June 10, 1957
MP 1997-

Avuncular Lancastrian former textile-printing business owner. Deputy speaker since 2010. Won acclaim for stealing the show during 2013 budget and was trending on Twitter. Clashed with Alex Salmond during Article 50 debate and reprimanded SNP MPs for singing Ode to Joy during the vote in 2017. Was in the Speaker's chair during Westminster terror attack and Commons lockdown 2017. Son of former Labour MP and peer Lord (Doug) Hoyle. Cllr, Chorley BC 1980-98; mayor, 1997-98. Divorced, remarried, two daughters. Ed: Lord's Coll, Bolton; Horwich FE Coll.

	Electorate	Turnout %	from 2010 % Change
	76,404	72.82	
*L Hoyle Lab	30,745	55.26	+10.16
C Moon C	23,233	41.76	+5.42
S Fenn LD	1,126	2.02	-0.59
P Lageard Green	530	0.95	-1.20

CHALLENGERS
Caroline Moon (C) Foster carer; worked in probation service and as a housing officer. Raised money for local sports facilities. Cllr, South Ribble BC 2010-.
Stephen Fenn (LD) Works in Manchester as a computer systems analyst. Cllr, Clayton-le-Woods PC. Contested: Chorley 2015, 2010, 2001; Blackburn 1997; Manchester Wythenshawe 1992.
Peter Lageard (Green) Retired clinical physiotherapist and lecturer, London South Bank University.

CONSTITUENCY PROFILE
Chorley is a southern Lancashire seat, situated between Preston and Wigan. The town itself, just to the west of the West Pennine Moors, is home to about 35,000 people and the seat is characterised by high levels of home ownership. House prices are about three quarters of the national average. The constituency's residents tend to be slightly more affluent than is average for the region. The seat was first won by Labour in 1945 and has been held by the party for most of its postwar history, with brief Conservative interregna from 1970 to 1974 and 1979 to 1997.

EU REFERENDUM RESULT

56.7% Leave   Remain 43.3%

Christchurch

CONSERVATIVE HOLD MAJORITY 25,171 (49.7%)

CHRISTOPHER CHOPE
BORN May 19, 1947
MP 1997-; 1983-92

Barrister and consultant, Ernst & Young. Abrasive carrier of the Thatcherite flame; honorary VP and former chairman of Conservative Way Forward. Climate change sceptic. Referred to Commons staff as servants in debate. Campaigned for Britain to stay in Europe in 1975 but later became a Eurosceptic; campaigned fervently for Brexit. Critic of John Bercow as Speaker. Voted against same-sex marriage. MP for Southampton Itchen 1983-92. Long-serving cllr, Wandsworth BC; leader 1979-83. Married, one daughter, one son. Ed: Marlborough Coll; University of St Andrews (LLB law).

	Electorate	Turnout %	from 2010 % Change
	70,329	71.99	
*C Chope C	35,230	69.58	+11.46
P Canavan Lab	10,059	19.87	+10.32
M Cox LD	4,020	7.94	+1.38
C Rigby Green	1,324	2.61	-1.71

CHALLENGERS
Patrick Canavan (Lab) Former trade union regional officer, including Amicus and Unite. Contested: Dorset PCC elections 2016; Dorset Mid & Poole North 2015; Torbay mayoral election 2011; Newton Abbot 2010.
Michael Cox (LD) Chartered accountant, set up and manages his own firm. Non-executive director for finance-based businesses. Previously a cllr and council leader. Contested Uxbridge and Ruislip South 2015 and 2010.

CONSTITUENCY PROFILE
The Dorset constituency of Christchurch stretches north and east along the coast from Bournemouth. Nearly a third of its residents are aged 65 or over, making it one of the oldest seats in the country. Nearly four fifths of houses in the seat are owned, with about half of homes owned outright, one of the highest proportions in the UK. The constituency and its various predecessors have been won by the Conservatives at every general election since 1910, although the Lib Dems won at a 1993 by-election before losing it at the subsequent general election.

EU REFERENDUM RESULT

60.0% Leave   Remain 40.0%

Cities of London & Westminster

CONSERVATIVE HOLD MAJORITY 3,148 (8.1%)

MARK FIELD
BORN Oct 6, 1964
MP 2001-

Former corporate lawyer at Freshfields; director, law employment agency. Minister for Asia and the Pacific 2017-. Opposed Brexit, but voted to trigger Article 50. Shadow SoS for CMS 2005-06; shadow financial secretary 2005; shadow minister for London 2003-05. Select cttees: constitutional affairs; intelligence and security. Contested Enfield North 1997. Cllr, Royal Borough of Kensington and Chelsea 1994-2001. Divorced after high-profile affair with Liz Truss. Remarried, two children. Ed: St Edmund Hall, Oxford (BA jurisprudence); The College of Law, Chester.

	Electorate	Turnout %	from 2010 Change %
	61,533	62.82	
*M Field C	18,005	46.58	-7.50
I Dogus Lab	14,857	38.44	+11.08
B Fox LD	4,270	11.05	+4.08
L McNally Green	821	2.12	-3.27
A Bhatti Ukip	426	1.10	-4.13
T Lord ND	173	0.45	
A The Maharaja of Kashmir Ind	59	0.15	
B Weenen Young	43	0.11	

CHALLENGERS
Ibrahim Dogus (Lab) Founder, Centre for Turkey Studies; restaurant owner. Set up the British Kebab Awards. Shot in Haringey in the early 2000s trying to combat drug crime. Son of Kurdish refugees. **Bridget Fox** (LD) Account director, Thorncliffe. London Assembly candidate 2010-12. Cllr, Islington BC 1998-2006.

CONSTITUENCY PROFILE
This seat contains the Houses of Parliament, Buckingham Palace, St. Paul's Cathedral and the Bank of England, and includes areas like Marylebone and Mayfair. By average income it is the second richest constituency in the country, after neighbouring Kensington. The rate of home ownership is lower than average, at about a third, while over two in five homes are rented privately. More than a third of residents hold a non-UK passport. The seat, created in 1950, has been held only by the Conservatives, except when it was the Speaker of the Commons' seat from 1959-65.

EU REFERENDUM RESULT

28.1% Leave   Remain 71.9%

Clacton

CONSERVATIVE GAIN MAJORITY 15,828 (35.9%)

GILES WATLING
BORN Feb 18, 1953
MP 2017-

Actor for theatre, television and adverts, best known as Vicar Oswald in the sitcom *Bread*. Theatre director, including local theatre. Stood against Douglas Carswell in 2015 general election and 2014 by-election. Cllr, Tendring DC 2007-; cabinet member for planning and regeneration. Supported Remain but Eurosceptic. Fundraiser providing opportunities for disabled children to sail. Married, two daughters.

CHALLENGERS
Natasha Osben (Lab)
Campaigner against cuts to schools and health services.

	Electorate	Turnout %	from 2010 Change %
	69,263	63.74	
G Watling C	27,031	61.23	+24.58
T Osben Lab	11,203	25.38	+10.98
P Oakley Ukip	3,357	7.60	-36.83
D Grace LD	887	2.01	+0.17
C Southall Green	719	1.63	-1.05
C Shearer Ind	449	1.02	
R Tilbrook Eng Dem	289	0.65	
N Martin Ind	210	0.48	

Fundraiser for the charity Mind. Researching the impact of austerity at University of Essex. **Paul Oakley** (Ukip) Barrister. Former Conservative activist: contested St Helens North 2005; chairman, Greater London Young Conservatives. Late replacement for Jeff Bray, who was involved in scandal over offensive tweets.

CONSTITUENCY PROFILE
This coastal Essex seat is dominated by Clacton-on-Sea with the smaller towns of Fricton-on-Sea and Walton-on-the-Naze farther up the coast. About a third of residents are aged 65 or over, and just one in twenty was recorded as not "White British" in the 2011 census. Clacton and its predecessor seat had been held by Labour from 1997 until Douglas Carswell won the seat in 2005. In 2014, Carswell defected from the Conservatives and became Ukip's first elected MP, but he left the party to sit as an independent a few months before the 2017 election.

EU REFERENDUM RESULT

73.0% Leave   Remain 27.0%

Cleethorpes

CONSERVATIVE HOLD MAJORITY 10,400 (21.7%)

MARTIN VICKERS
BORN Sep 13, 1950
MP 2010-

Background in printing industry and retail trade. Constituency agent to Edward Leigh MP. Cllr, North East Lincolnshire Council 1999-2011; Great Grimsby BC 1980-94. Cabinet member for environmental services. Contested Cleethorpes 2005. Backbench rebellion: voted in favour of EU referendum 2011, and supported Leave in the EU referendum. Voted against same-sex marriage. Select cttees: transport 2013-; procedure 2012-15. Married, one daughter. Ed: Havelock Comp, Grimsby; Grimsby College; University of Lincoln (BA politics), which he studied for part-time 2004-10.

	Electorate	Turnout %	from 2010 %	Change
	73,047	65.50		
*M Vickers C	27,321	57.10	+10.47	
P Keith Lab	16,921	35.37	+6.24	
T Blake Ukip	2,022	4.23	-14.31	
R Horobin LD	1,110	2.32	-0.67	
L Emmerson Green	470	0.98	-1.26	

CHALLENGERS
Peter Keith (Lab) Head of sales, Asset International. Contested Cleethorpes 2015. The husband of Shona McIsaac, who was MP for Cleethorpes from 1997 until 2010. **Tony Blake** (Ukip) Retired civil engineer. Founded and ran a construction firm. Chairman of Ukip Grimsby. Stood for Park ward in North East Lincolnshire Council election. **Roy Horobin** (LD) Secondary school teacher and local campaigner. Contested Cleethorpes 2015.

CONSTITUENCY PROFILE
About 40,000 people live in the north Lincolnshire town of Cleethorpes itself, but the seat stretches north along a more rural area on the southern side of the Humber estuary. The town, like neighbouring Grimsby, is an old fishing town, although only a few hundred residents still work in the industry. About a fifth of residents are aged 65 or over, and nearly three quarters of households are owner-occupied, both well above average. The seat had a Labour MP from 1997 until 2010, but the Conservatives have increased their majority in successive elections.

EU REFERENDUM RESULT

69.5% Leave	Remain 30.5%

Clwyd South

LABOUR HOLD MAJORITY 4,356 (11.6%)

SUSAN ELAN JONES
BORN Jun 1, 1968
MP 2010-

Former fundraiser. Critic of Jeremy Corbyn; she resigned from Labour front bench in 2016. Voted Remain in the 2016 EU referendum and has campaigned on military issues. Advocated the publication of all MPs' expenses. Shadow minister, Wales 2015-16; opposition whip 2011-15. PPS to Harriet Harman 2010-11. Contested Surrey Heath 1997. Cllr, London Borough of Southwark 2006-09; deputy leader of the opposition 2007-09. Select cttees: standards 2016-17; privileges 2016-17; Welsh affairs 2010-12. Fluent Welsh speaker; also speaks Japanese. Ed: University of Bristol (BA

	Electorate	Turnout %	from 2010 %	Change
	54,341	68.96		
*S Jones Lab	19,002	50.71	+13.49	
S Baynes C	14,646	39.08	+8.71	
C Allen PC	2,293	6.12	-4.21	
J Bassford-Barton Ukip	802	2.14	-13.49	
B Roberts LD	731	1.95	-1.90	

English); University of Cardiff (MA English language)

CHALLENGERS
Simon Baynes (C) Welsh Assembly candidate, Clwyd South 2016. Voted Leave. Organised petition to save the maternity services at Wrexham Maelor Hospital. Founder, Concertina - Music for the Elderly. **Christopher Allen** (PC) Engineer, Mail Solutions. Worked for Wrexham Borough Council's economic dev dept.

CONSTITUENCY PROFILE
Clwyd South is a rural north Wales seat to the south and west of Wrexham. Much of it lies along Wales's border with Shropshire. Manufacturing is a common source of jobs and residents' incomes are in line with the Welsh average. Home ownership in Clwyd South is lower than the Welsh average, with just under a quarter of households in the social-rented sector. Fewer than one in fifty residents in the seat is non-white. The constituency has been Labour since its creation in 1997, and its predecessor Clwyd South West also elected Labour MPs continuously from 1987.

EU REFERENDUM RESULT

59.9% Leave	Remain 40.1%

Clwyd West

CONSERVATIVE HOLD MAJORITY 3,437 (8.5%)

DAVID JONES
BORN Mar 22, 1952
MP 2005-

Qualified solicitor who set up law practice, David Jones & Co, where he was a senior partner. Appointed minister of state for exiting the European Union after his successful leadership of Vote Leave in Wales. SoS for Wales 2012-14; first Conservative to hold post and represent a Welsh constituency since 1987. AM for North Wales 2002-03. Contested: City of Chester 2001; Conwy 1997. Parly under-sec Wales 2010-12; shad min Wales 2006-10. Honorary life fellow, Cancer Research UK. Declared Freemason. Married, two sons. Ed: Ruabon GS; UCL (LLB law); Coll of Law, Chester.

	Electorate	Turnout %	from 2010 %	Change
	58,263	69.78		
*D Jones C	19,541	48.07	+4.77	
G Thomas Lab	16,104	39.61	+14.02	
D Roberts PC	3,918	9.64	-2.59	
V Babu LD	1,091	2.68	-0.96	

CHALLENGERS
Gareth Thomas (Lab) Barrister specialising in personal injury law. Formerly in insurance industry and manager of loss-adjusting firm in West Indies. MP for Clwyd West 1997-2005, didn't stand in 2010 due to all-woman shortlist. PPS to Paul Murphy 2001-05. Cllr, Flintshire CC 1995-97. **Dilwyn Roberts** (PC) Founded North Wales Economic Ambition Board. Cllr, Conwy CBC 2004-17; leader 2008-17; awarded Entrepreneurial Council of the

Year. Threatened with court action after not paying his council tax.

CONSTITUENCY PROFILE
The residents of this large rural north Wales seat are disproportionately older and whiter than the UK average. Its biggest town, Colwyn Bay, on Wales's northern coast, is home to 31,000 people and has a significant tourism industry. The constituency elected Labour MPs with modest majorities in 1997 and 2001. The Conservatives won the seat from Labour in 2005, and have increased their vote tally at every election since.

EU REFERENDUM RESULT
53.0% Leave   Remain 47.0%

Coatbridge, Chryston & Bellshill

LABOUR GAIN MAJORITY 1,586 (3.5%)

HUGH GAFFNEY
BORN Aug 10, 1963
MP 2017-

A Royal Mail postman who grew up in the area, still works there, and retook the seat for Labour. Scottish political officer for Communication Workers Union and North Lanarkshire TUC secretary. Won a seat on North Lanarkshire Council just a month before becoming an MP. Labour activist Paul Cruikshanks ran a lap around the Emirates Arena to celebrate Gaffney's election. Famously wore his ParcelForce shirt into parliament after the general election, and when asked what he was meant to be delivering he answered: "Justice for workers." Ed: Holy Cross HS, Hamilton.

	Electorate	Turnout %	from 2010 %	Change
	71,198	63.26		
H Gaffney Lab	19,193	42.61	+8.70	
*P Boswell SNP	17,607	39.09	-17.51	
R Halbert C	7,318	16.25	+9.92	
D Bennie LD	922	2.05	+0.96	

CHALLENGERS
Phil Boswell (SNP) MP for Coatbridge, Chryston and Bellshill 2015-17. Formerly a quantity surveyor and contracts engineer. **Robyn Halbert** (C) Contested Scottish Parliament elections 2016. Worked in Scottish parliament for Conservative Party. **David Bennie** (LD) Estate agent. Formerly a businessman and director of PR and communications company. Contested South Lanarkshire council 2017.

CONSTITUENCY PROFILE
This North Lanarkshire constituency immediately to Glasgow's east contains the old industrial towns of Coatbridge and Bellshill, along with a more rural area to their north. In the 2011 census, 72 per cent identified themselves as Christian, compared with the Scottish average of 54 per cent. Coatbridge has suffered long-term industrial decline due to the exhaustion of local iron deposits. The last ironworks closed in 1967. The constituency had been Labour since 1935 until the SNP landslide of 2015, but was one of the six SNP seats to return to Labour two years later.

EU REFERENDUM RESULT
38.8% Leave   Remain 61.2%

Colchester

CONSERVATIVE HOLD MAJORITY 5,677 (10.6%)

WILL QUINCE
BORN Dec 27, 1982
MP 2015-

	Electorate	Turnout %	from 2010 %	Change
	79,996	66.93		
*W Quince C	24,565	45.88	+6.94	
T Young Lab	18,888	35.28	+19.12	
B Russell LD	9,087	16.97	-10.49	
M Goacher Green	828	1.55	-3.60	
R Rennie CPA	177	0.33	+0.11	

Solicitor at Thompson Smith and Puxton 2013-15; customer development manager, Britvic 2007-10. Contested Colchester 2010. Campaigned for extra funding for the upkeep of war graves and for women's health charities. Campaigned against cuts to maternity services. Member, transport select cttee 2015-. Cllr, Colchester BC 2011-16; East Herts DC 2007-09. Elected to students' union during university. Married, two daughters. Ed: The Windsor Boys' School, Berks; Aberystwyth University (LLB law); University of the West of England (PgDip. legal practice).

CHALLENGERS
Tim Young (Lab) Cllr, Colchester BC 1992-; deputy leader; portfolio holder for culture and regeneration. Colchester Labour group leader. Chairman, Colne Housing. Non-exec dir, Southend Hospital University NHS Foundation Trust. Married to the Mayor of Colchester. **Bob Russell** (LD) MP for Colchester 1997-2015. Cllr, Colchester BC 1978-2002. Former mayor of Colchester. Contested Colchester 1979 as a Labour candidate,

before defecting to the SDP in 1981. Appointed high steward of Colchester 2015. Knighted in 2012.

CONSTITUENCY PROFILE
Colchester is the second largest town in Essex after Southend-on-Sea. Although the campus of the University of Essex is located in another constituency, many of its students live in Colchester. Income is significantly below average for the east of England. The constituency has elected a Labour MP once, at the 1945 general election. It was a Liberal Democrat seat from 1997 to 2015, but has been Conservative for most of its recent history.

EU REFERENDUM RESULT
51.5% Leave   Remain 48.5%

Colne Valley

LABOUR GAIN MAJORITY 915 (1.5%)

THELMA WALKER
BORN Apr 7, 1957
MP 2017-

	Electorate	Turnout %	from 2010 %	Change
	84,381	71.60		
T Walker Lab	28,818	47.70	+12.72	
*J McCartney C	27,903	46.18	+1.73	
C Burke LD	2,494	4.13	-1.87	
S King Green	892	1.48	-1.90	
P Sadio Ind	313	0.52		

Self-employed education consultant who spent 34 years in teaching. Former headteacher: Flockton First Sch; Overthorpe CofE Sch. Member, Kirklees Fairtrade Forum. Enjoys hill walking and is learning Italian. Married to Labour cllr Rob Walker, two sons. Ed: Marple Hall GS; Manchester Polytechnic (BEd education).

CHALLENGERS
Jason McCartney (C) MP for Colne Valley 2010-17. RAF officer turned broadcast journalist. Reached flight lieutenant after serving in Las Vegas, Turkey and Iraq. Reporter: BBC Radio Leeds;

ITV Calendar News. Contested Leeds CC as a Lib Dem 2006. Brexiteer. Member, 1992 exec cttee, 2013-17. Select cttee, CMS 2015-17. Divorced, two daughters. **Cahal Burke** (LD) Part-time teacher. Cllr, Kirklees C 2010-. Founder and chairman, Lindley community group. Marathon runner and fundraiser. Contested Colne Valley 2015. **Sonia King** (Green) Private maths tutor. Contested local elections 2015. **Patricia Sadio** (Ind) Director of Combating Obesity non-profit

organisation. Previously worked in finance.

CONSTITUENCY PROFILE
Containing some of Huddersfield's western suburbs and part of the eastern Pennines, this large and mostly rural seat is characterised by high levels of income. Education and finance are among the main industries. The BBC sitcom *Last of the Summer Wine* was set and filmed in Holmfirth. The seat alternated between Liberal and Labour for years, before being won from Labour by the Conservatives in 1987. It has swung between the two since, with Labour holding the seat from 1997-2010.

EU REFERENDUM RESULT
50.1% Leave   Remain 49.9%

Congleton

CONSERVATIVE HOLD MAJORITY 12,619 (22.4%)

FIONA BRUCE
BORN Mar 26, 1957
MP 2010-

	Electorate	Turnout %	from 2010 %	Change
	76,694	73.32		
*F Bruce C	31,830	56.61	+3.32	
S Corcoran Lab	19,211	34.16	+13.78	
P Hirst LD	2,902	5.16	-3.91	
M Davies Ukip	1,289	2.29	-11.29	
A Heath Green	999	1.78	-1.90	

Solicitor who owns firm Fiona Bruce & Co. Set up free legal advice service. Women in Business award winner 2015. Co-author, *There is Such a Thing as Society*. Supported Brexit. Strong interest in human rights: member, select cttee human rights 2015-17; draft modern slavery bill 2014. Co-founded a homelessness support project and works with a school in Tanzania. Member, APPG for North Korea. Evangelical Christian. Chairwoman. APPG pro-life; has said priority in Westminster was fighting for the sanctity of human life. Contested Warrington South 2005. Cllr,

Warrington BC 2004-10. Married, two sons. Ed: Burnley HS; Howell's School, Llandaff, University of Manchester (LLB law).

CHALLENGERS
Sam Corcoran (Lab) Chartered accountant and tax adviser. Cllr, Cheshire East BC 2011-. Worked as a teacher in rural Kenya.
Peter Hirst (LD) Retired doctor and lecturer. Cllr, Middlewich TC 1999-2015. Council member, Unlock Democracy. Member,

Electoral Reform Society. Contested Congleton 2015, 2010; Stroud 2005. **Mark Davies** (Ukip) Works in IT sales.

CONSTITUENCY PROFILE
This Cheshire constituency is older than average, and has high levels of home ownership and retirement among its residents, a high proportion of whom work in managerial jobs. The biggest town in the constituency is Congleton with 27,000 residents, but the region also contains the smaller towns of Sandbach and Middlewich. The seat has been Conservative since its inception in 1983; Ann Winterton held the seat from 1983 until 2010.

EU REFERENDUM RESULT

52.6% Leave   Remain 47.4%

Copeland

CONSERVATIVE HOLD MAJORITY 1,695 (3.9%)

TRUDY HARRISON
BORN Apr 19, 1976
MP 2017-

	Electorate	Turnout %	from 2010 %	Change
	61,751	69.52		
*T Harrison C	21,062	49.06	+13.27	
G Troughton Lab	19,367	45.12	+2.85	
R Hanson LD	1,404	3.27	-0.18	
H Crossman Ukip	1,094	2.55	-12.96	

Catapulted into politics after joining the Conservative Party in the autumn of 2016, and won Copeland from Labour at a by-election in February 2017. Pro-nuclear, campaigned to safeguard existing Sellafield site and supports the possible construction of Moorside Nuclear Power Station. Supported Brexit. Various roles in community planning and regeneration, including at Copeland BC. Project manager of Bootle2020, a local campaign to promote a sustainable rural community. Cllr, Bootle PC 2004-07. School governor. Married, four children. Ed:

Salford University (FdSc sustainable communities).

CHALLENGERS
Gillian Troughton (Lab) Active health campaigner and member of Cumbria Health Scrutiny cttee. St John blue light ambulance driver. Former doctor. Pro-nuclear. Remain campaigner. Cllr, Copeland BC 2011-2017. **Rebecca Hanson** (LD) Mathematics education consultant. Formerly a lecturer at the Open University and Manchester Met. Cllr, Cumbria

CC 2017-; Cockermouth TC 2016-.

CONSTITUENCY PROFILE
This large Cumbrian constituency consists of Lake District National Park land, including England's highest peak, Scafell Pike. Its largest town, Whitehaven, is home to about 23,000 people. The nuclear reprocessing plant Sellafield, which employs 10,000 people, is located further down the coast. Copeland and its predecessor, Whitehaven, had elected Labour MPs since 1931, but Labour lost it at a by-election in early 2017, as a result of the former MP Jamie Reed taking a job at Sellafield.

EU REFERENDUM RESULT

59.2% Leave   Remain 40.8%

Corby

CONSERVATIVE HOLD MAJORITY 2,690 (4.5%)

TOM PURSGLOVE
BORN Nov 5, 1988
MP 2015-

Before being elected as an MP, Pursglove was parly assistant to Chris Heaton-Harris and Peter Bone. He co-founded Grassroots Out!, which advocated Britain leaving the EU in the referendum. Came under fire for paying himself £20,000 for the campaign. Director, Together Against Wind, anti-wind farm campaign. PPS to Robert Goodwill, minister of state for immigration 2016-. APPG vice-chairman: sport; steel and metal related industries. The youngest Conservative MP 2015-17. Cllr, Wellingborough BC 2007-15. Ed: Sir Christopher Hatton Sch, Northants; Queen

	Electorate	Turnout %	from 2010 % Change
	82,439	72.78	
*T Pursglove C	29,534	49.23	+6.46
B Miller Lab	26,844	44.74	+6.27
C Stanbra LD	1,545	2.58	-0.02
S Watts Ukip	1,495	2.49	-11.23
S Scrutton Green	579	0.97	-1.48

Mary, University of London (BA politics).

CHALLENGERS
Beth Miller (Lab) Works in corporate governance policy at the Bank of England. Stakeholder relations manager, Britain Stronger in Europe 2016. Parly researcher to Vernon Coaker 2013-16; parly assistant to David Blunkett 2012-13. **Chris Stanbra** (LD) Bookkeeper and accountant. Cllr, Northamptonshire CC 2009-.

CONSTITUENCY PROFILE
This east Northamptonshire seat consists of Corby, a former iron and steelworks town, and several much smaller towns. Corby is thought to be "the most Scottish place in England," after significant migration from Scotland to Corby during the decline of the Clyde shipyards. Over 8,000 residents in this constituency were born north of the border, and many children have been born in Corby to Scottish parents. Almost a fifth of residents work in manufacturing. Corby is a bellwether, although Labour won it at a 2012 by-election after the resignation of Louise Mensch.

EU REFERENDUM RESULT
60.1% Leave   Remain 39.9%

Cornwall North

CONSERVATIVE HOLD MAJORITY 7,200 (14.1%)

SCOTT MANN
BORN Jun 24, 1977
MP 2015-

Former Royal Mail postman. Campaigned to Leave the EU. Keen to protect UK fishing and farming. PPS, dept for transport ministerial team 2017-. APPG vice-chairman, state-pension inequality for women. Backed Liam Fox in Conservative leadership race 2016. Typically toes the party line but voted for Assisted Dying Bill 2015. Cllr, North Cornwall DC 2009-16. Almost drowned in 2016 when he was embarrassed to admit he could not swim, was saved by MP Johnny Mercer. Honorary vice-president, Wadebridge Cricket Club. Married, one child. Ed: Wadebridge Sch.

	Electorate	Turnout %	from 2010 % Change
	68,850	73.99	
*S Mann C	25,835	50.71	+5.76
D Rogerson LD	18,635	36.58	+5.35
J Bassett Lab	6,151	12.07	+6.64
J Allman CPA	185	0.36	
R Hawkins Soc Lab	138	0.27	

CHALLENGERS
Daniel Rogerson (LD) MP for North Cornwall 2005-15. Campaigns officer, Devon & Cornwall Lib Dems 2002-04. Shadow minister: office of the deputy prime minister 2006; communities and local government 2006-10; culture, media and sport 2007. Opposition whip 2007-10. Parly under-sec, Defra 2013-15. Cllr, Bedford BC 1999-2002. Contested North East Bedfordshire 2001. **Joy Bassett**

(Lab) Small retail-business owner. Campaigned to oppose the privatisation of the Land Registry. Cllr, Bodmin TC 2017-.

CONSTITUENCY PROFILE
The largest Cornwall seat, Cornwall North contains the towns of Bude, Bodmin, Launceston and Wadebridge. It is mainly rural, containing much of Cornwall's Bodmin Moor. About a quarter of its population is aged over 65 and its working residents are more likely than elsewhere in the UK to be self-employed. The seat was held by Lib Dem MPs from 1992 to 2015, but was won by the Conservatives in 2015.

EU REFERENDUM RESULT
60.2% Leave   Remain 39.8%

Cornwall South East

CONSERVATIVE HOLD MAJORITY 17,443 (32.8%)

SHERYLL MURRAY
BORN Feb 4, 1956
MP 2010-

Worked as a part-time doctor's receptionist for 20 years. Passionate fishing industry campaigner, wife of a trawler skipper who died in an accident at sea in 2011. Fishing industry rep: spokeswoman, Save Britain's Fish; dir, the Fishermen's Assoc; Looe Fishermen's Protection Assoc; chairwoman, South West Fish Producers' Org. Voted Leave. Member, Objective One programme monitoring cttee. Member, 1922 exec cttee 2017-. Cllr: Caradon DC 2003-09, Conservative group leader 2003-07; Cornwall CC 2001-05. Widowed, one daughter, one son. Ed: Torpoint CS.

	Electorate	Turnout %	from 2010 %	Change
	71,896	74.02		
*S Murray C	29,493	55.42	+4.89	
G Derrick Lab	12,050	22.64	+13.35	
P Hutty LD	10,336	19.42	+2.55	
M Corney Green	1,335	2.51	-2.87	

CHALLENGERS
Gareth Derrick (Lab) Commodore in the Royal Navy. Served in Iraq wars 1991 and 2003. Awarded US Bronze Star 2004. British Embassy, Tokyo diplomat 2007-10. Contested Devon and Cornwall PCC 2016; came second. **Phil Hutty** (LD) Social work manager and child protection specialist. Contested: Cornwall SE 2015; Central Devon 2010. **Martin Corney** (Green) Cllr, St Ives PC 2013-; chairman. Former computer programmer.

CONSTITUENCY PROFILE
This is a large rural seat encompassing the Tamar towns of Saltash, which the Tamar Bridge connects to Plymouth, and Torpoint in its east, with Liskeard farther west and Looe to its south. More than half of residents in work are aged over 45 and are more likely to be self-employed than elsewhere in the UK. About one in seventy residents is non-white. Home ownership is well above average. Since its inception in 1983, the seat has elected Conservatives whenever they have been the largest electoral party, but Cornwall SE voted Lib Dem during the New Labour years.

EU REFERENDUM RESULT
55.1% Leave   Remain 44.9%

Cotswolds, The

CONSERVATIVE HOLD MAJORITY 25,499 (42.7%)

GEOFFREY CLIFTON-BROWN
BORN Mar 23, 1953
MP 1992-

Veteran and eccentric MP. Family history of parliamentary service. Chartered surveyor and farmer. Pro-Brexit MP who did not expect to win. Instrumental in schools' funding rebellion 2017, voicing concerns about under-funding. Shadow SoS, int dev 2007-10. Opp whip 2004-05; assist chief whip 2005. Shadow min: FCO 2005-07. Shadow spokesman: CLG 2001-04; Defra 2001. Finance cttee 2005-. Chairman, Con Party int office 2010-15. Vice-pres, AECR. APPG chairman: trade and investment; shooting and conservation. Chairman, Con Friends of the Chinese. Exec member, 1922

	Electorate	Turnout %	from 2010 %	Change
	80,446	74.21		
*G Clifton-Brown C	36,201	60.64	+4.09	
M Huband Lab	10,702	17.93	+8.68	
A Gant LD	9,748	16.33	-2.32	
S Poole Green	1,747	2.93	-1.71	
C Harlow Ukip	1,197	2.00	-8.91	
S Steel ND	107	0.18		

cttee. Divorced, two children. Ed: Eton Coll; Royal Agricultural College.

CHALLENGERS
Mark Huband (Lab) Former parly and foreign correspondent for *Guardian* and *FT*. Managing dir and co-founder, Livingstone & Co; manages research and business intelligence reporting. Remain campaigner. **Andrew Gant** (LD) Accomplished singer. Has authored books on musical

history. Music tutor, St Peter's Coll, Oxford. Cllr, Oxford CC 2014-; leader of Lib Dem group.

CONSTITUENCY PROFILE
The largest town in this sparse Gloucestershire seat is Cirencester, originally a Roman town, now with a population of about 19,000. Over half of its population is aged 45 or above, and overrepresented industries include real estate, tourism and forestry. The seat and its predecessor have elected only Conservative MPs since 1918, with the exception of the 1955 general election, when its MP William Morrison was the Speaker.

EU REFERENDUM RESULT
47.9% Leave   Remain 52.1%

Coventry North East

LABOUR HOLD MAJORITY 15,580 (33.5%)

COLLEEN FLETCHER
BORN Nov 23, 1954
MP 2015-

Previously customer services officer at the Orbit Housing Group. First woman to represent Coventry North East. Called on Jeremy Corbyn to resign and stepped down from her role as PPS to Kerry McCarthy 2016 in protest at his leadership. Remain campaigner. Recorded in hostile exchange on doorstep when canvassing in Coventry 2015. Cllr, Coventry CC at various times between 1992-2011. Previously a member of National Policy Forum. West Midlands Regional Board officer. Daughter of former cllr. Married, two sons. Ed: Lyng Hall Comprehensive Sch; Henley Coll, Coventry.

	Electorate	Turnout %	from 2010 % Change
	75,792	61.36	
*C Fletcher Lab	29,499	63.43	+11.27
T Mayer C	13,919	29.93	+6.84
A Taggar Ukip	1,350	2.90	-11.96
R Field LD	1,157	2.49	-2.26
M Handley Green	502	1.08	-1.87
A Mahmood Ind	81	0.17	

CHALLENGERS
Timothy Mayer (C) Cllr, Coventry CC 2016-. Cabinet member for adult services. **Avtar Taggar** (Ukip) IT consultant and engineer. Worked overseas in Bahrain and UAE. **Russell Field** (LD) Computer programmer for local building society. Cllr, Coventry CC 2008-12, 2004-07. The only Lib Dem on council 2008-12. Chaired council's scrutiny board for education and social sciences.

CONSTITUENCY PROFILE
About a quarter of Coventry North East residents are aged under 18. It is the most diverse Coventry seat, with an Asian population of more than 22,000 and over 11,000 black and mixed race residents. Islam and Sikhism are prominent, with 11,000 Muslims and 7,000 Sikhs recorded in the 2011 census. It is a deprived constituency: average income is under £20,000 and unemployment is high. Coventry North East has been Labour since its inception in 1974; Labour's majority is the biggest of the three Coventry seats. Only 1983 and 2010 saw Labour receive less than half of the vote.

EU REFERENDUM RESULT
57.8% Leave   Remain 42.2%

Coventry North West

LABOUR HOLD MAJORITY 8,580 (17.2%)

GEOFFREY ROBINSON
BORN May 25, 1938
MP 1976-

Wealthy industrialist close to the New Labour project. Chairman, Coventry City FC 2005-07. Owner, *New Statesman* 1996-2008. Chief exec, Triumph Motorcycles 1978-80; Jaguar Cars 1973-75. Joined Labour after meeting Harold Wilson at Yale. Reinstated as 2015 candidate after local party found no one to replace him. Resigned as Paymaster General (1997-98) after loan to Peter Mandelson was revealed. Faced questions over collapse of engineering firm TransTec. Married, two children. Emmanuel Sch, London; Clare Coll, Cambridge; Yale (Wolf's Head Society).

	Electorate	Turnout %	from 2010 % Change
	75,214	66.28	
*G Robinson Lab	26,894	53.95	+12.94
R Kotecha C	18,314	36.74	+5.69
M Gee Ukip	1,525	3.06	-12.63
A Hilton LD	1,286	2.58	-1.42
C Norris Ind	1,164	2.34	
S Gray Green	666	1.34	-3.00

CHALLENGERS
Resham Kotecha (C) Analyst, Farsight Consulting Ltd 2016-. Chief operating officer, Women2Win 2012-. Parly researcher to Baroness (Anne) Jenkin 2012-13. Governor, Breakspeare Sch 2013-15. Contested Dulwich & West Norwood 2015. Volunteer, Tower Hamlets Coll 2011-12. **Mick Gee** (Ukip) Contested Meriden 2015. **Andrew Hilton** (LD) IT service management consultant. **Ciaran**

Norris (Ind) Formerly dir, Global Rising Peace Forum.

CONSTITUENCY PROFILE
Coventry North West, on most demographic and economic issues, lies somewhere between its neighbours to the west and south. About a third of its residents are aged under 25. At around 4,000 each, it has a roughly equal population of Muslims and Sikhs. Like the other Coventry seats, it has lower than average levels of home ownership and high levels of private renting. It has been Labour since its creation in 1974, the party never having received less than two fifths of votes cast.

EU REFERENDUM RESULT
58.4% Leave   Remain 41.7%

Coventry South

LABOUR HOLD MAJORITY 7,947 (16.9%)

JIM CUNNINGHAM
BORN Feb 4, 1941
MP 1992-

Former Rolls-Royce engineer, where he was a shop floor steward. Selected after expulsion of his predecessor Dave Nellist from Labour. Called for the Queen to pay income tax in 1992. Campaigned to prevent Jaguar Cars closing its Browns Lane assembly plant. PPS to Mike O'Brien 2005-10. Select cttees: Scottish affairs 2015-17; procedures 2005-06; constitutional affairs 2003-05; trade and industry 1997-01; home affairs 1993-97. Cllr, Coventry CC 1972-1992; leader 1988-92. Married, two children. Ed: Columbia HS, Coatbridge; Trade Union College, Tillicoultry.

	Electorate	Turnout %	from 2010 %	Change
	70,754	66.44		
*J Cunningham Lab	25,874	55.04	+12.77	
M Lowe C	17,927	38.14	+3.16	
G Judge LD	1,343	2.86	-1.21	
I Rogers Ukip	1,037	2.21	-10.86	
A Challenor Green	604	1.28	-2.65	
S Findlay Ind	224	0.48		

CHALLENGERS
Michelle Lowe (C) Cllr, Sevenoaks DC 2007-; deputy council leader and cabinet member for housing and health. Ran on platform to protect the green belt. **Greg Judge** (LD) Public affairs officer, Brain Tumour Research. Parly asst to LD House of Lords members 2013-16. Contested Coventry South 2015. School governor. **Ian Rogers** (Ukip) Chairman, Coventry Ukip branch. **Aimee**

Challenor (Green) Equalities spokeswoman, Green Party.

CONSTITUENCY PROFILE
Contains the city centre and cathedral as well as Coventry University and most of its student halls of residence, hence the high population of 16 to 24 year-olds. It is the most affluent of the three Coventry seats, with its residents earning more than the regional average. The seat elected a Conservative in 1959 and a Coventry South West seat with different boundaries elected a Conservative MP during Labour's "wilderness years" (1979-1997). It remains Labour's least safe Coventry seat.

EU REFERENDUM RESULT

50.4% Leave   Remain 49.6%

Crawley

CONSERVATIVE HOLD MAJORITY 2,457 (4.9%)

HENRY SMITH
BORN May 14, 1969
MP 2010-

Advocate for English votes for English laws; co-authored *Direct Democracy*, arguing for devolution of powers. Owned property investment company. Ardent supporter of Brexit: Ukip did not field a candidate in Crawley in 2017. European scrutiny select cttee 2010-15. Animal welfare campaigner; co-chairman of the APPG for animal welfare. Contested Crawley 2005, 2001. PPS to Greg Clark 2015-16. Chairman, APPG for blood cancer. Cllr, West Sussex CC 1997-10; leader 2003-10. He was the youngest council leader in the UK: Crawley BC 2002-04. Endorsed

	Electorate	Turnout %	from 2010 %	Change
	73,424	68.47		
*H Smith C	25,426	50.58	+3.55	
T Lunnon Lab	22,969	45.69	+12.11	
M Scepanovic LD	1,878	3.74	+0.98	

by Brian May. Called Vladimir Putin a "tosser" on Twitter. School governor. Married, one daughter, one son. Ed: Frensham Heights Sch, Farnham; UCL (BA philosophy).

CHALLENGERS
Tim Lunnon (Lab) Career as an aircraft engineer for Virgin Atlantic; keen to protect the air industry in the Brexit negotiations. Cllr, Crawley BC 2014-; chairman, budget advisory group. **Marko Scepanovic** (LD) Training to be a barrister at City University. Has had several legal

internships, including the Royal Courts of Justice. Chairman, Crawley Lib Dems 2015-.

CONSTITUENCY PROFILE
This Sussex seat contains Gatwick Airport, the source of about 21,000 local jobs. The town of Crawley itself has a 13,000-strong population of Asian descent and significant Muslim and Hindu communities. The constituency is more affluent than the UK average, but slightly less than the southeast average. It is a Labour and Conservative marginal, and a bellwether since its creation in 1983, although Labour won the seat by just 37 votes in 2005.

EU REFERENDUM RESULT

58.4% Leave   Remain 41.6%

Crewe & Nantwich

LABOUR GAIN MAJORITY 48 (0.1%)

LAURA SMITH
BORN Mar 16, 1985
MP 2017-

Schools campaigner who spearheaded protests against education-funding cuts in Cheshire East; led parents in a 1,000-strong demonstration opposing the National Funding Formula. Former teacher and education entrepreneur. Founded tutoring business One-to-One Learning UK. Partner, two children. Ed: Brine Leas School; South Cheshire Coll; Manchester Metropolitan University.

CHALLENGERS
Edward Timpson (C) MP for Crewe and Nantwich 2008-17. Former family law barrister.

	Electorate	Turnout %	Change from 2010 %
	78,895	69.75	
L Smith Lab	25,928	47.12	+9.39
*E Timpson C	25,880	47.03	+2.05
M Stanley Ukip	1,885	3.43	-11.11
D Crowther LD	1,334	2.42	-0.33

Father runs Timpson shoe repair stores. Campaigned to Remain in the EU; voted to trigger Article 50. PPS to Theresa May 2010-12. Parly under-sec, education 2012-15. Minister of state, education 2015-17. Children, schools & families cttee 2008-10. Minister of the Year 2014. Ed: Uppingham Sch; Durham University (BA politics); College of Law, London (GDL). **Michael Stanley** (Ukip) On-board train operative. Cllr, Minshull Vernon and District PC. **David Crowther** (LD) Former cllr, St Helens MBC;

representative, Mersey Waste Disposal Authority. Contested Makerfield, 2001.

CONSTITUENCY PROFILE
This Cheshire seat consists primarily of the railway town of Crewe and the much smaller Roman town of Nantwich. The Conservatives won the seat in a 2008 by-election after the death of long-serving MP Gwyneth Dunwoody. Before this it had been held by Labour since 1983, with the predecessor Crewe seat electing Labour MPs continuously since 1945. It is now one of the most marginal seats in the country, Timpson having lost by just 48 votes.

EU REFERENDUM RESULT

60.3% Leave   Remain 39.7%

Croydon Central

LABOUR GAIN MAJORITY 5,652 (9.9%)

SARAH JONES
BORN Dec 20, 1972
MP 2017-

Former parly assistant to Mo Mowlam and Geraint Davies. Comms strategist: former head of campaigns, Shelter; deputy comms dir, London Olympics and Paralympics 2008-11. Spearheaded the Zone 4 Croydon campaign. Contested Croydon Central 2015. Supported Owen Smith in the 2016 leadership contest. Married, four children. Ed: Benson Primary Sch; Old Palace Sch; Durham University (BA history).

CHALLENGERS
Gavin Barwell (C) MP for Croydon Central 2010-17. Author, *How to Win a Marginal Seat*.

	Electorate	Turnout %	Change from 2010 %
	80,045	71.32	
S Jones Lab	29,873	52.33	+9.66
*G Barwell C	24,221	42.43	-0.55
G Hickson LD	1,083	1.90	-0.28
P Staveley Ukip	1,040	1.82	-7.26
T Hague Green	626	1.10	-1.65
J Boadu CPA	177	0.31	
D Locke Ind	71	0.12	

Chief of staff to Theresa May 2017-. COO 2003-2006; head of local government 1998-2003; special adviser 1995-97; researcher 1993-95. Cllr, Croydon BC 1998-2010. PPS to: Michael Gove 2012-13; Greg Clark 2011-12. Housing min 2016-17. Comptroller 2015-16. Treasury lord commissioner 2015-16; asst whip 2013-14. Subject to criminal investigation for 2015 election expenses. **Gill Hickson** (LD)

Community activist. Contested Croydon South 2015.

CONSTITUENCY PROFILE
Two thirds of this south London seat's residents are aged under 45. Although less diverse than other parts of London, the constituency has a significant Caribbean community of about 21,000. This seat contains the large New Addington estate, which was at one stage a place of significant BNP activity. Croydon's only marginal constituency, it has mainly elected Conservative MPs with Labour only claiming the seat under Blair (1997, 2001) and Corbyn (2017).

EU REFERENDUM RESULT

50.3% Leave   Remain 49.7%

Croydon North

LAB CO-OP HOLD MAJORITY 32,365 (54.3%)

STEVE REED
BORN Nov 12, 1963
MP 2012-

	Electorate	Turnout %	from 2010 %	Change
	87,461	68.17		
*S Reed Lab Co-op	44,213	74.15	+11.54	
S Kasumu C	11,848	19.87	-2.83	
M Pindar LD	1,656	2.78	-0.81	
P Underwood Green	983	1.65	-3.05	
M Swadling Ukip	753	1.26	-4.15	
L Berks Ind	170	0.29	+0.02	

Former educational publisher; now editor, *Inside Croydon*. Won 2012 by-election after death of Malcolm Wicks. Wanted to make Lambeth Britain's first co-op council, with residents running services. Resigned as shadow min for local govt in protest at Jeremy Corbyn in 2016. Campaigned to Remain; believed Brexit would increase unemployment in Croydon. Voted for Article 50. Shadow min: civil society 2016-; communities and local govt 2015-16; home affairs 2013-15. Chairman, Central London Forward 2010-11; Vauxhall Nine Elms regeneration strategy board. Member: FRSA; GMB; Unite. Awarded OBE 2013. Cllr, Lambeth BC 1998-2012; leader 2006-12. Partner. Ed: University of Sheffield (BA English).

CHALLENGERS
Samuel Kasumum (C) Founder, Elevation Networks, tackling graduate and youth unemployment. Winner of Barclays business enterprise award 2011. **Maltby Pindar** (LD) FE college lecturer. Cllr,

Lambeth Council 2002-06, 1994-98. **Peter Underwood** (Green) Former civil servant turned charity worker. Chairman, Croydon and Sutton Greens.

CONSTITUENCY PROFILE
A young constituency; less than a third of residents are aged over 45. This constituency has one of the largest black and mixed race populations of any seat in the UK. All three Croydon seats have significant Hindu and Muslim populations, but Croydon North has the largest of them. Labour candidates have consistently been returned with large majorities since this seat's creation in 1997.

EU REFERENDUM RESULT

41.2% Leave   Remain 58.9%

Croydon South

CONSERVATIVE HOLD MAJORITY 11,406 (18.6%)

CHRIS PHILP
BORN Jul 6, 1976
MP 2015-

	Electorate	Turnout %	from 2010 %	Change
	83,518	73.35		
*C Philp C	33,334	54.42	-0.07	
J Brathwaite Lab	21,928	35.80	+11.00	
A Jones LD	3,541	5.78	-0.19	
C Shelley Green	1,125	1.84	-1.90	
K Garner Ukip	1,116	1.82	-8.69	
D Omamogho CPA	213	0.35		

Serial entrepreneur who founded finance and travel businesses. Self-made millionaire. Founder, Next Big Thing charity, which provides mentors for young entrepreneurs. Cllr, Camden BC 2006-10. Author, *Work for the Dole: A Proposal to Fix Welfare Dependency* (2013) Led campaign to award compensation to disrupted Southern Rail passengers. Does not rebel against party whip. Backed Remain, voted to trigger Article 50. Married, one daughter, one son. Ed: St Olave's GS. Orpington; University Coll, Oxford (BA physics; MA theoretical quantum mechanics).

CHALLENGERS
Jennifer Brathwaite (Lab) Housing solicitor. Cllr, Lambeth BC. **Anna Jones** (LD) Travel company HR director. Previously set up a leadership and training business. **Catherine Shelley** (Green) Church of England minister. Charities' and church lawyer. **Kathleen Garner** (Ukip) Controversially described child ADHD sufferers as "naughty". Contested Croydon South 2015. **David Omamogho** (CPA) One

of two CPA candidates standing in Croydon constituencies.

CONSTITUENCY PROFILE
The seat consists of affluent, leafy, middle-class dormitory suburbs, with the north of the seat containing Waddon, which has a large council estate and tower blocks and sometimes returns Labour councillors. This is a safe Conservative seat, held by them since its creation in 1974. EU migration is no different to the national average. It is a multiracial constituency, with Hindu, Muslim and Buddhist communities. Employment rates are high in the financial sector and science.

EU REFERENDUM RESULT

45.8% Leave   Remain 54.2%

Cumbernauld, Kilsyth & Kirkintilloch East

SNP HOLD MAJORITY 4,264 (9.7%)

STUART MCDONALD
BORN May 2, 1978
MP 2015-

Human rights solicitor for Immigration Advisory Service 2005-09. Criticised Theresa May's migration policies for splitting up families. Began political career as researcher for Shirley-Anne Somerville MSP and Jim Eadie MSP. Head of information, Yes Scotland. Former parliamentary and public affairs officer, Coalition for Racial Equality and Rights. Parliamentary SNP spokesman on immigration, asylum and border control 2015-17. Select cttees: home affairs 2015-17; draft investigatory powers bill 2015-16. Member, Unite. Football fan. Grew up in constituency. Ed:

	Electorate	Turnout %	Change from 2010 %
	66,554	65.86	
*S McDonald SNP	19,122	43.62	-16.26
E Fisher Lab	14,858	33.90	+3.89
S Johnston C	8,010	18.27	+10.39
R Ackland LD	1,238	2.82	+0.60
C Pearson Ukip	605	1.38	

Craighead Primary; Kilsyth Academy; Edinburgh University; University of Leuven, Belgium.

CHALLENGERS
Elisha Fisher (Lab) Supports school leavers' transition from education into employment. **Stephen Johnston** (C) Spent 25 years in Royal Corps of Signal. Since then has worked in IT sector. **Rod Ackland** (LD) Retired. Cllr, E Dunbartonshire C 2017-. Contested: Renfrewshire North and West 2016;

Cumbernauld 2010. **Carl Pearson** (Ukip) Contested North Lanarkshire C 2017.

CONSTITUENCY PROFILE
This seat encompasses towns in North Lanarkshire and East Dunbartonshire. Cumbernauld is home to more than 50,000 people, with higher levels of home ownership and lower levels of unemployment than the Scottish average, although income tends to be below average. The seat had been Labour since its creation in 2005. The SNP won it with a majority of nearly 15,000 in 2015, and held on to it in 2017 with a reduced majority.

EU REFERENDUM RESULT

37.0% Leave   Remain 63.0%

Cynon Valley

LABOUR HOLD MAJORITY 13,238 (41.6%)

ANN CLWYD
BORN Mar 21, 1937
MP 1984-

Former journalist and broadcaster. Author, *Rebel With A Cause*. Contested: Gloucester 1974; Denbigh 1970. MEP, Mid and West Wales 1979-84. Campaigned to Remain, voted against triggering Article 50. Shadow minister: culture 1992-93; education 1987-88. Shadow SoS: Wales 1992; int dev 1989-92. Shadow spokeswoman: foreign affairs 1994-95; work and pensions 1993-94. Select cttees: foreign affairs 2010-17; arms export controls 2016-17, 2010-15; int dev 1997-2005; European legislation 1985-88. Special envoy to PM on human rights in Iraq 2003-10. Chairwoman, PLP

	Electorate	Turnout %	Change from 2010 %
	51,332	61.95	
*A Clwyd Lab	19,404	61.02	+13.33
K Dewhurst C	6,166	19.39	+7.33
L Walters PC	4,376	13.76	-3.06
I McLean Ukip	1,271	4.00	-12.33
N Knight LD	585	1.84	-0.88

2005-06. Married. Ed: Holywell GS; The Queen's Sch, Chester; Bangor University.

CHALLENGERS
Keith Dewhurst (C) Chairman of equality charity, Diverse Cymru. Former BBC engineer; lead co-ordinator in Freeview set-up. Former magistrate, Manchester. Contested Cynon Valley 2015. **Liz Walters** (PC) NHS worker. Former cllr, Rhondda Cynon Taff BC. Welsh Assembly candidate

2007. **Ian McLean** (Ukip) BT network planner. Former flight lieutenant, RAF Volunteer Reserve. Contested Rhondda Cynon Taf BC 2017. **Nicola Knight** (LD) Freelance marketing consultant.

CONSTITUENCY PROFILE
Former coal mining and iron works towns make up this south Wales seat. Unemployment is not unusually high in this seat, but levels of economic inactivity are well above average. Earnings are slightly higher than the Welsh average. Cynon Valley has elected Labour MPs since 1983, as did its predecessor seat from 1922.

EU REFERENDUM RESULT

56.7% Leave   Remain 43.3%

Dagenham & Rainham

LABOUR HOLD MAJORITY 4,652 (10.1%)

JON CRUDDAS
BORN Apr 7, 1962
MP 2001-

Policy officer, Labour Party policy directorate 1989-94. Deputy political secretary to Tony Blair 1997-2001. Visiting Professor: Nuffield Coll, Oxford 2016-; University of Leicester 2016-; University of Wisconsin 1987-89. Rebelled on tuition fees 2004. Nominated Jeremy Corbyn in 2015 leadership race; supported Owen Smith in 2016. Campaigned to Remain in the EU, voted to trigger Article 50. Labour dep leader contender 2007. Labour policy review co-ordinator 2010-15. Member, public accounts cttee 2003-10. APPG chairman, wellbeing economics. Married, one

	Electorate	Turnout %	from 2010 % Change
	70,620	64.92	
*J Cruddas Lab	22,958	50.08	+8.66
J Marson C	18,306	39.93	+15.56
P Harris Ukip	3,246	7.08	-22.77
D Breading Green	544	1.19	-0.69
J Fryer LD	465	1.01	-0.65
P Sturdy BNP	239	0.52	+0.17
T London Concordia	85	0.19	

child. Ed: Oaklands RC Comp, Portsmouth; Warwick University (BSc economics; MA industrial relations; PhD philosophy).

CHALLENGERS
Julie Marson (C) Former banker. Cllr, Thanet DC 2011-15. MEP candidate 2014. Contested Dagenham & Rainham 2015. Peter Harris (Ukip) Owner, car service and repair centre. Chairman, Barking & Dagenham

Ukip. London Assembly candidate, 2016. **Denis Breading** (Green) Former Ford worker. **Jonathan Fryer** (LD) Writer, broadcaster and lecturer. Vice-chairman, London4Europe.

CONSTITUENCY PROFILE
Average earnings in this east London seat are in line with the UK average, but about 16 per cent below London's. The BNP held council seats in the area in the 2000s and peaked in parliamentary elections in 2010, winning 11.2 per cent of the vote. The old Ford plant in Dagenham was the scene of a 1968 strike, which was a catalyst for equal pay for women.

EU REFERENDUM RESULT
70.3% Leave   Remain 29.7%

Darlington

LABOUR HOLD MAJORITY 3,280 (7.3%)

JENNY CHAPMAN
BORN Sep 25, 1973
MP 2010-

Worked as prison psychologist during university placements at HMP Frankland and Dartmoor. Had part-time job in local MP's office 1993-95. Took six years out as a stay-at-home mother. Resigned from shadow cabinet over Corbyn's leadership 2016. Nominated Liz Kendall as leader 2015. Shadow min: exiting the EU 2016-; education Jan-Jun 2016; justice 2011-16. Patron, YMCA Tees Valley. Cllr, Darlington BC 2003-10. Married to MP Nick Smith: two children from previous partner. Ed: Brunel University (BSc psychology). Durham University (MA medieval archaeology).

	Electorate	Turnout %	from 2010 % Change
	66,341	67.56	
*J Chapman Lab	22,681	50.61	+7.74
P Cuthbertson C	19,401	43.29	+8.10
K Brack Ukip	1,180	2.63	-10.47
A Curry LD	1,031	2.30	-2.48
M Snedker Green	524	1.17	-2.34

CHALLENGERS
Peter Cuthbertson (C) Healthcare PR consultant. Unsuccessfully contested Durham and Darlington PCC election 2016. Was heavily criticised during the election campaign when controversial blog posts he wrote about rape and homosexuality in 2002 were exposed in the press; was defended by Theresa May. **Kevin Brack** (Ukip) Former HGV driver and army sgt. **Anne-Marie Curry** (LD) Buyer,

National Savings Durham and London. Former Durham City Harriers coach. Cllr, Darlington BC 2008-; Lib Dem group leader. Contested Darlington 2015. **Matthew Snedker** (Green) Green Party Darlington co-ordinator. Environmental campaigner.

CONSTITUENCY PROFILE
Darlington is the biggest town in Co Durham. Average earnings are below both the UK and regional average, and its residents are more likely to have part-time work or an apprenticeship. The seat has swung between Labour and the Conservatives for 90 years.

EU REFERENDUM RESULT
58.1% Leave   Remain 41.9%

Dartford

CONSERVATIVE HOLD MAJORITY 13,186 (24.3%)

GARETH JOHNSON
BORN Oct 12, 1969
MP 2010-

Defence solicitor and son of a milkman. Campaigned against Dartford Crossing tolls. Contested: Dartford 2005; Lewisham West 2001. Backed Leave but did not actively campaign. PPS to: Matthew Hancock 2015-; David Gauke 2014-15. Particularly interested in justice issues: member, select cttees human rights 2014-15 and justice 2013-14. Chairman, APPG Dominican Republic. Honorary Pres, Dartford Valley Rugby Club. Pres, Greenhithe and Swanscombe Branch of Royal British Legion. Cllr, Bexley 1998-2002. Married: two children. Ed: Dartford GS; Coll of Law (LPC);

	Electorate	Turnout %	from 2010 % Change
	78,506	69.07	
*G Johnson C	31,210	57.56	+8.59
B Kaini Lab	18,024	33.24	+7.82
B Fryer Ukip	2,544	4.69	-15.21
S Beard LD	1,428	2.63	-0.14
A Blatchford Green	807	1.49	-1.04
O Adewunmi Ind	211	0.39	

UWE (PgDipLaw).

CHALLENGERS
Bachchu Kaini (Lab) Clinical governance manager, Queen Elizabeth Hospital, Woolwich. Associate lecturer, Greenwich School of Management. Selected as PPC after Daisy Page stood down for personal reasons. Cllr, Dartford BC 2015-. **Ben Fryer** (Ukip) Child stage actor, now account manager at consultancy firm and Ukip Dartford

Chairman. Unsuccessful local council candidate 2015. **Simon Beard** (LD) Researcher, Cambridge University's Centre for the Study of Existential Risk. Registered blind in both eyes. Contested Dartford 2015.

CONSTITUENCY PROFILE
Overrepresented industries include construction and transport. Dartford enjoys low levels of unemployment and higher average earnings than the UK. Dartford was a safe Labour seat in the aftermath of the Second World War, but has been a bellwether since 1970, with Labour holding on by only 706 votes in 2005.

EU REFERENDUM RESULT

64.0% Leave	Remain 36.0%

Daventry

CONSERVATIVE HOLD MAJORITY 21,734 (39.0%)

CHRIS HEATON-HARRIS
BORN Nov 28, 1967
MP 2010-

Received more tickets than any other MP for 2012 Olympics. Accepted tickets and hospitality for four events and the closing ceremony, worth £11,750, from Coca-Cola. Described himself as a fierce Eurosceptic. Advocate of small government. Contested Leicester S 2004, 1997. MEP, East Midlands 1999-2009. Chairman, EU sports platform 2009-10. Asst whip 2016-17. Select cttees: European scrutiny 2010-15; public accounts 2010-15. Anti-wind farms; helped to compose a letter to David Cameron asking for a cut to wind farm subsidies. Ran family's wholesale fruit and vegetables company before

	Electorate	Turnout %	from 2010 % Change
	75,335	73.89	
*C Heaton-Harris C	35,464	63.71	+5.54
A Ramsey Lab	13,730	24.67	+6.59
A Simpson LD	4,015	7.21	+2.73
I Gibbins Ukip	1,497	2.69	-13.11
J Wildman Green	957	1.72	-1.76

entering politics. Married, two children. Ed: Tiffin GS for Boys; Wolverhampton Polytechnic (did not complete degree).

CHALLENGERS
Aiden Ramsey (Lab) Cllr, Daventry TC 2016-. Student community co-ordinator at Coventry University's student union. Chairman, Devantry CLP 2016-. Youth leader, Phoenix Youth Centre. **Andrew Simpson** (LD) Chairman, Daventry Liberal Democrats. Cllr,

Northampton BC 1995-2011; dep leader of Lib Dem opposition group 1999-2004. Contested Northamptonshire CC 2017.

CONSTITUENCY PROFILE
A very homogeneous seat in east Northamptonshire where nearly half of the residents are aged over 45. The area is characterised by high levels of home ownership and low unemployment. The seat has many jobs in retail, with transport and agriculture among other overrepresented industries for residents. Daventry has elected a Conservative MP at every election since the Second World War.

EU REFERENDUM RESULT

58.6% Leave	Remain 41.4%

Delyn

LABOUR HOLD MAJORITY 4,240 (10.8%)

DAVID HANSON
BORN Jul 5, 1957
MP 1992-

	Electorate	Turnout %	from 2010	Change
	54,116	72.84		
*D Hanson Lab	20,573	52.19	+11.65	
M Wright C	16,333	41.44	+8.71	
P Rowlinson PC	1,481	3.76	-1.06	
T Rippeth LD	1,031	2.62	-1.07	

Spent 17 years on Labour's front bench in middle-management positions. Quit in 2015 to chair debates. Supported Remain. Nominated Yvette Cooper 2015 and Owen Smith 2016; now fairly neutral to Jeremy Corbyn. Contested: Delyn 1987; Eddisbury 1983. PPS to: Tony Blair 2001-05; Alistair Darling 1997-98. Shadow positions held: min FCO Sep-Oct 2015; immigration min 2013-15; policing min 2011-13; exchequer sec 2010-11. Min: crime and policing 2009-10; justice 2007-09; NI office 2005-07. Parly under-sec for Wales 1999-2001. Asst whip, Treasury 1998-99.

Appointed to Privy Council 2007. Cllr, Vale Royal BC 1983-91, leader 1989-91; Northwich TC 1987-91. Manager, Plymouth Co-operative. Married, four children. Ed: Verdin Comp, Cheshire; University of Hull (BA drama, Cert Ed).

CHALLENGERS
Matt Wright (C) Public affairs consultant. Campaign manager, Vale of Clwyd Conservatives 2004-15. Former cllr, Flintshire CC. Contested Vale of Clwyd 2010. **Paul Rowlinson** (PC)

Former teacher. Contested Delyn 2015, 2001; Welsh Assembly 2016, 2003. **Tom Rippeth** (LD) Professor of ocean physics, Bangor University.

CONSTITUENCY PROFILE
This constituency is one of the whitest seats in the country and has a significant population of retirees. Unemployment is below the average level in Wales while earnings are above the Welsh average. This north Wales constituency was created in 1983 from parts of two safe Labour and Conservative seats. It elected a Conservative MP in 1983 and 1987, but has been a Labour seat since 1992.

EU REFERENDUM RESULT
54.4% Leave   Remain 45.6%

Denton & Reddish

LABOUR HOLD MAJORITY 14,077 (35.5%)

ANDREW GWYNNE
BORN Jun 4, 1974
MP 2005-

	Electorate	Turnout %	from 2010	Change
	65,751	60.23		
*A Gwynne Lab	25,161	63.54	+12.71	
R Kana C	11,084	27.99	+4.34	
J Seddon Ukip	1,798	4.54	-14.14	
C Ankers LD	853	2.15	-0.32	
G Hayes Green	486	1.23	-2.56	
F Dave Loony	217	0.55		

Labour's GE campaign chief 2017. Famously told Boris Johnson to "calm down" during heated debate. Campaigned to Remain. Contradicted Jeremy Corbyn by stating he would authorise a drone strike to kill the leader of ISIL during GE campaign. PPS to: Ed Balls 2009-10; Jacqui Smith 2007-09; Baroness Scotland 2005-07. Shadow min: without portfolio 2016-17; health 2011-16; public health 2015-16; transport 2010-11. Select cttees: Crossrail bill 2007; procedure 2005-10. European co-ordinator for Arlene McCarthy MEP. Researcher to Andrew Bennet MP. Cllr, Tameside MBC 1996-

2008. Member: Unite; Christian Socialists. Married, one daughter, two sons. Ed: Tameside Coll; North East Wales Institute (HND business & finance); University of Salford (BA politics and history).

CHALLENGERS
Rozila Kana (C) Project manager, Association of Chief Police Officers. Former NHS worker now in counter-terrorism. Contested Workington

2015. **Josh Seddon** (Ukip) RTT Validation Officer, Stepping Hill Hospital. Sec, Ukip Stockport. **Catherine Ankers** (LD) IT industry worker.

CONSTITUENCY PROFILE
Situated in the south-east outskirts of Manchester, crossing into Stockport. A safe Labour seat where residents earn less than the UK average. The local industry used to area used to consist of cotton spinning and engineering, and the seat still retains many manual and skilled workers, although unemployment levels are slightly higher than national figures. Part of the M60 investment corridor.

EU REFERENDUM RESULT
61.0% Leave   Remain 39.0%

Derby North

LABOUR GAIN MAJORITY 2,015 (4.1%)

CHRIS WILLIAMSON
BORN Sep 16, 1956
MP 2017-; 2010-15

	Electorate	Turnout %	from 2010 % Change
	69,919	69.61	
C Williamson Lab	23,622	48.53	+11.97
*A Solloway C	21,607	44.39	+7.74
L Care LD	2,262	4.65	-3.92
B Piper Ukip	1,181	2.43	-12.17

Regained the seat after losing it to the Conservatives in 2015. Social worker and animal rights' officer. Trustee and former chairman, League Against Cruel Sports. Former market trader and bricklayer. Non-exec dir, Greater Derby NHS PCT. Cllr, Derby CC 1991-2011. Ally and vocal supporter of Jeremy Corbyn. Described 2017 campaign in Derby North as a "test case for Corbynism"; said New Labour was a "regrettable chapter of our history". Shadow min: home affairs 2017-; CLG 2010-13. Failed to gain nomination for Oldham W by-election 2015. Vegan for 41 years, tee-total and vociferously outspoken against blood sports. Twice divorced, once widowed. One daughter, one son. Ed: Castle Donington HS; Thomas More RC Sch; Leicester Polytechnic (CQSW).

CHALLENGERS
Amanda Solloway (C) MP for Derby North 2015-17. PPS to Rory Stewart 2016-17. Background in management consultancy. Cllr: Ockbrook and Borrowash PC 2011-15. **Lucy Care** (LD) Chartered engineer.

Contested 2015, 2010; Derby South 2005. Cllr Derbyshire CC 1997-2010. **Bill Piper** (Ukip) Former mayor of Lutterworth. Contested Loughborough 2015, 2010.

CONSTITUENCY PROFILE
This seat contains the University of Derby. Nearly a fifth of the voting-age population are aged under 25 largely due to the student population of about 10,000. About six sevenths of the population is white; the seat is less ethnically diverse than Derby South. Average income is also substantially higher. Labour won by 613 votes in 2010 before losing the seat for 7 years.

EU REFERENDUM RESULT
54.3% Leave   Remain 45.7%

Derby South

LABOUR HOLD MAJORITY 11,248 (24.8%)

DAME MARGARET BECKETT
BORN Jan 15, 1943
MP 1983-; 1974-79

	Electorate	Turnout %	from 2010 % Change
	69,918	64.80	
*M Beckett Lab	26,430	58.34	+9.32
E Williams C	15,182	33.51	+6.12
A Graves Ukip	2,011	4.44	-11.10
J Naitta LD	1,229	2.71	-1.49
I Sleeman Green	454	1.00	-1.96

The longest-serving female MP in history. Nominated Jeremy Corbyn for the 2015 Labour leadership, but has since been a frequent critic. Called herself a "moron" for nominating Corbyn; urged the leader to step down in 2016 to allow the party to "get its act together"; described Corbyn supporters as "members of a fan club", not of Labour. Remainer, voted for Article 50 bill. Leader, Labour Party 1994; deputy leader 1992-94. MP for Lincoln 1974-79. Minister of state, communities and local government 2008-09. Foreign secretary 2006-07; secretary of state for environment, food and rural affairs 2001-06. Member, Labour Party NEC 2012-15, 1980-81. Member, select cttees: national security strategy 2010-17; intelligence and security 2008. Married. Ed: Notre Dame HS, Norwich; UMIST.

CHALLENGERS
Evonne Williams (C) Spent six years in the Army Intelligence Corps, serving in the UK, Bosnia and Northern Ireland. Cllr, Derby CC 2000-. Contested Derby South 2015. **Alan Graves** (Ukip) Left the Labour Party to be an independent cllr in 2009. Cllr, Derby CC 2014-. **Joe Naitta** (LD) Cllr, Derby CC 2008-. Contested Derby South 2015.

CONSTITUENCY PROFILE
This seat contains the city centre as well as Derby's southern suburbs. More than 20 per cent of its population is of Asian descent, and about 15 per cent were born outside the EU. Unlike its neighbour to the north, Derby South has mostly been a safe seat, won by Labour at every election since its creation in 1950, although the Conservatives came close in 1983 and 1987.

EU REFERENDUM RESULT
61.4% Leave   Remain 38.6%

Derbyshire Dales

CONSERVATIVE HOLD MAJORITY 14,327 (28.9%)

SIR PATRICK MCLOUGHLIN
BORN Nov30, 1957
MP 1986-

Straight-talking and working class former miner. Relatively low-profile. Loyal to party lines. Early jobs including farm work and catering. HS2 advocate. Supported Remain. Said GE2017 was "most important in British history". Received knighthood in David Cameron's resignation honours. Contested Wolverhampton SE 1983. PPS to: Lord Young 1988-89; Angela Rumbold 1987-88. Chancellor of the duchy of Lancaster 2016-. Transport secretary 2012-16. Parly sec to Treasury and chief whip 2010-12. Opposition whip: chief 2005-10; dep chief 1998-2005; pairing 1997-98.

	Electorate	Turnout %	Change from 2010 %
	64,418	76.95	
*P McLoughlin C	29,744	60.00	+7.63
A Botham Lab	15,417	31.10	+8.38
A Hollyer LD	3,126	6.31	-2.07
M Buckler Green	1,002	2.02	-2.57
R Greenwood Humanity	282	0.57	+0.25

Govt whip: 1996-97; asst 1995-96. Parly under-sec: trade & industry 1993-94; employment 1992-93; transport 1989-92. Chairman, Conservative Party 2016-. Member, National Union of Mineworkers. Cllr, Channock Chase DC 1980-87; Staffordshire CC 1981-87. Married: two children. Ed: Staffs Agriculture Coll.

CHALLENGERS
Andy Botham (Lab) Train driver. Cllr, Derbyshire CC

2013-. Aslef union rep. **Andrew Hollyer** (LD) Joined party over Iraq war. Diagnosed with cancer 2013. **Matthew Buckler** (Green) Manager, Moors for the Future.

CONSTITUENCY PROFILE
Derbyshire Dales is a large sparse seat to the northwest of Derby itself, stretching up to the Peak District. More than half of its residents are over 45. 45 per cent of residents own their homes outright. The seat was created in 2010, but its predecessor of West Derbyshire elected Conservative MPs from 1950, having only elected a Labour MP in the 1945 general election.

EU REFERENDUM RESULT

51.2% Leave	Remain 48.8%

Derbyshire Mid

CONSERVATIVE HOLD MAJORITY 11,616 (23.1%)

PAULINE LATHAM
BORN Feb 4, 1948
MP 2010-

Local government warhorse. Dir, Michael St Development. Proprietor, Humble Plc. Led social action projects to Uganda. Admitted to a poor choice of words after dismissing those who wanted to offer child refugees sanctuary as "sentimental". Advocates greater support for children with diabetes. Worked to make new melanoma treatments available to patients. Lobbied the East Midlands Drugs Fund to alter its funding for various types of cancer. Leave voter. Contested: East Midlands Euro elections 2005, 1999; Broxstowe 2001. Member, 1922 exec cttee 2017-. Select cttee, int

	Electorate	Turnout %	Change from 2010 %
	67,466	74.66	
*P Latham C	29,513	58.59	+6.40
A Martin Lab	17,897	35.53	+10.11
A Wain LD	1,793	3.56	-1.24
S Macfarlane Green	1,168	2.32	-1.66

dev 2010-17. Cllr, Ecclesbourne CC 1998-2010, 1992-96; mayor 2007-08; Derbyshire CC 1987-93. OBE 1995. Married, three children. Ed: Bramcote Hill Technical GS.

CHALLENGERS
Alison Martin (Lab) French language senior lecturer, Nottingham Trent University. Cllr, Derby CC 2012-. **Adam Wain** (LD) IT professional. Contested Derbyshire CC 2017. **Sue MacFarlane** (Green) Freelance singer-songwriter

and voice coach. Contested Derbyshire CC 2017.

CONSTITUENCY PROFILE
Mostly covering the east and north of Derby itself, this seat also contains several suburban areas of the city. Over a fifth of the seat's residents are aged 65 or above, and it has high levels of home ownership. The University of Derby lies in the new Oakwood and Allstree development. Thorntons was once based in Belper. Mid Derbyshire was created in 2010, and has been held by the Tories since then. However, its predecessor seat, Amber Valley, was a New Labour stronghold.

EU REFERENDUM RESULT

52.5% Leave	Remain 47.5%

Derbyshire North East

CONSERVATIVE GAIN MAJORITY 2,861 (5.7%)

LEE ROWLEY
BORN Sep 11, 1980
MP 2017-

	Electorate	Turnout %	from 2010 %	Change
	72,097	69.88		
L Rowley C	24,784	49.19	+12.48	
*N Engel Lab	21,923	43.51	+2.87	
J Bush Ukip	1,565	3.11	-12.81	
D Lomax LD	1,390	2.76	-1.42	
D Kesteven Green	719	1.43	-0.78	

First non-Labour MP to take this seat since 1935. Son of a milkman who spent his early years in the family business. Left milk delivery for a career in finance: former senior manager of corporate change, Santander; also KPMG, Barclays, Co-op. Eurosceptic, voted Leave. Contested: Derbyshire NE 2015; Bolsover 2010. Formerly worked for the Centre for Social Justice. Cllr, Westminster CC 2006-14; former transport cabinet member who steered doomed parking charges in London's West End. Ed: St Mary's High School, Chesterfield; Lincoln College, Oxford (BA history); University of Manchester (MA history).

CHALLENGERS
Natascha Engel (Lab) MP for Derbyshire NE 2005-17. Berlin-born linguist. Campaigned to modernise the Commons; named backbencher of the year by *The House* 2011. Deputy speaker 2015-17. PPS to: John Denham 2009-10; Liam Byrne 2008-09; Peter Hain 2007-08. Chairwoman, business select cttee 2010-15. Founder, trade union co-ordinating cttee. **James Bush** (Ukip) Senior process engineer, PM Group. Contested Derbyshire NE 2015, 2010. **David Lomax** (LD) Retired special needs teacher. Cllr, High Peak BC 1991-.

CONSTITUENCY PROFILE
Derbyshire North East is a rural constituency spread around the town of Chesterfield. Its biggest town is Dronfield, with a population of more than 21,000. Over half of residents are aged 45 or over and incomes are above the UK and East Midlands' average. This is one of the six seats won by Labour in 2015 that were lost in 2017.

EU REFERENDUM RESULT

62.1% Leave   Remain 37.9%

Derbyshire South

CONSERVATIVE HOLD MAJORITY 11,970 (22.7%)

HEATHER WHEELER
BORN May 14, 1959
MP 2010-

	Electorate	Turnout %	from 2010 %	Change
	76,341	68.94		
*H Wheeler C	30,907	58.72	+9.34	
R Pearson Lab	18,937	35.98	+9.20	
L Johnson LD	1,870	3.55	-0.16	
M Kats Green	917	1.74	-0.65	

Former Lloyd's broker and the Chartered Institute associate. Interested in economic regeneration. Contested Coventry South 2005, 2001. Conservative Party A list 2006. Voted against same-sex marriage. Sparked backlash when she shared an image on Twitter suggesting that the British Empire won the Olympics. One of 79 Conservative MPs to support rebel Brexit bill 2011. Leave campaigner. PPS: John Whittingdale 2015-16; Jeremy Wright 2014-15. Asst whip 2016-. Select cttees: standards and privileges 2010-13; communities and local govts 2011-15. Dir, Brety Inns. Manager, Rics Insurance. Indemnity insurance broker, Lloyds. Cllr: South Derbyshire DC 1995-2010, leader 2007-10; Wandsworth BC 1982-86. Married: one daughter. Ed: Grey Coat Hospital, London.

CHALLENGERS
Robert Pearson (Lab) Senior assistant registrar, Loughborough University. Cllr, Derbyshire DC 2011-. **Lorraine Johnson** (LD) BT worker. Passionate about mental health due to own experiences. Contested Derbyshire S 2015. **Marten Kats** (Green) Export finance worker and local campaigner.

CONSTITUENCY PROFILE
A large, mostly rural seat to the south and west of Derby. The largest settlement, Swandlicote, is a town which 32,000 people call home. It is relatively young for such a rural seat, but a high proportion, around three quarters, own their homes and earnings are slightly higher than the East Midlands' average. Effectively a bellwether seat, it was held by Edwina Currie from its 1983 creation until Labour's 1997 win.

EU REFERENDUM RESULT

60.4% Leave   Remain 39.6%

Devizes

CONSERVATIVE HOLD MAJORITY 21,136 (41.8%)

CLAIRE PERRY
BORN Apr 3, 1964
MP 2010-

Career in finance: Credit Suisse First Boston; McKinsey & Co; Bank of America. Min, BEIS 2017-. Assistant whip 2013-14; parly under-sec, transport 2014-16. In 2016 said that she was "often ashamed" to be rail minister. Campaigned to Remain, wants to retain maximum possible access to the single market. Voted for amendment that parliament should have final say on Brexit deal – one of only seven Conservative MPs to do so. Won first selection attempt. Two daughters, one son. Ed: Brasenose Coll, Oxford (BA geography); Harvard Business School (MBA).

	Electorate	Turnout %	from 2010 %	Change
	72,184	70.09		
*C Perry C	31,744	62.74	+5.01	
I Shaikh Lab	10,608	20.97	+7.99	
C Coleman LD	4,706	9.30	+1.23	
T Page Ukip	1,706	3.37	-12.02	
E Dawnay Green	1,606	3.17	-2.65	
J Gunter Wessex Reg	223	0.44		

CHALLENGERS
Imtiyaz Shaikh (Lab) Supervisor at an electronics company. Contested local elections 2016. **Christopher Coleman** (LD) Solicitor. Deputy leader Cheltenham BC, cabinet member for green environment. Rep on National Adoption Leadership Board. **Timothy Page** (Ukip) Counsel at law firm Latham and Watkins and former Clifford Chance partner. **Emma Dawnay** (Green) Political

economist. Contested Devizes 2015. Interested in local public transport and infrastructure.

CONSTITUENCY PROFILE
A rural seat in Wiltshire which encompasses the town of Devizes – home to about 12,000 people – in its west. Unemployment and earnings are lower than the UK averages. This seat contains Larkhill Artillery Range and part of Salisbury Plain. More of Devizes' residents work in public administration and defence than in any other seat. Devizes has elected Conservative MPs since 1924, and has never returned a Labour member to parliament.

EU REFERENDUM RESULT
53.5% Leave   Remain 46.5%

Devon Central

CONSERVATIVE HOLD MAJORITY 15,680 (27.1%)

MEL STRIDE
BORN Sep 30, 1961
MP 2010-

Set up business in 1987, which specialised in trade exhibitions, conferences and publishing. Mild Eurosceptic opposed to Brexit. PPS to John Hayes 2012-14. Involved in the creation of the 2013 Energy Bill. Conservative party A list in 2006. Financial sec to Treasury and paymaster general 2017-. Pairing whip 2016-17; whip 2015-16; asst whip 2014-15. NI affairs cttee 2010-2011. Privy council member 2017. Ed: St Edmund Hall, Oxford (BA PPE; pres, Oxford Union).

CHALLENGERS
Lisa Robillard Webb (Lab) Runs small business. Chairwoman,

	Electorate	Turnout %	from 2010 %	Change
	74,370	77.78		
*M Stride C	31,278	54.07	+1.85	
L Robillard Webb Lab	15,598	26.97	+14.14	
A White LD	6,770	11.70	-0.50	
A Williamson Green	1,531	2.65	-6.29	
T Matthews Ukip	1,326	2.29	-10.88	
J Dean NHAP	871	1.51		
L Knight Lib	470	0.81		

Central Devon Labour Party 2013-. **Alex White** (LD) IT consultant. Stood in 2015 GE, where he was the youngest candidate in the southwest. **Andy Williamson** (Green) Musician, choir dir and teacher. Contested Devon Central 2015; increased the Green vote by 400 per cent. Interest in protecting A&E services and schools funding. **Tim Matthews** (Ukip) Music teacher. Charity work:

Hospiscare, ELF and Balloons. Contested Devon County Council 2017.

CONSTITUENCY PROFILE
Central Devon is a sparse, rural constituency with a chunk of the east of Dartmoor National Park, and Exeter to its east. More than half of its residents are aged 45 or older, while fewer than one in 60 is non-white. The seat has one of the highest rates of self-employment in the country and unemployment is far lower than average. The seat was created from other Devon seats in 2010, and the Conservatives have increased their vote share in every election since then.

EU REFERENDUM RESULT
50.9% Leave   Remain 49.1%

Devon East

CONSERVATIVE HOLD MAJORITY 8,036 (13.3%)

SIR HUGO SWIRE
BORN Nov 30, 1959
MP 2001-

	Electorate	Turnout %	from 2010 %	Change
	82,382	73.30		
*H Swire C	29,306	48.53	+2.11	
C Wright Ind	21,270	35.23		
J Ross Lab	6,857	11.36	+1.14	
A Eden LD	1,468	2.43	-4.36	
B Graham Ukip	1,203	1.99	-10.56	
P Faithfull Ind	150	0.25		
M Val Davies Ind	128	0.21		

Varied career pre-politics: the armed forces; financial consultant; dir, Sotheby's; head of development at the National Gallery. Eurosceptic prior to the referendum, but voted to Remain. Sacked from the shadow cabinet in 2007 after suggesting that free museum entry could be scrapped. Min: FCO 2012-16; Northern Ireland 2010-12.Boycotted Irish summit after it was held at a Brighton hotel which had been bombed by the IRA. Chairman, Conservative Middle East Council 2016-. Knighted in 2016. Two daughters. Ed: Eton Coll; University of St Andrew's; RMA Sandhurst.

CHALLENGERS
Clare Wright (Ind) Columnist for the *Express & Echo*. Contested Devon East 2015; came second. Cllr: Devon CC 2013-; East Devon DC 2011-15. **Janet Ross** (Lab) Lives in Exmouth. Stood for District CC in Broadclyst 2017. **Alison Eden** (LD) Healthcare comms specialist. Cllr: Teignmouth Central C 2016-; Teignbridge DC

2016-. **Brigitte Graham** (Ukip) Weaver, reseats antique chairs. Contested local elections 2017.

CONSTITUENCY PROFILE
East Devon is mostly rural, the largest town being coastal Exmouth. It also contains two of the Conservative areas in Exeter. More than a quarter of constituents are aged 65 or older and a greater than average proportion of its residents are employed in the tourism sector. The seat has been comfortably represented by Conservatives since its inception in 1997, but Swire's majority has twice been dented by Claire Wright since 2015.

EU REFERENDUM RESULT

50.4% Leave	Remain 49.6%

Devon North

CONSERVATIVE HOLD MAJORITY 4,332 (7.8%)

PETER HEATON-JONES
BORN Aug 2, 1963
MP 2015-

	Electorate	Turnout %	from 2010 %	Change
	75,784	73.50		
*P Heaton-Jones C	25,517	45.81	+3.11	
N Harvey LD	21,185	38.03	+8.59	
M Cann Lab	7,063	12.68	+5.61	
S Crowther Ukip	1,187	2.13	-12.62	
R Knight Green	753	1.35	-4.42	

Former journalist; interviewed Tony Blair in 2006 for BBC Swindon & Wiltshire. Worked in Australia as head of marketing for ABC's national radio stations and as policy adviser and press sec to New South Wales parliament. Campaign dir for Conservative candidates in 2010 general election. Cllr, Swindon BC 2010-14; retired after criticism of holding council seat in separate ward to where he lived. Supported Remain. PPS to Penny Mordaunt 2016-17. Ed: University of London.

CHALLENGERS
Sir Nick Harvey (LD) MP for

Devon North 1992-2015; lost his seat in the 2015 Lib Dem wipeout. Min, armed forces 2010-12. LD shadow SoS, defence 2006-10. **Mark Cann** (Lab) Retired politics teacher. Contested Devon North 2015, 2010, 2005. Chairman, North Devon Labour. Former cllr. **Stephen Crowther** (Ukip) Retired writer and owner of advertising agency. Appointed as interim Ukip leader after the 2017 election. Ukip chairman 2010-16. Contested Devon

N 2015, 2010. **Ricky Knight** (Green) Retired. Spent 30 years as a language teacher. Contested Devon North 2015, 2005.

CONSTITUENCY PROFILE
North Devon's biggest towns are Barnstaple and Ilfracombe, both coastal, with populations of 24,000 and 11,000 respectively. The seat has a significant tourist industry, low unemployment and an older than average population. A Liberal/Conservative swing seat: for 20 years, Devon North was the seat of the Liberal leader Jeremy Thorpe, before a Conservative gain in 1979 and a Liberal Democrat gain in 1992.

EU REFERENDUM RESULT

57.0% Leave	Remain 43.0%

Devon South West

CONSERVATIVE HOLD MAJORITY 15,816 (29.9%)

GARY STREETER
BORN Oct 02, 1955
MP 1992-

Spent 14 years as a local solicitor. Cllr, Plymouth CC 1986-92. Evangelical Christian; among MPs who signed a letter to the ASA in 2012 which called to overturn a ban on adverts that claimed God could heal people. Interested in human rights and the developing world. Remainer, voted to trigger Article 50. Vice-chairman, Conservative Party 2001-2002. Select cttees: speaker's cttee on the electoral commission 2006-; panel of chairs 2009-; ecclesiastical 2010-. Grew up on a dairy farm in east Devon. Married, two children. Ed: King's College London (BA law).

Electorate	Turnout %	from 2010 %	Change
71,262	74.17		
*G Streeter C	31,634	59.85	+3.27
P Davey Lab Co-op	15,818	29.93	+13.27
C Voaden LD	2,732	5.17	-2.31
I Ross Ukip	1,540	2.91	-11.59
W Scutt Green	1,133	2.14	-2.64

CHALLENGERS
Philippa Davey (Lab) Cllr, Plymouth CC 2009-. Member, Devon and Cornwall police and crime panel. Full time trade union official, University and College Union. **Caroline Voaden** (LD) Former Reuters journalist and small business owner; currently freelance editor. **Ian Ross** (Ukip) Defence industry engineer, Royal Navy. **Win Scutt** (Green) Properties curator, English Heritage. Former archaeologist with the BBC.

CONSTITUENCY PROFILE
This seat, with Dartmoor in its north and the Devon coastline along its southern edge, borders the two seats which comprise Devon's biggest city, Plymouth, but also contains two of its suburban areas, Plymstock and Plympton. Like other mostly rural Devon seats, demographically it is older than the local and national averages. Like much of the southwest, levels of home ownership are much higher than average. The seat has been Conservative since its creation in 1997. It's a safe seat for the party, although 2017 was Labour's strongest performance since 2001.

EU REFERENDUM RESULT
55.1% Leave   Remain 44.9%

Devon West & Torridge

CONSERVATIVE HOLD MAJORITY 20,686 (34.8%)

GEOFFREY COX
BORN Apr 30, 1960
MP 2005-

Barrister and QC. Co-founder, Thomas More Chambers. Formerly served as standing counsel to Mauritius; defence attorney in Operation Elveden trial. Forced to apologise to the House and resign from standards cttee for missing deadline to declare £400,000 of outside earnings from legal work 2015. Brexiteer. Serial backbencher. Rarely rebels but defied whip to vote to bring 3,000 refugee children to UK 2016. President, Tavistock football club. Anglican. Married, two sons, one daughter. Ed: King's Coll, Taunton; Downing Coll, Cambridge (BA English and law).

Electorate	Turnout %	from 2010 %	Change
80,527	73.86		
*G Cox C	33,612	56.51	+5.66
V Barry Lab Co-op	12,926	21.73	+11.10
D Chalmers LD	10,526	17.70	+4.47
C Jordan Green	1,622	2.73	-4.24
R Julian Ind	794	1.33	

CHALLENGERS
Vince Barry (Lab Co-op) University student. Local organiser, Co-operative Party. **David Chalmers** (LD) Former advertising and sales manager, *The Economist*. Co-founder, Kaleidoscope Trust. Cllr, Fremington PC 2015-. **Chris Jordan** (Green) Nurse. Environmental campaigner. **Robin Julian** (Ind) Contested Devon West and Torridge for Ukip 2010. Cllr: Torridge DC 2015-; Devon CC 2013-17.

CONSTITUENCY PROFILE
Situated to the north of Plymouth, this is a sparse and rural seat with a long border with Cornwall. The constituency has a large retired population and nearly three quarters of residents are homeowners. A greater than average proportion work in agriculture, forestry and fishing although earnings are lower than elsewhere in the region. The constituency was held by the Lib Dems for ten years after its Conservative MP, Emma Nicholson, defected in 1995. 2017 was the first time the Lib Dems have been beaten to second place by Labour since the seat was created in 1983.

EU REFERENDUM RESULT
57.2% Leave   Remain 42.8%

Dewsbury

LABOUR HOLD MAJORITY 3,321 (5.9%)

PAULA SHERRIFF
BORN Apr 16, 1975
MP 2015-

First opposition MP to have a budget amendment passed concerning the tampon tax. Worked in victim support for the police and the NHS. Active in Save Dewsbury Hospital campaign. Cllr, Wakefield C 2012-15. Shad min, women and equalities 2016-. Health cttee, 2015-16. Supported Yvette Cooper in the 2015 Labour leadership contest. Remainer, voted for Article 50. Pulled out of a 2016 fundraising event in aid of Palestine as men and women were to be seated separately. Unison. Campaigned for greater access to NHS dentistry in Dewsbury. Sister, Lee Sherriff,

	Electorate	Turnout %	from 2010 Change %
	81,338	69.52	
*P Sherriff Lab	28,814	50.96	+9.18
B Prescott C	25,493	45.08	+6.01
E Hussain LD	1,214	2.15	-1.44
S Cope Green	1,024	1.81	-0.74

contested Carlisle 2015. Left school at 18. Ed: Morton Sch, Carlisle.

CHALLENGERS
Beth Prescott (C) Youth leader; church minister. Twitter account once branded Beth4PM. Contested Normanton, Pontefract & Castleford 2015. **Ednan Hussain** (LD) Team leader, PC World. Son of former Kirklees mayor. Contested Dewsbury 2015. **Simon Cope** (Green) Said he would consider dropping out of the election if

Paula Sherriff gave concessions. Co-ordinator, Kirklees Green Party. Former chairman, Scarborough Athletic FC.

CONSTITUENCY PROFILE
This west Yorkshire seat consists of the old mill town of Dewsbury, home to 63,000 people, the smaller town of Mirfield, and a large rural sector south of the two towns. The area was a centre of the Luddite and Chartist revolts. More than 20 per cent of residents are of Asian descent. Dewsbury has elected Labour MPs since 1935, except for Conservatives in 1983 and 2010; Sayeeda Warsi contested the seat for the party in 2005.

EU REFERENDUM RESULT

57.1% Leave	Remain 42.9%

Don Valley

LABOUR HOLD MAJORITY 5,169 (11.2%)

CAROLINE FLINT
BORN Sep 20, 1961
MP 1997-

Combative campaigner, seen as part of Labour's "old right". Made frequent media appearances during Ed Miliband's leadership. Claimed Jeremy Corbyn was unfit to lead 2016. Europe min 2008-09; quit after attacking Gordon Brown's use of women as "window dressing". Secured the only non-government amendment to the Finance Bill 2016. Shadow SoS: DECC 2011-15; CLG 2010-11. Remainer. Vice-chairwoman APPG children of alcoholics; her mother died from alcoholism. Born to a 17-year-old single mother. First in her family to attend university. Married, three children. Ed: Twickenham

	Electorate	Turnout %	from 2010 Change %
	73,988	62.16	
*C Flint Lab	24,351	52.95	+6.77
A Bell C	19,182	41.71	+16.44
S Manion Yorkshire	1,599	3.48	
A Smith LD	856	1.86	-1.64

Girls Sch; Richmond Coll; University of East Anglia (BA American history, literature and film).

CHALLENGERS
Aaron Bell (C) Winner of the 2009 series of *The Krypton Factor*. Trading dev manager, Bet365. Senior business analyst for a financial tech firm. Brexiteer. **Stevie Manion** (Yorkshire) Production planner, Wabtec Rail Ltd. Contested Sheffield Brightside and Hillsborough by-election 2016.

Anthony Smith (LD) Works for a financial services company. Contested Rochdale BC 2015.

CONSTITUENCY PROFILE
This seat encompasses Doncaster's southern outskirts and several smaller south Yorkshire towns, such as Hatfield and Coinsbrough. It has a large retired population, numbering about 12,000, and the highest rate of home ownership of the three Doncaster constituencies. Unemployment is lower and wages higher than in neighbouring seats. It has elected only Labour MPs since 1922, with the majority falling to its lowest, 3,595, in 2010.

EU REFERENDUM RESULT

68.5% Leave	Remain 31.5%

Doncaster Central

LABOUR HOLD MAJORITY 10,131 (23.5%)

DAME ROSIE WINTERTON
BORN Aug 10, 1958
MP 1997-

	Electorate	Turnout %	from 2010 %	Change
	71,716	59.99		
*R Winterton Lab	24,915	57.91	+8.82	
T Hunt C	14,784	34.36	+13.62	
C Whitwood Yorkshire	1,346	3.13		
E Todd Ind	1,006	2.34		
A Breslford LD	973	2.26	-1.99	

Career politician who started as a constituency assistant to John Prescott 1980-86. Became Prescott protégée; head of his office 1994-97. Parly officer: Royal Coll of Nursing 1988-90; Southwark Council 1986-88. Later MD, Connect Public Affairs consultancy firm. Member: TGWU, NUJ. Did not nominate a candidate for Labour leadership in 2015 or 2016. Regarded as a moderate. Floated proposals for shadow cabinet elections but sacked as chief whip by Jeremy Corbyn in 2016. Campaigned Remain; voted for Article 50. Deputy speaker 2017-; opp chief whip 2010-16.

Min: regional affairs 2008-10; transport 2007-08; health 2003-07. Ed: Doncaster GS; Hull University (BA history).

CHALLENGERS
Tom Hunt (C) Press officer, Countryside Alliance. Contested European election 2014. Cllr, East Cambridgeshire CC 2011-. **Chris Whitwood** (Yorkshire) Teacher. Dep leader, Yorkshire party. Contested Doncaster mayoralty 2017. **Eddie Todd** (Ind) Businessman and inventor; owns a motorcycle park. **Alison Brelsford** (LD) Bookkeeper. Radio presenter. Cllr: Stocksbridge TC, 2003-15; Sheffield CC, 2004-14, 1995-2003.

CONSTITUENCY PROFILE
Doncaster Central covers most of the town of Doncaster. It is the most ethnically diverse of the three Doncaster seats, even though about 90 per cent of its residents are white. It has the fewest retirees and the lowest average earnings. Doncaster Central has elected Labour MPs since its inception in 1983, as the old Doncaster seat had done since 1964.

EU REFERENDUM RESULT
66.7% Leave   Remain 33.3%

Doncaster North

LABOUR HOLD MAJORITY 14,024 (33.1%)

ED MILIBAND
BORN Dec 24, 1969
MP 2005-

	Electorate	Turnout %	from 2010 %	Change
	72,372	58.46		
*E Miliband Lab	25,711	60.77	+8.34	
S Adoh C	11,687	27.62	+9.31	
K Parkinson Ukip	2,738	6.47	-16.13	
C Bridges Yorkshire	741	1.75		
R Adamson LD	706	1.67	-0.88	
F Calladine Ind	366	0.87		
D Allen Eng Dem	363	0.86	-0.28	

Leader of the Opposition 2010-15. Brownite who managed to unite Labour despite persistent concerns about his leadership and the public not seeing him as PM material. Researcher and speechwriter for Harriet Harman MP 1993-94; adviser to Gordon Brown MP 1997-2002. Cabinet Office min 2007-08. SoS ECC 2008-10. Youngest Labour leader. Gained cult following during leadership. Yet to rebel on a vote since Jeremy Corbyn became Labour leader. Jewish atheist. Son of Marxist academic Ralph Miliband; brother of former foreign sec David, whom he beat in 2010 leadership contest.

Married, two sons. Ed: Corpus Christi Coll, Oxford (BA PPE); LSE (MSc economics).

CHALLENGERS
Shade Adoh (Con) Nurse. Volunteer, Healthwatch Buckinghamshire. Cllr, Wycombe DC 2011-. **Kim Parkinson** (Ukip) Self-employed management consultant in chemicals industry. **Charlie Bridges** (Yorkshire) Fighting to devolve power from Westminster. **Robert Adamson** (LD) Former civil servant and carer. Has MS. Contested: Yorkshire East 2015, 2010; Darlington 2005; 2001.

CONSTITUENCY PROFILE
Doncaster North is more the area to the north of Doncaster than an area in the north of Doncaster, and it is even sparser than its mirror seat, Don Valley. Of the three Doncaster seats, its residents are least likely to have high qualification levels, although unemployment is not as high as in Doncaster Central. Labour MPs have held the seat since its creation in 1983.

EU REFERENDUM RESULT
71.7% Leave   Remain 28.3%

Dorset Mid & Poole North

CONSERVATIVE HOLD MAJORITY 15,339 (31.8%)

MICHAEL TOMLINSON
BORN Oct 1, 1977
MP 2015-

Barrister, 3PB Chambers. Campaign manager for 2010 Conservative candidate. Led delegation of Poole MPs to minister on fair funding for schools 2016. Brexiteer. APPG chairman: youth employment; vice-chairman, broadband and digital communications. Member, European scrutiny cttee 2016-17. Dep chairman, European Research Group. Member of the Lords and Commons cricket club. Participated in Conservative Party's project Umubano 2011, 2009. Married, three children. Ed: King's College London (BA classics); Coll of Law (PgDip).

Electorate	Turnout %	from 2010 % Change
65,054	74.18	
*M Tomlinson C	28,585	59.24	+8.40
V Slade LD	13,246	27.45	-0.74
S Brew Lab	6,423	13.31	+7.36

CHALLENGERS
Vikki Slade (LD) Regional financial services manager. Also works for regional disability charity. Contested Dorset Mid and Poole North 2015. Cllr, Poole BC 2011-16; LD council group support officer 2013-14. Pledged to support the building of affordable housing, challenge the downgrading of Poole Hospital, support rural businesses and oppose fracking. **Steve Brew** (Lab) Supply chain project manager for the RNLI. Contested Poole BC 2015.

CONSTITUENCY PROFILE
Mainly rural with the exception of the northern suburban areas of Poole in its east, the constituency has older residents than the average, with a fifth at retirement age or beyond. It is characterised by high levels of home ownership and part-time employment. Dorset Mid and Poole North was held by the Liberal Democrats between 2001 and 2015, but the Conservatives increased their vote share significantly at every election from 2010 and took the seat back in 2015. It is a reasonably affluent consituency that is economically active with sizeable working and middle classes.

EU REFERENDUM RESULT
57.1% Leave   Remain 42.9%

Dorset North

CONSERVATIVE HOLD MAJORITY 25,777 (46.3%)

SIMON HOARE
BORN June 28, 1969
MP 2015-

Previously worked at the advertising agency Charles Barker; head of property at Ketchum. Contested Cardiff South and Penarth 2010; Cardiff West 1997. Eurosceptic prior to the 2016 referendum but supported the Remain campaign. Lobbied for the building of a freight terminal near St Albans in 2011. Member: Speaker's advisory committee on works of art 2015-; regulatory reform select committee 2015-; procedure committee 2015-2016. PPS to farming minister George Eustice 2016-. Three daughters. Ed: Greyfriars Coll, Oxford (BA modern history).

Electorate	Turnout %	from 2010 % Change
76,385	72.95	
*S Hoare C	36,169	64.91	+8.29
P Osborne Lab	10,392	18.65	+9.69
T Panton LD	7,556	13.56	+1.90
J Tutton Green	1,607	2.88	-2.81

CHALLENGERS
Patrick Osborne (Lab) Cllr, Blandford Forum TC 2016-; Member, planning and recreation, and amenities cttee. Contested Dorset CC 2017. **Thomas Panton** (LD) Lives in the Blackmore Vale. Researcher in the Commons. Was parliamentary assistant to Alistair Carmichael 2015-2016; Jo Winson 2014-2015. **John Tutton** (Green) Mental health support worker. Grew up in Poole. Took part in a Save Dinah's Hollow Demonstration 2017.

CONSTITUENCY PROFILE
Just three towns in Dorset North – Verwood, Gillingham and Blandford Forum – have a population of more than 10,000. It is a large constituency that borders Somerset, Wiltshire and Hampshire. One in five residents are aged 65 or more and just one in 50 is non-white. Average earnings are slightly lower than the national and local averages. Its economy is largely dependent on livestock farming and food. The seat has elected a Conservative MP at every election since 1950, although by small majorities between 1997 and 2010, when the Liberal Democrats targeted the seat.

EU REFERENDUM RESULT
56.6% Leave   Remain 43.4%

Dorset South

CONSERVATIVE HOLD MAJORITY 11,695 (22.5%)

RICHARD DRAX
BORN Jan 29, 1958
MP 2010-

Spent nine years in the Coldstream Guards. Former reporter: *The Yorkshire Evening Press, Tyne Tees TV, Daily Telegraph, Daily Express, BBC South Today.* Campaigned to Leave. Said that pro-Remain MPs should resign in a letter to the *Daily Telegraph.* Voted against same-sex marriage. Falsely accused of sexual harassment by a former employee in 2013. Helped to secure the release of Marine A from prison 2017. Select cttees: European scrutiny 2015-; environment, food and rural affairs 2010-15. Four children. Ed: Harrow School; Royal

	Electorate	Turnout %	from 2010 % Change
	72,323	71.77	
*R Drax C	29,135	56.13	+7.25
T Warr Lab	17,440	33.60	+9.40
H Legg LD	3,053	5.88	-0.09
J Orrell Green	2,278	4.39	-0.29

Agricultural College (Dip rural land management); Westminster (Dip journalism).

CHALLENGERS
Tashi Warr (Lab) Campaign organiser for South Dorset Labour Party 2013-15; constituency asst to Clare Moody MEP 2014-15. Contested Weymouth and Portland BC 2014. **Howard Legg** (LD) Experience as a teacher and chartered electrical engineer. Cllr, Weymouth & Portland BC 1988-2012. **Jon Orrell** (Green)

GP. Cllr, Weymouth and Portland BC 2016-; first Green cllr to be elected here.

CONSTITUENCY PROFILE
Weymouth dominates the constituency and has a population of more than 52,000. Nearly a quarter of the seat's residents are over 65 and a greater than average proportion of residents work part-time. Home ownership levels are lower than in comparable constituencies. South Dorset was one of just two seats the Labour Party gained in 2001, Tony Blair's second landslide election, and Labour held it until the Conservatives won it in 2010.

EU REFERENDUM RESULT

59.4% Leave	Remain 40.6%

Dorset West

CONSERVATIVE HOLD MAJORITY 19,091 (32.0%)

SIR OLIVER LETWIN
BORN May 19, 1956
MP 1997-

Adviser, Margaret Thatcher's policy unit 1983-86. Banker, NM Rothschild 1986-91; dir, 1991-2003. Contested: Hampstead and Highgate 1992; Hackney North and Stoke Newington 1987. Campaigned to Remain. David Cameron's chief policy wonk during coalition and majority years; knighted in 2016 dissolution honours. Chancellor of the Duchy of Lancaster 2014-16. Gaffe-prone. Planned to retire in 2020 but contested snap election. Married, two children. Ed: Eton Coll; Trinity Coll, Cambridge (PhD philosophy); Princeton University; London Business Sch.

	Electorate	Turnout %	from 2010 % Change
	79,043	75.40	
*O Letwin C	33,081	55.51	+5.33
A Canning LD	13,990	23.47	+1.87
L Rhodes Lab	10,896	18.28	+8.31
K Clayton Green	1,631	2.74	-3.01

CHALLENGERS
Andy Canning (LD) Cllr, Dorchester TC 1999-; West Dorset DC 2003-; Dorset CC 2013-. Chairman, Dorchester Lib Dems; Dorchester transport & environment working group; heritage; audit cttee. Mayor of Dorchester 2012-13. **Lee Rhodes** (Lab) Former factory worker. Accountant, Dorset CC 2005-. Contested local elections 2015, 2011. **Kelvin Clayton** (Green) Ethics lecturer, Staffordshire University. Cllr, Bridport TC. Chairman, West and South

Dorset Green party. Trustee, Bridport youth and community centre.

CONSTITUENCY PROFILE
A large, sparse seat where the largest town, Dorchester, is home to about 19,000. Over a quarter of West Dorset's population are aged 65 and above; many are homeowners. Self-employment and part-time employment are significantly higher than the UK average; tourism is a large employer. The seat has only ever elected Conservative MPs and it is a safe seat, although Letwin's majority over the Lib Dems was never more than 4,000 until 2015.

EU REFERENDUM RESULT

51.0% Leave	Remain 49.0%

Dover

CONSERVATIVE HOLD MAJORITY 6,437 (12.4%)

CHARLIE ELPHICKE
BORN Mar 14, 1971
MP 2010-

Keen on stronger borders for post-Brexit Britain. Successfully campaigned against privatisation of Port of Dover in 2012, going against his party's 2005 stance. Chairman, APPG FairFuel 2016-. PPS to: Iain Duncan Smith 2014-15; David Lidington 2012-14. Lord commissioner, Treasury whip 2015-16. Select cttees: public accounts 2016-17; consolidation bills 2010-15; public admin 2010-13. Former tax lawyer and research fellow at Centre for Policy Studies. Brother-in-law of Mark Field, MP for Cities of London and Westminster. Married, two children. Ed: Felstead Sch, Essex; University of

	Electorate	Turnout %	from 2010 % Change
	74,564	69.69	
*C Elphicke C	27,211	52.36	+9.08
S Blair Lab	20,774	39.98	+9.23
P Wauchope Ukip	1,722	3.31	-16.95
S Dodd LD	1,336	2.57	-0.56
B Sawbridge Green	923	1.78	-0.80

Nottingham (LLB law); Inns of Court Sch of Law.

CHALLENGERS
Stacey Blair (Lab) Works in elderly care social service. Anti-austerity. Secretary for Deal West Labour branch. Contested Dover DC 2015. **Piers Wauchope** (Ukip) Barrister. Former Conservative Party member. Contested North Thanet 2015; Hampstead and Highgate for Con Party 2005. Ukip cllr, Tunbridge Wells

2012-15. Chairman, society of Ukip lawyers. Faced charges for breaching injunction order against his ex-wife in 2013, but these were later dropped.

CONSTITUENCY PROFILE
This east Kent seat is best known for its port town's connections to Calais. Dover and Deal have about 30,000 residents, and the remaining inland area of the seat is rural. Earnings are higher than the UK average, but lower than the southeast's. The seat was Conservative from its reconstitution in 1983. It elected Labour MPs during the New Labour years, but reverted to Conservative in 2010.

EU REFERENDUM RESULT
63.0% Leave   Remain 37.0%

Down North

INDEPENDENT HOLD MAJORITY 1,208 (3.1%)

LADY SYLVIA HERMON
BORN Aug 11, 1955
MP 2001-

The only independent elected to this Parliament, originally sat for UUP but quit over the party's links to the Conservatives in 2010. Appointed law lecturer at Queen's University Belfast aged 21. Expert on European and constitutional law. Author. From a Co Tyrone farming family. Socially liberal but voted against same-sex marriage. Campaigned to Remain, voted against Article 50. Member, NI affairs select cttee 2015-. Presbyterian. Widow of former RUC chief constable Sir Jack Hermon, two sons. Ed: Dungannon HS for Girls; Aberystwyth University (LLB law).

	Electorate	Turnout %	from 2010 % Change
	64,334	60.91	
*S Hermon Ind	16,148	41.21	
A Easton DUP	14,940	38.13	+14.52
A Muir Alliance	3,639	9.29	+0.70
S Agnew Green	2,549	6.51	+1.06
F Shivers C	941	2.40	-2.03
T McCartney SF	531	1.36	+0.60
C McNeill SDLP	400	1.02	+0.03
G Reynolds Ind	37	0.09	

CHALLENGERS
Alex Easton (DUP) Orangeman who worked in healthcare. Cllr, Down North BC 2001-14. Contested Down North 2015. **Andrew Muir** (Alliance) Ticketing systems manager, Translink. Pres, Alliance Party 2015-16. Cllr, Ards and Down North BC 2010-; mayor 2013-14. Contested Down North 2015. **Steven Agnew** (Green) MLA,

Down North 2011-. Leader, NI Green Party 2011-.

CONSTITUENCY PROFILE
Down North is centred around the town of Bangor, which has a population of over 60,000. According to the 2011 census there are approximately 67,000 Protestants and 11,000 Catholics in the seat. Nearly three quarters of homes are owned, and unemployment is below the Northern Irish average. Since Sylvia Hermon is an Independent unionist, Down North is the only parliamentary seat in Northern Ireland not held by the DUP or Sinn Fein after the 2017 general election.

EU REFERENDUM RESULT
47.6% Leave   Remain 52.4%

Down South

SINN FEIN GAIN MAJORITY 2,446 (4.8%)

CHRIS HAZZARD
BORN Aug 20, 1984
MP 2017-

MLA for Down South 2012-; youngest MLA at selection. Campaigned for local infrastructure projects and served as minister for infrastructure in NI Assembly, 2016-17. Sinn Fein spokesman on education. Community activist focusing on rural areas. Member of Drumaness GAC. Ed: Our Lady & St Patrick's Coll, Knock; Queen's University Belfast (PhD international studies and political philosophy).

CHALLENGERS
Margaret Ritchie (SDLP) MP for Down South 2010-17. Former social worker who launched

	Electorate	Turnout %	from 2010 % Change
	75,685	67.24	
C Hazzard SF	20,328	39.94	+11.40
*M Ritchie SDLP	17,882	35.14	-7.20
D Forsythe DUP	8,867	17.42	+9.26
H McKee UUP	2,002	3.93	-5.35
A McMurray Alliance	1,814	3.56	-0.23

the New Housing Agenda scheme 2008, aiming to tackle homelessness. Failed one-year SDLP leadership 2010-11. Served as SDLP spokeswoman. MLA for Down South 2003-12; minister for social development 2007-10. Cllr, Down DC 1985-2009. Parly assistant and political researcher to Eddie McGrady 1987-2003. Ed: Queen's University Belfast (BA geography and political science). **Diane Forsythe** (DUP) Accountant and former teacher. Father is a councillor. **Harold**

McKee (UUP) Farmer. MLA Down South 2016-.

CONSTITUENCY PROFILE
A large, sparse coastal seat in the southeast of Northern Ireland, Down South is home to the burial site of St Patrick and resident to about 79,000 Catholics and 29,000 Protestants. Over a third of its residents are aged under 25. It is also one of only a handful of seats where fewer than one in a hundred residents are non-white. Down South was Enoch Powell's constituency while he was an UUP MP, but the SDLP gained it from him in 1987 and held it for the next 30 years.

EU REFERENDUM RESULT

32.8% Leave   Remain 67.2%

Dudley North

LABOUR HOLD MAJORITY 22 (0.1%)

IAN AUSTIN
BORN Mar 6, 1965
MP 2005-

Former journalist, *Midland Sport magazine*. Long Labour career: press officer, West Midlands Labour Party 1995-98; adviser to Gordon Brown 1999-2005. Remain supporter. PPS to Gordon Brown 2007-08. Assistant whip 2008-09. Shadow min: work and pensions 2011-13; CMS 2010-11; communities and local govt 2010. Parly under-sec, planning 2009-10. West Midlands regional affairs minister 2008-10. Member, education select cttee 2015-2017. Heckled Jeremy Corbyn in 2016. Criticised over expense claims in 2009. Cllr, Dudley MBC 1991-95. Married, three children.

	Electorate	Turnout %	from 2010 % Change
	62,043	62.71	
*I Austin Lab	18,090	46.49	+4.68
L Jones C	18,068	46.44	+15.63
B Etheridge Ukip	2,144	5.51	-18.48
B France LD	368	0.95	-0.31
A Nixon Green	240	0.62	-0.74

Ed: University of Essex (BA government and politics).

CHALLENGERS
Les Jones (C) Dir, Mary Stevens Hospice. Cllr, Dudley Metropolitan BC 1999-; leader 2011-12. Contested West Midlands PCC 2016, 2014. **Bill Etheridge** (Ukip) Running for Ukip leadership a second time. MEP for West Midlands 2014-; member, regional development cttee. Cllr, Dudley Metropolitan BC 2014-. Contested: Dudley

North 2015; Ukip leadership, 2016; West Midlands PCC 2012. Criticised in 2014 for praising Hitler's public speaking. **Ben France** (LD) Chairman, Dudley Liberal Democrats.

CONSTITUENCY PROFILE
Dudley sits just to the south of Wolverhampton and west of Birmingham. Dudley North contains more of the town of Dudley than its neighbour seat to the south, and is more ethnically diverse and slightly less affluent than Dudley South. It has elected Labour MPs since 1997, but is now ultra-marginal. Ian Austin won by 649 votes in 2010 and by just 22 in 2017.

EU REFERENDUM RESULT

71.4% Leave   Remain 28.6%

Dudley South

CONSERVATIVE HOLD MAJORITY 11,695 (20.2%)

MIKE WOOD
BORN Mar 17, 1976
MP 2015-

Nearly died from sepsis in 2017; has since urged Theresa May to improve treatment of the condition. Introduced riot compensation private members' bill in 2015. Parly asst, Commons 2011-14. Caseworker for Andrew Griffiths 2010-11. Senior researcher, JDS Associates 2006-08. Cllr, Dudley MBC 2014-16. Voted Leave. Member, European scrutiny select cttee 2016-. Former policy adviser to European parliament in internal market legislation and environmental regulation. Asst to Earl of Stockton MEP 1999-2002. Married, two children. Ed: University of Aberystwyth

Electorate	Turnout %	from 2010 % Change
61,323	62.36	
*M Wood C	21,588	56.45 +12.68
N Millward Lab	13,858	36.24 +3.64
M Bolton Ukip	1,791	4.68 -14.25
J Bramall LD	625	1.63 -0.53
J Maxwell Green	382	1.00 -1.54

(BSc economics and law); University of Cardiff (PG Dip bar vocational course).

CHALLENGERS
Natasha Millward (Lab) Local area organiser, Unison. Formerly a student development officer at an FE college. Contested Dudley South 2015. Governor at Dudley College. **Mitch Bolton** (Ukip) Claimed he would take only £30,000 of his salary and donate the rest to charity if elected. Contested Dudley MBC

2016. Distribution manager. **Jon Bramall** (LD) Former bank manager. Works in apprentice and training industry.

CONSTITUENCY PROFILE
Dudley South contains much of the residential area outside the town of Dudley, but also includes areas still in the metropolitan district, such as Kingswinford. Residents here earn slightly more, on average, than in Dudley North, and unemployment is also lower. It elected Labour MPs from 1997 to 2010 but has been Conservative since then, with the Conservative vote-share growing at each election since the seat's creation.

EU REFERENDUM RESULT

70.4% Leave   Remain 29.6%

Dulwich & West Norwood

LABOUR HOLD MAJORITY 28,156 (50.2%)

HELEN HAYES
BORN Aug 8, 1974
MP 2015-

Background in planning and architectural practice. Dir, Allies and Morrison: Urban Practitioners 2011-15, created from merger of A&M of Urban Practitioners, of which she was a director 1998-2012. Cllr, Southwark BC 2010-16. Co-sponsor of the homelessness reduction bill 2017. Founding member of the APPG on Southern Rail. Campaigned to Remain in the EU, voted against Article 50. Member, CLG select cttee 2015-. Married, two children. Ed: Ormskirk Grammar School, Lancs; Balliol Coll, Oxford (BA PPE); LSE (MA social policy and administration).

Electorate	Turnout %	from 2010 % Change
77,947	72.03	
*H Hayes Lab	39,096	69.64 +15.57
R Wolf C	10,940	19.49 -3.20
G Kent LD	4,475	7.97 -1.87
R Nix Green	1,408	2.51 -6.92
R Lambert Ind	121	0.22
Y Chong Ind	103	0.18

CHALLENGERS
Rachel Wolf (C) Founder and dir, New Schools Network, which aims to increase the number of free schools, 2009-13; SVP, Amplify 2013-15; technology, innovation, education adviser to the PM 2015-16. Founder, Public First 2016-. **Gail Kent** (LD) Dir of resources and support, European Commission 2014-. Worked at the national crime agency. **Rashid Nix** (Green) Filmmaker and educator.

CONSTITUENCY PROFILE
This south London constituency, consisting of areas in Lambeth and Southwark, was the seventh highest voting Remain seat in the 2016 EU referendum. Levels of social and private renting are much higher than average, and about a third of residents are black or mixed race. The seat has been Labour since its creation in 1997, although its predecessor seats of Dulwich and Norwood had been held by the Conservatives at various times since the Second World War. Dulwich and West Norwood is the old seat of Labour former minister for the Olympics, Dame Tessa Jowell.

EU REFERENDUM RESULT

22.9% Leave   Remain 77.1%

Dumfries & Galloway

CONSERVATIVE GAIN MAJORITY 5,643 (10.9%)

ALISTER JACK
BORN Jul 15, 1963
MP 2017-

	Electorate	Turnout %	from 2010 %	Change
	74,206	69.53		
A Jack C	22,344	43.30	+13.40	
*R Arkless SNP	16,701	32.37	-9.05	
D Goodare Lab	10,775	20.88	-3.82	
J Mitchell LD	1,241	2.41	+0.72	
Y Hongmei Jin ND	538	1.04		

Entrepreneur specialising in self-storage marketing, with an estimated £20 million fortune; he sold two self-storage businesses for a total of £54 million in 2017. Co-founder of tent-hire firm, Field & Lawn. Farmer of 1,200 acres near Lockerbie. Campaign based on improving transport infrastructure and communications. Opposes Scottish independence and a second referendum. Former vice-chairman, Scottish Conservatives. Scottish Conservative spokesman for industry, 1998. Chairman: Fulling Mill; River Annan Fishery Board and Trust; Galloway Woodlands. Married, three children. Ed: Glenalmond Sch; Heriot-Watt University.

CHALLENGERS
Richard Arkless (SNP) MP for Dumfries and Galloway 2015-17. Previously worked as a solicitor in consumer litigation for ULL, and now runs own online-based business, LED Warehouse UK. Married, two children. **Daniel Goodare** (Lab) A&E doctor at Galloway Community Hospital and specialist in remote medicine. Worked as a doctor around the world, including in Calais refugee camp and also in Antarctica.

CONSTITUENCY PROFILE
This, the southernmost constituency in Scotland, is a large, sparse seat where more than half the population is aged over 45. There remains a significant fishing industry. Created in 2005 from parts of the longstanding Conservative seat of Galloway and Dumfries, which had been Labour since 1997, it was held by Labour until 2015, when it was won by the SNP in their 2015 landslide.

EU REFERENDUM RESULT
45.1% Leave   Remain 54.9%

Dumfriesshire, Clydesdale & Tweeddale

CONSERVATIVE HOLD MAJORITY 9,441 (19.3%)

DAVID MUNDELL
BORN May 27, 1962
MP 2005-

	Electorate	Turnout %	from 2010 %	Change
	67,672	72.35		
*D Mundell C	24,177	49.38	+9.56	
M McAllan SNP	14,736	30.10	-8.19	
D Beattie Lab	8,102	16.55	+1.76	
J Ferry LD	1,949	3.98	+1.31	

Qualified solicitor; legal adviser, BT. MSP for South of Scotland 1999-2005. The only Scottish Conservative MP between 2015 and 2017 elections. Came out as gay in 2016, making him the first openly gay Conservative cabinet minister. SoS for Scotland 2015-; shadow SoS for Scotland 2005-10. Presbyterian. Member, Scottish affairs select cttee 2005-10. Cllr, Dumfries and Galloway 2986-87 (for the SDP); Annandale and Eskdale 1984-86. Divorced, one daughter, two sons. Ed: Lockerbie Academy; University of Edinburgh (LLB law); Strathclyde University Business School (MBA).

CHALLENGERS
Mairi McAllan (SNP) Trainee commercial solicitor. Contested Scottish parliament 2016. Campaigner for Scottish independence. **Douglas Beattie** (Lab) Communications officer, Student Action for Refugees; media and parliamentary officer, ForcesWatch; press officer, Unite the Union. Journalist: BBC News; PA; STV Group. Cllr, Camden BC 2014-. Backed Yes campaign 2014. Criticised in 2017 for saying that British troops have blood on their hands over Northern Ireland. **John Ferry** (LD) Financial journalist.

CONSTITUENCY PROFILE
Mostly further inland and much less coastal than its neighbouring seat of Dumfries and Galloway, Dumfriesshire, Clydesdale and Tweeddale is also huge and sparse with a relatively old population. A large number of residents are employed in fishing. It is more affluent than its neighbour. Contains Lockerbie, site of the 1988 bombing. Held by the Conservatives since its creation in 2005, this was one of the three Scottish seats that wasn't won by the SNP in 2015.

EU REFERENDUM RESULT
44.6% Leave   Remain 55.4%

Dunbartonshire East

LIBERAL DEMOCRAT GAIN MAJORITY 5,339 (10.3%)

JO SWINSON
BORN Feb 5, 1980
MP 2017-; 2005-2015

	Electorate	Turnout %	from 2010 %	Change
	66,300	78.13		
J Swinson LD	21,023	40.58	+4.27	
*J Nicolson SNP	15,684	30.28	-9.99	
S Mechan C	7,563	14.60	+5.99	
C McNally Lab	7,531	14.54	+2.23	

Marketing manager. Was the bookies' favourite to replace Tim Farron as Lib Dem leader but opted to run for dep leader instead. Pro-EU. Deputy leader, LD 2017-. Contested: Dunbartonshire East 2015; Hull East 2001. PPS to Nick Clegg 2012. Min: employment relations and consumer affairs 2012-15; women and equalities 2012-15. Shadow min: FCO 2008-10; women and equalities 2007. Shadow SoS Scotland 2006-07. Opp whip 2005-06. Shadow spokeswoman CMS 2005-06. Dep leader of Scottish Lib Dems 2010-12. Founded own consultancy business specialising in workplace diversity 2015. Married to former Lib Dem MP Duncan Hames, one son. Ed: LSE (BSc management).

CHALLENGERS
John Nicolson (SNP) MP for Dubartonshire East 2015-17. Shadow SNP spokesman CMS 2015-17. Select cttees: CMS 2015-17; speaker's advisory on works of art 2015-17. BBC journalist; presented live coverage of 9/11. **Sheila Mechan** (C) Employment lawyer. Former general secretary of Scottish Secondary Teacher's Association. Was sacked after 11 days in the role. **Callum McNally** (Lab) Student. Former member, Scottish youth parliament.

CONSTITUENCY PROFILE
The seat lies just north of Glasgow. The population centre Bearsden is effectively a suburb of the city. The constituency is one of the more affluent seats in Scotland, with average incomes higher than in any of the other Glasgow seats. East Dunbartonshire had been held by Jo Swinson from its creation in 2005 and was won by the SNP in 2015, albeit with one of their smaller majorities.

EU REFERENDUM RESULT
26.9% Leave   Remain 73.1%

Dunbartonshire West

SNP HOLD MAJORITY 2,288 (5.2%)

MARTIN DOCHERTY-HUGHES
BORN Jan 21, 1971
MP 2015-

	Electorate	Turnout %	from 2010 %	Change
	67,602	65.21		
*M Docherty-Hughes SNP	18,890	42.85	-16.20	
J Mitchell Lab	16,602	37.66	+6.32	
P Hutton C	7,582	17.20	+10.17	
R Plenderleith LD	1,009	2.29	+0.69	

Left school with no qualifications and worked in a sweet factory. Later went to university and spent a decade in voluntary sector: West Dunbartonshire community and volunteering services; Volunteer Scotland. Was Scotland's youngest cllr when elected to Clydebank DC 1992-96. Cllr, Glasgow CC 2012-15. Read out names of all 520 victims of Clydebank Blitz during Commons debate. Voted against Article 50 bill. SNP shadow spokesman, voluntary sector, 2016-. Took his partner's name when they married, 2016. Ed: Glasgow Coll of Food Technology (HND business administration); University of Essex (BA politics); Glasgow Sch of Art (MPhil).

CHALLENGERS
Jean-Anne Mitchell (Lab) MD, charity development consultancy business. Works with stillbirth charity Sands after losing one of her own children. Formerly Scottish head of sales, Mirror Group. Trained dentist. **Penny Hutton** (C) Volunteer, NSPCC Schools Service. Formerly: co-owner, marine retail business; adviser, Prince's Trust Scottish youth business programme. Contested local elections, 2017.

CONSTITUENCY PROFILE
West Dunbartonshire is less affluent and suffers much higher unemployment than its neighbour to the east. Clydebank, the largest town in the seat, was once the main home of Upper Clyde Shipbuilders, and BAE systems remains one of the largest employers in the area. The seat had been Labour since its reconfiguration in 2005, its main predecessor having elected Labour MPs since 1936, but was won by the SNP in their 2015 landslide.

EU REFERENDUM RESULT
38.0% Leave   Remain 62.0%

Dundee East

SNP HOLD MAJORITY 6,645 (15.5%)

STEWART HOSIE
BORN Jan 3, 1963
MP 2005-

Veteran SNP activist who spent 20 years in IT. First SNP youth convener 1986-89. SNP organisation convenor 2003-05; national secretary 1999-03. Contested: Dundee East 2001; Kirkcaldy 1997, 1992. Long-time ally of Alex Salmond. Advocates tax cuts and fiscal probity. Resigned as SNP deputy leader after extramarital affair came to light. He and his wife, Shona Robison, became first married couple to represent same seat at Westminster and Holyrood in 2005. Voted against triggering Article 50. SNP Westminster economy spokesman 2015-. Separated, one daughter. Ed:

	Electorate	Turnout %	from 2010 %	Change
	65,854	65.19		
*S Hosie SNP	18,391	42.84	-16.86	
E Price C	11,746	27.36	+12.41	
L Brennan Lab	11,176	26.03	+6.10	
C McIntyre LD	1,615	3.76	+0.88	

Carnoustie HS; Dundee Institute of Technology (HD computer studies).

CHALLENGERS
Eleanor Price (C) High-yield asset manager, Baillie Gifford. Previously Citi, UBS. **Lesley Brennan** (Lab) Economist and business analyst specialising in healthcare, turned professional politician. MSP for ten weeks after resignation of Richard Baker 2016. Parly asst, Neil Findlay MSP 2016-. Cllr, Dundee CC 2012-. Contested Dundee

East 2015 and rejected donation from Tony Blair during election campaign.

CONSTITUENCY PROFILE
Dundee was the authority which voted more for Scottish independence than any other, but both Dundee seats stretch slightly beyond the city itself, with Dundee East containing the towns of Monifieth and Carnoustie. Its residents are older on average than Dundee West's and home ownership is far higher. It has been a Labour seat for most of its history, but Dundee East has been held by the SNP since 2005, they having also held it from 1974 to 1987.

EU REFERENDUM RESULT
38.4% Leave   Remain 61.6%

Dundee West

SNP HOLD MAJORITY 5,262 (13.6%)

CHRIS LAW
BORN Oct 21, 1969
MP 2015-

Ponytailed financial adviser. Owns Mortgage Doctor loan brokering company. Once nearly drowned in Mozambique. Spent ten years leading motorcycle expeditions in the Himalayas. Trained French chef. Led flamboyant Spirit of Independence fire engine tour during referendum campaign, 2014; questioned by police but later cleared of all wrongdoing over financial arrangements in 2016. Romantic nationalist. Voted against Article 50 bill. Attempted to take over the front-bench seat traditionally occupied by Dennis Skinner at start of 2015 parliament. Member,

	Electorate	Turnout %	from 2010 %	Change
	62,644	61.74		
*C Law SNP	18,045	46.66	-15.26	
A Cowan Lab	12,783	33.05	+9.36	
D Cormack C	6,257	16.18	+7.56	
J Blain LD	1,189	3.07	+0.71	
S Dobson Ind	403	1.04		

Scottish affairs select cttee 2015-. Ed: Madras College; University of St Andrews (MA cultural and social anthropology).

CHALLENGERS
Alan Cowan (Lab) Development officer, Citizens Advice Scotland. Co-ordinator, Dundee Festival for Peace. Secretary, Tayside CND. Member, Co-operative Party. Formerly caseworker: Marlyn Glen MSP; Jim McGovern MP. GMB union activist. Corbynite. **Darren**

Cormack (C) Policy and communications asst, European Parliament. Formerly banking adviser, Lloyds group.

CONSTITUENCY PROFILE
Dundee West contains the University of Dundee, and has a much greater student population than Dundee East, and is a slightly more affluent seat, too. It does, however, have higher levels of unemployment than its neighbour. Home ownership is low, but social and private renting are higher than typical. The seat elected only Labour MPs from 1950 until 2015, the original Dundee seat having first turned red in 1906.

EU REFERENDUM RESULT
40.7% Leave   Remain 59.3%

Dunfermline & West Fife

SNP HOLD MAJORITY 844 (1.7%)

DOUGLAS CHAPMAN
BORN Jan 5, 1955
MP 2015-

Career in finance and business development. Spent 12 years in retail banking, then ran youth training scheme, TSB. Later education convener, Convention of Scottish Local Authorities. Cllr, Fife C 2007-15, 1997-98. Contested: Kirkcaldy & Cowdenbeath 2010; Dunfermline & Fife West 2006 by-election, 2005. Campaigns against defence cuts. Named parliamentarian of the month by road safety charity Brake, due to work on local campaigns 2016. Censured for taking selfie on Commons bench 2015. Voted against triggering Article 50. Member, defence select cttee 2015-. Married, two

	Electorate	Turnout %	from 2010 % Change
	75,672	67.41	
*D Chapman SNP	18,121	35.52	-14.75
C Hilton Lab Co-op	17,277	33.87	+2.12
B Hacking C	12,593	24.69	+12.84
J Calder LD	3,019	5.92	+1.92

children. Ed: West Calder HS; Edinburgh Napier University (BA personnel management).

CHALLENGERS
Cara Hilton (Lab Co-op) MSP 2013-16. Member: executive committee, Scottish Labour. Won Scottish Parliament by-election after SNP's Bill Walker was convicted of assaulting ex-wives. Cllr, Fife C 2012-13. Daughter of Cathy Peattie, MSP 1999-2011. **Belinda Hacking** (C) Clinical psychologist. Contested Dunfermline & Fife

West 2010. **James Calder** (LD) Customer support for Aviit, aircraft IT company. Competes in international fencing competitions. Cllr, Fife C 2017-.

CONSTITUENCY PROFILE
Consists of the town of Dunfermline, the smaller coastal towns of Rosyth and Inverkeithing to its south, and the more rural area around it. Affluent. Dunfermline seats have elected Labour MPs in almost every election since 1935. This incarnation, created in 2005, elected Labour MPs then and in 2010, but was also won by Scottish Lib Dem leader Willie Rennie in a 2006 by-election.

EU REFERENDUM RESULT

39.4 Leave	Remain 60.6%

Durham, City of

LABOUR HOLD MAJORITY 12,364 (25.6%)

ROBERTA BLACKMAN-WOODS
BORN Aug 16, 1957
MP 2005-

Social policy academic. Former professor and associate dean, Northumbria University; previously at Ruskin Coll, Oxford. Nominated Yvette Cooper for Labour leadership 2015; Owen Smith 2016. Resigned from front bench to protest Jeremy Corbyn; was reappointed in Oct 2016. Shadow min, int dev 2017-. Remainer, voted to trigger Article 50. Rarely rebels. Co-chairwoman, APPG on universities. Shadow min: housing 2015-17; CLG 2011-15; cabinet office 2010-11. PPS to: David Lammy 2008-10; Des Browne 2007-08; Hilary Armstrong 2006-07. Cllr, Oxford

	Electorate	Turnout %	from 2010 % Change
	71,132	67.94	
*R Blackman-Woods Lab	26,772	55.40	+8.11
R Lawrie C	14,408	29.82	+7.57
A Hopgood LD	4,787	9.91	-1.38
M Bint Ukip	1,116	2.31	-9.15
J Elmer Green	797	1.65	-4.23
J Clark Ind	399	0.83	-0.60
J Collings Young	45	0.09	

CC 1996-2000; Newcastle CC 1982-85. Member, Fabian Society. Married, one daughter. Ed: Methodist Coll, Belfast; Ulster University (BSc, PhD social sciences).

CHALLENGERS
Richard Lawrie (C) Vice-master and senior tutor, University Coll, Durham. Brexiteer. **Amanda Hopgood** (LD) Cllr, Durham CC 2008-; Lib Dem leader

2013-. Trustee, Xcel academy partnership. **Malcolm Bint** (Ukip) Contested North Durham 2015.

CONSTITUENCY PROFILE
The seat consists of the City of Durham and a significant rural expanse, including mining collieries, surrounding the city. It contains the medieval city centre, the University of Durham's many colleges, most of its 18,000 students, and about 7,000 residents who work in the education sector. Its constituents earn the highest average pay of any of the County Durham seats and the constituency has elected only Labour MPs since 1935.

EU REFERENDUM RESULT

43.3% Leave	Remain 56.7%

Durham North

LABOUR HOLD MAJORITY 12,939 (29.9%)

KEVAN JONES
BORN Apr 25, 1964
MP 2001-

Campaign co-ordinator in Stockton South 1997. Officer, GMB 1999; led the union's campaign for compensation for the industrial victims of asbestos. His private member's bill, the Christmas Day Trading Act 2004, got passed by parliament. Jeremy Corbyn critic. Spoke in parliament about his struggles with depression and the stigmatisation of mental illness 2012. Was told by Ken Livingstone he "might need some psychiatric help" in 2015 after Jones criticised Livingstone's appointment as a chairman of Labour's defence review. Shadow min:defence 2010-16; veterans

	Electorate	Turnout %	from 2010 %	Change
	66,970	64.63		
*K Jones Lab	25,917	59.88	+4.96	
L Glossop C	12,978	29.98	+9.05	
K Rollings Ukip	2,408	5.56	-10.39	
C Martin LD	1,981	4.58	-0.52	

2010. Cllr, Newcastle CC 1990-2001. Ed: Newcastle Polytechnic, University of Southern Maine (BA government and public policy).

CHALLENGERS
Laetitia Glossop (C) Partner, Crewdson and Parters 2016-. Contested Durham North 2015. **Kenneth Rollings** (Ukip) Rep for the RMT trade union for five years. Stood in the Durham CC election 2013. **Craig Martin** (LD) Scout leader, teacher and finance worker for a further education

provider. Contested Durham PCC 2016.

CONSTITUENCY PROFILE
Slightly smaller and denser than the City of Durham, the biggest towns in Durham North are Stanley, once a mining town, and Chester-le-Street, with populations of 32,000 and 24,000 respectively, both only slightly closer to Durham than to nearby Gateshead or Sunderland. Unemployment in the seat is above average, and pay is below the regional average. The seat has elected only Labour MPs since 1906 if you include its predecessor, Chester-le-Street.

EU REFERENDUM RESULT

60.3% Leave	Remain 39.7%

Durham North West

LABOUR HOLD MAJORITY 8,792 (18.4%)

LAURA PIDCOCK
BORN Jun 18, 1988
MP 2017-

Fresh-faced and keen activist who has spoken at rallies with Jeremy Corbyn and John McDonnell. Manager of education team at UK's largest anti-racism charity. Cllr, Northumberland CC 2013-17. Community campaigner and trade unionist who has taken over the seat held since 2010 by retired Labour MP Pat Glass. Worked as mental health support worker during her degree. Criticised parliament in her maiden speech, saying: "I believe that the intimidating nature of this place is not accidental. The clothes, the language, and the obsession

	Electorate	Turnout %	from 2010 %	Change
	71,982	66.55		
L Pidcock Lab	25,308	52.83	+5.95	
S Hart C	16,516	34.48	+11.08	
O Temple LD	3,398	7.09	-2.00	
A Breeze Ukip	2,150	4.49	-12.48	
D Horsman Green	530	1.11	-2.55	

with hierarchies, control and domination are symbolic of the system at large." Ed: Manchester Metropolitan University (BA politics).

CHALLENGERS
Sally-Ann Hart (C) Solicitor and magistrate. Cllr, Rother DC, in the southeast of England. Cabinet member for tourism and culture. **Owen Temple** (LD) Cllr, Durham CC, 2008-. Contested: Durham North West 2015, 2010; European elections 2014.

Chartered financial planner, former schoolteacher. **Alan Breeze** (Ukip) Website developer and CCTV installer.

CONSTITUENCY PROFILE
A large, sparse constituency, mostly to the City of Durham's west, and with a large area of the North Pennines in its west. Its biggest town, Consett, was once home to a large steel industry which declined in the 1970s and 1980s. Durham North West has elected Labour MPs since its creation in 1950. Both Theresa May and Tim Farron stood against former MP and one-time chief whip Hilary Armstrong in this seat in 1992.

EU REFERENDUM RESULT

55.0% Leave	Remain 45.0%

Dwyfor Meirionnydd

PLAID CYMRU HOLD MAJORITY 4,850 (16.0%)

LIZ SAVILLE ROBERTS
BORN Dec 16, 1964
MP 2015-

Former news reporter in London and North Wales, and further education lecturer. Plaid Cymru's first female MP. Elected party's leader in House of Commons 2017. Voted against triggering Article 50. Shadow PC spokeswoman 2015-: energy and natural resources; local govt; women and equalities; environment, food and rural affairs; health; education; home affairs. Member, Welsh affairs select cttee 2015–17. Cllr, Gwynedd CC 2004–15. Originally from London, learnt Welsh at University. Married, two daughters. Ed: University of Aberystwyth (BA languages)

	Electorate	Turnout %	from 2010 %	Change
	44,699	67.89		
*L Saville Roberts PC	13,687	45.10	+4.25	
N Fairlamb C	8,837	29.12	+6.46	
M Norman Lab	6,273	20.67	+7.17	
S Churchman LD	937	3.09	-0.90	
F Wykes Ukip	614	2.02	-8.79	

CHALLENGERS
Neil Fairlamb (C) Clergyman. Co-ordinates local meals-on-wheels service. Contested Ynys Mon assembly seat in 2013 by-election. Former Classics teacher. **Mathew Norman** (Lab) Lawyer specialising in defending workers with permanent medical injuries due to workplace negligence. **Stephen Churchman** (LD) Former railway track design engineer and shopkeeper. Seasoned campaigner. Cllr: Gwynedd CC 2004-; Barking

and Dagenham BC 1994-1999, 1986-1990. Contested: Dwyfor Meirionnydd 2010; Barking 1992.

CONSTITUENCY PROFILE
The main body of this seat is covered by Snowdonia National Park, making it a mountainous and isolated area. The constituency is mostly rural and its largest towns Porthmadog and Pwllheli are home to fewer than 5,000 people each. More than one in four residents are aged 65 or above, and nearly half of residents own their homes outright. The seat, and its main predecessor Meirionnydd Nant Conwy, have elected Plaid Cymru MPs since 1983.

EU REFERENDUM RESULT

47.4% Leave | Remain 52.6%

Ealing Central & Acton

LABOUR HOLD MAJORITY 13,807 (24.9%)

RUPA HUQ
BORN Apr 2, 1972
MP 2015-

Former researcher and lecturer at Kingston University. Deputy mayor, Ealing BC 2010-11. Contested Chesham & Amersham 2005. Voted against triggering Article 50 after 71 per cent of her constituency voted to Remain in the EU. Initially nominated Jeremy Corbyn in leadership election but later supported Yvette Cooper. Shadow minister, crime and prevention 2016-. Select cttees: regulatory reform 2015-17; justice 2015-16. DJ. Sister of broadcaster Konnie Huq. Married, one son. Ed: Montpelier Primary Sch; Ealing & Notting Hill High Sch; Newnham Coll, Cambridge (BA

	Electorate	Turnout %	from 2010 %	Change
	74,200	74.58		
*R Huq Lab	33,037	59.70	+16.47	
J Morrissey C	19,230	34.75	-7.95	
J Ball LD	3,075	5.56	-0.55	

political & social sciences and law); University of East London (PhD cultural studies).

CHALLENGERS
Joy Morrissey (C) Has done humanitarian work in Albania, China, Kosovo, India. Now works for the Centre for Social Justice. Cllr, Ealing BC 2014-; shadow portfolio holder for health and adult social services. Staffer for Will Quince MP. Polyglot. **Jon Ball** (LD) MD film and TV production & lighting business. Cllr Ealing Common ward 2002-. Contested: Ealing Central and

Acton 2015, 2010; Hayes and Harlington 2005.

CONSTITUENCY PROFILE
While all three Ealing seats are very ethnically diverse, Ealing Central's residents are the most likely to be white, although a significant proportion of these are non-British. About 15 per cent of residents were born in EU nations outside the UK. It is also by far the most affluent Ealing constituency, the only one whose residents earn more than the London average. Created in 2010, the seat was gained by the Conservatives from Labour, but Labour won it back in 2015 with a majority of 274.

EU REFERENDUM RESULT

29.2% Leave | Remain 70.8%

Ealing North

LABOUR HOLD MAJORITY 19,693 (37.5%)

STEVE POUND
BORN Jul 3, 1948
MP 1997-

Public service career including spells as sailor, bus conductor and hospital porter. Went to LSE with trade union sponsorship; defeated Lord (Daniel) Finkelstein of Pinner for students' union presidency. Critical Blairite. Nominated Yvette Cooper for leader 2015; Owen Smith 2016. Christened "Jester of Westminster" by Quentin Letts for his wit. Sponsored private members' bill authorising people to use any means to defend homes from intruders, as suggested by *Today* programme listeners 2004. Voted against Article 50. Shadow NI min 2010-. Resigned

	Electorate	Turnout %	from 2010 %	Change
	74,764	70.24		
*S Pound Lab	34,635	65.95	+10.82	
I Grant C	14,942	28.45	-1.27	
H Sanders LD	1,275	2.43	-0.82	
P Mcilvenna Ukip	921	1.75	-6.33	
M Hans Green	743	1.41	-1.96	

as PPS three times to vote against foundation hospitals, Trident renewal and Gurkha visa restrictions. Voted against gay marriage. Catholic. Married, three children, one long-lost daughter who tracked him down in 2005. Ed: LSE (Dip trade union studies; BSc economics).

CHALLENGERS
Isobel Grant (C) Chartered civil engineer. Cllr, Ealing BC 2010-14. **Humaira Sanders** (LD) City fund manager and analyst.

Peter Mcilvenna (Ukip) Devout Christian. Chairman, Ealing & Hounslow Ukip. **Meena Hans** (Green) Adult education tutor. Contested: Ealing North 2015; London Assembly 2016.

CONSTITUENCY PROFILE
More than a quarter of Ealing North's residents are of Asian descent; another sixth are black or mixed race. Its residents are far less likely than average to own their homes, and far more likely to rent. For much of its postwar history it was a swing seat, which Eden, Wilson, Thatcher and Blair gained from their opponents, but it is now a safe Labour seat.

EU REFERENDUM RESULT

46.3% Leave	Remain 53.7%

Ealing Southall

LABOUR HOLD MAJORITY 22,090 (48.9%)

VIRENDRA SHARMA
BORN Apr 5, 1947
MP 2007-

Previously a bus conductor and day services manager for people with learning disabilities. Indian born. Campaigned against closure of children's unit at Ealing Hospital. Campaigned to Remain in the EU; tweeted that "Brexit would be an act of arson on the foreign order". Nominated Yvette Cooper in leadership bid. PPS to Phil Woolas 2008-09. Resigned in protest at building of third runway at Heathrow. APPGs: chairman, Indo-British; Gurkha welfare; Nepal; tuberculosis group; hepatitis group; British Hindus. Cllr, Ealing BC 1982-2010. Two children. Ed: LSE (MA).

	Electorate	Turnout %	from 2010 %	Change
	65,188	69.25		
*V Sharma Lab	31,720	70.26	+5.29	
F Conti C	9,630	21.33	-0.34	
N Bakhai LD	1,892	4.19	+0.61	
P Ward Green	1,037	2.30	-2.34	
J Poynton Ukip	504	1.12	-2.97	
A Thiara WRP	362	0.80		

CHALLENGERS
Fabio Conti (C) NHS GP. Volunteer mentor to child refugeees. Cllr, Ealing BC 2015-. Chairman, Ealing Southall Conservative Association. Pledged to eliminate fly-tipping. **Nigel Bakhai** (LD) Institute of Logistics and Transport, global printing company. Contested Ealing Southall 2010, 2007 by-election, 2005. Opposed to Heathrow expansion. **Peter Ward** (Green) Barrister, anti-

discrimination law; property developer. Chairman, Ealing Green Party. **John Poynton** (Ukip) Chartered accountant and management consultant.

CONSTITUENCY PROFILE
Southall is one of the few seats in the country where more than half of residents are of Asian descent, about two thirds of this half being Indian or of Indian descent. Indeed, it is the seat with the largest proportion of Sikh residents in Britain. Its socio-economic profile is more similar to Ealing North than Central, and the seat has elected Labour MPs at every election since 1983.

EU REFERENDUM RESULT

41.8% Leave	Remain 58.2%

Easington

LABOUR HOLD MAJORITY 14,892 (41.0%)

GRAHAME MORRIS
BORN Mar 13, 1961
MP 2010-

Medical lab scientific officer and former constituency worker to predecessor John Cummings. One of 16 Labour MPs who wrote to Ed Miliband in 2015 demanding greater opposition to austerity. Pioneered recognition of Palestine statehood as party policy. Nominated Jeremy Corbyn as leadership candidate 2015. Received treatment for lymphatic cancer 2016. Shadow SoS CLG 2016. Cllr, Easington DC 1987-2002. Chairman: Labour Friends of Palestine and the Middle East; parly Unite Group. Two sons. Ed: Newcastle Polytechnic BTec higher national medical laboratory sciences).

	Electorate	Turnout %	from 2010 %	Change
	62,385	58.29		
*G Morris Lab	23,152	63.67	+2.63	
B Campbell C	8,260	22.71	+9.78	
S McDonnell NE Party	2,355	6.48	+4.14	
A Roberts Ukip	1,727	4.75	-14.00	
T Hancock LD	460	1.26	-1.14	
M Warin Green	410	1.13	-0.99	

CHALLENGERS
Barney Campbell (C) Army officer 2006-12; author of *Rain*. Policy and comms officer, Conservative Middle East council 2013-14. **Susan McDonnell** (NE Party) Formed the North East Party 2014. Ex-Labour Party member. Cllr, Durham CC 2017-. **Allyn Roberts** (Ukip) Telecomms company project manager. **Tom Hancock** (LD) Local campaigner in Gateshead and Berwick-upon-Tweed. Involved in Yes to Fairer Votes. **Martie Warin** (Green) Data management asst, Durham and Darlington NHS trust. Cllr, Easington Village PC 2013-.

CONSTITUENCY PROFILE
A coastal Durham seat between Sunderland and Hartlepool, Easington was once a thriving area for coalmining, and the area is partly known for having inspired the film *Billy Elliot*. The largest towns are Seaham and Peterlee, which have populations of about 20,000 each. The seat is poorer, in terms of earnings, than the regional average. It has elected Labour MPs at every election since 1950.

EU REFERENDUM RESULT

66.0% Leave   Remain 34.0%

East Ham

LABOUR HOLD MAJORITY 39,883 (70.4%)

STEPHEN TIMMS
BORN Jul 29, 1955
MP 1997-

Former manager at Logica 1978-86; Ovum 1986-94. Survived stabbing in constituency in 2010. Threatened to resign from front bench if party did not grant free vote on same-sex marriage act 2013. Labour Party's faith envoy. Only MP to poll more than 40,000 votes in 2015 GE. Shadow min, work and pensions 2010-2015. Evangelical Christian. Married. Ed: Emmanuel Coll, Cambridge (MA mathematics, MPhil operational research).

CHALLENGERS
Kirsty Finlayson (C) Trainee solicitor. Worked for MP Anne Milton. Dep chairwoman,

	Electorate	Turnout %	from 2010 %	Change
	83,827	67.56		
*S Timms Lab	47,124	83.21	+5.64	
K Finlayson C	7,241	12.79	+0.72	
D Oxley Ukip	697	1.23	-3.78	
G Williams LD	656	1.16	-0.48	
C Oti-Obihara Green	474	0.84	-1.65	
C Afzal Friends	311	0.55		
M Rahman Ind	130	0.23		

Vincent Square Conservatives and Bethnal Green & Bow Conservatives. **Daniel Oxley** (Ukip) Former chairman, Ukip in Newham. **Glanville Williams** (LD) Founder, Inclusion Query; Country dir, Ian Dodds Consulting West Africa. Vice-chairman, ethnic minority Lib Dems 2016-. Contested Drury ward in Essex CC election 2017. **Chidi Oti-Obihara** (Green) Investment banker turned whistle-blower; now an independent financial consultant.

CONSTITUENCY PROFILE
East Ham is a young and ethnically diverse constituency. Less than a quarter of residents are aged over 45, and more than half of its residents are of Asian descent, including significant Indian, Pakistani and Bengali populations. This seat contains most of London City Airport. Stephen Timms won the largest numerical majority of any MP in 2010, and East Ham is one of three seats, all Labour, where more than 47,000 people voted for the party's candidate in 2017.

EU REFERENDUM RESULT

46.3% Leave   Remain 53.7%

East Kilbride, Strathaven & Lesmahagow

SNP HOLD MAJORITY 3,886 (7.1%)

LISA CAMERON
BORN Apr 8, 1972
MP 2015-

Former NHS consultant psychologist. Accredited risk assessor in historical abuse cases, Scottish court service. Chairwoman, APPG disabilities. Spoke out about receiving death threats in the aftermath of assassination of Jo Cox. Faced calls to resign after it emerged she owned a portfolio of ex-council houses; denied any wrongdoing and supported by SNP Westminster leadership. Remainer, voted against Article 50. SNP spokeswoman, climate change 2015-. Married, two daughters. Ed: University of Strathclyde (BA psychology); University of Stirling (MSc

	Electorate	Turnout %	from 2010 %	Change
	80,442	67.26		
*L Cameron SNP	21,023	38.86	-16.77	
M McAdams Lab	17,157	31.71	+3.38	
M McGeever C	13,704	25.33	+13.55	
P McGarry LD	1,590	2.94	+1.22	
J MacKay Ukip	628	1.16	-0.86	

psychology and health); University of Glasgow (PhD clinical psychology).

CHALLENGERS
Monique McAdams (Lab) Chief exec, East Kilbride Community Trust. Owner, marketing consultancy. Cllr, S Lanarkshire C 2017-. Endorsed by ex-footballers Ally McCoist and John Hartson. **Mark McGeever** (C) Media consultant: Scottish Fire and Rescue; Renfrewshire Council. Cllr, S Lanarkshire

C 2017-. **Paul McGarry** (LD) Marketing manager, St Andrew's First Aid. **Janice MacKay** (Ukip) Contested Rutherglen and Hamilton West 2015, 2010, 2005.

CONSTITUENCY PROFILE
This South Lanarkshire seat is located just south of Glasgow. The town of East Kilbride is home to 74,000 people, about three quarters of the seat's population. Nearly three quarters of its residents own their homes, but there is a significant imbalance towards those still paying for a mortgage compared with other seats. Until 2015 the seat had been Labour since its creation in 2005.

EU REFERENDUM RESULT

36.9% Leave   Remain 63.1%

East Lothian

LABOUR GAIN MAJORITY 3,083 (5.5%)

MARTIN WHITFIELD
BORN Aug 12, 1965
MP 2017-

Personal injury lawyer who retrained as a primary school teacher. Decided to stand so that an outsider wasn't parachuted into constituency. Took unpaid leave from teaching job to campaign. Chairman, Prestonpans Community Council 2016-17. Married, two sons. Ed: Huddersfield Polytechnic (BA business law); Newcastle Polytechnic (Law Society finals course); University of Edinburgh (PGCE).

CHALLENGERS
George Kerevan (SNP) MP for East Lothian 2015-17. Senior lecturer in economics; associate

	Electorate	Turnout %	from 2010 %	Change
	79,093	70.65		
M Whitfield Lab	20,158	36.08	+5.06	
*G Kerevan SNP	17,075	30.56	-11.98	
S Low C	16,540	29.60	+10.09	
E Wilson LD	1,738	3.11	+0.54	
M Allan Ind	367	0.66	+0.39	

editor, *The Scotsman*; chief exec, What If Productions. Contested Edinburgh East 2010. Cllr, Edinburgh CC 1984-96. Member, International Marxist Group. **Sheila Low** (C) Dir, Caledon Group 2012-; business development dir, Baker Tilly 2008-10. Former vice-chairwoman, Turning Point Scotland. School governor. **Elisabeth Wilson** (LD) Former social worker. Volunteers with Unesco. Founding member, Treesponsibility climate change

activism group. School governor. Quaker.

CONSTITUENCY PROFILE
Just to Edinburgh's east, East Lothian is a large coastal seat made up of fairly small towns, the largest of which are Musselburgh and Tranent, both in the constituency's west, and close to Edinburgh. The seat is fairly diverse, but average earnings are higher than in most other Scottish seats. East Lothian was solely a Labour seat from its creation in 1983, and its predecessors had regularly elected Labour MPs long before that, until the SNP landslide in 2015.

EU REFERENDUM RESULT

35.4% Leave   Remain 64.6%

Eastbourne

LIBERAL DEMOCRAT GAIN MAJORITY 1,609 (2.8%)

STEPHEN LLOYD
BORN Jun 15, 1957
MP 2017-; 2010-15

Former commodity broker, Cominco 1977-80; business development dir, Grass Roots Group 1998-2005; business development consultant, Federation of Small Businesses 2005-10. Contested: Eastbourne 2005; Beaconsfield 2001. MP for Eastbourne 2010-15. Voted against increasing tuition fees. Lobbied for reforms to student visas in 2010. Lib Dem spokesman for Northern Ireland 2010-15. Chairman, APPG: citizens advice; apprenticeships; microfinance. Founded APPG on religious education in schools. Sued for libel over election leaflets in 2011 (overturned in

	Electorate	Turnout %	from 2010 %	Change
	78,754	72.91		
S Lloyd LD	26,924	46.89	+8.71	
*C Ansell C	25,315	44.09	+4.52	
J Lambert Lab	4,671	8.13	+0.30	
A Hough Green	510	0.89	-1.67	

2013). Hearing impaired. Ed: St. George's Coll, Weybridge.

CHALLENGERS
Caroline Ansell (C) MP for Eastbourne 2015-17. French teacher. Cllr, Eastborne BC 2012-15. First female MP in Eastbourne. Voted Leave. Theresa May supporter. Criticised for accepting an intern from Christian Action Research and Education, which is thought to support gay conversion therapies. Christian. Married, three children. **Jake Lambert**

(Lab) Secondary school teacher. Contested Eastbourne 2015. President, East Sussex National Union of Teachers.

CONSTITUENCY PROFILE
Coastal Sussex and Victorian seaside town stereotyped for its geriatric population. Indeed, about a quarter of its residents are aged 65 or over, compared to about a sixth in the UK overall. It is also a notable south coast tourist destination. Eastbourne was won by the Lib Dems at a 1990 by-election after the assassination of Ian Gow by the IRA. It has flipped between the Conservatives and the Lib Dems at recent elections.

EU REFERENDUM RESULT
57.5% Leave   Remain 42.5%

Eastleigh

CONSERVATIVE HOLD MAJORITY 14,179 (24.8%)

MIMS DAVIES
BORN Jun 2, 1975
MP 2015-

Media, events and communications background, including as radio producer and journalist for West Sussex Today and the BBC. Worked with the police on road safety communications in the county. Shareholder of New River Retail, a company which owns 29 shopping centres. Voted to Leave the EU. PPS to Matt Hancock 2016-17. Cllr: Eastleigh BC 2015-; Haywards Heath TC 2012-15; Mid Sussex DC 2011-15. Chairwoman, southern region CWO. Select cttee, women and equalities 2015-16. First in family to go to university. Separated, two daughters. Ed: Royal Russell

	Electorate	Turnout %	from 2010 %	Change
	81,213	70.53		
*M Davies C	28,889	50.43	+8.16	
M Thornton LD	14,710	25.68	-0.11	
J Payne Lab	11,454	20.00	+7.06	
M Jones Ukip	1,477	2.58	-13.25	
R Meldrum Green	750	1.31	-1.42	

Sch; Swansea University (BA politics with international relations).

CHALLENGERS
Mike Thornton (LD) MP for Eastleigh 2013-15, elected in by-election following charge of sitting MP Chris Huhne for perverting the course of justice. Worked in hotel management, retail and marketing. Cllr: Eastleigh BC 2007-13; Bishopstoke PC 2008-13. Lib Dem transport spokesman.

Jill Payne (Lab) Customer service officer at local bank, Unite workplace representative. Corbynite. **Malcolm Jones** (Ukip) Builder. Contested Fareham 2015.

CONSTITUENCY PROFILE
This Hampshire seat consists of several towns to the north and east of Southampton, and is younger and more affluent than the UK average. It was the seat of the Lib Dem cabinet minister Chris Huhne until he resigned after pleading guilty to perverting the course of justice, causing a 2013 by-election won by the Lib Dems. They lost it to the Conservatives in 2015.

EU REFERENDUM RESULT
54.3% Leave   Remain 45.7%

Eddisbury

CONSERVATIVE HOLD MAJORITY 11,942 (23.3%)

ANTOINETTE SANDBACH
BORN Feb 15, 1969
MP 2015-

Former barrister; left the Bar to run family farm in Elwy Valley, north Wales. Previously researcher for David Jones MP. Taught English in Indonesia. North Wales AM 2011-15, resigned after election to Westminster. Contested Delyn 2010. Gave emotional Commons speech about sudden death of her five-day-old baby, Sam. Campaigns to increase funding for Cheshire schools and re-route HS2. Member, 1922 exec cttee. Remainer, voted to trigger Article 50. One rebellion, voting to require parly approval for new post-Brexit deal with EU. Divorced, remarried, one

	Electorate	Turnout %	from 2010 % Change
	70,272	73.03	
*A Sandbach C	29,192	56.88	+5.85
C Reynolds Lab	17,250	33.61	+9.98
I Priestner LD	2,804	5.46	-3.59
J Bickley Ukip	1,109	2.16	-10.04
M Green Green	785	1.53	-1.90
M Hill Pirate	179	0.35	

daughter, one deceased son. Ed: University of Nottingham (LLB law).

CHALLENGERS
Cathy Reynolds (Lab) Dir of business consultancy, Oakleaf. Former social services dir, Cheshire CC. **Ian Priestner** (LD) Dir of renewable energy firm ASC. Former oil and gas lobbyist and SDP press officer. Cllr, Utkinton PC 2013-. Married, one child. **John Bickley** (Ukip)

Retired IT tycoon; used EU cash for business that went bust. Retweeted cartoon saying "if you want a jihadi for a neighbour, vote Labour" 2017.

CONSTITUENCY PROFILE
Eddisbury is the largest and sparsest constituency in Cheshire. About half of its residents are aged 45 or above. Earnings are about 20 per cent more than the regional average. About three quarters of residents own their homes, and the seat has only elected Conservative MPs since it was reconstituted in 1983, although Labour came within 1,200 votes at its electoral peak in 1997.

EU REFERENDUM RESULT
52.2% Leave   Remain 47.8%

Edinburgh East

SNP HOLD MAJORITY 3,425 (7.9%)

TOMMY SHEPPARD
BORN Mar 6, 1959
MP 2015-

Outspoken SNP spokesman. As member of the standards cttee, heavily criticised Osborne's decision to take second job. Select cttees: privileges 2015-; standards 2015-. Cllr, Hackney BC 1986-93; as Labour. Former deputy general secretary of Scottish Labour Party. Deputy leader of local authority for second term. Edinburgh South organiser of the Yes Scotland campaign. Contested Bury St Edmunds 1992. Vice-president of NUS for two terms. Member, Scottish Comedy Agency. Joined SNP in Sep 2014. Founded and ran Edinburgh comedy club and fringe stalwart The Stand.

	Electorate	Turnout %	from 2010 % Change
	65,896	66.05	
*T Sheppard SNP	18,509	42.53	-6.72
P King Lab	15,084	34.66	+4.75
K Mackie C	8,081	18.57	+8.65
T Gray LD	1,849	4.25	+1.43

Ed: University of Aberdeen (BA politics and sociology).

CHALLENGERS
Patsy King (Lab) Community worker in East Lothian. Born and brought up in Craigmillar. **Katie Mackie** (C) Cllr, Musselburgh 2017-. Formerly worked for a brewing company. Public affairs adviser, Scottish Grocers' Federation 2008-11. **Tristan Gray** (LD) Retraining as software specialist. Cttee assistant, Scottish Parliament 2016-. Women's rugby coach.

CONSTITUENCY PROFILE
This compact urban seat contains the Holyrood Palace, the site of the Scottish Parliament, as well as some of the city's major tourist attractions and most of the University of Edinburgh's campus. It has the largest population aged 16 to 24 and student population of any Edinburgh seat. Its residents are also much more likely than average to rent their homes in the private sector. The seat was Labour from its creation in 1974 until the SNP landslide in 2015. Labour veteran Gavin Strang was the constituency's MP for over 40 years.

EU REFERENDUM RESULT
27.6% Leave   Remain 72.4%

Edinburgh North & Leith

SNP HOLD MAJORITY 1,625 (2.9%)

DEIDRE BROCK
BORN Dec 8, 1961
MP 2015-

Popular local figure in the Edinburgh North and Leith area. Formerly deputy lord provost of Edinburgh C. Raised in Perth, Australia, moved to Scotland in 1996. Ran parly office of Rob Gibson MSP. Board member: Edinburgh International Festival Council; the Centre for the Moving Image (Edinburgh International Film Festival/Filmhouse); Creative Edinburgh. Select cttees: Scottish affairs 2016-; public accounts 2015-16. Cllr, Edinburgh CC 2007-15. Two daughters. Ed: John Curtin University (BA English); West Australian Academy of Performing Arts.

	Electorate	Turnout %	from 2010 % Change
	79,473	71.16	
*D Brock SNP	19,243	34.03	-6.90
G Munro Lab Co-op	17,618	31.15	-0.13
I McGill C	15,385	27.21	+11.04
M Veart LD	2,579	4.56	+0.02
L Slater Green	1,727	3.05	-2.36

CHALLENGERS
Gordon Munro (Lab Co-op) Cllr, Edinburgh CC 2003-; housing spokesman 2007-10; culture and leisure spokesman 2010-. **Iain McGill** (C) Dir, Harmony Employment Agency. Cllr, New Town & Broughton CC. Contested: Edinburgh C 2011; Edinburgh North and Leith 2010; Midlothian 2005; Airdrie and Shots 2007; Forth by-election 2008. **Martin Veart** (LD) Studying for MSc in renewable energy at Heriot-Watt

University. Formerly senior tech adviser, ICOE research. **Lorna Slater** (Green) Chartered engineer.

CONSTITUENCY PROFILE
North and Leith is the densest and most exclusively urban Edinburgh seat. Containing the Imperial Dock and the Port of Leith, it is the Edinburgh seat with the highest unemployment and the largest proportion of EU citizens. It is also the seat with the highest proportion of private renting in the city. It elected Labour MPs from 1950, if you include predecessor seats, but fell to the SNP in their 2015 landslide.

EU REFERENDUM RESULT

21.8% Leave   Remain 78.2%

Edinburgh South

LABOUR HOLD MAJORITY 15,514 (32.4%)

IAN MURRAY
BORN Aug 10, 1976
MP 2010-

Labour's only Scottish MP in the 2015 parliament. Shadow SoS for Scotland 2015-16; resigned from Jeremy Corbyn's shadow cabinet live on television after the EU referendum result. Minister, trade & investment 2011-15. PPS to Ivan Lewis 2010-15. Select cttees: foreign affairs 2016-; Scottish affairs 2016-; public accounts 2015-; arms export controls 2010-11; BIS 2010-11; environmental audit 2010-12. Came through recount in 2010 to hold off Lib Dem challenge and admitted he didn't expect to win. Cllr, Edinburgh CC 2003-10. Spokesman: finance; social inclusion. Partner, Aspen

	Electorate	Turnout %	from 2010 % Change
	64,553	74.11	
*I Murray Lab	26,269	54.91	+15.77
J Eadie SNP	10,755	22.48	-11.31
S Smith C	9,428	19.71	+2.21
A Beal LD	1,388	2.90	-0.80

Bar & Grill. Campaign manager, Edinburgh Pentlands 2001, 1997. USDAW. Supporter, Care for the Wild. Edinburgh-born and raised. Local businessman. Has partner. Ed: Wester Hailes Ed Centre; Edinburgh (social policy & law).

CHALLENGERS
Jim Eadie (SNP) MSP, Edinburgh Southern constituency 2011-16. Formerly ran own consultancy firm. Gay. Divorced, two sons. Ed: University of Strathclyde.

Stephanie Smith (C) Cllr, Edinburgh council. **Alan Beal** (LD) Energy consultant. Formerly convenor of Edinburgh South Lib Dems.

CONSTITUENCY PROFILE
Edinburgh South has the lowest unemployment of the Edinburgh constituencies. It has the second highest student population after Edinburgh East and is the most affluent seat in Edinburgh in terms of average income. It has been a Labour seat since it was won from the Conservatives in 1987. Indeed, it was the only Scottish seat to elect a Labour MP in 2015, despite Ian Murray's majority being just 316 in 2010.

EU REFERENDUM RESULT

22.2% Leave   Remain 77.8%

Edinburgh South West

SNP HOLD MAJORITY 1,097 (2.2%)

JOANNA CHERRY
BORN Mar 18, 1966
MP 2015-

Nicola Sturgeon devotee; forced to apologise after tweeting false claims about nurse who questioned the party leader in an election debate. SNP group leader, justice and home affairs 2015-. Member, cttee on exiting the EU 2016-. Co-founder and leader of Lawyers for Yes. Convenor, Faculty of Advocates Law Reform cttee 2013-15. Previously standing junior counsel to Scottish government 2003-08. Identifies as LGBT. Author. Legal advocate; took silk in 2009. Formerly tutor, University of Edinburgh. Member Scottish Women's Rights Centre Advisory Group.

Electorate	Turnout %	from 2010 %	Change
71,178	69.39		
*J Cherry SNP	17,575	35.58	-7.38
M Briggs C	16,478	33.36	+13.12
F Choudhury Lab	13,213	26.75	-0.44
A Mir LD	2,124	4.30	+0.58

Ed: University of Edinburgh (LLB law; LLM, Vans Dunlop scholar; Dip LP).

CHALLENGERS
Miles Briggs (C) MSP, Lothian region 2016-. Conservative spokesman for mental health and public health in Scottish parliament. Lived in Canada. Contested: Edinburgh South 2015; North East Fife 2010. **Foysol Choudhury** (Lab) Bangladeshi-born businessman. Chairman, Bangladesh Samity Edinburgh 2010-. **Aisha Mir** (LD) Financier. Panel member, Children's Hearings Scotland.

CONSTITUENCY PROFILE
Edinburgh South West contains a large rural area beyond Edinburgh. While smaller than East and South's, it still has a significant student population and more than five per cent of residents are of Asian descent. A significant proportion of residents rent privately. It has been Labour since its creation in 2005, having been the seat of Alistair Darling, the Chancellor and Better Together chairman, although it has been won by the SNP twice since Darling's retirement in 2015.

EU REFERENDUM RESULT

27.9% Leave   Remain 72.1%

Edinburgh West

LIBERAL DEMOCRAT GAIN MAJORITY 2,988 (5.7%)

CHRISTINE JARDINE
BORN Nov 24, 1960
MP 2017-

Background in journalism and broadcasting: BBC, *Deeside Piper*, *The Scotsman*; Scotland editor, Press Association. Later taught journalism at University of the West of Scotland and Scottish Centre for Journalism Studies. No 10 adviser during coalition government; liaised between Downing St and Scotland Office. Contested: Gordon 2015; Aberdeen Donside by-election 2013. LD spokeswoman, CMS 2017-. Widowed, one daughter. Ed: University of Glasgow (MA modern history & politics).

CHALLENGERS
Toni Giugliano (SNP) Policy

Electorate	Turnout %	from 2010 %	Change
71,500	73.84		
C Jardine LD	18,108	34.30	+1.18
T Giugliano SNP	15,120	28.64	-10.33
S Batho C	11,559	21.89	+9.62
M Telford Lab	7,876	14.92	+3.21
M Whittet Referendum	132	0.25	

and public affairs manager, Mental Health Foundation in Scotland. Italian-born. Previously worked for European University Association. Member, SNP national exec cttee. **Sandy Batho** (C) HR dir, Babcock International. Previously ran SME consultancy business. Board dir, Edinburgh Zoo. Contested Linlithgow and Falkirk East 2015. **Mandy Telford** (Lab) President, NUS 2002-04. Cllr, Cumbria CC 2013-15. Former adviser to Tessa Jowell. Ex-wife of John Woodcock MP.

CONSTITUENCY PROFILE
In many senses, Edinburgh West is the city's outlier seat, since it contains the least of Edinburgh itself and is dissimilar to the other four seats. It contains the greatest proportion of residents who are aged 65 or above, and is the least diverse, with nine in ten residents being white British. The seat also contains Edinburgh Airport and the coastal town of Queensferry. It elected Liberal Democrats at every election from 1997, other than 2015, and Conservatives from 1931.

EU REFERENDUM RESULT

28.8% Leave   Remain 71.2%

Edmonton

LAB CO-OP HOLD MAJORITY 21,115 (48.3%)

KATE OSAMOR
BORN Aug 15, 1968
MP 2015-

One of the 36 MPs to nominate Jeremy Corbyn as a candidate for the Labour leadership election 2015. Worked for *The Big Issue*. Spent 15 years in the NHS; Enfield NHS GP practice manager. Active in campaigns: Women for Refugee Women; Set Her Free, to end the detention of women asylum seekers in the UK. Campaigned to Remain in the EU. Supports fuller representation of BME communities in political bodies. NEC 2014-. Unite. Shadow SoS for international development 2016-. Select cttees: consolidation bills joint cttee 2015-17; petitions 2015-16;

	Electorate	Turnout %	Change from 2010 %
	65,705	66.48	
*K Osamor Lab Co-op	31,221	71.48	+10.06
G Daniels C	10,106	23.14	-0.98
N Sussman Ukip	860	1.97	-6.17
D Schmitz LD	858	1.96	-0.21
B Gill Green	633	1.45	-1.84

education 2015-16. One son. Ed: University of East London (third world studies).

CHALLENGERS
Gonul Daniels (C) Contested Edmonton 2015. Systems engineer. Created South primary school provision campaign West Enfield Action Team; vice-chairwoman, Ashmole Academy Trust. Conservative Women's Organisation member. **Nigel Sussman** (Ukip) Managing dir, High Court Collections. Former

commercial dir, JBW Group.
David Schmitz (LD) Barrister. School governor. Contested Tottenham 2010.

CONSTITUENCY PROFILE
A North London seat in the borough of Enfield. Over a quarter of the population is aged under 16. About half of its residents are white and a third are black or mixed race, but the seat also has a large European population, especially from the post-2000 accession states. The constituency was won by the Conservatives from 1983 but has become a Labour safe seat since the party gained Edmonton in 1997.

EU REFERENDUM RESULT

45.5% Leave   Remain 54.5%

Ellesmere Port & Neston

LABOUR HOLD MAJORITY 11,390 (22.4%)

JUSTIN MADDERS
BORN Nov 22, 1972
MP 2015-

Former employment solicitor 1998-2015, legally represented high-profile sports personalities, Ian Sibbit and Andrew Henderson. Shadow health minister 2015-. Member, petitions select cttee 2015. Campaigned to remain in the EU. Backs a rise in corporation tax. Cllr, Cheshire West and Chester BC 2008-15, Labour group leader 2011-14; Ellesmere Port and Neston BC 1998-2009, leader 2007-09. Opp and Labour leader, Cheshire West and Chester BC 2011-14. Contested Tatton 2005. Married, three sons. First in family to attend university. Ed: University of Sheffield (LLB law).

	Electorate	Turnout %	Change from 2010 %
	68,666	74.18	
*J Madders Lab	30,137	59.16	+11.40
N Jones C	18,747	36.80	+2.47
E Gough LD	892	1.75	-1.59
F Fricker Ukip	821	1.61	-10.36
S Baker Green	342	0.67	-1.45

CHALLENGERS
Nigel Jones (C) Parly assistant, Graham Evans MP 2013-. Cllr, Little Neston and Burton Ward, Cheshire West and Chester Council. Previously solicitor. **Ed Gough** (LD) Software engineer, worked on projects including NHS systems and car plants. Volunteer scout leader and canoe instructor. Interested in social equality and outdoor education. **Ed Fricker** (Ukip) Ex-mine rescue worker and cllr. Currently lifestyle coach. **Steven Baker**

(Green) Trade unionist educator and researcher.

CONSTITUENCY PROFILE
Just north of Chester, Ellesmere Port lies on the southern banks of the River Mersey, below the Wirral peninsula. The port town has a population of more than 55,000, compared with neighbouring Neston's 15,000. Its residents enjoy higher than average home ownership but lower than average median pay. The Stanlow oil refinery and the Vauxhall car plan are major employers. The seat was held by the Conservatives from its creation in 1983 until 1992, but has been a Labour seat since.

EU REFERENDUM RESULT

58.3% Leave   Remain 41.7%

Elmet & Rothwell

CONSERVATIVE HOLD MAJORITY 9,805 (16.5%)

ALEC SHELBROOKE
BORN Jan 10, 1976
MP 2010-

	Electorate	Turnout %	from 2010 % Change
	80,291	74.16	
*A Shelbrooke C	32,352	54.33	+5.93
D Nagle Lab	22,547	37.87	+4.15
S Golton LD	2,606	4.38	-0.19
M Clover Yorkshire	1,042	1.75	
D Brown Green	995	1.67	-0.51

Former kitchen and bathroom fitter. Later project manager, University of Leeds; became researcher and assistant to pro-vice-chancellor. Cllr, Leeds CC 2004-10. Contested Wakefield 2005. Conservative trade unionist. Member, Blue Collar Conservatism group. Campaigns for trade union reform. Introduced private members' bill to ban unpaid internships. Member, 1922 exec cttee. Loyal backbencher. Remainer, voted for Article 50. Partially deaf; received apology from BBC *Newsbeat* after they tweeted suggesting him leaning in his seat to listen to an inbuilt bench speaker was actually him resting his eyes in Commons. PPS to: Hugo Swire 2014-15; Mike Penning 2012-14; Theresa Villiers 2010-12. Married. Ed: Brunel University (BEng mechanical engineering).

CHALLENGERS
David Nagle (Lab) Manager, ISS cleaning and security services company. School governor. Cllr, Leeds CC 2012-. **Stewart Golton** (LD) Dir, The Fair Exchange social enterprise.

Cllr, Leeds CC 1998-; LD group leader. Contested Elmet & Rothwell 2015. **Matthew Clover** (Yorkshire) Manager in hospitality industry.

CONSTITUENCY PROFILE
Elmet and Rothwell is a large seat encompassing numerous towns to the east of Leeds. Nearly half of its residents are aged 45 or above and there are high levels of home ownership. Income is also well above average for Yorkshire and the Humber. The seat has elected a Conservative MP since its creation in 2010, although both of the seats from which it was made were Labour since 1997.

EU REFERENDUM RESULT
56.8% Leave | Remain 43.2%

Eltham

LABOUR HOLD MAJORITY 6,296 (13.6%)

CLIVE EFFORD
BORN Jul 10, 1958
MP 1997-

	Electorate	Turnout %	from 2010 % Change
	64,474	71.59	
*C Efford Lab	25,128	54.44	+11.82
M Hartley C	18,832	40.80	+4.42
D Hall-Matthews LD	1,457	3.16	+0.13
J Clarke BNP	738	1.60	

Former London taxi driver. Previously a youth worker who set up a job club for young people. Cllr, Greenwich BC 1986-1997. Contested Eltham 1992. Made a formal complaint to the Police Complaints Authority after Stephen Lawrence was murdered in constituency. Voted against UK intervention in Iraq. One of Jeremy Corbyn's nominees in 2015 Labour leadership contest but resigned from his position as shadow min for culture, media and sport 2011-16 amid mass resignations from the shadow cabinet. PPS to: John Healey 2009-10; Margaret Beckett 2008-09. Married, three daughters. Ed: Southwark College.

CHALLENGERS
Matt Hartley (C) Head of public affairs at Money Advice trust. Previously worked as a media manager and parly researcher for Chris White MP. Contested Greenwich and Woolwich 2015. Cllr, Greenwich BC 2014-; opposition leader. School governor. **David Hall-Matthews** (LD) International development academic, previously lecturer at the University of Leeds and policy adviser to the Lib Dems. Strategy and policy adviser for Bounce Back Project offering training to ex-offenders. Contested three general elections.

CONSTITUENCY PROFILE
Located in the borough of Greenwich, Eltham has leafy, Conservative Bromley to its south and compact, ever-Labour Lewisham to its west. One of the less diverse London seats, with about two thirds of its residents identifying as white British. It was won by the Conservatives when it was created in 1983, but it has been held by Labour since 1997.

EU REFERENDUM RESULT
51.8% Leave | Remain 48.2%

Enfield North

LABOUR HOLD MAJORITY 10,247 (21.1%)

JOAN RYAN
BORN Sep 8, 1955
MP 2015-; 1997-2010

	Electorate	Turnout %	from 2010 %	Change
	68,454	70.95		
*J Ryan Lab	28,177	58.02	+14.30	
N De Bois C	17,930	36.92	-4.45	
N Da Costa LD	1,036	2.13	-0.16	
D Cairns Ukip	848	1.75	-7.21	
B Linton Green	574	1.18	-1.64	

Former teacher and charity worker. Exposed in expenses scandal, claimed £173,691, the most of any MP in 2006-07 tax year; caught in second-homes controversy and asked to repay £5,121 in mortgage expenses. Remainer, but voted for Article 50. Urged constituents to vote for her whatever their misgivings about the Labour leadership. Backbencher, served on a number of select cttees. MP for Enfield North 1997-2010. Special rep to Cyprus 2007-08. Parly under-sec, home office 2006-07. Whip, Treasury 2003-06. Vice-chairwoman, Labour Party 2007-08. School governor.

Married. Ed: City of Liverpool Coll (BA history and sociology); Polytechnic of the South Bank (MSc sociology).

CHALLENGERS
Nick De Bois (C) MP Enfield North 2010-15. Managing dir of marketing communications business Rapiergroup. Contested: Enfield North 2005, 2001; Stalybridge & Hyde 1997. Secretary, 1922 backbench cttee 2012-15. Chairman, UK Events Industry Board. Divorced, remarried. Three daughters, one son from first marriage. **Nicholas Da Costa** (LD) Remainer. Works in healthcare. Contested GLA 2016.

CONSTITUENCY PROFILE
It is the northernmost seat in Greater London, and the M25 runs along its northern border. A young and diverse seat, where a quarter of its residents are too young to vote, nearly two thirds are aged under 45, and about a fifth are black or mixed race. Joan Ryan and Nick de Bois have faced off against each other for this constituency in every election since 2001, with de Bois victorious just once.

EU REFERENDUM RESULT
49.2% Leave   Remain 50.8%

Enfield Southgate

LABOUR GAIN MAJORITY 4,355 (9.0%)

BAMBOS CHARALAMBOUS
BORN Dec 2, 1967
MP 2017-

	Electorate	Turnout %	from 2010 %	Change
	65,137	74.19		
B Charalambous Lab	24,989	51.71	+12.70	
*D Burrowes C	20,634	42.70	-6.69	
P Morgan LD	1,925	3.98	+0.67	
D Flint Green	780	1.61	-2.08	

First MP of full Cypriot descent. Qualified solicitor. Housing lawyer for Hackney BC. Contested: Enfield Southgate 2015, 2010; Epping Forest 2005. Cllr, Enfield BC 2014-. Member of Unison and GMB. Trustee of charity Positive Women. Founder of Chair of Enfield Law Centre. Formerly director of London Arts Board. Married, two children. Ed: Liverpool Polytechnic (LLB law); University of North London (LPC law).

CHALLENGERS
David Burrowes (C) MP for Enfield Southgate, 2005-17. Solicitor and consultant. Campaigned to Leave the EU. Railed against government on cuts to housing benefits for under-22s. Faced embarrassment after campaigners accidentally canvassed in neighbouring constituency, Edmonton, during GE 2015. Contested Edmonton 2001. School governor. Christian. Married, six children. **Pippa Morgan** (LD) Heads the education and skills team for a business group. Previously worked for Vince Cable. **David Flint** (Green) Retired IT expert. Author of two IT books. Chairman, Enfield Green Party.

CONSTITUENCY PROFILE
Enfield Southgate is a diverse north London constituency with more than over 10,000 Muslims, 4,000 Hindus and 3,000 Jews. It's a semi-rural seat, including the Middlesex University campus and Trent Park. One of the less affluent seats in London, it has higher than UK average levels of income and of private renting. It is also the seat where the "Portillo moment" occurred in 1997, when Conservative defence secretary Michael Portillo lost his seat to Labour's Stephen Twigg.

EU REFERENDUM RESULT
37.9% Leave   Remain 62.1%

Epping Forest

CONSERVATIVE HOLD MAJORITY 18,243 (35.9%)

ELEANOR LAING
BORN Feb 1, 1958
MP 1997-

Former solicitor. Special adviser to John MacGregor 1989-94. Contested Paisley North 1987. Not active in Brexit campaign; voted to Leave but did not vote on Article 50. Actively involved in constitutional reform before becoming deputy speaker 2013-. Served in several positions on the shadow front bench when the Conservatives were in opposition. One son. Ed: St Columba's Sch; University of Edinburgh (BA LLB; first female president, Students' Union).

CHALLENGERS
Liam Preston (Lab) Parly and policy officer, YMCA

	Electorate	Turnout %	from 2010 % Change
	74,737	67.94	
*E Laing C	31,462	61.96	+7.19
L Preston Lab	13,219	26.03	+9.90
J Whitehouse LD	2,884	5.68	-1.31
P O'Flynn Ukip	1,871	3.68	-14.65
S Heap Green	1,233	2.43	-1.18
T Hall Young	110	0.22	+0.05

England. Former chairman for the British Youth Council. Member, Advisory Council on Youth, Council of Europe 2014-. Contested Brentwood and Ongar 2015. **Jon Whitehouse** (LD) Active local campaigner. Regional development officer for East England Lib Dems. Contested the seat in 2015. Served as councillor on Epping Forest DC, Epping Forest TC and Essex CC. Epping Town mayor 2012-13. **Patrick O'Flynn**

(Ukip) Formerly chief political commentator for the *Daily Express* and a key proponent of its anti-EU campaign. Outspoken critic of Nigel Farage. MEP for East of England 2014-. Contested Cambridge 2015.

CONSTITUENCY PROFILE
A west Essex constituency bordering London. The seat is characterised by higher than average levels of home ownership and income. It also has a fairly large Jewish population of nearly 4,000. This seat has been won by the Conservatives since its creation in 1974.

EU REFERENDUM RESULT

61.0% Leave   Remain 39.0%

Epsom & Ewell

CONSERVATIVE HOLD MAJORITY 20,475 (34.5%)

CHRIS GRAYLING
BORN Apr 1, 1962
MP 2001-

Formerly worked in television production and as European marketing director of communications firm Burson Marsteller. A post-Thatcherite thinker. Contested Warrington South 1997. Cllr, Merton BC 1998-2002. Broke ranks to campaign for Brexit; one of six ministers to support Leave. Campaign manager for Theresa May's leadership bid. SoS for transport 2016-; leader of the HoC 2015-16. MoS for DWP 2010-12. Controversial spell as justice sec 2012-15 included tribunal fees, banning books for prisoners, and a deal with Saudi Arabia to sell prison training.

	Electorate	Turnout %	from 2010 % Change
	80,029	74.06	
*C Grayling C	35,313	59.58	+1.29
E Mayne Lab	14,838	25.04	+9.52
S Gee LD	7,401	12.49	+3.73
J Baker Green	1,714	2.89	-0.81

Married, one daughter, one son. Ed: Royal Grammar Sch; Sidney Sussex Coll, Cambridge (BA history).

CHALLENGERS
Ed Mayne (Lab) Train driver for South West Trains. Former constituency officer for Robert Evans MEP. Cllr, Hounslow BC 2010-. **Steve Gee** (LD) Trained in quantity surveying. Contested: Epsom & Elwell 2015; Wimbledon 2005. Former chairman, Epsom & Ewell Liberal Dems. **Janice Baker**

(Green) English language teacher. Former politics lecturer in Africa.

CONSTITUENCY PROFILE
This seat in northern Surrey is most recognisable for hosting the Epsom Derby. It is an affluent constituency where many residents commute to work by train, and many working in managerial and professional-level jobs. Incomes are also well above average. The seat has high levels of property ownership and among one of the smallest proportion of residents renting from the council in the country. Conservative MPs have been elected since its creation in 1974.

EU REFERENDUM RESULT

47.8% Leave   Remain 52.2%

Erewash

CONSERVATIVE HOLD MAJORITY 4,534 (9.1%)

MAGGIE THROUP
BORN Jan 27, 1957
MP 2015-

Marketing consultant for her own business, Maggie Throup Marketing, and previously for a pharmaceutical company. Former medical laboratory scientist who is an advocate for wider use of diagnostic testing. Chairwoman of the APPG on obesity and member of the health select cttee 2015-17. Remain supporter. Rarely rebels. Contested: Solihull 2010, lost by fewer than 200 votes; Colne Valley 2005. Ed: Bradford Girls' GS; University of Manchester (BSc biology).

CHALLENGERS
Catherine Atkinson (Lab)

	Electorate	Turnout %	from 2010 %	Change
	72,991	68.20		
*M Throup C	25,939	52.11	+9.40	
C Atkinson Lab	21,405	43.00	+7.71	
M Garnett LD	1,243	2.50	-0.93	
R Hierons Green	675	1.36	-1.09	
R Dunn Ind	519	1.04		

Barrister specialising in personal injury and employment law. Awarded the Lincoln's Inn Gluckstein prize. Contested: Erewash 2015; Kensington and Chelsea 2005. Cllr, Kensington and Chelsea BC 2006-10. Chairwoman, Erewash Labour. **Martin Garnett** (LD) Medical background. Served on the strategy team for Engineering and Physical Sciences Research Council. Associate professor in pharmacy, University of Nottingham. Cllr, Draycott PC

1995-99. Contested Erewash 2015, 2010, 2005, 2001, 1997. **Ralph Hierons** (Green) Internet designer and website administrator. **Roy Dunn** (Ind) Retired rail engineer.

CONSTITUENCY PROFILE
A slim seat in Derbyshire, between Derby and Nottingham. Routine-level jobs are overrepresented among the workforce, partly due to the now declined iron works and coal mines. The average income in the seat is slightly higher than the East Midlands average, but lower than the UK average. Erewash has been a bellwether since its creation in 1983.

EU REFERENDUM RESULT

63.2% Leave   Remain 36.8%

Erith & Thamesmead

LABOUR HOLD MAJORITY 10,014 (22.5%)

TERESA PEARCE
BORN Feb 1, 1955
MP 2010-

Tax specialist, formerly worked at Inland Revenue and as a senior manager at PwC. On the left of the party. Campaigned to Remain in the EU. Served on the shadow cabinet as: SoS for CLG 2016-17; housing minister 2015-16. Select cttees: treasury 2011-15; work and pensions 2010-15; public accounts 2015. Backed as candidate in 2010 selection by predecessor John Austin, despite national party support for Georgia Gould, the daughter of Blair's pollster Lord (Philip) Gould. Cllr, Bexley BC 1998-2002. Lancashire-born but London-raised. Became single mother aged 18, two daughters.

	Electorate	Turnout %	from 2010 %	Change
	69,724	63.77		
*T Pearce Lab	25,585	57.54	+7.77	
E Baxter C	15,571	35.02	+7.60	
R Johnson Ukip	1,728	3.89	-13.40	
S Waddington LD	750	1.69	-0.59	
C Letsae Green	507	1.14	-1.07	
T Olodu CPA	243	0.55	-0.05	
D Oddiri Ind	80	0.18		

Ed: St Thomas More Sch, Eltham.

CHALLENGERS
Edward Baxter (C) Management consultant. Chairman, Cities of London and Westminster Conservative Association 2015-. **Ronnie Johnson** (Ukip) Chief exec of a regional charity working with young offenders. Formerly Labour. **Simon Waddington** (LD) Works in

international comms. Contested Erith and Thamesmead, 2015.

CONSTITUENCY PROFILE
This seat in southeast London is split between the boroughs of Bexley and Greenwich. About a third of its residents are black, Afro-Caribbean or mixed race, and about half are white British. A quarter of the population is aged under 15. Earnings are approximately a sixth less than the average in London and home ownership levels are much lower than the UK average. A fairly safe Labour seat. Pearce's majority was reduced to below 6,000 in 2010, but has recovered since.

EU REFERENDUM RESULT

54.6% Leave   Remain 45.4%

Esher & Walton

CONSERVATIVE HOLD MAJORITY 18,243 (38.9%)

DOMINIC RAAB
BORN Feb 25, 1974
MP 2010-

Former international lawyer at Linklaters who worked on secondment at the London-based human rights NGO Liberty. Has written books on human rights and the coalition, including *The Assault on Liberty – What Went Wrong With Rights*. Joined FCO in 2000, led team in The Hague to bring war criminals to justice. Chief of staff to shadow home and justice secretaries. Won Newcomer of the Year at *The Spectator's* Parliamentarian of the Year Awards 2011. Ed: Dr Challoners GS, Amersham; Lady Margaret Hall, Oxford (BA law); Jesus Coll, Cambridge (LLM law).

	Electorate	Turnout %	from 2010 %	Change
	80,938	73.94		
*D Raab C	35,071	58.61	-4.31	
L Hylands Lab	11,773	19.67	+6.99	
A Davis LD	10,374	17.34	+7.91	
O Palmer Green	1,074	1.79	-2.34	
D Ions Ukip	1,034	1.73	-8.01	
B Badger Loony	318	0.53		
D Reynolds Ind	198	0.33	-0.07	

CHALLENGERS
Lana Hylands (Lab) Law student at the Open University. Previously worked in intercultural dialogue and refugee support. Volunteer for health and disability charities. **Andrew Davis** (LD) Co-founded business which promotes environmental transport. Has campaigned against Heathrow expansion. Cllr, Elmbridge BC 2012-; deputy leader. **Olivia**

Palmer (Green) Charity worker. Contested Esher and Walton 2015.

CONSTITUENCY PROFILE
This north Surrey seat borders the southwest London seats of Twickenham and Kingston and Surbiton. It is well connected to London by rail and many of its residents are commuters with young children. In terms of income and socio-economic classification, it is one of the most affluent seats in the country, with finance, real estate and communications among the overrepresented industries. Esher and Walton is a safe Conservative seat.

EU REFERENDUM RESULT
41.6% Leave   Remain 58.4%

Exeter

LABOUR HOLD MAJORITY 16,117 (29.1%)

BEN BRADSHAW
BORN Aug 30, 1960
MP 1997-

Journalist for BBC Radio 4, won the Sony News Reporter Award 1993. BBC correspondent at fall of Berlin Wall. Member of the executive from 2000 to 2010, but failed to be elected to Ed Miliband's shadow cabinet and has spent the time since on backbenches and select cttees. Came last in 2015 Labour deputy leadership election. Jeremy Corbyn critic. Member, Lab Campaign for Electoral Reform. Remainer; member of Open Britain. Rarely rebels, but did vote against triggering Article 50. Civil partnership. Ed: Thorpe St Andrew Sch, Norwich; University of Sussex

	Electorate	Turnout %	from 2010 %	Change
	77,329	71.67		
*B Bradshaw Lab	34,336	61.95	+15.56	
J Taghdissian C	18,219	32.87	-0.23	
V Newcombe LD	1,562	2.82	-1.48	
J Levy Green	1,027	1.85	-4.61	
J West Ind	212	0.38		
J Bishop ND	67	0.12		

(BA German).

CHALLENGERS
James Taghdissian (C) Barrister at Colleton Chambers. Contested Cardiff West 2015. Cllr, Exeter CC 2008-12. Chairman of Exeter Central Conservatives. **Vanessa Newcombe** (LD) Campaigner for education and adult social services; involved in the construction of a local outdoor education centre. Governor of a school and children's centre.

Former cllr for Exeter CC and Devon CC. **Joe Levy** (Green) Works for University of Exeter student information. Fundraising officer, Exeter Green Party.

CONSTITUENCY PROFILE
Situated in southwest England, an area with historically few Labour MPs. The three largest employers in the city are the university, the Met Office's weather forecasting headquarters and the county council offices. The student population is large, at just under a fifth of all residents. Home to a significant Chinese community. It was held by the Conservatives almost continuously from 1911.

EU REFERENDUM RESULT
44.8% Leave   Remain 55.2%

Falkirk

SNP HOLD MAJORITY 4,923 (9.1%)

JOHN MCNALLY
BORN Feb 1, 1951
MP 2015-

Barber, owns a barbershop in his constituency. Cllr, Falkirk C 2005-15. Contested Falkirk 2010. Won the largest SNP majority in 2015; received the highest number of votes for any SNP candidate in election history. Member, environmental audit select committee 2015-17. Chairman of APPGs on flood prevention and the hair industry. Remainer: voted against triggering Article 50. Married, two children.

CHALLENGERS
Dr Craig Martin (Lab) Cllr, Falkirk C 2007-; former Labour leader. Was researcher to

Electorate	Turnout %	from 2010 % Change
82,240	65.43	
*J McNally SNP	20,952	38.94 -18.79
C Martin Lab	16,029	29.79 +4.71
C Laidlaw C	14,088	26.18 +14.04
A Reid LD	1,120	2.08 +0.05
D Pickering Green	908	1.69
S Martin Ukip	712	1.32 -1.71

Michael Connarty MP. MSP candidate, Falkirk East 2016. **Callum Laidlaw** (C) Corporate communications consultant. Campaigned against Scottish independence. Chairman, Tory Reform Group Scotland. MSP candidate 2016. Cllr, Edinburgh CC 2017-. **Austin Reid** (LD) Educational consultant who has worked in Zambia, Mexico and Bhutan. International observer, overseing Turkish elections, 2015. **Debra Pickering** (Green)

Trained psychotherapist who specialises in addictions.

CONSTITUENCY PROFILE
On the southern bank of the River Forth, Falkirk once had significant iron and steel industries, which have receded in recent years. Earnings are lower than the Scottish average. Falkirk was a strong Labour seat, having elected only Labour MPs from 1935 if you include its predecessors, but it was won by the SNP in 2015. Accusations of vote-rigging in the Labour selection process in Falkirk led the constituency party to be placed in special measures in 2015.

EU REFERENDUM RESULT
42.1% Leave   Remain 57.9%

Fareham

CONSERVATIVE HOLD MAJORITY 21,555 (37.8%)

SUELLA FERNANDES
BORN Apr 3, 1980
MP 2015-

Barrister specialising in planning and public law, No 5 Chambers. Defended Home Office in immigration cases and MoD in Guantanamo Bay inquiry. Former parly researcher to Dominic Grieve MP. Co-founder, Africa Justice Foundation. Set up a free school in Wembley. Contested Leicester East 2005. Ally of Boris Johnson. Leave campaigner. Became chairwoman of influential pro-Brexit European research group of backbenchers after incumbent Steve Baker made a Brexit minister following 2017 election. Daughter of Kenyan and Mauritian immigrants. Ed:

Electorate	Turnout %	from 2010 % Change
79,495	71.72	
*S Fernandes C	35,915	62.99 +6.89
M Randall Lab	14,360	25.19 +10.93
M Winnington LD	3,896	6.83 -1.97
T Blewett Ukip	1,541	2.70 -12.70
M Grindey Green	1,302	2.28 -1.61

Queen's Coll, Cambridge (MA law; president CUCA); Université de Paris Panthéon Sorbonne (LLM); New York Bar.

CHALLENGERS
Matthew Randall (Lab) 22-year-old history and politics graduate. Former chairman, Keele Labour Students. Volunteered in Africa with International Citizen Service. **Matthew Winnington** (LD) Support worker at local children and families charity. Former manager, DWP.

Cllr, Portsmouth CC, 2012-. Contested Fareham 2015.

CONSTITUENCY PROFILE
Fareham is a coastal Hampshire constituency named after its largest town. About four in five homes are owned or mortgaged. There are low levels of social housing. It is a relatively affluent constituency where jobs are skewed towards managerial and professional occupations over low-skilled and routine jobs. However, incomes are lower than the southeast average. Since its creation in 1885, Fareham has been held by the Conservatives with sizeable majorities.

EU REFERENDUM RESULT
55.5% Leave   Remain 44.5%

Faversham & Kent Mid

CONSERVATIVE HOLD MAJORITY 17,413 (35.0%)

HELEN WHATELY
BORN June 23, 1976
MP 2015-

Electorate	Turnout %	Change from 2010 %		
76,008	65.45			
*H Whately C	30,390	61.09	+6.73	
M Desmond Lab	12,977	26.08	+9.92	
D Naghi LD	3,249	6.53	-0.10	
M McGiffin Ukip	1,702	3.42	-14.58	
A Gould Green	1,431	2.88	-0.98	

Worked at PwC, AOL, and NHS as a healthcare consultant. Conservative parly rep to Trump inauguration; faced backlash after tweeting it had been incredible. Campaigned against Brexit. Member, health select cttee 2015-. PPS to Greg Hands 2016-. Vice-chairwoman, Women in Parliament. Married, three children. Ed: Lady Margaret Hall, Oxford (BA PPE).

CHALLENGERS
Michael Desmond (Lab) Volunteer: founder of community festival Edgware Week; founder, Clean Up Clapton; chairman, think tank Society Syndrome; founded House the Homeless, a homelessness project. Cllr, Hackney BC 2001-, 1990-98; speaker 2013-14. Managing dir, On The House estate agents. **David Naghi** (LD) Business owner. Chairman of Maidstone Sea Cadets. Contested Faversham and Kent Mid 2010, 2005. Cllr, Maidstone BC 2002-; deputy mayor 2017-18. **Mark McGiffin** (Ukip) Career in construction industry, working locally and overseas. **Alastair Gould** (Green) NHS

GP in Faversham for 26 years. Passionate about cycling.

CONSTITUENCY PROFILE
The seat contains Faversham in its east and some suburbs of Maidstone in its west. It is fairly affluent with relatively high levels of home ownership. The population is predominantly white and UK born. A quarter of residents are employed in retail or construction. Held by the Conservatives since its creation in 1997, the majority was just over 4,000 in 1997 and 2001, but has recovered considerably since then. The predecessor seat of Faversham was won by Labour in 1945 and held until 1970.

EU REFERENDUM RESULT
58.7% Leave   Remain 41.3%

Feltham & Heston

LAB CO-OP HOLD MAJORITY 15,603 (29.4%)

SEEMA MALHOTRA
BORN Aug 7, 1972
MP 2011-

Electorate	Turnout %	Change from 2010 %		
81,707	64.90			
*S Malhotra Lab Co-op	32,462	61.22	+8.91	
S Jassal C	16,859	31.79	+2.68	
S Agnew Ukip	1,510	2.85	-9.72	
H Malik LD	1,387	2.62	-0.58	
T Firkins Green	809	1.53	-1.29	

Former freelance business and public service adviser in video games and film industries. Worked in strategy and IT systems at Accenture and PWC. Shadow chief secretary to the Treasury 2015-16; resigned in protest at Jeremy Corbyn's leadership. PPS to Yvette Cooper 2012-14. Shadow min, preventing violence against women and girls 2014-2015. Actively involved in the Fabian Society; former chairwoman and co-founder and dir of Fabian Women's Network. Married. Ed: University of Warwick (BA politics and philosophy); Aston University (MSc business IT).

CHALLENGERS
Samir Jassal (C) Businessman. Founding chairman of East Ham Conservative Future group. Criticised for unpaid court orders during 2017 campaign. Assisted Priti Patel MP with PM's UK-India Diaspora Champion campaign and advises government on relations with Indian community. Cllr, Gravesham BC 2007-2011. **Stuart Agnew** (Ukip) Farmer. Former teacher in Kashmir and soil and water conservation officer in Rhodesia. Rejects man-made global warming. Contested: Broadland 2015, 2010; North Norfolk 2005; Mid-Norfolk 2001. Ukip spokesman for agriculture. MEP for East of England 2009-.

CONSTITUENCY PROFILE
Feltham and Heston lies just east of Heathrow Airport along Greater London's western border, characterised by high levels of social and private renting and income substantially lower than the London average. About two-fifths of residents are Asian, mostly of Indian descent. The seat has voted Labour in all but two elections since its 1974 creation; the Thatcher landslides.

EU REFERENDUM RESULT
55.9% Leave   Remain 44.1%

Fermanagh & South Tyrone

SINN FEIN GAIN MAJORITY 875 (1.6%)

MICHELLE GILDERNEW
BORN Mar 28, 1970
MP 2017-

MP for Fermanagh & South Tyrone 2001-15, held her seat by four votes in 2010 before losing out to the UUP in 2015. MLA for Fermanagh & South Tyrone 2016-17, 1998-2011. Dealt with the spread of bluetongue disease during her time as agriculture and rural development min 2007-11. Sinn Fein health spokeswoman. Anti-Brexit. Part of the first Sinn Fein delegation to visit Downing St. Married, three children. Ed: St Catherine's College, Armagh; University of Ulster.

CHALLENGERS
Tom Elliott (UUP) MP for

	Electorate	Turnout %	from 2010 %	Change
	70,601	75.75		
M Gildernew SF	25,230	47.18	+1.80	
*T Elliott UUP	24,355	45.54	-0.87	
M Garrity SDLP	2,587	4.84	-0.53	
N Campbell Alliance	886	1.66	+0.36	
T Jones Green	423	0.79	-0.76	

Fermanagh & South Tyrone 2015-17; contested seat in 2005. Spent 18 years as a part-time member of the Ulster Defence Regiment and the Royal Irish Regiment. Previously County Grand Master of the Orange Order within Fermanagh; assistant secretary to the Grand Lodge of Ireland. Leader of UUP 2010-12, resigned after hostility he faced as leader. MLA for Fermanagh & South Tyrone 2003-15; UUP spokesman for justice. Cllr, Fermanagh

DC 2001-10. **Mary Garrity** (SDLP) Worked as a Post Office manager and for British Telecom. Cllr, Fermanagh and Omagh DC 2014-; chairwoman 2016-.

CONSTITUENCY PROFILE
This sparse and largely rural seat shares a long border with the Republic. Its residents are about 58 per cent Catholic and 32 per cent Protestant. It has higher unemployment than the Northern Ireland average. Sinn Fein held this seat from 2001. The UUP won with a majority of 530 in 2015. It was represented by Bobby Sands, who died on hunger strike in 1981.

EU REFERENDUM RESULT

41.4% Leave   Remain 58.6%

Fife North East

SNP HOLD MAJORITY 2 (0.0%)

STEPHEN GETHINS
BORN Mar 28, 1976
MP 2015-

Held the seat by just two votes. Shadow SNP spokesman for Europe and international affairs 2017-; Europe 2015-17. Previously consultant on international development in the Balkans and South Caucasus and on democratisation in Africa. Former special adviser to Alex Salmond, advising on European and international affairs. European Parliament candidate 2014. Worked at Scotland Europa, helping Scottish organisations to gain influence and funding from the EU. Worked in the office of SNP MSP Andrew Wilson. Married, one daughter. Ed: Perth

	Electorate	Turnout %	from 2010 %	Change
	58,685	71.27		
*S Gethins SNP	13,743	32.86	-8.06	
J Riches LD	13,741	32.86	+1.53	
T Miklinski C	10,088	24.12	+7.83	
R Garton Lab	4,026	9.63	+1.95	
M Scott-Hayward Sovereign	224	0.54		

Academy; University of Dundee (LLB law); University of Kent (MA).

CHALLENGERS
Elizabeth Riches (LD) Former secondary school teacher. Cllr, Fife DC; dep leader 2007-2012; leader of the opposition 1997-2007. Spent two years living in the Arctic Circle. **Tony Miklinski** (C) Former teacher and marine. Awarded CBE 2006. Volunteers with autism improvement groups; son has autism. **Rosalind**

Garton (Lab) Geology tutor at the University of St Andrews. Teaches yoga.

CONSTITUENCY PROFILE
North East Fife is a large rural seat containing the coastal, university town of St Andrews, which is also famous as the home of the Royal and Ancient Golf club. Education and tourism are important industries for the local economy. Former Liberal Democrat leader Sir Menzies Campbell held the seat for 28 years. As with all but three Scottish seats it was won by the SNP in 2015, and is now the most marginal seat in the UK parliament.

EU REFERENDUM RESULT

36.3% Leave   Remain 63.7%

Filton & Bradley Stoke

CONSERVATIVE HOLD MAJORITY 4,182 (8.3%)

JACK LOPRESTI
BORN Aug 23, 1969
MP 2010-

	Electorate	Turnout %	from 2010 % Change
	72,569	69.86	
*J Lopresti C	25,331	49.97	+3.29
N Rylatt Lab	21,149	41.72	+15.08
E Fielding LD	3,052	6.02	-1.27
D Warner Green	1,162	2.29	-2.30

Strong voice for the TA; served a five-month tour in Afghanistan as gunner, Gloucester Volunteer Artillery. Passionate about social mobility having left school at 15. Was diagnosed with bowel cancer in 2013; said that he had a "lucky escape" after a tumour was untreated following a delay of three months. PPS to Desmond Swayne 2014-15. Select cttees: armed forces bill 2015, 2011; NI affairs 2010-17. Cllr, Bristol CC 1999-2007. Contested Bristol East 2001; European Parliament 2004. Member: Freedom Association; Conservative Way Forward. Consultant and manager in financial services and residential property sectors. Worked in family ice-cream and catering business. Interested in military and political history: member, International Churchill Society, General George Patton Historical Society – cites George Patton as hero. Married, one daughter, two sons. Ed: Brislington Comp Sch.

CHALLENGERS
Naomi Rylatt (Lab) Works in motor claims for an insurance company. Cllr, Bristol CC 2014- 16. **Eva Fielding** (LD) Works for Gloucestershire County Council. Formerly engineering apprentice. Liberal Democrat constituency campaign organiser for Bath during the 2015 GE.

CONSTITUENCY PROFILE
A mostly suburban seat characterised by low unemployment and a modest skew towards professional and managerial-level jobs, with finance and insurance among the overrepresented industries. Filton and Bradley Stoke has Labour leaning areas such as Filton and Patchway but mostly consists of Conservative-leaning wards.

EU REFERENDUM RESULT
48.8% Leave   Remain 51.2%

Finchley & Golders Green

CONSERVATIVE HOLD MAJORITY 1,657 (3.2%)

MIKE FREER
BORN May 29, 1960
MP 2010-

	Electorate	Turnout %	from 2010 % Change
	73,138	71.62	
*M Freer C	24,599	46.96	-3.94
J Newmark Lab	22,942	43.79	+4.05
J Davies LD	3,463	6.61	+3.34
A Ward Green	919	1.75	-0.92
A Price Ukip	462	0.88	-2.53

Fervent Thatcherite. Pioneer of new easyCouncil local government model as cllr, Barnet BC 2001-10, 1990-94; leader 2006-09. Faced criticism over council's deposits in Icelandic banks. PPS to: Eric Pickles 2013-14; Nick Boles 2014, resigned that year to vote against recognition of Palestinian state. Contested Harrow West 2005. Self-employed consultant on regeneration and local gov't and marketing adviser. Keen cyclist. Gay; civil partnership. Ed: Chadderton GS; St Aidan's Sch, Carlisle; University of Stirling (accountancy and business law – did not take finals); BT Vital Vision exec MBA (Harvard, Stanford, Berkeley).

CHALLENGERS
Jeremy Newmark (Lab) Associate, Champollion Group. Chairman of the Jewish Labour Movement. Chief exec, Jewish Leadership Council 2006-13. Director of communications for the chief rabbi 1999-2004. **Jonathan Davies** (LD) Retired solicitor. Contested Finchley and Golders Green 1997. Treasurer, Golders Green synagogue. Vice-chairman Lib Dem Friends of Israel. Member, Board of Deputies of British Jews.

CONSTITUENCY PROFILE
This northwest London seat has the largest Jewish population of any parliamentary seat in the country, at over a fifth of residents. It also has a significant Muslim population, about ten per cent. There are above average levels of self-employment and degree-level qualifications. Private renting is significantly higher than both the UK and London averages. Although Margaret Thatcher held the seat from 1959 to 1992, Labour won under Tony Blair.

EU REFERENDUM RESULT
31.1% Leave   Remain 68.9%

Folkestone & Hythe

CONSERVATIVE HOLD MAJORITY 15,411 (26.2%)

DAMIAN COLLINS
BORN Feb 4, 1974
MP 2010-

Focused and smooth. Former chief of staff to Michael Howard, whose seat he inherited. Heads an international coalition of football reform activists, New FIFA Now. Trustee: Shepway Sports Trust; Folkestone Youth Project. Chairman: Step Short, a heritage charity; Conservative Arts and Creative Industries Network. Chairman, culture, media and sport select committee 2016-. Occasionally plays for the Lords and Commons rugby and cricket clubs. Manchester United fan. Born in Northampton. Married, two children. Ed: St Mary's High School, Lugwardine; Belmont

	Electorate	Turnout %	from 2010 % Change
	84,090	70.01	
*D Collins C	32,197	54.69	+6.84
L Davison Lab	16,786	28.51	+14.08
L Beaumont LD	4,222	7.17	-1.70
S Priestley Ukip	2,565	4.36	-18.41
M Whybrow Green	2,498	4.24	-1.13
D Plumstead Ind	493	0.84	
N Slade Ind	114	0.19	

Abbey School, Hereford; St Benet's Hall, Oxford (BA modern history).

CHALLENGERS
Laura Davison (Lab) National organiser, National Union of Journalists. Former radio journalist. **Lynne Beaumont** (LD) School governor. Active campaigner against fuel duty rises with FairFuelUK. Co-founder and member, Gurkha

justice. **Stephen Priestley** (Ukip) Mental health professional. **Martin Whybrow** (Green) Journalist. Cllr, Kent CC 2013-. **David Plumstead** (Ind) Former engineer.

CONSTITUENCY PROFILE
A southeast Kent seat bordering the English Channel, Folkestone and Hythe is older than average, with a fifth of its residents aged 65 or over. It is also characterised by higher than average levels of private sector renting and lower than average wages. Held by the Conservatives since its creation in 1950, it seated party leader Michael Howard 1983-2010.

EU REFERENDUM RESULT

61.6% Leave	Remain 38.4%

Forest of Dean

CONSERVATIVE HOLD MAJORITY 9,502 (18.4%)

MARK HARPER
BORN Feb 26, 1970
MP 2005-

Campaigned to Remain in Brexit referendum despite past Euro-scepticism. Strong supporter of Israel. Chartered accountant at KPMG until 1995. Worked in finance, business and operations with Intel Corporation until 2002. Established own chartered accountancy business. Chief whip 2015-16. Minister: work and pensions 2014-15; immigration 2012-14, resigned after his cleaner was revealed to be an illegal immigrant. Shadow minminister: work and pensions 2007-10; defence 2005-07. Governor, Newent Community School 2000-05. Married. Ed: Headlands Sch, Swindon;

	Electorate	Turnout %	from 2010 % Change
	70,898	73.02	
*M Harper C	28,096	54.27	+7.44
S Stammers Lab	18,594	35.92	+11.27
J Ellard LD	2,029	3.92	-1.39
J Greenwood Green	1,241	2.40	-3.06
E Warrender Ukip	1,237	2.39	-15.36
J Burrett Ind	570	1.10	

Swindon Coll; Brasenose Coll, Oxford (BA PPE).

CHALLENGERS
Shaun Stammers (Lab) Teacher. Campaigned to Remain in the EU. **Janet Ellard** (LD) Volunteer manager for homeless charity. Former modern languages teacher. **James Greenwood** (Green) Formerly worked, researched and raised money for international charities. Campaigned to stop the

proposed nuclear power station at Oldbury.

CONSTITUENCY PROFILE
Situated in rural west Gloucestershire with Gloucester and Stroud to its east, this seat only has towns with populations of no more than 10,000. More than half of its residents are over 45, and fewer than two per cent are non-white. About 75 per cent of homes are owner-occupied, well above the national average. The area has a rich industrial and mining history. Labour held the seat from its creation in 1997 to 2005; in its preceding form the seat was held by Labour from 1918 until 1979.

EU REFERENDUM RESULT

57.9% Leave	Remain 42.1%

Foyle

SINN FEIN GAIN MAJORITY 169 (0.4%)

ELISHA MCCALLION
BORN Jan 1, 1982
MP 2017-

First Sinn Fein MP for Foyle, took seat by just 169 votes. Community activist on welfare and housing issues: dir, Greater Shantallow Area Partnership; member, Off the Streets youth initiative. Helped to launch the bid for European Youth Capital which led to the northwest region becoming year of youth in 2019. First SF MP to attend a First World War commemoration service. MLA for Foyle 2017. Cllr, Derry CC 2005-; mayor 2015. Married, three children.

CHALLENGERS
Mark Durkan (SDLP) MP for

	Electorate	Turnout %	from 2010	Change %
	70,324	65.36		
E McCallion SF	18,256	39.72	+8.15	
*M Durkan SDLP	18,087	39.35	-8.55	
G Middleton DUP	7,398	16.09	+3.74	
S Harkin PBP	1,377	3.00		
J Doherty Alliance	847	1.84	-0.41	

Foyle 2005-17. Started career as campaign organiser and asst to John Hume MP. Prominent member of SDLP: leader 2001-10; deputy first minister 2001-02; chairman 1990-95; spokesman for a range of departments. MLA for Foyle 1998-2010. Member, SDLP talks team 1996-98, 1991-92. Cllr, Derry CC 1993-2000. Married, one daughter. **Gary Middleton** (DUP) Former youth co-ordinator and asst to MLA William Hay. MLA for Foyle 2015-; dep chairman, health cttee

2016-. Cllr, Derry CC 2011-15; dep mayor 2013-15.

CONSTITUENCY PROFILE
Despite containing Northern Ireland's second largest city Londonderry, Foyle has the second highest unemployment rate of any seat in the UK, and below average levels of income. The city was the UK's inaugural Capital of Culture in 2013, partly to attract investment to the area. Foyle was the most anti-Brexit constituency in Northern Ireland. Although the old seat of Londonderry elected unionists until 1983, Foyle has been held by nationalists since; it was considered an SDLP stronghold.

EU REFERENDUM RESULT

21.7% Leave   Remain 78.3%

Fylde

CONSERVATIVE HOLD MAJORITY 11,805 (25.4%)

MARK MENZIES
BORN May 18, 1971
MP 2010-

Marketing career for Asda and Morrisons. Contested: Selby 2005; Glasgow Govan 2001. Campaigned: liberalisation of Sunday trading; Remain; against fox hunting. PPS to: Alan Duncan 2013-14; Mark Prisk 2012-13; Charles Hendry 2010-12. Resigned as PPS to Alan Duncan over allegations of paying a male escort for sex and drugs. Select cttees: regulatory reform 2017; finance 2016-17; transport 2015-17. Member of the Armed Forces Parliamentary Scheme. Raised by mother after merchant navy father died before his birth. Ed: University of Glasgow (MA economics and social history).

	Electorate	Turnout %	from 2010	Change %
	65,937	70.47		
*M Menzies C	27,334	58.82	+9.68	
J Sullivan Lab	15,529	33.42	+14.63	
F Van Mierlo LD	2,341	5.04	+1.31	
T Rothery Green	1,263	2.72	-0.45	

CHALLENGERS
Jed Sullivan (Lab) Unite convenor, Blackpool Council. Trustee of Blackpool Boys and Girls Club. Anti-fracking. Criticised for jokes about gay people, women and Liverpudlians on Twitter. **Freddie Van Mierlo** (LD) Career in public affairs consultancy, Harwood Levitt Consulting 2014-. Campaigned to Remain in the EU. Volunteer, Hillary for America 2016. Fluent in three languages. **Tina Rothery** (Green) Freelance writer. Contested

Tatton 2015; the first Green candidate to do so. Campaigner for Frack Free UK; opposed to effect of industrialisation on tourism and farming. Educated in Australia and Hong Kong.

CONSTITUENCY PROFILE
Situated in Lancashire, Fylde lies between Preston and Blackpool, on the north bank of the River Ribble. Nearly a quarter of its residents are of pensionable age, well above average, compared with a similar number aged under 25. Unemployment is low and, on average, residents enjoy incomes greater than those earned in neighbouring seats. Conservative since 1918.

EU REFERENDUM RESULT

56.7% Leave   Remain 43.3%

Gainsborough

CONSERVATIVE HOLD MAJORITY 17,023 (33.1%)

SIR EDWARD LEIGH
BORN Jul 20, 1950
MP 1983-

	Electorate	Turnout %	from 2010 % Change
	75,893	67.76	
*E Leigh C	31,790	61.82	+9.14
C Tite Lab	14,767	28.72	+7.40
L Rollings LD	3,630	7.06	+0.38
V Pearson Green	1,238	2.41	-0.21

Former barrister, Goldsmiths Chambers. Fellow, Chartered Institute of Arbitrators. Private sec to Margaret Thatcher 1974-81. Contested Teesside Middlesbrough 1974. Campaigned to Leave the EU. Parly under-sec, trade and industry 1990-93: sacked for opposition to Maastricht treaty. Select cttees include: panel of chairs 2010-; int trade 2016-17; public accounts 2011-17, 2000-10; member's expenses 2011-15; liaison 2001-10. APPG chairman: France; Italy; Russia. Co-chairman: Holy See; rowing. Cllr, Richmond BC; Greater London C 1974-81. Knighted 2013.

Married, six children. Ed: The Oratory School, Berkshire; Lycée Français, London; University College, Durham (BA modern history).

CHALLENGERS
Catherine Tite (Lab) Political researcher, Ipsos Mori 2011-. Cllr, North East Derbyshire DC 2015-. Assistant professor, University of Regina, Canada 2004-11. Lecturer, University of Manchester 1998-2001. Member, Fabian Society 2013-17. **Lesley Rollings** (LD) Teacher,

Gainsborough Academy. Former mayor of Gainsborough. Cllr, West Lindsey DC 2000-; Lincolnshire CC 2013-. **Vicky Pearson** (Green) Cllr, Bardney parish council. Chairwoman, West Lindsey Green Party.

CONSTITUENCY PROFILE
A town in the West Lindsey district of Lincolnshire gives its name to this agricultural seat. Diversity is limited: 98.2 per cent of the population is white and immigration levels are low. Nearly 20 per cent of residents are pensioners. The seat has above-average levels of home ownership and is known for pig farming and RAF Scampton.

EU REFERENDUM RESULT
62.0% Leave   Remain 38.0%

Garston & Halewood

LABOUR HOLD MAJORITY 32.149 (60.1%)

MARIA EAGLE
BORN Feb 17, 1961
MP 1997-

	Electorate	Turnout %	from 2010 % Change
	75,248	71.13	
*M Eagle Lab	41,599	77.72	+8.64
A Marsden C	9,450	17.66	+3.99
A Martin LD	1,723	3.22	-1.43
L Brown Green	750	1.40	-2.05

Former third-sector worker and lawyer. Longstanding Hillsborough justice campaigner. Staunch sceptic of Jeremy Corbyn: resigned from frontbench following Brexit; voted no confidence in Labour leader. Twin sister of Angela Eagle. Contested Crosby 1992. Campaigned to Remain; voted against Article 50. Public accounts cttee 1997-99. PPS to John Hutton 1999-2001. Parly sec, equalities 2008-09. Min: equalities 2009-10; justice 2009-10. Shadow min: justice 2010; solicitor general 2010; equalities 2010. Shadow SoS: transport 2010-13; environment, food &

rural affairs 2013-15; defence 2015-16; CMS 2016. Reshuffled to CMS as Eagle supports Trident renewal; Corbyn does not. Vice-chairwoman of APPGs: Hillsborough disaster and oral hormone pregnancy tests. Ed: St Peter's CofE Sch; Formby HS; St John's Coll, Oxford (BA PPE); College of Law, London.

CHALLENGERS
Adam Marsden (C) Investment consultant. Contested Liverpool Walton 2010; Liverpool CC 2008. **Anna Martin** (LD)

Secretary, Liverpool Liberal Democrats. Contested: Garston and Halewood 2015; Liverpool CC 2016, 2014, 2012. **Lawrence Brown** (Green) Contested Liverpool Riverside 1992.

CONSTITUENCY PROFILE
The area is largely deprived, although the suburb Woolton in the north is one of Liverpool's most affluent. Over 17,000 adults in households are unemployed. The number of residents paid below the Living Wage is slightly above the regional average. It was last won by the Conservatives in 1979 and it is almost twenty years since the Tories won even a cllr here.

EU REFERENDUM RESULT
48.0% Leave   Remain 52.0%

Gateshead

LABOUR HOLD MAJORITY 17,350 (41.2%)

IAN MEARNS
BORN Apr 21, 1957
MP 2010-

Formerly worked for Northern Gas. Backbencher with considerable local govt experience. Brief spell as PPS to Ivan Lewis; resigned in protest at the party's line on welfare sanctions 2013. One of 16 Labour MPs who wrote to Ed Miliband in 2015 demanding greater opposition to austerity. Rebelled in voting against Jobseekers (Back to Work schemes) Bill 2013. Member, Unison; Unite. Select cttees: chairman, backbench business 2016-; education, skills and the economy sub-cttee 2015-; liaison 2015-; education 2015-. Cllr, Gateshead C 1983-2010.

	Electorate	Turnout %	from 2010 %	Change
	65,186	64.59		
*I Mearns Lab	27,426	65.14	+8.45	
L Hankinson C	10,076	23.93	+9.30	
M Bell Ukip	2,281	5.42	-12.38	
F Hindle LD	1,709	4.06	-2.74	
A Redfern Green	611	1.45	-2.62	

Two children. Ed: St Mary's RC Technical College.

CHALLENGERS
Lauren Hankinson (C) Political adviser, Conservative Party 2017-. Senior parly assistant, SoS for Scotland 2014-16. Lawyer, Dentons. Contested Glasgow North 2015. **Mark Bell** (Ukip) Contested Blaydon, 2015. **Frank Hindle** (LD) IT development worker and former head of computing, Northumbria University 2001-10.

Cllr, Gateshead C 1991-2016; leader of the opposition 2011-15. Chairman, Gateshead Liberal Democrats 2016-. **Andy Redfern** (Green) Technical dir, Venture Stream 2016-. Contested Gateshead 2015, 2010.

CONSTITUENCY PROFILE
The town lies along the southern bank of the River Tyne opposite Newcastle. Just short of 90,000 residents are white and from the UK. The town centre has a new lease of life after recent re-development. The seat was re-created in 2010, having previously been split into eastern and western parts which both had a strong Labour history.

EU REFERENDUM RESULT
56.2% Leave   Remain 43.8%

Gedling

LABOUR HOLD MAJORITY 4,694 (9.1%)

VERNON COAKER
BORN Jun 17, 1953
MP 1997-

History teacher and deputy headmaster. First Labour MP to win Gedling. Critical of Jeremy Corbyn. Toured the country in 2017 compiling voters' opinions on where the Labour Party should improve. Remainer; voted for Article 50. Supports multilateral disarmament. Shadow SoS: N Ireland 2015-16, 2011-13; defence 2013-15. Shadow min: home affairs 2010-11; education 2010. min: schools and learners 2009-10; policing, crime and security 2008-09. Govt whip 2005; asst whip 2003-05. Parly under-sec: crime reduction 2007-08; home office 2006-07. Cllr, Nottinghamshire DC 1983-97;

	Electorate	Turnout %	from 2010 %	Change
	71,221	72.57		
*V Coaker Lab	26,833	51.92	+9.61	
C Abbott C	22,139	42.84	+6.75	
L Waters Ukip	1,143	2.21	-12.23	
R Swift LD	1,052	2.04	-1.94	
R Connick Green	515	1.00	-2.20	

leader of Labour group 1987-97. Was one of Unicef's special friends in Parliament. Married, two children. Ed: University of Warwick (BA economics and politics); Trent Polytechnic (PGCE).

CHALLENGERS
Carolyn Abbott (C) Runs wrought iron manufacturing business and worked in financial sector. Contested: Gedling 2015; Chesterfield 2010; Barnsley East and Mexborough 2005; Sheffield

Heeley 2001. School governor. **Lee Waters** (Ukip) Contested Gedlin 2015. Deputy chairman, Ukip Gedling. **Robert Swift** (LD) Consultant. Formerly worked in marketing, specialising in mobile phones.

CONSTITUENCY PROFILE
An urban town in Nottinghamshire where residents, 94 per cent of whom were born in the UK, enjoy high levels of home ownership and economic activity. Historically, Gedling and its predecessor Carlton used to be regarded as safe Conservative seats. However, it has been held by Labour since 1997.

EU REFERENDUM RESULT
56.3% Leave   Remain 43.7%

Gillingham & Rainham

CONSERVATIVE HOLD MAJORITY 9,430 (19.3%)

REHMAN CHISHTI
BORN Oct 4, 1978
MP 2010-

Barrister, Goldsmith Chambers. Contested Horsham 2005 as a Labour Party candidate; defected to the Conservatives and became adviser to Francis Maude 2006. Political adviser to Benazir Bhutto 1999–2007. Private members' bills on road safety and mental health successfully passed in 2014 and 2015. Voted to Leave the EU. PPS to Jeremy Wright 2015; Nick Gibb 2014-15. Select cttees: justice 2012-15; human rights 2011-14; draft defamation bill 2011. Cllr, Medway C 2003-07. Born in Pakistan. Ed: Aberystwyth University (LLB law); Inns of Court School of Law.

	Electorate	Turnout %	from 2010 %	Change
	72,903	67.03		
*R Chishti C	27,091	55.44	+7.45	
A Stamp Lab	17,661	36.14	+10.52	
M Cook Ukip	2,097	4.29	-15.25	
P Chaplin LD	1,372	2.81	-0.82	
C Gregory Green	520	1.06	-1.34	
R Peacock CPA	127	0.26		

CHALLENGERS
Andy Stamp (Lab) Cllr, Medway Council 2007-. Campaigner against cuts to local organisations. Senior environmental regulator; has prosecuted companies for environmental reasons. **Martin Cook** (Ukip) Chartered accountant. Involved in local Leave campaign. **Paul Chaplin** (LD) Auditor to medical profession. Contested Gillingham and Rainham 2015. Treasurer,

Medway Lib Dems. **Clive Gregory** (Green) Freelance musician and sound engineer. Contested Rochester and Strood 2014 by-election.

CONSTITUENCY PROFILE
This constituency was created in 2010 to replace Gillingham. The old seat had been consistently Conservative, other than in 1945 and from 1997 to 2010. Local retail, industry, business parks, trades and professions and convenient access to the City of London provide constituents with a high level of employment, in mostly professional occupations, on moderate to middle incomes.

EU REFERENDUM RESULT

63.6% Leave	Remain 36.4%

Glasgow Central

SNP HOLD MAJORITY 2,267 (6.3%)

ALISON THEWLISS
BORN Sep 13, 1982
MP 2015-

Previously worked as a researcher for Bruce McFee MSP. SNP spokeswoman, land and environmental services. Campaigned against third-child tax credit policy and called for changes to rape clause. Shadow SNP spokeswoman for cities 2015-; Treasury 2017-. Member, select cttee CLG 2015-17. Campaigned to Remain in the EU. Member of Scottish CND and believes passionately in the scrapping of nuclear weapons. Cllr, Glasgow CC 2007-2015. Married, two children. Ed: Carluke High School; University of Aberdeen (BA politics and international relations).

	Electorate	Turnout %	from 2010 %	Change
	64,346	55.92		
*A Thewliss SNP	16,096	44.73	-7.81	
F Hameed Lab	13,829	38.43	+5.38	
C Fairbanks C	5,014	13.93	+7.93	
I Nelson LD	1,045	2.90	+1.35	

CHALLENGERS
Faten Hameed (Lab) Project manager, Glasgow CC. Born in Iraq and led drive to help Iraqi refugees. Founder, Scottish Iraqi Association. **Charlotte Fairbanks** (C) Committed unionist; opposed to second Scottish independence referendum. **Isabel Nelson** (LD) Worked in the University of Strathclyde's department of architecture and building science on research into dampness in Glasgow's council housing. Founding member of Heatwise

Glasgow, a conservation and training company.

CONSTITUENCY PROFILE
The economic renewal of Glasgow since the 1990s has led to rapidly rising property prices and gentrification in the areas closest to the city centre, Merchant City and Glasgow Green. This makes it the most educated and affluent of the Glasgow seats, but there is still poverty. North of the Clyde, the Calton area suffers severe deprivation with unemployment and high levels of crime. A quarter of residents are students. This was a safe Labour seat until the 2015 SNP landslide.

EU REFERENDUM RESULT

28.8% Leave	Remain 71.2%

Glasgow East

SNP HOLD MAJORITY 75 (0.2%)

DAVID LINDEN
BORN May 14, 1990
MP 2017-

	Electorate	Turnout %	from 2010 % Change
	66,242	54.61	
D Linden SNP	14,024	38.77	-18.09
K Watson Lab	13,949	38.56	+6.19
T Kerr C	6,816	18.84	+12.84
M Clark LD	576	1.59	+0.84
J Ferguson Ukip	504	1.39	-1.21
K Finegan Ind	158	0.44	
S Marshall Soc Dem	148	0.41	

Career in financial sector as an underwriter at Access Loans & Mortgages and Glasgow Credit Union. Ran the office of Alison Thewliss MP for Glasgow Central, prior to being elected. Former caseworker at Glasgow East constituency office. Campaign organiser and policy researcher for SNP in the Scottish, European and UK parliaments. Married, one son. Ed: Bannerman HS, Baillieston.

CHALLENGERS
Kate Watson (Lab) Unionist and former dir of operations for the Better Together campaign. **Thomas Kerr** (C) 20-year-old PR and advertising student. Cllr, Glasgow CC 2017-. Better Together campaigner. **Matthew Clark** (LD) History and business management student at the University of Glasgow. Visually impaired. Charity trustee of VICTA, supporting blind and partially sighted children.

CONSTITUENCY PROFILE
Like many of the Glasgow seats, this has been safely held by Labour since the 1930s. The 2008 by-election that followed the death of David Marshall was won by the SNP on a swing of 22 per cent, and although Labour regained the seat in 2010, the SNP won it back in their 2015 landslide. The winning MP, Natalie McGarry, resigned the party whip in 2015 after an investigation into fraud, for which she was later charged. The seat is one of the most deprived in the UK and ranked as the second worst constituency for residents' health. Unemployment is well above the national average and more than 30,000 residents have no qualifications.

EU REFERENDUM RESULT

43.8% Leave   Remain 56.2%

Glasgow North

SNP HOLD MAJORITY 1,060 (3.2%)

PATRICK GRADY
BORN Feb 5, 1980
MP 2015-

	Electorate	Turnout %	from 2010 % Change
	53,863	62.14	
*P Grady SNP	12,597	37.63	-15.48
P Duncan-Glancy Lab	11,537	34.47	+6.53
S Cullen C	4,935	14.74	+6.89
P Harvie Green	3,251	9.71	+3.53
C Shepherd LD	1,153	3.44	+0.70

Advocacy manager, Scottish Catholic International Aid Fund. Contested Glasgow North 2010. National sec, SNP 2012-16. Campaigned for Scottish independence. Interested in international development. SNP Westminster spokesman, international development 2015-17. Select cttee, procedures 2015-17. Joined the SNP in 1997. Originally from Inverness. Ed: University of Strathclyde.

CHALLENGERS
Pam Duncan-Glancy (Lab) Senior communications and engagement officer, NHS Scotland 2015-; policy officer, Independent Living in Scotland 2009-. Campaigns for disability rights. Wheelchair user. **Stuart Cullen** (C) Former president of Oxford Union. Followed parents into legal profession. **Patrick Harvie** (Green) Co-convener of Scottish Green Party. MSP, Glasgow region 2003-. Campaigned to repeal section 2A of Local Govt Act. Proposed civil partnership legislation in Scottish parliament. **Calum Shepherd** (LD) MA student, University of Liverpool.

CONSTITUENCY PROFILE
Outskirts include large council estates; however, in the centre are middle-class Victorian houses and Glasgow University, which makes it one of the best-educated seats in the city. Residents dominate largely managerial and professional occupations. Even in the days of Scottish Labour hegemony this seat was not as overwhelmingly Labour as the others, its predecessor Glasgow Hillhead having been won by the Conservatives from 1918 until Roy Jenkins's SDP by-election victory of 1982. It was represented by Labour from 1987 until the SNP landslide in 2015.

EU REFERENDUM RESULT

21.6% Leave   Remain 78.4%

The 2017 House of Commons

Seats by party

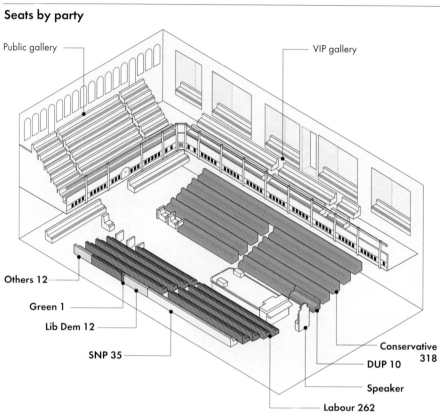

Public gallery

VIP gallery

Others 12

Green 1

Lib Dem 12

SNP 35

Conservative 318

DUP 10

Speaker

Labour 262

Vote share, %

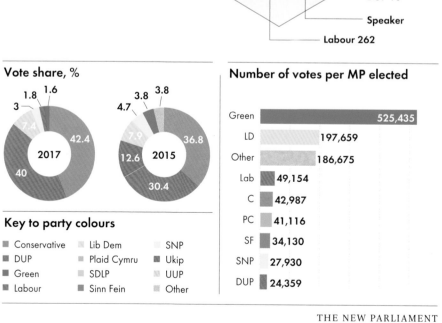

2017

1.8
1.6
3
7.4
42.4
40

2015

3.8
3.8
4.7
7.9
36.8
12.6
30.4

Number of votes per MP elected

Green	525,435
LD	197,659
Other	186,675
Lab	49,154
C	42,987
PC	41,116
SF	34,130
SNP	27,930
DUP	24,359

Key to party colours

- Conservative
- DUP
- Green
- Labour
- Lib Dem
- Plaid Cymru
- SDLP
- Sinn Fein
- SNP
- Ukip
- UUP
- Other

The political map of the United Kingdom 2017

2015 results

Orkney & Shetland

Glasgow

Northern Ireland

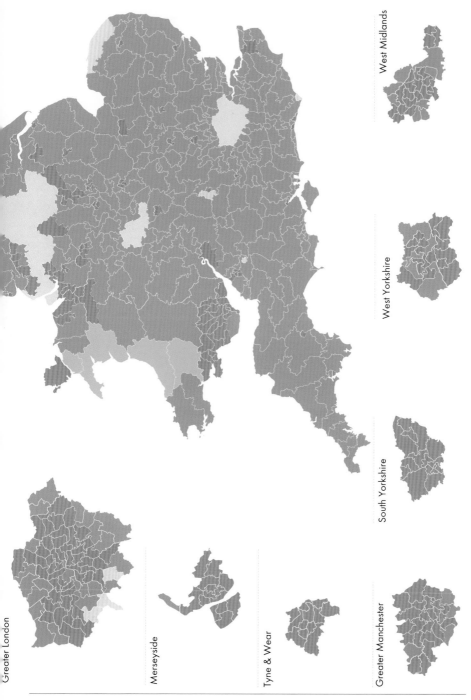

Greater London

Merseyside

Tyne & Wear

Greater Manchester

South Yorkshire

West Yorkshire

West Midlands

Anatomy of the election

Voters

Gender

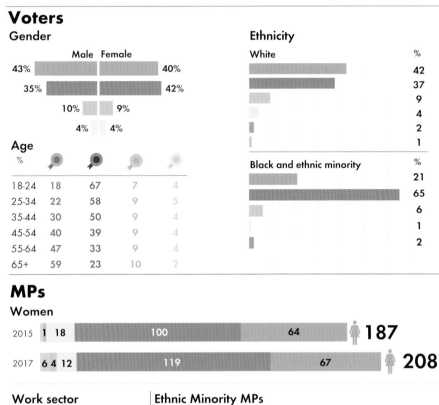

	Male	Female
	43%	40%
	35%	42%
	10%	9%
	4%	4%

Age

%				
18-24	18	67	7	4
25-34	22	58	9	5
35-44	30	50	9	4
45-54	40	39	9	4
55-64	47	33	9	4
65+	59	23	10	2

Ethnicity

White	%
	42
	37
	9
	4
	2
	1

Black and ethnic minority	%
	21
	65
	6
	1
	2

MPs

Women

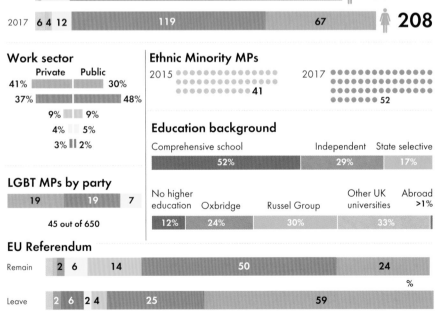

2015	1	18	100	64	187
2017	6 4	12	119	67	208

Work sector

	Private	Public
	41%	30%
	37%	48%
	9%	9%
	4%	5%
	3%	2%

Ethnic Minority MPs

2015 — 41

2017 — 52

Education background

Comprehensive school	Independent	State selective
52%	29%	17%

No higher education	Oxbridge	Russel Group	Other UK universities	Abroad >1%
12%	24%	30%	33%	

LGBT MPs by party

19 | 19 | 7

45 out of 650

EU Referendum

Remain	2	6	14	50	24
Leave	2 6	2 4	25		59

%

Source: British Future, House of Commons Library, Sutton Trust Data, Times research

Glasgow North East

LAB CO-OP GAIN MAJORITY 242 (0.8%)

PAUL SWEENEY
BORN Jan 16, 1989
MP 2017 -

Senior account manager, Scottish Enterprise. Former operations strategy co-ordinator, BAE systems. Young, from a shipbuilding family. Community activist: founded Springburn Winter Gardens restoration project. TA Reservist 2006-. Contested Holyrood elections 2016. Shadow min, Scotland 2017-. Self-professed champion of Glasgow's architectural heritage; founded project to restore Glasgow Winter Gardens. Ed: Turnbull HS; University of Stirling (CertHE economics and politics); University of Glasgow (MA economic history and politics).

	Electorate	Turnout %	from 2010 % Change
	59,932	53.02	
P Sweeney Lab Co-op	13,637	42.92	+9.23
*A McLaughlin SNP	13,395	42.16	-15.89
J Wyllie C	4,106	12.92	+8.25
D Donaldson LD	637	2.00	+1.21

CHALLENGERS
Anne McLaughlin (SNP) MP for Glasgow NE 2015-17. Former charity adviser. MSP, Glasgow 2009-11. Contested Inverclyde, 2011. Campaigned to Remain; voted against Article 50 being triggered. Shadow SNP spokeswoman, civil liberties 2015-17. **Jack Wyllie** (C) Speechwriter for Alexander Burnett MSP 2016-. **Daniel Donaldson** (LD) Solicitor and founder, social enterprise law centre, Legal Spark. Contested local elections 2017.

CONSTITUENCY PROFILE
As with most of Glasgow, the seat was Labour but fell to the SNP in 2015. Between 2000 and 2009 the constituency was represented by Michael Martin, the Speaker of the Commons, and by convention was not opposed by the main parties. After the Speaker stood down in 2009 it went to Labour. Almost half of all residents in this area live in social housing, while crime and unemployment are pressing issues. This constituency ranks first for the number of residents with no qualifications in Scotland. It was one of the six seats won back by Labour from the SNP in 2017.

EU REFERENDUM RESULT

40.7% Leave   Remain 59.3%

Glasgow North West

SNP HOLD MAJORITY 2,561 (6.6%)

CAROL MONAGHAN
BORN Aug 2, 1972
MP 2015-

Former physics teacher. Joined SNP after the Scottish independence referendum. Staunch devotee of Nicola Sturgeon. Previously SQA consultant. Former university lecturer training future teachers. Novice stonemason who aimed to pursue a career in stonemasonry until she was selected as the candidate for Glasgow NW. Has spoken openly about the challenges of balancing motherhood with life as an MP in Westminster. Shadow SNP Westminster group leader for public services and education 2015-. Member, science and technology select

	Electorate	Turnout %	from 2010 % Change
	63,773	60.91	
*C Monaghan SNP	16,508	42.50	-12.02
M Shanks Lab	13,947	35.91	+5.02
C Land C	7,002	18.03	+9.61
J Speirs LD	1,387	3.57	+0.85

cttee 2015-. Married, three children. Ed: University of Strathclyde (BSc laser physics and optoelectronics); St Andrew's Coll, Bearsden (PGCE).

CHALLENGERS
Michael Shanks (Lab) Charity worker for vulnerable children and young people with disabilities. **Chris Land** (C) Political risk consultant. Adviser to Liz Smith MSP in Scottish parliament. Contested Edinburgh C 2017. **James Speirs** (LD) Mental health and learning

disabilities charity worker. Contested local elections 2017.

CONSTITUENCY PROFILE
One of the seven Glasgow seats, this constituency lies on the north bank of the Clyde and covers contrasting areas to the city's north-west, encompassing the deprived Drumchapel housing estate as well as the more affluent areas of Scotstoun and Jordanhill. Over 20,000 homes are owned, however the social rented sector does not fall far behind with more than 15,000 households. While unemployment is lower than in other parts of Glasgow, residents are not well qualified.

EU REFERENDUM RESULT

31.5% Leave   Remain 68.5%

Glasgow South

SNP HOLD MAJORITY 2,027 (4.5%)

STEWART MCDONALD
BORN Aug 24, 1986
MP 2015-

Worked as a retail manager and holiday rep in Tenerife before becoming a parliamentary caseworker for Anne McLaughlin MSP and James Dornan MSP. Campaign manager, SNP Glasgow and Cathcart 2011. Remainer, voted against Article 50. SNP spokesman for defence 2017-. Lodged a private members' bill against unpaid trial shifts. Backbencher, member of transport select cttee 2015-17. Human rights and LGBTQ+ equality campaigner: supported "Yes" vote in Irish same-sex marriage referendum; attacked Donald Trump's proposed ban

	Electorate	Turnout %	from 2010 %	Change
	69,126	64.45		
*S McDonald SNP	18,312	41.10	-13.78	
E Dinning Lab	16,285	36.55	+6.82	
T Muir C	8,506	19.09	+9.35	
E Hoyle LD	1,447	3.25	+1.16	

on transgender people in the US military 2017. Ed: Govan HS.

CHALLENGERS
Eileen Dinning (Lab) Equalities officer, Unison. Member, Show Racism the Red Card advisory group. **Taylor Muir** (C) Works in telecoms customer service. Contested: Rutherglen and Hamilton West 2015, aged 19; Holyrood 2016. **Ewan Hoyle** (LD) Campaigner for the legalisation of cannabis. Founder of Liberal Democrats for Drug Policy Reform. Contested:

Glasgow South 2015; Holyrood 2011.

CONSTITUENCY PROFILE
Covering the southern part of Scotland's most populated city, this constituency consists of leafy, residential areas as well as the sprawling housing estates built for families displaced by Glasgow's slum clearances. The area has a growing Pakistani community. Typical of Glasgow, a relatively high proportion of residents live in social housing. Wages outstrip the national average and residents are typically well qualified. This was a safe Labour seat, gained by the SNP in 2015.

EU REFERENDUM RESULT
28.2% Leave   Remain 71.8%

Glasgow South West

SNP HOLD MAJORITY 60 (0.2%)

CHRIS STEPHENS
BORN Mar 20, 1973
MP 2015-

Former local government officer for Glasgow City Council. Trade unionist: senior Unison activist; sec, SNP trade union group. Shadows SNP spokesman, trade unions and workers' rights 2017-. Contested: Glasgow SW 2010; European parliament 2014; Scottish parliament 2011, 2007. Campaigned to Remain; voted against triggering of Article 50. Member, European scrutiny select cttee 2017. APPG vice-chairman: Botswana; South Africa; shipbuilding. Member, SNP national executive cttee. Convenor, Glasgow Pollok Constituency Assoc. Married. Ed: Trinity HS, Renfrew.

	Electorate	Turnout %	from 2010 %	Change
	62,991	56.16		
*C Stephens SNP	14,386	40.66	-16.49	
M Kerr Lab Co-op	14,326	40.49	+7.66	
T Haddow C	5,524	15.61	+10.64	
B Denton-Cardew LD	661	1.87	+0.88	
S Hemy Ukip	481	1.36	-1.01	

CHALLENGERS
Matt Kerr (Lab Co-op) Former postman. Cllr, Glasgow CC 2007- . Prominent local govt figure: moved a successful motion to condemn the UK Border Agency refugee policy; led efforts to introduce basic income to Glasgow - the pilot scheme is to begin in 2017. **Thomas Haddow** (C) Store manager, Tesco. Contested Scottish parliament 2016. **Ben Denton-Cardew** (LD) Politics student at University of Glasgow. Former member of UK

youth parliament. **Sarah Hemy** (Ukip) Former retail manager. Contested Glasgow South West 2015.

CONSTITUENCY PROFILE
This area is blighted with crime, poor health and deprivation. Residents tend to have low levels of qualifications and unemployment is high. Historically a Labour stronghold, the seat was lost in 2015 to the SNP with 57 per cent of the vote during the SNP's landslide victory in Scotland. The 60 votes separating the SNP from Labour in 2017 makes the seat the seventh most marginal in parliament.

EU REFERENDUM RESULT
40.9% Leave   Remain 59.1%

Glenrothes

SNP HOLD MAJORITY 3,267 (8.1%)

PETER GRANT
BORN Oct 12, 1960
MP 2015-

Former teacher. Retrained as an NHS accountant. Recovered in excess of £93,000 for constituents wrongly assessed by the DWP. Cllr, Fife CC 1992-2015; leader 2007-12. Contested Glenrothes by-election 2008. SNP spokesman for Europe 2017-. Select cttees: exiting the European Union 2016-17; consolidation 2015-17; European scrutiny 2015-16. Member of SNP's international affairs team. Brought up in Lanarkshire in a working-class Labour household. Married.

CHALLENGERS
Altany Craik (Lab) Worked

	Electorate	Turnout %	from 2010 %	Change
	66,378	60.86		
*P Grant SNP	17,291	42.80	-16.99	
A Craik Lab	14,024	34.71	+4.12	
A Brown C	7,876	19.50	+11.75	
R Bell LD	1,208	2.99	+1.12	

as an economics lecturer and in advertising. Cllr, Fife CC 2012-. Anti-fracking; launched a motion which opposed fracking and UGE in Fife 2016. **Andrew Brown** (C) Former head of office to the Conservative digital economy spokesman. Political aide to Jamie Greene MSP 2016-17; head of office 2017-. **Rebecca Bell** (LD) Radio and TV journalist specialising in business and political news. Previously: news editor, Kingdom FM; asst producer, BBC News. Press officer, Liberal Democrats 2017-.

CONSTITUENCY PROFILE
Glenrothes is the administrative centre of Fife. Traditionally a mining town, the constituency is now a successful centre for technology and industry. For those in work, the area demonstrates a relatively balanced variety of managerial, administrative, skilled trade and technical occupations. Glenrothes and its predecessor, Fife Central, were both safe Labour seats. However, the Fife Central seat in the Scottish Parliament, now contested on different boundaries, was in 2007 won by the SNP. Glenrothes was taken by the SNP in their landslide victory of 2015.

EU REFERENDUM RESULT

47.6% Leave   Remain 52.4%

Gloucester

CONSERVATIVE HOLD MAJORITY 5,520 (10.2%)

RICHARD GRAHAM
BORN Apr 4, 1958
MP 2010-

Career as an investment banker, diplomat and airline manager. Previously general manager of Cathay Pacific in France and the Philippines; first secretary, British Embassy Peking; British trade commissioner China; consul for Macau. Dir, The Greater China Fund 1995-2005. Cllr, Cotswold DC 2003-07. Remainer, has stated Brexit poses a trade conundrum. Voted for Article 50. Keen interest in foreign relations and served as PM's trade envoy to: Indonesia 2012-; Malaysia 2016-; Philippines 2016-. PPS to: Hugo Swire 2012-14; Lord Howell 2010-12. Select cttee, work and

	Electorate	Turnout %	from 2010 %	Change
	82,963	65.17		
*R Graham C	27,208	50.32	+4.98	
B Kirby Lab	21,688	40.11	+8.56	
J Hilton LD	2,716	5.02	-0.36	
D Woolf Ukip	1,495	2.76	-11.49	
G Hartley Green	754	1.39	-1.43	
G Ridgeon Loony	210	0.39	-0.04	

pensions 2010-17. Married, three children. Ed: Eton Coll; Christ Church, Oxford (BA history).

CHALLENGERS
Barry Kirby (Lab) Owner of research business. Cllr, Gloucestershire CC 2013-17. Founding member, Kingsway Residents Association. **Jeremy Hilton** (LD) Cllr, Gloucester CC 2002-, 1990-93, 1982-86. Contested Gloucester 2015. **Daniel Woolf** (Ukip)

Contested Gloucestershire CC 2017. Freelance web designer. Conservative defector.

CONSTITUENCY PROFILE
Famous for its cathedral, this city and district in the south-west of England has been a bellwether between Labour and Conservative since 1979. After nearly three decades as a Conservative seat, it was held by Labour from 1997 to 2010 before returning to the Conservatives. A relatively affluent area, unemployment is slightly below the national average, and levels of health and home ownership are higher. Income is below average for the southwest.

EU REFERENDUM RESULT

58.9% Leave   Remain 41.1%

Gordon

CONSERVATIVE GAIN MAJORITY 2,607 (4.9%)

COLIN CLARK
BORN Feb 12, 1968
MP 2017-

Businessman and fresh produce farmer. Chairman, Nessgro. Cllr, Aberdeenshire CC 2016-17; vice-chairman, business services cttee. Contested: Gordon 2015; Holyrood, Aberdeenshire East 2016. Married, two sons. Ed: Turriff Academy; Heriot-Watt University.

CHALLENGERS
Alex Salmond (SNP) First Minister of Scotland 2007-14. SNP leader 2004-14, 1990-2000. MP: Gordon 2015-17, Banff and Buchan 1987-2010. Former Scottish Office and RBS economist. Visiting professor of economics, University of

	Electorate	Turnout %	from 2010	Change %
	78,531	68.36		
C Clark C	21,861	40.72	+29.02	
*A Salmond SNP	19,254	35.86	-11.79	
K Muat Lab	6,340	11.81	+5.89	
D Evans LD	6,230	11.60	-21.11	

Strathclyde. MSP: Banff and Buchan 1999-2001; Gordon 2007-10; Aberdeenshire East 2011-16. Resigned as First Minister after Indyref "No" result. Campaigned to Remain; voted against Article 50. SNP Westminster foreign affairs spokesman 2015-17. Married. Ed: Edinburgh Coll of Commerce (HNC business studies); University of St Andrews (MA economics and medieval history). **Kirsten Muat** (Lab) Undergraduate politics student. Vice-chairwoman, Scottish

Labour Students. **David Evans** (LD) Information governance assistant, NHS Grampian. Contested Banff and Buchan 2015.

CONSTITUENCY PROFILE
The semi-rural Gordon constituency covers central Aberdeenshire and a northern part of the city of Aberdeen. This area, with many affluent households, was traditionally a Liberal/Conservative marginal. In the SNP's 2015 landslide election Alex Salmond gained the constituency with a large majority, however, he lost his seat to the Conservatives in the 2017 election.

EU REFERENDUM RESULT

38.8% Leave   Remain 61.2%

Gosport

CONSERVATIVE HOLD MAJORITY 17,211 (34.8%)

CAROLINE DINENAGE
BORN Oct 28, 1971
MP 2010-

Former director of Dinenages, a small business supplying corporate identity products. Contested Portsmouth South 2005. Campaigned to Remain, voted to trigger Article 50. Parly under-sec for: work and pensions 2017-; education 2016-17; justice 2015-16. Minister for equalities 2015-16. PPS to Nicky Morgan 2014-15. Select cttees: science & technology 2012-13; business, innovation & skills 2012-15. Cllr, Winchester CC 1998-2003. Married, two children. Ed: Oaklands RC Comp, Waterlooville; University of Wales, Swansea (BA politics and english).

	Electorate	Turnout %	from 2010	Change %
	73,886	66.97		
*C Dinenage C	30,647	61.94	+6.63	
A Durrant Lab	13,436	27.15	+12.62	
B Tennent LD	2,328	4.70	-2.21	
C Palmer Ukip	1,790	3.62	-15.82	
M Cassidy Green	1,024	2.07	-1.51	
J Roberts Ind	256	0.52		

CHALLENGERS
Alan Durrant (Lab) Semi-retired tutor. Secretary, Gosport Labour Party. Member, Momentum. Contested Gosport 2015. **Bruce Tennent** (LD) Former manager, British American Tobacco. Cllr: Eastleigh BC 2006-; West End PC 2007-; Hampshire CC 2009-. Contested European elections 2014. **Chloe Palmer** (Ukip) Runs café relying on food waste. Former carer for elderly and disabled. Chairwoman,

Ukip Gosport. **Monica Cassidy** (Green) Former teacher. Contested Gosport 2015.

CONSTITUENCY PROFILE
Gosport, comprising of a few small villages in southeast England, has been held by the Conservatives since its creation in 1974. Many of the working residents hold managerial and professional occupations and unemployment sits below the national average. The MP until 2010, Sir Peter Viggers, was forced to retire after being responsible for one of the most iconic claims in the MPs' expenses scandal – a £1,600 floating duck house.

EU REFERENDUM RESULT

61.8% Leave   Remain 38.2%

Gower

LABOUR GAIN MAJORITY 3,269 (7.2%)

TONIA ANTONIAZZI
BORN Oct 5, 1971
MP 2017-

Spent more than 20 years as a language teacher: head of languages, Bryngwyn School, Llanelli. Had a stint as a tighthead prop for Welsh national rugby team; won nine caps in three years. Voted Remain. Daughter of Italian immigrants who make ice cream and run a chain of cafés. Divorced, one child. Ed: St John Lloyd RC Sch, Llanelli; Gower Coll, Swansea; University of Exeter (BA French and Italian); Cardiff University (PGCE).

CHALLENGERS
Byron Davies (C) MP for Gower 2015-17. Retired Metropolitan

	Electorate	Turnout %	from 2010 %	Change
	62,163	73.32		
T Antoniazzi Lab	22,727	49.87	+12.83	
*B Davies C	19,458	42.69	+5.60	
H Roberts PC	1,669	3.66	-3.47	
H Evans LD	931	2.04	-1.59	
R Ford Ukip	642	1.41	-9.75	
J Winstanley Pirate	149	0.33		

Police officer. Welsh assembly member for southwest Wales 2011-15. Contested Gower 2010. Campaigned to Remain in the 2016 EU referendum; voted to trigger Article 50. Member, home affairs cttee 2016-17. **Harri Roberts** (PC) IT and business consultant. Contested Welsh assembly elections 2016. **Howard Evans** (LD) Deputy head teacher. Formerly chairman, Mawr Development Trust. Contested Gower 1997.

CONSTITUENCY PROFILE
This seat consists of the Gower peninsula, including the popular coastal resort of The Mumbles, and the former mining towns of Gorseinon and Pontarddulais. The area is middle class: wages are relatively high; many dwellers are homeowners and constituents are educated to a high level. There is a sizeable retired population: about a fifth of residents are pensioners. Gower is an occasionally marginal Labour stronghold that unexpectedly returned a Conservative for the first time in 100 years in 2015, with a majority of just 27: the smallest of that election.

EU REFERENDUM RESULT
49.3% Leave   Remain 50.7%

Grantham & Stamford

CONSERVATIVE HOLD MAJORITY 20,094 (35.5%)

NICK BOLES
BORN Nov 2, 1965
MP 2010-

Entrepreneur. Founder, DIY manufacturing company Longwall Holdings and dot com business. Founding dir, Policy Exchange. Cllr, Westminster CC 1998-2002. Boris Johnson's interim chief of staff 2008. CCHQ staffer responsible for planning policy implementation before 2010 election. Contested: Hove 2005; London mayoral primary 2007, withdrew after Hodgkin's Lymphoma diagnosis. Campaigned to Remain; left cancer ward to vote for Article 50. Managed leadership campaign of former flatmate Michael Gove 2016. Caught up in plot to keep Andrea Leadsom

	Electorate	Turnout %	from 2010 %	Change
	81,762	69.22		
*N Boles C	35,090	62.00	+9.17	
B Fairbairn Lab	14,996	26.50	+9.63	
A Day LD	3,120	5.51	-0.56	
M King Ukip	1,745	3.08	-14.42	
T Mahmood Ind	860	1.52	-0.37	
B Thackray Green	782	1.38	-2.10	

off members' ballot. Minister: skills & equalities 2014-16; planning 2012-14. PPS to Nick Gibb 2010-12. Rarely rebels. Civil partnership. Ed: Winchester Coll; Magdalen Coll, Oxford (BA PPE); Harvard University (Kennedy scholarship).

CHALLENGERS
Barrie Fairbain (Lab) Criminal law solicitor and practice owner. Contested Grantham and Stamford 2015. **Anita Day**

(LD) Chartered accountant; consultancy firm partner.

CONSTITUENCY PROFILE
Grantham, in the south of this Lincolnshire seat, is associated with Margaret Thatcher who grew up there. Unemployment is below the national average and income is high for the east Midlands. Historically Conservative, it briefly changed hands after Quentin Davies's defection to Labour in 2007, although the seat has never elected a Labour MP. The Conservatives held their seat with 62 per cent of the votes in 2017, a 9.2 per cent increase from the last election.

EU REFERENDUM RESULT
61.0% Leave   Remain 39.0%

Gravesham

CONSERVATIVE HOLD MAJORITY 9,347 (19.1%)

ADAM HOLLOWAY
BORN Jul 29, 1965
MP 2005-

Former ITN journalist: foreign affairs correspondent in Sarajevo and undercover investigative reporter. Grenadier Guards 1991-97. Rebel: voted against military action in Syria 2014; abstained on vote for RAF airstrikes in Syria 2015. Campaigned to Leave the EU; voted to trigger Article 50. PPS to David Lidington 2010-11. Select cttees: foreign affairs 2015-17; public administration 2014-15; defence 2006-10, 2012-14. APPG vice-chairman: Belize; governance and inclusive leadership. Ed: Cranleigh Sch, Surrey; Magdalene Coll, Cambridge (BA theology; MA social and political science);

	Electorate	Turnout %	from 2010 Change %
	72,948	67.17	
*A Holloway C	27,237	55.59	+8.74
M Garford Lab	17,890	36.51	+6.37
E Feyisetan Ukip	1,742	3.56	-15.00
J Willis LD	1,210	2.47	+0.25
M Gilligan Green	723	1.48	-0.77
M Rogan Ind	195	0.40	

Imperial Coll, London (MBA); RMA Sandhurst.

CHALLENGERS
Mandy Garford (Lab) Primary school teacher and autism awareness activist: organised Dartford exhibition *Art of Autism*. Cllr, Stone PC. **Emmanuel Feyisetan** (Ukip) Dir, real estates consultancy 1 Stop Realty. Former home office compliance manager. **James Willis** (LD) Head of printing business Managed Print Services. Contested Dartford 2010. Cllr, Maidstone BC 2014-.

CONSTITUENCY PROFILE
On the south bank of the Thames, this constituency is under large-scale regeneration. Traditionally, the area is poorer, more ethnically diverse and has a higher proportion of council housing than other Kent seats. The Labour-voting commercial Gravesend is countered by firmly Conservative villages to the south. Considered a bellwether seat between the Second World War and 2005, the Conservatives have held the seat since 2010.

EU REFERENDUM RESULT
65.4% Leave   Remain 34.6%

Great Grimsby

LABOUR HOLD MAJORITY 2,565 (7.2%)

MELANIE ONN
BORN Jun 19, 1979
MP 2015-

Worked in Labour Party head office for ten years, including as head of compliance unit. Former regional organiser, Unison. Contested European elections 2009. Sceptical of Jeremy Corbyn: nominated Yvette Cooper 2015; voted no confidence 2016. Campaigned to Remain, voted to trigger Article 50. Shadow: housing min 2017-; deputy Commons leader 2015-16. Select cttees: procedure 2016-17; CLG 2016-17; energy and climate change 2015. One child. Ed: Healing Comp Sch; Middlesex University (BA politics, philosophy and international studies).

	Electorate	Turnout %	from 2010 Change %
	61,743	57.53	
*M Onn Lab	17,545	49.39	+9.63
J Gideon C	14,980	42.17	+15.86
M Hookem Ukip	1,648	4.64	-20.31
S Beasant LD	954	2.69	-2.29
C McGilligan-Fell Ind	394	1.11	-0.05

CHALLENGERS
Jo Gideon (C) Small business owner. Dir of fundraising, the Ella foundation 2009-11. Cllr, Thanet DC 2003-15. Contested Scunthorpe 2015. **Mike Hookem** (Ukip) MEP, Yorkshire and the Humber 2014-. Ukip spokesman: fisheries 2016-; defence 2014-16. Contested Hull East 2010. Famously involved in EU parliament altercation with Steven Woolfe 2016. Bill Etheridge's running mate, Ukip leadership race 2016.

CONSTITUENCY PROFILE
Located in northeast Lincolnshire, this market town and port is a major industrial centre for fishing, manufacturing and wholesale trade. Historically it has been a Labour seat. However, the constituency now demonstrates a strong two-party divide, as the Conservatives followed closely behind after making dramatic gains from the decline in the Ukip vote compared with 2015. A small percentage of residents have qualifications beyond GCSE level. The unemployment rate is one of the highest in the country at 7.9 per cent, and is especially high among young people.

EU REFERENDUM RESULT
71.4% Leave   Remain 28.6%

Great Yarmouth

CONSERVATIVE HOLD MAJORITY 7,973 (18.1%)

BRANDON LEWIS
BORN Jun 20, 1971
MP 2010-

Barrister called to the bar in 1995. Formerly dir, Woodlands Schools, which runs private primary schools. Contested Sherwood 2001. Campaign manager for Eric Pickles during 2005 election campaign; formerly hosted *The Eric and Brandon Show* on local radio with Pickles. Remainer, voted to trigger Article 50. Handful of minor rebellions during coalition years. Min: immigration 2017-; policing and fire service 2016-17; housing and planning 2014-16. Parly under-sec CLG 2012-14. Cllr, Brentwood BC 1998-2009; leader 2004-09. Member, Carlton Club. Married,

Electorate	Turnout %	from 2010 % Change
71,408	61.82	
*B Lewis C	23,901	54.14 +11.21
M Smith-Clare Lab	15,928	36.08 +6.99
C Blaiklock Ukip	2,767	6.27 -16.83
J Joyce LD	987	2.24 -0.08
H Webb Green	563	1.28 -0.92

two children. Ed: Forest Sch, Walthamstow; University of Buckingham (BSc economics; LLB law); King's Coll London (LLM commercial law).

CHALLENGERS
Mike Smith-Clare (Lab) Co-founder, the Bread Kitchen skills charity; received an MBE for community work in 2017 New Year's Honours. Cllr, Norfolk CC 2017-. **Catherine Blaiklock** (Ukip) Runs charity, Nepal in Need. Formerly an investment

banker. **James Joyce** (LD) Cllr, Broadland DC 2004-11. Contested Great Yarmouth 2015.

CONSTITUENCY PROFILE
This seaside and ferry port on the Norfolk coast is known for its oil industry and offshore natural gas rigs. The area is comprised of a relatively high proportion of EU residents. Much of the working population lacks qualifications and unemployment is high. Home to a considerable retired population, more than one fifth of residents are aged over 65. A bellwether seat since 1979, Great Yarmouth has been held by the Conservatives since 2010.

EU REFERENDUM RESULT
71.5% Leave   Remain 28.5%

Greenwich & Woolwich

LABOUR HOLD MAJORITY 20,714 (39.0%)

MATTHEW PENNYCOOK
BORN Oct 29, 1982
MP 2015-

Background in charities and low pay campaigns. Previously worked for Child Poverty Action Group and the Fair Pay Network. Researcher: Resolution Foundation; Institute of Public Policy Research. Member, Living Wage Foundation advisory board. Cllr, Greenwich BC 2010-15. Nominated Yvette Cooper 2015; Owen Smith 2016. Remainer, voted to trigger Article 50. Signed EDM to deny Donald Trump a Westminster invitation. Shadow Brexit min 2016-. PPS to John Healey 2015-16. One time rebel: voted to legalise assisted dying. Raised by single mother; first person in

Electorate	Turnout %	from 2010 % Change
77,190	68.80	
*M Pennycook Lab	34,215	64.43 +12.23
C Attfield C	13,501	25.42 -1.20
C Adams LD	3,785	7.13 +1.47
D Garrun Green	1,605	3.02 -3.38

family to go to university. Lives with partner, one son. Ed: LSE (BSc history and international relations); Balliol Coll, Oxford (MPhil international relations).

CHALLENGERS
Caroline Attfield (C) Banker. Dir of sales and risk at management consultancy. RBS, Citibank. Contested European elections 2014. **Chris Adams** (LD) Academic historian; former tutor, Aberystwyth University. Presidential aide and governance officer, Lib Dems. Parly asst,

Mark Williams 2011-15. **Dan Garrun** (Green) Managing editor of GlobalData.

CONSTITUENCY PROFILE
This southeast London seat is mostly inner city and working class, with a quarter of people in council properties and above-average rates of unemployment, although there are some affluent areas. Home to a significant ethnic minority population, particularly of African descent. It has a large student population and almost three quarters of residents are below the age of 44. A safe Labour seat, the party increased its vote-share by 12.2 per cent in 2017.

EU REFERENDUM RESULT
35.7% Leave   Remain 64.3%

Guildford

CONSERVATIVE HOLD MAJORITY 17,040 (30.7%)

ANNE MILTON
BORN Nov 3, 1955
MP 2005-

NHS nurse politicised during 25-year career. Pioneered scheme to look after people who were sent home early from hospital. Previously a union steward, Royal Coll of Nursing; vice-chairwoman, Conservative Medical Society; chairwoman, National Childbirth Trust Hackney and Islington branch. Cllr, Reigate and Banstead BC 1999-2004; Surrey CC 2000-03. Campaigned to reduce stigma around mental illness while in opposition. Did not reveal she voted to Remain until after referendum, voted to trigger Article 50. Dep chief whip, treasurer of HM household,

	Electorate	Turnout %	from 2010 % Change
	75,454	73.57	
*A Milton C	30,295	54.58	-2.48
Z Franklin LD	13,255	23.88	+8.40
H Smith Lab	10,545	19.00	+6.89
M Bray-Parry Green	1,152	2.08	-2.66
J Morris Peace	205	0.37	-0.06
S Essessi ND	57	0.10	

2012-. Parly under-sec, health 2010-12. Rarely rebels but voted against same-sex marriage. Four children. Ed: Haywards Heath GS; St Bartholomew's Hospital (RGN); South Bank Polytechnic (Dip district nursing).

CHALLENGERS
Zoë Franklin (LD) Career in publishing and administration. Manager, village community centre. Cllr, Guildford BC 2008-15. **Howard Smith** (Lab) Former

drummer, new-wave power-pop band the Vapors. Runs music promotion company.

CONSTITUENCY PROFILE
This large Surrey constituency includes the towns of Guildford, Godalming and Farnham. A significant proportion of residents are highly qualified in professional occupations and own their homes. This area is historically a Conservative stronghold, held by the Conservatives in every parliament since 1910, other than 2001, when it was held by the Liberal Democrats, whose vote-share has since receded significantly.

EU REFERENDUM RESULT
41.2% Leave   Remain 58.8%

Hackney North & Stoke Newington

LABOUR HOLD MAJORITY 35,139 (62.4%)

DIANE ABBOTT
BORN Sep 27, 1953
MP 1987-

Britain's first black female MP. Former home office civil servant, now shadow home secretary 2016-. Subject of mockery due to a poor interview during campaign. Race relations officer, National Council for Civil Liberties (now Liberty). Cllr, Westminster CC 1982-86. Firebrand left-winger with interests in police reform and anti-racism. Serial backbench rebel during New Labour years; defied Jeremy Corbyn to vote against replacing Trident. Remainer, voted for Article 50. Close Corbyn ally, nominated him for leadership 2015 and campaigned for his re-election

	Electorate	Turnout %	from 2010 % Change
	83,955	67.06	
*D Abbott Lab	42,265	75.07	+12.22
A Gray C	7,126	12.66	-2.07
J Richards LD	3,817	6.78	+1.78
A Binnie-Lubbock Green	2,606	4.63	-9.97
J Homan AWP	222	0.39	-0.05
A Spielmann Ind	203	0.36	
C Corlis-Khan Friends	59	0.10	

2016. Contested Labour leadership 2010. Shadow: SoS for international development 2015-16; min, public health 2010-13. Divorced, one son. Ed: Harrow County GS; Newnham Coll, Cambridge (BA history).

CHALLENGERS
Amy Gray (C) Dir of communications, Policy Exchange. Contested Hackney North and Stoke Newington

2015. **Joe Richards** (LD) Co-founder of Economy, a public education charity.

CONSTITUENCY PROFILE
Hackney North and Stoke Newington is one of the smallest and most compact seats in parliament. It is a young and diverse seat: less than a quarter of its residents are aged over 45, about a quarter are black or mixed race and more than 25 per cent were born outside the EU. The seat has only elected Labour MPs since its creation in 1950, and is now one of the safest in parliament. Abbott is one of just ten MPs, all Labour, whose new majority is more than 35,000.

EU REFERENDUM RESULT
20.5% Leave   Remain 79.5%

Hackney South & Shoreditch

LAB CO-OP HOLD MAJORITY 37,931 (68.5%)

MEG HILLIER
BORN Feb 14, 1969
MP 2005-

Former journalist. Remainer, voted against Article 50. Sceptical of Jeremy Corbyn, particularly after Brexit. PPS to Ruth Kelly 2006-07. Select cttees: public accounts 2011-17, chairwoman 2015-17; commons liaison 2015-17. Parly under-sec, home office 2009-10, 2007-08. Shadow min, home office 2010. Shadow SoS, energy and climate change 2010-11. Cllr, Islington BC 1994-98; mayor 1998-9. GLA, 2000-04. Member, Fabian Society. Married, three children. Ed: Portsmouth HS; St Hilda's Coll, Oxford (BA PPE); City, University of London (Dip newspaper journalism).

	Electorate	Turnout %	from 2010 Change %
	82,004	67.50	
*M Hillier Lab Co-op	43,974	79.44	+15.04
L Parker C	6,043	10.92	-2.57
D Raval LD	3,168	5.72	+1.13
R Johnson Green	1,522	2.75	-8.84
V Hudson AWP	226	0.41	
R Higgs Ind	143	0.26	
A Watt CPA	113	0.20	-0.29
J Leff WRP	86	0.16	+0.02
H Sugg Ind	50	0.09	
D Kalamazad Ind	29	0.05	

CHALLENGERS
Luke Parker (C) Worked in sales management: IBM; Logica; Hewlett Packard. Contested Brent North 2015. **Dave Raval** (LD) Chief exec, green technology business LoftZone. Contested: Leicester East 2015; Hackney South and Shoreditch 2010. **Rebecca Johnson** (Green)

Contested Hampstead and Kilburn 2015.

CONSTITUENCY PROFILE
This seat stretches from Old Street in the west to Stratford's Olympic Park in the east. Residents earn slightly more than the residents of Hackney North, and are more likely to be in social rented housing. Half of Hackney South and Shoreditch's homes are rented socially, although less than three fifths of these are rented from the local authority. It is a young, diverse seat that, including its predecessors, has returned Labour MPs to parliament at every election since 1950.

EU REFERENDUM RESULT

22.8% Leave   Remain 77.2%

Halesowen & Rowley Regis

CONSERVATIVE HOLD MAJORITY 5,253 (11.8%)

JAMES MORRIS
BORN Feb 4, 1967
MP 2010-

Entrepreneur who started a string of software companies. Founding dir, London Policy Institute. Staunch advocate of localism: former chief exec, Localis think tank. Previously dir, Mind the Gap. Resigned as PPS to vote for law change to require planning permission to demolish local pubs. Campaigned to Remain; voted to trigger Article 50. APPG chairman, mental health 2010-17. PPS: Jeremy Hunt 2016-; Esther McVey 2014-15. Married, two children. Ed: Nottingham HS; University of Birmingham (BA English literature); Wadham Coll, Oxford (postgraduate

	Electorate	Turnout %	from 2010 Change %
	68,856	64.45	
*J Morris C	23,012	51.85	+8.65
I Cooper Lab	17,759	40.02	+3.84
S Henley Ukip	2,126	4.79	-11.82
J Scott LD	859	1.94	-0.13
J Robertson Green	440	0.99	-0.95
T Weller Ind	183	0.41	

research); Cranfield School of Management (MBA).

CHALLENGERS
Ian Cooper (Lab) Community development manager, Sandwell MBC. Member, GMB. Cllr, Dudley MBC 2014-; cabinet member for children's services. **Stuart Henley** (Ukip) Firefighter. Fire Brigades Union rep. Former RAF auxiliary. Cllr, Dudley MBC 2014-. **Jamie Scott** (LD) Criminal barrister, Citadel

Chambers. Former housing and homelessness caseworker in Brixton. **James Robertson** (Green) Social media marketing manager.

CONSTITUENCY PROFILE
This West Midlands seat, a metropolitan area between the urban centres of Birmingham and Dudley, is less ethnically diverse and slightly older than most of the seats in the area, and while median pay is lower than the regional average, levels of home ownership are slightly higher. The seat was held by Labour between 1997 and 2010, but has elected James Morris in each election since then.

EU REFERENDUM RESULT

66.6% Leave   Remain 33.4%

Halifax

LABOUR HOLD MAJORITY 5,376 (11.1%)

HOLLY LYNCH
BORN Oct 8, 1986
MP 2015-

Halifax born and bred former fast-food shopworker. Worked for a technology business. Former asst to Linda McAvan MEP. Champions Protect the Protectors initiative to impose tough punishments on people who assault police officers. Covered Batley and Spen after the murder of Jo Cox. Remainer; voted to trigger Article 50. Labour leadership nominations: Andy Burnham 2015; Owen Smith 2016. Shadow min, Defra 2017-. Opposition whip 2015-16, resigned when Rosie Winterton was sacked. Founder and co-chairwoman, APPG for Fairtrade. Married. Ed: Brighouse

	Electorate	Turnout %	from 2010 %	Change
	71,224	67.78		
*H Lynch Lab	25,507	52.84	+12.82	
C Pearson C	20,131	41.70	+2.67	
M Weedon Ukip	1,568	3.25	-9.60	
J Baker LD	1,070	2.22	-1.51	

HS; Lancaster University (BA politics and history).

CHALLENGERS
Chris Pearson (C) Owns disability services business, CJP Outreach. Cllr, Calderdale MBC 2015-. Contested Hemsworth 2015. Born in Halifax. **Mark Weedon** (Ukip) Wants foreign aid money to be invested in Halifax instead. **James Baker** (LD) Professional campaigner; ran anti-identity cards group NO2ID. Development officer, Association of Liberal Democrat

Cllrs. Cllr, Calderdale MBC 2012-.

CONSTITUENCY PROFILE
This west Yorkshire seat contains the town of Halifax and the nearby town of Sowerby Bridge. It has a young population and over a fifth of residents are aged under 16. Although Halifax is four fifths white, it also has a large Asian community. Manufacturing and finance are among the overrepresented industries. The seat has only elected Labour MPs since 1964, with the exception of Margaret Thatcher's 1983 landslide, when it became Conservative for a single term.

EU REFERENDUM RESULT

58.8% Leave   Remain 41.2%

Haltemprice & Howden

CONSERVATIVE HOLD MAJORITY 15,405 (29.9%)

DAVID DAVIS
BORN Dec 23, 1948
MP 1987-

Breezy Eurosceptic catapulted onto front line by Brexit. Former senior exec, Tate & Lyle. Member of Territorial SAS during business career. Defender of civil liberties. Resigned as shadow home secretary to fight by-election over 42-day terrorism detention 2008. Initiated, along with Tom Watson, successful legal challenge to bulk data retention in snooper's charter at ECJ. Contested Tory Party leadership 2005, 2001. Frequent critic of coalition govt on Europe, civil liberties and ISIS airstrikes. Brexit secretary 2016-; Europe minister 1994-97. Shadow home

	Electorate	Turnout %	from 2010 %	Change
	71,520	71.92		
*D Davis C	31,355	60.95	+6.78	
H Devanney Lab	15,950	31.01	+10.05	
D Nolan LD	2,482	4.83	-1.44	
D Wallis Yorkshire	942	1.83		
C Needham Green	711	1.38	-2.33	

sec 2003-08. Born to single mother. Married, three children. Ed: Tooting Bec GS; University of Warwick (BSc molecular and computer sciences); London Business Sch (MSc business); Harvard (advanced management programme).

CHALLENGERS
Hollie Devanney (Lab) Writing PhD. Teacher. Previously worked for NHS in local prison. **David Nolan** (LD) Owns market research business. Cllr: Hessle

TC 2013-; East Riding CC 1991-2007.

CONSTITUENCY PROFILE
This east Yorkshire constituency is a large and mostly rural region to the north of the Humber estuary, and to the west of Hull, encompassing the city's middle-class suburbs. Characterised by one of the highest levels of home ownership in the country, around four fifths of households are owner-occupied. A fifth of residents are aged over 65 and incomes are higher than in the neighbouring areas. It has been a safe Tory seat since its creation in 1997, and its predecessor was also safely held by the party.

EU REFERENDUM RESULT

55.2% Leave   Remain 44.8%

Halton

LABOUR HOLD MAJORITY 25,405 (51.3%)

DEREK TWIGG
BORN Jul 9, 1959
MP 1997-

	Electorate	Turnout %	from 2010 %	Change
	73,457	67.41		
*D Twigg Lab	36,115	72.93	+10.09	
M Lloyd C	10,710	21.63	+3.84	
G Redican Ukip	1,488	3.00	-11.06	
R Bate LD	896	1.81	-0.63	
V Turton Ind	309	0.62	+0.01	

Previously a civil servant in the Department for Education and Employment 1975-94. Became branch secretary, CPSA union aged 18. Campaigned to Remain, voted to trigger Article 50. Apparently neutral about Jeremy Corbyn. Voted against same-sex marriage in 2013. PPS to: Helen Liddell; Stephen Byers. Defence min 2006-08; parly under-sec for transport 2004-06; Govt whip 2002-04. Interested in housing, social inclusion and education. Select cttees: liaison 2015-17; statutory instruments 2015-17. Cllr, Cheshire CC 1980-85. Interested in military history. Married, one daughter, one son. Ed: Bankfield HS, Widnes; Halton Coll of FE.

CHALLENGERS
Matthew Lloyd (C) CEO, Omniplex eLearning Software. Cllr, Alderley Edge PC 2010-15. Primary school governor. **Glyn Redican** (Ukip) Former Labour cllr, Halton BC; mayor 2002-03. Landlord, The Wine Bar, Runcorn. Currently dir, The Wilsons Project. Defected to Ukip in 2013. **Ryan Bate** (LD) Head of geography at secondary school. Cllr, Grappenhall and Thelwall PC 2012-.

CONSTITUENCY PROFILE
Halton is a small, mostly urban north Cheshire seat to the southwest of Liverpool. It consists of the town of Widnes and most of the railway town of Runcorn. Just one in fifty residents is non-white and about a third of residents' jobs, well above average, are routine and semi-routine jobs. Incomes in Halton are well below the average in Cheshire, but only slightly lower than the North West average. The constituency has never elected an MP from a party other than Labour.

EU REFERENDUM RESULT
57.7% Leave   Remain 42.3%

Hammersmith

LABOUR HOLD MAJORITY 18,651 (35.7%)

ANDY SLAUGHTER
BORN Sep 29, 1960
MP 2005-

	Electorate	Turnout %	from 2010 %	Change
	72,803	71.77		
*A Slaughter Lab	33,375	63.87	+13.87	
C Dewhirst C	14,724	28.18	-8.23	
J Onstad LD	2,802	5.36	+0.73	
A Horn Green	800	1.53	-2.86	
J Bovill Ukip	507	0.97	-3.42	
J Hauzaree Ind	44	0.08		

Trained as a barrister, specialising in housing and personal injury law. Previously researcher for the BBC and Michael Meacher MP. Campaigned for locals to take in refugees from Syria and Calais. Shadow min: housing 2016-; justice 2010-16. Resigned as justice minister following Leave vote and in protest against Jeremy Corbyn's leadership. Campaigned to Remain in the EU and defied Labour leadership by voting against triggering Article 50. PPS to: Lord Malloch-Brown 2007-09; Lord Jones 2007-08; Stephen Ladyman 2005-07. Cllr, Hammersmith and Fulham BC 1986-2005; leader 1996-2005. Contested Uxbridge 1997. Strong interest in the Middle East, particularly Palestine. Ed: Latymer Upper Sch; University of Exeter (BA English).

CHALLENGERS
Charlie Dewhirst (C) Works for England Rugby, previously UK Sport. Former sports journalist. Cllr, Hammersmith and Fulham BC 2010-. **Joyce Onstad** (LD) Worked in international development for Christian Aid and ActionAid. **Alex Horn** (Green) HR professional, Charing Cross Hospital.

CONSTITUENCY PROFILE
A slim compact seat in west London, with Kensington to its east and Ealing to its west. Two fifths of residents are white British and under half were born outside of the UK. House prices in the seat have soared in recent years; the average price of a terraced house is over a million pounds. Hammersmith was reconstituted in 2010, and Andy Slaughter has increased his majority in every election since.

EU REFERENDUM RESULT
31.3% Leave   Remain 68.7%

Hampshire East

CONSERVATIVE HOLD MAJORITY 25,852 (46.7%)

DAMIAN HINDS
BORN Nov 27, 1969
MP 2010-

	Electorate	Turnout %	from 2010 %	Change
	74,148	74.73		
*D Hinds C	35,263	63.64	+2.98	
R Dasgupta Lab	9,411	16.98	+6.88	
R Robinson LD	8,403	15.17	+4.07	
R Knight Green	1,760	3.18	-2.97	
S Jerrard JACP	571	1.03		

Previously had a career in pubs, brewing and hotels as a strategist and marketer: Greene King; Intercontinental Hotels; Holiday Inn Worldwide. Contested Stretford and Urmston 2005. Former council member, Bow Group. Particular interests in business, the economy, tackling disadvantage and widening opportunity. Campaigned to Remain in the EU; voted to trigger Article 50. Min, DWP 2016-; exchequer secretary 2015-16; asst whip 2014-15. Formerly APPG chairman: social mobility, credit unions. Married, three children. Ed: St Ambrose GS, Altrincham; Trinity Coll, Oxford (BA PPE; president, student union).

CHALLENGERS
Rohit Dasgupta (Lab) From Calcutta, India. First Bengali to contest UK general election. Media and cultural studies lecturer, Loughborough University, with interest in South Asia and queer identities. **Richard Robinson** (LD) Chartered accountant, AGI Media, previously British Council. Cllr, Burton PC 2002-04. Married, three children. **Richard Knight** (Green) Runs a business developing custom database systems. **Susan Jerrard** (JACP) Cllr, Greatham PC 2011-.

CONSTITUENCY PROFILE
The biggest towns in Hampshire East are Petersfield, Bordon and Alton. Home ownership levels and average incomes in this very homogeneous, white seat are above both the national and regional averages. Almost half of the residents are aged over 45. It is held by the Conservatives and has been since its creation in 1983, while its predecessor, Petersfield, was held by the Conservatives from 1892.

EU REFERENDUM RESULT
49.3% Leave   Remain 50.7%

Hampshire North East

CONSERVATIVE HOLD MAJORITY 27,772 (48.2%)

RANIL JAYAWARDENA
BORN Sep 3, 1986
MP 2015-

	Electorate	Turnout %	from 2010 %	Change
	75,476	76.35		
*R Jayawardena C	37,754	65.51	-0.36	
B Jones Lab	9,982	17.32	+7.53	
G Cockarill LD	6,987	12.12	+1.65	
C Spradbery Green	1,476	2.56	-1.82	
M Gascoigne Ukip	1,061	1.84	-6.92	
R Blay Ind	367	0.64		

Background in financial services: government relations manager, Lloyds Banking Group; lobbied MEPs in Brussels on European financial regulation. Cllr, Basingstoke and Deane BC 2008-15; deputy leader 2012-15. Won open primary to take over from James Arbuthnot in 2015. Campaigned for Brexit. Select cttees: international trade 2016-17; home affairs 2015-17. Freeman, City of London. Member, Carlton Club. Interested in local history and shooting. Married, two daughters. Christian. Ed: Robert May's Sch; Alton College; LSE (BSc government).

CHALLENGERS
Barry Jones (Lab) Cllr, Rushmoor BC 2012-, 1996-2000. Labour group deputy leader. **Graham Cockarill** (LD) Insurance broker, Willis Group Holdings. Former telemarketing executive. Cllr: Hart DC 2002-; Yateley TC. **Chas Spradbery** (Green) Works in offshore energy industry designing renewable energy projects and as a consultancy manager. **Mike Gascoigne** (Ukip) Chemical engineer and fitness instructor. Contested local elections 2017, 2016, 2015.

CONSTITUENCY PROFILE
Sprawling around the town of Basingstoke, about three quarters of households in the constituency are owner-occupied, well above the national and regional averages. The information and communication sector is overrepresented and Hampshire North East has one of the largest proportions of managers and directors of any seat. It is one of the most affluent areas in the country. It has long been held by the Conservatives.

EU REFERENDUM RESULT
46.2% Leave   Remain 53.8%

Hampshire North West

CONSERVATIVE HOLD MAJORITY 22,679 (38.6%)

KIT MALTHOUSE
BORN Oct 27, 1966
MP 2015-

Qualified chartered accountant who worked for Deloitte & Touche. Founder and majority shareholder, County Finance Group. Former MS charity patron, resigned after voting in favour of disability benefit cuts. London Assembly member 2008-16; appointed by Boris Johnson to deputy mayor for policing. Cllr, Westminster CC 1998-2006; deputy leader 2000-06. Contested Liverpool Wavertree 1997. Eurosceptic who was claimed there would be an election for a president of Europe; said he fears the "elimination of the nation state". Married, three children.

	Electorate	Turnout %	from 2010 % Change
	81,430	72.17	
*K Malthouse C	36,471	62.06	+3.98
A Fitchet Lab	13,792	23.47	+10.17
A Payton LD	5,708	9.71	+0.38
R Clark Ukip	1,467	2.50	-12.20
D Hill Green	1,334	2.27	-2.33

Ed: Liverpool Coll; Newcastle University (BA economics and politics).

CHALLENGERS
Andy Fitchet (Lab) Minister, Whitchurch Baptist Church. Cllr, Andover TC 2010-; vice-chairman 2013-14. Helped form Andover Youth Council. **Alex Payton** (LD) Cllr: Newbury TC 2013-15; West Berkshire C 2003-07. Former Thatcham cllr; mayor 2006-07. Contested: Hampshire North West 2015; Havant 2010.

Roger Clark (Ukip) Claimed current fascism "comes from the liberal elite centre". Contested Northamptonshire South 2015. **Dan Hill** (Green) Reuters manager. Contested Hampshire North West 2015.

CONSTITUENCY PROFILE
The biggest town in this large and mostly rural seat is Andover. Home ownership and average earnings are lower than in Hampshire North East, but the seats are very similar demographically. Hampshire North West is a very safe Conservative seat, and its previous MP was one-time chief whip Sir George Young.

EU REFERENDUM RESULT

54.8% Leave   Remain 45.2%

Hampstead & Kilburn

LABOUR HOLD MAJORITY 15,560 (26.6%)

TULIP SIDDIQ
BORN Sep 16, 1982
MP 2015-

Worked in charity and private sectors: Amnesty Int; Save the Children; Brunswick Group LLP. Cllr, Camden BC 2010-14. Former policy adviser to Tessa Jowell; deputy field dir for Ed Miliband's leadership campaign. Nominated Jeremy Corbyn in 2015 Labour leadership contest but not particularly pro-Corbyn. Shadow education min 2016-17, resigned in opposition to Labour's three-line whip for Article 50 vote. PPS to Michael Dugher 2015-16. Aunt is the current prime minister of Bangladesh. Vocal supporter of her imprisoned British-Iranian constituent Nazanin Zaghari-

	Electorate	Turnout %	from 2010 % Change
	82,957	70.41	
*T Siddiq Lab	34,464	59.01	+14.58
C Leyland C	18,904	32.37	-9.96
K Allan LD	4,100	7.02	+1.39
J Mansook Green	742	1.27	-3.15
H Easterbrook Ind	136	0.23	
R Weiss Ind	61	0.10	

Ratcliffe. Married, one daughter. Ed: UCL (BA English); King's Coll, London (MA politics, policy and government).

CHALLENGERS
Claire-Louise Leyland (C) University lecturer and psychotherapist. Contested West Tyrone 2015. Cllr, Camden BC 2010-. Deputy chairwoman, Conservative Women's Organisation 2012-16. **Kirsty Allan** (LD) Press dir for

Norman Lamb's unsuccessful Lib Dem leadership campaign 2015. Contested Westminster North 2015.

CONSTITUENCY PROFILE
The constituency of Hampstead and Kilburn in north London combines wards from Camden and Brent councils. Compared to other London seats, there are far fewer aged under 25, and a much greater proportion of 25-44-year-olds. House prices are high, although there is significant inequality. It is also diverse: about two fifths of residents are white British. It has been Labour since its creation in 2010.

EU REFERENDUM RESULT

23.7% Leave   Remain 76.3%

Harborough

CONSERVATIVE HOLD MAJORITY 12,429 (21.6%)

NEIL O'BRIEN
BORN Nov 6, 1978
MP 2017-

Dir: Policy Exchange 2008-12; Open Europe 2005-08. Eurosceptic of long vintage. Campaigned against Britain joining the Euro while an economics researcher. Was campaign dir, Vote 2004, which advocated for an EU referendum. Author, *Reforming the EU for the 21st Century: Roadmaps for Reform*. Lead adviser on industrial strategy and the Northern Powerhouse in David Cameron's policy unit. Special adviser to George Osborne 2012-16, credited with improving Osborne's retail offer to working-class voters. Succeeds Sir Edward Garnier, who served

	Electorate	Turnout %	from 2010 Change %
	78,647	73.24	
N O'Brien C	30,135	52.32	-0.42
A Thomas Lab	17,706	30.74	+15.41
Z Haq LD	7,286	12.65	-0.76
T Khong Ukip	1,361	2.36	-12.01
D Woodiwiss Green	1,110	1.93	-2.22

as MP since 1992. Ed: Oxford University (BA PPE).

CHALLENGERS
Andy Thomas (Lab) Worked in Leicestershire CC and Leicester CC 1992-2013. Remainer. **Zuffar Haq** (LD) Businessman and founder of international aid charity. **Teck Khong** (Ukip) GP. Cllr, Oadby and Wigston BC. Contested Bradford North 2005 for Conservatives. **Darren Woodiwiss** (Green) Agile software engineer,

Travis Perkins. Sustainability campaigner.

CONSTITUENCY PROFILE
This south Leicestershire seat has the town of Market Harborough, on the Northamptonshire border, to its south, and Oadby and Wigston, two small towns just south of Leicester, to its north. About a seventh of its population is Asian or of Asian descent, mostly Indian. Home ownership levels in the constituency are well above the national average. Harborough elected a Labour MP in 1945, but has been represented only by Conservative MPs since 1950.

EU REFERENDUM RESULT

52.4% Leave   Remain 47.6%

Harlow

CONSERVATIVE HOLD MAJORITY 7,031 (15.7%)

ROBERT HALFON
BORN Mar 22, 1969
MP 2010-

Career politician who extols blue-collar conservatism and published pamphlet urging more Tories to join trade unions. Former chief of staff to Oliver Letwin MP. Member, Conservative Way Forward. Board member, Centre for Social Justice. Contested Harlow 2005, 2001. Tireless backbencher before ministerial career: organised petition to make St George's Day a public holiday. Ran Petrol Promise campaign, which successfully lobbied govt to lower fuel duty and cut petrol and diesel costs. Named *Spectator* Campaigning MP of the Year 2013. Min: education

	Electorate	Turnout %	from 2010 Change %
	67,697	66.25	
*R Halfon C	24,230	54.03	+5.16
P Waite Lab	17,199	38.35	+8.36
M Gough Ukip	1,787	3.98	-12.30
G Seeff LD	970	2.16	+0.12
H Clare Green	660	1.47	-0.68

2016-17; without portfolio, Cabinet Office 2015-16. PPS to George Osborne 2014-15. Chairman, education select cttee 2017-. Jewish. Lives with partner. Ed: University of Exeter (BA politics; MA Russian and eastern European politics).

CHALLENGERS
Phil Waite (Lab) Trade official, Usdaw. Cllr, Harlow DC 2012-. Remainer. **Mark Gough** (Ukip) Suspended from Conservative party in 2012 and defected to

Ukip soon after. Cllr, Harlow DC 2008-10. **Geoffrey Seeff** (LD) Contested Harlow 2015.

CONSTITUENCY PROFILE
Comprised of the Essex town of Harlow and some of the rural area around it. Overrepresented industries in the seat include retail and construction. The seat is characterised by much higher than average levels of local authority renting and incomes are skewed to below the national and east of England averages. Harlow was held by Labour from its creation in 1974 until 1983. It has since been a bellwether, although Labour's majority at the 2005 election was just 97.

EU REFERENDUM RESULT

67.7% Leave   Remain 32.3%

Harrogate & Knaresborough

CONSERVATIVE HOLD MAJORITY 18,168 (32.0%)

ANDREW JONES
BORN Nov 28, 1963
MP 2010-

Proud Yorkshireman. Prior to election worked in sales and marketing: Bettys and Taylors of Harrogate; M & C Saatchi; Going Places; Kingfisher; Superdrug; B&Q. Chairman, Bow Group 1999-2000. Cllr, Harrogate BC 2003-11. Contested Harrowgate and Knaresborough 2001. Campaigns on environmental issues and champions renewable energy and recycling. Campaigned to Remain; voted to trigger Article 50. Treasury min 2017-. Parly under-sec for transport 2015-17. Enjoys cricket and squash. Ed: Bradford GS; University of Leeds (BA English).

	Electorate	Turnout %	from 2010 % Change
	77,265	73.44	
*A Jones C	31,477	55.48	+2.73
H Flynn LD	13,309	23.46	+1.38
M Sewards Lab	11,395	20.08	+9.95
D Fraser Ind	559	0.99	

CHALLENGERS
Helen Flynn (LD) Local businesswoman. Cllr, Harrogate BC 2012-16. Member, federal policy cttee. Chairwoman, Social Liberal Forum. Exec member, Lib Dem Education Association. Worked in publishing. Runs a retail and mail order business. Contested Skipton and Ripon 2010. **Mark Sewards** (Lab) Maths teacher who previously worked in finance. **Donald Fraser** (Ind) Runs a marketing company and works as a freelance designer. Brexiteer who aligned himself with Liberal Leave. Previously campaigned for the Lib Dems but left the party over second EU referendum policy.

CONSTITUENCY PROFILE
Harrogate and Knaresborough is the smallest seat in England's largest county with a 95 per cent white population. Home ownership in this north Yorkshire region is relatively high, and incomes tend to be slightly higher than the Yorkshire and Humber average. The predecessor seat of Harrogate elected Conservative MPs since 1950 but Harrogate and Knaresborough was held by the Lib Dems from 1997 to 2010.

EU REFERENDUM RESULT
47.2% Leave   Remain 52.8%

Harrow East

CONSERVATIVE HOLD MAJORITY 1,757 (3.5%)

BOB BLACKMAN
BORN Apr 26, 1956
MP 2010-

Career in sales and management, including as regulatory compliance manager for BT. Cllr, Brent BC 1986-2010; deputy leader 2006-10; leader 1991-96. London Assembly member 2004-08. Contested: Brent North 2005; Bedford and Kempston 1997; Brent South 1992. Backbencher from mainstream Conservative right. Brexit supporter. Member, backbench business cttee 2012-17. Voted against equal marriage "on principle". School governor. Christian. Married. Ed: Preston Manor HS; University of Liverpool (BSc physics and maths).

	Electorate	Turnout %	from 2010 % Change
	71,757	70.86	
*B Blackman C	25,129	49.42	-0.92
N Shah Lab	23,372	45.97	+5.33
A Bernard LD	1,573	3.09	+0.98
E Wallace Green	771	1.52	-0.21

CHALLENGERS
Navin Shah (Lab) Born in India, moved to UK to take scholarship at UCL. Architect. Cllr, Harrow BC 1994-2014; leader 2004-06. First Indian London Assembly member 2008-. Won 2006 Asian Achievers Award. Founder and trustee, Harrow Anti-Racist Alliance. **Adam Bernard** (LD) Researcher in computer science, medicine and linguistics at Queen Mary UoL. **Emma Wallace** (Green) School librarian. Campaigned to protect libraries, health services and children's centres. Contested Harrow East 2015.

CONSTITUENCY PROFILE
This northwest London seat has one of the largest proportions of Hindu residents of any seat, and is also home to large Muslim and Jewish communities. Home ownership in Harrow East is higher not only than the London average, but the UK average too, although earnings are slightly lower than the London average. The area has a significant student population and low unemployment. A bellwether since 1979, majorities are often small and the Conservatives' majority fell by 3,000 in 2017.

EU REFERENDUM RESULT
47.5% Leave   Remain 52.5%

Harrow West

LAB CO-OP HOLD MAJORITY 13,314 (26.4%)

GARETH THOMAS
BORN Jul 15, 1967
MP 1997-

Former teacher. Long-standing chairman of the Co-operative Party 2000-17. Cllr, Harrow BC 1990-97. Remainer; voted to trigger Article 50. Former parly under-sec for trade and Dfid. Promoted to ministerial roles under Gordon Brown's government: international development 2008-10; BERR 2008-09. Shadow minister: CLG 2016-; FCO 2013-15. Sought Labour Party candidacy for 2016 London mayoralty, but came last. PPS to Charles Clarke 1999-2003. Married, two children. Ed: Hatch End HS; Aberystwyth University (BSc economics and politics); King's

Electorate	Turnout %	from 2010 % Change
69,798	72.14	
*G Thomas Lab Co-op	30,640	60.85 +13.89
H David C	17,326	34.41 -7.81
C Noyce LD	1,267	2.52 -0.85
R Langley Green	652	1.29 -1.52
R Alagaratnam Ukip	470	0.93 -3.46

Coll, London (MA imperial and commonwealth studies); Thames Polytechnic (PGCE).

CHALLENGERS
Hannah David (C) Restaurant owner. Non-practising solicitor. Founder, Planning Futures think tank focused on town and country planning. Cllr, Hertsmere BC 2004-13. Chairwoman, Hendon Ward Conservatives. Contested Harrow West 2015. **Christopher Noyce** (LD) Solicitor. Cllr,

Harrow BC 2006-, 1986-2002. Contested: Harrow West 2015, 2010, 2005, 2001, 1992; Bedford 1997.

CONSTITUENCY PROFILE
A slightly younger seat than its neighbour, with two thirds of its residents aged 45 or under. More than two fifths of residents are either Asian or of Asian descent, and the seat has large Hindu and Muslim communities. A minority of the population is white. Home ownership is lower and private-sector renting higher than its counterpart. Harrow West returned Conservative MPs from 1945 to 1997, but has been Labour since.

EU REFERENDUM RESULT

45.1% Leave   Remain 54.9%

Hartlepool

LABOUR HOLD MAJORITY 7,650 (18.3%)

MIKE HILL
BORN May 12, 1963
MP 2017-

Library worker turned union official. Regional organiser and political lead officer, Unison; former branch sec, Rochdale Unison; sec, TULO. Active campaigner on health issues, including to protect local assisted fertility units and GP practices. Previously vice-chairman, Labour North. Contested Richmond (Yorks) 2015. Voted Remain in EU referendum. Married, two sons. Ed: Sutherland Road HS, Heywood; Lancaster University (BA drama and English literature).

CHALLENGERS
Carl Jackson (C) Qualified

Electorate	Turnout %	from 2010 % Change
70,718	59.16	
M Hill Lab	21,969	52.51 +16.87
C Jackson C	14,319	34.23 +13.32
P Broughton Ukip	4,801	11.48 -16.51
A Hagon LD	746	1.78 -0.14

solicitor. Dir, MSB Consultancy. Former policy adviser to David Davis MP. Co-editor, *Future of Conservatism*. Former guest political columnist, *Yorkshire Post*. Cllr, Chiltern DC 2015-. Contested Don Valley 2015. **Phillip Broughton** (Ukip) Supervisor at Tesco. Former semi-professional wrestler; runs a small business promoting the sport. Contested Hartlepool 2015. Stood for Ukip leader in 2016, finished fourth out of five. **Andy Hagon** (LD) Background in education as a history teacher,

specialist leader in education and education officer at Hartlepool Local Education Authority.

CONSTITUENCY PROFILE
Hartlepool is a coastal northeast town between Redcar and Easington, and the seat extends a little way beyond it. Less than one in forty residents is non-white and although incomes are in line with the rest of the region, unemployment is well above average. Like its predecessor, Hartlepool has only elected Labour MPs since 1964. It was Peter Mandelson's seat between 1992 and 2004. The seat had the highest Leave vote in the North East.

EU REFERENDUM RESULT

69.6% Leave   Remain 30.4%

Harwich & Essex North

CONSERVATIVE HOLD MAJORITY 14,356 (28.1%)

BERNARD JENKIN
BORN Apr 9, 1959
MP 1992-

Former venture capital manager. Eurosceptic rightwinger and avid Brexit campaigner. Policy adviser to Leon Brittan 1986-88. MP for Essex North 1997-2010; Colchester North 1992-97. Contested Glasgow Central 1987. Embroiled in 2009 expenses scandal for paying rent for property to his sister-in-law. Chairman, public administration and constitutional affairs select cttee 2010-; led select cttee inquiry into collapse of Kids Company charity. Member, 1922 exec cttee 2015-. Long-time friend of screenwriter Richard Curtis, who regularly names characters Bernard. Married,

	Electorate	Turnout %	from 2010 %	Change
	71,294	71.73		
*B Jenkin C	29,921	58.51	+7.46	
R Scott Lab	15,565	30.44	+10.72	
D Graham LD	2,787	5.45	-1.93	
A Hammond Ukip	1,685	3.29	-14.18	
B Roberts Green	1,042	2.04	-2.34	
S Todd CPA	141	0.28		

two sons. Ed: William Ellis Sch; Corpus Christi Coll, Cambridge (BA English).

CHALLENGERS
Rosalind Scott (Lab) Former science teacher. Cllr, Colchester CC 2014-. Local chairwoman, Refugee Action. **Dominic Graham** (LD) Cllr, Colchester CC 2014-17. Contested Harwich and Essex North 2015. **Aaron Hammond** (Ukip) Aged 18 at time of election. Acting

membership secretary for local Ukip branch.

CONSTITUENCY PROFILE
This seat contains the University of Essex's Colchester campus. Education is an overrepresented industry among residents, although most students in the area live in neighbouring Colchester. Over a fifth of residents are aged 65 or above, around three quarters of households are owner-occupied, and the seat has relatively high levels of self-employment. It is a safe Conservative seat, as was its predecessor. Jenkin first won Essex North in 1997, Labour's high watermark, by 5,000 votes.

EU REFERENDUM RESULT
59.0% Leave   Remain 41.0%

Hastings & Rye

CONSERVATIVE HOLD MAJORITY 346 (0.6%)

AMBER RUDD
BORN Aug 1, 1963
MP 2010-

Home sec 2016-. Previously worked in investment banking and venture capital. Appointed by Richard Curtis as aristocracy co-ordinator for party scenes in Four Weddings and a Funeral. Contested Liverpool Garston 2005. Filled in for Theresa May in seven-way BBC election debate just days after her father died. Prominent Remain campaigner who attacked Boris Johnson for being misleading during ITV debate. Speech about foreign workers to the 2016 Conservative party conference was reported as a hate incident to police. SoS, ECC 2015-16; Parly under-sec, ECC 2014-

	Electorate	Turnout %	from 2010 %	Change
	78,298	69.95		
*A Rudd C	25,668	46.87	+2.32	
P Chowney Lab	25,322	46.24	+11.11	
N Perry LD	1,885	3.44	+0.27	
M Phillips Ukip	1,479	2.70	-10.62	
N Wilson Ind	412	0.75		

15; govt whip 2013-14; PPS to George Osborne 2012-13. Was married to the late restaurant critic AA Gill, who referred to her as the "Silver Spoon" in his columns. Two children. Ed: Cheltenham Ladies' Coll; University of Edinburgh (BA history).

CHALLENGERS
Peter Chowney (Lab) First elected cllr, Hastings BC; leader 2015-. Worked in scientific research. **Nicholas Perry** (LD)

Trained social worker. Contested Hastings and Rye 2015, 2010. **Michael Phillips** (Ukip) Cllr, E Sussex CC 2013-17.

CONSTITUENCY PROFILE
Hastings and Rye are coastal Sussex towns. The seat is characterised by relatively high levels of self-employment and lower than average wages, and its overrepresented industries include health and social care and construction. The seat has been a bellwether since its creation in 1983, although both the old individual seats of Hastings and Rye had been consistently Conservative since the Second World War.

EU REFERENDUM RESULT
55.9% Leave   Remain 44.1%

Havant

CONSERVATIVE HOLD MAJORITY 15,956 (34.5%)

ALAN MAK
BORN Nov 19, 1983
MP 2015-

Former lawyer at Clifford Chance. Family ran a small shop in York. Elected through an open primary in 2015. Has campaigned for the Tories since sixth form. Non-executive dir and investor in a range of businesses. Former president, Magic Breakfast, a charity for disadvantaged children. Criticised for U-turn on Brexit, originally told Havant select cttee he was Eurosceptic but campaigned to Remain in 2016. Member, Conservative Christian Fellowship. Ed: St Peter's Sch, York (assisted-place scholarship); Peterhouse, Cambridge (BA law; won ECS Wade Prize); Oxford

	Electorate	Turnout %	from 2010 % Change
	72,464	63.91	
*A Mak C	27,676	59.76	+8.10
G Giles Lab	11,720	25.31	+9.36
P Gray LD	2,801	6.05	-0.49
J Perry Ukip	2,011	4.34	-16.27
T Dawes Green	1,122	2.42	-2.82
A Buckley Ind	984	2.12	

Institute of Legal Practice (PgDip law & business).

CHALLENGERS
Graham Giles (Lab) Founded international development charity, Europe to Europe in 1991. Developed probation schemes across Europe. Former justice consultant, World Bank. Assisted dissidents in Eastern Bloc nations. **Paul Gray** (LD) Worked in financial services, mostly in the City of London.

Staunchly opposed to Brexit. **John Perry** (Ukip) Retired accountant, auditor and electronic design engineer. Chairman, Ukip Havant branch. Cllr, Havant BC 2014-.

CONSTITUENCY PROFILE
More than a fifth of the constituency's residents are aged 65 or above. While home ownership is average for the southeast, there is a disproportionate number of households in the social rented sector. Unemployment is low and pay is below average. Havant is a safe Conservative seat, held by the party since 1950.

EU REFERENDUM RESULT
62.6% Leave   Remain 37.4%

Hayes & Harlington

LABOUR HOLD MAJORITY 18,115 (37.9%)

JOHN MCDONNELL
BORN Sep 8, 1951
MP 1997-

Softly spoken left-winger whose time has come. Condemned for his use of language in the past, particularly with regard to the IRA, Margaret Thatcher and Grenfell. Close ally of Jeremy Corbyn: campaign agent to Corbyn during 2015 Labour leadership contest, shadow chancellor of the exchequer 2015-. History of rebelling on numerous issues including Iraq, tuition fees, and ID cards. Chief exec, assoc of London Authorities 1987-95. Cllr, GLC 1981-86. Editor, *Labour Herald*. Chairman of Socialist Campaign Group during New Labour. Campaigned to Remain but

	Electorate	Turnout %	from 2010 % Change
	73,268	65.24	
*J McDonnell Lab	31,796	66.52	+6.94
G Smith C	13,681	28.62	+3.89
C Dixon Ukip	1,153	2.41	-9.55
B Newton Dunn LD	601	1.26	-0.71
J Bowman Green	571	1.19	-0.57

caused controversy when he later said that Brexit offered enormous opportunities. Married, three children. Ed: Brunel University London (BSc government and politics); Birkbeck, London (MSc politics and sociology).

CHALLENGERS
Greg Smith (C) Runs a marketing and campaigns business. Cllr, Hammersmith & Fulham BC 2006-. Campaigned for a Leave vote. **Cliff Dixon**

(Ukip) Communications and consumer electronics professional. Resigned from English Democrats in 2011.

CONSTITUENCY PROFILE
This west London seat contains Heathrow airport, a significant source of local jobs, and the built-up residential area to the north of it. About a quarter of residents are aged under 16, more than a third are of Asian descent and the seat contains large Muslim and Sikh communities. Incomes and house prices are below the London average. The seat was Conservative from 1983 to 1997, and has been Labour since.

EU REFERENDUM RESULT
58.2% Leave   Remain 41.8%

Hazel Grove

CONSERVATIVE HOLD MAJORITY 5,514 (12.5%)

WILLIAM WRAGG
BORN Dec 11, 1987
MP 2015-

	Electorate	Turnout %	from 2010 %	Change
	62,684	70.40		
*W Wragg C	20,047	45.43	+4.05	
L Smart LD	14,533	32.93	+6.72	
N Mishra Lab	9,036	20.47	+2.93	
R Lee Green	516	1.17	-1.47	

Former primary school teacher who mentored children with special educational needs. Teach First graduate. Caseworker for David Nuttall MP. Cllr, Stockport MBC 2011-15; first Conservative elected to serve Hazel Grove ward since 1992. School governor. Member, 1922 exec cttee. Right-winger who backed Andrea Leadsom's leadership bid. Made headlines when he moved in with his parents so he could save for a deposit 2016. Brexiteer. Rebelled to vote against liberalising Sunday trading law. Openly gay. Ed: Poynton HS; University of Manchester (BA history).

CHALLENGERS
Lisa Smart (LD) Energetic charity and community activist. Dir: Stockport Credits Union; Joseph Rowntree Reform Trust. Member, HS2 Community and Business Funds independent panel. Previously worked in international investment management. School governor. Cllr, Stockport MBC 2016-. Contested Hazel Grove 2015. **Nav Mishra** (Lab) Works at John Lewis. Founder, Momentum Stockport. Member, Unite. **Robbie Lee** (Green) 18-year-old sixth form student. Co-convenor, North West Young Greens.

CONSTITUENCY PROFILE
This Greater Manchester seat, just east of Stockport, is partly rural and partly metropolitan. It was created in 1974 and absorbed parts of what was the Cheadle constituency. About half of its residents are aged over 45. About three quarters of homes are owner-occupied, well above the UK average, and median pay is slightly above the North West average. The seat elected a Liberal Democrat from 1997 until 2015, but had elected Conservative MPs for the preceding 23 years.

EU REFERENDUM RESULT

52.2% Leave   Remain 47.8%

Hemel Hempstead

CONSERVATIVE HOLD MAJORITY 9,445 (18.1%)

MIKE PENNING
BORN Sep 29, 1957
MP 2005-

	Electorate	Turnout %	from 2010 %	Change
	75,011	69.70		
*M Penning C	28,735	54.96	+2.08	
M Tattershall Lab	19,290	36.90	+13.07	
S Symington LD	3,233	6.18	+1.34	
S Hassan Green	1,024	1.96	-1.39	

Former grenadier guardsman, fireman and journalist. Political reporter, *Express* and freelance. Served in the army in Northern Ireland, Kenya and Germany. A populist right-winger. Long-standing supporter of Brexit although he did not join any of the Leave campaign groups. Contested Thurrock 2001. Media adviser to several members of the William Hague shadow cabinet and deputy head of media for Conservative Central Office 2000-04. Min: armed forces 2016-17; policing 2014-16; disabled people 2013-14; Northern Ireland 2012-13. Married, two daughters. Ed:

Appleton Comp; King Edmund Comp, Essex.

CHALLENGERS
Mandi Tattershall (Lab) Works in housing management. Previously a citizens advice volunteer and employment tribunal rep. School governor. **Sally Symington** (LD) Trustee of Pepper Foundation, funding hospice-at-home care for children. Previously an institutional fund manager and researcher at constitution unit, UCL. Chairwoman, Great Gaddesdon PC. **Sherief Hassan** (Green) Works in media. Has been employed by the Ministry of Defence and NHS.

CONSTITUENCY PROFILE
This Hertfordshire seat, just north of Watford and south of Luton, consists of the town of Hemel Hempstead and some of the more rural areas to its north. Council renting is well above average, and pay is slightly above the regional average. A high proportion of residents are employed in communication and administration. The seat was held by Labour from 1997 to 2005, but has otherwise mostly elected Conservative MPs.

EU REFERENDUM RESULT

55.5% Leave   Remain 44.5%

Hemsworth

LABOUR HOLD MAJORITY 10,174 (22.1%)

JON TRICKETT
BORN Jul 2, 1950
MP 1996-

Electorate	Turnout %	from 2010 %	Change
71,870	63.93		
*J Trickett Lab	25,740	56.02	+4.68
M Jordan C	15,566	33.88	+11.02
D Dews Ukip	2,591	5.64	-14.56
M Roberts Yorkshire	1,135	2.47	
J MacQueen LD	912	1.99	-1.21

Previously worked as a plumber and builder. Leading figure in grassroots left organisation Compass. Committed and loyal to Jeremy Corbyn but removed as his campaign co-ordinator before two crucial by-elections in 2017 after allegations of a spat with Corbyn's office manager, Karie Murphy. Among the first to call for Tony Blair's resignation. Eurosceptic, leaked emails revealed he sought permission from Corbyn to vote Leave in the EU referendum and was accused of undermining the Remain campaign. On shadow front bench as lord president of the council 2017- and minister for the cabinet office 2017-, 2010-13.. PPS to: Gordon Brown 2008-10; Peter Mandelson 1997-98. Cllr, Leeds CC 1984-96; leader 1989-96. Married, two daughters, one son. Ed: Roundhay GS, Leeds; University of Hull (BA politics); University of Leeds (MA political sociology).

CHALLENGERS
Mike Jordan (C) Chemist. Cllr, Selby DC 2007-. **David Dews** (Ukip) Cllr, Wakefield DC 2014- Contested: Morley and Outwood 2015; Pudsey 2010. **Martin Roberts** (Yorkshire) Interest in social care, sceptical about HS2.

CONSTITUENCY PROFILE
Hemsworth is a west Yorkshire seat made up of former coalmining towns and villages. Many of its residents commute to Wakefield and Leeds. Over a fifth of the workforce are employed in wholesale and retail (well above the UK average) and there is a prevalence of routine-level jobs. The seat has only elected Labour MPs since its creation in 1918, although in 2017 the Conservatives won their largest share of the vote in Hemsworth.

EU REFERENDUM RESULT
68.1% Leave   Remain 31.9%

Hendon

CONSERVATIVE HOLD MAJORITY 1,072 (2.1%)

MATTHEW OFFORD
BORN Sep 3, 1969
MP 2010-

Electorate	Turnout %	from 2010 %	Change
76,329	68.41		
*M Offord C	25,078	48.03	-0.99
M Katz Lab	24,006	45.98	+4.46
A Hill LD	1,985	3.80	+1.61
C Legarda Green	578	1.11	-0.94
S Warsame Ukip	568	1.09	-4.14

Former political analyst at the BBC. Investigated by police in 2016 for swearing at a Labour candidate and a former fire officer from his office window. Campaigned to Leave the EU. Contested Barnsley East and Mexborough 2001. Cllr, Barnet BC 2002-; as deputy leader he introduced the first compulsory recycling scheme in the UK. Member, environmental audit select cttee 2016-17, 2012-15. Fellow, Royal Geographical Society. Ed: Amery Hill Sch, Alton; Nottingham Trent University; Lancaster University (MA environment, culture and society); King's College London (PhD rural governance).

CHALLENGERS
Mike Katz (Lab) Worked for rail union TSSA. Cllr, Kilburn BC 2010-14. Contested Cities of London and Westminster 2001. Former chairman: Cities of London and Westminster CLP; Hampstead and Highgate CLP. **Alasdair Hill** (LD) Director of studies at a comprehensive secondary school. Studied tropical environmental science and worked on malaria research before teaching. Led the successful Save Barnet Libraries petition group. Contested Hendon 2015.

CONSTITUENCY PROFILE
This northwest London area is home to Middlesex University and is a relatively young seat with a large student community. It is very ethnically diverse and has the second biggest Jewish population of any seat after neighbouring Finchley and Golders Green. Income is slightly below the London average. The seat was re-created in 1997 and was held by Labour until 2010 when Andrew Dismore lost it by 106 votes.

EU REFERENDUM RESULT
41.6% Leave   Remain 58.4%

Henley

CONSERVATIVE HOLD MAJORITY 22,294 (39.0%)

JOHN HOWELL
BORN Jul 27, 1955
MP 2008-

Former partner, Ernst & Young. Led attempts to establish UK trading links with eastern Europe; awarded OBE for efforts 2000. Business reporter, BBC World Service 1994-95. Has published books on archaeology and international affairs. Campaigned to Remain in the EU. PPS to: Andrew Lansley 2012-14; Sir George Young 2010-12; Greg Clark 2010-11. Select cttees: justice 2014-17; work and pensions 2008-10. Member, Council of Europe. Married, three children. Ed: University of Edinburgh (MA archaeology); St John's Coll, Oxford (DPhil prehistoric archaeology).

	Electorate	Turnout %	from 2010 %	Change
	74,987	76.15		
*J Howell C	33,749	59.11	+0.64	
O Kavanagh Lab	11,455	20.06	+7.54	
L Coyle LD	8,485	14.86	+3.63	
R Bennett Green	1,864	3.26	-3.64	
T Scott Ukip	1,154	2.02	-8.85	
P Gray Radical	392	0.69		

CHALLENGERS
Oliver Kavanagh (Lab) Lawyer. Former barman. Football referee for local club. **Laura Coyle** (LD) Housing solicitor, Turpin & Miller. Cllr, Haringey BC 2004-10. Former volunteer, Citizens Advice Bureau. **Robin Bennett** (Green) Guitarist, St Etienne. Co-founder, green living festival Woodfest. Former songwriting tutor, Oxford Brookes University. **Tim Scott** (Ukip) Ex-army, Christian and pro-Israel.

CONSTITUENCY PROFILE
A large, affluent and overwhelmingly rural Oxfordshire seat, stretching from north of Oxford down to the north of Reading. Famous for its annual royal regatta. Median income in the constituency is far above the national average and Henley's workforce is skewed towards managers, directors and other professional occupations. Home ownership is above average, just shy of three quarters, and unemployment rate is one of the lowest in the UK. The seat's two previous MPs have been cabinet ministers Michael Heseltine and Boris Johnson.

EU REFERENDUM RESULT

43.1% Leave   Remain 56.9%

Hereford & Herefordshire South

CONSERVATIVE HOLD MAJORITY 15,013 (29.7%)

JESSE NORMAN
BORN Jun 23, 1962
MP 2010-

Previously a philosophy researcher and teacher, UCL. Worked at Barclays 1991-97. Ran an educational project giving away textbooks in eastern Europe. Refused to make public his referendum vote on Brexit. Sacked as govt adviser by David Cameron for abstaining from Syrian intervention vote. Parly under-sec: transport 2017-; BIS 2016-17. Friend and Eton contemporary of Boris Johnson. Policy adviser to Johnson during mayoral campaign and George Osborne when shadow chancellor. Has written a number of books and pamphlets; shortlisted for prestigious awards

	Electorate	Turnout %	from 2010 %	Change
	71,088	71.02		
*J Norman C	27,004	53.49	+0.92	
A Coda Lab	11,991	23.75	+10.97	
J Kenyon Ind	5,560	11.01		
L Hurds LD	3,556	7.04	-3.54	
D Toynbee Green	1,220	2.42	-4.81	
G Price Ukip	1,153	2.28	-14.55	

for biography of Edmund Burke. Dir, Hay Festival of Literature and the Arts. Married, three children. Ed: Eton Coll; Merton Coll, Oxford (MA classics); UCL (MPhil; PhD philosophy).

CHALLENGERS
Anna Coda (Lab) Retired chemistry teacher, lives on small family farm. Chairwoman, Hereford and Herefordshire South Labour. Voluntary worker, Oxfam. Previously

representative: NUT, NASUWT. **Jim Kenyon** (Ind) Served in armed forces for 14 years.

CONSTITUENCY PROFILE
A large and mostly rural seat, except for the towns of Hereford and Ross-on-Wye on the Welsh border. Nearly a fifth of residents are aged 65 or over and about one in fifty residents is non-white. Among the most overrepresented industries are manufacturing, forestry and agriculture. Before Norman won the seat back, the old Hereford seat was held by a Lib Dem MP between 1997 and 2010, although previously it had been Conservative since 1931.

EU REFERENDUM RESULT

60.4% Leave   Remain 39.6%

Herefordshire North

CONSERVATIVE HOLD MAJORITY 21,602 (43.1%)

BILL WIGGIN
BORN Jun 4, 1966
MP 2001-

	Electorate	Turnout %	from 2010 %	Change
	67,751	74.06		
*B Wiggin C	31,097	61.97	+6.34	
R Page Lab	9,495	18.92	+7.52	
J Falconer LD	5,874	11.71	-0.30	
E Chowns Green	2,771	5.52	-1.43	
S Norris Ind	577	1.15		
A Devine Ind	363	0.72		

Former financier and TA officer with Royal Welsh Fusiliers reaching platoon commander. Particular interest in agriculture; named Countryside Alliance's first Westminster champion and owns a farm stocked with Hereford cattle. Pro-Brexit. Apologised for mistakenly claiming £11,000 for a phantom mortgage. Contested Burnley 1997. Treasury whip 2010-12. Member, 1992 exec cttee 2015-. Son of former Tory MP Sir Jerry Wiggin. Contemporary of David Cameron at Eton. Married, two sons, one daughter. Ed: Eton Coll; University Coll of North Wales (BA economics).

CHALLENGERS
Roger Page (Lab) Planning consultant and chairman, Bromyard Chamber of Commerce and Industry. Cllr, Bromyard PC. Vice-chairman, North Hertfordshire Labour Party. **Jeanie Falconer** (LD) Former European public affairs consultant working in London and Brussels. Runs a farm and vineyard. Married, three children. Contested Herefordshire North 2015. **Ellie**

Chowns (Green) Spent 20 years working in charities.

CONSTITUENCY PROFILE
Herefordshire North is a large and very sparse seat along the English border with Wales. Nearly a quarter of its residents are of pensionable age and fewer than one in seventy residents is non-white. The seat is characterised by relatively high levels of home ownership, and incomes are above average. The seat has a substantially self-sufficient population. It has been Conservative since its creation in 2010; its predecessor Leominister had voted only Conservative since 1910.

EU REFERENDUM RESULT
58.0% Leave   Remain 42.0%

Hertford & Stortford

CONSERVATIVE HOLD MAJORITY 19,035 (31.7%)

MARK PRISK
BORN Jun 12, 1962
MP 2001-

	Electorate	Turnout %	from 2010 %	Change
	82,429	72.78		
*M Prisk C	36,184	60.31	+4.18	
K Chibah Lab	17,149	28.59	+10.67	
M Argent LD	4,845	8.08	+0.28	
D Woollcombe Green	1,814	3.02	-1.74	

Chartered surveyor and businessman. Set up own marketing consultancy. Founder, East Hertfordshire Business Forum. Voted Remain. Has held ministerial roles in business, innovation and enterprise, as well as housing 2012-13. Tweeted that he had been asked to make way for a younger generation when sacked as housing minister. Prime minister's investment envoy to Nordic and Baltic nations 2014-; Brazil 2016-. Criticised for taking on second job as strategic adviser for a private property developer in 2014. Founding chairman, Youth for Peace through Nato.

Member, Prince's Trust. Married. Ed: Truro Sch; University of Reading (BSc land management).

CHALLENGERS
Katherine Chibah (Lab) Music teacher, accomplished viola player. Cllr Enfield BC 2014-. Member: Musicians Union; Unite; Co-operative Party. **Mark Argent** (LD) Background in web design, publishing and organisational consultancy. Ran his own business. Secretary of the East of England Faiths Council 2001-06. Regular

contributor to *Independent Voices*. **David Woollcombe** (Green) Co-founder of international climate change charity.

CONSTITUENCY PROFILE
Hertford and Stortford is a wide seat that runs along Hertfordshire's border with Essex, with Hertford to the southwest and Bishop's Stortford to the northeast. Workers in the constituency are more likely to be in managerial and professional occupations and tend to be higher paid than average. A safe Conservative seat which the party has comfortably held since 1983.

EU REFERENDUM RESULT
49.2% Leave   Remain 50.8%

Hertfordshire North East

CONSERVATIVE HOLD MAJORITY 16,835 (30.3%)

SIR OLIVER HEALD
BORN Dec 15, 1954
MP 1992-

Former barrister and QC. Solicitor general 2012-14; led the digital modernisation of the criminal justice system. Soft Tory, EU Remain campaigner. Argued for tightening of female genital mutilation laws. Contested Southwark and Bermondsey 1987. Justice min 2016-17; was asked to make way for a younger person. Vociferously opposed House of Lords Reform Bill. Shadow min: justice 2004-07; work and pensions 2002-03. Leader of Commons 2003-05. Exec chairman, Society of Conservative lawyers 2008-. Married, three children. Ed:

	Electorate	Turnout %	from 2010 %	Change
	75,967	73.16		
*O Heald C	32,587	58.63	+3.27	
D Swanney Lab	15,752	28.34	+9.47	
N Shepard LD	4,276	7.69	+0.14	
T Lee Green	2,965	5.33	+0.00	

Reading Sch; Pembroke Coll, Cambridge (BA, law); City Law School.

CHALLENGERS
Doug Swanney (Lab) Secretary for the Methodist Church. Worked as a children's development officer. Campaigner for child protection and care issues. **Nicky Shepard** (LD) Former business owner, now works in PR for a housing association. Former community campaigner. **Tim Lee** (Green) Runs a consultancy company.

CONSTITUENCY PROFILE
The biggest towns in this large and mostly rural constituency are Letchworth and Royston. Many London commuters reside in the south of the seat and it is close to Stansted airport. The population is predominantly UK-born and white but also contains a larger than average Sikh community. The workforce in this seat is more likely to work in professional and managerial jobs. Median pay is well above average while unemployment is low. Home ownership is high and residents tend to enjoy good health. The seat has voted Conservative since its creation in 1997.

EU REFERENDUM RESULT
51.4% Leave   Remain 48.6%

Hertfordshire South West

CONSERVATIVE HOLD MAJORITY 19,550 (32.2%)

DAVID GAUKE
BORN Oct 8, 1971
MP 2005-

Former solicitor who worked in financial services for Macfarlanes. Researcher for Barry Legg MP while a university student. Contested Brent East 2001. Safe pair of hands who capably firefights in the media. Campaigned to Remain in the EU, voted to trigger Article 50. Work and pensions sec 2017-; chief sec to Treasury 2016-17; financial sec 2014-16; exchequer sec 2010-14; shadow Treasury 2007-10. Tends not to rebel. Patron, the Hospice of St Francis. Married, three sons. Ed: Northgate HS, Ipswich; St Edmund Hall, Oxford (BA law); Chester Coll of Law.

	Electorate	Turnout %	from 2010 %	Change
	80,293	75.54		
*D Gauke C	35,128	57.92	+0.98	
R Wakely Lab	15,578	25.68	+9.37	
C Townsend LD	7,078	11.67	+1.42	
P De Hoest Green	1,576	2.60	-1.91	
M Anderson Ukip	1,293	2.13	-9.40	

CHALLENGERS
Ron Wakely (Lab) Works for the Department for Transport, focusing on reducing the environmental impact of transport fuels. Previously worked at DWP. **Christopher Townsend** (LD) Career in the City: dir of capital markets, RBC; quantitative analyst, Credit Suisse. Open University tutor. Has a PhD in computer science and mathematics. Cllr: Tring TC 2015-; Dacorum BC 2007-15. **Paul de Hoest** (Green) Career in finance and public sectors. **Mark Anderson** (Ukip) Contested Hertfordshire South West 2015.

CONSTITUENCY PROFILE
This seat stretches north from Ruislip in northwest London and lies along the border with Buckinghamshire. It is home to a small Asian community, mostly Indian, making up about one in sixteen residents, and a Jewish community of over a thousand. Pay is well above average, and many residents commute into London for work; managerial and professional occupations are prevalent. The seat has elected only Conservative MPs since 1950.

EU REFERENDUM RESULT
46.2% Leave   Remain 53.8%

Hertsmere

CONSERVATIVE HOLD MAJORITY 16,951 (32.4%)

OLIVER DOWDEN
BORN Aug 1, 1978
MP 2015-

Born and raised in Hertsmere. Prior to his parliamentary career he worked for the Conservative research dept and for a PR company. Returned to Conservative Party to work as David Cameron's deputy chief of staff; he was awarded a CBE in recognition of his work in 2015. Opposed Brexit in the lead-up to the referendum. Promoted to SoS for Sir Michael Fallon MP in 2017 reshuffle. Select committees: petitions 2015-17; public administration and constitutional affairs 2015-16. Co-chairs APPG on British Jews; passionate about preventing antisemitism and

	Electorate	Turnout %	from 2010 % Change
	73,554	71.04	
*O Dowden C	31,928	61.10	+1.82
F Smith Lab	14,977	28.66	+6.23
J Jordan LD	2,794	5.35	-0.20
D Hoy Ukip	1,564	2.99	-9.75
S Summerhayes Green	990	1.89	

anti-Israel sentiment. Married, two children. Ed: Parmiters' Sch, Watford; Trinity Hall, Cambridge (BA law).

CHALLENGERS
Fiona Smith (Lab) Works for an independent think tank. Served in the police and RAF. **Joe Jordan** (LD) Scientist and software engineer. Campaigning for referendum on final Brexit deal. **David Hoy** (Ukip) Chairman of Hertsmere's Ukip branch.

CONSTITUENCY PROFILE
The biggest towns in this seat on Greater London's northern border are Borehamwood, home of Elstree Studios, and Potters Bar. One of the most Jewish constituencies in the country, with about 14,000 Jews out of 100,000 residents; there is also a significant Asian and Asian-British population. The seat is characterised by high levels of self-employment and good levels of health and education, while pay is well above average. The seat has elected Conservative MPs since its creation in 1983 and was once the seat of Lord Cecil Parkinson, a former chairman of the party.

EU REFERENDUM RESULT
50.8% Leave   Remain 49.2%

Hexham

CONSERVATIVE HOLD MAJORITY 9,236 (20.0%)

GUY OPPERMAN
BORN May 18, 1965
MP 2010-

Vocal and on the left of his party. Former barrister, won 2007 Bar Pro Bono Award for Free Representation Unit work, judicial review challenge and campaign against local hospital closures. Entered politics after leading a campaign against the closure of a hospital that he credited with saving his mother's life. Tireless advocate for the NHS. Whip: 2016-; assistant 2015-16. Contested: Caernarfon 2005; Swindon North 1997; . One of the first MPs to take on an apprentice. Author and blogger. Amateur jockey. Long-term partner. Ed: Harrow Sch; University of Buckingham (LLB

	Electorate	Turnout %	from 2010 % Change
	61,012	75.76	
*G Opperman C	24,996	54.08	+1.40
S Powers Lab	15,760	34.09	+9.17
F Hall LD	3,285	7.11	+0.28
W Foot Green	1,253	2.71	-2.93
F Miles Ukip	930	2.01	-7.91

law); University of Lille, France (Diploma).

CHALLENGERS
Stephen Powers (Lab) Cllr, Newcastle CC 2012-. Vice-chairman, Co-operative Councils' Innovation Network. Has a sign language qualification. **Fiona Hall** (LD) MEP 2004-14; leader of the Lib Dems 2009-14. As an MEP she took a particular interest in climate change and energy policy. **Wesley Foot** (Green)

Heating engineer. Parish councillor for Warden.

CONSTITUENCY PROFILE
A huge and sparse Northumberland seat on the Scottish border. Hexham's residents are older than average, with more than half the population aged over 45. One in fifty residents is non-white. The seat is characterised by higher than average self-employment and is one of the richest seats in terms of typial incomes in the region. Hexham has elected only Tory MPs at every election since 1951, although Labour came within a few hundred votes of winning Hexham in 1997.

EU REFERENDUM RESULT
45.3% Leave   Remain 54.7%

Heywood & Middleton

LABOUR HOLD MAJORITY 7,617 (15.3%)

LIZ MCINNES
BORN Jan 1, 1957
MP 2014-

Worked as a clinical scientist for the NHS from 1981 until becoming an MP. Senior biochemist, Pennine Acute Hospitals NHS Trust. Won by-election after death of Jim Dobbin. Supported Jeremy Corbyn in the vote of no confidence against him, but resigned from position as shad min for CLG 2015-16 as she believed Corbyn should stand down in response to vote. Re-joined frontbench later that year as shad foreign minister 2016-. Campaigned to Remain in the EU. Cllr, Rossendale BC 2010-14; chairwoman, overview and scrutiny. Partner, one son.

	Electorate	Turnout %	from 2010 % Change
	79,901	62.41	
*L McInnes Lab	26,578	53.30	+10.19
C Clarkson C	18,961	38.02	+18.93
L Seville Ukip	3,239	6.50	-25.70
B Winlow LD	1,087	2.18	-1.13

Ed: Hathershaw CS; St Anne's Coll, Oxford (BSc biochemistry); University of Surrey (MSc clinical biochemistry).

CHALLENGERS
Chris Clarkson (C) Trained as lawyer. Corporate development consultant at Virgin. Leave campaigner. Cllr, Salford CC 2011-. Contested Wallasey 2015. Member, Countryside Alliance. **Lee Seville** (Ukip) Worked for NHS Blood and Transplant for 16 years. Chairman, Ukip Rochdale. **Bill Winlow** (LD)

Specialist in neuroscience and UCL professor. Cllr: Lancashire CC 2009-17; Leeds CC 1986-99.

CONSTITUENCY PROFILE
This seat comprises of the Greater Manchester towns of Heywood and Middleton and some of the rural area to their north. Many of its residents' work in routine and semi-routine occupations, and its workforce is slightly worse off in terms of income than the average northwest seat. The seat has elected only Labour MPs since its creation in 1983, although it nearly fell to Ukip in the 2014 by-election which Labour won by 617 votes.

EU REFERENDUM RESULT

62.4% Leave	Remain 37.6%

High Peak

LABOUR GAIN MAJORITY 2,322 (4.3%)

RUTH GEORGE
BORN Nov 27, 1969
MP 2017-

Trained as a tax accountant and founded local accountancy business. Worked as parly officer for shopworkers' union Usdaw, for past 18 years; campaigned to raise the minimum wage and improve rights for new parents. Helped to set up Freedom from Fear campaign which addresses abuse of retail staff. Set up group to produce neighbourhood plan. Previously school governor. Married, four children. Ed: Millfield Sch; University of Manchester (BA politics and modern history).

CHALLENGERS
Andrew Bingham (C) MP for

	Electorate	Turnout %	from 2010 % Change
	73,254	73.52	
R George Lab	26,753	49.68	+14.35
*A Bingham C	24,431	45.37	+0.40
C Lawley LD	2,669	4.96	+0.25

High Peak 2010-17. Frequently rebellious while in parliament, including over plain cigarette packaging. Cllr, High Peak BC 1999-2011; keen to develop local tourism trade. Formerly director of family firm distributing engineering equipment. Brexiteer. PPS: Justine Greening 2015-17; Mark Francois 2014-15. Select cttee, CMS 2015-17. Contested High Peak 2005. Married. **Charles Lawley** (LD) Humanitarian aid worker. Previously managed a pub and war memorial club, and worked in TV. Campaigned against local

hospital closures and for better rural policing.

CONSTITUENCY PROFILE
This large north Derbyshire seat contains the towns of Glossop, Boxton and New Mills, and stretches across a large rural and largely uninhabited area of the Peak District. Just one in fifty residents is non-white. Typical incomes are slightly higher than the East Midlands average and unemployment is below average. Labour held the seat between 1997 and 2010, although the Tories had previously held it since 1970. This is the first time Labour has held High Peak in opposition.

EU REFERENDUM RESULT

50.5% Leave	Remain 49.5%

Hitchin & Harpenden

CONSERVATIVE HOLD MAJORITY 12,031 (20.5%)

BIM AFOLAMI
BORN Feb 11, 1986
MP 2017-

Senior exec, HSBC. Worked in corporate law before moving into finance: Freshfields Bruckhaus Deringer; Simpson, Thacher and Bartlett. Worked for George Osborne. Former treasurer, Bow Group. School governor. Contested Lewisham Deptford 2015. His parents are Nigerian, although his mother was born in Britain. His father came to Britain in the 1980s and is an NHS doctor, and his mother is a pharmacist. Married, two sons. Ed: Eton Coll; University Coll, Oxford (BA modern history; vice-president Oxford Union); BPP Law Sch, London (PGdip law).

	Electorate	Turnout %	from 2010 %	Change
	75,916	77.43		
B Afolami C	31,189	53.06	-3.81	
J Hayes Lab	19,158	32.59	+11.94	
H Annand LD	6,236	10.61	+2.51	
R Cano Green	1,329	2.26	-3.25	
R Blake Ind	629	1.07		
S Cordle CPA	242	0.41		

CHALLENGERS
John Hayes (Lab) Primary school head teacher in north London. Member, National Union of Teachers. Chairman, Hitchin Labour Party. **Hugh Annand** (LD) Senior translator, European Commission. Previously taught English in eastern Siberia. Contested Hertfordshire North East 2010. **Richard Cano** (Green) Primary school head teacher. Born and raised in Hitchin. Campaigned on local issues such as community centre closure and school budget cuts.

CONSTITUENCY PROFILE
Hitchin and Harpenden is a fairly large Hertfordshire seat that sprawls around Luton and has a long border with Bedfordshire. Median pay is well above average. Overrepresented industries in its workforce include information, communication, real estate and finance. The seat has elected only Conservatives since it was created in 1997; the previous MP was Peter Lilley, a cabinet minister under Margaret Thatcher and John Major.

EU REFERENDUM RESULT
39.8% Leave   Remain 60.2%

Holborn & St Pancras

LABOUR HOLD MAJORITY 30,509 (51.7%)

SIR KEIR STARMER
BORN Sep 2, 1962
MP 2015-

Mild-mannered, distinguished human rights' lawyer. Co-founder, Doughty Street Chambers. Appointed Queen's Counsel 2002. Director of public prosecutions 2008-13. Drafted a victims' law with Doreen Lawrence that was in Labour's 2015 manifesto. Mentioned as possible candidate for 2015 Labour leadership election; he declined to run, supporting Andy Burnham. Nominated Owen Smith 2016. Remainer, voted to trigger Article 50. Shadow SoS for Exiting the European Union 2016-; shadow Home Office min, 2015-16. Member, home affairs select cttee 2015. Married, two

	Electorate	Turnout %	from 2010 %	Change
	88,088	66.98		
*K Starmer Lab	41,343	70.08	+17.16	
T Barnes C	10,834	18.36	-3.51	
S Crosher LD	4,020	6.81	+0.34	
S Berry Green	1,980	3.36	-9.41	
G Game Ukip	727	1.23	-3.76	
J Polenceus Eng Dem	93	0.16		

children. Ed: Reigate Grammar School; University of Leeds (law); St Edmund Hall, Oxford (BCL).

CHALLENGERS
Tim Barnes (C) Runs a small business that supports new businesses as they grow. Founded Citrus Saturday, a charity project that teaches school children about business. Former chairman, Tory Reform Group. **Stephen Crosher** (LD) Founder, Fleet Renewables clean technology consultancy. Member, Energy and Climate Change and New Economy LD policy development groups.

CONSTITUENCY PROFILE
Holborn and St Pancras is a slim central London seat stretching from Holborn tube station in the south to the area around Hampstead Heath in the north, encompassing King's Cross, Camden Town and Kentish Town. Incomes and house prices are well above even the London average. More than half its residents are aged 16 to 45, and more than a third are non-white. It has elected Labour MPs since its creation in 1983.

EU REFERENDUM RESULT
26.7% Leave   Remain 73.3%

Hornchurch & Upminster

CONSERVATIVE HOLD MAJORITY 17,723 (31.6%)

JULIA DOCKERILL
BORN Jun 4, 1984
MP 2017-

Author and political adviser. Former chief of staff to Mark Field. Photographed entering Downing Street with handwritten "have cake and eat it" Brexit strategy notes on display in November 2016. Co-authored *The Best of Times* and *Between the Crashes* with Field. Currently researching and writing a book called *London in the Noughties*. Former trustee, Inspire Malawi nonprofit organisation. Cllr, Tower Hamlets BC 2014-. Voted Leave. Engaged. Ed: Herts & Essex HS, Bishop's Stortford; Queens' Coll, Cambridge (BA social and political sciences).

	Electorate	Turnout %	from 2010 % Change
	80,821	69.42	
J Dockerill C	33,750	60.15	+11.18
R Gill Lab	16,027	28.57	+8.46
L Webb Ukip	3,502	6.24	-19.06
J Mitchell LD	1,371	2.44	-0.27
P Caton Green	1,077	1.92	-0.63
D Furness BNP	380	0.68	+0.33

CHALLENGERS
Rocky Gill (Lab) Former non-executive director, Barking & Dagenham NHS primary care trust. Previously worked at JP Morgan, Morgan Stanley and 3M. Member, Co-operative party. Cllr, Barking and Dagenham BC 2006-. Son of Punjabi immigrants. Sikh. Supported Brexit. **Lawrence Webb** (Ukip) Former electrician and nightclub manager. Spent eight years in the TA. First Ukip councillor

elected in London. Political asst to Gerard Batten MEP. Contested London mayoralty 2012. Cllr, Havering BC 2013-.

CONSTITUENCY PROFILE
Hornchurch and Upminster is London's easternmost constituency. It is culturally more similar to Essex than to much of London, being both older and more ethnically homogeneous. Overrepresented industries among its workforce include construction and finance. It is currently a fairly safe Conservative seat, although Labour did hold Upminster from 1997 to 2001. UKIP came second in 2015.

EU REFERENDUM RESULT

69.5% Leave	Remain 30.5%

Hornsey & Wood Green

LABOUR HOLD MAJORITY 30,738 (49.3%)

CATHERINE WEST
BORN Sep 14, 1966
MP 2015-

Formerly worked helping migrants to secure welfare and housing. Taught English in Nanjing. Caseworker for David Lammy. Cllr, Islington BC 2002-14; leader 2010-13. Nominated Jeremy Corbyn 2015 and supported him again in 2016. Anti-Trident renewal. Voted against Article 50 bill. Voted for Chuka Umunna's single market amendment, and sacked from frontbench. Shadow FCO minister 2015-17. Reportedly agreed to canvass Stop the War Coalition on Syria policy. Australian-born. Quaker. Speaks five languages. Married, two children. Ed: Ravenswood

	Electorate	Turnout %	from 2010 % Change
	79,944	77.92	
*C West Lab	40,738	65.40	+14.49
D Barnes LD	10,000	16.05	-15.72
E Lane C	9,246	14.84	+5.59
S Hall Green	1,181	1.90	-3.55
N Ali Women	551	0.88	
R Price Ukip	429	0.69	-1.51
H Spiby-Vann CPA	93	0.15	-0.05
A Athow WRP	55	0.09	-0.05

Sch for Girls, Sydney; SOAS (BA social science and languages; MA Chinese studies).

CHALLENGERS
Dawn Barnes (LD) Career in marketing and PR: KCL, UCL, Islington BC. Trustee, Booktrust reading charity. Contested Witney 2010. **Emma Lane** (C) Banker. Risk division, Lloyds; relationship director, Barclays.

Cllr: New Forest DC 2015-; Ellingham, Harbridge and Ibsley PC 2007-. Contested Swansea West 2015.

CONSTITUENCY PROFILE
Hornsey and Wood Green is a compact north London seat between Finchley, Golders Green and Tottenham and includes Alexandra Palace. More than two thirds of its residents are white. Levels of private renting are particularly high while home ownership is low. The seat was won by the Conservatives in 1983, gained by Labour in 1992, and then won and held for ten years by the Liberal Democrat, Lynne Featherstone.

EU REFERENDUM RESULT

25.0% Leave	Remain 75.0%

Horsham

CONSERVATIVE HOLD MAJORITY 23,484 (37.9%)

JEREMY QUIN
BORN Sep 24, 1968
MP 2015-

Selected to stand for Horsham after Francis Maude announced his decision to stand down. Former company adviser at NatWest Securities (now Deutsche Bank). Seconded to HM Treasury 2008-09. Contested Meirionnydd Nant Conway 1997. Volunteer: City UK; Debate Mate; Countryside Alliance Foundation; Aylesbury Homeless Shelter. Involved in establishing a free school for children with autism. Supporter of Heathrow expansion rather than Gatwick. A Remainer who has subsequently embraced Brexit. Cttees: regulatory reform 2015-17; DWP 2015-16.

	Electorate	Turnout %	from 2010 % Change
	82,773	74.89	
*J Quin C	36,906	59.54	+2.22
S Brady Lab	13,422	21.65	+10.24
M Millson LD	7,644	12.33	+0.65
C Ross Green	1,844	2.97	-0.89
R Arthur Ukip	1,533	2.47	-11.53
J Smith S New	375	0.60	-0.05
J Duggan Peace	263	0.42	-0.12

Married. Church of England. Ed: St Albans Sch; Hertford Coll, Oxford (BA history; president, Oxford Union).

CHALLENGERS
Susannah Brady (Lab) Small business owner, local campaigner and Open University student. Contested West Sussex CC 2017. Local resident born in Horsham. **Morwen Millson** (LD) Cllr, West Sussex CC 1989-. Director,

4TheYouth charity. Former teacher. Contested Horsham 2015, 1997.

CONSTITUENCY PROFILE
The majority of residents in this constituency live in the town of Horsham itself, with just under half living in the rural areas of Sussex around the town. The seat is just south of Gatwick airport, where a significant number of its residents work. The seat is characterised by low unemployment and relatively high levels of home ownership. Horsham and its predecessors have elected only Conservative MPs since 1880, making it one of the country's safest seats.

EU REFERENDUM RESULT

49.5% Leave   Remain 50.5%

Houghton & Sunderland South

LABOUR HOLD MAJORITY 12,341 (29.8%)

BRIDGET PHILLIPSON
BORN Dec 19, 1983
MP 2010-

Formerly managed a women's refuge and worked on regeneration projects for Sunderland CC. She was aged 26 when first elected. Select committees: home affairs 2010-13; procedure 2010-11; electoral commission 2010-; public accounts 2015-. PPS to Jim Murphy 2010-13. Whip 2013-15. Local campaigns on transport, schools and anti-social behaviour. Remain supporter, but voted for Article 50 bill. Critic of Jeremy Corbyn's EU stance; reportedly told him to resign at a PLP meeting. Member, GMB. Married, two children. Ed: St Robert of Newminster RC Sch,

	Electorate	Turnout %	from 2010 % Change
	68,123	60.89	
*B Phillipson Lab	24,665	59.46	+4.33
P Howell C	12,324	29.71	+11.25
M Joyce Ukip	2,379	5.74	-15.78
P Edgeworth LD	908	2.19	+0.13
R Bradley Green	725	1.75	-1.10
M Watson Ind	479	1.15	

Washington; Hertford College, Oxford (BA modern history; chairwoman, OULC).

CHALLENGERS
Paul Howell (C) Accountant and former financial director. Cllr, Aycliffe North and Middridge, Durham CC 2017-. **Michael Joyce** (Ukip) Regimental company quartermasters sergeant. Joined the army in 1989. Served in Northern Ireland, Bosnia and Iraq. Has

worked as a volunteer driver for local community bus.

CONSTITUENCY PROFILE
This seat consists of Sunderland's southern suburbs and the towns of Houghton-le-Spring and Hetton-le-Hole. About 98 per cent of its residents are white and three quarters are Christian. There is a skew in the workforce towards routine and semi-routine jobs, although average pay in the constituency is not much less than the regional average. Including its predecessors, Houghton and Sunderland South has elected Labour MPs consistently since 1935.

EU REFERENDUM RESULT

62.4% Leave   Remain 37.6%

Hove

LABOUR HOLD MAJORITY 8,757 (32.6%)

PETER KYLE
BORN Sep 9, 1970
MP 2015-

Co-founder of Fat Sand, Brighton-based video company. Chief exec, Working for Youth, a charity aiming to tackle youth unemployment 2013-15. Won in 2015 after the sitting Tory MP Michael Weatherley stepped down. Member, BIS/BEIS select cttee 2015-. Campaigned to Remain in the EU; voted against Article 50 bill. Former trustee, Pride. Former adviser to cabinet office on social exclusion. Aid worker in Eastern Europe and the Balkans in 1990s. Ed: University of Sussex (BA human geography and international development; DPhil community economic development).

	Electorate	Turnout %	from 2010 %	Change
	74,236	77.58		
*P Kyle Lab	36,942	64.14	+21.85	
K Adams C	18,185	31.57	-8.35	
C Hynds LD	1,311	2.28	-1.29	
P Mac Cafferty Green	971	1.69	-5.15	
C Sabel Ind	187	0.32	-0.29	

CHALLENGERS
Kristy Adams (C) Linked to a church accused of attempting to cure LGBT people. Claimed to have healed a man's deafness through prayer. Campaigns against modern slavery. Cllr, Bedford BC. Director of a design business. **Caroline Hynds** (LD) Editor and proofreader. First experience of political campaigning was to research and write a Lib Dem report called *Europe is working in Brighton & Hove*. **Phelim Mac Cafferty**

(Green) Cllr, Brighton and Hove CC 2011-.

CONSTITUENCY PROFILE
Hove is Brighton's neighbouring town, immediately to its west. This west Sussex seat has fewer children and pensioners than the UK average, and more than a third of its residents are aged between 24 and 45. The average income is slightly higher than in Brighton Pavillion and Kemptown. Levels of private sector renting are almost double the average. Although Labour had never held Hove until 1997, the Conservatives have only held the seat for one term since then, from 2010 to 2015.

EU REFERENDUM RESULT

32.9% Leave   Remain 67.1%

Huddersfield

LAB CO-OP HOLD MAJORITY 12,005 (27.4%)

BARRY SHEERMAN
BORN Aug 17, 1940
MP 1979-

Unlikely leader of attempt to overthrow Gordon Brown in 2009. Charity entrepreneur. Hopes to remain an MP into his 80s. Voted no confidence in Jeremy Corbyn 2016. Contested Taunton 1974. Shadow spokesman: disability rights 1992-94; home affairs 1988-92; education and employment 1983-88. Cttees: education, 2001-10; liaison 1999-2010; public accounts 1981-83. Chairman, skills commission. Former lecturer. Supported Remain but voted for the Article 50 bill. Married, three daughters, one son. Ed: Hampton GS; Kingston Tech Coll; LSE (BSc economics);

	Electorate	Turnout %	from 2010 %	Change
	67,033	65.39		
*B Sheerman Lab Co-op	26,470	60.39	+15.46	
S Benton C	14,465	33.00	+6.22	
A Cooper Green	1,395	3.18	-3.73	
Z Ali LD	1,155	2.63	-3.21	
B Katenga Yorkshire	274	0.63		
M Thokkudubiyyapu Ind	75	0.17		

University of London (MSc political sociology).

CHALLENGERS
Scott Benton (C) Former teacher. Cllr, Calderdale C 2016-. Leader of Conservative group. Urged council to make every school fly the Union flag and sing the national anthem. Parly asst to Craig Whittaker. **Andrew Cooper** (Green) Works for a company developing energy-saving schemes. Cllr, Kirklees C

1999-. Contested Huddersfield 2015.

CONSTITUENCY PROFILE
This west Yorkshire seat contains the former wool-making and large working class town of Huddersfield, although some of its western areas are in Colne Valley. The constituency includes the University of Huddersfield and most of its 20,000 students. The average income is below the Yorkshire and Humber average. Huddersfield has been Labour since its 1983 creation, although the old seat of Huddersfield West was held by the Liberals, Labour and the Conservatives between 1950 and 1983.

EU REFERENDUM RESULT

51.9% Leave   Remain 48.1%

Hull East

LABOUR HOLD MAJORITY 10,396 (28.4%)

KARL TURNER
BORN Apr 15, 1971
MP 2010-

Born to seafaring family. A working-class role model who sold antiques before returning to education and becoming a barrister. Remainer, but vowed not to block Brexit after Hull voted Leave. Brought his baby daughter to the Article 50 vote. Initially a Jeremy Corbyn critic: nominated Andy Burnham 2015; Owen Smith 2016. Tends not to rebel. Shadow min: transport 2017-; attorney general 2016; justice 2015-16; solicitor general 2014-16. Opposition whip 2017. First Hull-born MP to represent the constituency since 1784. Involved in the Bransholme HS. Ed: University of Hull (LLB law).

	Electorate	Turnout %	from 2010 %	Change
	65,959	55.55		
*K Turner Lab	21,355	58.29	+6.56	
S Burton C	10,959	29.91	+14.00	
M Fox Ukip	2,573	7.02	-15.35	
A Marchington LD	1,258	3.43	-3.09	
J Brown Green	493	1.35	-0.95	

CHALLENGERS
Simon Burton (C) Adviser to the government's chief whip. Former adviser to secretary of state for transport. Former constituency assistant to Huntingdon MP Jonathan Djanogly. **Mark Fox** (Ukip) Former builder, currently studying construction management. **Andrew Marchington** (LD) Maths and computing teacher teacher in secondary and primary schools. Former cllr, Kirklees C. Contested West Yorkshire

PCC 2012. **Julia Brown** (Green) Teacher.

CONSTITUENCY PROFILE
This east Yorkshire seat contains several middle-class suburbs of Hull as well as deprived areas such as Marfleet and Drypool. Hull East is the least affluent of the Hull seats ranked by income, although it has a slightly lower unemployment rate than its neighbours. A significant portion of constituents have no qualifications. Hull East has consistently returned a Labour MP since 1935; it was held for 31 years by deputy prime minister and Labour Party stalwart John Prescott.

EU REFERENDUM RESULT
72.8% Leave   Remain 27.2%

Hull North

LABOUR HOLD MAJORITY 14,262 (38.6%)

DIANA JOHNSON
BORN Jul 25, 1966
MP 2005-

Former barrister specialising in employment and welfare. Resigned from front bench 2016. Hull's first female MP. Launched Reproductive Health Bill to remove some criminal sanctions facing women and doctors under current abortion rules. Cllr, Tower Hamlets BC 1994-2002. Contested Brentwood and Ongar 2001. Visiting legal member of Mental Health Act Commission. PPS to Stephen Timms 2005-07. Asst whip 2007-09. Junior min: education 2009-10. Shadow min: FCO 2015-16; home 2010-15; health 2010. Ed: Northwich County GS; Brunel University (Law).

	Electorate	Turnout %	from 2010 %	Change
	64,666	57.37		
*D Johnson Lab	23,625	63.68	+10.87	
L Nici-Townend C	9,363	25.24	+10.22	
M Ross LD	1,869	5.04	-3.95	
J Kitchener Ukip	1,601	4.32	-11.99	
M Deane Green	644	1.74	4.11	

CHALLENGERS
Lia Nici-Townend (C) Runs local television channel, Estuary TV. Former director at St Margaret's Pre-school Laceby. **Mike Ross** (LD) Moved to Hull in 2000. Cllr, Hull CC 2002-; leader of Lib Dem group. Led campaign to save local swimming pools with some success and oversaw a school rebuilding programme. Contested Hull West and Hessle 2010. **John Kitchener** (Ukip) Originally from Gateshead. Contested: Howden and

Haltemprice 2015; local elections 2016.

CONSTITUENCY PROFILE
The University of Hull is based in Hull North and the seat has a much greater proportion of 18-to-24-year-olds and students than the other two Hull constituencies. It is also characterised by slightly higher average pay than the other two Hull seats, although all three are below the regional average. However, its residents also have the lowest level of home ownership of the three. Including its predecessors, Hull North has been represented by Labour MPs since 1964.

EU REFERENDUM RESULT
59.8% Leave   Remain 40.2%

Hull West & Hessle

LABOUR HOLD MAJORITY 8,025 (23.2%)

EMMA HARDY
BORN Jul 17, 1979
MP 2017-

Former primary school teacher, Willerby Carr Lane Primary Sch. Deputy gen sec, Socialist Education Association. Member, Unite. Previously member, Labour housing policy forum. Replaces former home sec Alan Johnson after beating Jeremy Corbyn's speechwriter and son of Lord (John) Prescott, David, to local party nomination. Interest in politics was "ignited" after Labour's 2010 loss and Michael Gove's tenure as education sec. Cllr, Hessle TC 2015-. PPS to Sir Keir Starmer 2017-. Methodist. Two daughters. Ed: University of Liverpool (BA politics); University of Leeds (PGCE).

	Electorate	Turnout %	from 2010 % Change
	60,181	57.44	
E Hardy Lab	18,342	53.07	+3.87
C Mackay C	10,317	29.85	+12.36
C Thomas LD	2,210	6.39	-3.57
M Dewberry Ind	1,898	5.49	
G Shores Ukip	1,399	4.05	-15.80
M Lammiman Green	332	0.96	-2.00
W Taylor Libertarian	67	0.19	

CHALLENGERS
Christine Mackay (C) Rep, MSD Pharmaceuticals. Chairwoman of charity supporting Burundi orphanage. Contested Hull East 2015, 2010. Branch chairwoman, Hull West and Hessle Conservative Party 2010-15. **Claire Thomas** (LD) Mental health charity worker; formerly employed by manufacturing company and University of Hull. Cllr, Hull CC 2008-. **Michelle**

Dewberry (Ind) Businesswoman; set up own consultancy. Winner of second series of *The Apprentice*. Sky News pundit; co-presenter, *The Pledge*. Brexiteer.

CONSTITUENCY PROFILE
The seat of Hull West and Hessle has the highest rate of unemployment of the three Hull seats, only slightly higher than Hull North's, although it retains a relatively high number of manufacturing jobs. The seat has been held by Labour, including its predecessors, since the creation of Hull West in 1955. Until this election Hull West and Hessle was the seat of the former home secretary Alan Johnson.

EU REFERENDUM RESULT

68.0% Leave   Remain 32.0%

Huntingdon

CONSERVATIVE HOLD MAJORITY 14,475 (24.2%)

JONATHAN DJANOGLY
BORN Jun 3, 1965
MP 2001-

Solicitor and former partner at commercial law firm, SJ Berwin LLP. Ran mail order retail business with wife. Wealthy son of multimillionaire textile magnate and philanthropist, Sir Harry Djanogly. Cllr, Westminster CC 1994-2001. Contested Oxford East 1997. In the shadow cabinet until 2010. Parliamentary under-secretary, justice 2010-12. Voted to Remain in the EU. His reputation was slightly damaged during the expenses scandal. Jewish. Married, one daughter, one son. Ed: University Coll Sch; Oxford Poly (BA law and politics); Coll of Law, Guildford.

	Electorate	Turnout %	from 2010 % Change
	84,320	70.83	
*J Djanogly C	32,915	55.12	+2.10
N Johnson Lab	18,440	30.88	+12.55
R Cantrill LD	5,090	8.52	+0.70
P Bullen Ukip	2,180	3.65	-13.29
T MacLennan Green	1,095	1.83	-2.06

CHALLENGERS
Dr Nik Johnson (Lab) Consultant paediatrician, Hinchingbrooke Hospital. Campaign focused on local NHS and social care. Contested Huntingdon 2015. Awarded local Community Inspiration award. **Rod Cantrill** (LD) Financial adviser and entrepreneur. Managing director, Millington Advisory Partners. Cllr, Cambridge CC 2004-. Trustee and former chairman, Wintercomfort charity for

the homeless. Contested Huntingdon 2015.

CONSTITUENCY PROFILE
The biggest towns in this west Cambridgeshire seat are St Neots and Huntingdon. It is demographically balanced, with neither home ownership nor average incomes as high as many similar neighbouring seats in East Anglia. It does, however, have very low levels of unemployment. It is a safe Conservative seat which was held by John Major between 1983 and 2001. The seat has been held by Conservative MPs since 1964, and has never been won by Labour.

EU REFERENDUM RESULT

53.5% Leave   Remain 46.5%

Hyndburn

LABOUR HOLD MAJORITY 5,815 (12.9%)

GRAHAM JONES
BORN Mar 3, 1966
MP 2010-

Worked as a graphic designer and lecturer specialising in prepress. Refuse collector, carer, home assistant and community transport driver for the council. Opposition assistant whip 2010-15, resigned in opposition to Jeremy Corbyn's election as Labour leader. Regards Corbyn as too far left and called for him to stand down after the no confidence vote in 2016. Claimed Corbyn "doesn't give a damn about the Labour Party". Remain voter. Cllr: Lancashire CC 2009-10; Hyndburn BC 2002-10, opposition leader 2005-10. Partner, one son, one daughter. Ed: St Christopher's CofE HS,

	Electorate	Turnout %	from 2010 %	Change
	73,110	61.83		
*G Jones Lab	24,120	53.36	+11.21	
K Horkin C	18,305	40.50	+8.61	
J Brown Ukip	1,953	4.32	-17.02	
L Jones LD	824	1.82	-0.18	

Accrington; Accrington and Rossendale Coll; University of Central Lancashire (BA applied social studies).

CHALLENGERS
Kevin Horkin (C) Businessman, owns opticians and country-wear stores. Pet consultant who appeared on TV and in magazines as a pet columnist. Founded a charity promoting responsible pet ownership. Cllr, Clitheroe TC 2011-, mayor 2013-14; Ribble Valley BC 2011-15; Hyndburn BC 1985-

89. Chairman, Ribble Valley Community Safety Partnership. Contested Hyndburn 2015. **Janet Brown** (Ukip) Manager at Slimming World. Contested Hyndburn 2015.

CONSTITUENCY PROFILE
The Hyndburn seat is a small collection of Lancashire towns to the east of Blackburn. The seat has a large Muslim population and nearly a third of its residents are aged under 25. About a sixth of the workforce work in manufacturing, and Hyndburn's residents receive lower than average pay. Conservatives held Hyndburn from 1983 until 1992, but it has been Labour since.

EU REFERENDUM RESULT
65.8% Leave   Remain 34.2%

Ilford North

LABOUR HOLD MAJORITY 9,369 (18.2%)

WES STREETING
BORN Jan 21, 1983
MP 2015-

Long-time activist interested in education. Formerly: consultant, PwC; chief exec, Helena Kennedy Foundation; head of education, Stonewall. President, National Union of Students 2008-10. Cllr, Redbridge BC 2010-; continues unpaid. Supported Liz Kendall 2015 and Owen Smith 2016. Critical of Jeremy Corbyn, including over complacency about antisemitism. Confronted Ken Livingstone on *Newsnight* over controversial Hitler comments. Remainer who voted for Article 50 but supported Chuka Umunna's single market amendment. He was endorsed at this election

	Electorate	Turnout %	from 2010 %	Change
	72,997	72.52		
*W Streeting Lab	30,589	57.78	+13.92	
L Scott C	20,950	39.57	-3.09	
R Clare LD	1,034	1.95	-0.36	
D Osen Ind	368	0.70	+0.52	

by Sir Ian McKellen. Openly gay. Ed: Westminster City Sch; Selwyn Coll, Cambridge (BA history; president, students' union).

CHALLENGERS
Lee Scott (C) MP for Ilford North 2005-15. Professional charity fundraiser. Formerly: director, Scott & Fishell; sales executive for companies including Toshiba. Contested Waveney 2001. Jewish. **Richard Clare** (LD) Advocacy officer, Cats Protection. Former intern:

Norman Baker and Lembit Opik. Contested Ilford North 2015.

CONSTITUENCY PROFILE
A northeast London seat bordering Essex, Ilford North is a diverse seat with a large Asian population, and large Muslim, Hindu, Jewish and Sikh populations. Many of its residents commute into London to work; overrepresented industries include finance and transport. Ilford North is a Labour/Conservative marginal, changing hands six times since 1945, although Wes Streeting's new majority is the largest any Ilford North MP has achieved for 20 years.

EU REFERENDUM RESULT
53.3% Leave   Remain 46.7%

Ilford South

LAB CO-OP HOLD MAJORITY 31,647 (54.9%)

MIKE GAPES
BORN Sep 4, 1952
MP 1992-

Briefly worked in the NHS and as an adult educator after graduating. Spent 15 years at Labour HQ, including spells as international secretary and national student organiser. Member, Labour national policy forum 1996-2005. Backbencher and Jeremy Corbyn critic who calls himself a "Kinnockite". Voted against Article 50 bill. Outspoken on Twitter. Said he would stand down in 2020 before election was called. Select cttees: panel of chairs 2017-; foreign affairs 2005-17, 1992-97, chair 2005-10; defence 2003-05, 1999-2001. PPS to: Lord Rooker 2001-02; Paul Murphy 1997-99.

	Electorate	Turnout %	from 2010 % Change
	85,358	67.55	
*M Gapes Lab Co-op	43,724	75.83	+11.82
C Chapman C	12,077	20.95	-4.97
F Ahmed LD	772	1.34	-0.61
R Warrington Green	542	0.94	-1.96
T Saeed Ukip	477	0.83	-4.38
K Khan Friends	65	0.11	

Contested Ilford North 1983. Divorced, three daughters (one died from a heart attack aged 19). Ed: Buckhurst County HS; Fitzwilliam Coll, Cambridge (MA economics); Middlesex Poly (Dip industrial relations).

CHALLENGERS
Chris Chapman (C) Content development manager at media company, Centaur Media. Cllr: Tower Hamlets BC 2014-, deputy leader Conservative

group; Runnymede BC 2008-12. Contested Ilford South 2015.

CONSTITUENCY PROFILE
Ilford South is denser, younger, and more ethnically diverse than Ilford North, with about a sixth of its residents considering themselves white British in the 2011 census; more than half the population are of Asian descent. More than half of its residents are Muslim. Levels of private renting are well above the UK average and mean incomes in the area are high. Ilford South may currently be a safe Labour seat, but it has changed hands between Labour and the Tories six times since 1945.

EU REFERENDUM RESULT
43.3% Leave   Remain 56.7%

Inverclyde

SNP HOLD MAJORITY 384 (1.0%)

RONNIE COWAN
BORN Sep 6, 1959
MP 2015-

IT consultant with his own firm. Ardent independence campaigner: joined the SNP aged 16; founded YES Inverclyde, a pro-independence organisation, in 2012. Select cttees: public administration and constitutional affairs 2015-. Campaigned to Remain in the EU and voted against the triggering of Article 50. Causes since 2015: welfare; broadband speed; gambling addiction; employment; drugs reform. Campaigning to save the Port Glasgow Jobcentre. Son of Scottish goalkeeper Jimmy Cowan. Three children. Ed: Greenock Academy.

	Electorate	Turnout %	from 2010 % Change
	58,853	66.42	
*R Cowan SNP	15,050	38.50	-16.62
M McCluskey Lab	14,666	37.52	+7.20
D Wilson C	8,399	21.48	+11.52
D Stevens LD	978	2.50	+0.02

CHALLENGERS
Martin McCluskey (Lab) Worked for the Equality & Human Rights Commission, 2008-10. VSO's parliamentary relations manager 2010-12. Adviser: Margaret Curran 2012-16. Policy dir, Scottish Labour 2016-. Contested Scottish parliament, West Scotland 2016. Trustee, Holocaust Memorial Day Trust 2011-. **David Wilson** (C) Former farmer who has worked for Rank Xerox, Unicom and Dow Jones Corp. Cllr, Inverclyde Council 2007-.

Contested: Renfrewshire North and West 2016; Inverclyde 2011, 2010.

CONSTITUENCY PROFILE
Perched on the banks of the Clyde, Inverclyde lies to Glasgow's west. Its biggest town, Greenock, was once a centre of Scotland's shipbuilding industry, but the industry has dwindled since the 1980s. About a third of its workers are in routine and semi-routine jobs, well above the UK average. Inverclyde had elected Labour MPs since 1936, dependent on which of its predecessor seats is considered, until the SNP won it for the first time in 2015.

EU REFERENDUM RESULT
36.2% Leave   Remain 63.8%

Inverness, Nairn, Badenoch & Strathspey

SNP HOLD MAJORITY 4,924 (9.3%)

DREW HENDRY
BORN May 21, 1964
MP 2015-

Background in retail, manufacturing and new technology. Founder, Teclan Ltd: the first private sector living wage employer in Inverness. Appointed to the board of Cairngorms National Park Authority 2007. Cllr, Highland C 2007-15; leader 2012-15. Contested European parliament 2009. Ousted Danny Alexander as MP in 2015. SNP transport spokesman 2015-; SNP Cosla leader 2015-. Campaigned for Remain. APPGs: digital economy, chairman; women in transport; smart cities. Married, four children. Ed: Grove Academy, Dundee; Dundee &

	Electorate	Turnout %	from 2010 %	Change
	76,844	68.71		
*D Hendry SNP	21,042	39.85	-10.20	
N Tulloch C	16,118	30.53	+24.61	
M Robb Lab	8,552	16.20	+8.71	
R Cunningham LD	6,477	12.27	-19.03	
D Boyd SCP	612	1.16	+0.43	

Angus Coll.

CHALLENGERS
Nicholas Tulloch (C) Corporate finance and corporate broking professional. Corporate FD at Cenkos Securities 2014-.**Mike Robb** (Lab) IT consultancy owner. Contested Inverness, Nairn, Badenoch and Strathspey 2015, 2010. **Ritchie Cunningham** (LD) Former head teacher and textbook author. Dir: Inverness and Nairn Enterprise 1998-2004; UHI Millennium Institute 2003-05. Contested Highland

C twice: 2017 (Lib Dem); 2012 (Independent).

CONSTITUENCY PROFILE
A huge, sparse seat in Scotland's highlands with the Cairngorms in the south and east. Average incomes here are slightly lower than the Scottish average. Inverness itself is home to about 47,000 people, and is also home to Scottish Natural Heritage. Nearly a tenth of working residents have jobs in tourism-related industries. The seat was gained by the Liberal Democrats upon its creation in 2005, and held by Danny Alexander for ten years until the SNP won it in 2015.

EU REFERENDUM RESULT

40.1% Leave   Remain 59.9%

Ipswich

LABOUR GAIN MAJORITY 831 (1.6%)

SANDY MARTIN
BORN May 2, 1957
MP 2017-

Local govt stalwart and self-described "democratic socialist". Cllr: Suffolk CC 1997-2017, Labour group leader; Ipswich BC 2001-14. Member of the LGBT Labour campaign. In a civil partnership. Has lived in Suffolk for most of his life. Said during the election campaign he would not seek ministerial office if elected. Ed: Merton Coll, Oxford (BA PPE).

CHALLENGERS
Ben Gummer (C) MP for Ipswich 2010-17. Entered parliament as his father, former cabinet minister John Gummer, left. Co-authored 2017

	Electorate	Turnout %	from 2010 %	Change
	74,799	68.37		
S Martin Lab	24,224	47.37	+10.28	
*B Gummer C	23,393	45.75	+0.99	
T Gould Ukip	1,372	2.68	-9.03	
A Hyyrylainen-Trett LD	1,187	2.32	-0.55	
C Armstrong Green	840	1.64	-1.92	
D Tabane Ind	121	0.24		

Conservative manifesto. Cabinet office min 2016-17. Worked for Sancroft, father's consultancy firm, and ran small engineering firm. Author of *The Scourging Angel*, a history of the Black Death. **Tony Gould** (Ukip) Chairman, Ukip Ipswich branch. **Adrian Hyyrylainen-Trett** (LD) Translator and translation consultant. The UK's first openly HIV-positive candidate. Leading Lib Dem campaigner on equalities and spearheaded equal

marriage policy in the party. Contested Vauxhall 2015.

CONSTITUENCY PROFILE
Most of the southeast Suffolk town of Ipswich is contained in this seat, although some of its suburban areas are in surrounding constituencies. The demography of the seat is young, being home to many of the University of Suffolk's 9,000 students. A Labour/Conservative swing seat, but not quite a bellwether, Ipswich was gained by the Conservatives in 1970, 1987 and 2010. Ben Gummer was the first Conservative to win Ipswich twice since the Second World War.

EU REFERENDUM RESULT

56.5% Leave   Remain 43.5%

Isle of Wight

CONSERVATIVE HOLD MAJORITY 21,069 (28.3%)

BOB SEELY
BORN 1966
MP 2017-

	Electorate	Turnout %	from 2010 % Change
	110,697	67.28	
B Seely C	38,190	51.28	+10.61
J Critchley Lab	17,121	22.99	+10.21
V Lowthian Green	12,915	17.34	+3.96
N Belfitt LD	2,740	3.68	-3.77
D Pitcher Ukip	1,921	2.58	-18.60
J Jones-Evans Ind	1,592	2.14	-2.41

Author and soldier. Started his career as foreign correspondent in eastern Europe for *The Times* and *Washington Post*. Served with TA in Iraq and Afghanistan. Worked as an adviser to Francis Maude and Sir Malcolm Rifkind, later for MTV Networks International. Cllr, Isle of Wight C 2013-. Contested Broxtowe 2005. Great-great-uncle, General Jack Seely, was MP for the Isle of Wight 1900-1906, 1923-24. Author, *The Deadly Embrace*, about Russia's role in Caucasus. Research associate, Oxford University, changing character of war programme. Ed: Arnold House Sch; Harrow Sch; King's Coll London (war studies; PhD in unconventional warfare, ongoing).

CHALLENGERS
John Critchley (Lab) Worked in the civil service at Whitehall: private secretary to Gillian Shephard and David Blunkett. Taught history and politics at a south London comprehensive. **Vix Lowthion** (Green) Lecturer in geology, geography and history in Newport.

CONSTITUENCY PROFILE
Just off the Hampshire coast, the Isle of Wight constituency has the largest electorate of any parliamentary seat. Nearly a quarter of its population are aged 65 or older, and tourism, health and social care are among the largest industries. Traditionally a Conservative/Liberal marginal, the Liberal Democrats last won this seat in 1997 but they fell to fifth place by 2015. New MP Bob Seely succeeds Andrew Turner, who stepped down after criticism for calling homosexuality "wrong" and "dangerous to society". Seely's majority is a record for the seat.

EU REFERENDUM RESULT

61.9% Leave   Remain 38.1%

Islington North

LABOUR HOLD MAJORITY 33,215 (60.5%)

JEREMY CORBYN
BORN May 26, 1949
MP 1983-

	Electorate	Turnout %	from 2010 % Change
	74,831	73.40	
*J Corbyn Lab	40,086	72.98	+12.74
J Clark C	6,871	12.51	-4.68
K Angus LD	4,946	9.00	+0.91
C Russell Green	2,229	4.06	-6.18
K Fraser Ukip	413	0.75	-3.25
M Foster Ind	208	0.38	
K Knapp Loony	106	0.19	
S Cameron-Blackie Ind	41	0.07	
B Martin SPGB	21	0.04	-0.19
A Mendoza Comm Lge	7	0.01	

Leader of the Opposition since 2015. Despite being widely believed to be leading Labour to electoral oblivion, in 2017 the party managed to gain 30 seats and its biggest swing in vote-share since 1945. Defied odds to be elected party leader twice, despite being seen as fringe candidate. Archetypal 1980s leftwinger who rebelled against New Labour govts many times. Long-time Eurosceptic: voted No in 1975 referendum, and against Maastricht and Lisbon treaties; campaigned for Remain in 2016. Cllr, Haringey BC 1974–83. Vegetarian since the age of 20, when he worked on a pig farm in Jamaica. Won highest share of votes in Islington North in constituency's history. Twice divorced, remarried. Three sons. Ed: Adams' GS.

CHALLENGERS
James Clark (C) Former army infantry officer. Awarded Joint Commanders' Commendation after serving in Helmand, 2012. **Keith Angus** (LD) Financial services project manager and local activist.

CONSTITUENCY PROFILE
The smallest constituency in the UK by size, and one of the densest, Islington North is a young and both ethnically and religiously diverse seat where four in ten homes are rented from the council and one in four from the private sector. Islington North has elected Labour MPs only since 1937, although Corbyn's immediate predecessor Michael O'Halloran briefly served as SDP and Independent.

EU REFERENDUM RESULT

21.6% Leave   Remain 78.4%

Islington South & Finsbury

LABOUR HOLD MAJORITY 20,263 (42.2%)

EMILY THORNBERRY
BORN Jul 27, 1960
MP 2005-

Practised as a barrister specialising in human rights law from 1985 until her election as MP for Islington South and Finsbury in 2005. Re-entered Labour front benches after she was forced to resign as shadow attorney general in 2014 after controversial "white van" tweet during Rochester and Strood campaign. Appointed as shadow foreign secretary 2016. Loyal Jeremy Corbyn supporter. Campaigned to Remain in the EU. Married, one daughter, two sons. Ed: CofE Secondary Modern, Guildford; Burlington Danes, Shepherd's Bush; University of Kent (BA law).

	Electorate	Turnout %	from 2010 %	Change
	69,534	69.10		
*E Thornberry Lab	30,188	62.83	+11.90	
J Charalambous C	9,925	20.66	-1.57	
A Desmier LD	5,809	12.09	+1.18	
B Hamdache Green	1,198	2.49	-5.12	
P Muswell Ukip	929	1.93	-5.69	

CHALLENGERS
Jason Charalambous (C) British-born Cypriot. Cllr, Enfield BC 2014-. Chairman of Trent Park Museum Trust. **Alain Desmier** (LD) Founded online marketing agency E-Finity Leads in 2012. Involved in Liberal Democrat activism since 2009. **Benali Hamdache** (Green) Worked for Britain Stronger in Europe campaign during the EU Referendum. Former Green Party equalities spokesperson and stood for London Assembly.

CONSTITUENCY PROFILE
Another small, dense, inner London seat; well over half of Islington South and Finsbury's residents are aged 16 to 45, and just under half of its residents are white British. It is one of a minority of seats where more households are owned and rented out by the local authority than owner-occupied, but mean income is significantly higher than the UK and London averages. Islington South has elected only Labour MPs since its creation in 1974, although Emily Thornberry only won her first election in 2005 with a majority of 484 over the Liberal Democrat candidate.

EU REFERENDUM RESULT

28.3% Leave   Remain 71.7%

Islwyn

LAB CO-OP HOLD MAJORITY 11,412 (31.6%)

CHRIS EVANS
BORN Jul 7, 1976
MP 2010-

Joined Labour Party aged 15. Former bookmaker and account manager, Lloyds TSB. Official, Union of Finance Staff. Marketing Exec, University of Glamorgan. Contested Cheltenham 2005. Researcher to Don Touhig MP. Pioneered a work placement scheme. Remainer. Initially rebelled and voted against triggering Article 50, but reversed his position. Critical of Jeremy Corbyn's EU campaigning; publicly called for him to resign and supported vote of no confidence. Select cttee, public accounts 2015-17. Member: Unite, Fabian Society, Co-op Party. Ed: Porth County

	Electorate	Turnout %	from 2010 %	Change
	56,256	64.16		
*C Evans Lab Co-op	21,238	58.84	+9.87	
D Thomas C	9,826	27.22	+12.07	
D Jones PC	2,739	7.59	-3.13	
J Smyth Ukip	1,605	4.45	-15.13	
M Kidner LD	685	1.90	-0.79	

CS; Pontypridd Coll; Trinity Coll Carmarthen (BA history).

CHALLENGERS
Dan Thomas (C) Works for building society. Cllr, Barnet C 2006-; deputy leader 2011-. Trustee, Finchley Charities. Contested Islwyn 2010. **Darren Jones** (PC) Cllr, Cardiff CC 1998-2004; youngest cabinet member in Wales in first Plaid Cymru administration. Mayor of Blackwood 2003-04. **Joe Smyth** (Ukip) Campaign manager

Euro, elections for Wales 2014. Chairman, Ukip Swansea branch 2013-14.

CONSTITUENCY PROFILE
The south Wales constituency of Islwyn consists of several smallish towns once dominated by the coalmining industry. Manufacturing is among the dominant industries in the area now, with nearly two fifths of the workforce in routine and semi-routine jobs. Islwyn and its predecessors have returned Labour MPs to parliament for more than a century, and the seat was represented by former Labour leader Neil Kinnock from 1970 until 1995.

EU REFERENDUM RESULT

58.9% Leave   Remain 41.1%

Jarrow

LABOUR HOLD MAJORITY 17, 263 (40.1%)

STEPHEN HEPBURN
BORN Dec 6, 1959
MP 1997-

Former builder and vocal supporter of Jeremy Corbyn's leadership, believing he had a "clear mandate to lead". Cllr, South Tyneside MBC 1985-97; deputy leader 1990-97. Research asst to predecessor, Don Dixon. Campaigned to Remain in EU; voted for Article 50. Campaigned for justice for mesothelioma sufferers. Select cttees: Northern Ireland 2015-17, 2004-10; Scotland 2015-17. APPGs: shipbuilding; football. Football-loving Geordie: president, Jarrow FC. Member, UCATT. Ed: Springfield CS, Jarrow; Newcastle University (BA politics).

Electorate	Turnout %	from 2010 %	Change
64,828	66.36		
*S Hepburn Lab	28,020	65.13	+9.47
R Gwynn C	10,757	25.00	+7.93
J Askwith Ukip	2,338	5.43	-14.23
P Maughan LD	1,163	2.70	-0.51
D Herbert Green	745	1.73	-1.67

CHALLENGERS
Robin Gwynn (C) Civil servant with prolific career at FCO, including senior posts overseas. Trustee chairman, Clean Sheet, a charity which finds employment for ex-offenders. Voted Leave. **James Askwith** (Ukip) Contested Newcastle CC 2016. **Peter Maughan** (LD) Solicitor. Cllr, Gateshead C 2012-. Contested Durham North 2015; Blaydon 2005, 2001, 1997. Member, Tyne and Wear Fire Authority Committee.

CONSTITUENCY PROFILE
On the southern bank of the Tyne, the seat of Jarrow consists of the town itself, the eastern edge of Gateshead, and the smaller town of Boldon in its southeast. Its residents are significantly more likely than average to have an apprenticeship or to work in manufacturing. The town lends its name to the famous Jarrow March against unemployment and destitution in 1936. Jarrow has elected Labour MPs in all but one election since 1922, and Labour's majority in the seat hasn't been less than 10,000 at any general election since the Second World War.

EU REFERENDUM RESULT

61.8% Leave   Remain 38.2%

Keighley

LABOUR GAIN MAJORITY 249 (0.5%)

JOHN GROGAN
BORN Feb 24, 1961
MP 2017-; 1997-2010

MP for Selby 1997-2010. Chairman of the Mongolian-British Chambers of Commerce. Former press officer. Voted against Jeremy Corbyn's whip in favour of Chuka Umunna's amendment to stay in the single market 2017. Chaired Labour Party Yorkshire and Humber Development Board. Contested: Keighley 2015; Selby 1992, 1987; York 1989. Member, Fabian Soc, IPPR. Ed: St Michael's RC Coll; St John's Coll, Oxford (BA history and economics, president of student union).

CHALLENGERS
Kristan Hopkins (C) MP

Electorate	Turnout %	from 2010 %	Change
71,429	72.41		
J Grogan Lab	24,066	46.53	+8.43
*K Hopkins C	23,817	46.05	+1.74
P Latham Ukip	1,291	2.50	-9.03
M Walker LD	1,226	2.37	-0.32
R Brown Green	790	1.53	-1.85
D Crabtree Ind	534	1.03	

for Keighley 2010-17. Brash former soldier. Parly under-sec, Northern Ireland 2016-17; CLG 2013-15. Housing min 2013-14. PPS to Andrew Robathan 2012-13. Member, Tory Reform Group. Married, one daughter. Education: Leeds (BA communications and cultural studies). **Paul Latham** (Ukip) Business consultant. Regional organiser, Ukip Yorkshire North Lincs. **Matt Walker** (LD) Works for a healthcare consultancy.

Formerly head of primary healthcare, Trafford CCG 2016.

CONSTITUENCY PROFILE
This West Yorkshire seat, in which more than 70,000 residents live in the town of Keighley itself, is characterised by high home ownership and incomes slightly higher than the Yorkshire average. It has a large Muslim community of over 12,000. The seat has changed hands between Labour and the Conservatives 10 times since 1945. 2017 is the first time since the 1979 that Labour has won the seat while in opposition. BNP leader Nick Griffin won over 4,000 votes here in 2005.

EU REFERENDUM RESULT

53.3% Leave   Remain 46.7%

Kenilworth & Southam

CONSERVATIVE HOLD MAJORITY 18,086 (35.2%)

JEREMY WRIGHT
BORN Oct 24, 1972
MP 2005-

	Electorate	Turnout %	from 2010 %	Change
	66,323	77.37		
*J Wright C	31,207	60.82	+2.46	
B Singh Lab	13,121	25.57	+10.26	
R Dickson LD	4,921	9.59	-0.48	
R Ballantyne Green	1,133	2.21	-1.80	
H Cottam Ukip	929	1.81	-9.39	

A relative unknown who rose through the ranks of the Conservative Party during the David Cameron premiership. Attorney-general 2014-; Parly under-sec: justice 2012-14. Govt whip 2010-12; opposition whip 2007-10. Remainer, led govt bid to use royal perogative to trigger Article 50. Member, constitutional affairs select cttee 2005-2007. Chairman, Warwick and Leamington Con Assoc 2002-03. MP for Rugby and Kenilworth 2005-10. Married, one son, one daughter. Ed: Trinity Sch, New York City; University of Exeter (LLB law); Inns of Court Sch (BVC).

CHALLENGERS
Bally Singh (Lab) Leadership development manager, NFU Mutual, 2014-. Cllr, Coventry CC 2010-. Contested Kenilworth and Southam 2015. Richard Dickson (LD) Trustee, Kenilworth Community Care. Previously dir, Bucks Community Foundation; development dir, Cord peace building charity. Contested Kenilworth and Southam 2015. Rob Ballantyne (Green) Runs a bookkeeping and management accounts practice. Harry Cottam (Ukip) Solicitor, owns a practice. Contested: Kenilworth and Southam 2015; Stratford upon Avon 2005.

CONSTITUENCY PROFILE
This Warwickshire seat consists of much of the rural area to the north, east and west of Warwick. More than a fifth of residents are aged 65 or above, over three quarters of homes are owner-occupied, a large proportion of the workforce are employed in managerial and director-level jobs. The seat has elected a Conservative MP since its creation in 2010, and the Conservatives have never won less than half the vote-share.

EU REFERENDUM RESULT

46.2% Leave   Remain 53.8%

Kensington

LABOUR GAIN MAJORITY 20 (0.1%)

EMMA DENT COAD
BORN Nov 2, 1954
MP 2017-

	Electorate	Turnout %	from 2010 %	Change
	60,594	63.83		
E Dent Coad Lab	16,333	42.23	+11.11	
*V Borwick C	16,313	42.18	-10.08	
A Mullin LD	4,724	12.21	+6.58	
J Nadel Green	767	1.98	-3.08	
J Torrance Ind	393	1.02		
P Marshall Ind	98	0.25		
J Lloyd Green Soc	49	0.13	-0.20	

Architectural historian, design writer and author. Part-way through PhD on architectural style and meaning in Franco's Spain. Kensington's first Labour MP, winning by 20 votes after three recounts. Blamed local council for Grenfell fire, which was subject of her maiden speech 2017. Campaigns against gentrification. Staunch supporter of Jeremy Corbyn and socialist policies. Cllr, Kensington and Chelsea BC 2006-. Member, London Fire and Emergency Planning Authority. Three children. Ed: Royal Coll of Art (MA design history); University of Liverpool (PhD).

CHALLENGERS
Victoria Borwick (C) MP for Kensington 2015-17. Replaced Sir Malcolm Rifkind after he resigned in wake of cash-for-access allegations. Brexiteer. Cllr, Kensington and Chelsea BC 2002-15. Failed to win Conservative nomination for London mayoralty 2008, 2004. Annabel Mullin (LD) Public service career: Met Police constable; NHS clinical psychologist. Worked in energy for PwC.

CONSTITUENCY PROFILE
This slim west London seat contains Notting Hill and Grenfell Tower. Kensington is one of only three seats where the mean salary is six figures. It had the highest average house prices of any seat in 2015. Despite this, child poverty is above average and the borough has among the highest rates of homelessness in the UK. The seat had never been held by Labour since its creation in 1974, although differently configured Kensington North seats have elected Labour MPs since 1945.

EU REFERENDUM RESULT

31.2% Leave   Remain 68.8%

Kettering

CONSERVATIVE HOLD MAJORITY 10,562 (21.4%)

PHILIP HOLLOBONE
BORN Nov 7, 1964
MP 2005-

Industry research analyst. Served in TA for eight years, latterly as a paratrooper. Contested Kettering 2001; Lewisham East 1997. With no staff and low expenses, Hollobone is Westminster's cheapest MP. Frequent rebel. Outspoken and prone to controversy. Campaigned to Leave EU and agreed a GE2017 electoral pact with Ukip: they fielded no candidate. Agreed with Ukip on Brexit, HS2, foreign aid target and burka ban. Cllr, Kettering BC 2003-; Bromley BC 1990-94. Deputy chairman, Conservative Assoc 2002-11. Divorced, two children. Ed: Dulwich Coll; LMH, Oxford

	Electorate	Turnout %	from 2010 %	Change
	71,523	69.07		
*P Hollobone C	28,616	57.92	+6.11	
M Scrimshaw Lab	18,054	36.54	+11.39	
S Austin LD	1,618	3.28	+0.12	
R Reeves Green	1,116	2.26	-1.20	

(BA Modern History and Economics).

CHALLENGERS
Mick Scrimshaw (Lab) Partner, online retail company. Cllr, Northamptonshire CC 2013-; Kettering BC 2015-, Labour leader. Voted Remain, but now embracing Brexit. Deputy pres, Kettering Chamber of Trade. Trustee, Kettering Community Unit. **Suzanna Austin** (LD) Small business owner with a background in logistics management. **Rob Reeves**

(Green) Self-employed tutor and poet. Contested Kettering 2015.

CONSTITUENCY PROFILE
Both house prices and incomes tend to be slightly lower than average in this Northamptonshire seat. Manufacturing and retail are among the largest local industries, and residents are slightly more likely to be aged under 45 and to own homes. Although Kettering was held by Labour between 1945 and 1983, it has mostly returned Conservatives since. Labour held the seat from 1997 to 2005, although Phil Sawford never won the seat by over 1,000 votes.

EU REFERENDUM RESULT

61.0% Leave   Remain 39.0%

Kilmarnock & Loudoun

SNP HOLD MAJORITY 6,269 (13.5%)

ALAN BROWN
BORN Aug 12, 1970
MP 2015-

Known for his thick accent which often has to be translated. Formerly a civil engineer. Shadow SNP spokesman transport 2017-; infrastructure and energy 2017-. Cllr, East Ayrshire C 2007-2015. Member, European scrutiny cttee 2016-. Cabinet member; chairman, grants cttee; spokesman, housing and strategic planning. Campaigned to Remain in the EU. Trustee and director roles: Kilmarnock Leisure Centre; Irvine Valley Regeneration Partnership. Married, two sons. Enjoys camping. Ed: Loudoun Academy; University of Glasgow (BEng: civil engineering).

	Electorate	Turnout %	from 2010 %	Change
	73,327	63.43		
*A Brown SNP	19,690	42.34	-13.32	
L Dover Lab	13,421	28.86	-1.50	
A Harper C	12,404	26.67	+14.14	
I Lang LD	994	2.14	+0.67	

CHALLENGERS
Laura Dover (Lab) One of the youngest candidates put forward by any of the parties at the age of 23. Vice-chairwoman, Scottish Young Labour. Glasgow University law graduate. Member, GMB. **Alison Harper** (C) Businessowner in East Ayrshire. Worked for tribunals service and Acas before moving to the private sector to work for a major bank. **Irene Lang** (LD) Former office manager and personal assistant for a small architecture firm. Retired.

CONSTITUENCY PROFILE
This seat covers the town of Kilmarnock and parts of rural Ayrshire in west Scotland. About half of its constituents live in Kilmarnock, a town known for the Johnnie Walker whisky bottled there until 2012, and Alexander Fleming, who attended Kilmarnock Academy. Like many former industrial towns, the area has seen economic decline: incomes are below average and unemployment is relatively high. A Labour stronghold since 1945, the constituency was a victim of the SNP's 2015 landslide. The Conservative vote-share is at its highest since 1979.

EU REFERENDUM RESULT

39.5% Leave   Remain 60.5%

Kingston & Surbiton

LIBERAL DEMOCRAT GAIN MAJORITY 4,124 (6.6%)

SIR ED DAVEY
BORN Dec 25, 1965
MP 2017-; 1997-2015

Re-elected after losing this
seat in 2015. Various business
consulting appointments
since losing office in 2015.
Management consultant. SoS:
ECC 2012-15; parly under-sec:
BIS 2010-12. Chairman of party's
2010 election campaign. Shadow
SoS: foreign and commonwealth
2007-10. Chief of staff to Sir
Menzies Campbell 2006-07. LD
whip 1997-2000. Spokesman:
ODPM 2002-05; London
2000-03; economy 1999-2001;
Treasury 1997-99. Member,
Federal Policy cttee. Economic
adviser to senior Liberal
Democrat MPs. Married, one
son. Ed: Nottingham HS; Jesus

	Electorate	Turnout %	from 2010 %	Change
	81,584	76.21		
E Davey LD	27,810	44.73	+10.27	
*J Berry C	23,686	38.09	-1.14	
L South Lab	9,203	14.80	+0.33	
G Matthews Ukip	675	1.09	-6.21	
C Walker Green	536	0.86	-3.06	
Chinners Loony	168	0.27		
M Basman Ind	100	0.16		

Coll, Oxford (BA PPE); Birkbeck
Coll, London (MSc economics).

CHALLENGERS
James Berry (C) MP for
Kingston & Surbiton 2015-17.
Liberal and open-minded,
favours a lowered voting age and
use of mindfulness practices in
schools. Member, home affairs
cttee 2015-17. Barrister, Serjeants'
Inn, specialising in healthcare
and police issues. Acted for

Surrey Police in Leveson
Inquiry. School governor.
Laurie South (Lab) Freelance
consultant. Former teacher.

CONSTITUENCY PROFILE
A southwest London seat that
borders Surrey and is younger
and more diverse than the UK
average. More than a sixth of
residents is Asian or of Asian
descent, and more than a fifth
live in private rented housing.
House prices are high, but
unlike some neighbouring seats,
they are not more than double
the UK average. The seat was
created in 1997 from Kingston
and Surbiton, which had both
been Conservative seats.

EU REFERENDUM RESULT
40.8% Leave   Remain 59.2%

Kingswood

CONSERVATIVE HOLD MAJORITY 7,500 (15.4%)

CHRIS SKIDMORE
BORN May 17, 1981
MP 2010-

Historian; wrote biography of
Edward VI, teaches part-time
at University of Bristol. Former
adviser and researcher for
Bristol's bid for European Capital
City of Culture. Journalist,
Western Daily Press. Previously
adviser to Michael Gove and
David Willets. Chairman
of the Bow Group 2007-08
and research fellow at Policy
Exchange. Loyal backbencher.
Campaigned to Remain in
the EU. Parly under-secretary
cabinet office 2016-. PPS to
George Osborne 2015-16.
Member, select cttees: education
2012-14; health 2010-13. Guitar
player. Education: Bristol GS;

	Electorate	Turnout %	from 2010 %	Change
	69,426	70.21		
*C Skidmore C	26,754	54.89	+6.57	
M Threlfall Lab	19,254	39.50	+9.90	
K Wilkinson LD	1,749	3.59	-0.21	
M Furey-King Green	984	2.02	-0.83	

Christ Church, Oxford (BA
history), St Cyre's and Dixon
Scholar.

CHALLENGERS
Mhairi Threlfall (Lab)
Development manager,
University of the West of
England. Cllr, Bristol CC 2013-.
Karen Wilkinson (LD) Director,
Parents Union. Ex-regional
planning consultant, Legal
Services Commission 2000-
04. Healthcare sales manager,
Scottish Mutual. **Matt Furey-
King** (Green) Aircraft engineer.

CONSTITUENCY PROFILE
Kingswood is a suburban seat
just to the east of Bristol, where
nearly three quarters of homes
are owner-occupied. Incomes
are slightly lower than the
regional average, and lower
than in nearby Bristol West and
Bristol North West. Kingswood
is characterised by significantly
above-average levels of
apprenticeship qualifications
among its residents, and
construction is one of the most
significant industries. The seat
has the highest proportion of
people in part-time employment
in the UK. Kingswood was a
Labour seat from 1992 until 2010
but has been Conservative since.

EU REFERENDUM RESULT
57.1% Leave   Remain 42.9%

Kirkcaldy & Cowdenbeath

LABOUR GAIN MAJORITY 259 (0.6%)

LESLEY LAIRD
BORN Nov 15, 1958
MP 2017-

Career in human resources for electronic, semiconductor and financial services companies. Senior talent manager, RBS 2009-12. Founder and former dir, Lesley Laird & Associates Ltd. Cllr, Fife C 2012-; deputy leader 2014-. Member, Unison. Board member, Fife Economy Partnership. Made shadow Scottish secretary six days after being elected to parliament. Married, one son. Ed: Caledonian University, Glasgow (Institute of personnel management); Napier University, Edinburgh (BA business management and human resources); Institute

	Electorate	Turnout %	from 2010 Change %
	72,721	63.52	
L Laird Lab	17,016	36.84	+3.46
*W Mullin SNP	16,757	36.28	-15.96
D Dempsey C	10,762	23.30	+13.42
M Wood LD	1,118	2.42	+0.25
D Coburn Ukip	540	1.17	-1.17

of Leadership & Management (executive coaching and leadership mentoring).

CHALLENGERS
Roger Mullin (SNP) MP for Kirkcaldy and Cowdenbeath 2015-17. Owner, UN culture studies provider Inter-Ed. Politics lecturer and thesis supervisor: University of Stirling, Open University. SNP Treasury spokesman 2015-17. **Dave Dempsey** (C) Teaches maths and IT in prisons. Previously

software engineer. Cllr, Fife C 2007-. Contested Kirkcaldy and Cowdenbeath 2015.

CONSTITUENCY PROFILE
Kirkcaldy and Cowdenbeath is a coastal seat along the northern side of the Firth of Forth. Incomes in this seat are below the Scottish average, and routine and semi-routine jobs are common. Unemployment is well above average, as are the levels of social renting, although home ownership is in line with the Scottish average. Kirkcaldy and Cowdenbeath was Gordon Brown's seat from 2005 to 2015, when it was won by the SNP following his retirement.

EU REFERENDUM RESULT
43.3% Leave   Remain 56.7%

Knowsley

LABOUR HOLD MAJORITY 42,214 (76.1%)

GEORGE HOWARTH
BORN Jun 29, 1949
MP 1986-

Former engineer 1966-75 and teacher. Chief exec, Wales Co-operative Centre, Cardiff 1982-86. Cllr: Knowsley BC 1975-86, dep leader 1982-83; Huyton DC 1971-75. MP for Knowsley and Sefton E 1997-2010; Knowsley N 1986-97. Jeremy Corbyn sceptic, supported vote of no confidence. Campaigned to Remain and abstained in vote to trigger Article 50. Opp spokesman: home 1994-97; environment 1989-94. Parly under-sec: NI 1999-2001; home 1997-99. Has served a number of select cttees, including: panel of chairs 2009-17; finance and services 2012-15; armed forces 2005-06; public

	Electorate	Turnout %	from 2010 Change %
	81,751	67.87	
*G Howarth Lab	47,351	85.34	+7.22
J Spencer C	5,137	9.26	+2.62
N Miney Ukip	1,285	2.32	-7.49
C Cashman LD	1,189	2.14	-0.79
S Baines Green	521	0.94	-1.56

accounts 2002-03. Married, three children. Ed: Huyton Secondary Sch; Kirkby Coll; Liverpool Polytechnic (BA social sciences).

CHALLENGERS
James Spencer (C) Comms manager for Catholic Education Service. **Neil Miney** (Ukip) Critical care nurse, NHS. Chairman, Ukip Knowsley branch. Contested Liverpool West Derby 2015; Liverpool Wavertree 2010. **Carl Cashman** (LD) Student. Cllr, Knowsley

MBC 2016-; Lib Dem leader. **Steve Baines** (Green) Events organiser.

CONSTITUENCY PROFILE
This Merseyside seat contains Kirby in the north and Huyton in the south. The area between the towns is home to a safari park. Knowsley is characterised by council estates, high unemployment and lower than average income. Well over a quarter of residents are in socially rented housing. This is the UK's most Christian constituency, according to the 2011 census. The predecessor seat of Huyton was held by Harold Wilson.

EU REFERENDUM RESULT
52.3% Leave   Remain 47.7%

Lagan Valley

DUP HOLD MAJORITY 19,229 (42.8%)

SIR JEFFREY DONALDSON
BORN Dec 7, 1962
MP 1997-

Lifelong political activist who joined the Orange Order in his youth. Later a member, Ulster Young Unionist council and Ulster Defence Regiment, reaching corporal. Agent to Enoch Powell MP 1982-84. NI assembly member: Down South 1985-86, representing UUP. MLA Lagan Valley 2003-10. Defected to the DUP from the UUP in 2004. DUP chief whip 2015-; was DUP signatory of confidence and supply pact with Conservatives in aftermath of general election. Campaigned to Leave the EU. DUP spokesman: defence, equality and energy and climate change 2010-15. First

Electorate	Turnout %	from 2010 %	Change
72,380	62.07		
*J Donaldson DUP	26,762	59.57	+11.69
R Butler UUP	7,533	16.77	+1.55
A McIntyre Alliance	4,996	11.12	-2.81
P Catney SDLP	3,384	7.53	+1.25
J Russell SF	1,567	3.49	+0.61
I Nickels C	462	1.03	-0.62
J Orr ND	222	0.49	

DUP member to be knighted, in 2016 Queen's birthday honours. Married, two daughters. Ed: Castlereagh Coll.

CHALLENGERS
Robbie Butler (UUP) Butcher who later became a fire and rescue officer. Cllr, Lisburn and Castlereagh CC 2014-16. MLA Lagan Valley 2016-. **Aaron McIntyre** (Alliance) Cllr, Lisburn & Castlereagh CC

2014-. Contested Belfast West by-election 2011. **Pat Catney** (SDLP) Retired pub owner. MLA Lagan Valley 2017-. Cllr, Lisburn CC 2011-.

CONSTITUENCY PROFILE
Lies southwest of Belfast. The largest town, Lisburn, is home to about 72,000 people. Protestants accounted for more than two thirds of Lagan Valley residents in 2011, and less than a fifth are Catholics. The seat is slightly more affluent than the Northern Ireland average. The seat has never elected a nationalist MP and the combined vote share of Sinn Fein and the SDLP hasn't reached 15 per cent since 1992.

EU REFERENDUM RESULT

53.1% Leave	Remain 46.9%

Lanark & Hamilton East

SNP HOLD MAJORITY 266 (0.5%)

ANGELA CRAWLEY
BORN Jun 3, 1987
MP 2015-

Named in the Forbes 30 Under 30 list for her work as an MP. Parly asst to: Bruce Crawford MSP; Clare Adamson MSP. Interned as a legal asst, Aamer Anwar & Co, solicitors. Former convenor, Young Scots for Independence. SNP NEC member. Volunteer, Royal Princess Trust for Young Carers. Cllr, South Lanarkshire C 2012-16. SNP spokeswoman: disabilities, child maintenance, housing, family support 2017-; equalities, women and children 2015-17. Openly gay. Ed: John Ogilvie HS; University of Stirling (BA politics); University of Glasgow (LLB law).

Electorate	Turnout %	from 2010 %	Change
77,313	65.28		
*A Crawley SNP	16,444	32.58	-16.24
P Corbett C	16,178	32.05	+16.18
A Hilland Lab	16,084	31.87	+1.33
C Robb LD	1,214	2.41	+0.23
D Mackay Ukip	550	1.09	-1.50

CHALLENGERS
Poppy Corbett (C) Finance and human resources manager in her family's electronics firm. Cllr, South Lanarkshire C 2017-. **Andrew Hilland** (Lab) Policy adviser, Policy and Research Commission. Senior policy adviser to the office of Gordon and Sarah Brown 2013-15. Director of research and secretary, Global Citizenship Commission 2014-16. Associate, Freshfields Bruckhaus Deringer 2012-13; left to work for 2014

Better Together campaign.. **Colin Robb** (LD) Works as a project manager for a utilities company.

CONSTITUENCY PROFILE
This south Scotland seat is demographically skewed slightly towards older people and is overwhelmingly white, with less than one in fifty ethnic minority residents. Both home ownership and local authority renting are higher than the Scotland average, as are typical incomes. Lanark and Hamilton East was held by Labour from 2005 until 2015, and although the SNP won by more than 10,000 votes in 2015, the constituency is now a genuine three-way marginal.

EU REFERENDUM RESULT

36.0% Leave	Remain 64.0%

Lancashire West

LABOUR HOLD MAJORITY 11,689 (21.5%)

ROSIE COOPER
BORN Sep 5, 1950
MP 2005-

Defected from Lib Dems in 1999 having been a Liverpool cllr 1973-2000; lord mayor of Liverpool 1992-93. Contested for the Lib Dems: Liverpool Broadgreen 1992; Knowsley N 1987, 1986 by-election; Liverpool Garston 1983. PR and comms professional, previously at Littlewoods Organisation. Disability advocate; both her parents were deaf. Vice-chairwoman, Liverpool Health Authority; chairwoman, Liverpool Women's Hospital. PPS to: Ben Bradshaw 2007-10; Lord Rooker 2006-07. Usdaw rep. Ed: Bellerive Convent GS; University of Liverpool.

	Electorate	Turnout %	Change from 2010 %
	73,258	74.24	
*R Cooper Lab	32,030	58.89	+9.62
S Currie C	20,341	37.40	+4.96
J Barton LD	1,069	1.97	-0.65
N Higgins Green	680	1.25	-1.93
D Braid WVPTFP	269	0.49	+0.19

CHALLENGERS
Sam Currie (C) Marketing adviser, Entwistle Green estate agent. Previously served in the Royal Navy, signals store operator. Cllr, West Lancashire BC 2016-. **Jo Barton** (LD) Cllr, Sefton MBC 2014-, member licensing and regulatory cttee; Barnstaple TC 2007-11. **Nate Higgins** (Green) 20-year-old musical theatre student at Edge Hill University. Describes himself as "Red-Green." LGBT campaigner.

CONSTITUENCY PROFILE
A seat just north of Liverpool and just inland from the coastal seats of Southport and Sefton Central, Lancashire West's biggest towns are Skelmersdale and Ormskirk. Ormskirk contains Edge Hill University, and more than 7,000 students live in the constituency. The seat is also characterised by high levels of home ownership, and typical incomes slightly above the northwest average. Lancashire West elected Conservative MPs from 1983 but the seat was gained by Labour in 1992, and Labour's smallest majority since gaining the seat was still over 4,000 in 2010.

EU REFERENDUM RESULT
55.0% Leave   Remain 45.0%

Lancaster & Fleetwood

LABOUR HOLD MAJORITY 6,661 (14.5%)

CAT SMITH
BORN Jun 16, 1985
MP 2015-

Background in social work as campaigns and policy officer for the British Association of Social Workers and trustee of local charity, Empowerment. Led campaigns defending the Royal Lancaster Infirmary and the Fleetwood Hospital. North West regional role on NUS national executive committee. Contested Wyre and Preston North 2010. Jeremy Corbyn supporter. Shadow: min for voter engagement and youth affairs 2016-; deputy Commons leader 2016-. Married. Ed: Barrow Sixth Form Coll; Lancaster University (BA sociology and gender studies).

	Electorate	Turnout %	Change from 2010 %
	67,171	68.47	
*C Smith Lab	25,342	55.10	+12.83
E Ollerenshaw C	18,681	40.62	+1.38
R Long LD	1,170	2.54	-0.79
R Novell Green	796	1.73	-3.28

CHALLENGERS
Eric Ollerenshaw (C) MP for Lancaster and Fleetwood 2010-15. Long-serving history teacher. PPS to Baroness Warsi 2012-15. Leader of the Tory group on GLA 2002-04; member, 2000-04. Cllr, Hackney BC 1990-2007; leader 2000-01. Awarded MBE 1991. **Robin Long** (LD) Physics researcher at Lancaster University. Contested Lancaster & Fleetwood 2015. **Rebecca Novell** (Green) Social worker and criminal justice researcher. Writes for *The Guardian*'s Social

Care Network. Cllr, Lancaster CC 2015-.

CONSTITUENCY PROFILE
A coastal seat with the area of Bowland Fells in its east. More than 14,000 students live in the constituency, which contains the University of Lancaster. At nearly one in ten, this seat has one of the greatest proportions of people living in communal areas of any constituency, and about one in five households is rented in the private sector. Created in 2010, this seat was won by the Conservatives on a narrow majority of 333 in that year, but was a Labour gain in 2015.

EU REFERENDUM RESULT
52.0% Leave   Remain 48.0%

Leeds Central

LABOUR HOLD MAJORITY 23,698 (49.7%)

HILARY BENN
BORN Nov 26, 1953
MP 1999-

The fourth-generation Benn in parliament. Special adviser to David Blunkett 1997-99. Cllr, Ealing BC 1979-99. MSF: research officer; head of policy and communications. Sacked from shadow cabinet after EU referendum amid rumours he was organising a campaign against Jeremy Corbyn. Made impassioned speech in favour of extending airstrikes to Syria that was applauded in the House. Shadow foreign sec 2015-16; shadow CLG SoS 2011-15; shadow Commons leader 2010-11. SoS: Defra 2007-10; int dev 2003-07. Widowed, remarried, one daughter, three sons. Ed:

	Electorate	Turnout %	from 2010 %	Change
	89,537	53.24		
*H Benn Lab	33,453	70.17	+15.21	
G Davies C	9,755	20.46	+3.17	
B Palfreman Ukip	2,056	4.31	-11.41	
E Carlisle Green	1,189	2.49	-5.40	
A Nash LD	1,063	2.23	-1.16	

University of Sussex (BA Russian & east European studies).

CHALLENGERS
Gareth Davies (C) Has worked in pension fund asset management for more than ten years. Contested Doncaster Central 2010. **Bill Palfreman** (Ukip) IT engineer. Secretary, Kingston-upon-Hull Ukip. **Ed Carlisle** (Green) Project manager at Leeds-based charity Together for Peace. Contested local elections 2016, 2015.

CONSTITUENCY PROFILE
The most densely populated Leeds seat, Leeds Central contains a large space around the city's centre and much of the urban area of Leeds to its immediate south. The University of Leeds is in the consituency, and about 25,000 residents are students. Renting, both social and private, is well above average, and it is one of few seats where unemployment is over 3,000. It is a diverse seat, since about a quarter of the population is non-white. It has returned Labour MPs since its re-creation in 1983 but, at 53 per cent, it had the lowest turnout of any English seat in 2017.

EU REFERENDUM RESULT
46.0% Leave   Remain 54.0%

Leeds East

LABOUR HOLD MAJORITY 12,752 (30.8%)

RICHARD BURGON
BORN Sep 19, 1980
MP 2015-

Employment rights lawyer and trade union activist. Socialist who nominated Jeremy Corbyn for leadership in 2015 and emerged as a key Corbyn ally in aftermath of shadow cabinet resignations 2016. Campaigned to Remain, voted to trigger Article 50. Shadow Treasury min 2015-16; shadow lord chancellor and justice secretary 2016-. Power metal enthusiast who has featured on a track with a local Leeds band. Nephew of Colin Burgon, MP for Elmet 1997-2010. Ed: Cardinal Heenan RC HS; St John's Coll, Cambridge (BA English literature; chairman, Labour Club).

	Electorate	Turnout %	from 2010 %	Change
	65,950	62.84		
*R Burgon Lab	25,428	61.36	+7.61	
M Robinson C	12,676	30.59	+9.65	
P Spivey Ukip	1,742	4.20	-14.79	
E Sanderson LD	739	1.78	-1.61	
J Moran Green	434	1.05	-1.88	
J Otley Yorkshire	422	1.02		

CHALLENGERS
Matthew Robinson (C) Education charity worker. Cllr, Leeds CC 2010-. Governor, Shadwell and Bramham School Federation. **Paul Spivey** (Ukip) Motor engineer and former mechanic. Cllr, Kippax PC. Chairman, Ukip Leeds. Contested Elmet and Rothwell 2015. **Ed Sanderson** (LD) Family law solicitor. Former vice-president, Liberal Youth. Previously policy and research

asst, Leeds & North Yorkshire Chamber of Commerce. Contested: Leeds East 2015; Doncaster North 2010.

CONSTITUENCY PROFILE
Leeds East has the lowest median income of any seat in Yorkshire and the Humber and about a third of households are in the social rented sector. It also has a particularly high rate of long-term unemployment. The seat has elected only Labour MPs since it was re-created in 1955 and for much of that time it was the seat of one-time defence secretary, chancellor of the exchequer and Labour deputy leader Denis Healey.

EU REFERENDUM RESULT
61.4% Leave   Remain 38.6%

Leeds North East

LABOUR HOLD MAJORITY 16,991 (32.1%)

FABIAN HAMILTON
BORN Apr 22, 1955
MP 1997-

Outspoken critic of the all-female Labour shortlists of the 90s; said that being "kept out of a job just because I'm a man offends me deeply". Cllr, Leeds CC 1989-1997. Contested Leeds NE 1992. Nominated Yvette Cooper for Labour leadership 2015; resigned front-bench role during attempt to oust Jeremy Corbyn as leader 2016. Remainer, voted to trigger Article 50. Rebellions over renewing Trident nuclear deterrent. Shadow minister: FCO 2016-; defence 2016-. Jewish. Married, three children. Ed: Brentwood Sch, Essex; University of York (BA social sciences).

	Electorate	Turnout %	from 2010 %	Change
	70,112	75.59		
*F Hamilton Lab	33,436	63.09	+15.18	
R Stephenson C	16,445	31.03	-1.87	
J Hannah LD	1,952	3.68	-1.64	
A Forsaith Green	680	1.28	-3.98	
T Seddon Yorkshire	303	0.57		
C Foote Green Soc	116	0.22	-0.72	

CHALLENGERS
Ryan Stephenson (C) Cllr, Leeds CC 2016-. Contested: Leeds E 2015; European parliament elections 2014. Chief of staff to Alec Shelbrooke MP 2010-. GE campaign manager, Elmet and Rothwell 2010. **Jon Hannah** (LD) Managing dir, Xytgeist Consulting. Chairman, Lib Dems East and North East Leeds. **Ann Forsaith** (Green) Retired school teacher. Formerly co-ordinator, Yorkshire and

the Humber Green Party. **Tess Seddon** (Yorkshire) Theatre director and writer.

CONSTITUENCY PROFILE
Demographically, Leeds North East is the most white British seat in Leeds, according to the 2011 census, but nearly 5,000 of the constituency's residents, about one in twenty, is Jewish. It is also the only Leeds seat where home ownership isn't well below the national average. Although this was once the seat of Thatcherite progenitor Keith Joseph, it has been consistently Labour since 1997, and Fabian Hamilton's majority has never fallen below 4,000.

EU REFERENDUM RESULT

37.4% Leave	Remain 62.6%

Leeds North West

LAB CO-OP GAIN MAJORITY 4,224 (9.1%)

ALEX SOBEL
BORN Apr 26, 1975
MP 2017-

General manager, Social Enterprise Yorkshire and the Humber 2009-. Former community development worker. On the team that lodged bid for Leeds' largest Surestart scheme. Cllr, Leeds CC 2012-. Helped to establish first new park in north Leeds in over 50 years. Contested Leeds NW 2015. Operations manager, Labour Yes to Fairer Votes during 2011 AV referendum. Organiser, Yorkshire and Humber Ed Miliband for Leader 2010. Member, Jewish Labour Movement. Born in Leeds. Married, two sons. Ed: University of Leeds (BSc information systems).

	Electorate	Turnout %	from 2010 %	Change
	68,152	67.92		
A Sobel Lab Co-op	20,416	44.11	+14.03	
*G Mulholland LD	16,192	34.98	-1.80	
A Lamb C	9,097	19.65	+1.01	
M Hemingway Green	582	1.26	-5.76	

CHALLENGERS
Greg Mulholland (LD) MP for Leeds NW 2005-17. Remainer; abstained from Article 50 vote. Shadow minister: health 2007-10; education 2006-07; international development 2005-06. Chairman, Lib Dem parliamentary campaigns 2015-16. Select cttees: public administration 2010-15; work and pensions 2005-10. Campaigned for an English national anthem. Cllr, Leeds CC 2003-05. Father was a Lib Dem cllr and parliamentary candidate.

Alan Lamb (C) Cllr, Leeds CC 2011-. Owns and runs restaurant and catering business. Born in Leeds.

CONSTITUENCY PROFILE
Contains Leeds Metropolitan University. Over a quarter of residents are aged 18 to 24, and about 20,000 residents are students. It has the lowest unemployment rate of any Leeds seat and, along with Leeds North East, is the most affluent. It is also the most ethnically diverse Leeds seat. It returned Conservative MPs from 1950 until 1997, when Labour gained it before Greg Mulholland's first victory in 2005.

EU REFERENDUM RESULT

35.4% Leave	Remain 64.6%

Leeds West

LABOUR HOLD MAJORITY 15,965 (37.8%)

RACHEL REEVES
BORN Feb 13, 1979
MP 2010-

Spent ten years as an economist at HBOS, Bank of England and the British Embassy, Washington. Junior chess champion. Contested Bromley and Chislehurst 2006, 2005. Spearheaded Labour's campaign against bedroom tax. Jeremy Corbyn sceptic who resigned front-bench post when he was elected; followed whip on Syria bombings and Article 50. Chairwoman, BEIS select cttee 2017-. Shadow chief sec to the Treasury 2011-13; shadow SoS DWP 2013-15. Married, two children. Ed: Cator Park Sch, Bromley; New Coll, Oxford (BA PPE); LSE (MSc economics).

Electorate	Turnout %	from 2010 %	Change
67,955	62.14		
*R Reeves Lab	27,013	63.97	+15.93
Z Metcalfe C	11,048	26.16	+6.05
M Thackray Ukip	1,815	4.30	-14.19
A Pointon Green	1,023	2.42	-5.95
A McGregor LD	905	2.14	-1.75
E Jones Yorkshire	378	0.90	
M Davies Green Soc	47	0.11	

CHALLENGERS
Zoe Metcalfe (C) Former educational practitioner. Trustee, Hollytree Foundation Charity. Public governor, Harrogate NHS trust. Cllr, Harrogate BC 2015-. Contested Doncaster Central 2015. **Mark Thackray** (Ukip) Dir, textile machine manufacturing firm Textronix. Contested Dewsbury 2015. **Andrew Pointon** (Green) IT support specialist, Leeds CC. Secretary,

Farnley and Wortley Green Party 2010-16. Contested Leeds West 2015. **Alisdair McGregor** (LD) IT service analyst at a Leeds communication firm. Contested Calder Valley 2015.

CONSTITUENCY PROFILE
Leeds West is a young constituency, with almost half of its residents aged between 16 and 45. Just over half of households are owner-occupied, and social renting is more likely than in much of the rest of the UK. This seat has been won by Labour at all but one postwar election, when a Liberal MP won it in Margaret Thatcher's 1983 landslide.

EU REFERENDUM RESULT

53.3% Leave   Remain 46.7%

Leicester East

LABOUR HOLD MAJORITY 22,428 (42.8%)

KEITH VAZ
BORN Nov 26, 1956
MP 1987-

Former barrister. Chairman, home affairs select cttee 2007-16; stepped down following newspaper sting alleging drug offences and that he paid for sex with male prostitutes. Prominent in the British-Indian community; first MP of Asian origin since 1929 when elected in 1987. Sister, Valerie Vaz, is MP for Walsall South. Member, Labour Party NEC. Board member, British Council. Remainer, voted to trigger Article 50. Did not nomiate leadership candidate in 2015 but backed Owen Smith 2016. Rarely rebels on substantive issues. Member, justice select cttee 2016-. Min:

Electorate	Turnout %	from 2010 %	Change
77,788	67.39		
*K Vaz Lab	35,116	66.98	+5.85
E He C	12,688	24.20	+1.25
S Barot Ind	1,753	3.34	
N Dave LD	1,343	2.56	-0.00
M Wakley Green	1,070	2.04	-1.01
I Fox Ind	454	0.87	

FCO 1999-2001. Parly under-sec, lord chancellor's dept 1999. Married, one daughter, one son. Ed: Latymer Upper Sch; Gonville and Caius Coll, Cambridge (BA Law; MA; MCFI); Coll of Law.

CHALLENGERS
Edward He (C) Aerospace manufacturing engineer. Worked in schools as Stem ambassador. **Sujata Barot** (Ind) Local community activist. Ex-BBC Radio Leicester presenter.

Nitesh Dave (LD) Special needs teacher. Vice-chairman, Leicester Liberal Democrats.

CONSTITUENCY PROFILE
Leicester East is the worst off of the city's constituencies in terms of median income. It has the highest proportion of Asian and British Asian residents of any seat in the country, about three fifths, with the local community including about 35,000 Hindus and 22,000 Muslims. A fifth of residents are employed in manufacturing. The seat has been won by Labour at all elections since 1974 except 1983, when a Conservative won the seat by under 1,000 votes.

EU REFERENDUM RESULT

54.1% Leave   Remain 45.1%

Leicester South

LAB CO-OP HOLD MAJORITY 26,261 (52.0%)

JONATHAN ASHWORTH
BORN Oct 14, 1978
MP 2011-

Professional politician. Former Labour staffer: econ and welfare policy officer 2002-04; political research officer 2001. Special adviser to Gordon Brown. Opposition whip 2011-13. Shadow health sec 2016-. Shadow min: without portfolio 2015-16; cabinet office 2013-15. Remainer. Backed Yvette Cooper's leadership bid 2015; did not declare support for Jeremy Corbyn or Owen Smith in second 2016 contest. Loyal: voted against airstrikes in Syria; voted for Article 50. Married, two children. Ed: Philips HS, Whitefield; Bury Coll; University of Durham (BA politics and philosophy).

	Electorate	Turnout %	from 2010 % Change
	75,534	66.88	
*J Ashworth Lab Co-op	37,157	73.55	+13.74
M Sonecha C	10,896	21.57	+0.62
H Bisnauthsing LD	1,287	2.55	-2.08
M Lewis Green	1,177	2.33	-3.18

CHALLENGERS
Meera Sonecha (C) Permanent asst to Sir Edward Garnier MP 2011-17. Exec officer, Conservative Friends of India. Former outreach manager, Andy Street for West Midlands Mayor. **Harrish Bisnauthsing** (LD) Former RAF radar engineer. Cllr: Stamford TC 1987-, mayor 2002-03; South Kesteven DC 2003-. Contested Grantham and Stamford 2015, 2010. **Mags Lewis** (Green) Green Party's disability spokeswoman. Contested local elections 2015.

CONSTITUENCY PROFILE
This seat contains the city centre and is the most affluent of Leicester's seats. It is home to the city's university and over 22,000 students. A diverse seat, with 33,000 Muslim residents, but fewer Hindus than Leicester East. Over 25 per cent of the population lives in private rented accommodation, well above average. It has mostly elected Labour MPs, but it was won by the Conservatives in 1974 and 1983, and by the Liberal Democrat Parmjit Singh Gill at a 2004 by-election. Ashworth became MP when Sir Peter Soulsby resigned to become mayor.

EU REFERENDUM RESULT
42.4% Leave   Remain 57.6%

Leicester West

LABOUR HOLD MAJORITY 11,060 (29.5%)

LIZ KENDALL
BORN Jun 11, 1971
MP 2010-

Contested Labour leadership on Blairite ticket in 2015, came last with four per cent of the vote. Remainer, voted for Article 50. Jeremy Corbyn sceptic. Shadow health min 2011-15. Primarily interested in early years policy, became associate dir, IPPR. Special adviser to Patricia Hewitt and Harriet Harman in early New Labour years. Later public health researcher, King's Fund. Formerly dir: Ambulance Services Network; Maternity Alliance. Member: Unite; Fabian Society. Regular panellist, BBC *This Week*. Ed: Watford Girls' GS; Queens' Coll, Cambridge (BA history).

	Electorate	Turnout %	from 2010 % Change
	64,834	57.86	
*L Kendall Lab	22,823	60.84	+14.35
J Hickey C	11,763	31.36	+5.73
S Young Ukip	1,406	3.75	-13.49
I Bradwell LD	792	2.11	-2.25
M Gould Green	607	1.62	-3.82
D Bowley Ind	121	0.32	

CHALLENGERS
Jack Hickey (C) Primary school teacher. Chairman, City of Leicester Conservatives 2016-. National cttee member, Conservative Education Society. Contested local elections 2015. **Stuart Young** (Ukip) Bookkeeper. Contested Leicester W 2015. **Ian Bradwell** (LD) Registered blind. Disability awareness trainer. Former chairman, Leicester Disabled Persons Access Group.

Contested: Leicester W 2015; local elections 2015, 2011, 2007.

CONSTITUENCY PROFILE
Leicester West is proportionally the least ethnically diverse of the three Leicester seats, with about two thirds of residents registering as white British in the 2011 census. There is also a significant prevalence of routine and semi-routine work compared with the UK average and the constituency has the highest proportion of socially rented households in Leicester, too. Unlike its two neighbours, Leicester West has only ever been represented by Labour MPs since its creation in 1974.

EU REFERENDUM RESULT
50.8% Leave   Remain 49.2%

Leicestershire North West

CONSERVATIVE HOLD MAJORITY 13,286 (24.8%)

ANDREW BRIDGEN
BORN Oct 28, 1964
MP 2010-

Trained in the Royal Marines, before co-founding and running an agricultural company. Former East Midlands chairman, Institute of Directors. Led campaign to decriminalise non-payment of the TV Licence. Critic of David Cameron: demanded a vote of no confidence that was later withdrawn in 2013. Lifelong Eurosceptic who campaigned for Leave. Cttees: regulatory reform 2010-17; Commons liaison 2015-17. Chairman, Uzbekistan APPG. Two children. Ed: The Pingle Sch, Swadlincote; University of Nottingham (BSc biological sciences).

	Electorate	Turnout %	from 2010 %	Change
	75,362	71.05		
*A Bridgen C	31,153	58.19	+8.71	
S Sheahan Lab	17,867	33.37	+5.96	
M Wyatt LD	3,420	6.39	+2.44	
M Woolley Green	1,101	2.06	-0.22	

CHALLENGERS
Sean Sheahan (Lab) Cllr, Leicestershire CC 2013-, 1997-2009. Governor, Moira Infant Sch. Dir, Ashby Canal Trust. Contested Charnwood 2001. **Michael Wyatt** (LD) Leicester micropub and café owner. Cllr, Leicestershire CC 2009-, 1993-97. Unlike most Lib Dems, supported Leave in the EU referendum. Anti-HS2. Contested Mansfield 2010. **Mia Woolley** (Green) Secondary school teacher. Contested local elections 2017.

CONSTITUENCY PROFILE
The biggest towns in this seat, which stretches along the border with Derbyshire, are Ashby-de-la-Zouch and Coalville. The latter is an old mining town. Incomes in the seat are slightly above the UK average, and its residents enjoy relatively high levels of home ownership. Prominent industries among the workforce include manufacturing and transport, partly because of the presence of East Midlands airport in the north of the seat. The seat had been a bellwether since its creation in 1983, but Bridgen has increased his majority at successive elections.

EU REFERENDUM RESULT

60.7% Leave   Remain 39.3%

Leicestershire South

CONSERVATIVE HOLD MAJORITY 18,631 (32.9%)

ALBERTO COSTA
BORN Nov 13, 1971
MP 2015-

Lawyer who worked in Whitehall. Consultant, Nicholas Woolf & Co, solicitors. Founded London-based law firm, Costa Carlisle. Grew up in Scotland. Contested Angus 2010. Voted to Remain and trigger Article 50. Loyal backbencher who served on justice select cttee 2015-17. Member, Institute of Directors. Freeman of the City of London. Married, one son, one daughter. Ed: University of Glasgow (MA LLB law); University of Strathclyde (PgDip legal practice).

CHALLENGERS
Shabbir Aslam (Lab) Runs own

	Electorate	Turnout %	from 2010 %	Change
	78,985	71.77		
*A Costa C	34,795	61.38	+8.16	
S Aslam Lab	16,164	28.51	+6.49	
G Webb LD	2,403	4.24	-3.15	
R Helmer Ukip	2,235	3.94	-13.42	
M Morgan Green	1,092	1.93		

accountancy business. Cllr, Blaby DC 2015-; Braunstone TC 2011-, mayor 2014-15. Police volunteer. **Gregory Webb** (LD) Software contractor and web developer. Children and youth worker volunteer. **Roger Helmer** (Ukip) Former business executive. MEP for East Midlands 1999-2017, defected from the Conservatives in 2012. Ukip spokesman for energy and industry. Contested 2014 Newark by-election. Published books and papers on Europe and the Conservative

Party. **Mary Morgan** (Green) Self-employed pilates instructor and active environmentalist.

CONSTITUENCY PROFILE
The seat contains Braunstone Town, a residential area to Leicester's immediate southwest but beyond the commuter villages and towns, the seat is mainly rural. Home ownership is very high, with about four fifths of households in the constituency owner-occupied, and incomes too tend to be above the regional average. Leicestershire South has never elected anything but a Conservative MP, and neither did its predecessor seat, Blaby.

EU REFERENDUM RESULT

58.1% Leave   Remain 41.9%

Leigh

LAB CO-OP HOLD MAJORITY 9,554 (20.4%)

JO PLATT
BORN Jun 16, 1973
MP 2017-

Leigh's first female MP. Won the hotly contested Labour selection following Andy Burnham's decision to stand down and focus on his successful Greater Manchester mayoral bid; gained Burnham's support after being his election agent in 2015. Previously worked in marketing and advertising. Volunteered as an advocacy worker for alcoholics' support group. School governor. Secretary, Leigh CLP. Cllr, Wigan BC 2012-; portfolio holder for young people 2014-17. PPS to Angela Rayner 2017-. Single mother, one son, one daughter. Ed: St Patrick's RC HS, Salford.

	Electorate	Turnout %	from 2010 Change %
	76,211	61.51	
J Platt Lab Co-op	26,347	56.21	+2.33
J Grundy C	16,793	35.83	+13.19
M Bradley Ukip	2,783	5.94	-13.79
R Kilpatrick LD	951	2.03	-0.52

CHALLENGERS
James Grundy (C) Cllr, Wigan BC 2008-; longest serving Conservative councillor in Leigh. Launched bid for Leigh to have its own council. Member, Greater Manchester Transport Authority. **Mark Bradley** (Ukip) Project manager in health and social care. Worked in the Royal Navy for 22 years. Campaigned for "Lexit", to make Leigh independent from Wigan. **Richard Kilpatrick** (LD) Senior account exec in healthcare company. Previously teacher

and campaign organiser for former Lib Dem MP John Leech. Contested Middlesbrough 2015.

CONSTITUENCY PROFILE
The three largest towns in this Greater Manchester seat, Leigh, Golborne and Tyldesley, account for nearly nine out of ten of its residents. The constituency is a former mining area and incomes are lower on average than in nearby seats such as Warrington North and Bolton West and Worsley. The seat has elected Labour MPs at every election since 1922. Leigh's previous MP was Andy Burnham, who was elected mayor of Greater Manchester in May 2017.

EU REFERENDUM RESULT

63.3% Leave   Remain 36.7%

Lewes

CONSERVATIVE HOLD MAJORITY 5,508 (10.2%)

MARIA CAULFIELD
BORN Aug 6, 1973
MP 2015-

Former NHS nurse and senior sister who led specialist breast cancer research team at Royal Marsden Hospital. Volunteer shepherd, Urban Shepherd. Part-owner and shareholder Lewes Football Club. Breast Cancer Now ambassador. Sussex No2AV co-ordinator, 2011. Non-executive director, BHT Sussex local housing charity. Cllr, Brighton and Hove CC 2007-11. Contested Caerphilly 2010. Brexiteer. One rebellion, over Sunday trading. Christian who accused progressive alliance campaigners of "preaching hate" for dressing up as nuns at a Lewes rally. Daughter of Irish

	Electorate	Turnout %	from 2010 Change %
	70,947	76.38	
*M Caulfield C	26,820	49.49	+11.49
K Blundell LD	21,312	39.33	+3.47
D Chapman Lab	6,060	11.18	+1.29

immigrant farmer, grew up on council estate in Wandsworth, London. Married to Steve Bell OBE, former NCC president.

CHALLENGERS
Kelly-Marie Blundell (LD) Fundraising and marketing professional who runs own consultancy firm for charities. Contested Guildford 2015. **Daniel Chapman** (Lab) Policy research analyst, National Association of Headteachers. Former asst to Des Turner MP. Labour election campaign organiser, Brighton Kemptown

2010. Cllr Brighton and Hove CC 2015-.

CONSTITUENCY PROFILE
Lewes is a coastal Sussex seat between Brighton and Eastbourne. Nearly a quarter of its residents are aged 65 or over and the seat has high levels of outright home ownership. Residents are more likely than average to be self-employed and are relatively affluent compared with the UK average. The seat had been Lib Dem from 1997, but was mainly Conservative before that. The town itself is thought to have voted Liberal Democrat, but the rural area around it voted Conservative.

EU REFERENDUM RESULT

47.1% Leave   Remain 52.9%

Lewisham Deptford

LABOUR HOLD MAJORITY 34,899 (63.3%)

VICKY FOXCROFT
BORN Mar 9, 1977
MP 2015-

Union career before parliament: finance sector officer, Unite 2009-15; political officer, Amicus 2005-09; research officer, AEEU 2002-05. Cllr, Lewisham BC 2010-14: spearheaded successful Save Lewisham Hospital campaign. Led establishment of cross-party youth violence commission 2016. Sceptical of Jeremy Corbyn. Remainer, voted against invoking Article 50. Labour whip 2015-17. Statutory instruments cttee 2016-17. APPGs: youth affairs, vice-chairwoman; domestic violence. Ed: De Montford University (BA business studies; chairwoman, Labour Students).

	Electorate	Turnout %	from 2010 %	Change
	78,472	70.23		
*V Foxcroft Lab	42,461	77.04	+16.80	
M McLean C	7,562	13.72	-1.16	
B Dean LD	2,911	5.28	+0.02	
J Coughlin Green	1,640	2.98	-9.53	
M Martin CPA	252	0.46	-0.18	
L McAnea AWP	225	0.41		
J Lawrence Realist	61	0.11		

CHALLENGERS
Melanie McLean (C) Small business owner. Contested Islington South and Finsbury 2005. **Bobby Dean** (LD) PR consultant at youth development charity. Communications officer, Liberal Youth 2011-12. First in his family to attend university. Contested Lewisham BC 2016. **John Coughlin** (Green) Freelance translator and musician. Manager, Brockley

Tenants' Co-op. Cllr, Lewisham BC 2014-.

CONSTITUENCY PROFILE
Deptford has the highest unemployment of the three Lewisham seats. On average, it is the youngest Lewisham seat, with more than two fifths of residents aged 25 to 44. About half of residents are white, and over a third are black or mixed race. Deptford's residents are more likely to be in privately and socially rented accommodation than the other Lewisham seats. This seat has elected Labour MPs since its creation in 1974, and is now one of the safest seats in the country.

EU REFERENDUM RESULT
24.4% Leave   Remain 75.6%

Lewisham East

LABOUR HOLD MAJORITY 21,213 (44.9%)

HEIDI ALEXANDER
BORN Apr 17, 1975
MP 2010-

Former Clothes Aid manager. Researcher for Joan Ruddock MP 1999-2005. Chairwoman, Greater London Enterprise 2007-09. Voted for Syria airstrikes 2015; resigned as SoS for health, voted no confidence in Jeremy Corbyn. Remainer, voted against Article 50. Whip 2013-15; shadow SoS, health 2015-16. Cttees: health 2016-17; selection 2013-16; regulatory reform 2010-15; CLG 2010-12. Cllr, Lewisham BC 2004-10; dep mayor regeneration cabinet min 2006-10. Ed: Churchfields Sch, Swindon; Durham University (BA geography; MA European urban and regional change).

	Electorate	Turnout %	from 2010 %	Change
	68,126	69.28		
*H Alexander Lab	32,072	67.95	+12.25	
P Fortune C	10,859	23.01	+0.70	
E Frith LD	2,086	4.42	-1.30	
S Poorun Green	803	1.70	-3.96	
K Forster Ukip	798	1.69	-7.36	
W Winston Ind	355	0.75		
M Martin CPA	228	0.48	-0.17	

CHALLENGERS
Peter Fortune (C) Training and development manager, Newsquest Media Group. Ex-Royal Yeomanry, Croydon. Cllr, Bromley BC 2014-. Contested Lewisham East 2015. **Emily Frith** (LD) Health adviser, Liberal Democrats 2002-06. Special adviser, health and welfare, to Nick Clegg 2013-15: oversaw introduction of waiting time standards in mental health.

Storm Poorun (Green) Chief exec Olan Trust 2005-. Contested: Lewisham East 2015; Southwark North & Bermondsey 2005. Green Party deputy leadership candidate 2016.

CONSTITUENCY PROFILE
Lewisham East is broadly similar to Lewisham Deptford, but with lower incomes and a greater proportion of black and mixed-race residents. Lewisham East has higher levels of home ownership, and unemployment is significantly lower than in Lewisham Deptford. The Conservatives won the seat in 1983, but the seat has been Labour since 1992.

EU REFERENDUM RESULT
35.4% Leave   Remain 64.6%

Lewisham West & Penge

LABOUR HOLD MAJORITY 23,162 (43.5%)

ELLIE REEVES
BORN Dec 11, 1980
MP 2017-

Employment law barrister, she represented employees against companies such as British Airways and Balfour Beatty. Previously at Monaco Solicitors and OH Parsons. Set up Working Mums Advisory service to provide legal assistance to women and families facing workplace discrimination. Labour national executive cttee member 2006-16. Vice-chairwoman, London Labour Party. Remain voter, campaigning to avoid hard Brexit. Younger sister of Rachel Reeves MP. Married to John Cryer, MP for Leyton and Wanstead, one son. Ed: Cator

	Electorate	Turnout %	from 2010 Change %
	72,902	72.97	
E Reeves Lab	35,411	66.57	+15.98
S Bailey C	12,249	23.03	-1.15
J Russell LD	3,317	6.24	-1.47
K Wheller Green	1,144	2.15	-6.32
H Cheah Ukip	700	1.32	-6.51
K Hortense CPA	325	0.61	
R White Populist	50	0.09	

Park Sch; New Coll, Oxford (BA jurisprudence).

CHALLENGERS
Shaun Bailey (C) Specialist in youth, crime and drug issues. Special adviser to David Cameron on youth and crime 2010-13. Research fellow, Centre for Policy Studies. Member, London Assembly 2016-; dep chairman, health cttee. Contested Hammersmith 2010.

John Russell (LD) Freelance photographer. Chairman, Wide Horizons charity. Cllr, Lewisham BC 2006-10.

CONSTITUENCY PROFILE
Lewisham West and Penge is demographically fairly similar to the other two Lewisham constituencies, but the Penge wards are from Bromley Borough Council. Therefore, partly because of Penge's inclusion, this is the most affluent seat in Lewisham; it is also the whitest, with just three in ten black or mixed-race residents. Labour has held this seat, including its predecessor Lewisham West, since 1992.

EU REFERENDUM RESULT
34.6% Leave   Remain 65.4%

Leyton & Wanstead

LABOUR HOLD MAJORITY 22,607 (49.0%)

JOHN CRYER
BORN Apr 11, 1964
MP 2010-; 1997-2005

Hard-left union official and former journalist at *Tribune*, *Morning Star*, *Labour Briefing* and *Guardian*. Son of ex-MPs Anne and Bob Cryer. Political officer: Unite, Aslef. MP for Hornchurch 1997-2005. Did not nominate a leadership candidate in 2015. Regular rebel under Tony Blair but he rarely rebelled under Ed Miliband. Eurosceptic, backed neither Leave nor Remain in referendum. PLP chairman 2015-. Member, Socialist Campaign Group. Married to Ellie Reeves, MP for Lewisham West and Penge. Ed: Oakbank Sch, Keighley; Hatfield Poly; London Coll of Printing.

	Electorate	Turnout %	from 2010 Change %
	65,285	70.73	
*J Cryer Lab	32,234	69.81	+11.20
L Farris C	9,627	20.85	-1.11
B Sims LD	2,961	6.41	+0.75
A Gunstock Green	1,351	2.93	-4.38

CHALLENGERS
Laura Farris (C) Discrimination barrister and former journalist for BBC and Reuters. Daughter of former Conservative MP Michael McNair-Wilson. Sought candidacy for Richmond Park in 2017. **Ben Sims** (LD) Ex-UN technology project leader in Africa and Latin America. Works as a data strategist and tech consultant. **Ashley Gunstock** (Green) Former actor on ITV's *The Bill*. Party member since 1989. Teacher, Tower Hamlets. Contested: Leyton and Wanstead

2015, 2010, 2005, 2001; Finchley and Golders Green 1997; Green Party leadership 2008.

CONSTITUENCY PROFILE
Almost 40 per cent of residents in this northwest London seat are aged 25 to 44. Just under half of the local population is white, and a quarter is Asian. A significant proportion are EU citizens, in particular those from post-2001 accession nations. About a tenth of residents are students. Private renting in the seat is even higher than London average, and the median income is below it. The seat, including its predecessor Leyton, has elected only Labour MPs since 1966.

EU REFERENDUM RESULT
34.8% Leave   Remain 65.2%

Lichfield

CONSERVATIVE HOLD MAJORITY 18,581 (34.7%)

MICHAEL FABRICANT
BORN Jun 12, 1950
MP 1992-

	Electorate	Turnout %	from 2010 % Change
	74,430	71.91	
*M Fabricant C	34,018	63.56	+8.40
C Worsey Lab	15,437	28.84	+9.02
P Ray LD	2,653	4.96	-0.29
R Pass Green	1,416	2.65	-1.19

Eccentric and outspoken blond bombshell. Chartered engineer. Worked as a broadcaster and economist. MP for Staffordshire Mid 1992-97. Contested South Shields 1987. Brexiteer. Led campaign to lift ban on gay men giving blood. Rebelled to vote against HS2 railway line and plain cigarette packaging. Vice-chairman, Conservative Party 2012-14; sacked after HS2 opposition and comments on Maria Miller's resignation from cabinet. Govt whip 2010-12; opposition whip 2005-10. Ed: Brighton, Hove and Sussex GS; Loughborough University (BSc economics and law); University of Sussex (MSc operations research).

CHALLENGERS
Chris Worsey (Lab) Employment and management consultant. Partnerships dir, Stepjockey fitness app. Cllr, Sandwell MBC 2012-. Member: Unite; Co-op Party. Contested Lichfield 2015. **Paul Ray** (LD) Solicitor specialising in banking and finance law. Partner, Browne Jacobson. Cllr, Lichfield CC. Contested Lichfield 2015. **Robert Pass** (Green) Dir, Fortress Recycling. Chairman, Lichfield Green Party. Contested Lichfield 2015.

CONSTITUENCY PROFILE
One fifth of residents are aged 65 or above and 97.5 per cent are white. In terms of average incomes, the seat is affluent compared with neighbouring seats and three quarters of households in the constituency are owner occupied. The former mining town Burntwood is more Labour-leaning than the constituency's rural villages, so Michael Fabricant won the seat by just 238 votes when it was re-created in 1997, but his majority has increased since.

EU REFERENDUM RESULT
57.5% Leave — Remain 42.5%

Lincoln

LABOUR GAIN MAJORITY 1,538 (3.2%)

KAREN LEE
BORN Jan 15, 1959
MP 2017-

	Electorate	Turnout %	from 2010 % Change
	73,111	66.64	
K Lee Lab	23,333	47.89	+8.34
*K McCartney C	21,795	44.74	+2.10
N Smith Ukip	1,287	2.64	-9.57
C Kenyon LD	1,284	2.64	-1.62
B Loryman Green	583	1.20	
P Gray Ind	312	0.64	
I Scott-Burdon Ind	124	0.25	

Nurse at Lincoln County Hospital. Mayor of Lincoln 2012-13. Helped to form Lincoln's anti-poverty strategy as chairwoman of the council's community leadership scrutiny cttee. Trade unionist; member: Unite, Unison. PPS to John McDonnell 2017-. Four children. Roman Catholic. Ed: St Hugh's RC Sch; South Park Sch; Lincoln Coll.

CHALLENGERS
Karl McCartney (C) MP for Lincoln 2010-17. Brexiteer. Former magistrate, director of a communications consultancy and PR manager. Conservative researcher and agent, including for Dame Angela Rumbold. Cllr, Wrothan PC 1997-2003. Contested Lincoln 2005. Investigated by police over alleged breach of spending rules in 2015. Member, 1922 exec cttee 2012-17. Married, two sons. **Nick Smith** (Ukip) Chairman, Lincoln Ukip. Contested Lincoln 2015, 2010, 2005. Served in the army. **Caroline Kenyon** (LD) Qualified barrister, magazine editor and entrepreneur. Owns PR agency promoting Lincolnshire produce. **Ben Loryman** (Green) Doctor, Lincoln hospital.

CONSTITUENCY PROFILE
This constituency is home to the University of Lincoln and many of its 12,000 students.. Lincoln is characterised by lower average incomes than the rest of UK and East Midlands. About a fifth of households rent privately, a figure significantly above the UK average. The seat had previously been a bellwether but Labour winning Lincoln at this election is the first time the party has won the seat when in opposition since the 1970s.

EU REFERENDUM RESULT
57.4% Leave — Remain 42.6%

Linlithgow & Falkirk East

SNP HOLD MAJORITY 2,919 (5.2%)

MARTYN DAY
BORN Mar 26, 1971
MP 2015-

Former worker at the Bank of Scotland. Member, Chartered Institute of Bankers in Scotland. Community campaigner. Took the seat from Labour's Michael Connarty who had held it in various incarnations since the 1992 election. Cllr, West Lothian CC 1999-2015. SNP spokesman, development and transport. Election agent: Falkirk East 2011; Linlithgow and Falkirk East 2010; Linlithgow 1999. Born in Falkirk, raised and educated in Linlithgow. Married. Ed: Linlithgow Academy.

CHALLENGERS
Joan Coombes (Lab) Born

	Electorate	Turnout %	from 2010 Change %
	86,186	65.08	
*M Day SNP	20,388	36.35	-15.69
J Coombes Lab	17,469	31.14	+0.10
C Kennedy C	16,311	29.08	+17.09
S Pattle LD	1,926	3.43	+1.40

and raised in Grangemouth. Former sales manager who sold Tuppaware in Falkirk. Cllr, Falkirk C 2017-; deputy leader. **Charles Kennedy** (C) Quantity surveyor and commercial manager. Born, raised and educated in West Lothian. Led the 2014 West Lothian Better Together campaign. **Sally Pattle** (LD) Former antisocial behaviour officer in Plymouth who went on to work for a publisher and became a bookseller. Founded book festivals in West Lothian.

CONSTITUENCY PROFILE
This seat, on the southern side of the Firth of Forth in eastern Scotland, is demographically skewed towards older people, with nearly half of its residents over the age of 45. Over a quarter of households are in the social-rented sector, a figure slightly higher than the Scottish average. Among the workforce there is an overrepresentation of routine and semi-routine occupations, and residents' incomes are slightly below the Scottish average. The seat and its predecessors had elected only Labour MPs going back as far as 1935 until the SNP landslide of 2015.

EU REFERENDUM RESULT

42.0% Leave	Remain 58.0%

Liverpool Riverside

LAB CO-OP HOLD MAJORITY 35,947 (74.9%)

LOUISE ELLMAN
BORN Nov 14, 1945
MP 1997-

Lectured at the Open University 1970-76. TGWU. Voted for Iraq War. Supports Trident renewal. Backbencher who has been a member of various select cttees, including: national policy statements 2017; transport 2002-17; liaison 2008-17. APPG: chairwoman, Britain-Israel; vice-president, against anti-Semitism. Vice-chairwoman, Labour friends of Israel. Nominated Liz Kendall for leader 2015; Owen Smith 2016. Cllr: Lancs CC 1970-97, leader 1981-97; W Lancs DC 1974-87. Married, one daughter, one son. Ed: Manchester HS for Girls; University of Hull (BA sociology & history); University

	Electorate	Turnout %	from 2010 Change %
	76,332	62.91	
*L Ellman Lab Co-op	40,599	84.55	+17.14
P Hall C	4,652	9.69	+0.10
S Pitchers Green	1,582	3.29	-8.84
T Sebire LD	1,187	2.47	-1.41

of York (MPhil social admin).

CHALLENGERS
Pamela Hall (C) Works in human resources for Sky UK. Cllr, Cheshire West and Chester C 2008-; member, staffing cttee. Trustee, City of Chester Charter Trustees. **Stephanie Pitchers** (Green) Born in South Africa and moved to the UK in 2005. Member of the Save Liverpool Women's Hospital campaign. **Tom Sebire** (LD) Management consultant for water and energy companies.

CONSTITUENCY PROFILE
Average incomes are higher in this seat than in the other Liverpool constituencies, although still slightly below the northwest average. A huge 30,000 students live in this seat, which contains almost all of the university campus buildings in Liverpool. Riverside contains the highest proportion of Northern Irish residents outside constituencies in Northern Ireland, and is also most ethnically diverse Liverpool seat. The seat has elected only Labour MPs. No other party has received more than 10,000 votes in this seat since its creation in 1983.

EU REFERENDUM RESULT

27.3% Leave	Remain 72.7%

Liverpool Walton

LABOUR HOLD MAJORITY 32,551 (77.1%)

DAN CARDEN
BORN Oct 28, 1986
MP 2017-

Former aide to Unite boss, Len McCluskey, who beat Liverpool mayor Joe Anderson in a controversial selection contest that caused the local party secretary to quit in protest. Former parly asst to John Cummings. Previously: youth officer, TGWU parly branch; treasurer, LSE Labour Club. Member, LGBT Labour. Socialist who joined Labour as a schoolboy. Jeremy Corbyn supporter. His father was a shop steward who was sacked during 1995-98 Liverpool dockers' strike. Ed: St Edward's Coll, Liverpool; London School of Economics (BSc international relations).

	Electorate	Turnout %	Change from 2010 %
	62,738	67.26	
D Carden Lab	36,175	85.73	+4.43
L Evans C	3,624	8.59	+3.90
T May Ind	1,237	2.93	+2.79
K Brown LD	638	1.51	-0.83
C Feeley Green	523	1.24	-1.25

CHALLENGERS
Laura Evans (C) Runs a fibre-optic cable business. Suffered from chronic obesity, lost 16 stone in two years. Cllr, Trafford MBC 2011-. **Terry May** (Ind) Local businessman who owns two bars that host autism community coffee mornings. Left school aged 15 with no qualifications. Regeneration advocate. **Kris Brown** (LD) Mental health care worker. Chairman, Liverpool LD. Contested Wallasey 2015. **Colm**

Feeley (Green) Events and sales manager.

CONSTITUENCY PROFILE
Liverpool Walton contains the stadiums of both of Liverpool's Premier League football teams. It is the poorest Liverpool seat based on average income, and of the Liverpool seats it has the highest unemployment rate and the greatest proportion of households in the social rented sector. The constituency has elected Labour MPs continuously since 1964; previous MPs include hard-left firebrand Eric Heffer, and Steve Rotheram, who was elected mayor of Liverpool City Region.

EU REFERENDUM RESULT

52.2% Leave   Remain 47.8%

Liverpool Wavertree

LAB CO-OP HOLD MAJORITY 29,466 (67.5%)

LUCIANA BERGER
BORN May 13, 1981
MP 2010-

At centre of local deselection row weeks after election. Formerly worked in govt strategy; at Accenture; and as govt and parly manager, NHS confederation. Member and former dir, Labour Friends of Israel. Resigned from NUS NEC in antisemitism dispute. Member: Unite; Co-op Party; Fabian Society; Progress. Shadow min public health 2013-16. Resigned after no confidence vote in Jeremy Corbyn. Ed: Haberdashers' Aske's Sch; University of Birmingham (BA commerce and Spanish); Birkbeck Coll, London (MSc government, politics and policy).

	Electorate	Turnout %	Change from 2010 %
	62,411	69.92	
*L Berger Lab Co-op	34,717	79.55	+10.24
D Haddad C	5,251	12.03	+2.03
R Kemp LD	2,858	6.55	+0.56
T Grant Green	598	1.37	-3.85
A Heatherington ND	216	0.49	

CHALLENGERS
Denise Haddad (C) Nurse who spent 25 years in NHS, now at Chetham's Sch of Music, Manchester. School governor. Dir, CNS Focus healthcare company. Cllr, Trafford MBC 2016-. **Richard Kemp** (LD) Partner in community business consultancy. Previously worked on overseas regeneration projects. Cllr, Liverpool CC 1992-; 1975-84. Appointed CBE 2011. Formerly vice-chairman, local government association.

CONSTITUENCY PROFILE
Liverpool Wavertree is home to some 10,000 students and, like Liverpool Riverside, it has a large Northern Irish population, albeit smaller than Riverside's. More than a quarter of households in privately rented accomodation. Having been reconstituted in 1997 from two seats, one Labour, one Lib Dem, Wavertree has only ever elected Labour MPs, although a previous incarnation of the seat elected only Conservative MPs at general elections from 1923 until it was redrawn and renamed in 1983. Labour has never won less than half of the votes in Wavertree since its constitution in 1997.

EU REFERENDUM RESULT

35.3% Leave   Remain 64.7%

Liverpool West Derby

LAB CO-OP HOLD MAJORITY 32,908 (72.9%)

STEPHEN TWIGG
BORN Dec 25, 1966
MP 2010-; 1997-
2005

Formerly: political consultant
at Rowland Sallingbury Casey;
research asst, Margaret Hodge
MP; parly officer, Amnesty Int;
pres, NUS. Chairman, Progress.
Beat Michael Portillo in Enfield
Southgate in 1997, but then
lost to the Conservatives in
2005. One of the first openly
gay MPs. Cllr Islington BC
1992-97. Nominated Liz Kendall
for leadership 2015. Several
education posts: shad SoS 2011-
13; min, schools 2004-05; parly
under-sec 2002-04. Shad min:
constitutional reform 2013-15;
FCO 2010-11. Dep leader of
HoC 2001-02. Ed: Southgate CS;
Balliol Coll, Oxford (BA politics

	Electorate	Turnout %	from 2010 %	Change
	65,164	69.31		
*S Twigg Lab Co-op	37,371	82.75	+7.58	
P Richardson C	4,463	9.88	+3.28	
S Radford Lib	2,150	4.76	-0.23	
P Parr LD	545	1.21	-1.13	
W Ward Green	329	0.73	-1.70	
G Hughes Ind	305	0.68		

and economics).

CHALLENGERS
Paul Richardson (C) Former
RAF officer, serving in the
Middle East, the Falklands and
Germany. Candidate for St
Helens North 2015. Banker.
Former chairman of a London
Chamber of Commerce.
Chairman of the London
regional forum of the Chartered
Management Institute. **Steve
Radford** (Lib) Cllr, Liverpool CC

1984-, 1981-83. Liverpool's first
openly gay councillor. Leader of
Liberal Party Group. Contested
every election since 1997.

CONSTITUENCY PROFILE
Liverpool West Derby is a
slightly more suburban seat than
the other Liverpool seats, and it
has a long border with Huyton
and Knowsley. Unemployment
and social renting in the
seat are both relatively high,
although not as high as in West
Derby's neighbour, Liverpool
Walton. Liverpool West Derby
has elected only Labour MPs
since the 1964 general election,
although it not done so at any
previous general election.

EU REFERENDUM RESULT

49.8% Leave   Remain 50.2%

Livingston

SNP HOLD MAJORITY 3,878 (7.4%)

HANNAH BARDELL
BORN Jun 1, 1983
MP 2015-

Persuaded by Alex Salmond to
work on SNP's 2007 Holyrood
election campaign, producing
SNP TV online. Previously
asst producer on *GMTV*.
Later became Salmond's office
manager 2007-10. Formerly
worked for US state dept in
Edinburgh Consulate managing
protocol and press; head of
comms and marketing, Stork
oil and gas service; comms
manager, Subsea 7, engineering
and construction contractors.
SNP group leader, fair work
and employment 2015-; small
business, enterprise and
innovation 2015-17. Previously
policy cttee member, Grampian

	Electorate	Turnout %	from 2010 %	Change
	81,208	64.65		
*H Bardell SNP	21,036	40.06	-16.82	
R Wolfson Lab	17,158	32.68	+5.06	
D Timson C	12,799	24.38	+14.07	
C Dundas LD	1,512	2.88	+0.74	

Chamber of Commerce. Won
Pushkin Prize as a teenager.
Musical theatre enthusiast. Ed:
Broxburn Academy; University
of Stirling (MA film & media;
politics & English).

CHALLENGERS
Rhea Wolfson (Lab) Former
youth worker. Constituency
representative on Labour NEC,
NEC, ally of Jeremy Corbyn.
Left-leaning. **Damian Timson**
(C) Former RAF serviceman and
Scottish Rugby Panel referee.
Cllr, West Lothian C 2017-.

CONSTITUENCY PROFILE
A West Lothian seat bordering
two of the Edinburgh
constituencies, Livingston is
skewed towards younger people,
with far fewer residents aged 65
and over than average. Incomes
are slightly below average and
residents are more likely than is
typical to work in routine-level
jobs. A new town built to ease
pressure on Glasgow in the
1960s, Livingston was held by
New Labour's foreign secretary
Robin Cook from 1983 until his
death in 2005. His successor Jim
Devine was suspended from the
party after he was charged and
convicted during the expenses
scandal.

EU REFERENDUM RESULT

43.3% Leave   Remain 56.7%

Llanelli

LABOUR HOLD MAJORITY 12,024 (29.8%)

NIA GRIFFITH
BORN Dec 4, 1956
MP 2005-

	Electorate	Turnout %	Change from 2010 %
	59,434	67.88	
*N Griffith Lab	21,568	53.46	+12.12
S Davies C	9,544	23.66	+9.31
M Arthur PC	7,351	18.22	-4.73
K Rees Ukip	1,331	3.30	-12.95
R Daniels LD	548	1.36	-0.59

Former language teacher and schools inspector. Member, NUT. Cllr, Carmarthen TC 1987-99. Carmarthen Sheriff 1997-98; deputy mayor 1998-99. Jeremy Corbyn sceptic who nominated Andy Burnham in 2015 and Owen Smith in 2016; clashed with Corbyn over Nato and Trident renewal. Remainer, voted to trigger Article 50. PPS to: Harriet Harman 2008-10; Hilary Benn 2007-08. Shadow min: Wales 2011-15; BIS 2010-11. Shadow SoS: defence 2016-; Wales 2015-16. Chairwoman, APPG on modern languages. Divorced, publicly came out as gay in 2016. Ed: Newland HS for Girls; Somerville Coll, Oxford (BA modern languages); University of Wales, Bangor (PGCE).

CHALLENGERS
Stephen Davies (C) Caseworker for Mohammad Asghar AM. Voluntary family support worker. Deputy chairman, Llanelli Conservative Association. Campaigned to Leave the EU. Contested Carmarthenshire C 2015. **Mari Arthur** (PC) Dir, Sustain Wales charity. Marketing and business strategist. Founder, Mari Arthur Marketing. Board member, Keep Wales Tidy.

CONSTITUENCY PROFILE
Llanelli is a coastal south Wales seat to the northwest of Swansea. Llanelli itself is home to about 50,000 people, and is a former mining town. Nowadays, routine and semi-routine jobs are well overrepresented in Llanelli's workforce and incomes are below the average in Wales. Llanelli has been held by Labour at every election since 1922 and is considered a safe seat although Labour hasn't won more than 50 per cent of the vote in Llanelli since 1997.

EU REFERENDUM RESULT
56.7% Leave   Remain 43.3%

Londonderry East

DUP HOLD MAJORITY 8,842 (21.6%)

GREGORY CAMPBELL
BORN Feb 15, 1953
MP 2001-

	Electorate	Turnout %	Change from 2010 %
	67,038	61.20	
*G Campbell DUP	19,723	48.07	+5.83
D Nicholl SF	10,881	26.52	+6.76
S Quigley SDLP	4,423	10.78	-1.51
R Holmes UUP	3,135	7.64	-7.72
C McCaw Alliance	2,538	6.19	-1.43
L St Clair-Legge C	330	0.80	-0.41

Former civil servant and director of publishing company, Causeway Press. Staunchly opposed to Irish Language Act and barred for two days from speaking in NI Assembly after yawning over Sinn Fein member speaking Irish. DUP spokesman: int dev; cabinet office. MLA for East Londonderry 1998-2016. NI Assembly min: culture, arts and leisure 2008-09; regional development 2000-01. Member, NI Forum for political dialogue 1996-98. Contested: Londonderry East 1997; Foyle 1992, 1987, 1983. Cllr, Londonderry CC 1981-2011. Married, one son, three daughters. Ed: Londonderry Tech Coll; Magree Coll (Extra Mural Cert political studies).

CHALLENGERS
Dermot Nicholl (SF) Cllr, Causeway Coast and Glens BC 2014-; Coleraine BC 2011-14. **Stephanie Quigley** (SDLP) Podiatrist, formerly at the Northern Health and Social Care Trust. Cllr, Causeway Coast and Glens BC 2014-; Coleraine BC 2013-14. Founder of Street Pastors Project, training volunteers to create safer neighbourhoods. **Richard Holmes** (UUP) Managing director of manufacturing firm based in Antrim. Cllr, Causeway Coast & Glens BC 2014-; Coleraine BC 2011-14. Brexit supporter, despite UUP leadership favouring Remain.

CONSTITUENCY PROFILE
Mainly rural northwest Northern Irish constituency with small Indian and Chinese communitites. High rates of economic inactivity for Northern Ireland, with a considerable number of retirees and students. Construction and agriculture are large employment sectors.

EU REFERENDUM RESULT
48.0% Leave   Remain 52.0%

Loughborough

CONSERVATIVE HOLD MAJORITY 4,269 (7.9%)

NICKY MORGAN
BORN Oct 10, 1972
MP 2010-

	Electorate	Turnout %	from 2010 % Change
	79,607	68.02	
*N Morgan C	27,022	49.90	+0.38
J Miah Lab	22,753	42.02	+10.15
D Walker LD	1,937	3.58	-0.52
A McWilliam Ukip	1,465	2.71	-8.26
P Leicester Green	971	1.79	-1.75

Remainer who voted for Article 50 but seen as one of the new backbench "awkward squad", having been openly critical of govt Brexit plans. Sacked from cabinet after Theresa May became PM. Criticised May for wearing £1,000 leather trousers in *Sunday Times* photoshoot. Supported Michael Gove's leadership bid. Education sec 2014-16. Min: women and equalities 2014-16. Treasury sec: financial 2014; economic 2013-14. Chairwoman, Treasury select cttee 2017-. Previously a corporate solicitor: Travers Smith; Allen & Overy; Theodore Goddard. Contested:

Loughborough 2005; Islington S and Finsbury 2001. Married, one son. Ed: Surbiton HS; St Hugh's Coll, Oxford (BA law, MA law); Coll of Law, Guildford (LPC).

CHALLENGERS
Jewel Miah (Lab) Of Bangladeshi origin. Previously resigned from party over Iraq. Cllr, Charnwood BC 2011-; Leicestershire CC 2009-. **David Walker** (LD) Retired university lecturer. Founder member, SDP. Cllr, Charnwood BC 2007-11.

Philip Leicester (Green)
Researcher, Loughborough University.

CONSTITUENCY PROFILE
This seat consists of the north Leicestershire town, Loughborough, and much of the rural area around it, including the smaller towns of Shepsed, Quorn and Barrow upon Soar. The seat contains Loughborough University; 16,000 residents are full-time students. Education and manufacturing are among the overrepresented industries. Loughborough elected Labour MPs consistently postwar but since 1979 has tracked the largest party in parliament.

EU REFERENDUM RESULT
50.1% Leave   Remain 49.9%

Louth & Horncastle

CONSERVATIVE HOLD MAJORITY 19,641 (37.2%)

VICTORIA ATKINS
BORN Mar 22, 1976
MP 2015-

	Electorate	Turnout %	from 2010 % Change
	79,006	66.79	
*V Atkins C	33,733	63.92	+12.76
J Speed Lab	14,092	26.70	+8.67
J Noble Ukip	2,460	4.66	-16.75
L Gabriel LD	1,990	3.77	-0.71
T Arty-Pole Loony	496	0.94	+0.42

Former criminal barrister. Serious organised crime specialist, Red Lion Chambers; added to Attorney General's regulators panel and serious Fraud Office's list of specialist fraud prosecutors. Contested Gloucestershire PCC 2012. Remainer, voted to trigger Article 50. One rebellion, to decriminalise abortion. Formerly vice-chairwoman of APPGs on diabetes and broadband. First in her family to go to university. Father is former Conservative minister and chief whip, Sir Robert Atkins. Married, one son. Ed: Corpus Christi Coll, Cambridge (BA law).

CHALLENGERS
Julie Speed (Lab) Retired after career in London commercial sector. Cllr, Louth TC 2016-. Volunteer, East Coast Homeless Outreach. **Jonathan Noble** (Ukip) Former secondary school teacher. Cllr, Boston BC 2015-. Contested local elections 2017. **Lisa Gabriel** (LD) Freelance composer and musician. Former guitar teacher. Contested: Lincoln 2005, 2001, 1997; Louth 2015; East Midlands European elections 2004, 1999.

CONSTITUENCY PROFILE
Louth and Horncastle is a large and sparse Lincolnshire seat facing out to the North Sea. Over a quarter of the population is aged 65 or above and the seat is one of the whitest in Britain. Home ownership, especially outright ownership, is above average and the seat retains a small fishing sector. Now a safe Conservative seat, with the party having gained the old seats of Louth and Horncastle separately from the Liberals in 1924. Ukip came second here in 2010 and Louth and Horncastle's previous MP was Sir Peter Tapsell, the 2010 parliament's Father of the House.

EU REFERENDUM RESULT
68.9% Leave   Remain 31.1%

Ludlow

CONSERVATIVE HOLD MAJORITY 19,286 (38.6%)

PHILIP DUNNE
BORN Aug 14, 1958
MP 2005-

	Electorate	Turnout %	from 2010 % Change
	68,034	73.45	
*P Dunne C	31,433	62.90	+8.61
J Buckley Lab	12,147	24.31	+12.03
H Kidd LD	5,336	10.68	-2.78
H Wendt Green	1,054	2.11	-2.96

Businessman and banker. Co-founded the book store Ottakar's. Former dir, Juvenile Diabetes Research Foundation. Remainer; voted for Article 50 bill. Minister: health 2016-; defence procurement 2015-16. Parly under-sec for MoD 2012-15. Asst whip 2010-12. Opposition whip 2008-10. Select cttees: treasury 2007-08; public accounts 2006-09; work and pensions 2005-06. Confirmed that the govt will carry out independent inquiry into NHS tainted blood scandal 2017. Co-founded the book store Ottakar's. Former dir, Juvenile Diabetes Research Foundation.

NFU member. Grandfather and great-grandfather were MPs. Married, two daughters, two sons. Ed: Eton Coll; Keble Coll, Oxford (BA PPE).

CHALLENGERS
Julia Buckley (Lab) Cllr, Bridgnorth TC 2017-. Funding officer, Wolverhampton CC. Campaigned to save a local maternity unit. **Heather Kidd** (LD) Former teacher. Cllr, Shropshire C 2009-. Contested Ludlow 2010. **Hilary Wendt** (Green) Contested Shropshire C

2017. Worked in mental health services.

CONSTITUENCY PROFILE
Ludlow is a large constituency made up of several small towns and a large area of rural Shropshire between them. Nearly a quarter of residents are aged 65 or over and, unusually, less than a quarter are under the age of 25. Home ownership is high, as is the proportion of Ludlow residents who are self-employed. With the exception of the 2001 election, when a Liberal Democrat won the seat, the constituency has returned Tory MPs at every election since the First World War.

EU REFERENDUM RESULT

57.9% Leave   Remain 42.1%

Luton North

LABOUR HOLD MAJORITY 14,364 (30.8%)

KELVIN HOPKINS
BORN Aug 22, 1941
MP 1997-

	Electorate	Turnout %	from 2010 % Change
	66,811	69.78	
*K Hopkins Lab	29,765	63.84	+11.59
C Kerswell C	15,401	33.03	+3.11
R Martins LD	808	1.73	-1.32
S Hall Green	648	1.39	-0.89

Union man: worked in TUC economic dept and for Unison. Later lectured in economics. Member: GMB; Socialist Campaign Group. Pro-Brexit, previously described the EU as "anti-working class". Nominated Jeremy Corbyn for leader 2015. Shadow SoS for culture, media and sport 2016. Select committees: public administration 2002-17; draft deregulation bill 2013; European scrutiny 2007-16; crossrail bill 2005-07. Married, one son, one daughter. Ed: Queen Elizabeth's GS, High Barnet; University of Nottingham (BA politics, economics and maths)

CHALLENGERS
Caroline Kerswell (C) Solicitor and barrister. Partner in West Midlands law firm, advises on post-Brexit rural economy. Board member, Conservative constitutional review panel. **Rabi Martins** (LD) Retired business consultant and human rights campaigner. Advises Lib Dems on diversity. Cllr, Watford BC 1994-; vice-chairman. Contested Luton North 2015, 2010. **Simon Hall** (Green) Runs a design and manufacturing company. Local Green Party treasurer for five

years. Contested: Luton South 2015; Luton North 2010.

CONSTITUENCY PROFILE
Just under half of its residents were white British in the 2011 census, with over a quarter of residents of Asian descent. Incomes are slightly higher in Luton North than in Luton South, although both figures are significantly lower than the east of England average. Transport-related jobs are among the overrepresented sources of work for Luton North's residents. The seat has been Labour since 1997, having originally elected a Conservative when the seat was first created in 1983.

EU REFERENDUM RESULT

59.2% Leave   Remain 40.8%

Luton South

LAB CO-OP HOLD MAJORITY 13,925 (30.2%)

GAVIN SHUKER
BORN Oct 10, 1981
MP 2010-

Church pastor. Former leader, City Life Church, Luton. Pro-EU, abstained on Article 50 vote. Shadow min: Defra 2013-15; international development 2013-15. Stepped down from front bench after citing differences with newly elected Labour leader Jeremy Corbyn. Nominated Owen Smith for leadership 2016; Liz Kendall 2015. Tends not to rebel. Chairman, Co-operative Party parliamentary group. Vice-chairman, Christians in Parliament. Married, one daughter. Ed: Icknield HS; Luton Sixth Form Coll; Girton Coll, Cambridge (BA social and political science).

	Electorate	Turnout %	from 2010 %	Change
	67,188	68.66		
*G Shuker Lab Co-op	28,804	62.44	+18.24	
D Russell C	14,879	32.25	+1.58	
A Strange LD	1,056	2.29	-5.25	
U Ub Ukip	795	1.72	-10.43	
M Scheimann Green	439	0.95	-1.98	
A Ali Ind	160	0.35	-1.79	

CHALLENGERS
Dean Russell (C) Runs his own digital strategy consultancy. Children's author. Former vice-chairman, NHS Health. Cllr, St Albans DC 2010-13. FRSA. Contested Luton North 2015.
Andy Strange (LD) Runs web development and technology consultancy in Luton. Cllr, Luton BC 2003-11. Board member, Luton Culture, which runs libraries and museums in the town. **Ujjawal Ub** (Ukip)

Entrepreneur who migrated to Britain from India in 1980.

CONSTITUENCY PROFILE
A campus of the University of Bedfordshire is in the seat, and about 12,000 students live in the constituency. The seat has a large Asian community, many of whom are of Pakistani heritage. Over a quarter of households rent in the private sector. Luton Airport is in this seat, and many residents work in the transport sector. Like Luton North, the seat was Conservative from 1983, but has been Labour since 1997. Esther Rantzen memorably stood here in the 2010 general election.

EU REFERENDUM RESULT

54.6% Leave   Remain 45.4%

Macclesfield

CONSERVATIVE HOLD MAJORITY 8,608 (15.9%)

DAVID RUTLEY
BORN Mar 7, 1961
MP 2010-

Career as a senior executive and marketing dir: Barclays; Halifax General Insurance; Asda Stores; Safeway Stores; PepsiCo. Special adviser to: cabinet office, MAFF, Treasury 1994-96. Member, Bow Group. Contested St Albans 1997. Mainly interested in business and the economy. Campaigned for Remain, voted to trigger Article 50. Tends not to rebel. PPS to: Amber Rudd 2016-; Stephen Crabb 2016; Iain Duncan Smith 2015-16. Immigration min 2010-12. Co-chairman, APPG on mountaineering; chairman, British-Danish APPG. One of three practising Mormons

	Electorate	Turnout %	from 2010 %	Change
	75,228	72.19		
*D Rutley C	28,595	52.65	+0.11	
N Puttick Lab	19,987	36.80	+14.12	
R Flowers LD	3,350	6.17	-1.58	
J Booth Green	1,213	2.23	-2.61	
M Johnson Ind	1,162	2.14		

in the Commons. Married, two daughters, two sons. Ed: Priory Sch, Lewes; LSE (BSc economics); Harvard (MBA).

CHALLENGERS
Neil Puttick (Lab) Works for science startup incubator company. Cllr, Macclesfield TC 2015-. Campaigns for community ownership of rural pubs.
Richard Flowers (LD) Former chartered accountant. Member, federal finance and resources committee. **James Booth**

(Green) Barrister specialising in industrial injury claims.

CONSTITUENCY PROFILE
A commuter town to neighbouring Manchester, Macclesfield used to be one of the world's biggest producers of finished silk. Its residents are mainly white and well educated. There is considerable inequality across the constituency, but little unemployment, high levels of home ownership and few are in social housing. Now has a thriving manufacturing industry and is home to AstraZeneca pharmaceuticals. A safe Tory seat that has been held by the party since 1918.

EU REFERENDUM RESULT

47.2% Leave   Remain 52.8%

Maidenhead

CONSERVATIVE HOLD MAJORITY 26,457 (45.4%)

THERESA MAY
BORN Oct 1, 1956
MP 1997-

Leader of the Conservative Party and prime minister 2016-. Called snap election hoping to increase majority but which resulted in a loss of 13 seats. Vicar's daughter with penchant for striking shoes. Contested: Barking 1994; Durham North West 1992. Longest-serving modern-day home secretary 2010-16. Minister for women and equalities 2010-12. Low-key Remainer during EU referendum. Chairwoman, Conservative Party 2002-03; coined "nasty party" while in conference speech. Married. Ed: St Hugh's Coll, Oxford (BA geography).

	Electorate	Turnout %	from 2010 %	Change %
	76,276	76.35		
*T May C	37,718	64.76	-1.07	
P McDonald Lab	11,261	19.34	+7.46	
T Hill LD	6,540	11.23	+1.32	
D Wall Green	907	1.56	-2.00	
G Batten Ukip	871	1.50	-6.93	
A Knight AWP	282	0.48		
L Buckethead ND	249	0.43		
G Smith Ind	152	0.26		
H Hope Loony	119	0.20		
E Victor CPA	69	0.12		
J Reid Just	52	0.09		
Y Hailemariam Ind	16	0.03		
B Smith ND	3	0.01		

CHALLENGERS
Pat McDonald (Lab) Cllr, White Waltham PC 1994-. Contested Maidenhead 2010. **Tony Hill** (LD) Retired school headmaster. Contested Maidenhead 2015,

2010. **Derek Wall** (Green) Political economy lecturer, Goldsmiths Coll, London. **Gerard Batten** (Ukip) MEP 2004-. Founding member, Ukip. Previously salesman, BT. **Andrew Knight** (AWP) Animal welfare and ethics lecturer.

CONSTITUENCY PROFILE
One of the safest Conservative seats in the country. Known as England's silicon corridor, along the M4 motorway, for its thriving software and informatics industries. Many residents commute to Slough, Reading and London. Striking inequality although low levels of unemployment.

EU REFERENDUM RESULT
45.0% Leave   Remain 55.0%

Maidstone & The Weald

CONSERVATIVE HOLD MAJORITY 17,704 (34.3%)

HELEN GRANT
BORN Sep 28, 1961
MP 2010-

The Conservatives Party's first female black MP. Solicitor who founded own firm; specialist in family law and clinical negligence. Sat on reform commission for Centre for Social Justice. Formerly non-exec dir, Croydon Primary Care Trust 2005-07. Special adviser to Oliver Letwin 2006-10. Campaigned to Remain, voted to trigger Article 50. Rarely rebels. Parly under-sec: sport and tourism 2013-15; women and equalities. Former youth judo champion. Brought up by single mother on council estate. Married, two sons. Ed: St Aidan's CS, Carlisle; University of Hull (LLB); Coll of Law.

	Electorate	Turnout %	from 2010 %	Change %
	75,334	68.62		
*H Grant C	29,136	56.36	+10.88	
A Simpson Lab	11,432	22.11	+11.58	
E Fermor LD	8,455	16.36	-7.71	
P Watts Ukip	1,613	3.12	-12.74	
S Jeffery Green	888	1.72	-1.07	
Y Kenward Ind	172	0.33	+0.23	

CHALLENGERS
Allen Simpson (Lab) Dir, public policy for Barclays Bank. Previously, PA manager London stock exchange. Chief operations officer Labour in the City. Former researcher for Keith Vaz MP. Contested Maidstone and The Weald 2015. **Emily Fermor** (LD) Public affairs consultant, Bell Pottinger. Cllr, Maidstone BC 2016-. **Pamela Watts** (Ukip) Financial dir, waste electronics company.

CONSTITUENCY PROFILE
Most of the electorate live in urban Maidstone, which is dominated by the service sector, although there are significant orchards and market gardens to the south. Many residents commute to London. The seat is demographically homogeneous, with about 93 per cent white residents in the 2011 census. Some inequality, although low levels of social rent and unemployment. Significant proportion of its population work in public administration and defence, as well as construction. The seat was held by Ann Widdecombe 1987-2010, and remains a Tory stronghold.

EU REFERENDUM RESULT
55.9% Leave   Remain 44.1%

Makerfield

LABOUR HOLD MAJORITY 13,542 (28.9%)

YVONNE
FOVARGUE
BORN Nov 29, 1956
MP 2010-

Inherited seat in 2010 from
Ian McCartney, for whom her
husband, Paul Kenny, was a
press officer. Chief exec, St
Helens Citizens Advice Bureau.
Formerly: housing officer in
Moss Side, Manchester; estate
manager, Manchester CC.
Cllr, Warrington BC 2004-
10. Member: Unite, Mensa.
Remainer, voted for Article
50. Shadow min: local govt
2017-; business 2015-16; defence
2013-14, 2015; education 2014-15;
transport 2013; opp whip 2011-13.
Citizens Advice parliamentarian
of the year 2011. Married, one
daughter. Ed: Sale GS; University
of Leeds (BA English).

	Electorate	Turnout %	from 2010 %	Change
	74,259	63.20		
*Y Fovargue Lab	28,245	60.18	+8.36	
A Carney C	14,703	31.33	+11.79	
B Brierley Ind	2,663	5.67		
J Skipworth LD	1,322	2.82	-0.84	

CHALLENGERS
Adam Carney (C) HR officer
in car industry. Formerly
constituency caseworker for
Esther McVey MP. **Bob Brierley**
(Ind) Former sawmill saw
servicer. Cllr, Wigan C 2004-07
as member of Community
Action Party; independent 2008-.
Contested Makerfield 2010.
John Skipworth (LD) Retired
education consultant. Formerly
worked at the Co-operative
Bank. Cllr, Harrow BC 1985-98.
Contested: Makerfield 2015; local
elections 2014.

CONSTITUENCY PROFILE
Considered one of the safest
Labour seats in the country,
Makerfield has been held by
the party since 1906. It contains
the west side of Wigan, the
second most populous borough
of Greater Manchester, and part
of St Helens in Merseyside. The
area is predominantly working
class and incomes tend to be
lower than average. It is much
less diverse than the rest of
the region, as it is 98 per cent
white. There are high levels
of home ownership and low
levels of social renting. Since
the decline of coalmining in the
area, construction has become a
significant industry.

EU REFERENDUM RESULT

64.9% Leave   Remain 35.1%

Maldon

CONSERVATIVE HOLD MAJORITY 23,430 (46.7%)

JOHN
WHITTINGDALE
BORN Oct 16, 1959
MP 1992-

Worked for NM Rothschild
between stints as a special
adviser. Was close to Baroness
Thatcher after serving as
her political secretary 1988-
90; awarded OBE in 1990
resignation honours. Prominent
cabinet Brexiteer. Secretary of
state for CMS 2015-16. Lead role
in phone-hacking investigation
and compelled Murdochs to
attend. *Spectator's* inquisitor of
the year 2011. Has described
BBC licence fee as regressive.
Vice-chairman, 1922 cttee 2010-
15. Shadow SoS: CMS 2004-05,
2002-03; Defra 2003-04; trade
and industry 2001-02. PPS to:
William Hague 1999-2001; Eric

	Electorate	Turnout %	from 2010 %	Change
	66,960	74.97		
*J Whittingdale C	34,111	67.95	+7.35	
P Edwards Lab	10,681	21.28	+9.43	
Z O'Connell LD	2,181	4.34	-0.15	
J Pryke Ukip	1,899	3.78	-10.87	
S Betteridge Green	1,073	2.14	-0.99	
R Perry BNP	257	0.51		

Forth 1994-96. Opp Treasury
spokesman 1998-99. Opp whip
1997-98. Divorced, one daughter,
one son. Ed: Winchester Coll;
UCL (BSc economics).

CHALLENGERS
Peter Edwards (Lab) Editor,
LabourList. Former press
secretary for Chris Leslie MP.
Former journalist *CityAM*,
Yorkshire Post. Chairman,
London Community Credit
Union. Contested Maldon 2015.

Zoe O'Connell (LD) IT engineer.
Secretary, LGBT Lib Dems.
Transgender activist. Served
five years as an army reservist.
Contested Maldon 2015.

CONSTITUENCY PROFILE
Renowned for Maldon sea salt,
which is produced in the area.
Has mostly been represented
by Conservatives since its
creation. Very homogeneous
middle-class demographic,
with generally high-skilled jobs
in a largely rural area. Has a
high proportion of older voters
aged 45 and above. High levels
of home ownership and very
low levels of social renting and
unemployment.

EU REFERENDUM RESULT

61.0% Leave   Remain 39.0%

Manchester Central

LAB CO-OP HOLD MAJORITY 31,445 (63.2%)

LUCY POWELL
BORN Oct 10, 1974
MP 2012-

Manchester's first female Labour MP. Joined the party aged 15. Formerly: dir, Britain in Europe; Manchester innovation project leader, Nesta. Contested Manchester Withington 2010. Chief of staff to Ed Miliband 2010-12; managed Miliband's 2010 leadership campaign. Elected in 2012 by-election after Tony Lloyd stepped down to become Greater Manchester PCC. Vice-chairwoman, Labour GE campaign 2015. Nominated Andy Burnham for leadership 2015; Owen Smith 2016; resigned from shadow cabinet in protest at Jeremy Corbyn's leadership. Remainer, voted for Article 50.

	Electorate	Turnout %	from 2010 %	Change
	90,261	55.08		
*L Powell Lab Co-op	38,490	77.41	+16.15	
X Wang C	7,045	14.17	+0.64	
J Bridges LD	1,678	3.37	-0.74	
K Chapman Ukip	1,469	2.95	-8.15	
R Shah Green	846	1.70	-6.77	
N Blackburn Pirate	192	0.39	-0.38	

Shadow education sec 2015-16. Shadow min: cabinet office 2014-15; education 2013-14. Married, one daughter, one son, one stepson. Ed: Xaverian Coll, Manchester; Somerville Coll, Oxford (BSc chemistry), King's Coll London (MSc chemistry).

CHALLENGERS
Xingang Wang (C) Senior manager, Scotiabank. Cllr, Claygate PC 2015-. Born and raised in China. **John Bridges**

(LD) Cllr, Manchester CC 1993-2010, 1987-88. Political officer, association of Lib Dem councillors.

CONSTITUENCY PROFILE
An ultra-safe Labour seat with a young, working-class electorate. The seat covers the University of Manchester and almost 30 per cent of the population are students. Labour increased its majority significantly in the 2017 election. An ethnically diverse population that is 15 per cent Asian and British Asian. Levels of social renting are among the highest in the country and unemployment is also very high.

EU REFERENDUM RESULT

36.4% Leave   Remain 63.6%

Manchester Gorton

LABOUR HOLD MAJORITY 31,730 (69.0%)

AFZAL KHAN
BORN Apr 5, 1958
MP 2017-

Former Greater Manchester Police officer who retrained as a solicitor and became a partner at Mellor & Jackson. North West MEP 2014-17. Cllr, Manchester CC 2000-14. Awarded a CBE in 2008 for work in local government and community cohesion. Selected for Gorton on an all-Asian shortlist. Manchester's first Asian Muslim and youngest, lord mayor 2005-06. Made shadow Home Office minister three weeks after being elected. Born in Pakistan, moved to Britain aged 11. Married, two sons, one daughter. Ed: Manchester Polytechnic (BA law).

	Electorate	Turnout %	from 2010 %	Change
	75,362	60.98		
A Khan Lab	35,085	76.35	+9.27	
S Jaradat C	3,355	7.30	-2.37	
G Galloway Ind	2,615	5.69		
J Pearcey LD	2,597	5.65	+1.41	
J Mayo Green	1,038	2.26	-7.52	
P Eckersley Ukip	952	2.07	-6.10	
K Abidogun CPA	233	0.51		
D Hopkins Ind	51	0.11		
P Clifford Comm Lge	27	0.06		

CHALLENGERS
Shaden Jaradat (C) Manages University of Manchester's relations and recruitment in Middle East and Africa. **George Galloway** (Ind) Ex-Labour MP expelled in 2003 over Iraq War comments. MP for: Bradford West 2012-15; Bethnal Green and Bow 2005-10; Glasgow Kelvin

1997-2005; Glasgow Hillhead 1987-97. **Jackie Pearcey** (LD) Holds PhD in nuclear physics. Cllr, Manchester CC 1991-2012.

CONSTITUENCY PROFILE
Gorton was held by the 2015 parliament's Father of the House Sir Gerald Kaufman for 34 years until his death in February 2017. A safe Labour seat since the 1930s, ground was lost to the Lib Dems after the Iraq War. Large student population. One of the most diverse seats in the country, only 50 per cent white and 30 per cent Asian. The Tories returned their lowest vote share for any seat in the UK at the 2017 election, with 7.3 per cent.

EU REFERENDUM RESULT

38.2% Leave   Remain 61.8%

Manchester Withington

LABOUR HOLD MAJORITY 29,875 (55.7%)

JEFF SMITH
BORN Jan 26, 1963
MP 2015-

Former DJ and nightclub promoter. Interested in devolution, human rights and climate change. Member: Unite; Socialist Education Association; Friends of the Earth; Withington Civic Soc. Opp Treasury and CMS whip 2015-. Nominated Owen Smith for Labour leadership 2016; Andy Burnham 2015. Remainer; defied his own whip to vote against triggering Article 50. Abstained on July 2015 welfare bill. Rebelled to vote against renewing Trident. Cllr, Manchester CC 1997-2015. Ed: Manchester GS; University of Manchester (BA politics and economics).

	Electorate	Turnout %	from 2010 Change %
	74,553	71.90	
*J Smith Lab	38,424	71.68	+17.96
J Leech LD	8,549	15.95	-8.01
S Heald C	5,530	10.32	+0.57
L Bannister Green	865	1.61	-6.49
S Carr Women	234	0.44	

CHALLENGERS
John Leech (LD) MP for Manchester Withington 2005-15. Serial rebel during coalition years: voted against raising tuition fees to £9,000, welfare and legal aid cuts. Cllr, Manchester CC 2016-; 1998-2008. Former assistant manager, McDonalds 1995-97. Named Lib Dem MP of the year 2013. Shadow transport minister 2006-10. **Sarah Heald** (C) Dir of corporate affairs and investor relations, Pennon Group

utilities company 2016-. Former investment banker at Bank of America Merrill Lynch and Canadian Bank of Montreal.

CONSTITUENCY PROFILE
A Conservative seat from its creation in 1918, but it turned red in 1987. Gained by the Lib Dems in 2005, in part due to post-Iraq upset, but won back in 2015. Large influx of young professionals to the area in recent years, and the population is about one fifth students. Ethnically diverse seat which is 12 per cent Asian and British Asian. Home ownership is lower than average, with a third of residents renting privately.

EU REFERENDUM RESULT

24.9% Leave   Remain 75.1%

Mansfield

CONSERVATIVE GAIN MAJORITY 1,057 (2.1%)

BEN BRADLEY
BORN Dec 11, 1989
MP 2017-

First-ever Tory to be returned for Mansfield in its 132-year history. Office manager, Mark Spencer MP 2015-17. Covered for Nick Boles MP while he was undergoing cancer treatment in 2016. Cllr, Ashfield DC 2015-; former Conservative group leader. Previous customer service roles in hotels and supermarkets, and Open University office manager before entering politics. Local school governor. Volunteer hockey coach. Married, two sons. Nottingham Trent University (BA politics).

CHALLENGERS
Sir Alan Meale (Lab) MP for

	Electorate	Turnout %	from 2010 Change %
	77,811	64.46	
B Bradley C	23,392	46.64	+18.48
*A Meale Lab	22,335	44.53	+5.11
S Pepper Ukip	2,654	5.29	-19.82
P Shields Ind	1,079	2.15	
A Prabhakar LD	697	1.39	-2.09

Mansfield 1987-2017. Former backbench stalwart and John Prescott ally. Came under fire during expenses scandal for claiming £13,000 for his garden over a four-year period. Listed as "negative" to Jeremy Corbyn's leadership in a leaked party document 2016. Knighted 2011. Opposition whip 1992-94. Parly under-sec, environment 1998-99. **Sid Pepper** (Ukip) Serial entrepreneur who founded his first business aged 16. MD, Arromax Structures. Formerly

a DJ. Contested Mansfield 2015. **Philip Shields** (Ind) Former Labour member who quit party after becoming disillusioned with professional politicians.

CONSTITUENCY PROFILE
In the 2017 election this former safe Labour seat, held by the party for nearly a century, turned blue by a narrow margin. A traditional former mining town on the western edge of Nottinghamshire, Mansfield's coal mines closed long ago and unemployment has been exacerbated by the closures of other local industries such as the Mansfield Brewery and the AG Barr factory.

EU REFERENDUM RESULT

70.9% Leave   Remain 29.1%

Meon Valley

CONSERVATIVE HOLD MAJORITY 25,692 (47.4%)

GEORGE HOLLINGBERY
BORN Oct 12, 1963
MP 2010-

Entrepreneur best known for founding Companion Care veterinary surgeries. Entered politics in 1997 to oppose a supermarket being opened in his village. Cllr, Winchester CC 1999-2009. Contested Winchester 2005. Particularly interested in planning reform and welfare. Remainer, voted to trigger Article 50. Infrequent rebel during coalition years. PPS to Theresa May 2016-, 2012-15. Govt whip 2015-16. Married, three children. Ed: Lady Margaret Hall, Oxford (BA human sciences); Wharton School, University of Pennsylvania (MBA).

	Electorate	Turnout %	from 2010 % Change
	74,246	72.99	
*G Hollingbery C	35,624	65.74	+4.68
S King Lab	9,932	18.33	+7.39
M Tod LD	5,900	10.89	+1.24
P Bailey Ukip	1,435	2.65	-12.17
A Hayward Green	1,301	2.40	-1.14

CHALLENGERS
Sheena King (Lab) Law graduate who went on to work in air traffic control. Does voluntary conservation work. Socialist. Representative, Meon Valley Trade Unions and Young People. Contested Yeovil 2015. **Martin Tod** (LD) Background in marketing. Chief exec, Men's Health Forum; previously worked at Procter and Gamble homeless charity Shelter. Cllr, Winchester CC 2012-. Contested Winchester 2010. **Paul Bailey**

(Ukip) Contested: local elections 2017; New Forest West 2015. **Andrew Hayward** (Green) Photography teacher.

CONSTITUENCY PROFILE
This Hampshire constituency was historically a swing seat between Conservatives and Lib Dems, but since the 2015 general election it has become one of the safest Conservative seats in the country. The seat is a fairly affluent area and has very low levels of unemployment. Largely older demographic and 97 per cent white. It is characterised by high levels of home ownership and particularly low levels of social renting.

EU REFERENDUM RESULT
51.9% Leave   Remain 48.1%

Meriden

CONSERVATIVE HOLD MAJORITY 19,198 (35.1%)

DAME CAROLINE SPELMAN
BORN May 4, 1958
MP 1997-

Received a damehood in David Cameron's resignation honours. Honest image tarnished by lengthy inquiry into "nanny-gate" affair, forced to repay money and apologise for inadvertent breach of rules. Resulted in demotion from Conservative Party chairwoman 2007-2009 to shadow SoS, CLG 2009-10. Second church estates commissioner 2015-; SoS, Defra 2010-12. Remainer, voted for Article 50. Vocal critic of the detainment of female asylum seekers. Frequently campaigns to protect the green belt. Contested Bassetlaw 1992. Fluent in French and German. Research fellow,

	Electorate	Turnout %	from 2010 % Change
	81,437	67.10	
*C Spelman C	33,873	61.99	+7.26
T McNeil Lab	14,675	26.86	+7.85
A Rogers LD	2,663	4.87	-0.14
L Kaye Ukip	2,016	3.69	-13.24
A Gavin Green	1,416	2.59	-1.53

University of Kent. Business consultant. Married, one daughter, two sons. Ed: Herts & Essex HS for Girls; Queen Mary, University of London (BA European studies).

CHALLENGERS
Thomas McNeil (Lab) Strategic adviser to West Midlands PCC. Former charity and social enterprise lawyer. Special constable, Metropolitan Police. **Antony Rogers** (LD) Business co-owner. **Leslie Kaye** (Ukip)

Condemned by local cllr for scaremongering about a proposed biomass plant.

CONSTITUENCY PROFILE
The seat covers Solihull and a number of neighbouring villages, including Meriden. There is significant inequality and high levels of unemployment, although wages are higher than the regional average. The area is relatively diverse, with many constituents from mixed ethnic groups. Previously considered a Labour/Tory marginal, but has become a Tory stronghold since the 1997 general election. The party has increased its majority in each election since.

EU REFERENDUM RESULT
58.8% Leave   Remain 41.2%

Merthyr Tydfil & Rhymney

LABOUR HOLD MAJORITY 16,334 (48.7%)

GERALD JONES
BORN Aug 21, 1970
MP 2015-

	Electorate	Turnout %	from 2010 %	Change
	55,463	60.48		
*G Jones Lab	22,407	66.80	+12.94	
P Jorgensen C	6,073	18.10	+8.04	
A Kitcher PC	2,740	8.17	-1.30	
D Rowlands Ukip	1,484	4.42	-14.24	
B Griffin LD	841	2.51	-1.62	

Labour activist politicised by 1984-85 miners' strike. Shadow min: defence 2017-; Wales 2016-17. Attracted controversy in 2017 for hiring his partner as his senior parly assistant. Listed as "neutral, but not hostile" towards Jeremy Corbyn in leaked party document 2016. Remainer, voted for Article 50. Former cllr, Caerphilly CBC; deputy leader 2014-15. Formerly development officer, Gwent Association of Voluntary Organisations. Trustee, Phillipstown Residents and Community Assoc. Volunteer dir, White Rose Resource Centre, set up as part of regeneration for New Tredegar. Secretary, New Tredegar Communities Partnership. Member, GMB. Ed: Bedwelty Comp Sch; Ystrad Mynach Coll.

CHALLENGERS
Pauline Jorgensen (C) Works at British Airways. Active on Twitter, tweeted "stop trying to be a trendy leftie Tim, you aren't" to Tim Farron in 2017. Cllr, Wokingham BC 2008-. Mayor, Earley TC 2012-13. **Amy Kitcher** (PC) Campaigns officer,

Alzheimer's Society 2013-17. Public affairs, League Against Cruel Sports 2011-13.

CONSTITUENCY PROFILE
Centred on the town of Merthyr in Glamorgan, Wales, this has been a solid and consistently Labour seat since the 1950s except when an independent Labour candidate won in 1970. At one time the greatest iron-producing centre in Britain, as well as a mining and railway hub, now manufacturing is a significant industry in the region. A white, working-class seat. Income is significantly below average for the region and unemployment is very high.

EU REFERENDUM RESULT
58.4% Leave   Remain 41.6%

Middlesbrough

LABOUR HOLD MAJORITY 13,873 (38.9%)

ANDY MCDONALD
BORN Mar 8, 1958
MP 2012-

	Electorate	Turnout %	from 2010 %	Change
	61,114	58.31		
*A McDonald Lab	23,404	65.67	+8.85	
J Young C	9,531	26.74	+10.27	
D Hodgson Ukip	1,452	4.07	-14.60	
T Lawton Ind	632	1.77		
D Islam LD	368	1.03	-2.70	
C Martinez Green	250	0.70	-3.60	

Lawyer, specialist in serious injuries. Advised defence select cttee on armed forces compensation. Elected in a by-election after death of Sir Stuart Bell. Appointed shadow minister for transport in 2016, after Jonathan Reynolds's resignation in January 2016, and made shad SoS after Lillian Greenwood's resignation. Member, justice select cttee 2012-16. Cllr, Middlesborough BC 1995-99. Middlesbrough Coll 2012-. Married, two daughters, two sons, one of whom has epilepsy and severe development delay. Another son died in 2006, aged 16. Ed: St George's SS, St Mary's Sixth Form Coll; Leeds Polytechnic (LLB).

CHALLENGERS
Jacob Young (C) Lead technician, Petrochemicals 2017-. Surprise winner of Coulby Newham council seat 2017. Contested Redcar 2015. **David Hodgson** (Ukip) Lecturer. Dir, Britannia Training Ltd.

CONSTITUENCY PROFILE
Middlesbrough is a large industrial town to the south of the River Tees. The constituency, a former centre for steel production, now has the fourth highest rate of unemployment in the country. About 44 per cent of households have no adults in employment, over 10 per cent higher than the UK average. Household income is lower than in the rest of the northeast and there are low levels of property ownership. The seat includes the University of Teesside and has a fairly high proportion of 16- to 24-year-olds. It is a safe Labour seat, but Ukip came second here in both the 2012 by-election at which Andy McDonald was first elected, and in 2015.

EU REFERENDUM RESULT
66.1% Leave   Remain 33.9%

Middlesbrough South & Cleveland East

CONSERVATIVE GAIN MAJORITY 1,020 (2.1%)

SIMON CLARKE
BORN Sep 28, 1984
MP 2017-

A former Slaughter and May solicitor born and raised in Middlesbrough. This constituency's first Conservative MP, although the predecessor seat of Langbaurgh turned blue under Margaret Thatcher and John Major. Policy adviser and head of media for Graham Stuart MP 2013-. Parliamentary assistant to Dominic Raab MP 2010-13. Contested Middlesbrough 2015. Married, one son. Ed: University Coll, Oxford (BA modern history); Oxford Brookes University (GD law); BPP Law Sch (LPC).

CHALLENGERS
Tracy Harvey (Lab) Cllr,

	Electorate	Turnout %	from 2010 %	Change
	72,336	65.83		
S Clarke C	23,643	49.65	+12.60	
T Harvey Lab	22,623	47.51	+5.49	
C Foote-Wood LD	1,354	2.84	-0.58	

Middlesbrough BC 2011-. Formerly a community worker for Middlesbrough Council 1986-2010. School governor. **Chris Foote-Wood** (LD) Property investment manager. Author. Cllr, Bishop Auckland TC 1967-2007. Formerly worked as a civil engineer. Brother of the late comedian Victoria Wood. Has contested about 10 general elections and multiple European elections.

CONSTITUENCY PROFILE
This North Yorkshire seat contains the southern outskirts

of the town of Middlesbrough, extending eastwards to the coast. This area has one of the highest proportions of residents employed in mining in any seat. Yet, the decline in mining and industrial production has hit the seat significantly, and unemployment is higher than the regional and national average. 97.5 per cent of residents are white. Formerly held by the Labour Party since its creation in 1997 but with much tighter majorities than the safe urban seat of Middlesbrough. Middlesbrough South and Cleveland East turned Conservative in 2017 with a majority of 1,020 votes.

EU REFERENDUM RESULT
65.3% Leave   Remain 34.7%

Midlothian

LABOUR GAIN MAJORITY 885 (2.0%)

DANIELLE ROWLEY
BORN Feb 25, 1990
MP 2017-

Labour's youngest MP. Campaigns and public affairs officer, Shelter Scotland 2016-17. Former comms officer, ACOSVO 2015-16. E-communications officer, Scottish parliament 2015. Constituency media manager for Gordon Brown MP 2014-15. Daughter of Scottish Labour deputy leader Alex Rowley. Came under fire when she travelled to Cuba during election campaign. Ed: Edinburgh Telford Coll; Edinburgh Napier University (BA journalism).

CHALLENGERS
Owen Thompson (SNP) MP for Midlothian 2015-17. Cllr,

	Electorate	Turnout %	from 2010 %	Change
	68,328	66.26		
D Rowley Lab	16,458	36.35	+6.16	
*O Thompson SNP	15,573	34.40	-16.20	
C Donnelly C	11,521	25.45	+13.53	
R Laird LD	1,721	3.80	+1.46	

Midlothian C 2005-; leader 2013-. Assistant to: Clare Adamson MSP; Rob Gibson MSP. Secretary, SNP Cosla Group. Honorary vice-pres, SNP students. Ed: Edinburgh Napier University (BA accounting and finance). **Chris Donnelly** (C) Barrister. Community engagement officer for RFU 2016-. Policy officer, Citizens Advice Scotland 2015-. **Ross Laird** (LD) Vice-chairman: YMCA Scotland; YMCA Penicuik. Head of Edinburgh-based communications company.

CONSTITUENCY PROFILE
A rural seat to the south of Edinburgh that contains former mining towns that are now increasingly home to Edinburgh commuters. A large proportion of the Midlothian population is UK-born and 98.2 per cent of residents are white. Unemployment is at the UK average. There are relatively high levels of social housing, well above those of the rest of Scotland. In 2017 Labour snatched back their former traditional heartland from the SNP, which had won it in 2015, with a slim 885-vote majority. In the 19th century it was the seat of William Gladstone.

EU REFERENDUM RESULT
37.9% Leave   Remain 62.1%

Milton Keynes North

CONSERVATIVE HOLD MAJORITY 1,915 (3.1%)

MARK LANCASTER
BORN May 12, 1970
MP 2005-

Former soldier; army officer then major with TA (Territorial Decoration, VRSM); undertook active service in Afghanistan in 2006 parliament summer recess. Armed forces minininister 2017-; parliamentary under secrecretary, defence 2015-17. Government whip 2012-15. PPS to Andrew Mitchell 2010-12. Shadow min, int dev 2007-10. Opposition whip 2006-07. Dir, Kimbolton Fireworks. Cllr, Huntingdon DC 1995-99. Plays for Commons cricket team. Married to Caroline Dinenage MP, one daughter from previous relationship. Ed: Kimbolton Sch, Huntingdon; RMA Sandhurst;

	Electorate	Turnout %	from 2010 %	Change
	89,272	71.54		
*M Lancaster C	30,307	47.46	+0.23	
C Pullen Lab	28,392	44.46	+14.14	
I Shepherd-Dubey LD	2,499	3.91	-2.28	
J Wyatt Ukip	1,390	2.18	-9.70	
A Francis Green	1,107	1.73	-2.18	
V Sams CPA	169	0.26		

University of Buckingham (BSc business studies; honorary PhD); University of Exeter (MBA).

CHALLENGERS
Charlynne Pullen (Lab) Head of workforce data, Education and Training Foundation 2014-. Formerly senior research fellow, IPPR 2016. Contested Bedfordshire Mid 2015. **Imogen Shepherd-Dubey** (LD) IT engineer. Cllr, Wokingham BC 2017-. Formerly

senior technology consultant. Interested in the environment.

CONSTITUENCY PROFILE
Contains the northern part of Milton Keynes, the biggest planned new town in Britain, and is the more rural of the towns two seats. It has an ethnically diverse population, with a large number of residents of African descent. It has low levels of home ownership, but the second-highest rate of shared ownership in the UK. More than 20 per cent of residents work in retail. Historically a Conservative/Labour marginal; the Tories had their majority reduced in 2017 to 1,915 votes.

EU REFERENDUM RESULT

49.7% Leave   Remain 50.3%

Milton Keynes South

CONSERVATIVE HOLD MAJORITY 1,725 (2.7%)

IAIN STEWART
BORN Sep 18, 1972
MP 2010-

Scottish-born former accountant, and board member of the headhunters Odgers, Ray & Berndtson. Ran research unit in Westminster analysing legislation for clients, including Conservatives. Gay; deputy chairman of the LGBT Conservative group 2009-11. PPS to: Liam Fox 2016-17; David Mundell 2015-16; Patrick McLoughlin 2013-15. Member of transport select cttee 2010-17. Campaigned to Leave the EU. Contested Milton Keynes South West 2005, 2001. Ed: Hutchesons' GS, Glasgow; University of Exeter (BA politics).

	Electorate	Turnout %	from 2010 %	Change
	92,494	69.72		
*I Stewart C	30,652	47.53	+0.65	
H O'Neill Lab	28,927	44.86	+12.79	
T Maher LD	1,895	2.94	-0.97	
V Peddle Ukip	1,833	2.84	-10.38	
G Findlay Green	1,179	1.83	-1.45	

CHALLENGERS
Hannah O'Neill (Lab) Cllr, Milton Keynes C 2008-; dep leader; cabinet member for housing and regeneration. Has led the largest house-building programme outside of London. **Tahir Maher** (LD) Works for Transport for London. Qualified management accountant. Head of finance, Imperial College London 2001-05. Muslim. **Vince Peddle** (Ukip) Senior design engineer. Contested Milton Keynes South 2015.

CONSTITUENCY PROFILE
Dominated by Milton Keynes, the seat is more densely populated than its northern neighbour. Average earnings are similar to the rest of the South East and above the UK average. An above-average number of people are employed in the retail sector as the seat contains the central shopping district and Amazon distribution. As with Milton Keynes in general the seat has a notably young population. Historically the area has been a Labour/Conservative marginal but it has been held by Iain Stewart for the Conservatives since the new seat was formed in 2010.

EU REFERENDUM RESULT

53.1% Leave   Remain 46.9%

Mitcham & Morden

LABOUR HOLD MAJORITY 21,375 (44.4%)

SIOBHAIN MCDONAGH
BORN Feb 20, 1960
MP 1997-

Committed backbencher but not afraid to stand out from the crowd; first MP to publicly call Gordon Brown's leadership into question in 2008. Remain campaigner. Rarely rebels but voted for 2015 Syria airstrikes. Joined Labour aged 15 and was elected as the party's youngest cllr in 1982. Contested Mitcham and Morden 1992, 1987. Assistant whip 2007-08. Select cttees: women and equalities 2015-16; education 2012-15. Lives with her sister, Baroness Margaret McDonagh, the only woman to hold the position of Labour general secretary. Ed: Essex University (BA politics).

	Electorate	Turnout %	from 2010 % Change
	68,705	70.04	
*S McDonagh Lab	33,039	68.66	+8.01
A Kearns C	11,664	24.24	+1.07
C Mathys LD	1,494	3.10	+0.05
R Hilton Ukip	1,054	2.19	-7.31
L Collins Green	644	1.34	-1.81
D Coke CPA	223	0.46	-0.02

CHALLENGERS
Alicia Kearns (C) Counter-terrorism expert and former civil servant. Led govt campaigns on Syria and Iraq. While at MoD led the dept's Scottish referendum campaign. **Claire Mathys** (LD) Qualified accountant, now works as a parliamentary adviser on housing and the environment. Played a key role in the successful campaign to end letting fees for tenants. Parly assistant to Baroness Shirley

Williams 2011-12. **Richard Hilton** (Ukip) Conservative defector. Caused uproar in 2015 when he suggested Jihadi John should have killed himself.

CONSTITUENCY PROFILE
Suburban, densely populated seat in South London. The area is increasingly multi-ethnic, with large black, Asian and Polish communities. Home to a young working population, many of whom are employed in the retail and social sectors. The income of residents is below the London average. A safe Labour seat with a majority of 21,375 in 2017, but was held by the Conservatives for much of the 1980s.

EU REFERENDUM RESULT
44.7% Leave   Remain 55.3%

Mole Valley

CONSERVATIVE HOLD MAJORITY 24,137 (42.6%)

SIR PAUL BERESFORD
BORN Apr 6, 1946
MP 1997-

Part-time dentist; came under scrutiny in 2009 MPs' expenses scandal when his west London surgery was found to be registered as his second home. Eurosceptic but campaigned to Remain in the EU. Cllr, Wandsworth 1978-92. MP for Croydon Central 1992-97. Parly under-sec, dept of environment 1994-97. Select cttees: Commons commission 2015-17; administration 2015-17; liaison 2015-17. Knighted for work on inner-city rehabilitation. Originally from New Zealand. Divorced, one child. Remarried, four children. Ed: University of Otago, New Zealand (dentistry).

	Electorate	Turnout %	from 2010 % Change
	74,545	76.10	
*P Beresford C	35,092	61.86	+1.23
P Kennedy LD	10,955	19.31	+4.84
M Green Lab	7,864	13.86	+5.58
J Fewster Green	1,463	2.58	-2.82
J Moore Ukip	1,352	2.38	-8.83

CHALLENGERS
Paul Kennedy (LD) Former barrister, accountant and actuary. Helped to develop the citizen's pension policy introduced by the Liberal Democrats during the coalition government. Strongly opposes fracking and the Tory plans for a new town in Surrey's green belt. Cllr, Mole Valley DC. Contested Mole Valley 2015. **Marc Green** (Lab) IT consultant and business owner. Former finance manager for the Anti-

Apartheid Movement. Bookham and Fetcham Labour Party. Contested local elections 2017.

CONSTITUENCY PROFILE
Rural seat in Surrey bordering Guildford that consists of affluent commuter towns and villages. It is home to a cluster of high-tech and research businesses and therefore a higher than average proportion of residents are employed in professional or technical occupations. Unemployment is low and there is relatively little social housing. More than half of households own two cars or more. A safe Conservative seat with a sizeable majority.

EU REFERENDUM RESULT
47.3% Leave   Remain 52.7%

Monmouth

CONSERVATIVE HOLD MAJORITY 8,206 (16.5%)

DAVID DAVIES
BORN Jul 27, 1970
MP 2005-

Former TA member who worked for British Steel and as a nightclub promoter and rickshaw driver in Australia, before returning to work as a lorry driver. Spent nine years as special constable with British Transport Police. On hard right of the party: vocal Brexit supporter; opposed same-sex marriage; climate change denier. Came under fire in 2016 for a tweet suggesting refugee children should be have their age verified using dental records. Contested Bridgend 1997. Appointed rep of UK deleg to parly assembly of Council of Europe 2012. Learnt Welsh when

	Electorate	Turnout %	from 2010 Change %
	64,909	76.62	
*D Davies C	26,411	53.10	+3.17
R Jones Lab	18,205	36.60	+9.81
V German LD	2,064	4.15	-1.11
C Damon PC	1,338	2.69	-1.26
I Chandler Green	954	1.92	-1.51
R Neale Ukip	762	1.53	-8.88

elected to National Assembly of Wales. Amateur boxer. Married, three children. Ed: Bassaleg Comprehensive School.

CHALLENGERS
Ruth Jones (Lab) NHS physiotherapist. Contested Monmouth 2015. **Veronica German** (LD) Former maths and science teacher. Welsh assembly member 2010-11. **Ian Chandler** (Green) Worked in international development for Oxfam.

CONSTITUENCY PROFILE
This rural, sparsely populated seat in the southeast of Wales borders Gloucestershire and Herefordshire. Has more in common with its English neighbours than with the Welsh, with one of the lowest proportions of Welsh speakers of any seat. A third of the seat's population were born in England and there is little support for Plaid Cymru. Average income is well above the rest of Wales. Predominantly white with a considerable retired population. A marginal that has been won by Labour only in its very best years and has been held by David Davies since 2005.

EU REFERENDUM RESULT
48.1% Leave   Remain 51.9%

Montgomeryshire

CONSERVATIVE HOLD MAJORITY 9,285 (26.6%)

GLYN DAVIES
BORN Feb 16, 1944
MP 2010-

Former farmer. Very interested in health issues after overcoming rectal cancer. Member, Welsh affairs select committee 2013-. PPS to Cheryl Gillan 2010-12. AM for Mid and West Wales 1999-2007. Cllr, Montgomeryshire DC 1979-89; chairman 1985-89. Contested Montgomeryshire 1997. Ousted Lembit Öpik in 2010. Chairman, Development Board for Rural Wales. Member: Wales Tourism Board; Welsh Development Agency. President, Campaign for Protection of Rural Wales. Recently learnt Welsh. Blogger. Keen golfer. Married, four children. Ed: Caereinon HS;

	Electorate	Turnout %	from 2010 Change %
	50,755	68.74	
*G Davies C	18,075	51.80	+6.76
J Dodds LD	8,790	25.19	-4.07
I Jones Lab	5,542	15.88	+10.26
A Hughes PC	1,960	5.62	+0.45
R Chaloner Green	524	1.50	-2.23

Aberystwyth University (Dip international law and politics).

CHALLENGERS
Jane Dodds (LD) Child protection social worker. Cllr, Richmond BC 2006-10. Previously worked for Refugee Council. Contested Montgomeryshire 2015. **Iwan Wyn Jones** (Lab) Recent Aberystwyth University graduate. **Aled Hughes** (PC) Former national chairman of Plaid Cymru Youth.

CONSTITUENCY PROFILE
A rural and sparsely populated seat in central Wales that includes the town of Welshpool. Agriculture is important and employs about a tenth of the population. Montgomeryshire contains the second highest proportion of self-employed residents in the country. Unemployment is low and average earnings below the Welsh and UK average. Like much of Wales the population is homogeneous and 98.9 per cent of its residents are white. There is a strong Liberal tradition in the seat, but it has been held by the Conservatives since 2010 with a growing majority.

EU REFERENDUM RESULT
55.8% Leave   Remain 44.2%

Moray

CONSERVATIVE GAIN MAJORITY 4,159 (8.7%)

DOUGLAS ROSS
BORN Apr 9, 1983
MP 2017-

Football referee. Cllr, Moray C 2012-; sacked from planning administration after high-profile controversy over school closures. Highlands and Islands MSP 2016-17. PPS to Mary Scanlon MSP. Governor, Milne's Institute Trust Scheme. Member, Scottish Senior Football Referee Association. Chairman, Sport Moray executive cttee. Contested Moray 2015, 2010. Ed: Alves Primary & Forres Academy; Scottish Agricultural Coll.

CHALLENGERS
Angus Robertson (SNP) MP for Moray 2001-17. Leader, SNP Westminster group 2007-17.

	Electorate	Turnout %	from 2010 Change %
	70,649	67.38	
D Ross C	22,637	47.55	+16.47
*A Robertson SNP	18,478	38.82	-10.67
J Kirby Lab	5,208	10.94	+1.00
A Linklater LD	1,078	2.26	-0.57
A Glen Ind	204	0.43	

Ran 2015 election campaign for SNP. SNP spokesman: foreign affairs and defence 2001-15. National organiser, Student Nationalists Federation. Member: SNP international bureau. European policy adviser, SNP group Scottish Parliament. Communications consultant. Ex-BBC World Service journalist. Ed: Aberdeen (MA politics and international relations). **Jo Kirby** (Lab) History and modern studies teacher. Previously worked for Harriet Harman.

CONSTITUENCY PROFILE
A large rural seat in northeast Scotland in which 98.9 per cent of residents are white. Agriculture, fishing, tourism and whisky distilling are important industries in the area. Defence is also highly represented in the seat as the RAF Lossiemouth base is located here. Some residents commute to neighbouring Aberdeenshire to work in the oil industry. The proportion of property owners is slightly higher than the Scottish and UK average. A Conservative/SNP marginal which was previously held by the deputy leader of the SNP, Angus Robertson, from 2001.

EU REFERENDUM RESULT
49.9% Leave   Remain 50.1%

Morecambe & Lunesdale

CONSERVATIVE HOLD MAJORITY 1,399 (3.1%)

DAVID MORRIS
BORN Jan 3, 1966
MP 2010-

Hairdresser who ran his own salon chain. Interested in tourism and business. Son of a lifeboat inspector from a nautical family. PPS to Stephen Crabb 2014-15. Remainer; voted for Article 50. Contested: Carmarthen West and South Pembrokeshire 2005; Blackpool South 2001. Member: Institute of Directors, National Hairdressing Council. Adviser to Greenwich University on study into effects of minimum wage. Former musician and songwriter, was in a band with Rick Astley; one of two MPs to have performed on *Top of the Pops*. Divorced, two sons. Ed: St Andrews

	Electorate	Turnout %	from 2010 Change %
	66,838	68.31	
*D Morris C	21,773	47.69	+2.15
V Singleton Lab	20,374	44.62	+9.70
M Severn LD	1,699	3.72	-0.01
R Gillespie Ukip	1,333	2.92	-9.47
C Sinclair Green	478	1.05	-2.18

Nassau, Bahamas; Lowton Sch, Lancashire.

CHALLENGERS
Vikki Singleton (Lab) Dir, Blackpool Housing Company. CLP secretary, Blackpool N and Cleveleys Labour Party 2016-. Cllr: Blackpool C 2015; Lancaster CC 2011-15. Formerly business development specialist, Inenco 2011-13. **Matt Severn** (LD) Insurance sales adviser, Marsh Limited. Cllr, South Lakeland DC 2014-. Methodist Church.

Contested Morecambe and Lunesdale 2015.

CONSTITUENCY PROFILE
Bellwether seat at the northern edge of Lancashire. It includes the seaside town of Morecambe and stretches into the Pennines in the east. Contains fairly high levels of property ownership and a small proportion of residents in social housing. Unemployment and average earnings are lower than the regional average. Three in ten residents are employed in retail or social work. Was a safe Conservative seat until it fell to Labour in 1997. Regained by the Conservatives in 2010 and has been held by them since.

EU REFERENDUM RESULT
58.2% Leave   Remain 41.8%

Morley & Outwood

CONSERVATIVE HOLD MAJORITY 2,104 (4.0%)

ANDREA JENKYNS
BORN Jun 16, 1974
MP 2015-

	Electorate	Turnout %	from 2010	Change %
	76,495	68.44		
*A Jenkyns C	26,550	50.71	+11.80	
N Dawson Lab Co-op	24,446	46.69	+8.65	
C Dobson LD	1,361	2.60	-0.36	

International business development manager before entering politics. Previously: music teacher; shop manager; soprano singer who released a charity single in 2015. Passionate about health: member health select cttee 2015-; trustee and regional representative, MRSA Action UK after father died of superbug in 2011. Cllr, Lincolnshire CC 2009-13. Select cttee, exiting the EU 2016-. Campaigned to Leave the EU. Yet to rebel against the party whip. Had a high-profile affair with fellow Tory backbencher Jack Lopresti, MP for Filton and Bradley Stoke. One son, with

Lopresti. Ed: Open University (Dip economics); University of Lincoln (BA international relations and politics).

CHALLENGERS
Neil Dawson (Lab) Accountant. Former pensions manager, Northern Power Grid. Cllr, Leeds CC 2011-. **Craig Dobson** (LD) GP. Medical adviser to the East Riding of Yorkshire Clinical Commissioning Group. Member, metical technologies cttee.

CONSTITUENCY PROFILE
This seat to the south of Leeds contains Morley, a former textile and coalmining town, and Outwood. The area has recovered from the decline in manufacturing and mining and has a low unemployment rate. It has experienced a huge expansion of housebuilding in the past few decades, and more than 70 per cent of residents are property owners. Morley and Outwood is less ethnically diverse than the rest of Yorkshire and the UK. Historically a safe Labour seat, it was held by Ed Balls until 2015 when his defeat became a symbol of Labour's downfall. The Conservatives increased their majority from 422 in 2015 to 2,104 in 2017.

EU REFERENDUM RESULT

59.8% Leave   Remain 40.2%

Motherwell & Wishaw

SNP HOLD MAJORITY 318 (0.8%)

MARION FELLOWS
BORN May 5, 1949
MP 2015-

	Electorate	Turnout %	from 2010	Change %
	68,215	61.46		
*M Fellows SNP	16,150	38.52	-18.02	
A Feeney Lab	15,832	37.76	+5.88	
M Gallacher C	8,490	20.25	+12.59	
Y Finlayson LD	920	2.19	+0.95	
N Wilson Ukip	534	1.27	-1.40	

Former business studies teacher and EIS trade union member. EU Remain campaigner. Senior figure in the Yes campaign during 2014 Scottish independence referendum, winning a majority in her future constituency. Cllr, Wishaw 2012-15. SNP whip 2015-17. SNP small business spokeswoman 2017-. Married, three children. Ed: Heriot-Watt University (BA accountancy and finance).

CHALLENGERS
Angela Feeney (Lab) NHS podiatrist with 20 years' experience. Socialist and trade unionist; Unison rep in her

workplace. Member, Campaign for Socialism. Jeremy Corbyn supporter. Set up Wishaw to Calais appeal for refugees with her daughter in 2015. Cllr, North Lanarkshire C 2017-. **Meghan Gallacher** (C) Customer relations manager for John Lewis. Anti-Scottish independence. Cllr, North Lanarkshire C 2017-. Contested: Scottish parliament 2016; Motherwell and Wishaw 2015. **Yvonne Finlayson** (LD) Business consultant, electronics industry.

Appeared on TV programme *Come Dine With Me.*

CONSTITUENCY PROFILE
A small seat in North Lanarkshire to the south east of Glasgow with a predominantly white, UK-born population. A third of residents have no qualifications and there are high levels of unemployment. Second highest proportion of residents renting from the council in the UK. Earnings are below the Sottish average. A safe seat for Labour who gained majorities of more than 10,000 here until Marion Fellows took the seat in 2015. The SNP majority was reduced to 318 votes in 2017.

EU REFERENDUM RESULT

37.7% Leave   Remain 62.3%

Na h-Eileanan an Iar

SNP HOLD MAJORITY 1,007 (6.8%)

ANGUS MACNEIL
BORN Jul 21, 1970
MP 2005-

Former BBC Radio Scotland reporter and primary school teacher. Part of "Super Six" SNP MPs elected before 2015 landslide. Known for Commons heckling. First person to call for investigation into "cash for honours" 2006. Locked himself into the Commons bathroom to avoid voting in EU referendum. Criticised for having an affair that included London hotel stays claimed on expenses 2016. Voted against Article 50. Rarely rebels. Contested Inverness East, Nairn and Lochaber 2001. Separated, three daughters. Ed: The Nicolson Institute, Stornoway; University of Strathclyde (BEng

	Electorate	Turnout %	from 2010 %	Change
	21,301	69.56		
*A MacNeil SNP	6,013	40.58	-13.77	
E MacDonald Lab	5,006	33.78	+5.17	
D McCroskrie C	2,441	16.47	+8.85	
J Cormack SCP	1,108	7.48	+0.92	
J Paterson LD	250	1.69	-1.17	

civil engineering); Jordanhill Coll (PGCE).

CHALLENGERS
Ealasaid MacDonald (Lab) Former research and policy officer, Renfrewshire C. Chairwoman, Meur Phaislig Gaelic group. **Dan McCroskie** (C) Full-time Tory activist. Manages office of Donald Cameron MSP. Co-ordinated Vote Leave ground campaign. **James Paterson** (LD) Stay-at-home dad. Formerly parly asst

to Jamie Stone MSP and John Farquahar Munro MSP.

CONSTITUENCY PROFILE
Gaelic for Western Isles, Na h-Eileanan an Iar is the smallest seat in parliament by population, with only 28,000 residents. More than a fifth of its population are aged 65 or above, fewer than one in a hundred is non-white, and nearly three quarters are Christian. Home ownership is high and the seat has one of the lowest rates of private renting in the UK. The seat first elected a Labour MP in 1935 and has since switched between Labour and the SNP.

EU REFERENDUM RESULT

43.9% Leave   Remain 56.1%

Neath

LAB CO-OP HOLD MAJORITY 12,631 (33.0%)

CHRISTINA REES
BORN Feb 21, 1954
MP 2015-

Former barrister and Justice of the Peace. Previously squash professional, national coach, Wales squash and racketball. Shadow SoS for Wales 2017-. Shadow justice minister 2016-17. Select cttees: justice 2015; Welsh affairs 2015-16. Contested European parliament 2014. Campaigned against Leaving the EU. Resigned from Jeremy Corbyn's shadow cabinet following vote of no confidence. Cllr, Bridgend BC 2012-15. Member: Unite; GMB. Divorced from former cabinet minister Ron Davies who resigned from the Blair government after his "moment of madness" with a

	Electorate	Turnout %	from 2010 %	Change
	55,859	68.54		
*C Rees Lab Co-op	21,713	56.71	+12.90	
O Lowe C	9,082	23.72	+8.40	
D Williams PC	5,339	13.95	-4.16	
R Pritchard Ukip	1,419	3.71	-12.70	
F Little LD	732	1.91	-1.25	

stranger on Clapham Common. One daughter. Ed: Cynffig Comp Sch; Ystrad Mynach Coll; University of Wales (LLB law).

CHALLENGERS
Orla Lowe (C) Solicitor. Senior adviser, Private Family Office. Previously worked at Adam Perry & Co LLP 2013-14. **Daniel Williams** (PC) Professor of English and dir of the Richard Burton Centre for the Study of Wales at Swansea University. Author. Saxophonist.

CONSTITUENCY PROFILE
The south Wales town of Neath, northeast of Swansea, is home to about 19,000 people, consisting of a rural area up to the edge of the Brecon Beacons. The workforce is skewed towards routine and semi-routine occupations and the average income is slightly below what is typical in Wales. However, home ownership in Neath is higher than average, mostly at the expense of private sector renting. The seat has elected a Labour MP at every election since 1922, and its former MP was New Labour cabinet minister and anti-apartheid campaigner Peter Hain.

EU REFERENDUM RESULT

54.0% Leave   Remain 46.0%

New Forest East

CONSERVATIVE HOLD MAJORITY 21,995 (42.8%)

JULIAN LEWIS
BORN Sep 26, 1951
MP 1997-

Former deputy dir, Conservative research dept. Defence consultant, political researcher. Royal Navy reservist. Author. Visiting senior research fellow, Centre for Defence Studies at King's Coll London. Infiltrated Labour party in 1970s to oust "Trotskyite" leftwingers. A vigorous rightwinger and leading Eurosceptic. Campaigned to Leave the EU. Passionate champion of nuclear defence and leading Conservative supporter of the Speaker, John Bercow. Rebelled to vote against military action in Syria. Chairman, defence select cttee 2015-. Select cttees: arms export

	Electorate	Turnout %	from 2010 %	Change
	72,602	70.75		
*J Lewis C	32,162	62.61	+6.35	
J Renyard Lab	10,167	19.79	+7.62	
D Harrison LD	7,786	15.16	+5.80	
H Mellor Green	1,251	2.44	-2.27	

controls 2016-17; NSS 2015-17. Ed: Dynevor GS, Swansea; Balliol Coll, Oxford (MA philosophy and politics); St Antony's Coll, Oxford (DPhil strategic studies).

CHALLENGERS
Julie Renyard (Lab) Retired secondary school maths teacher. **David Harrison** (LD) Town, district and Hampshire county cllr 1994-. Worked in local government for 30 years. Former chartered insurer. **Henry Mellor** (Green) Currently a Makaton tutor. Cllr, Brockenhurst PC.

CONSTITUENCY PROFILE
The largest town in this Hampshire seat is Totton, which sits on the River Test just to the west of Southampton and is home to about 28,000 people. The seat also contains most of the New Forest National Park. More than one in five residents is aged 65 or above and 19 out of 20 are white British. Home ownership is well above average, with about three quarters of households owner-occupied. New Forest East has been Conservative at every election since its creation in 1997 and its predecessors had elected Conservatives going as far back as 1910.

EU REFERENDUM RESULT
60.2% Leave   Remain 39.8%

New Forest West

CONSERVATIVE HOLD MAJORITY 23,431 (47.2%)

SIR DESMOND SWAYNE
BORN Aug 20, 1956
MP 1997-

School teacher 1981-87 then became manager of risk management systems at RBS 1987-97. Dir, property development company. Army officer in the reserves for 30 years. TA officer, served in Iraq July-December 2003. Knighted in 2016. Opposed Britain's EEC membership in 1975 referendum. Campaigned for Brexit. Close to David Cameron. Min, int dev 2014-16. Govt whip 2012-14. Privy Counsellor. PPS to: David Cameron 2005-12; Michael Howard 2004-05. Married, two daughters, one son. Ed: Bedford Sch; University of St Andrews (MA theology).

	Electorate	Turnout %	from 2010 %	Change
	68,787	72.15		
*D Swayne C	33,170	66.84	+6.89	
J Graham Lab	9,739	19.62	+8.80	
T Scriven LD	4,781	9.63	+2.69	
J Richards Green	1,454	2.93	-2.87	
D Hjerling Pirate	483	0.97		

CHALLENGERS
Jo Graham (Lab) Trained as a primary teacher. Set up her own business, Learning Unlimited, in 1999. **Terry Scriven** (LD) Previously a colonel in the Royal Military Police. Service took him to Cyprus, Gurkhas, Northern Ireland and Bosnia. Chairman, UK national defence medal campaign. Former cllr: Hyde PC; Ringwood TC. Contested New Forest East 2010. **Janet Richards** (Green) Worked in telecommunications for 19 years.

Co-founder of local food co-operative and community farm.

CONSTITUENCY PROFILE
New Forest West contains less of New Forest itself than its neighbour. Its biggest settlements are the coastal town of New Milton and Ringwood. Nearly three in ten are aged 65 or over, and about three quarters of households are owner-occupied. Incomes in both New Forest seats are in line with the Hampshire average, but median income in New Forest West is higher than its eastern neighbour. Like New Forest East, this has been a safe Conservative seat since its creation in 1997.

EU REFERENDUM RESULT
55.3% Leave   Remain 44.7%

Newark

CONSERVATIVE HOLD MAJORITY 18,149 (33.0%)

ROBERT JENRICK
BORN Jan 9, 1982
MP 2014-

	Electorate	Turnout %	Change from 2010 %
	75,526	72.88	
*R Jenrick C	34,493	62.67	+5.62
C Lee Lab	16,344	29.69	+7.97
D Watts LD	2,786	5.06	+0.50
X Arundel Ukip	1,419	2.58	-9.46

Formerly a solicitor and international MD, Christie's. Elected in 2014 after Patrick Mercer's resignation during "cash for questions" furore. The police later took no action in response to claims of overspending during the campaign. A leading proponent of flood defences. Campaigned to Remain in the EU. Attended Donald Trump's presidential inauguration 2017. PPS to: Amber Rudd 2017-, 2014-15; Liz Truss 2016-17; Michael Gove 2015-16. Contested Newcastle-under-Lyme 2010. Married, three daughters. Ed: Wolverhampton GS; St John's Coll, Cambridge (BA history);

University of Pennsylvania (Thouron fellow); Coll of Law (Grad Dip law); BPP Law Sch (LPC).

CHALLENGERS
Chantal Lee (Lab) Works for a women's refuge charity. Former senior education worker. **David Watts** (LD) Former solicitor and lecturer. Contested: Newark 2014; Broxtowe 2010, 2005, 2001. Cllr, Broxtowe BC 1995-2015; leader 2010-11. **Xandra Arundel** (Ukip) Cognitive behavioural psychotherapist.

CONSTITUENCY PROFILE
A large east Nottinghamshire seat bordering Lincolnshire. It has an ageing population, with nearly a fifth of residents aged 65 or over, and more than 70 per cent of households owner-occupied. The workforce is skewed towards more affluent professions but incomes are roughly in line with the regional average. Newark was represented by Labour MPs from 1950 to 1979 and again throughout the 1997 parliament but has otherwise elected Conservative MPs for the last 100 years, including at a 2014 by-election at which Ukip won a quarter of the vote.

EU REFERENDUM RESULT

55.7% Leave   Remain 44.3%

Newbury

CONSERVATIVE HOLD MAJORITY 24,380 (40.1%)

RICHARD BENYON
BORN Oct 21, 1960
MP 2005-

	Electorate	Turnout %	Change from 2010 %
	82,923	73.38	
*R Benyon C	37,399	61.46	+0.43
J Bunting LD	13,019	21.40	+6.38
A Skirvin Lab	8,596	14.13	+5.69
P Field Green	1,531	2.52	-1.54
D Yates AD	304	0.50	+0.10

Former army officer, farmer and chartered surveyor. Archetypal rural, ex-military man. Son of the former MP Bill Benyon and great-great-grandson of prime minister Lord Salisbury. Wealth estimated at £110 million, making him one of the richest MPs. Campaigned to Remain in the EU. Controversy in 2014 when Benyon's family firm bought an affordable housing estate and increased rent to market rate. Parly under-sec, Defra 2010-13. Shadow min Defra 2009-10. Interested in defence, health, rural issues and African affairs. Privy Council 2017. Cllr, Newbury DC 1991-95; led

Conservative group. Contested Newbury 2001, 1997. Divorced, remarried, five children. Ed: Bradfield Coll; Royal Agricultural Coll (Dip real estate management, land economy).

CHALLENGERS
Judith Bunting (LD) Scientist and television producer. Exec at a deaf-run production house, Remark. Contested Newbury 2015. **Alex Skirvin** (Lab) Aged 23, works for corporate and external affairs dept, Vodafone.

Paul Field (Green) Head teacher, worked in education for 25 years. Contested Newbury 2015.

CONSTITUENCY PROFILE
Just to the west of Reading in Berkshire. The town itself, in the south of the seat, is home to about 39,000 residents. There is a slight skew towards working-age people and children in the profile of the seat. Only five per cent of residents are non-white and average incomes are above what is typical in the South East, one of Britain's more affluent regions. The seat has returned a Tory MP in every election since 1924 except for 1993, 1997 and 2001, when it voted Lib Dem.

EU REFERENDUM RESULT

47.8% Leave   Remain 52.2%

Newcastle-under-Lyme

LABOUR HOLD MAJORITY 30 (0.1%)

PAUL FARRELLY
BORN Mar 2, 1962
MP 2001-

Former journalist, *Reuters* and *Observer*, and corporate financier. He has managed to cling on to his seat with an ever-depleting majority. On the left of the Labour party. Played lead role in opposition to higher university fees. Jeremy Corbyn sceptic; backed Andy Burnham 2015. Did not include Corbyn's policies on campaign leaflets. Rebellious streak: voted against triggering Article 50; was one of 13 MPs to vote against a snap election 2017. Contested Chesham and Amersham 1997. Married, three children. Ed: Wolstanton County GS; St Edmund Hall, Oxford (BA PPE).

	Electorate	Turnout %	from 2010 %	Change
	65,540	66.89		
*P Farrelly Lab	21,124	48.18	+9.76	
O Meredith C	21,094	48.11	+11.20	
N Jones LD	1,624	3.70	-0.54	

CHALLENGERS
Owen Meredith (C) Dir, Professional Publishers Association. Community campaigner. Previously worked for a Staffordshire MP. Stood for Welsh assembly. Deputy chairman, Tory Reform Group. LGBT Conservatives council member. **Nigel Jones** (LD) MP for Cheltenham 1992-2005. Made peer in dissolution honours 2005. Former computer industry worker. Cllr, Gloucester CC 1989-92. Contested Cheltenham 1979. Served as spokesman while in the Commons.

CONSTITUENCY PROFILE
Part of the same metropolitan area as Stoke-on-Trent, Newcastle-under-Lyme is home to about 75,000 people. The seat also extends west into a more rural area that contains Keele University, so about 9,000 students live in the constituency. Average incomes are below what is typical in the West Midlands. It has been represented by Labour MPs since 1919, when its then-MP, Josiah Wedgewood, defected to Labour from the Liberals, although the Labour majority in the seat has fallen from 17,000 in 1997 to double figures now. It is, numerically, Labour's third smallest majority.

EU REFERENDUM RESULT
61.6% Leave   Remain 38.4%

Newcastle upon Tyne Central

LABOUR HOLD MAJORITY 14,937 (40.3%)

CHI ONWURAH
BORN Apr 12, 1965
MP 2010-

Chartered engineer. Former head of telecoms technology for Ofcom. Mixed race with working-class origins in the North East. Spent two years living in Nigeria but fled with mother during Biafran civil war. Voted no confidence in Jeremy Corbyn. Made loose claims implying Corbyn discriminated against her and another BME MP 2016. Backed Remain. Shad min: industrial strategy 2016-; BIS 2015-16, 2010-13; CMA 2015-16; Cabinet Office 2013-15. Former nat exec, Anti-Apartheid Movement. Member: Fabian Soc; Co-op Party; Institute of Engineering and Technology.

	Electorate	Turnout %	from 2010 %	Change
	55,571	66.75		
*C Onwurah Lab	24,071	64.89	+9.88	
S Kyte C	9,134	24.62	+5.73	
N Cott LD	1,812	4.88	-1.44	
D Muat Ukip	1,482	4.00	-10.87	
P Thomson Green	595	1.60	-3.31	

Ed: Kenton Comp; Imperial Coll, London (BEng electrical engineering); Manchester Business Sch (MBA).

CHALLENGERS
Steve Kyte (C) Public sector worker. Served in RAF. Editor, local Gosforth Matters newsletter. **Nick Cott** (LD) History lecturer, Open University. Teacher, Newcastle University. PhD in modern history. Cllr, Newcastle CC 2000-.

CONSTITUENCY PROFILE
Has a sizeable student population of 13,000, about a seventh of the population, only a third of which is aged over 45. A quarter of residents are non-white, mainly of Asian descent, and the seat is home to about 13,000 Muslims, making it the most diverse of the three Newcastle seats. Home ownership is low, at just two in five households, and social renting is well above average at nearly one third of households. This seat has the highest unemployment rate of the three. Postwar it has elected a Tory MP once, in Margaret Thatcher's landslide of 1983.

EU REFERENDUM RESULT
48.0% Leave   Remain 52.0%

Newcastle upon Tyne East

LABOUR HOLD MAJORITY 19,261 (46.3%)

NICK BROWN
BORN Jun 13, 1950
MP 1983-

Tough enforcer loyal to party line. Proctor & Gamble advertiser. Previously worked for a dry-cleaning company. GMW regional research officer 1978-83. Outed by the *News of the World* in 1998. Spent years as whip trying to get Jeremy Corbyn to toe the line; was asked by him to keep rebels in check 2016. Backed Yvette Cooper 2015. Good friends with Gordon Brown. Min: North East 2007-10; DWP 2001-03. SoS, agriculture, fisheries, food 1998-2001. Shadow dep leader Commons 1992-94. Shadow solicitor general 1985-92. Multiple shadow spokesman roles. Cllr, Newcastle

	Electorate	Turnout %	from 2010 % Change
	62,333	66.80	
*N Brown Lab	28,127	67.55	+18.15
S Kitchen C	8,866	21.29	+3.74
W Taylor LD	2,574	6.18	-4.86
T Sanderson Ukip	1,315	3.16	-9.36
A Ford Green	755	1.81	-6.92

CC 1980-84. Privy cllr 1997. Awarded freedom of Newcastle 2001. Ed: Tunbridge Wells Tech HS; Manchester University (BA).

CHALLENGERS
Simon Kitchen (C) Alzheimer's Society worker; involved with development of Dementia Alliance. Senior adviser, Sustainable Development Commission. Splits time between Newcastle and London. **Wendy Taylor** (LD) Breast cancer consultant, Freeman Hospital.

Cllr, Newcastle CC 1988-. Awarded MBE 2015 for public and political service.

CONSTITUENCY PROFILE
Newcastle upon Tyne East is the smallest, densest and most urban Newcastle seat. It is home to 24,000 students, who make up about a quarter of the population. Home ownership is low, with over a quarter of households privately rented and nearly a third socially rented. By median income, however, it is the most affluent seat in the city. Including its predecessor of the same name, the seat has only elected Labour MPs since 1959, when it elected a Conservative.

EU REFERENDUM RESULT

41.1% Leave   Remain 58.9%

Newcastle Upon Tyne North

LABOUR HOLD MAJORITY 10,349 (21.4%)

CATHERINE MCKINNELL
BORN Jun 8, 1976
MP 2010-

Former employment solicitor. One of eight children. Newcastle born and raised. First shadow cabinet member to resign over Jeremy Corbyn's leadership 2016. Nominated Yvette Cooper 2015. Staunch Remainer; only North East MP to vote against triggering Article 50. Shadow attorney general 2015-16. Shadow: economic and exchequer secretary to Treasury 2013-15; minister for children and young families 2011-13; solicitor general 2010-11. Married, three children. Ed: University of Edinburgh (MA politics and history); Northumbria University (law).

	Electorate	Turnout %	from 2010 % Change
	66,312	72.82	
*C McKinnell Lab	26,729	55.35	+9.27
D Crute C	16,380	33.92	+10.45
A Lower LD	2,533	5.25	-4.48
T Marron Ukip	1,780	3.69	-12.90
A Whalley Green	513	1.06	-2.31
B Moore North	353	0.73	

CHALLENGERS
Duncan Crute (C) Businessman, runs tailoring company Crutes la Mar. Previously a marketing consultant. Trustee, Newcastle Conservatives. Contested Newcastle East 2015. **Anita Lower** (LD) Cllr, Newcastle CC 1994-; Lib Dem group leader 2013-. **Timothy Marron** (Ukip) Former shopkeeper, completing training at Newcastle Coll to be teacher's assistant. Motorbike enthusiast.

CONSTITUENCY PROFILE
This constituency stretches beyond the city of Newcastle, and while it still contains a significant portion of the city, it is much more rural and less dense. Unlike the other two, student numbers are in line with the national average and the age profile is much more balanced. It is also the least ethnically diverse of the three. Home ownership in the seat is about average. It had been represented by Conservative MPs from 1918 to 1983, but was won by Labour in 1983 following significant boundary changes, and has been represented by Labour MPs ever since.

EU REFERENDUM RESULT

56.8% Leave   Remain 43.2%

Newport East

LABOUR HOLD MAJORITY 8,003 (21.7%)

JESSICA MORDEN
BORN May 29, 1968
MP 2005-

Professional Labour activist. General sec, Welsh Labour. Previously worked for GMB and as a researcher for MPs Huw Edwards and Llew Smith. First female MP in SE Wales. Labour leadership nominations: Owen Smith 2016; Liz Kendall 2015. Does not rebel. Remainer; voted for Article 50. Opposition whip 2015-. PPS to: Owen Smith 2015-16; Peter Hain 2009-10, 2007-08; Paul Murphy 2008-09. Partner, two children. Ed: Croesyceiliog Sch; University of Birmingham (BA history).

CHALLENGERS
Natasha Asghar (C) TV

	Electorate	Turnout %	from 2010 % Change
	57,233	64.33	
*J Morden Lab	20,804	56.50	+15.80
N Asghar C	12,801	34.77	+7.46
I Gorman Ukip	1,180	3.20	-15.21
P Brown LD	966	2.62	-3.79
C Wixcey PC	881	2.39	-1.11
N Ahmed ND	188	0.51	

presenter, Zee TV. Author, *Me, Myself and My Arranged Marriage*. Formerly retail banker, Barclays. Daughter of Mohammad Asghar AM. Contested Newport East 2015. **Ian Gorman** (Ukip) Founding director, P3MA digital media start-up. Previously worked in Texas local government. Treasurer, Ukip Caerphilly. **Pete Brown** (LD) Archaeologist, university lecturer, prison teacher.

CONSTITUENCY PROFILE
Divided from Newport West by the River Usk, this seat is larger and more rural than its Newport neighbour, expanding out further towards Wales' border with England. The seat contains the Llanwern Steelworks, which employs about 1,600 people. There is an above average proportion of manufacturing jobs and a lot of routine and semi-routine jobs taken up by Newport West's residents. About 5,000 students make up the demographic. Only Labour MPs have been elected since its creation in 1983, and the same is true of its predecessor seat since 1945.

EU REFERENDUM RESULT
59.3% Leave   Remain 40.7%

Newport West

LABOUR HOLD MAJORITY 5,658 (13.0%)

PAUL FLYNN
BORN Feb 9, 1935
MP 1987-

Former industrial chemist in Welsh steel factory. Later researcher for Llew Smith MEP. Cllr: Newport BC 1972-81; Gwent CC 1974-82. Contested Denbigh 1974. Veteran left-winger and outspoken anti-war campaigner. Author, *How to be an MP* and *Commons Knowledge: How to be a Backbencher*. Nominated Liz Kendall for leadership 2015. Became the oldest MP in over a century to hold a shadow cabinet post when appointed shadow SoS for Wales in 2016. Shadow leader, HoC 2016. Serial backbench rebel. Remainer, voted for Article 50. Married, three children, one deceased. Ed:

	Electorate	Turnout %	from 2010 % Change
	64,399	67.45	
*P Flynn Lab	22,723	52.31	+11.09
A Jones-Evans C	17,065	39.29	+6.76
S Edwards Ukip	1,100	2.53	-12.67
M Bowler-Brown PC	1,077	2.48	-1.50
S Lockyer LD	976	2.25	-1.67
P Bartolotti Green	497	1.14	-2.01

St Illtyd's Coll; University Coll, Cardiff.

CHALLENGERS
Angela Jones-Evans (C) Comms and strategy officer for Kay Swinburne MEP. Owns training business. Previously university lecturer. Contested Cardiff West 2010. **Stan Edwards** (Ukip) Chartered surveyor. Visiting lecturer in retail planning and development, Cardiff University. Chairman, Ukip Newport.

CONSTITUENCY PROFILE
Newport West contains Newport Docks and stretches across the south Wales coast towards Cardiff. It contains the University of South Wales campus and about 5,000 full-time students live here. There is a greater proportion of residents in Newport West than East in higher-paid, managerial-level jobs, however the seats' average incomes are fairly similar and both are roughly in line with the average in Wales. The seat has only ever been represented by a Conservative MP for one term, which started in 1983. Paul Flynn then gained the seat for Labour in 1987.

EU REFERENDUM RESULT
53.7% Leave   Remain 46.3%

Newry & Armagh

SINN FEIN HOLD MAJORITY 12,489 (23.3%)

MICKEY BRADY
BORN Oct 7, 1950
MP 2015-

Former welfare rights officer, working as a benefits and housing campaigner. MLA, Newry and Armagh 2007-15. Sinn Fein spokesman, welfare and older people. Deputy chairman, social development cttee. APPGs: trade unions 2013-, vice-chairman; mental health 2012-; football 2012-. As an abstentionist, never votes. Campaigned to Remain, fighting the case for designated special status for the North within the EU. Faced death threats in 2015. Enjoys hurling. Married, four children. Ed: Abbey Christian Brothers' Grammar School; University of Liverpool.

	Electorate	Turnout %	from 2010 %	Change
	78,266	68.46		
*M Brady SF	25,666	47.90	+6.83	
W Irwin DUP	13,177	24.59		
J McNulty SDLP	9,055	16.90	-7.21	
S Nicholson UUP	4,425	8.26	-24.45	
J Coade Alliance	1,256	2.34	+0.66	

CHALLENGERS
William Irwin (DUP) Dairy farmer who got involved in politics after his son drowned. Orangeman. MLA, Newry and Armagh 2007-. Cllr, Armagh City and DC 2005-14. **Justin McNulty** (SDLP) Former Gaelic footballer and manager; part of Armagh team that won All-Ireland championship 2002. Later a financial engineer. MLA, Newry & Armagh 2016-. Contested Newry and Armagh 2015. **Sam Nicholson**
(UUP) Chartered architect. Orangeman. Son of UUP MEP and former MP Jim Nicholson.

CONSTITUENCY PROFILE
Newry and Armagh is a Northern Irish seat on the border with the Republic. While the town of Armagh itself is home to more Catholics than Protestants, much of the area around Armagh is dominated by large Protestant populations. The seat is roughly two thirds Catholic and three tenths Protestant, and has elected Sinn Féin MPs since 2005, having elected nationalists for over 30 years. UUP MPs were elected here between 1922 and 1983.

EU REFERENDUM RESULT

37.1% Leave   Remain 62.9%

Newton Abbot

CONSERVATIVE HOLD MAJORITY 17,160 (33.2%)

ANNE MARIE MORRIS
BORN Jul 5, 1957
MP 2010-

Suspended from the Conservative Party after describing the prospect of leaving EU without a deal as a "real n***er in the woodpile" at at a report launch in the East India Club, July 2017. Corporate lawyer. Later marketing director: PwC; Ernst & Young. Set up consultancy mentoring small businesses in the South West. Cllr, West Sussex DC 2005-07. Publicly criticised chancellor for proposed NIC rise 2016. Brexiteer. Rebelled on minor Europe votes during coalition years. One of 30 Tory rebels against Isis airstrikes 2013. PPS to Jo Johnson 2015-16. Partner,

	Electorate	Turnout %	from 2010 %	Change
	71,722	72.00		
*A Morris C	28,635	55.45	+8.16	
J Osben Lab	11,475	22.22	+12.40	
M Chadwick LD	10,601	20.53	-3.34	
K Driscoll Green	926	1.79	-2.80	

stepchildren. Ed: Hertford Coll, Oxford (BA jurisprudence); Coll of Law, London; Open University (MBA).

CHALLENGERS
James Osben (Lab) NHS mental health nurse. Chairman, Newton Abbot CLP. **Marie Chadwick** (LD) Campaigns officer, RNIB. Formerly constituency office manager, Nick Harvey MP. Former cllr: Teignbridge DC 2007-11; Newton Abbot TC. **Kathryn Driscoll** (Green) Occupational therapy student.

CONSTITUENCY PROFILE
The Devon town of Newton Abbot is home to about 26,000 people. The other large towns in this seat are Teignmouth and Dawlish, which lie along the railway line between Torquay and Exeter on the coast. Nearly 25 per cent of residents are 65 or over and just one in 50 is non-white. Incomes in the area are below the regional average. The predecessor seat of Teignbridge was held by the Liberal Democrats from 2001 to 2010. The Conservatives beat them in this seat by 523 votes in 2010. The Tory vote has grown while the Lib Dem vote has receded in the elections since.

EU REFERENDUM RESULT

56.0% Leave   Remain 44.0%

Norfolk Mid

CONSERVATIVE HOLD MAJORITY 16,086 (28.9%)

GEORGE FREEMAN
BORN Jul 12, 1967
MP 2010-

Previously a venture capitalist, founded consultancy 4D Biomedical, MD 2003-10. Campaigned to Remain in the EU but did see Brexit as an opportunity to rethink the economic model. First UK minister for life sciences 2014-16. Govt adviser on life sciences to David Willets 2011-13. PPS to Greg Barker 2010-12. Co-founder, 2020 group of Con MPs. Under-sec of BIS and health 2014-16. Sparked outrage by saying benefits should only go to "really disabled" people in 2017. Adviser, Norwich Research Park. Contested Stevenage 2005. Married, one son, one daughter.

	Electorate	Turnout %	from 2010 %	Change
	80,026	69.56		
*G Freeman C	32,828	58.97	+6.86	
S Simpson Lab	16,742	30.07	+11.72	
F Tod LD	2,848	5.12	-1.20	
T Knowles Ukip	2,092	3.76	-15.26	
H Lester Green	1,158	2.08	-2.12	

Ed: Radley Coll; Girton Coll, Cambridge (BA geography).

CHALLENGERS
Sarah Simpson (Lab) Grew up in a forces family. Operations dir of an engineering consultancy in Norwich. **Fionna Tod** (LD) Parliamentary policy adviser specialising in foreign affairs and Brexit. Field organiser, Barack Obama's re-election campaign. **Tracy Knowles** (Ukip) Career in industrial manufacturing after studying chemistry. **Hannah**

Lester (Green) 22-year-old law student, training to be a solicitor.

CONSTITUENCY PROFILE
A rural seat to the west of Norwich containing a mixture of villages and market towns. The population is predominantly white and UK-born. A significant number of people move here to retire, the proportion of residents aged over 65 is well above average. Income is slightly lower than the rest of the region. Over 70 per cent of residents are property owners and the constituency contains little social housing. A safe Conservative seat, not held by another party since its creation in 1983.

EU REFERENDUM RESULT

60.6% Leave   Remain 39.4%

Norfolk North

LIBERAL DEMOCRAT HOLD MAJORITY 3,512 (6.7%)

NORMAN LAMB
BORN Sep 16, 1957
MP 2001-

Employment solicitor. Formerly worked as parly asst to Labour MP Greville Janner. Cllr, Norwich CC 1987-91. Contested Norfolk North 1997, 1992. Tireless mental health campaigner after sister's suicide and diagnosis of son's OCD. Architect of part-privatisation of Royal Mail. Ran for Liberal Democrat leadership 2015; declined to do so again in 2017. Lib Dem health spokesman 2015-. Defends Lib Dems' coalition record. Remainer; abstained on Article 50 vote. Minister: care 2012-15; employment 2012. PPS: Nick Clegg 2010-12; Charles Kennedy 2003-05. Chairman,

	Electorate	Turnout %	from 2010 %	Change
	69,263	75.35		
*N Lamb LD	25,260	48.40	+9.35	
J Wild C	21,748	41.67	+10.80	
S Burke Lab	5,180	9.93	-0.28	

science and technology select cttee 2017-. Remortgaged house to help launch career of rapper Tinchy Stryder. Married, two sons. Ed: University of Leicester (LLB).

CHALLENGERS
James Wild (C) Adviser to Sir Michael Fallon MP. Formerly a lobbyist for T-Mobile. Worked in Conservative Research Department. Married to Lords leader Baroness Evans of Bowes Park. **Stephen Burke** (Lab) Career in health and the third sector career.

CONSTITUENCY PROFILE
A rural and coastal seat made up of small towns and fishing villages. It has one of the highest proportions of older people in the UK, and as a result of this 45 per cent of households have no-one in employment. It is sparsely populated and fairly remote. Retail, agriculture and tourism are important industries. The constituency contains a lot of self-employed residents and small business owners. Over 70 per cent of Norfolk North's population are property owners. In 2001 Norman Lamb became the first Liberal to represent the seat since 1918, after it had been Conservative for 31 years.

EU REFERENDUM RESULT

58.4% Leave   Remain 41.6%

Norfolk North West

CONSERVATIVE HOLD MAJORITY 13,788 (28.2%)

SIR HENRY BELLINGHAM

BORN Mar 29, 1955
MP 2001-; 1983-97

Worked as a barrister for eight years. Knighted in 2016. Campaigned to Leave the EU. Parly under-sec, FCO 2010-12. Opposition whip 2005-06. MP for Norfolk North West 1983-97. Ran consultancy firm 1997-2001. PPS to Malcolm Rifkind 1991-97. Controversy in 2014 when it emerged he was being paid £1,300 an hour by an African mining company he had once lobbied for. Passionate about rural issues. Opposed to the ban on fox hunting. Distant ancestor shot PM Spencer Perceval dead in 1812. Enthusiastic member of Lords and Commons cricket team. Married, one son. Ed: Eton

Electorate	Turnout %	from 2010 % Change
72,062	67.73	
*H Bellingham C	29,408	60.25 +8.05
J Rust Lab	15,620	32.00 +9.25
M Stone Ukip	1,539	3.15 -14.60
R Moss-Eccardt LD	1,393	2.85 -0.68
A De Whalley Green	851	1.74 -2.01

Coll; Magdalene Coll, Cambridge (BA law).

CHALLENGERS
Joanne Rust (Lab) Early years and child development officer at Norfolk CC. Secondment as Norfolk campaigns organiser for Unison. **Rupert Moss-Eccardt** (LD) IT security consultant. Cllr, Cambridgeshire CC 2005-11. Contested: Cambridgeshire CC 2017; Norfolk South West 2015. Served on Cambridge Fire Authority.

CONSTITUENCY PROFILE
This East Anglia seat stretches from the coast to the regional centre of Kings Lynn and it contains the surrounding farmland and small villages. The royal estate of Sandringham is situated here. Norfolk North West is a popular location to retire to: almost a quarter of residents are over 65. Employment is focused on tourism, retail and manufacturing. Earnings are well below the regional and national averages. In recent elections the Conservatives have gained comfortable majorities, although Labour briefly held it after the 1997 landslide.

EU REFERENDUM RESULT

65.8% Leave   Remain 34.2%

Norfolk South

CONSERVATIVE HOLD MAJORITY 16,678 (27.3%)

RICHARD BACON
BORN Dec 3, 1962
MP 2001-

Formerly worked as an investment banker, financial journalist and associate partner of Brunswick PR consultancy. Set up own business, English Word Factory, advising companies on comms. Select cttees: public accounts 2001-; European scrutiny 2001-07. Trenchant critic of financial mismanagement and fraud in the EU; tried to introduce a bill to repeal the human rights act in 2012. Campaigned to Leave the EU. Co-author of *Conundrum: Why every government gets things wrong and what we can do about it.* Consistently rebelled against military action in Middle

Electorate	Turnout %	from 2010 % Change
83,056	73.58	
*R Bacon C	35,580	58.22 +3.96
D Glavin Lab	18,902	30.93 +12.55
C Brown LD	5,074	8.30 +0.09
C Rowett Green	1,555	2.54 -2.86

East, including 2003 invasion of Iraq. Contested Vauxhall 1997. Married, two children. Ed: King's Sch, Worcester; LSE (BSc politics and economics).

CHALLENGERS
Danielle Glavin (Lab) Senior press officer at Cancer Research UK, lives on a smallholding. Former BBC journalist 2002-2013, went undercover to reveal poor hygiene at NHS hospital. **Christopher Brown** (LD) Chartered PR practitioner and business owner. Former cllr,

Reading BC. Previously a trustee of a homeless charity.

CONSTITUENCY PROFILE
Situated just south of Norwich, this largely rural area includes the market towns of Diss and Harleston, as well as several villages. It is homogeneous: most residents are white and British. There is a significant retired population – nearly 20 per cent of residents are pensioners – and there are high levels of home ownership. It is a safe Conservative seat. The Liberal Democrats have traditionally come second, although in the last two elections the Labour Party has been runner up.

EU REFERENDUM RESULT

50.9% Leave   Remain 49.1%

Norfolk South West

CONSERVATIVE HOLD MAJORITY 18,312 (34.9%)

ELIZABETH TRUSS
BORN July 26, 1975
MP 2010-

	Electorate	Turnout %	from 2010 Change %
	77,874	67.31	
*E Truss C	32,894	62.76	+11.84
P Smith Lab	14,582	27.82	+10.56
D Williams Ukip	2,575	4.91	-18.34
S Gordon LD	2,365	4.51	+0.09

Former economics dir, Cable & Wireless; commerical analyst, Shell. Dir, Reform think tank 2008-09. Founder, Free Enterprise Group. Cllr, Greenwich BC 2006-10. Contested: Calder Valley 2005; Hemsworth 2001. Chief secretary to the Treasury after post-election reshuffle in what was seen as a demotion. Lord chancellor and justice sec 2016-17; criticised by some in legal community for not defending judicial independence following Supreme Court Article 50 verdict. SoS, Defra 2014-16. Education min 2012-14. Youngest-ever female cabinet minister upon appointment. Campaigns for retention of RAF bases. Remainer, voted for Article 50. Co-author: *After the Coalition* and *Britannia Unchained*. Married, two daughters. Ed: Roundhay Sch, Leeds; Merton Coll, Oxford (BA PPE).

CHALLENGERS
Peter Smith (Lab) Former teacher and community worker. Union rep. Contested Norfolk SW 2015, 2010. **Stephen Gordon** (LD) Homeopath and trained osteopath. Previously general secretary to European Central Council of Homeopaths.

CONSTITUENCY PROFILE
A sparsely populated, rural and predominantly white seat. Local economy is mainly driven by agriculture and forestry. A significant number work in public admin and defence as the seat includes the army's Stanford Training Area. Unemployment is below national average with 15 per cent of residents in skilled trade occupations. There are high levels of home ownership. A safe Tory seat, with the party winning a 35 per cent majority in 2017.

EU REFERENDUM RESULT
66.7% Leave   Remain 33.3%

Normanton, Pontefract & Castleford

LABOUR HOLD MAJORITY 14,499 (29.5%)

YVETTE COOPER
BORN Mar 20, 1969
MP 1997-

	Electorate	Turnout %	from 2010 Change %
	81,641	60.25	
*Y Cooper Lab	29,268	59.50	+4.56
A Lee C	14,769	30.02	+9.17
L Thompson Ukip	3,030	6.16	-15.16
D Gascoigne Yorkshire	1,431	2.91	
C Roberts LD	693	1.41	-1.49

A 2015 Labour leadership candidate, considered a Brownite. Shadow home secretary 2011-15; shadow foreign secretary 2010-11. Held various ministerial positions under New Labour, culminating in SoS for work and pensions 2009-10. Before parliament: chief economic correspondent, *The Independent* 1995-1997; research associate, Centre for Economic Performance 1994; policy adviser, Harriet Harman 1992; economic policy researcher for John Smith 1990-92. Campaigned to Remain, but voted in favour of triggering Article 50. Now chairwoman, home affairs select cttee 2016-.

Married to Ed Balls; first married couple to sit in cabinet together. Three children. Ed: Balliol Coll, Oxford (BA PPE); LSE (MSC economics); Harvard (Kennedy scholar).

CHALLENGERS
Andrew Lee (C) Cllr, North Yorkshire CC. Voted Leave. Contested Sheffield Central 2010. **Lewis Thompson** (Ukip) Urged voters to vote Labour in seats where no Ukip candidate was running.

CONSTITUENCY PROFILE
In addition to the three closely-connected towns in its name to the southwest of Leeds, this seat also contains the town of Knottingley, home to a further 14,000 people. About one in 40 in the constituency is non-white. A former coalmining area, its main industries now include manufacturing and retail. Two fifths of jobs are in routine and semi-routine occupations, well above average, and typical incomes are lower than both Yorkshire and national averages. A safe seat, its predecessors of Pontefract and Normanton have been represented only by Labour since 1935.

EU REFERENDUM RESULT
69.3% Leave   Remain 30.7%

Northampton North

CONSERVATIVE HOLD MAJORITY 807 (2.0%)

MICHAEL ELLIS
BORN Oct 13, 1967
MP 2010-

Criminal barrister, worked on legal aid cases. Regular contributor for broadcast media on constitution and monarchy. Member, Society of Conservative Lawyers. Lifelong Northampton man, selected by open primary. Cllr, Northampton CC 1997-2001. Treasury whip and deputy Commons leader 2016-. Campaigned for extra funds to reduce potholes, granted in the 2014 budget. Remainer, voted for Article 50. Chairman, APPG for Queen's Diamond Jubilee 2010-13. Ed: Wellingborough Sch; University of Buckingham (LLB); Inns of Court School of Law, City University (BVC).

	Electorate	Turnout %	from 2010 %	Change
	58,183	69.40		
*M Ellis C	19,065	47.22	+4.84	
S Keeble Lab	18,258	45.22	+11.08	
J Bullock Ukip	1,404	3.48	-12.65	
G Smid LD	1,015	2.51	-1.04	
S Miller Green	636	1.58	-2.24	

CHALLENGERS
Sally Keeble (Lab) MP, Northampton North 1997-2010. Former journalist and comms dir. Leader, Southwark BC 1990-93. Hon fellow, South Bank University. Parly under-sec: international development 2002-03; transport 2001-02. PPS to Hilary Armstrong 1999-2001. **Jonathan Bullock** (Ukip) Told Michael Ellis he would not stand if he admitted that Brexit "was right". Contested Kettering 2015 as independent.

CONSTITUENCY PROFILE
Northampton North is more densely populated than its southern neighbour. It contains most of the campuses of the University of Northampton and about 7,000 students live in the constituency. Just over a sixth of Northampton North's residents are non-white, while income in the seat is below both the East Midlands and the national averages, but about the same as in Northampton South. House prices and home ownership in the area are both low. It is a classic bellwether, having been held by whichever party has been in government since its creation in 1974.

EU REFERENDUM RESULT
60.3% Leave   Remain 39.7%

Northampton South

CONSERVATIVE HOLD MAJORITY 1,159 (2.8%)

ANDREW LEWER
BORN Jul 18, 1971
MP 2017-

Worked in publishing before entering politics. MEP 2014-17; spokesman on education and culture. Awarded MBE for services to local govt in 2014. Campaigned for Brexit on the basis that David Cameron's renegotiation was not good enough. Cllr, Derbyshire CC 2005-15; council leader 2009-13. Governor, University of Derby. Dir, Derbyshire Historic Buildings Trust. Vice-chairman, Millbank Club. Interested in the arts. Married, one son. Ed: Queen Elizabeth's Grammar School; Newcastle University (BA history); Downing Coll, Cambridge (MA history).

	Electorate	Turnout %	from 2010 %	Change
	60,993	67.28		
A Lewer C	19,231	46.87	+5.30	
K McKeever Lab	18,072	44.04	+12.23	
R Gibbins Ukip	1,630	3.97	-14.32	
J Hope LD	1,405	3.42	-0.88	
S Mabbutt Green	696	1.70	-1.91	

CHALLENGERS
Kevin McKeever (Lab) Qualified barrister. PR consultant, quit as a partner of Portland in 2017 to launch a new reputation and political risk advisory agency. Jeremy Corbyn sceptic. Contested: Northampton South 2015; Harborough 2010. **Rose Gibbins** (Ukip) Civil servant who has worked for NHS and Foreign Office. Contested Northampton South 2015. **Jill Hope** (LD) Corporate banker: Barclays; HSBC. Instrumental in team

that relocated Barclaycard from London to Northampton.

CONSTITUENCY PROFILE
Containing the city centre, Northampton South is a young seat in which a low proportion of residents are over 65 and almost two thirds are under the age of 45. It is a diverse seat, since about a fifth of residents are non-white. Home ownership is below average, while more than a fifth of households are privately rented. The seat has been held by the Conservatives for most of its history. Since its creation in 1974, it has only been held by Labour between 1997 and 2005.

EU REFERENDUM RESULT
59.0% Leave   Remain 41.0%

Northamptonshire South

CONSERVATIVE HOLD MAJORITY 22,840 (35.1%)

ANDREA LEADSOM
BORN May 13, 1963
MP 2010-

Leading Brexiteer who reached the final two in the 2016 Tory leadership contest; dropped out after telling *The Times* being a mother made her a better choice for PM than Theresa May because it meant she had a "very real stake" in Britain's future. Previously had a career in the City, including at Barclays and Invesco Perpetual. Contested Knowsley South 2005. Leader of the House of Commons 2017-. SoS, Defra 2016-17; energy minister 2015-16. Treasury economic sec 2014-15. Mocked for referring to Jane Austen as a "living author" in parliament. Devout Christian.

	Electorate	Turnout %	from 2010 Change %
	85,756	75.79	
*A Leadsom C	40,599	62.46	+2.31
S Johnson Lab	17,759	27.32	+10.58
C Lofts LD	3,623	5.57	-0.36
N Wickens Ukip	1,363	2.10	-11.38
D Donaldson Green	1,357	2.09	-1.60
J Phillips Ind	297	0.46	

Wants to repeal foxhunting ban. Cllr, South Oxon DC 2003-07. Married, two sons, one daughter. Ed: Tonbridge Girls' GS; University of Warwick (BA political science).

CHALLENGERS
Sophie Johnson (Lab) Founder, Big Eye Dear healthcare comms consultancy. Freelance medical writer and translator. Chairwoman, Northamptonshire South CLP. **Chris Lofts**

(LD) Retired. Cllr, South Northamptonshire C 2015-.

CONSTITUENCY PROFILE
A sprawling rural seat, Northamptonshire South's biggest settlements are the market towns of Brackley and Towcester, although its largest population centre is suburban Northampton. It has the largest number of homeowner mortgages in the country. The mean income in the seat is well above average. Silverstone race course straddles the border with Buckinghamshire. Since it was recreated in 2010, the Tories have not received less than half of the vote.

EU REFERENDUM RESULT

53.3% Leave	Remain 46.7%

Norwich North

CONSERVATIVE HOLD MAJORITY 507 (1.1%)

CHLOE SMITH
BORN May 17, 1982
MP 2009-

Former management consultant at Deloitte. Seconded to Conservatives' implementation unit. Gained seat in 2009 by-election to become the youngest member of the Commons, youngest Conservative MP for more than 30 years and youngest Conservative woman ever in the Commons. Assistant whip 2017-; parly under-sec NI office 2017. Ruffled feathers among more experienced Conservative MPs as govt whip 2010-11. Treasury economic sec 2011-12; parly sec, Cabinet Office 2012-13, quit to focus on constituency role. Remainer, voted to trigger Article 50. Married, one child.

	Electorate	Turnout %	from 2010 Change %
	66,924	68.58	
*C Smith C	21,900	47.72	+4.01
C Jones Lab	21,393	46.61	+13.15
H Lanham LD	1,480	3.22	-1.12
A Holmes Green	782	1.70	-2.74
L Matthews Pirate	340	0.74	

Ed: Swaffham Sixth Form Coll; University of York (BA English literature).

CHALLENGERS
Chris Jones (Lab) Retired NHS psychiatric consultant who worked with mentally ill offenders in prison, hospital and the community. Works for a local charity supporting people appealing against cuts to disability benefits. Contested Norfolk PCC 2016. **Hugh Lanham** (LD) Founder of his

own chartered accountancy business.

CONSTITUENCY PROFILE
Norwich North is a sparser and more residential area than its southern neighbour. Nearly a fifth of residents are 65 or older. Home ownership is much higher than in Norwich South, although incomes tend to be lower on average than in Norwich South. The seat was Labour from its creation in 1950 until the Tories won it in 1983. Labour regained it in 1997 and held onto it until 2009, when Chloe Smith won the by-election triggered by Ian Gibson's resignation following the expenses controversy.

EU REFERENDUM RESULT

56.7% Leave	Remain 43.3%

Norwich South

LABOUR HOLD MAJORITY 15,596 (30.4%)

CLIVE LEWIS
BORN Sep 11, 1971
MP 2015-

	Electorate	*Turnout %*	*Change from 2010 %*
	74,182	69.23	
*C Lewis Lab	31,311	60.96	+21.69
L Hempsall C	15,715	30.60	+7.12
J Wright LD	2,841	5.53	-8.10
R Bearman Green	1,492	2.91	-11.02

Grew up on a council estate in Northampton, first in family to go to university. Former BBC eastern region's chief political reporter and army reservist who toured Afghanistan in 2009. Spoken of as a possible future Labour leader. Campaigned against Brexit, and resigned from shad cab to vote against triggering Article 50. Describes himself as a "proud socialist". Rebelled over nuclear weapons, tuition fees and immigration. Shadow SoS: BEIS 2016-17; defence 2016. Described Chris Leslie, long-time critic of Jeremy Corbyn, as a "lonely, bitter man" after he criticised Labour for not winning the election. Ed: University of Bradford (BA economics; SU president).

CHALLENGERS
Lana Hempsall (C) Businesswoman in energy markets sector. Set up physiotherapy practice in 1999. Registered blind and uses a guide dog. Contested Denton and Reddish 2015. **James Wright** (LD) Worked in the IT industry for 20 years, including for BBC. Runs his own IT consultancy. **Richard Bearman** (Green) Cllr,

Norwich CC 2009-17; former Green group leader.

CONSTITUENCY PROFILE
Norwich South is the denser and more urban of the two Norwich seats, and contains the city centre. Home to over 18,000 16-24 year-olds, it contains the University of East Anglia and Norwich University of the Arts. Over 50 per cent of residents are in either social or private rented accommodation. From its creation in 1950 until 1987 the seat was a Labour/Conservative marginal. The only party other than Labour to have held it since 1987 was the Liberal Democrats between 2010 and 2015.

EU REFERENDUM RESULT
40.5% Leave   Remain 59.5%

Nottingham East

LAB CO-OP HOLD MAJORITY 19,590 (49.8%)

CHRIS LESLIE
BORN Jun 28, 1972
MP 2010-; 1997-2005

	Electorate	*Turnout %*	*Change from 2010 %*
	61,762	63.68	
*C Leslie Lab Co-op	28,102	71.46	+16.90
S Murray C	8,512	21.64	+0.87
B Holliday LD	1,003	2.55	-1.64
R Hall-Palmer Ukip	817	2.08	-7.87
K Boettge Green	698	1.77	-8.09
D Bishop Elvis	195	0.50	

MP for Shipley 1997-2005. Became dir, New Local Government Network after losing seat. Member, GMB. Remainer opposed to leaving single market; voted against triggering Article 50. Founding member, Open Britain. Vocally sceptical of Jeremy Corbyn: nominated Owen Smith for leadership 2015. Shadow: chancellor of the exchequer May-Sep 2015; chief sec to Treasury 2013-15; Treasury min 2010-13. Cllr, Bradford MBC 1994-98. Married. Ed: University of Leeds (BA politics and parliamentary studies; MA industrial and labour studies).

CHALLENGERS
Simon Murray (C) Barrister. Chairman, Sherwood Conservative Association. **Barry Holliday** (LD) Former IT support worker who retrained as a history teacher. Held roles in Unison and ATL. **Robert Hall-Palmer** (Ukip) Owns and operates string of car parks in Newark. Previously contested parish council elections. **Kat Boettge** (Green) Psychotherapist.

CONSTITUENCY PROFILE
A varied region, comprising some of the city of Nottingham and a number of its suburbs. Average house prices fall significantly below the average for the East Midlands. A young electorate, due in large part to the large student population, and much more ethnically diverse that the rest of the East Midlands, with 17 per cent Asian and Asian British and 9 per cent BAC population. Very low levels of home ownership, at 40 per cent with high levels of social and private renting. A safe Labour seat, which has been held by the party since 1992, with a record 19,590 majority in 2017.

EU REFERENDUM RESULT
42.9% Leave   Remain 57.1%

Nottingham North

LAB CO-OP HOLD MAJORITY 11,160 (29.1%)

ALEX NORRIS
BORN Feb 4, 1984
MP 2017-

Trade union organiser, Unison. Cllr, Nottingham CC 2011-; held adults and health portfolio. Member: Co-op party; GMB. Chairman of governors, Rosslyn Park Primary Sch. Close ally of outgoing MP Graham Allen, who stepped down citing ill health. Signed a letter calling on Jeremy Corbyn to resign and supported Owen Smith's 2016 leadership bid. Anglican. Married. Ed: Manchester GS; University of Nottingham (BA politics).

CHALLENGERS
Jack Tinley (C) Corporate banker, Lloyds. Trustee of a

	Electorate	Turnout %	from 2010 %	Change
	66,894	57.28		
A Norris Lab Co-op	23,067	60.20	+5.64	
J Tinley C	11,907	31.07	+10.07	
S Crosby Ukip	2,133	5.57	-12.94	
T Jones LD	674	1.76	-0.64	
K Jones Green	538	1.40	-1.67	

charity that works with at-risk children. Brexiteer. Fostered several children. Contested Hackney South and Shoreditch 2015. **Stephen Crosby** (Ukip) Manufacturing engineer in aerospace industry. **Tad Jones** (LD) Works in the healthcare research sector, with interest in science policy. Member, ALDE. **Kirsty Jones** (Green) Paediatric critical care nurse, Queen's Medical Centre, Nottingham. Chairwoman, Nottingham Green Party.

CONSTITUENCY PROFILE
Containing a significant proportion of urban Nottingham, this is a relatively young area, in which more than three fifths are aged under 45 and nearly a quarter under 16. About three quarters of residents are white British, with black and mixed-race residents accounting for most of the rest. It has the highest median income of the three main Nottingham seats, although it is lower than in nearby Gedling. Nottingham North has elected Labour MPs since its creation in 1955, with the sole exception of 1983, when it elected a Conservative MP by a mere 362 votes.

EU REFERENDUM RESULT

63.8% Leave	Remain 36.2%

Nottingham South

LABOUR HOLD MAJORITY 15,162 (31.5%)

LILIAN GREENWOOD
BORN Mar 26, 1966
MP 2010-

Career as a Unison regional organiser, manager and officer. Nominated Owen Smith for leadership 2016; Andy Burnham 2015. Shadow transport sec 2015-16; resigned from shad cab after feeling ignored and undermined by Jeremy Corbyn, and believing he did not have what it takes to be leader. Remainer; voted against triggering Article 50. Member: Fabian Society; Fawcett Society. Married, three daughters. Ed: Canon Slade Sch, Bolton; St. Catherine's Coll, Cambridge (BA economics and social and political science); Southbank Polytechnic (MSc sociology and social policy).

	Electorate	Turnout %	from 2010 %	Change
	71,178	67.62		
*L Greenwood Lab	30,013	62.36	+14.74	
J Hunt C	14,851	30.86	-0.80	
T Sutton LD	1,564	3.25	-0.28	
D Hollas Ukip	1,103	2.29	-8.98	
A McGregor Green	598	1.24	4.15	

CHALLENGERS
Jane Hunt (C) Caseworker for Nicky Morgan MP. Previously worked in sales management for a telecoms company. Cllr, Charnwood BC 2011-15. Contested: Nottingham South 2015; Leicester East 2010, 2005. **Tony Sutton** (LD) Manager at Unilever, later worked for Boots. Cllr, Nottingham CC 2005-11. Contested Nottingham South 2005. **David Hollas** (Ukip) Retired army officer. Military historian.

CONSTITUENCY PROFILE
A large degree of economic inequality in the constituency, encompassing both high and low income areas. It is thus the most marginal of all the Nottingham seats, although it has remained Labour since 1992 and Lilian Greenwood secured a 15,162 majority in the 2017 election. A strikingly young demographic, due in large part to the fact that it has the second largest student population in the country. The seat contains the University of Nottingham campus and one site of Nottingham Trent University. Ethnically diverse with a 17 per cent Asian and 5 per cent BAC demographic.

EU REFERENDUM RESULT

46.5% Leave	Remain 53.5%

Nuneaton

CONSERVATIVE HOLD MAJORITY 4,739 (10.3%)

MARCUS JONES
BORN Apr 5, 1974
MP 2010-

Entrepreneur who ran a string of small and micro businesses prior to entering politics. Interested in local government and housing. Campaigned against fuel duty increases and to scrap beer duty escalator. One of 24 MPs to not declare battlebus expenses in 2015. CPS took no action. Parly under-sec, DCLG 2015-. PPS to Sajid Javid 2013-15. Occasional backbench rebel. Remainer, voted to trigger Article 50. Cllr, Nuneaton and Bedworth BC 2005-10; leader 2008-09. Married, one son, one daughter. Keen angler. Anglican. Ed: St Thomas More RC School, Nuneaton; King Edward VI Coll.

	Electorate	Turnout %	from 2010 %	Change
	69,201	66.57		
*M Jones C	23,755	51.57	+6.04	
P Johnson Lab	19,016	41.28	+6.43	
C Carpenter Ukip	1,619	3.51	-10.87	
R Brighton-Knight LD	914	1.98	+0.20	
C Brookes Green	763	1.66	-1.14	

CHALLENGERS
Philip Johnson (Lab)
Environmental consultant. Cllr, Warwickshire CC 2013-17; criticised Jeremy Corbyn's "unpopular leadership style" after 2017 local election losses. **Craig Carpenter** (Ukip) Contested local elections 2016. **Richard Brighton-Knight** (LD) Aesthetic doctor based in Warwick, Milton Keynes and Harley Street. Chairman, LD health policy working group 2004.

CONSTITUENCY PROFILE
This north Warwickshire seat, just north of Coventry, is characterised by higher than average home ownership but lower than average earnings. Overrepresented sectors in terms of residents' employment include manufacturing, retail and transport. Nuneaton has become in recent years an archetypal bellwether seat, having been the first key marginal to declare in 2015. It was gained by the Conservatives from Labour in 2010, and in 2015 they increased their majority from 2,000 to nearly 5,000, indicating that the Conservatives might win an overall majority.

EU REFERENDUM RESULT

64.5% Leave   Remain 35.5%

Ochil & Perthshire South

CONSERVATIVE GAIN MAJORITY 3,359 (6.2%)

LUKE GRAHAM
BORN Jun, 1985
MP 2017-

Chartered accountant. Dir and co-founder, Tech & The Beancounters accountancy firm for startups and SMEs. Formerly dir, Amplecom. Previously worked in finance at Tesco, the University of Sheffield and Marks & Spencer. Stint working in planning for Tough Mudder. Contested Ochil and Perthshire South 2015. Ed: University of Sheffield (BA economics and social policy); Chartered Institute of Management Accountants (ACMA accountancy).

CHALLENGERS
Tasmina Ahmed-Sheikh (SNP) MP for Ochil and Perthshire

	Electorate	Turnout %	from 2010 %	Change
	76,767	70.56		
L Graham C	22,469	41.48	+20.77	
*T Ahmed-Sheikh SNP	19,110	35.28	-10.72	
J Ross Lab	10,847	20.02	-8.40	
I Stefanov LD	1,742	3.22	+0.66	

2015-17. Solicitor and partner, Hamilton Burns WS. Awarded an OBE in 2014 for services to business and the Asian community. Formerly actress who starred in Asian TV serials. Winner, Scottish Asian businesswoman of the year award 2010. Investigated over professional standards during legal career by Law Society 2017. Member, SNP NEC. Advisory board member, Yes Scotland. Stood in elections for the Conservatives before defecting to the SNP in 2000. **Joanne Ross**

(Lab) Community education worker and Applied Theatre tutor. Former Alloa councillor.

CONSTITUENCY PROFILE
The largest town in this large and mostly rural seat is Alloa, home to around 19,000 people. Residents' average income is slightly above the Scottish average, and home ownership is about 5 per cent ahead of the Scottish average in this constituency. Labour held this seat from its creation in 2005 until the SNP landslide of 2015. Despite their victory in 2017, the Conservatives finished a fairly distant third here in the three previous elections.

EU REFERENDUM RESULT

39.5% Leave   Remain 60.5%

Ogmore

LABOUR HOLD MAJORITY 13,871 (37.3%)

CHRIS ELMORE
BORN Dec 23, 1983
MP 2016-

Former butcher's apprentice who won May 2016 by-election after Huw Irranca-Davies stepped down to seek election to Welsh Assembly. Worked in further education after graduating from university. Cllr, Vale of Glamorgan CC 2008-17. Contested Vale of Glamorgan 2015. Campaigned to Remain in the EU, voted to trigger Article 50. Opposition whip 2016-17. Yet to rebel. Chairman, APPG for the coalfield communities. Member: Barry Communities First; Barry YMCA Hub. Lives with partner. Ed: Cardiff Metropolitan University (BA history and culture).

	Electorate	Turnout %	from 2010 % Change
	56,661	65.66	
*C Elmore Lab	23,225	62.43	+9.48
J Wallis C	9,354	25.14	+9.20
H Marshall PC	2,796	7.52	-2.57
G Davies Ukip	1,235	3.32	-12.06
G Francis LD	594	1.60	-1.44

CHALLENGERS
Jamie Wallis (C) MD, Fields Associates digital forensic consultancy. Cllr, Pencoed TC. Contested Welsh Assembly elections 2016. **Huw Marshall** (PC) Runs digital media consultancy. Former head of digital development, S4C. Member, CSAS; Digital Teaching Council for Wales. **Glenda Davies** (Ukip) Contested Ogmore by-election 2016. Qualified nurse and teacher. **Gerald Francis** (LD) Plumber

and plumbing teacher. Former county and district cllr.

CONSTITUENCY PROFILE
Ogmore is a rural south Wales seat located between Swansea and Cardiff, named after the river that runs through it. Its largest town is Pencoed, which has fewer than 10,000 residents. Home ownership is well above average, mainly at the expense of privately rented accommodation. Manufacturing is a significant source of local jobs in a seat where residents are likely to do routine and semi-routine work. The seat has returned a Labour MP at every election since its creation in 1918.

EU REFERENDUM RESULT

58.9% Leave	Remain 41.1%

Old Bexley & Sidcup

CONSERVATIVE HOLD MAJORITY 15,466 (32.2%)

JAMES BROKENSHIRE
BORN Jan 8, 1968
MP 2005-

Lawyer. Former partner, Jones Day Gouldens. MP for Hornchurch 2005-10 when constituency was dissolved. Worked on John Major's 1996 European election campaign. Previously vice-chairman, Young Conservatives. Campaigned to Remain, voted to trigger Article 50. SoS for Northern Ireland 2016-; faced some criticism for failing to broker restoration of Stormont power-sharing executive. Home Office minister who negotiated Abu Qatada's deportation 2012. Married, three children. Ed: Cambridge Centre for Sixth Form Studies; University of Exeter (LLB).

	Electorate	Turnout %	from 2010 % Change
	66,005	72.79	
*J Brokenshire C	29,545	61.50	+8.70
D Hackett Lab	14,079	29.31	+10.31
F Vachha Ukip	1,619	3.37	-14.87
D Heffernan LD	1,572	3.27	-0.24
D Moran Green	820	1.71	-1.15
M Jones BNP	324	0.67	+0.21
C Nwadikeduruibe CPA	83	0.17	

CHALLENGERS
Danny Hackett (Lab) Cllr, Bexley BC 2014-; the youngest councillor ever elected to Bexley Council; shadow cabinet member for regeneration and growth. Previously warned that "lifelong Labour voters cannot support us with the leadership team we have". **Freddy Vachha** (Ukip) London regional chairman, Ukip. Contested Chingford and Woodford Green 2015.

CONSTITUENCY PROFILE
Old Bexley and Sidcup is a southeast London seat on the border with Kent. It is demographically one of the older seats in London, with 19 per cent of residents aged 65 and over, compared to the London average of 11 per cent. Home ownership is well above average, with nearly four fifths of households owner-occupied. Among the overrepresented industries in the area are finance and construction. It is a safe Conservative seat, although in 1997 Labour came within 7 per cent of gaining it from Edward Heath, who held the seat from its creation in 1983 until 2001.

EU REFERENDUM RESULT

62.4% Leave	Remain 37.6%

Oldham East & Saddleworth

LABOUR HOLD MAJORITY 8,182 (17.4%)

DEBBIE ABRAHAMS
BORN Sep 15, 1960
MP 2011-

Public health consultant, and former director of public health research group at University of Liverpool. Chairwoman, Rochdale Primary Care Trust 2002-07; resigned over the use of private health companies in the NHS. Was chairwoman of Labour Party health cttee and organised an inquiry into the effectiveness of international health systems. Shadow SoS DWP 2016-. Shadow min disabled people 2015-16. PPS to Andy Burnham 2011-15. Contested Colne Valley 2010. Married, two daughters. Ed: University of Salford (BSc biochemistry and physiology);

	Electorate	Turnout %	from 2010 % Change
	72,223	65.13	
*D Abrahams Lab	25,629	54.49	+15.08
K Ali C	17,447	37.09	+11.18
I Bond Ukip	2,278	4.84	-14.39
J Smith LD	1,683	3.58	-9.28

University of Liverpool (MEd health education and public health).

CHALLENGERS
Kashif Ali (C) Barrister and former law tutor at University of Manchester. Former dep chairman, Manchester Conservative Federation. Contested Oldham East and Saddleworth 2011, 2010. **Ian Bond** (Ukip) Law student, campaign clashed with his final year exams. **Jonathan Smith** (LD) Former dir of social services in Tameside and NHS chief exec in North West.

CONSTITUENCY PROFILE
This seat, on the eastern edge of Greater Manchester, contains the eastern outskirts of Oldham and stretches to the Pennines. It is more rural and affluent, and less ethnically diverse, than its neighbour Oldham West. The Lib Dems came within 103 votes of unseating former MP Phil Woolas in 2010, but their vote has receded in successive elections. The seat is relatively new, created in 1997, but no Oldham seat has elected an MP from any party other than Labour at an election since 1955.

EU REFERENDUM RESULT

59.9% Leave	Remain 40.1%

Oldham West & Royton

LAB CO-OP HOLD MAJORITY 17,198 (37.6%)

JIM MCMAHON
BORN Jul 7, 1980
MP 2015-

Varied career as a town centre manager, technician at the University of Manchester and a delivery driver. Extensive experience in local government; was involved in devolution negotiations for Greater Manchester. Cllr, Oldham MBC 2003-16; leader 2011-16. Centre-left Remain supporter who was elected in the December 2015 by-election following the death of Michael Meacher. Voted for the Article 50 bill. PPS to Tom Watson 2016. Shadow minister for devolution 2016-. Awarded OBE for leading regeneration of Oldham 2015. Leader of Labour group and vice-chairman of

	Electorate	Turnout %	from 2010 % Change
	72,418	63.23	
*J McMahon Lab Co-op	29,846	65.18	+10.40
C Glenny C	12,648	27.62	+8.64
R Keating Ukip	1,899	4.15	-16.47
G Harkness LD	956	2.09	-1.60
A King Green	439	0.96	-0.99

Local Government Association 2015-.. Fellow, RSA. Married, two children.

CHALLENGERS
Christopher Glenny (C) Consultant, PA Consulting Group. Former home affairs adviser to the Conservative Party. School governor. Married, two children. **Garth Harkness** (LD) Maths teacher and support worker for SEN students. Cllr: Oldham MBC 2012-, shadow cabinet member for education and skills; Saddleworth PC 2011-15. Former caseworker for Gordon Birtwistle MP. School governor.

CONSTITUENCY PROFILE
Oldham West is a diverse seat, with over a quarter of the population being Asian or of Asian descent. It is a less affluent seat than the North West average and about a quarter of households live in the social rented sector. The seat has elected Labour MPs since it was created in 1997. The 2015 by-election in which Jim McMahon was elected was seen as Jeremy Corbyn's first electoral test as leader of the Labour Party.

EU REFERENDUM RESULT

61.3% Leave	Remain 38.7%

Orkney & Shetland

LIBERAL DEMOCRAT HOLD MAJORITY 4,563 (19.6%)

ALISTAIR CARMICHAEL
BORN Jul 15, 1965
MP 2001-

Combative, media-friendly figure from the Lib Dems' centre-left, now their chief whip. Career began in the hotel industry. Studied law and practised as a solicitor. SoS for Scotland 2013-15. Quit the frontbench to vote for a referendum on EU membership in 2008, but campaigned to Remain in 2016. Taken to election court in 2015 after leaking a memo, and later admitted to lying. Successfully campaigned against deportation of Sakchai Makao, a Thai Shetlander 2006. Married, two sons. Ed: Islay HS; University of Aberdeen (Scots law LLB, Dip LP).

	Electorate	Turnout %	from 2010 Change %
	34,164	68.13	
*A Carmichael LD	11,312	48.60	+7.21
M Brett SNP	6,749	28.99	-8.80
R Barton Lab	2,664	11.44	+4.30
J Halcro Johnston C	2,024	8.70	-0.21
R Smith Ukip	283	1.22	-3.54
S Hill Ind	245	1.05	

CHALLENGERS
Miriam Brett (SNP) Aged 25 at time of campaign. Worked in policy research and as a senior economic adviser to SNP's Westminster group. Prominent role in Yes campaign 2014. **Robina Barton** (Lab) Has worked in social care, administration, heritage, tourism and as an HGV driver. **Jamie Halcro Johnston** (C) Member of Scottish parliament for Highlands and Islands region

2017-. Self-employed freelance consultant. Contested Moray 2005. **Robert Smith** (Ukip) Orkney fisherman. Contested Orkney and Shetland 2015, 2010. **Stuart Hill** (Ind) Pensioner.

CONSTITUENCY PROFILE
Orkney and Shetland is the second smallest seat by population. There is a high rate of part-time work and unemployment is very low. Main industries include construction, transport, agriculture, forestry and fishing. The seat has been held by Liberal candidates for all but 15 years since 1937, and was former Liberal Leader Jo Grimond's seat for 33 years.

EU REFERENDUM RESULT

40.3% Leave   Remain 59.7%

Orpington

CONSERVATIVE HOLD MAJORITY 19,461 (38.6%)

JO JOHNSON
BORN Dec 23, 1971
MP 2010-

Worked as: a corporate financier for Deutsche Bank; a journalist, associate editor of the *Financial Times*. Brother of Boris Johnson. On the left of the party and unostentatious. Minister for universities, science, research and innovation 2015-. Head of Number 10 policy unit 2013-15 under David Cameron, helped develop the Conservative manifesto. Assistant whip to Treasury 2012-14. Pro-European; campaigned to Remain in the EU. Particular interest in India and improving trade connections. Married to award-winning *Guardian* writer, two children. Ed: Balliol Coll, Oxford

	Electorate	Turnout %	from 2010 Change %
	67,906	74.31	
*J Johnson C	31,762	62.94	+5.53
N de Gruchy Lab	12,301	24.38	+8.79
A Feakes LD	3,315	6.57	-0.22
B Philp Ukip	2,023	4.01	-12.66
T Galloway Green	1,060	2.10	-1.43

(BA modern history); Institut d'Etudes Européennes.

CHALLENGERS
Nigel de Gruchy (Lab) Born in Nazi German-occupied Jersey. Worked as EFL teacher in Spain and France and became active in NASUWT. **Alex Feakes** (LD) Physics teacher, previously accountant and finance director. Cllr for eight years. Contested Lewisham and Penge 2015. **Brian Philp** (Ukip) Father of Chris Philp, MP for Croydon South.

Tamara Galloway (Green) Statistician and computer scientist.

CONSTITUENCY PROFILE
Orpington is a southeast London seat within the borough of Bromley. Nine in 10 residents in the seat are white. Mean incomes are well above the national average, if slightly below the London average, and four in five households are owner-occupied. The seat has elected Conservative MPs since 1945 except for when it was held by the Liberals between 1962 and 1970. The 2017 election is the first time Labour has finished second in the seat since 1959.

EU REFERENDUM RESULT

57.5% Leave   Remain 42.5%

Oxford East

LAB CO-OP HOLD MAJORITY 23,284 (43.2%)

ANNELIESE DODDS
BORN Mar 16, 1978
MP 2017-

Former senior lecturer in public policy at Aston University. Took over from Andrew Smith, former Labour Oxford East MP who held the seat for 30 years. Scottish. South East MEP 2014-, member: conference of delegation chairs; economic and monetary affairs cttee; special cttee on tax rulings. Delivered a speech on tax avoidance in the European parliament while cradling young daughter in solidarity with working mothers. Former acting dir, National Institute for Health Research, Patient Safety, King's Coll. Previously invited professor at Kosovan universities. Shadow

	Electorate	Turnout %	from 2010 %	Change
	78,360	68.78		
A Dodds Lab Co-op	35,118	65.16	+15.14	
S Bartington C	11,834	21.96	+2.08	
K Johnson LD	4,904	9.10	-1.66	
L Sanders Green	1,785	3.31	-8.31	
C Artwell Ind	255	0.47	+0.16	

Treasury min 2017-. Married, two children. Ed: St Hilda's Coll, Oxford (BA PPE); University of Edinburgh (MA social policy); LSE (PhD government).

CHALLENGERS
Suzanna Bartington (C) Clinical researcher, University of Birmingham. Cllr: Oxfordshire CC 2017; Witney TC 2015-. Remain campaigner. **Kirsten Johnson** (LD) International concert pianist, recorded 14 albums. Contested Chesham

and Amersham 2015. Cllr, Oxfordshire CC 2017-.

CONSTITUENCY PROFILE
This seat contains most of Oxford itself, including the city centre, many of Oxford University's colleges and Oxford Brookes University. About 26,000 students live in the seat, over a quarter of the population. More than half of residents are aged between 18 and 44 and home ownership is low, with social and private renting each accounting for about half of households. Although the seat was won by the Tories when it was created in 1983, it has only elected Labour MPs since 1987.

EU REFERENDUM RESULT

32.5% Leave   Remain 67.5%

Oxford West & Abingdon

LIBERAL DEMOCRAT GAIN MAJORITY 816 (1.4%)

LAYLA MORAN
BORN Sep 12, 1982
MP 2017-

Former maths and physics teacher. Works for an education company providing revision courses. First MP of Palestinian descent. Pro-EU. Roots in community action, led a campaign to save a local community centre. Contested: Oxford West and Abingdon 2015; Battersea 2010. International background, her father is a British EU ambassador; her mother is Palestinian. Polyglot. Ed: Imperial Coll, London (BSc physics); Brunel University (MA comparative education).

CHALLENGERS
Nicola Blackwood (C) MP for

	Electorate	Turnout %	from 2010 %	Change
	79,289	75.70		
L Moran LD	26,256	43.75	+14.80	
*N Blackwood C	25,440	42.39	-3.30	
M Tidball Lab	7,573	12.62	-0.09	
A Harris Ukip	751	1.25	-5.67	

Oxford West and Abingdon 2010–17. South African born musician. Voted against same-sex marriage in 2013 after suggesting she would vote in favour. Health min 2016-17. PPS to Matthew Hancock MP 2013-15. Vice-chairwoman, Conservative Party 2010-13. Ed: St Anne's Coll, Oxford; Emmanuel Coll, Cambridge. **Marie Tidball** (Lab) Disability law researcher, disabled rights activist, established Oxford Labour Disability Network. Cllr, Oxford CC.

CONSTITUENCY PROFILE
Oxford West and Abingdon is less dense and urban than its neighbour, taking in a rural area around Oxford which contains Abingdon to the south and Kidlington to the north. The seat is on average older and less ethnically diverse than Oxford East, with considerably higher incomes. The constituency is home to about 10,000 full-time students, a figure still much higher than average although less than the number in Oxford East. Created in 1983, the seat had a Conservative MP until 1997, followed by a Liberal Democrat representative until 2010.

EU REFERENDUM RESULT

38.0% Leave   Remain 62.0%

Paisley & Renfrewshire North

SNP HOLD MAJORITY 2,613 (5.6%)

GAVIN NEWLANDS
BORN Feb 2, 1980
MP 2015-

Electorate	Turnout %	from 2010 Change %
67,436	69.12	
*G Newlands SNP	17,455	37.45 -13.29
A Taylor Lab	14,842	31.84 -0.91
D Gardiner C	12,842	27.55 +15.30
J Boyd LD	1,476	3.17 +1.08

Business manager of restaurant chain. Campaigned for Remain. Has demonstrated support for Jeremy Corbyn on social media. Shadow SNP spokesman for sport 2016-. Select cttee, backbench business 2015-17. Cllr, Renfrewshire C 2011-15. Was forced to defend claiming £15,000 in expenses for Business UK flights to and from London in 2016. Former treasurer, St James' Pre-5 Centre. Rugby fan; played for Paisley RFC for 17 years. Married, two daughters. Ed: Trinity HS; James Watt Coll.

CHALLENGERS
Alison Taylor (Lab) Senior dir, national property consulting firm, and chartered surveyor. Joined Labour in 1998 having campaigned for a Yes vote in the devolution referendum 1997. Campaigned to Remain in the EU. **David Gardiner** (C) Worked as a civil servant in the Scotland office, and as a policy adviser for the Scottish Conservatives. Served as deputy dir of desearch for the Better Together campaign 2014. **John Boyd** (LD) Retired businessman. Campaigned on improving NHS and education standards.

CONSTITUENCY PROFILE
A homogeneous northwest Glasgow seat consisting of a 97 per cent white British and 60 per cent Christian population with generally low levels of education. There are a significant proportion of homeowners. A varied constituency, ranging from Glasgow airport through former industrial shipping and tannery areas to the more leafy and affluent edges of Glasgow. Home to engineering company Doosan Babcock. The working-class centre of Paisley still provides the bulk of the electorate, the seat was previously a Labour stronghold and switched to SNP in 2015.

EU REFERENDUM RESULT

35.5% Leave   Remain 64.5%

Paisley & Renfrewshire South

SNP HOLD MAJORITY 2,541 (6.1%)

MHAIRI BLACK
BORN Sep 12, 1994
MP 2015-

Electorate	Turnout %	from 2010 Change %
61,344	68.00	
*M Black SNP	16,964	40.67 -10.27
A Dowling Lab	14,423	34.58 4.07
A Thomson C	8,122	19.47 +11.84
E McCartin LD	1,327	3.18 +1.00
P Mack Ind	876	2.10

The UK's youngest MP since 1832: elected at the age of 20 while an undergraduate. Called Westminster "old and defunct" and an "old boys' club". Viral maiden speech criticised the government for dismantling the welfare state, declared "Food banks are not part of the welfare state. They are a symbol that the welfare state is failing". Voted to Remain but had misgivings, said she "held her nose" while voting. Labelled a "champagne nationalist" for claiming almost £13,500 for Business UK flights to and from London. Very positive about Jeremy Corbyn's anti-austerity politics. Select cttee, work and pensions 2015-17. Ed: University of Glasgow (BA politics and public policy).

CHALLENGERS
Alison Dowling (Lab) Anti-poverty campaigner. **Amy Thomson** (C) Previously worked in civil service and at Deloitte. **Eileen McCartin** (LD) Scottish Lib Dem culture spokeswoman 2016-. Cllr, Renfrewshire C 1988-, dep leader 2007-12. Contested: Scottish parliament 2003; Paisley and Renfrewshire South 1997. **Paul Mack** (Ind) Cllr, Renfrewshire C 2012-, 1995-99. Known for controversial outbursts.

CONSTITUENCY PROFILE
Modelled on the old Paisley South seat, this seat has a diverse electorate. There are high levels of unemployment and a significant number of long-term sick and disabled people. Almost 28 per cent of households are socially rented. The seat, and its Paisley South predecessor, had only elected Labour MPs for more than 30 years until Mhairi Black's victory over Labour's shadow foreign secretary Douglas Alexander in 2015.

EU REFERENDUM RESULT

34.8% Leave   Remain 65.2%

Pendle

CONSERVATIVE HOLD MAJORITY 1,279 (2.9%)

ANDREW STEPHENSON
BORN Feb 17, 1981
MP 2010-

Former self-employed insurance broker. Particularly interested in jobs and employment: holds an annual job fair; campaigned for the National Living Wage. National dep chairman, Conservative Future 2001-02. PPS to four ministers including Boris Johnson. Campaigned to Leave the EU. Campaigned against hospital and healthcare cuts. Appointed government whip after 2017 general election. Chairman, Conservative Assoc 2006. Cllr, Macclesfield BC 2003-07. Volunteer ambulance first responder. President, Nelson Brass Band 2010-13. Patron, railway campaign group Selrap.

	Electorate	Turnout %	from 2010 %	Change
	64,963	69.05		
*A Stephenson C	21,986	49.02	+1.82	
W Blackburn Lab	20,707	46.17	+11.24	
G Lishman LD	941	2.10	-1.25	
B Parker BNP	718	1.60		
I Barnett Green	502	1.12	-1.23	

Methodist. Ed: Poynton County HS; Royal Holloway, University of London (BSc business management).

CHALLENGERS
Wayne Blackburn (Lab) Caseworker for Labour MP Kate Green. Cllr, Pendle BC 2015-. Born with cerebral palsy. **Gordon Lishman** (LD) Former DG of Age Concern charity. Led campaigns on issues that affect older people; awarded CBE for contribution to improving pensions, particularly for older women.

CONSTITUENCY PROFILE
A Pennine seat, straddling the traditional boundary between Yorkshire and Lancashire. The textile industry is long gone, leaving small commuter and tourist towns of terraced Victorian housing. A marginal between Labour and the Tories, although the Lib Dems also have significant strength and had an overall majority on the council until 2008. Largely working class. The population is 80 per cent white with a significant Pakistani and Muslim population.

EU REFERENDUM RESULT
63.2% Leave   Remain 36.8%

Penistone & Stocksbridge

LABOUR HOLD MAJORITY 1,322 (2.7%)

ANGELA SMITH
BORN Aug 16, 1961
MP 2005-

Born in Grimsby. Father was a printer and former fisherman. Worked for NHS, then became English lecturer at Dearne Valley Coll. Campaigned to remain. Staunch Jeremy Corbyn critic, reportedly told him to quit. Shadow min: Defra 2014-15; dep leader of the commons 2011-14. Opp asst whip 2010-11. PPS to Yvette Cooper 2005-08. Came to brink of resignation over abolition of 10p tax 2008. MP for Sheffield Hillsborough 2005-10. Came under fire during expenses scandal 2009, submitted claims for four beds for a one bedroom flat. Cllr, Sheffield CC. Member, Unison. Married, two

	Electorate	Turnout %	from 2010 %	Change
	71,293	69.83		
*A Smith Lab	22,807	45.81	+3.78	
N Wilson C	21,485	43.15	+15.48	
J Booker Ukip	3,453	6.94	-15.98	
P Baker LD	2,042	4.10	-2.21	

stepchildren. Supports Sheffield Wednesday. Ed: Toll Bar Sch; University of Nottingham (BA English).

CHALLENGERS
Nicola Wilson (C) Co-founder, steel business. Contested Leeds Central 2015. **John Booker** (Ukip) Dir, Ace domestics, domestic appliance retailer and engineer 1985-. Cllr, Sheffield CC 2014-. **Penny Baker** (LD) Worked in NHS for 28 years. Cllr, Stannington 2012-, 2007-11; dep leader, Lib Dem group.

CONSTITUENCY PROFILE
The seat is most heavily populated on its eastern fringe, occupied mostly by commuters to Sheffield, Leeds and Manchester, with the Peak District National Park to the west. Almost all residents are white and a fifth are in retirement, with high levels of home ownership and low levels of social rent. By the standards of South Yorkshire, one of Labour's most reliable bedrocks in England, this counts as a marginal. Division of opposition support between the Conservatives and Liberal Democrats keeps Penistone and Stocksbridge in Labour hands.

EU REFERENDUM RESULT
60.7% Leave   Remain 39.3%

Penrith & The Border

CONSERVATIVE HOLD MAJORITY 15,910 (34.2%)

RORY STEWART
BORN Jan 3, 1973
MP 2010-

	Electorate	Turnout %	from 2010 % Change
	65,139	71.34	
*R Stewart C	28,078	60.42	+0.76
L McEvoy Lab	12,168	26.18	+11.82
N Hughes LD	3,641	7.84	-0.69
K Wilde Ukip	1,142	2.46	-9.73
D Lawson Green	1,029	2.21	-3.05
J Davies Ind	412	0.89	

Former soldier, diplomat, author and Harvard professor. Dir of Havard's Carr Centre for Human Rights. Founded Afghanistan NGO Turquoise Mountain. Tutor to Prince William and Harry. Former Labour supporter who began his parliamentary career on select committee; appointed to cabinet after 2015 election. Rarely rebels. Supported Remain campaign but now wants to make a success of Brexit; voted for Article 50 bill. In 2011, his campaign convinced OFCOM to ensure mobile phone companies would provide 98 per cent 4G coverage. Episcopalian. Married, one son. Ed: Eton Coll;

Balliol Coll, Oxford (BA history and philosophy).

CHALLENGERS
Lola McEvoy (Lab) Campaigns and communications manager for Living Wage Foundation. Previously a campaign organiser for Labour. **Neil Hughes** (LD) Teacher. Cllr, Eden DC 2003-. Member of Michael Apted's 7UP group. **Keryanne Wilde** (Ukip) Founder and CEO of CERT UK Ltd, a community emergency

response team. Won Spirit of Cumbria award 2015.

CONSTITUENCY PROFILE
Nestled between the Pennines and the Lake District, this Cumbrian seat is mostly farmed terrain, with a few small towns. More than half the population is aged over 45 and there are high levels of home ownership. The 2011 census showed that 99 per cent of constituents are white and there is a large Christian contingent. The 2001 foot-and-mouth epidemic resulted in a large swing to the Conservatives, which they maintain. Their majority has increased in each election since 2010.

EU REFERENDUM RESULT

55.2% Leave   Remain 44.8%

Perth & Perthshire North

SNP HOLD MAJORITY 21 (0.0%)

PETE WISHART
BORN Mar 9, 1962
MP 2001-

	Electorate	Turnout %	from 2010 % Change
	71,743	71.82	
*P Wishart SNP	21,804	42.32	-8.20
I Duncan C	21,783	42.28	+9.55
D Roemmele Lab	5,349	10.38	+2.24
P Barrett LD	2,589	5.02	+1.23

First MP to appear on Top of the Pops; he played the keyboard in Runrig from the late 1980s until his election in 2001. Formerly a trained community worker and columnist for Scots independent newspaper. SNP chief whip 2001-07. Shadow SNP Westminster group leader 2015-. Scottish affairs cttee chairman 2015-. "Foul-mouthed", humorous tweet attacking unionist opponents caused controversy in 2017. Westminster Public Affair's 'Parliamentary Tweeter of the Year' 2015. Remainer. Generally toes party line but was against renewing Trident and UK air strikes in Iraq. Musicians' Union.

Member of parliamentary rock band MP4. Married but separated, one son. Education: Queen Anne HS, Dunfermline; Moray House Coll of Education (Dip CommEd).

CHALLENGERS
Ian Duncan (C) Appointed peer and Scotland office minister 2017. MEP 2014-17. Before becoming MEP was head of Scottish EU office and EU parly adviser. **David Roemmele** (Lab) Building surveyor. **Peter Barrett** (LD) Recruitment, press officer and

council group leader Perth and Kinross C 2003-.

CONSTITUENCY PROFILE
Covers a huge swathe of remote Scottish mountains, forest and moorlands as well as the city of Perth itself, where most of the electorate lives. It is an affluent area with earnings above the national average, although there are pockets of deprivation, mostly in and around the city of Perth itself. Residents of Perth and Perthshire North are predominantly white. While it is historically a Tory/SNP battleground, the SNP have held the seat since 1995, but it is now an ultra-marginal.

EU REFERENDUM RESULT

39.9% Leave   Remain 60.1%

Peterborough

LABOUR GAIN MAJORITY 607 (1.3%)

FIONA ONASANYA
BORN Aug 23, 1983
MP 2017-

Electorate	Turnout %	from 2010	Change %
71,522	66.75		
F Onasanya Lab	22,950	48.07	+12.47
*S Jackson C	22,343	46.80	+7.11
B Sellick LD	1,597	3.35	-0.42
F Radic Green	848	1.78	-0.81

Solicitor with expertise in property development, DC Law. Formerly worked at Nockolds LLP, Eversheds and Howes Percival. Cllr, Cambridgeshire CC 2014-17. Has said she wants to become Britain's first black female prime minister and a "modern day Esther". Evangelical Christian; participates in Evangelical Alliance's public leadership initiatives. Ed: Netherhall Sch; University of Hertfordshire (LLB); Coll of Law (LPC).

CHALLENGERS
Stewart Jackson (C) MP for Peterborough 2005-17. Appointed chief of staff to David Davis 2017. Previously: vice-president, Local Government Association; bank manager, Lloyds TSB. Cllr, Ealing BC 1990-98. Vigorous Brexiteer. Helped set up Conservative Voice. PPS to Owen Paterson 2010-11. Shadow communities and local government min 2008-10. Opposition whip 2007-08. Contested: Peterborough 2001; Brent South 1997. Married, one daughter. **Beki Sellick** (LD) Dir, SellickRail Ltd. Previously engineering manager for British Rail and its successors 1986-2016.

Fiona Radic (Green) Works in university administration in Cambridge.

CONSTITUENCY PROFILE
A Victorian industrial town, Peterborough is now a thriving retail and services centre. Proximate to London and with below average earnings, it has an encouraging business climate and was the fastest growing city in the UK between 2001 and 2011. The city has a sizeable Asian population and 13.7 per cent of the population are Muslim. It is a key Labour/ Conservative marginal, reclaimed by Labour in 2017 after it lost the seat in 2005.

EU REFERENDUM RESULT

61.3% Leave   Remain 38.7%

Plymouth Moor View

CONSERVATIVE HOLD MAJORITY 5,019 (11.1%)

JOHNNY MERCER
BORN Aug 17, 1981
MP 2015-

Electorate	Turnout %	from 2010	Change %
69,342	65.50		
*J Mercer C	23,567	51.89	+14.29
S Dann Lab	18,548	40.84	+5.65
W Noble Ukip	1,849	4.07	-17.41
G Reed LD	917	2.02	-0.95
J Pope Green	536	1.18	-1.22

Eccentric former army captain and Afghanistan veteran. Opposed Brexit. Entered politics with a view to improving veterans' physical and mental healthcare. Select cttee, defence 2015-. Attracted media attention following radio interview in which he responded, "You don't put diesel in a Ferrari" to an enquiry as to whether he had ever taken drugs. First parly campaign was subject to police investigation following allegations he breached spending regs, no charges pressed. Sleeps on boat in east London to avoid "obscene" house prices in capital. Married, two daughters.

Ed: Eastbourne Coll; RMA Sandhurst.

CHALLENGERS
Sue Dann (Lab) Cllr, Plymouth CC 2015-. Former lecturer at South Devon College. National employment manager, Working Links 2007-16. **Graham Reed** (LD) Consultant and founder, Sci-Glass consultancy. Cllr, Stirling Council 2007-12. Former master glassblower and fellow, British Society of Scientific Glassblowers 1970-2010.

CONSTITUENCY PROFILE
Plymouth is home to the largest naval base in Europe. For Plymouth Moor View, this remains an important industry: 10 per cent of those employed work in public administration and defence. The population is largely white British. The proportion of people without any qualifications exceeds the national average, as does the quantity of people living in social housing. Average wages are significantly lower than the UK average. It is a Labour/ Conservative marginal. Before 2015 it had been held by Labour since 1992, when former SDP leader David Owen stood down.

EU REFERENDUM RESULT

66.4% Leave   Remain 33.6%

Plymouth Sutton & Devonport

LAB CO-OP GAIN MAJORITY 6,002 (13.3%)

LUKE POLLARD
BORN Apr 10, 1980
MP 2017-

Adviser on construction projects. Former head of public affairs, ABTA travel association. Born and raised in Plymouth. Contested: Plymouth Sutton and Devonport 2015; Devon South West 2010. Member of GMB and Unite. Plymouth Argyle supporter. Ale enthusiast, member of the Campaign for Real Ale. Ed: Christleton HS; University of Exeter (BA politics; student union president).

CHALLENGERS
Oliver Colvile (C) MP for Plymouth Sutton and Devonport 2010-17. Former communications consultant. Contested Plymouth

	Electorate	Turnout %	from 2010 %	Change
	76,584	58.26		
L Pollard Lab Co-op	23,808	53.36	+16.67	
*O Colvile C	17,806	39.90	+2.13	
R Ellison Ukip	1,148	2.57	-11.46	
H Bewley LD	1,106	2.48	-1.71	
D Sheaff Green	540	1.21	-5.88	
D Bamping Ind	213	0.48		

Sutton 2005, 2001. Became renowned in parliament for his interest in hedgehogs. Proprietor, Oliver Colvile & Associates. Account dir, Saatchi & Saatchi. Conservative Party agent. Member, Barbican Arts Centre. Cricketer. Ed: Stowe Sch, Buckingham. **Richard Ellison** (Ukip) Charity administrator. Mariner who represents UK on World Sailing Speed Record Council. **Henrietta Bewley** (LD) Freelance singing teacher.

Formerly business analyst for British Airways. Executive board member, Hammersmith and Fulham Lib Dems.

CONSTITUENCY PROFILE
Located on the southwest coast, Plymouth Sutton and Devonport covers Plymouth city centre, but also includes Devonport naval base, home to seven nuclear submarines. It has a large student population; about 17,000 of its residents are students. Earnings and home ownership levels are below the national average. It is a Labour/Conservative marginal, with Labour regaining the seat in 2017 after a narrow loss in 2015.

EU REFERENDUM RESULT

54.4% Leave   Remain 45.6%

Pontypridd

LABOUR HOLD MAJORITY 11,448 (28.7%)

OWEN SMITH
BORN May 2, 1970
MP 2010-

Former producer of the *Today* programme, BBC Radio 4. Resigned from the shadow cabinet to mount controversial leadership challenge 2016. Interested in urban regeneration and welfare reform. Contested Blaenau Gwent by-election 2006. Shadow SoS: Northern Ireland 2017-; Wales 2012-15. Shadow min: work and pensions 2015-16; Wales 2010-11. Special adviser to Paul Murphy as sec of state for Wales and NI. Dir, Amgen. Son of Professor Dai Smith. Member, Unite. Cites Jean Jaures among political heroes. Local man, Pontypridd RFC fan. Married, two sons,

	Electorate	Turnout %	from 2010 %	Change
	60,566	65.87		
*O Smith Lab	22,103	55.40	+14.35	
J Ash C	10,655	26.71	+9.37	
F Elin PC	4,102	10.28	-1.20	
M Powell LD	1,963	4.92	-8.02	
R Hunter-Clarke Ukip	1,071	2.68	-10.74	

one daughter. Ed: University of Sussex (BA history and French).

CHALLENGERS
Juliette Ash (C) Dir of training and development consultancy. Previously worked at Centre for Social Justice 2006-12. Development consultant, MaST International Group Ltd 2002-06. **Fflur Elin** (PC) Partner, Darwin Gray law firm. Policy coordinator, Plaid Cymru 1998-99. **Michael Powell** (LD) Plumbing and heating engineer.

Had to apologise for using the term "retards" to describe council officers and contractors in a Facebook post. Cllr, Rhondda Cynon Taff CBC 1999-. Contested Pontypridd 2010.

CONSTITUENCY PROFILE
Covers the Taf and Ely valleys and is home to a large middle-class population, a strong service sector and the University of South Wales. There are high levels of home ownership and wages are above the regional average. According to the 2011 census, 96.2 per cent of residents are white. Pontypridd is a safe Labour seat and has been held by Labour since the 1920s.

EU REFERENDUM RESULT

46.5% Leave   Remain 53.5%

Poole

CONSERVATIVE HOLD MAJORITY 14,209 (28.5%)

ROBERT SYMS
BORN Aug 15, 1956
MP 1997-

Former managing director of family plant hire firm. Contested Walsall North 1992. Campaigned to Leave the EU. Shadow spokesman environment, transport and the regions 1999-2001. Opposition whip 2003. Shadow minister: communities and local government 2005-07; office of the deputy PM 2003-05. Lord Commissioner, Treasury 2016-; assistant whip 2012-13. Vice-chairman, Conservative Party 2001-02. Select committees include: admin 2016-17; finance and services 2013-15; regulatory reform 2010-12; health 2007-10, 1997-2000. Cllr: Wiltshire CC 1985-97; North Wiltshire DC

	Electorate	Turnout %	from 2010 %	Change
	73,811	67.54		
*R Syms C	28,888	57.95	+7.85	
K Taylor Lab	14,679	29.45	+16.57	
M Plummer LD	4,433	8.89	-2.86	
A Oliver Green	1,299	2.61	-2.03	
M Caine DDI	551	1.11		

1984-87. Separated, two children. Ed: Colston's Sch, Bristol.

CHALLENGERS
Kate Taylor (Lab) Teacher. Chairwoman, Poole Labour Party. **Mike Plummer** (LD) Business and management lecturer, Bournemouth and Poole College. Former Cllr, Poole BC. Contested: Bournemouth West 2015; New Forest West 2010. **Adrian Oliver** (Green) Former bookkeeper and bank clerk. Cllr, Camden BC 2006-10.

Contested: Poole 2015; Holborn and St Pancras 2005.

CONSTITUENCY PROFILE
Poole is an affluent town on England's south coast. The area covers the Sandbanks peninsula, which has the largest concentration of expensive properties outside of London. The proportion of homeowners, particularly those who own their properties outright, significantly exceeds the national average. There is a considerable elderly population, with 20,000 over the age of 65. It is a safe Conservative seat, and has been held by the party since its recreation in 1950.

EU REFERENDUM RESULT

57.4% Leave   Remain 42.6%

Poplar & Limehouse

LABOUR HOLD MAJORITY 27,712 (47.1%)

JIM FITZPATRICK
BORN Apr 4, 1952
MP 1997-

Glaswegian former firefighter. Publicly condemned the segregation of men and women at Muslim weddings in 2009. Shadow minister: transport 2010-13; environment 2010. Environment minister 2009-10. Junior minister: transport 2007-09; employment relations and postal services 2006-07. Whip 2001-05. Select cttees: Defra 2013-17; transport 2013-15. Keen interest in sport: president of Millwall Rugby Club, Poplar and Blackwall Rowing Club and Poplar Bowls. Divorced, remarried. One daughter and one son from first marriage. Ed: Holyrood RC Sch.

	Electorate	Turnout %	from 2010 %	Change
	87,274	67.39		
*J Fitzpatrick Lab	39,558	67.26	+8.71	
C Wilford C	11,846	20.14	-5.25	
E Bagshaw LD	3,959	6.73	+2.52	
O Rahman Ind	1,477	2.51		
B Lant Green	989	1.68	-3.14	
N McQueen Ukip	849	1.44	-4.68	
D Barker ND	136	0.23		

CHALLENGERS
Christopher Wilford (C) Head of policy, Chartered Institute of Arbitrators. Ran for Tower Hamlets mayor 2014. Contested Poplar and Limehouse 2015. **Elaine Bagshaw** (LD) Consultant in the City. Contested Poplar and Limehouse 2015. Parly assistant to Lynne Featherstone 2008. **Oliur Rahman** (Ind) Cllr, Tower Hamlets C 2010. Bangladeshi.

CONSTITUENCY PROFILE
Covering deprived parts of Tower Hamlets and the gleaming skyscrapers of Canary Wharf, Poplar and Limehouse is a constituency of extremes: 20 per cent of those in employment work in the financial sector and earnings are well above the regional average yet a significant proportion of residents live in social housing. The constituency is young – more than 80 per cent of residents are under the age of 45. It is diverse, with 42.2 per cent of residents of Asian descent, many of them Bangladeshi. It is a safe Labour seat, and its predecessor seat was once held by Clement Attlee.

EU REFERENDUM RESULT

34.2% Leave   Remain 65.8%

Portsmouth North

CONSERVATIVE HOLD MAJORITY 9,965 (21.1%)

PENNY MORDAUNT
BORN Mar 4, 1973
MP 2010-

Former magician's assistant from a military family who pursued a career in business and comms. Known to court publicity, most notably her participation in the second series of ITV diving show *Splash!* in 2014. Accused of trivialising the Commons when she made a speech on poultry using rude language as a dare. Minister: work and pensions 2016-; defence and armed forces 2015–16. Parly under-sec, communities and local government 2014–15. Royal Navy reservist. Divorced, lives with her partner. Ed: Oaklands RC Comp; University of Reading (BA philosophy).

	Electorate	Turnout %	from 2010 Change %
	71,374	66.14	
*P Mordaunt C	25,860	54.78	+7.76
R Khan Lab	15,895	33.67	+9.86
D Sanders LD	2,608	5.52	-0.71
M Fitzgerald Ukip	1,926	4.08	-15.00
K Hawkins Green	791	1.68	-1.52
J Jenkins Libertarian	130	0.28	

CHALLENGERS
Rumal Khan (Lab) Worked as a project director for Portsmouth ,CC. Elected ethnic minority officer for Portsmouth Labour Party 2015. **Darren Sanders** (LD) Account manager in public affairs and consultation. Cllr: Portsmouth CC 2012-; previously Lambeth BC. Contested: Portsmouth North 2015, 2010, 2001; Streatham 2005. **Mike Fitzgerald** (Ukip) International manager for Hewlett Packard.

Contested Portsmouth North 2015, 2010.

CONSTITUENCY PROFILE
Portsmouth North contains the Navy Command Headquarters on Whale Island. A key Conservative/Labour marginal and bellwether seat, it has been won by the party that obtained the largest number of seats at every election since its creation in 1974. High proportion of children and teenagers and low proportion of people aged over 65. Below average levels of education and quality of jobs, particularly compared to the region; however, enjoys low levels of unemployment.

EU REFERENDUM RESULT

63.7% Leave   Remain 36.3%

Portsmouth South

LABOUR GAIN MAJORITY 1,554 (3.5%)

STEPHEN MORGAN
BORN Jan 17, 1981
MP 2017-

The first Labour MP for Portsmouth South in its 99-year history. Former charity chief exec. Previously worked for the Royal Borough of Kensington and Chelsea and Basingstoke Voluntary Action, commuting from Portsmouth. Cllr, Portsmouth CC 2016-; Labour group leader. PPS to Andrew Gwynne 2017-. Called for Jeremy Corbyn to stand down in June 2016, but says Labour's leader now has his "full backing". Ed: Priory Sch, Southsea; Portsmouth Coll; University of Bristol (BSc politics & sociology); Goldsmiths, University of London (MA politics).

	Electorate	Turnout %	from 2010 Change %
	69,785	63.86	
S Morgan Lab	18,290	41.04	+21.51
*F Drummond C	16,736	37.55	+2.75
G Vernon-Jackson LD	7,699	17.28	-5.02
K Chippindall-Higgin Ukip	1,129	2.53	-10.82
I McCulloch Green	712	1.60	-5.91

CHALLENGERS
Flick Drummond (C) MP for Portsmouth South 2015-17. Former insurance broker, Ofsted inspector and TA intelligence officer. Contested: Portsmouth South 2010; Southampton Itchen 2005. Select cttee, women and equalities 2015-17. Married, four children. **Gerald Vernon-Jackson** (LD) Cllr, Portsmouth CC 2003-.

CONSTITUENCY PROFILE
Portsmouth has a long naval history as the home of the largest Royal Navy base, with defence among the main local industries. Portsmouth South contains the principal naval base, the docks and shipyards and many postwar council estates. It also contains Portsmouth University, and is the more student-heavy of the two Portsmouth seats with a high proportion of young people. It is less homogeneous than the rest of the South East, with more ethnic diversity. Low levels of home ownership and very high levels of private renting. Higher unemployment than its neighbour but still below the national average.

EU REFERENDUM RESULT

51.8% Leave   Remain 48.2%

Preseli Pembrokeshire

CONSERVATIVE HOLD MAJORITY 314 (0.7%)

STEPHEN CRABB
BORN Jan 20, 1973
MP 2005-

Former marketing consultant and policy manager at the London Chamber of Commerce. Interested in energy policy and human rights; election observer in Bosnia-Herzegovina 1998. Hit by sexting scandal during his 2016 Conservative leadership bid, after which he was not reappointed to the cabinet. SoS for: work and pensions 2016; Wales 2014-16. Whip and parly under-sec for Wales 2012-14. Select cttees: Treasury 2008-09; Welsh affairs 2005-07. Leader of Project Umubano, the Conservatives' social action project in Rwanda and Sierra Leone. Contested Preseli

	Electorate	Turnout %	from 2010 % Change
	58,540	72.08	
*S Crabb C	18,302	43.37	+2.98
P Thompson Lab	17,988	42.63	+14.48
O Williams PC	2,711	6.42	+0.22
C Overton Ind	1,209	2.87	
B Kilmister LD	1,106	2.62	+0.70
S Bale Ukip	850	2.01	-8.48
R Maile Worth	31	0.07	+0.02

Pembrokeshire 2001. Raised by a single mother in council housing. Married, one daughter, one son. Ed: Tasker Milward Sch, Haverfordwest; University of Bristol (BSc politics); London Business Sch (MBA).

CHALLENGERS
Philippa Thompson (Lab) Media and policy adviser to Eluned Morgan AM. Deputy registrar, Pembrokeshire CC. **Owain**

Williams (PC) Leader of Welsh nationalist political party Llais Gwynedd. Cllr, Gwynedd CC 2012-.

CONSTITUENCY PROFILE
Wales' most westerly seat, at the tip of the Pembrokeshire peninsula. Contains Milford Haven port, key to Britain's energy network with its oil refineries and natural gas terminal. Southern Pembrokeshire is very English in its culture and language, long known as "little England beyond Wales". The seat has mostly returned Conservative MPs since 1970, but is hardly safe, falling to Labour in 1992.

EU REFERENDUM RESULT

55.3% Leave   Remain 44.7%

Preston

LAB CO-OP HOLD MAJORITY 15,723 (44.2%)

MARK HENDRICK
BORN Nov 2, 1958
MP 2000-

Engineer and college lecturer. MEP for Central Lancashire 1994-99. Particular interest in foreign affairs and defence. Select cttees: foreign affairs 2012-17; int dev 2009-10; European scrutiny 2001-04. Chairman and vice-chairman of several APPGs, including on China and Romania. Opp asst whip 2010-13. PPS to: Ivan Lewis 2009-10; Jack Straw 2007-08; Margaret Beckett 2003-07. Cllr, Salford CC 1987-95. Chairman, Eccles Labour Party 1990-94. Member: Co-operative Party; GMB. Married. Ed: Salford GS; Liverpool Poly (BSc electrical and electronic engineering);

	Electorate	Turnout %	from 2010 % Change
	57,791	61.60	
*M Hendrick Lab Co-op	24,210	68.01	+11.97
K Beaty C	8,487	23.84	+3.86
S Platt Ukip	1,348	3.79	-11.57
N Darby LD	1,204	3.38	-0.33
A Power Green	348	0.98	-3.93

University of Manchester (MSc computer science; Cert Ed); Volkshochschule, Hanau (German).

CHALLENGERS
Kevin Beaty (C) Farmer. Owns green waste composting business. Cllr, Eden DC 2015-; council leader. Contested European parliament 2014. **Simon Platt** (Ukip) Self-employed chartered engineer. Former lecturer at University of Central Lancashire.

CONSTITUENCY PROFILE
The middle slice of the city of Preston, the administrative centre for Lancashire. The old textile and manufacturing industries have disappeared; the major employment sectors now include retail, distribution, call centres and the defence industry. There is a significant Asian and Muslim demographic in the seat. Long-term unemployment is quite high and health, job quality and social mobility are below national and regional averages. Since the creation of a single Preston seat and the removal of the more affluent suburbs into neighbouring seats it has been a reliable Labour constituency.

EU REFERENDUM RESULT

55.7% Leave   Remain 44.3%

Pudsey

CONSERVATIVE HOLD MAJORITY 331 (0.6%)

STUART ANDREW
BORN Nov 25, 1971
MP 2010-

	Electorate	Turnout %	from 2010 % Change
	72,622	74.30	
*S Andrew C	25,550	47.35	+0.94
I McCargo Lab Co-op	25,219	46.74	+9.16
A Nixon LD	1,761	3.26	-0.52
B Buxton Yorkshire	1,138	2.11	
M Wharton Ind	291	0.54	

Experienced charity fundraiser, previously at British Heart Foundation and Martin House Children's Hospice, where he led a team that raised £4m in a year. Member, Institute of Fundraisers. Contested Wrexham 1997. Cllr, Leeds CC 2003-10. Brexit supporter. Interested in health: chairman, APPG on heart disease; former patron, Westminster Health Forum. PPS to: Patrick McLoughlin 2015-17; Francis Maude 2012-15. Vice-chairman, Conservative Party 2016-. Grew up on a council estate in Wales. Patron, LGBTory. Partner. Ed: Ysgol David Hughes, Anglesey.

CHALLENGERS
Ian McCargo (Lab Co-op) Project manager at healthcare software company, EMIS Health. Contested Leeds CC 2016. Vice chairman, Pudsey CLP. Trustee, Rosebank Millenium Green Trust. **Allen Nixon** (LD) Works in administration at the University of Leeds. Former stockbroker. Public speaker and specialist in radio broadcasting. Arts enthusiast: supports local arts venues and serves on the Lib Dems Arts Advisory Group.

CONSTITUENCY PROFILE
A long spindly seat between Leeds and Bradford and is mostly an affluent residential area for commuters to these cities. Pudsey has a homogeneous 93 per cent white demographic, boasting good health, high quality jobs, social mobility, and high levels of education. Home ownership is prevalent and few live in social housing. Finance, insurance and education are big areas of economic output. Held by the Conservatives for most of its history, but often by narrow margins. In the 1997 landslide election it fell to Labour and was regained by the Tories in 2010.

EU REFERENDUM RESULT

48.6% Leave	Remain 51.4%

Putney

CONSERVATIVE HOLD MAJORITY 1,554 (3.3%)

JUSTINE GREENING
BORN Apr 30, 1969
MP 2005-

	Electorate	Turnout %	from 2010 % Change
	65,026	72.12	
*J Greening C	20,679	44.10	-9.67
N Patil Lab	19,125	40.78	+10.80
R Mercer LD	5,448	11.62	+5.27
B Fletcher Green	1,107	2.36	-2.47
P Ward Ukip	477	1.02	-3.63
L Quizeen Ind	58	0.12	

Trained accountant. Rising star of the party with quick ascent to the front bench. First openly LGBT female cabinet minister, after coming out on Twitter in 2016. Resolute EU Remain campaigner. Contested Ealing, Acton and Shepherd's Bush 2001. Appointed SoS for education and min for women and equalities 2016-. Economic sec, HM Treasury 2010-11. SoS for: international development 2012-16; transport 2011-12. Select cttees: public accounts 2010-11; work and pensions 2005-07. Vice-chairwoman, Conservative Party 2005-10. Daughter of steel workers from Rotherham.

Partner. Ed: University of Southampton (MA economics); London Business School (MBA).

CHALLENGERS
Dr Neeraj Patil (Lab) Doctor, worked in NHS for over 20 years. Foundation governor for Guy's and St Thomas' Hospital, and King's College Hospital. Cllr, Lambeth BC 2006-14; mayor 2010-11. Shortlisted for London Mayor in 2015, losing out on nomination to Sadiq Khan.

Born in India. **Ryan Mercer** (LD) Policy adviser, The Royal Society. Former caseworker to Simon Wright MP.

CONSTITUENCY PROFILE
Situated on the south bank of the Thames opposite Fulham, Putney is a largely affluent, owner-occupied suburbia. However, it is also home to a substantial amount of social housing, particularly in Roehampton. Boasting excellent health and job satisfaction and with 52 per cent educated to degree level, Putney has very low unemployment. Historically a Conservative seat that fell briefly to Labour in 1997.

EU REFERENDUM RESULT

27.8% Leave	Remain 72.2%

Rayleigh & Wickford

CONSERVATIVE HOLD MAJORITY 23,450 (42.4%)

MARK FRANCOIS
BORN Aug 14, 1965
MP 2001-

Served as a territorial army infantry officer during the Cold War with local Royal Anglican Regiment. Worked as self-employed consultant before first being elected. Contested Brent East 1997. Failed to secure nomination for Kensington-Chelsea by-election 1999. Cllr, Basildon DC 1991-95. Tends to be found on the right of the party, a long-time Eurosceptic who campaigned for Brexit. Notably pro-armed forces. Held a range of shadow ministerial positions 2004-10. Minister of state for: communities and local government 2015-16; defence 2012-15. Divorced. Ed: University

	Electorate	Turnout %	from 2010	Change %
	78,556	70.42		
*M Francois C	36,914	66.72	+12.07	
M Daniels Lab	13,464	24.34	+11.74	
P Smith Ukip	2,326	4.20	-18.08	
R Tindall LD	1,557	2.81	-0.23	
P Hill Green	1,062	1.92	-0.95	

of Bristol (BA history); King's Coll London (MA war studies).

CHALLENGERS
Mark Daniels (Lab) Worked as a train driver for 25 years. Trustee, ASLEF. Contested Essex CC 2016. Secretary, Rayleigh and Wickford CLP. **Peter Smith** (Ukip) Spent career working in transport sector, IT, and small businesses. Earnestly pro-Brexit. Accused Mark Francois MP of being too lazy to get as many Facebook likes as himself.

Deputy regional organiser, Essex. Cllr, Thurrock BC 2015-. **Ron Tindall** (LD) Former trade union organiser. Cllr: Dacroum BC 2013-; Hertfordshire CC 2009-. Began history degree at the age of 60.

CONSTITUENCY PROFILE
Seat in rural Essex consisting of small towns. Wickford is undergoing regeneration through the Thames Gateway project. Fairly affluent with low levels of unemployment and income higher than the region's average. The third highest rate of home ownership in the country. A safe Conservative seat created from Rayleigh in 2010.

EU REFERENDUM RESULT
67.7% Leave   Remain 32.3%

Reading East

LABOUR GAIN MAJORITY 3,749 (6.8%)

MATT RODDA
BORN Dec 15, 1966
MP 2017-

Education specialist. Worked on the academies programmes as a civil servant at the department for education. Former journalist, including at *The Independent*. Project manager and consultant for the voluntary sector. Cllr, Reading BC 2011-; campaigned to prevent closure of local centre for disabled adults. Contested: Reading East 2015; East Surrey 2010. Decided to become involved in public service after surviving 1999 Ladbroke Grove rail crash. Married, two children. Ed: University of Sussex.

CHALLENGERS
Rob Wilson (C) MP for Reading

	Electorate	Turnout %	from 2010	Change %
	75,522	73.14		
M Rodda Lab	27,093	49.05	+15.98	
*R Wilson C	23,344	42.26	-3.72	
J Woods LD	3,378	6.12	-1.25	
K Johannessen Green	1,093	1.98	-4.39	
M Turberville Ind	188	0.34		
A Kirkwood Active Dem	142	0.26		

East 2005-17. Entrepreneur. Published two books about the coalition and ministerial scandals. First MP selected by an open primary. Minister for civil society 2014-16. Parly under-sec to CMS 2016-17. Remainer but did not actively campaign; voted in favour of Article 50. PPS to: George Osborne 2013-14; Jeremy Hunt 2010-12. Cllr, Reading BC 2003-06, 1992-96; successfully campaigned for expansion of Reading station. **Jenny Woods**

(LD) Contested Reading East 2015.

CONSTITUENCY PROFILE
An affluent commercial centre and commuter town in Berkshire. Home to high tech and service industries, it has the second highest percentage of residents working in information and communication nationally. Contains the University of Reading and the majority of its students. Ethnically diverse with a large number of Indian and Pakistani residents. Labour overturned decades of Tory representation in 1997, but lost in 2005. Matt Rodda reclaimed the seat for Labour in 2017.

EU REFERENDUM RESULT
38.3% Leave   Remain 61.7%

Reading West

CONSERVATIVE HOLD MAJORITY 2,876 (5.6%)

ALOK SHARMA
BORN Sep 6, 1967
MP 2010-

Chartered accountant, Coopers & Lybrand Deloitte. Later went into banking: Nikko Securities, SE Banken. Previously chairman, Bow Group's economic affairs cttee. Inspired by Margaret Thatcher to deliver Conservative leaflets aged 11. Former Conservative vice-chairman for BME communities. Vocal supporter of Crossrail, HS2 and Heathrow expansion. Campaigned to Remain; voted to trigger Article 50. Minister for housing and planning 2017-. FCO parliamentary under-secretary 2016-17. PPS to: Oliver Letwin 2015-16; Mark Hoban 2010-12. Served as

	Electorate	Turnout %	from 2010 %	Change
	74,518	69.47		
*A Sharma C	25,311	48.90	+1.21	
O Bailey Lab	22,435	43.34	+9.39	
M O'Connell LD	3,041	5.87	+1.01	
J Whitham Green	979	1.89	-1.01	

David Cameron's infrastructure envoy for India. Married, two daughters. Ed: Reading Blue Coat Sch; University of Salford (BSc applied physics with electronics).

CHALLENGERS
Olivia Bailey (Lab) Research dir, Fabian Society. Formerly: political analyst, BBC News; adviser, Angela Eagle MP. Chairwoman, Labour Women's Network. **Meri O'Connell** (LD) Gum and sweets taster, Mondelez International. Cllr,

Reading BC 2012-. Contested Reading West 2015. **Jamie Whitham** (Green) Opposed to cuts to public services and favours greater investment.

CONSTITUENCY PROFILE
Slightly less affluent than its neighbour Reading East and has areas of deprivation, but average earnings of full-time employees are above the regional and national averages. The seat has benefitted from town centre regeneration and investment. A classic marginal, held by the Conservatives from its creation in 1983 until the Labour landslide of 1997. It remained Labour until 2010.

EU REFERENDUM RESULT
51.5% Leave   Remain 48.5%

Redcar

LAB CO-OP HOLD MAJORITY 9,485 (22.3%)

ANNA TURLEY
BORN Oct 9, 1978
MP 2015-

Long-time civil servant, having worked in cabinet office and DWP. Failed to receive nomination for Durham North West 2010. Strong supporter of animal rights, tabled a private members' bill in 2017 to introduce harsher sentences for animal cruelty. Hostile to Jeremy Corbyn: backed Andy Burnham 2015; resigned from shadow cabinet in 2016. One of 14 MPs singled out by Corbyn's 2016 campaign team and accused of abusing Corbyn and his allies. Remain supporter; voted to trigger Article 50. Attended an independent school on an academic scholarship but drove

	Electorate	Turnout %	from 2010 %	Change
	66,836	63.68		
*A Turley Lab Co-op	23,623	55.51	+11.65	
P Gibson C	14,138	33.22	+17.02	
J Mason LD	2,849	6.69	-11.78	
C Gallacher Ukip	1,950	4.58	-13.79	

Labour's bid to make private and state schools share facilities. Married. Ed: Ashford School.

CHALLENGERS
Peter Gibson (C) Former worker for Iron Trades Insurance company. Qualified solicitor; owns legal practice. **Josh Mason** (LD) Parly asst to previous Redcar MP Ian Swales. Publically apologised after taking a selfie in a crematorium and uploading it to Facebook and dating app Tinder. Cllr, Redcar and Cleveland BC 2011-; Lib

Dem group leader. Contested Redcar 2015.

CONSTITUENCY PROFILE
An industrial seat on the southern bank of the Tees estuary, which neighbours Middlesbrough. The majority of the population is English and 98.4 per cent is white. There are high levels of unemployment, especially among those aged between 50 and 74. Previously a safe Labour seat, held since its creation in 1974. The closure of the steelworks in 2009 was the cause of an immense swing in 2010, when the Lib Dems took the seat. Labour won it back in 2015.

EU REFERENDUM RESULT
67.7% Leave   Remain 32.3%

Redditch

CONSTITUENCY HOLD MAJORITY 7,363 (16.3%)

RACHEL MACLEAN
BORN Oct 3, 1965
MP 2017-

Technology entrepreneur and sales manager. Founded small businesses specialising in publishing IT content and HR software. Founder and director of charity Skilled and Ready, to help young people prepare for the world of work. Regional council member of the Confederation of British Industry. Co-chairwoman of West Midlands Combined Authority Mayoral Campaign for former John Lewis chief exec Andy Street. Contested Birmingham Northfield 2015. Fundraiser and community worker; volunteer consultant for LoveBrum. Married, four

	Electorate	Turnout %	from 2010 %	Change
	64,334	70.26		
R Maclean C	23,652	52.32	+5.22	
R Blake Lab	16,289	36.04	+4.93	
N Stote NHAP	2,239	4.95		
P Swansborough Ukip	1,371	3.03	-13.14	
S Juned LD	1,173	2.59	-0.46	
K White Green	380	0.84	-1.34	
S Woodhall Ind	99	0.22	-0.16	

children. Ed: St Hugh's Coll, Oxford (BSc psychology); Aston University (MSc work and organisational psychology); Stanford GSB (EPGC cert).

CHALLENGERS
Rebecca Blake (Lab) Teacher in adult learning. Cllr, Redditch BC 2011-16, 2003-07. Contested Redditch 2015. Co-founder and vice-chairwoman, Redditch Mental Health Action Group.

Neal Stote (NHAP) Runs family business. Alexandra Hospital campaigner.

CONSTITUENCY PROFILE
The seat is located in East Worcestershire. Redditch itself expanded after becoming a new town in the 1960s. This saw new housing developments spring up to home Birmingham's overspill population. Over a third of the population is employed in the manufacturing or retail industries. Redditch was won by Jacqui Smith on its creation in 1997, whose expenses and troubled stint as home sec led to defeat in 2010, and the Tories have since held this seat.

EU REFERENDUM RESULT

61.0% Leave   Remain 39.0%

Reigate

CONSTITUENCY HOLD MAJORITY 17,614 (32.7%)

CRISPIN BLUNT
BORN Jul 15, 1960
MP 1997-

Army officer, 1979-90; resigned commission as captain in order to stand for parliament. Worked as a political consultant and as special adviser to Malcolm Rifkind 1993-97. Contested West Bromwich East 1991. Pro-Brexit. Announced his use of party drug poppers during Commons debate in 2016. Anti-Trident - a public critic and rebel MP. Held a number of shadow ministerial roles from 2001 to 2010. Parly under-sec for prisons and probations 2010-12. Former chairman, Conservative Middle East Council. In 2010, ended marriage and came out as gay. Uncle of actress Emily Blunt. Ed:

	Electorate	Turnout %	from 2010 %	Change
	74,628	72.12		
*C Blunt C	30,896	57.40	+0.63	
T Brampton Lab	13,282	24.68	+11.87	
A Tarrant LD	5,889	10.94	+0.49	
J Essex Green	2,214	4.11	-2.57	
J Fox Ukip	1,542	2.86	-10.41	

Wellington College; Sandhurst; Durham University (BA politics); Cranfield University School of Management (MBA).

CHALLENGERS
Toby Brampton (Lab) Account manager for an automotive emission control technology company. **Anna Tarrant** (LD) Lib Dems campaigner since she was a teenager. Has worked as a probation officer, teacher, and tutor for Surrey Council's family learning team. Regional

co-ordinator of the Southeast Lib Dems. Cllr, Reigate and Banstead BC 2008-12. Contested Reigate 2015.

CONSTITUENCY PROFILE
Very affluent seat in eastern Surrey. Has good transport links to London, Brighton and the south coast so it is popular with commuters. Unemployment is low, and income is well above the regional and national averages. The demand for housing here has led to a 42 per cent rise in house prices between 2005 and 2015. Safe Conservative seat held by Crispin Blunt since 1997, although Labour gained an 11.9 per cent swing in 2017.

EU REFERENDUM RESULT

48.0% Leave   Remain 52.0%

Renfrewshire East

CONSERVATIVE GAIN MAJORITY 4,712 (8.8%)

PAUL MASTERTON
BORN Sep 2, 1985
MP 2017-

Former solicitor specialising in pensions law; worked for McGregors and then Pinsent Masons. Contested Scottish parliament 2016. The region's first Conservative MP for two decades. Voted to Remain, believes priority in the wake of Brexit is looking after business and protecting free trade. Strong policy interest in pensions, long-term savings and secure family units. Ed: George Watson Coll; University of Dundee (LLB).

CHALLENGERS
Kirsten Oswald (SNP) MP for Renfrewshire East 2015-17. Head of human resources, South

	Electorate	Turnout %	from 2010 %	Change
	70,067	76.70		
P Masterton C	21,496	40.00	+18.03	
*K Oswald SNP	16,784	31.23	-9.33	
B McDougall Lab	14,346	26.70	-7.32	
A Morton LD	1,112	2.07	+0.18	

Lanarkshire Coll. Previously worked in human resources for Motherwell Coll. Shadow SNP spokeswoman for armed forces and veterans 2015-17. Remainer. Unionist husband joined the Labour Party after 2015 election. Married, two sons. **Blair McDougall** (Lab) Senior Labour backroom figure, former leader of Better Together campaign. Worked as Labour special adviser, oversaw David Miliband's campaign. Openly critical of Jeremy Corbyn's politics. **Aileen Morton** (LD)

Cllr, Argyll and Bute CC 2012-; policy lead for economic development 2015-. Professional background in IT.

CONSTITUENCY PROFILE
The seat is located to the south of Glasgow. An affluent, middle-class commuter area with a high proportion of owner-occupiers and professionals. Has the largest Jewish population of any seat in Scotland, with almost half of Scotland's Jewish population living here. The SNP ousted Scottish Labour leader, Jim Murphy, in 2015. However, the Tories, who last held Renfrewshire East in 2005, won a majority of 4,712 in 2017.

EU REFERENDUM RESULT
25.7% Leave   Remain 74.3%

Rhondda

LABOUR HOLD MAJORITY 13,746 (41.7%)

CHRIS BRYANT
BORN Jan 11, 1962
MP 2001-

Former clergyman; stopped being a vicar when he realised he was gay, aged 25. Worked as Frank Dobson's election agent and as Labour's local govt development officer. Author of several political biographies and a book about the history of Christian socialism. Head of European affairs at the BBC 1998-2000. PPS to: Harriet Harman 2007-08; Lord Falconer 2005-06. Shadow leader of HoC 2015-16; resigned in protest to Jeremy Corbyn's leadership, warning the leader would be remembered as the man who broke the Labour Party. Contested Wycombe

	Electorate	Turnout %	from 2010 %	Change
	50,513	65.20		
*C Bryant Lab	21,096	64.05	+13.40	
B Cennard PC	7,350	22.32	-4.70	
V Crosbie C	3,333	10.12	+3.41	
J Kenrick Ukip	880	2.67	-10.00	
K Roberts LD	277	0.84	-0.66	

1997. Cllr, Hackney BC 1993-98. Chairman: Lab Movement for Europe; Christian Socialist Movement. First MP to hold civil partnership. Ed: Cheltenham Coll; Mansfield Coll, Oxford (BA English); Ripon Coll, Cuddesdon (MA cert theol).

CHALLENGERS
Branwen Cennard (PC) Local company director and TV producer for S4C, Tinopolis, Boomerang and BBC. Produced TV series *Iechyd Da* and

currently working on *Byw Celwydd*. Founder, Tarian. **Virginia Crosbie** (C) Maths teacher. Dir, Conservative Women's Organisation.

CONSTITUENCY PROFILE
A former coalmining territory which suffered economic deprivation with the departure of the mines. Predominantly white seat containing one of the highest proportions of UK-born residents nationally. Only 52 per cent of residents are in employment and average earnings are below the Welsh and UK-wide average. Safe Labour seat, held by Chris Bryant since 2001.

EU REFERENDUM RESULT
60.4% Leave   Remain 39.6%

Ribble Valley

CONSERVATIVE HOLD MAJORITY 13,199 (23.9%)

NIGEL EVANS
BORN Nov 10, 1957
MP 1992-

Pro-Brexit Welsh former convenience store owner. Spent one year as an independent backbencher after being charged with rape and sexual assault against seven men, was acquitted in 2014. Faced similar allegations 2016-17, but no charges brought. Supported Independence Day on June 23. Came out as gay in 2010, involved in LGBT group ParliOut. Worked on three US Presidential campaigns in 1980s; led Tory 2001 general election campaign in Wales. Contested: Ribble Valley 1991; Pontypridd 1989; Swansea West 1987. PPS to: William Hague 1997; Tony Baldry 1995-96; David

	Electorate	Turnout %	from 2010 %	Change
	77,968	70.80		
*N Evans C	31,919	57.82	+9.20	
D Hinder Lab	18,720	33.91	+11.33	
A Knox LD	3,247	5.88	+0.61	
G Sowter Green	1,314	2.38	-1.82	

Hunt 1993-95. Vice-chairman, Conservative Party 1999-2001. Shadow SoS for Wales 2001-03. Cllr, West Glamorgan CC 1985-91. Ed: University Coll, Swansea (BA politics).

CHALLENGERS
David Hinder (Lab) Retired businessman and finance worker. Winning contestant on ITV's *The Chase*. Contested: Ribble Valley 2015; Altrincham and Sale 1987. **Allan Knox** (LD) Worked in oil industry. Former agent for Chris Davies MP. Clitheroe mayor

2005-07. Cllr: Lancashire CC 2009-13; Ribble Valley BC 1999-.

CONSTITUENCY PROFILE
A predominantly rural seat to the northeast of Preston containing a considerable commuter and retired population. High levels of property ownership and low unemployment. Manufacturing is a key employer. Boundary changes in 2010 added more urban areas from South Ribble, and hence, a large number of Labour voters. Safe Tory seat, briefly won by the Lib Dems on a huge swing in the 1991 by-election, but was reclaimed in 1992.

EU REFERENDUM RESULT
58.7% Leave   Remain 41.3%

Richmond (Yorks)

CONSERVATIVE HOLD MAJORITY 23,108 (40.5%)

RISHI SUNAK
BORN May 12, 1980
MP 2015-

Businessman: director, Catamaran Ventures; co-founded an investment firm. Worked for charity hedge fund The Children's Investment. Was head of the BME Research Unit. Leave campaigner. Member of Cameron's secret 'A-list' 2015. Select cttee, environment, food and rural affairs 2015-17. Married, two daughters. Ed: Lincoln Coll; Oxford (BA PPE); Stanford University (MBA, Fulbright scholar).

CHALLENGERS
Dan Perry (Lab) Lead mechanical engineer for GE Power, formerly Alstom. Has

	Electorate	Turnout %	from 2010 %	Change
	80,920	70.46		
*R Sunak C	36,458	63.95	+12.57	
D Perry Lab	13,350	23.42	+10.22	
T Abel LD	3,360	5.89	-0.52	
C Pearson Yorkshire	2,106	3.69		
F Yorke Green	1,739	3.05	-1.23	

spent over 10 years working in the energy industry. Cllr, Newcastle CC 2015-. **Tobie Abel** (LD) IT contractor who works with a number of businesses in Europe and the US. Initially trained as an accountant. **Chris Pearson** (Yorkshire) Mental health nurse for 35 years; now a part-time support worker for an out-of-hours GP service. Concerned with the spending difference between Yorkshire and Westminster, and is campaigning for the creation

of a Yorkshire Parliament.
Fiona Yorke (Green) Learning consultant.

CONSTITUENCY PROFILE
A geographically vast seat that covers several small villages and hamlets in rural North Yorkshire. Residents are predominantly white and a significant number - nearly 14,000 - are retired. Defence is an important industry for the local economy because the seat includes the army base at Catterick Garrison. Average earnings match the regional average. It is one of the safest Conservative seats in the country and was held by William Hague from 1989 to 2015.

EU REFERENDUM RESULT
54.7% Leave   Remain 45.3%

Richmond Park

CONSERVATIVE GAIN MAJORITY 45 (0.1%)

ZAC GOLDSMITH
BORN Jan 20, 1975
MP 2017-, 2010-16

Journalist and former editor of *The Ecologist*. Left the party in rebellion over plans for the Heathrow runway, losing at the by-election as an independent candidate in 2016. Re-elected as a Conservative in 2017. Ran for London Mayor, losing to Labour's Sadiq Khan in 2016. Brexit supporter. Born into wealthy banking family who have strong roots to Conservative Party. Famously expelled from Eton College when cannabis was found in his room. Divorced, three children. Remarried, two children. Ed: Eton Coll; Cambridge Centre for Sixth Form Studies.

Electorate	Turnout %	from 2010 % Change
80,025	79.14	
Z Goldsmith C	28,588	45.14 -13.07
*S Olney LD	28,543	45.07 +25.80
C Tuitt Lab	5,773	9.12 -3.23
P Jewell Ukip	426	0.67 -3.50

CHALLENGERS
Sarah Olney (LD) MP for Richmond Park 2016-17. Qualified accountant. Finance manager at National Physical Laboratory. Firmly against govt plans for a third runway at Heathrow Airport. Married, two children. Ed: King's College, London (BA English language and literature). **Cate Tuitt** (Lab) Co-op activist and trained lawyer. Board member, London community land trust. Cllr, Tower Hamlets BC 1998-2002. **Peter Jewell** (Ukip) Former

magistrate. Ukip spokesman for justice 2016-.

CONSTITUENCY PROFILE
An affluent, middle-class suburban seat in southwest London. It consists of the residential areas bordering Richmond Park: Richmond, Kew and Kingston upon Thames. Characterised by low unemployment and a high proportion of residents employed in managerial or professional positions. Less ethnically diverse than the rest of London. Tory/Lib Dem marginal. Sarah Olney took the seat in the 2016 by-election. However, Goldsmith regained the seat in 2017.

EU REFERENDUM RESULT

28.7% Leave   Remain 71.3%

Rochdale

LABOUR GAIN MAJORITY 14,189 (29.6%)

TONY LLOYD
BORN Feb 25, 1950
MP 2017-; 1983-2012

Labour stalwart. MP for Stretford 1983-97 and Manchester Central 1997-2012, before becoming Greater Manchester's police and crime commissioner in 2012. He acted as Manchester's interim mayor 2015-17. Ran for Rochdale after Simon Danczuk was barred from standing due to sending explicit texts to a 17-year-old. Voted against Iraq war. Cllr, Trafford BC 1979-84. Shadow housing min 2017-. Chairman, PLP 2006-10. Married, four children. Ed: University of Nottingham (BSc mathematics); Manchester Business School (MA business administration).

Electorate	Turnout %	from 2010 % Change
78,064	64.11	
T Lloyd Lab	29,035	58.02 +11.88
J Howard C	14,216	28.41 +11.37
A Kelly LD	4,027	8.05 -2.23
C Baksa Ukip	1,641	3.28 -15.47
*S Danczuk ND	883	1.76
A Littlewood GM Homeless	242	0.48

CHALLENGERS
Jane Howard (C) Works in communications for Salford University. Cllr, Rochdale BC 2006-. **Andy Kelly** (LD) Youth and community worker. Runs a not-for-profit company which has raised over £1.3m for organisations in the north of England. Holds the UK record for TV game and quiz show appearances. Cllr, Rochdale BC 2010-. **Christopher Baksa** (Ukip) Was in the Navy. Former vice-

chairman, Todmorden Patients Participation Group.

CONSTITUENCY PROFILE
In the northeast of Greater Manchester. More diverse than the rest of the region with large Pakistani and Muslim communities. It has not yet recovered from the decline of the textile industry. The proportion of residents that are long-term unemployed is higher than the national average. The addition of Labour-supporting areas in 2010 helped the seat change hands to MP Simon Danczuk. Historically, a Lab/Lib marginal but the Lib Dems were pushed into fourth place in 2015.

EU REFERENDUM RESULT

57.5% Leave   Remain 42.5%

Rochester & Strood

CONSERVATIVE HOLD MAJORITY 9,850 (18.3%)

KELLY TOLHURST
BORN Aug 23, 1978
MP 2015-

Background in marine sales and consultancy. Dir, marine surveyors and consultancy business. Formerly sales dir, Skippers UK. Vocal critic of Israel. Remainer, but not ardent campaigner. Contested Rochester and Strood 2014 by-election, caused by Mark Reckless's defection to Ukip. Defeated Reckless with a comfortable majority 2015. Backbencher, member of BIS cttee 2015-17. Cllr, Medway BC 2011-. Volunteer supervisor for SFS Northfleet, a fostering charity. Father ran a boatbuilding business. Ed: Old Chapter HS.

	Electorate	Turnout %	from 2010 % Change
	82,702	65.02	
*K Tolhurst C	29,232	54.37	+10.30
T Murray Lab	19,382	36.05	+16.25
D Allen Ukip	2,893	5.38	-25.10
B Ricketts LD	1,189	2.21	-0.17
S Hyner Green	781	1.45	-1.43
S Benson CPA	163	0.30	
P Chiguri Ind	129	0.24	

CHALLENGERS
Teresa Murray (Lab) Former teacher, now deputy head of education at Maidstone Prison. Cllr, Medway BC 2007-; dep leader, Labour group. **David Allen** (Ukip) Frequently writes for UKIPDaily.com. Varied career as IT consultant, musician, engineer and therapist. Author, *The Sophisticated Alcoholic.* **Bart Ricketts** (LD) Contested Bromsgrove 2015.

Cllr, Kingston BC 2002-10; dep mayor 2007-08.

CONSTITUENCY PROFILE
A largely industrial seat in northern Kent. Contains a mixed demographic of middle and working classes; similar average earnings to the rest of the South East. Part of the London commuter belt, house prices are above the national average. Rochester and Strood was formed in 2010. It was gained by Mark Reckless who defected to Ukip in 2014, causing a by-election which he won. However, in 2015, the seat was claimed by incumbent Kelly Tolhurst.

EU REFERENDUM RESULT

63.7% Leave   Remain 36.3%

Rochford & Southend East

CONSERVATIVE HOLD MAJORITY 5,548 (11.7%)

JAMES DUDDRIDGE
BORN Aug 26, 1971
MP 2005-

Barclays banker 1993-2003, ran operations in Botswana. Founder member, YouGov. Leave supporter. Parly under-sec, FCO 2014-16; lord commissioner 2010-12. Opposition whip 2008-10. Select cttees: procedure 2016-17; draft deregulation bill 2013; liaison 2012-14; regulatory reform 2012-14; international development 2006-08; EFRA 2005-07. Contested Rother Valley 2001. Southend United supporter. Bristol-born. Married, three children. Ed: University of Essex (BA government).

CHALLENGERS
Ashley Dalton (Lab) Manager,

	Electorate	Turnout %	from 2010 % Change
	73,501	64.28	
*J Duddridge C	23,013	48.71	+2.29
A Dalton Lab	17,465	36.96	+12.28
R Woodley Ind	2,924	6.19	
N Hookway Ukip	1,777	3.76	-16.76
P Gwizdala LD	1,265	2.68	-0.67
S Cross Green	804	1.70	-3.33

South Essex Active Travel programme 2017-. Project manager, Southend BC 2016-. Treated for breast cancer in 2014, now volunteers for Macmillan Cancer Support. **Ron Woodley** (Ind) First independent leader of Southend Council. Stormed out of a Southend Council budget meeting in 2014 after the leader claimed he sold a senior position to his rival. **Neil Hookway** (Ukip) Cllr, Great Wakering and Foulness 2014-. **Peter Gwizdala**

(LD) Major in the Royal Artillery, army reserve.

CONSTITUENCY PROFILE
Includes the town of Rochford and the central and eastern part of the Georgian seaside resort of Southend. As with most British seaside towns it has declined since its heyday, but tourism remains a major part of the economy. Levels of home ownership are lower than the regional and national averages. Held by the Conservatives since its creation in 1997, but Labour increased their vote share by 12.3 per cent in 2017, making it the second most marginal seat in Essex.

EU REFERENDUM RESULT

60.9% Leave   Remain 39.1%

Romford

CONSERVATIVE HOLD MAJORITY 13,778 (27.6%)

ANDREW ROSINDELL
BORN Mar 17, 1966
MP 2001-

Far-right Conservative who has seen his fair share of controversy. Was distanced by David Cameron after he doubted Rachel Reeves's ability to be a mother and shadow minister. Brexiteer. Tabled an early day motion in 2016 calling for the national anthem to be played daily on BBC One to celebrate Brexit. Referred to burgundy EU passports as a source of humiliation. Advocate of death penalty. Former journalist. Contested: Thurrock 1997; Glasgow Provan 1992. Shadow minister, home affairs 2007-10; opposition whip 2005-07; vice-chairman, Conservative Party

	Electorate	Turnout %	from 2010 %	Change %
	73,516	67.94		
*A Rosindell C	29,671	59.41	+8.44	
A Leatherbarrow Lab	15,893	31.82	+10.94	
A Beadle Ukip	2,350	4.71	-18.09	
I Sanderson LD	1,215	2.43	-0.44	
D Hughes Green	815	1.63	-0.85	

2004-05. Member, Conservative Christian Fellowship. Cllr, Havering BC 1990-2002. Ed: Marshalls Park Comp, Romford.

CHALLENGERS
Angela Leatherbarrow (Lab) NHS worker. Chairwoman, Romford Labour. Remainer. Father was Maltese migrant. **Andrew Beadle** (Ukip) Contested Ukip leadership after Diane James's resignation. Contested: Sutton C 2015 by-election; Bermondsey 2015.

Ian Sanderson (LD) Contested Romford 2015.

CONSTITUENCY PROFILE
Part of Greater London but has historic links to Essex. A major office and retail centre for north London, construction and secretarial jobs are overrepresented in the constituency. Less ethnically diverse than the rest of London. Property ownership above the national average, and considerably higher than the London average. Historically a Conservative/Labour marginal but has been held by Andrew Rosindell since 2001 with a comfortable majority.

EU REFERENDUM RESULT

69.3% Leave   Remain 30.7%

Romsey & Southampton North

CONSERVATIVE HOLD MAJORITY 18,006 (36.0%)

CAROLINE NOKES
BORN Jun 26, 1972
MP 2010-

Got her first taste of politics at home as father was Conservative politician Roy Perry; worked as a policy adviser to him. Remain-supporting backbencher, but rebelled in 2011 to vote for an EU referendum. Parly under-sec: cabinet office 2017-; department of work and pensions 2016-17. Cllr, Test Valley BC 1999-2011. Contested: Romsey 2005; Southampton Itchen 2001. Claimed she was told she was too pretty to be in politics. Had an affair with a Conservative cllr, which led to breakdown of her marriage. Attached her name to the declaration of Christian conscience shortly before news

	Electorate	Turnout %	from 2010 %	Change %
	67,186	74.67		
*C Nokes C	28,668	57.14	+2.83	
C Royce LD	10,662	21.25	+3.54	
D Paffey Lab	9,614	19.16	+7.29	
I Callaghan Green	953	1.90	-2.81	
D Jerrard JACP	271	0.54		

of this broke. Divorced, one child. Ed: Peter Symonds Coll, Winchester; University of Sussex (BA politics and international relations).

CHALLENGERS
Catherine Royce (LD) Works in medicine. Recently returned from work in an Ethiopian hospital. Member, Lib Dem Women Exec. **Darren Paffey** (Lab) Cllr, Southampton CC 2011-. Contested Romsey and Southampton North 2015.

Worked for 2010 Labour GE campaign. **Ian Callaghan** (Green) Former Morgan Stanley employee. Contested Romsey and Southampton North 2015.

CONSTITUENCY PROFILE
An affluent, predominantly white Hampshire seat. Mostly consists of the towns and villages of the Test Valley, stretching northwards from Southampton. The proportion of residents aged 16-24 is well above average due to the large student population. Unemployment is low and income is close to the national average. Safe Conservative seat, held by Caroline Nokes since it was created in 2010.

EU REFERENDUM RESULT

46.1% Leave   Remain 53.9%

Ross, Skye & Lochaber

SNP HOLD MAJORITY 5,919 (15.4%)

IAN BLACKFORD
BORN May 14, 1961
MP 2015-

Business and banking background. Former managing dir, Deutsche Bank in Scotland and Holland. Non-exec chairman, Commsworld. SNP Westminster leader 2017-. Was sacked as treasurer for SNP through a vote of no confidence 2000. Defeated Charles Kennedy for seat in 2015. Remain campaigner. SNP spokesman, pensions 2015-. Select cttee, petitions 2015-16. Contested: Paisley South 1997 by-election; Ayr 1997. Managing dir, investor relations consultancy First Seer. Married, three children, three stepchildren. Ed: Royal HS, Edinburgh.

	Electorate	Turnout %	from 2010 % Change
	53,638	71.69	
*I Blackford SNP	15,480	40.26	-7.86
R Mackenzie C	9,561	24.86	+18.65
J Davis LD	8,042	20.91	-14.95
P O'Donnghaile Lab	4,695	12.21	+7.32
R Campbell Ind	499	1.30	+0.84
S Sturrock S New	177	0.46	

CHALLENGERS
Robert Mackenzie (C) Farmer. Qualified solicitor, left the legal profession to set up a business which exports rapeseed oil. **Jean Davis** (LD) Cllr, Highland DC 2015-17. Worked as a campaigner for Charles Kennedy. Retired doctor. Occupational physician and senior manager at a global chemical company. **Peter O'Donnghaile** (Lab) Runs: B&B in Skye; small agricultural enterprise. Formerly: worked

in the fish farming industry; contract engineer, British Rail; school technician.

CONSTITUENCY PROFILE
Vast rural seat: geographically the largest in the UK. Most of the constituency is extremely remote and sparsely populated and Ben Nevis, the highest mountain in the UK, is within its boundaries. Tourism and agriculture are important industries, and there is low unemployment. Previously a safe Liberal Democrat seat held by Charles Kennedy, Ross, Skye and Lochaber was gained by the SNP in 2015. In 2017, the Lib Dems slipped into third place.

EU REFERENDUM RESULT

43.5% Leave   Remain 56.5%

Rossendale & Darwen

CONSERVATIVE HOLD MAJORITY 3,216 (6.4%)

JAKE BERRY
BORN Dec 29, 1978
MP 2010-

Solicitor and specialist in property and development law. Worked for: City Law Partnership; DWF; Halliwells. Interested in social housing and supporting manufacturing. Parly under-sec to DCLG 2017-. Advised David Cameron on housing, regional growth and local government as member of No 10 policy unit. Remainer. PPS to: Greg Hands 2015-17; Grant Shapps 2010-. Agent to Amber Rudd 2005. Select cttee, finance 2015-17. Shareholder, Tung Sing Housing Assoc. Partner, one son. Ed: Liverpool Coll; University of Sheffield (LLB); Coll of Law, Chester.

	Electorate	Turnout %	from 2010 % Change
	72,495	69.19	
*J Berry C	25,499	50.84	+4.24
A Barnes Lab	22,283	44.43	+9.36
S Bonner LD	1,550	3.09	+1.45
J Payne Green	824	1.64	-0.49

CHALLENGERS
Alyson Barnes (Lab) Worked in the housing and charity sector. Cllr, Rossendale BC 1999-; council leader 2011-, campaigned to secure funding for town development and flooding defences. Member, LGA environment, economy, housing and transport board. **Sean Bonner** (LD) Advisory intern at New Schools Network, an education charity. Former campaign assistant for Tim Farron. **John Payne** (Green) Worked in manufacturing;

developed environmentally sustainable products. Previously: coll lecturer; school governor.

CONSTITUENCY PROFILE
The constituency covers the West Pennine Moors south of Blackburn and the towns of Rawtenstall, Bacup and Darwen. These former textile towns are fast becoming commuter towns into Greater Manchester. It is a relatively homogeneous area of the North West; only 3.6 per cent of residents do not hail from the UK or Ireland. The seat is a Conservative/Labour marginal: it was gained by Labour in 1992, before falling to the Conservatives in 2005.

EU REFERENDUM RESULT

58.9% Leave   Remain 41.1%

Rother Valley

LABOUR HOLD MAJORITY 3,882 (7.8%)

SIR KEVIN BARRON
BORN Oct 26, 1946
MP 1983-

Former miner and trade unionist. Resigned as chairman of standards cttee after inadvertent breach of code of conduct rules in hosting parliament event for a drugs firm 2016. Remain campaigner. Jeremy Corbyn critic, said he was "not a leader". PPS to Neil Kinnock 1985-88. Backbencher since 1998. Shad spokesman: health 1995-98; DWP 1993-95; ECC 1988-93. Has been member of 11 select cttees, most recently: standards 2013-; privileges 2013-17; liaison 2015-17. Knighted in 2014. Chairman, Yorkshire group of Labour MPs 1987-. Member, General Medical Council. Pres, Rotherham Trades

	Electorate	Turnout %	from 2010 %	Change
	75,230	65.78		
*K Barron Lab	23,821	48.13	+4.53	
B Eddy C	19,939	40.29	+17.01	
L Hunter Ukip	3,704	7.48	-20.60	
K Pruszynski LD	1,155	2.33	-1.90	
P Martin Green	869	1.76		

Union Congress. Member, NUM, expelled for disloyalty due to work on Tony Blair's Clause IV. Widowed and remarried, three children, three stepchildren. Ed: Maltby Hall Sch; University of Sheffield (Dip social sciences); Ruskin Coll, Oxford.

CHALLENGERS
Bethan Eddy (C) Conservative Party campaign manager, including Marcus Jones MP 2013-15. Former asst manager Sports Direct. **Lee Hunter**

(Ukip) Waterjet profiler. Contested Barnsley C 2015. Cllr, Rotherham MBC 2014-. **Katie Pruszynski** (LD) Parly asst Chloe Smith MP.

CONSTITUENCY PROFILE
Situated in the south Yorkshire coalfield, Rother Valley consists of towns and villages that flourished with the expansion of coalmining. The last mine in the area, Maltby Main Colliery, closed in 2013. Bucks the trend of declining pit towns: unemployment is average and three quarters own their own homes. One fifth of residents are retired. Held by Labour since its creation in 1918.

EU REFERENDUM RESULT

66.7% Leave   Remain 33.3%

Rotherham

LABOUR HOLD MAJORITY 11,387 (30.0%)

SARAH CHAMPION
BORN Jul 10, 1969
MP 2012-

Rotherham's first female MP. Began her career in the arts before succeeding Denis MacShane, who resigned during expenses scandal. Resigned from shadow frontbench in 2016; voted no confidence in Jeremy Corbyn. Remain supporter; voted for Article 50. Was arrested and cautioned by police after assaulting her former husband. Resigned as SoS women and equalities 2016-17, apologised for "extremely poor choice of words" in *Sun* article about child abuse. Advocate for women's rights and domestic abuse victims: shad min for preventing abuse 2015-16; chairwoman APPG

	Electorate	Turnout %	from 2010 %	Change
	63,237	59.97		
*S Champion Lab	21,404	56.44	+3.93	
J Bellis C	10,017	26.41	+14.10	
A Cowles Ukip	3,316	8.74	-21.43	
A Carter LD	1,754	4.63	+1.74	
M Bower Yorkshire	1,432	3.78		

victims and witnesses 2014-15. PPS to Tristram Hunt 2013-15. Chief exec, Chinese Arts Centre, Manchester. Adviser, Arts Council of England. Divorced. Ed: Prince William CS, Oundle; University of Sheffield (BA psychology).

CHALLENGERS
James Bellis (C) Economist and consultant specialising in telecommunications. Contested Lambeth BC 2014, 2010. **Allen Cowles** (Ukip) Director of

IT consultant business, CC Technology. Cllr, Rotherham MBC 2014-. **Adam Carter** (LD) NHS junior doctor. Cllr, Rotherham MC 2017-.

CONSTITUENCY PROFILE
Just north of Sheffield, this constituency covers Rotherham, a working-class town still haunted by the child sex abuse scandal that toppled the local council. 30 per cent of people live in social housing and one third have no qualifications. Unemployment is higher than average after the decline of heavy industry. One tenth of residents are Muslim. Labour held since 1933.

EU REFERENDUM RESULT

68.3% Leave   Remain 31.7%

Rugby

CONSERVATIVE HOLD MAJORITY 51,336 (16.0%)

MARK PAWSEY
BORN Jan 16, 1957
MP 2010-

	Electorate	Turnout %	from 2010 %	Change
	72,175	71.13		
*M Pawsey C	27,872	54.29	+5.24	
C Edwards Lab	19,660	38.30	+10.35	
J Roodhouse LD	2,851	5.55	-0.11	
G Bliss Green	953	1.86	-1.03	

Former successful businessman. Started a multimillion pound catering supply business with his brother. Cllr, Rugby BC 2002-07. Contested Nuneaton 2005. Interested in land issues and agriculture. Relatively quiet backbencher. Remainer, voted to trigger Article 50. Member, 1922 exec cttee. PPS to: Damian Green 2016-; Anna Soubry 2014-16. Founder and chairman APPG for e-cigarettes 2015 and district councils 2016. Son of former Conservative MP James Pawsey, who held this seat 1979-97. Married, four children. Ed: University of Reading (BSc estate management).

CHALLENGERS
Claire Edwards (Lab) Charity trustee working in the voluntary sector. Previously worked for a Warwickshire MP and MEP. Cllr, Rugby Borough Council 2002-; council Labour group leader. Contested Rugby 2015.
Jerry Roodhouse (LD) Self-employed businessman and local campaigner. Cllr: Rugby Borough Council 1990-; Warwickshire County Council 1993-. **Graham Bliss** (Green) Media production teacher and singer in hard-rock band 'Wounded Cross'. Ran

Rugby Green Party's 2015 GE campaign.

CONSTITUENCY PROFILE
The town itself is far more industrial and working class than its public history may suggest. An engineering and industrial town, producing turbines and cement. Outside Rugby the seat encompasses the countryside to the north including many affluent commuter villages. Although it is home to a significant Indian population, the seat has a very homogeneous white demographic. Since its recreation in 2010, the seat has remained in Conservative hands.

EU REFERENDUM RESULT

58.6% Leave   Remain 41.4%

Ruislip, Northwood & Pinner

CONSERVATIVE HOLD MAJORITY 13,980 (26.2%)

NICK HURD
BORN May 13, 1962
MP 2005-

	Electorate	Turnout %	from 2010 %	Change
	73,425	72.70		
*N Hurd C	30,555	57.24	-2.35	
R Lury Lab	16,575	31.05	+10.95	
A Cunliffe LD	3,813	7.14	+2.19	
S Green Green	1,268	2.38	-1.14	
R Braine Ukip	1,171	2.19	-8.74	

Latest MP in a Conservative dynasty; fourth successive generation of his family to serve as MP. Fuels the Conservative stereotype - Old Etonian, Oxonian, member of the Bullingdon Club and son of former foreign secretary Lord Hurd. Environmentally minded – chairman of APPG for environment and served on environment audit committee. Took sustainable communities act through parliament as a private members' bill. Voted to Remain in EU referendum. Publically criticised after saying young people lacked the "grit and character" needed to get a

job 2013. Divorced, four children, remarried, two children. Ed: Eton Coll; Exeter Coll, Oxford (BA classics).

CHALLENGERS
Rebecca Lury (Lab) Financial technology worker. Labour Party activist for over 10 years. Worked on: 2006 local election campaign; 2010, 2015 GE campaigns. Cllr, Southwark C 2012-. **Alex Cunliffe** (LD) Practising barrister and former solicitor. Contested: Eltham

2015; Erith and Thamesmead 2010. Former school governor. **Sarah Green** (Green) Operates passenger boat business on the Grand Union Canal. **Richard Braine** (Ukip) Managed Grassroots Out and Vote Leave campaigns in Kensington and Chelsea 2016. Anti-HS2.

CONSTITUENCY PROFILE
The most northwesterly seat in London, made up of wealthy, middle-class suburbia. An affluent commuter area with a high proportion of people aged 45 and above and a much higher white demographic than the rest of London. Unemployment is low. Safe Conservative seat.

EU REFERENDUM RESULT

49.5% Leave   Remain 50.5%

Runnymede & Weybridge

CONSERVATIVE HOLD MAJORITY 18,050 (35.0%)

PHILIP HAMMOND
BORN Dec 4, 1955
MP 1997-

	Electorate	Turnout %	from 2010 %	Change
	74,887	68.92		
*P Hammond C	31,436	60.91	+1.17	
F Dent Lab	13,386	25.94	+10.42	
J Vincent LD	3,765	7.30	+0.58	
N Wood Ukip	1,675	3.25	-10.64	
L Lawrance Green	1,347	2.61	-1.53	

Private, careful and straight-edged (some would say dull) Conservative often likened to an accountant. Made his own millions from various entrepreneurial schemes. Illustrious career on the front-bench since 2010. SoS: foreign 2014-16; defence 2011-14; transport 2010-11. Promoted to chancellor of the exchequer at the expense of George Osborne in 2016. As foreign sec he worked on the Iran nuclear deal and supported Saudi-led intervention in Yemen. Eurosceptic who supported Remain. Critic of gay marriage legislation. Reported to have said "public-sector workers are overpaid" in 2017 Cabinet meeting. Contested Newham North East 1994. Married, three children. Ed: Shenfield High Sch; University Coll, Oxford (BA PPE).

CHALLENGERS
Fiona Dent (Lab) Artist and campaigner. Unison, Artists Union of England, Labour campaign for human rights. Contested Windsor 2015. **John Vincent** (LD) Chief exec, International Federation of Airworthiness. Contested: Runnymede and Weybridge 2015; Crawley 2010; Epsom and Elwell 2001. Cllr, Reigate and Banstead BC 1997-2000. **Nicholas Wood** (Ukip) Principal pharmacy and chemistry lecturer, Kingston University.

CONSTITUENCY PROFILE
With good transport links into London it provides a home to major company headquarters. Constituents enjoy very good health and relatively high levels of education. Many work in the transport and storage sector and over 15 per cent have senior managerial roles, while unemployment is very low.

EU REFERENDUM RESULT

49.8% Leave   Remain 50.2%

Rushcliffe

CONSERVATIVE HOLD MAJORITY 8,010 (13.7%)

KENNETH CLARKE
BORN Jul 2, 1940
MP 1970-

	Electorate	Turnout %	from 2010 %	Change
	74,740	78.02		
*K Clarke C	30,223	51.83	+0.43	
D Mellen Lab	22,213	38.09	+11.76	
J Phoenix LD	2,759	4.73	-0.31	
R Mallender Green	1,626	2.79	-3.66	
M Faithfull Ukip	1,490	2.56	-8.22	

Tory big beast and current Father of the House. Strong-minded and combative veteran with unrivalled frontbench career and experience. Barrister, appointed QC in 1980. Former non-exec dir, BAT 1998-2008. Contested: Mansfield 1966, 1964. Enthusiastic cigar-smoker. Notorious Europhile; only Tory rebel on 2017 Article 50 vote. One of 15 Conservative MPs to vote against Iraq War 2003. Regards Margaret Thatcher as the best Prime Minister he ever worked with. Lost three leadership bids — 1997, 2001, 2005 — in part due to his love for the EU. Had suggested prior to 2017 election he would step down in 2020. Widower, two children. Ed: Gonville & Caius Coll, Cambridge (BA LLB).

CHALLENGERS
David Mellen (Lab) Church children's worker. Previously primary sch headteacher. Cllr, Nottingham CC 2007-. Contested Rushcliffe 2015. **Jayne Phoenix** (LD) Runs a business that raises awareness of Asperger's syndrome. **Richard Mallender** (Green) Nottingham CC transport strategy worker; previously IT and telecommunications worker. Cllr, Rushcliffe BC 2007-. Contested Rushcliffe 2015.

CONSTITUENCY PROFILE
Near-homogeneous area which is 93 per cent white. Enjoys good health, high levels of home ownership and minimal social rent and unemployment. Levels of education are very high for the region, with 40 per cent of residents educated to degree level, and many residents occupying senior positions. Almost 15 per cent of the local population work in education. A safe Conservative seat.

EU REFERENDUM RESULT

41.5% Leave   Remain 58.5%

Rutherglen & Hamilton West

LAB CO-OP GAIN MAJORITY 265 (0.5%)

GED KILLEN
BORN May 1, 1986
MP 2017-

Founded his own construction company after leaving university. Cllr, South Lanarkshire C 2013-; elected at the age of 26. Contested Scottish parliament 2012. Member: Co-op Party, GMB. Catholic. Gay, active LGBT campaigner who criticised Conservative-DUP confidence and supply deal. Married. Ed: Trinity HS, Rutherglen; Glasgow Caledonian University (BA occupational safety and health).

CHALLENGERS
Margaret Ferrier (SNP) MP for Rutherglen and Hamilton West 2015-17. Trained teacher. Former volunteer for Citizens

	Electorate	Turnout %	from 2010 % Change
	80,098	63.51	
G Killen Lab Co-op	19,101	37.55	+2.31
*M Ferrier SNP	18,836	37.03	-15.53
A Le Blond C	9,941	19.54	+11.99
R Brown LD	2,158	4.24	+2.43
C Santos Ukip	465	0.91	-1.34
A Dixon Ind	371	0.73	

Advice Bureau. Worked as a sales manager in blue chip manufacturing construction company before being elected. Shadow SNP spokeswoman for Scotland office 2015-17. **Ann Le Blond** (C) Development and estates surveyor, The Co-operative Group. Previously asset manager, Serco. Cllr, South Lanarkshire DC 2017-. **Robert Brown** (LD) Qualified solicitor and former partner at Ross Harper & Murphy. Cllr: South

Lanarkshire DC 2012-; Glasgow DC 1977-1992. MSP, Glasgow 1999-2011; dep min for education and young people 2005-07. Awarded CBE for political service 2014.

CONSTITUENCY PROFILE
Scotland's oldest burgh. Suburban area which carries echoes of heavy industry and is dominated by high-density housing. Very homogeneous, in keeping with region, with a 94 per cent white British population. High levels of social housing, particularly council accommodation, and unemployment coupled with generally low levels of education.

EU REFERENDUM RESULT

37.6% Leave   Remain 62.4%

Rutland & Melton

CONSERVATIVE HOLD MAJORITY 23,104 (40.1%)

SIR ALAN DUNCAN
BORN Mar 31, 1957
MP 1992-

Outspoken millionaire former oil trader. Social and economic libertarian and progressive Tory moderniser. Has written two books on politics; in one he called for legalisation of drugs and state disengagement with education. Resigned as PPS to Brian Mawhinney 1994 due to a home-buying scandal. William Hague's campaign chief 1997 and former roommate. Made his own leadership bid in 2005; dropped out due to lack of support and publically denounced the outdated attitudes of the "Tory Taliban". Notoriously Eurosceptic in the 1990s, but backed Remain. First sitting Conservative MP to

	Electorate	Turnout %	from 2010 % Change
	78,463	73.37	
*A Duncan C	36,169	62.83	+7.18
H Peto Lab	13,065	22.69	+7.34
E Reynolds LD	4,711	8.18	+0.11
J Scutter Ukip	1,869	3.25	-12.65
A McQuillan Green	1,755	3.05	-1.21

both come out and enter a civil partnership. Contested Barnsley West and Penistone 1987. Ed: Merchant Taylors' School; St John's Coll, Oxford (BA PPE; pres, Oxford Union); Harvard University.

CHALLENGERS
Heather Peto (Lab) Melton's first transgender candidate. Suffers from Kleine Levin syndrome. Was homeless for a time in the 1990s. **Ed Reynolds** (LD) Renewable energy worker at a

local biomass company. **John Scutter** (Ukip) Contested council elections 2017, 2015. **Alastair McQuillan** (Green) Works in a local pub, previously a biological researcher in Latin America and Indonesia. Contested Rutland and Melton 2015.

CONSTITUENCY PROFILE
Enjoys high levels of home ownership and very low levels of social rent. Manufacturing and education are big employers in the seat and unemployment is very low. Very homogeneous constituency which is 94 per cent white British, with a large Christian population. It has been Conservative since 1945.

EU REFERENDUM RESULT

53.9% Leave   Remain 46.1%

Saffron Walden

CONSERVATIVE HOLD MAJORITY 24,966 (41.0%)

KEMI BADENOCH
BORN Jan, 1980
MP 2017-

	Electorate	Turnout %	from 2010 %	Change
	83,690	72.78		
K Badenoch C	37,629	61.78	+4.58	
J Berney Lab	12,663	20.79	+8.99	
M Hibbs LD	8,528	14.00	+3.44	
L Howe Ukip	2,091	3.43	-10.35	

Born in Wimbledon, grew up in Nigeria and USA. Had a career in the City, business analyst, RBS; associate director and vice-president, Coutts. Later head of digital, *The Spectator*. Board member, Centre for the Study of British Politics and Public Life. Deputy leader, Conservative London Assembly group 2016-17. Formerly non-executive director, Charlton Triangle Homes housing association. London AM 2015-17. Assisted on Zac Goldsmith's unsuccessful mayoral campaign 2016. Member, 1922 exec cttee 2017-. Passionate about access to education, particularly for BME groups. Contested Dulwich and West Norwood 2010. Voted Leave. Previously a governor of two inner city schools. Supports The Dogs Trust and the Birkbeck Alumni fund. Chess and poker player. Married, one son, one daughter. Ed: University of Sussex (MEng engineering); Birkbeck Coll, University of London (LLB).

CHALLENGERS
Jane Berney (Lab) Chartered accountant, auditor in the City. School governor. PhD in history.

Contested Saffron Walden 2015. **Mike Hibbs** (LD) Architect. Founding partner, Hibbs & Walsh Associates. Cllr, Saffron Walden TC 1987-; mayor 2008-09, 1993-94. Contested Saffron Walden 2015.

CONSTITUENCY PROFILE
A large, middle class and rural seat containing the historic market towns of Saffron Walden and Great Dunmow. It serves an affluent population, with the most cars per household in the country. Stansted airport is the constituency's biggest recruiter. The area once relied on saffron farming. It has been a safe Tory seat since the 1940s.

EU REFERENDUM RESULT
51.2% Leave   Remain 48.8%

St Albans

CONSERVATIVE HOLD MAJORITY 6,109 (10.7%)

ANNE MAIN
BORN May 17, 1957
MP 2005-

	Electorate	Turnout %	from 2010 %	Change
	72,811	78.28		
*A Main C	24,571	43.11	-3.54	
D Cooper LD	18,462	32.39	+13.88	
K Pollard Lab	13,137	23.05	-0.21	
J Easton Green	828	1.45	-2.28	

Former English and drama teacher who taught at inner London comprehensive school. Enthusiastic Commons performer. Held a parly debate on the "foul practice of lobbing [dog] poo bags into hedges and trees" in 2017. Brexiteer. Rebelled against coalition govt 75 times; has been more loyal since 2015. Bruised by expenses controversy but comfortably survived local deselection bid 2009. Chairwoman, Britain-Bangladesh APPG 2009. Cllr: Beaconsfield PC 1999-2002; South Bucks DC. Widowed, remarried, two daughters, two sons. Ed: Bishop of Llandaff Sch; Swansea University (BA English); University of Sheffield (PGCE).

CHALLENGERS
Daisy Cooper (LD) Joint exec dir for pro-press regulation group Hacked Off. Freelance campaigns adviser. Former stakeholder manager. Dir, Commonwealth Advisory Bureau. Contested: Sussex Mid 2015; Suffolk Coastal 2010. **Kerry Pollard** (Lab) PR consultant. MP for St Albans 1997-2005. Chairman, Labour housing group. Former housing association director. Cllr: Herts CC 1989-97; St Albans 1982-97. Contested St Albans 2015.

CONSTITUENCY PROFILE
Affluent seat consisting of the eponymous cathedral city and its surrounding countryside. The population is well educated, with the number of people with at least level 4 qualifications 20 per cent higher than the national average. The city's iconic cathedral is often used in films. Unemployment is low and major industries include retail, science and technology and education. Solidly Conservative, although it returned a Labour MP under New Labour.

EU REFERENDUM RESULT
37.8% Leave   Remain 62.2%

St Austell & Newquay

CONSERVATIVE HOLD MAJORITY 11,142 (20.6%)

STEVE DOUBLE
BORN Dec 19, 1966
MP 2015-

Former pastor and evangelical Christian. Noted for an affair with one of his married case workers in 2016. Publicly apologised and reconciled with his wife. Ironically had made traditional fabric of family values a key issue in his 2015 campaign. Pro-Brexit. Select cttees: European scrutiny 2016-17; petitions 2015-17. Former dir: Phoenix Corporate events company; Bay Direct Media marketing org. Cllr: St Austell TC 2009-15, mayor 2013-14; Cornwall CC 2009-13. Married, two sons. Ed: Poltair Sch; Cornwall Coll (BTEC business studies).

Electorate	Turnout %	from 2010 % Change
78,618	68.96	
*S Double C	26,856 49.54	+9.33
K Neil Lab	15,714 28.99	+18.76
S Gilbert LD	11,642 21.47	-2.51

CHALLENGERS
Kevin Neil (Lab) Unite member and Momentum activist. Homelessness campaigner. Local political roles have included chairman of CLP and trade union shop steward. **Stephen Gilbert** (LD) MP for St Austell and Newquay 2010-15. Vocally opposed to proposed pasty tax 2012. PPS to Ed Davey 2012-15. Lib Dem spokesman, defence 2011-12. Works in finance, former researcher for Lembit Opik MP and Robert Teverson MEP. Cllr: Haringey BC 2002-05; Restormel BC 1998-2002.

CONSTITUENCY PROFILE
This constituency combines the South Cornwall market town of St Austell and seaside town of Newquay. The area is home to multiple china clay pits, with the second highest number of mining and quarrying employees in the country. The seat contains the Eden Project and tourism is crucial to the local economy; one tenth of people work in accommodation and food services. The previous incarnation of the seat returned Liberal MPs from 1974 but became a Conservative/Lib Dem marginal in 2010, although the Conservative majority has increased since 2015.

EU REFERENDUM RESULT
64.1% Leave   Remain 35.9%

St Helens North

LABOUR HOLD MAJORITY 18,406 (36.6%)

CONOR MCGINN
BORN Jul 31, 1984
MP 2015-

Former voluntary sector worker specialising in mental health and prison work. Northern Irish. Father was Sinn Fein cllr and mayor. Vehemently anti-Jeremy Corbyn. Claimed Corbyn considered phoning his father to "bully [him] into submission" after McGinn publicly doubted Corbyn's abilities. Supported Remain. Opp whip 2015-16, stood down after sacking of Dame Rosie Winterton. Member, defence select cttee 2015. Socialist society representative, Labour NEC. Former special adviser to Vernon Coaker. Vice-chairman, Fabian Society 2011-12. Married: two children.

Electorate	Turnout %	from 2010 % Change
76,088	66.01	
*C McGinn Lab	32,012 63.74	+6.71
J Ng C	13,606 27.09	+7.45
P Peers Ukip	2,097 4.18	-10.92
T Morrison LD	1,287 2.56	-1.86
R Parkinson Green	1,220 2.43	-1.38

Ed: St Pauls HS, Bessbrook; London Metropolitan University (BA history and politics).

CHALLENGERS
Jackson Ng (C) Partner, Chan Neill Solicitors. Adviser to Lord Wei of Shoreditch 2011-. Dir, Conservative Friends of the Chinese. Contested Liverpool Riverside 2015. **Peter Peers** (Ukip) Former chairman, Ukip St Helens. Accused Ukip of rigging votes after he was unsuccessful in gaining party nomination

2015. **Tim Morrison** (LD) Account dir at communications agency Remarkable Group. Former community engagement political adviser to LD MPs. Cllr, Liverpool CC 2010-14.

CONSTITUENCY PROFILE
A working-class constituency and one of the country's whitest and most Christian areas. Unemployment levels are slightly higher than average. The seat has an industrial reputation in part due to former coal, gas and chemical works, although agriculture is also important to the local economy. Staunchly Labour, it's been held by the party since its creation in 1983.

EU REFERENDUM RESULT
58.4% Leave   Remain 41.6%

St Helens South & Whiston

LABOUR HOLD MAJORITY 24,343 (46.0%)

MARIE RIMMER
BORN Apr 27, 1947
MP 2015-

Formerly Pilkington's glass factory worker, rising up the ranks from work in accounts to procurement. Awarded CBE in 2005 for services to local government. Cllr, St Helens MBC 1978-2016 and leader for almost 20 years; brought two new hospitals to area. Registered as disabled due to deafness. Shadow min: disabled people 2017-. Member, justice select cttee 2015-17. Arrested and charged for assault while campaigning against Scottish independence at a Glasgow polling station in 2014; later cleared of charges. Divorced. Ed: Lowe House Girls Sch.

	Electorate	Turnout %	Change from 2010 %
	79,036	66.91	
*M Rimmer Lab	35,879	67.84	+8.02
E McRandal C	11,536	21.81	+5.89
B Spencer LD	2,101	3.97	-1.68
M Hitchen Ukip	1,953	3.69	-10.29
J Northey Green	1,417	2.68	-1.94

CHALLENGERS
Ed McRandal (C) Associate director, Four Communications. Formerly: policy adviser, Recruitment and Employment Confederation; aide to Andrew Lansley. Contested Liverpool West Derby 2015. Ed: Bristol University (MSc international relations). **Brian Spencer** (LD) Former electrician for NBC. Previously branch sec, NUM. Cllr, St Helens MBC 1990-2012, 1983-96, 1980-82; leader 2006-10. Fined for assaulting

Labour candidate after losing seat. Contested St Helens and Whiston 2010.

CONSTITUENCY PROFILE
St Helens is a white middle-class Merseyside town with the country's fifth highest number of Christians. An old industrial seat which was once home to the first railway trials, it has been hit hard by the decline of coalmining. One fifth live in social housing. The area is known for its historical glass production, with Pilkington and the former Ravenhead both operating in the seat. Unsurprisingly, it has been held by Labour since its 2010 creation.

EU REFERENDUM RESULT
56.1% Leave   Remain 43.9%

St Ives

CONSERVATIVE HOLD MAJORITY 312 (0.6%)

DEREK THOMAS
BORN Jul 20, 1972
MP 2015-

Former development manager for Cornwall-based voluntary organisation Mustard Seed. Contested St Ives 2010. Campaigned to Leave the EU. Particular interest in health and housing. Member, science and tech cttee 2015-. Parish cllr. Community worker, church volunteer. School governor. Born to missionary parents. Grew up in West Cornwall, qualified as a Cornish Mason in the construction industry. Married, three children.

CHALLENGERS
Andrew George (LD) MP for St Ives 1997-2015. First person

	Electorate	Turnout %	Change from 2010 %
	67,462	75.93	
*D Thomas C	22,120	43.18	+4.91
A George LD	21,808	42.57	+9.41
C Drew Lab	7,298	14.25	+4.91

to speak the Cornish language in parliament. Believes the Lib Dem anti-Brexit stance hindered the party. Staunchly against the coalition. LD shadow SoS DFID 2005-06. LD shadow min: rural affairs 2002-05; disabilities 2000-01; fisheries 1997-2001. PPS to Charles Kennedy 2001-02. Select cttees: health 2010-15; CLG 2007-10; agriculture 1997-2000. Contested St Ives 1992. Rural community devt council 1994-97. **Christopher Drew** (Lab) Spanish and Arabic student at the University of Manchester. Asst at The Centre, Newlyn.

CONSTITUENCY PROFILE
Seat covering the southwestern tip of England, including Penzance, The Lizard, Land's End and a number of coastal villages. The industries that dominated were tin-mining and fishing, but the decline of these has meant the economy has turned to tourism. One tenth of residents now work in accommodation and food services. The seat also includes the Isles of Scilly, 28 miles off the Cornish coast with a population of 2,000. St Ives returned Conservative MPs until the 1997 election when the Lib Dems gained the seat. It was reclaimed by the Tories in 2015.

EU REFERENDUM RESULT
54.8% Leave   Remain 45.2%

Salford & Eccles

LABOUR HOLD MAJORITY 19,132 (40.2%)

REBECCA LONG-BAILEY
BORN Sep 22, 1979
MP 2015-

Solicitor specialising in NHS procurement contracts and estates. Formerly worked in call centres, a furniture factory, and as a postwoman. Socialist who nominated Jeremy Corbyn for Labour leadership in 2015 and 2016. Protégé of John McDonnell, talked of as future leader and keeper of the Corbynite flame. Replaced Hilary Benn on Labour NEC, September 2015. Remainer, voted to trigger Article 50. Rebelled to vote against renewing Trident. Shadow: business sec 2017-; Treasury chief sec 2016-17; Treasury min 2015-16; . Daughter of Salford dock worker. Married,

	Electorate	Turnout %	from 2010 %	Change
	78,082	60.99		
*R Long-Bailey Lab	31,168	65.45	+16.07	
J Sugarman C	12,036	25.28	+4.88	
C Barnes Ukip	2,320	4.87	-13.17	
J Reid LD	1,286	2.70	-1.03	
W Olsen Green	809	1.70	-3.50	

one son. Ed: Chester Catholic HS; Manchester Metropolitan University (BA politics and sociology).

CHALLENGERS
Jason Sugarman (C) Barrister and QC, Foundry Chambers. Specialist in prosecuting rape and white-collar commercial fraud. Cllr, Lewes DC 1995-2003. Contested: Lewes 2010; Dudley South 2001. **Christopher Barnes** (Ukip) Contested local elections 2016.

CONSTITUENCY PROFILE
With over 74,000 residents, the Greater Manchester seat of Salford and Eccles covers Ellesmere Park, Salford and Pendlebury. The University of Salford campus is located within it and, as a result, the area has a large number of 16-24-year-olds. Home ownership is well below average, as a high proportion of people live in rented accommodation and wages sit beneath regional and national averages. Levels of unemployment among 16-24-year-olds match those regionally. The seat has returned a Labour MP in every election since 1945.

EU REFERENDUM RESULT
53.6% Leave   Remain 46.4%

Salisbury

CONSERVATIVE HOLD MAJORITY 17,333 (32.5%)

JOHN GLEN
BORN Apr 1, 1974
MP 2010-

Compassionate Conservative but anti-immigration and a tough Eurosceptic who backed Remain. Practical environmentalist. Sits on Policy Board. Played significant role in APPG for hunger and food poverty's inquiry Feeding Britain. Has been member of Conservative Christian Fellowship. Prior to becoming MP swapped between consultancy and politics. Stints at Conservative Research dept: head of political section under William Hague; director 2004-06. Magistrate (JP) at Horseferry Road 2006-12. PPS to: Philip Hammond 2016-17; Sajid Javid 2015-16; Eric Pickles

	Electorate	Turnout %	from 2010 %	Change
	72,892	73.14		
*J Glen C	30,952	58.06	+2.46	
T Corbin Lab	13,619	25.55	+10.22	
P Sample LD	5,982	11.22	+1.16	
D Palethorpe Ukip	1,191	2.23	-9.90	
B Oubridge Green	1,152	2.16	-3.29	
K Pendragon Ind	415	0.78	-0.66	

2012-14. Contested Plymouth Devonport 2001. Married: two stepchildren. Ed: King Edward's Sch, Bath; Mansfield Coll, Oxford (BA history); Judge Institute, Cambridge (MBA); King's College London (MA international security and strategy).

CHALLENGERS
Tom Corbin (Lab) Train driver and union representative, Aslef. Treasurer, Salisbury & District

TUC. Cllr, Salisbury CC 2013-. Contested Salisbury 2015.

CONSTITUENCY PROFILE
Located in the South West, Salisbury is home to Stonehenge, the River Avon and Salisbury Cathedral. Predominantly white and Christian, it has few people from minority backgrounds. While median wages are low, the proportion of people in full-time employment is more than 5 per cent higher than national and regional averages. The MoD is a key employer here with several military bases located nearby. Salisbury has returned a Conservative MP in every election since the 1920s.

EU REFERENDUM RESULT
49.9% Leave   Remain 50.1%

Scarborough & Whitby

CONSERVATIVE HOLD MAJORITY 3,435 (6.8%)

ROBERT GOODWILL
BORN Dec 31, 1956
MP 2005-

Long-time Eurosceptic, but eventually supported Remain. NFU member, has 250-acre family farm. Former MD of company providing environmentally friendly burials. MEP for Yorkshire and the Humber 1999-2004; spokesman for environment 2001-04. Contested: NW Leicestershire 1997; Redcar 1992. Minister of state: education 2017-; immigration 2016-17. Parly under-sec for transport 2013-16. Shadow minister, transport 2007-10. Has served in several whip roles. Member, Cornerstone Group. Married, one daughter, two sons. Ed: Bootham Sch,

Electorate	Turnout %	Change from 2010 %		
73,593	68.55			
*R Goodwill C	24,401	48.37	+5.19
E Broadbent Lab	20,966	41.56	+11.37
S Cross Ukip	1,682	3.33	-13.76
R Lockwood LD	1,354	2.68	-1.84
D Malone Green	915	1.81	-2.76
J Freeman Ind	680	1.35	
B Black Yorkshire	369	0.73	
G Johnson Ind	82	0.16	

York; Newcastle University (BSc agriculture).

CHALLENGERS
Eric Broadbent (Lab) Former coach builder, apprentice with Plaxtons. Cllr: North Yorkshire CC 2001-09; Scarborough BC 1991-. **Sam Cross** (Ukip) Property landlord. Chartered insurer. Cllr: N Yorkshire CC 2013-; Scarborough BC

2007-. **Robert Lockwood** (LD) Engineer, runs own business.

CONSTITUENCY PROFILE
Scarborough and Whitby is a predominantly white seat located on the east coast, south of Middlesbrough. Retirees account for 19.4 per cent of the constituency's population. Home ownership is high, but wages are significantly lower than national levels. Over 22 per cent of people travel to work on foot – almost twice the average for Yorkshire and the Humber. Historically a safe Conservative seat, it was gained by Labour in their 1997 landslide but the Conservatives reclaimed it in 2005.

EU REFERENDUM RESULT
61.3% Leave   Remain 38.7%

Scunthorpe

LABOUR HOLD MAJORITY 3,431 (8.5%)

NIC DAKIN
BORN Jul 10, 1955
MP 2010-

Former council leader with long career in teaching: principal, John Leggott Sixth Form Coll, Scunthorpe; previously English teacher in Hull and Sweden. Cllr, N Lincs 1996-2007; leader 1997-2003. Campaigned to Remain in the EU. Lukewarm support for Jeremy Corbyn, who he said would make a "decent" leader and was on a "big learning curve". Opp whip 2011-. Shad min, education 2015-16. Select cttees: procedure 2011-17; education 2010-11. Member of over 20 APPGs. Christian. Member: NUT; Friends of the Earth; Child Poverty Action Group. Married, two daughters,

Electorate	Turnout %	Change from 2010 %	
61,578	65.29		
*N Dakin Lab	20,916	52.03	+10.36
H Mumby-Croft C	17,485	43.49	+10.31
A Talliss Ukip	1,247	3.10	-14.03
R Downes LD	554	1.38	-0.71

one son. Ed: Longslade Upper Sch, Birstall; University of Hull (BA history); King's College London (PGCE).

CHALLENGERS
Holly Mumby-Croft (C) Broughton town cllr and North Lincolnshire cllr, chairwoman of health scrutiny cttee. Previous mayor of Boughton. School governor. **Andy Talliss** (Ukip) Aircraft certification and project manager for Eastern Ariways. Cllr, Hibaldstow PC. School governor. **Ryk Downes** (LD)

Church caretaker. Launched company organising ultra-marathons in Yorkshire. Cllr, Leeds CC 2004-.

CONSTITUENCY PROFILE
Strongly pro-Brexit, the constituency of Scunthorpe has over 90,000 residents. The proportion of people from ethnic minorities is less than half the national average. Just 10.6 per cent of Scunthorpe's population is in a professional occupation – more than 6 per cent lower than the national figure. A leading employer in the area is British Steel, which has a workforce of over 4,000 people. At £113,875, the average house price is low.

EU REFERENDUM RESULT
68.7% Leave   Remain 31.3%

Sedgefield

LABOUR HOLD MAJORITY 6,059 (14.6%)

PHIL WILSON
BORN May 31, 1959
MP 2007-

Aide to Tony Blair, whom he helped to win the selection as Labour's candidate for Sedgefield in 1983. Trade unionist. Shop assistant, clerical worker. Adviser, Gala Coral. Rarely rebels, but did vote to join US-led coalition air strikes against Isil in Syria 2015. In 2017 he posted on Facebook that he was not a supporter of either Theresa May or Jeremy Corbyn and that any votes were for him, not for a potential PM. He said he was "for Labour... not Corbyn". Voted to trigger Article 50. Opp asst whip 2010-15. PPS to: Andy Burnham 2009-10; Vernon Coaker 2008-09. Select cttees:

	Electorate	Turnout %	from 2010 %	Change
	63,890	65.10		
*P Wilson Lab	22,202	53.38	+6.18	
D Davison C	16,143	38.81	+9.29	
J Grant Ukip	1,763	4.24	-12.36	
S Psallidas LD	797	1.92	-1.62	
M Wilson Green	686	1.65	-1.48	

panel of chairs 2015-; defence 2015-17; public accounts 2007-10; regulatory reform 2007-10. Board member, Progress. Partner, two children, three stepchildren. Ed: Trimdon Secondary Modern; Sedgefield Comp.

CHALLENGERS
Dehenna Davison (C) Studying politics and legislative studies at the University of Hull. Chairwoman, Hull University Conservative Future. Contested Hull North 2015. Former asst

to MP Jacob Rees-Mogg. **John Grant** (Ukip) Contested Durham CC 2017.

CONSTITUENCY PROFILE
A pro-Brexit former mining seat in the North East which was previously represented by Tony Blair. With a small ethnic minority population, 98.6 per cent of constituents are white. Residents of Sedgefield earn £30 more than the national weekly average for full-time employees. House prices are half the England and Wales average of £219,000 and the numbers of people in social rented accommodation is high. It is a safe Labour seat.

EU REFERENDUM RESULT
59.4% Leave   Remain 40.6%

Sefton Central

LABOUR HOLD MAJORITY 15,618 (30.0%)

BILL ESTERTON
BORN Oct 27, 1966
MP 2010-

Small business advocate. Director of training consultancy firm. Introduced bill to improve labelled drinking guidelines for pregnant women 2015. Voted against military intervention in Syria 2014. Remain MP and one of only 40 to vote full confidence in Jeremy Corbyn 2016. Cites Dennis Skinner as his political hero. PPS to Stephen Twigg 2011-13. Shadow min: international trade 2016-; BEIS 2016-; small business 2015-16. Cllr, Medway 1995-2010. Married: two children. Ed: Rochester Mathematical Sch; University of Leeds (BSc maths and philosophy).

	Electorate	Turnout %	from 2010 %	Change
	69,019	75.46		
*B Esterton Lab	32,830	63.04	+9.27	
J Marsden C	17,212	33.05	+3.44	
D Lewis LD	1,381	2.65	-1.60	
M Carter Green	656	1.26	-1.16	

CHALLENGERS
Jade Marsden (C) Housewife and mother. Previously employed by high-voltage engineering company. Daughter of nurse and second-generation Polish immigrant. Deputy chairwoman, Merseyside Conservatives. Contested Bootle 2015. **Daniel Lewis** (LD) Mortage broker and former sales and retention representative. Dementia and Alzheimer's Research campaigner. Parly assistant to John Pugh 2012-14. Cllr, Sefton BC 2014-. **Mike**

Carter (Green) Cllr, Aintree Village PC.

CONSTITUENCY PROFILE
A safe Labour seat located on the west coast between Liverpool and Southport. Over 67,000 people reside in Sefton Central and almost 55 per cent of them are aged over 45. Has the second highest proportion of owner-occupation of any seat in the UK and the percentage of people in rented accommodation is among the lowest in the country. Child poverty is half the national and regional average. The constituency is home to the Aintree racecourse and Grand National.

EU REFERENDUM RESULT
44.1% Leave   Remain 55.9%

Selby & Ainsty

CONSERVATIVE HOLD MAJORITY 13,772 (24.6%)

NIGEL ADAMS
BORN Nov 30, 1966
MP 2010-

Businessman from working-class background; son of school cleaner and caretaker. Left school aged 17. Sales worker who then started his own telecommunications business. Dir, NGC Networks. Biomass advocate – chairman of biomass APPG although criticised for accepting £50,000 in political donations and tips from biomass industry 2017. Apologised in 2016 for voting against gay marriage. Pro-Brexit. Member of Number 10 Policy Board; responsible for economic affairs prior to 2015. PPS to: Lord Hill 2013-14; Lord Strathclyde 2010-13. Cricket fan: played for Lords and Commons

	Electorate	Turnout %	from 2010 % Change
	75,765	74.01	
*N Adams C	32,921	58.71	+6.20
D Bowgett Lab	19,149	34.15	+7.32
C Delhoy LD	2,293	4.09	+0.45
T Pycroft Ukip	1,713	3.05	-10.94

CC; member, cricket APPG. Contested Rossendale and Darwen 2005. Married, four children. Ed: Selby High Sch.

CHALLENGERS
David Bowgett (Lab) Freelance animator and film-maker. Cllr, Tadcaster TC 2015-; vice-chairman town environment cttee. **Callum Delhoy** (LD) Politics student at the University of York; chairman of the university Lib Dems 2016-17. Non-portfolio officer, Young Liberals 2015-16. Contested

Daventry 2015. **Tony Pycroft** (Ukip) Businessman. Came under national scrutiny and Ukip investigation for racist and sexist content shared on Twitter.

CONSTITUENCY PROFILE
This rural area, formerly renowned for shipbuilding, is sandwiched between York and Leeds. Currently, much of its economy centres on agriculture. An affluent part of Yorkshire and the Humber, child poverty levels are low and home ownership high. Its greater than 96,000 residents are predominantly white Christians. Voted Conservative since its creation in 2010.

EU REFERENDUM RESULT

57.7% Leave   Remain 42.3%

Sevenoaks

CONSERVATIVE HOLD MAJORITY 21,917 (42.8%)

SIR MICHAEL FALLON
BORN May 14, 1952
MP 1997-; 1983-92

Former director of multiple businesses: Bannatyne Fitness, Quality Care Homes, Just Learning (nurseries). Member of advisory council, Social Market Foundation 1994-2000. MP for Darlington 1983-92, during the miners' strike he was threatened and once assaulted. Thought of as David Cameron's "attack dog" in 2015 election and EU referendum; awarded knighthood in Cameron's dissolution honours 2016. Left red-faced during 2017 campaign when criticising what he thought was a Jeremy Corbyn quote about the Iraq War, before learning it was said by Boris

	Electorate	Turnout %	from 2010 % Change
	71,061	72.08	
*M Fallon C	32,644	63.74	+6.81
C Clark Lab	10,727	20.94	+8.08
A Bullion LD	4,280	8.36	+0.50
G Cushway Ukip	1,894	3.70	-14.20
P Dodd Green	1,673	3.27	-1.20

Johnson. Remainer, voted for Article 50. SoS for defence 2014-. Held a range of ministerial positions. Deputy chairman, Conservative Party 2010-12. Pres, Royal Society for Blind Children. Married: two sons. Ed: Epsom Coll, Surrey; University of St Andrews (MA classics and ancient history).

CHALLENGERS
Chris Clark (Lab) Rail industry worker in both public and private sector. Contested Sevenoaks

2015. **Alan Bullion** (LD) Senior agricultural policy analyst. Contested: Sevenoaks 2015, 2010; Hammersmith and Fulham 2005.

CONSTITUENCY PROFILE
Popular commuter area covering many Kent villages and a large amount of Green Belt land; development is an important local issue. Historic market town with higher than average white and UK-born population. Low rate of unemployment. According to 2011 census, 72.9 per cent of residents are homeowners. Tory-held since its 1885 creation, except for 1923-24 when it was Liberal.

EU REFERENDUM RESULT

54.0% Leave   Remain 46.0%

Sheffield Brightside & Hillsborough

LABOUR HOLD MAJORITY 19,143 (45.7%)

GILL FURNISS
BORN Mar 14, 1957
MP 2016-

Elected in 2016 by-election to replace her late husband, Harry Harpham. Was part-time researcher for Harpham 2015-16. Former library assistant and hospital administrator who left school aged 16. Daughter of steel worker. Shop steward for NALGO, now Unison. Supported Remain. First shadow minister for steel 2016-. Member, women and equalities select cttee 2016. Contested Sheffield Hallam 2001. Cllr, Sheffield CC 1999-2016. Widowed: three children, two stepchildren. Ed: Chaucer Comp, Sheffield; Leeds Metropolitan University (BA library and information studies).

	Electorate	Turnout %	from 2010 Change %
	70,344	59.52	
*G Furniss Lab	28,193	67.33	+10.75
M Naughton C	9,050	21.61	+10.61
S Harper Ukip	2,645	6.32	-15.79
S Clement-Jones LD	1,061	2.53	-1.97
C Gilligan Kubo Green	737	1.76	-2.51
M Driver WRP	137	0.33	
M Rahman Soc Dem	47	0.11	

CHALLENGERS
Michael Naughton (C) Youth group leader, volunteer. Govt policy adviser. Worked for MEP Martin Callanan 2011-13. Contested: Wentworth and Dean 2015; European parliament 2014. **Shane Harper** (Ukip) DJ. Contested local elections 2016. **Simon Clement-Jones** (LD) Former steel industry worker turned businessman. MD, CDE Systems. Cllr, Sheffield CC 2004-

15. Contested Sheffield Heeley 2010.

CONSTITUENCY PROFILE
The most working-class Sheffield seat with the city's highest levels of unemployment. Nearly two fifths live in social housing. Residential area consisting of inter and postwar housing estates. Large Pakistani population and high numbers of black and Arab constituents. Seat includes Hillsborough stadium, scene of the 1989 disaster. Strong Labour seat. New Labour veteran David Blunkett represented the seat and its pre-2010 incarnation for 28 years.

EU REFERENDUM RESULT
60.0% Leave   Remain 40.0%

Sheffield Central

LABOUR HOLD MAJORITY 27,748 (58.0%)

PAUL BLOMFIELD
BORN Aug 25, 1953
MP 2010-

Advocate of education reform. General manager, Sheffield Student's Union 2003-10; former governor, Sheffield Polytechnic. Voted Inspiring Leader at the *Guardian* University Awards 2015. Anti-apartheid campaigner. Chairman: Sheffield Labour Party 1993-2009; Sheffield City Trust 1997-2008. Remain MP who called for Jeremy Corbyn's resignation post-referendum. Brought back into fold and made shadow min for Brexit 2016-. PPS to Hilary Benn 2010-16. Founder and chairman, APPG students 2014-; sec, APPG universities. Member: Unison; Unite; GMB; Co-op Party.

	Electorate	Turnout %	from 2010 Change %
	77,560	61.73	
*P Blomfield Lab	33,963	70.94	+15.91
S Roe C	6,215	12.98	+1.85
N Bennett Green	3,848	8.04	-7.81
S Mohammed LD	2,465	5.15	-4.54
D Cook Ukip	1,060	2.21	-5.25
J Carrington Yorkshire	197	0.41	
R Moran Pirate	91	0.19	-0.07
J Westridge Soc Dem	38	0.08	

Married to Labour MEP Linda McAvan, one son. Ed: Tadcaster GS; St John's Coll, York (BA theology).

CHALLENGERS
Stephanie Roe (C) Solicitor. Contested Sheffield Central 2015. **Natalie Bennett** (Green) Journalist and former Green Party leader 2012-16. Editor of *Guardian Weekly* 2001-12.

Contested Holborn and St Pancras 2015, 2010.

CONSTITUENCY PROFILE
Covering the University of Sheffield and Sheffield Hallam campuses, 38.1 per cent of the population are students, the highest proportion in the country according to 2011 census. The seat includes the city centre and working-class neighbourhoods. High mixed Asian population. Just over a third of people are home owners and a quarter live in social housing. Safe Labour seat, although the Liberal Democrats were strong contenders in 2005 and 2010.

EU REFERENDUM RESULT
31.9% Leave   Remain 68.1%

Sheffield Hallam

LABOUR GAIN MAJORITY 2,125 (3.7%)

JARED O'MARA
BORN Nov 15, 1981
MP 2017-

Disability rights campaigner who ousted the former deputy PM in one of the most shocking results of the night. Reportedly had to run out and buy a suit in the middle of the night when he discovered he had won. Remainer. Cerebral palsy sufferer and one of only five disabled MPs. Former press, parly and campaigns officer of a disability rights charity. Trustee of a Sheffield-based disability charity. Former DJ. Ed: Tapton Sixth Form; Staffordshire University (BA journalism).

CHALLENGERS
Nick Clegg (LD) MP for

	Electorate	Turnout %	from 2010 % Change
	73,455	77.63	
J O'Mara Lab	21,881	38.37	+2.57
*N Clegg LD	19,756	34.65	-5.39
I Walker C	13,561	23.78	+10.19
J Thurley Ukip	929	1.63	-4.81
L Robin Green	823	1.44	-1.75
S Winstone Soc Dem	70	0.12	

Sheffield Hallam 2005-17. Deputy PM 2010-15. Lib Dem party leader 2007-15, resigned after crushing defeat for Lib Dems in GE 2015. Europhile polyglot. Former journalist, *FT*. Lectured at University of Sheffield and Cambridge. Lib Dem spokesman: international trade 2016-17; exiting the EU 2016-17; home affairs 2006-07. Lord president of the council 2010-15. Married, three sons.
Ian Walker (C) Engineer. MD,

Rotary Electrical UK. Former chairman, air sub-committee, NHS North of England. Dir, South Yorkshire strategic health authority 2000-13.

CONSTITUENCY PROFILE
Aside from the west of Sheffield, this seat covers a largely rural area stretching into the Peak District. A wealthy and affluent population with the second highest proportion of people in professional occupations, and nearly 80 per cent owning their own home. Least ethnically diverse Sheffield constituency. Claimed by Labour for the first time after 20 years of Lib Dems. Traditionally Tory before that.

EU REFERENDUM RESULT

34.0% Leave   Remain 66.0%

Sheffield Heeley

LABOUR HOLD MAJORITY 13,828 (31.3%)

LOUISE HAIGH
BORN Jul 22, 1987
MP 2015-

Previously Aviva Policy manager and has worked in a call centre. Former political researcher to Lisa Nandy MP. Unite shop steward. Replaced long-serving MP Meg Munn but has already made a name for herself in Commons debates and questions. Named hardest working of 2015's new MPs by Independent HoC Library Research 2016. Speaker John Bercow has commented on her "terrier-like" intensity. Remain supporter who voted for Article 50. Nominated Jeremy Corbyn for party leadership in 2015, voted for Owen Smith 2016. Helped set up APPG international

	Electorate	Turnout %	from 2010 % Change
	68,040	65.00	
*L Haigh Lab	26,524	59.97	+11.77
G Gregory C	12,696	28.71	+12.55
J Otten LD	2,022	4.57	-6.72
H Denby Ukip	1,977	4.47	-12.93
D Walsh Green	943	2.13	-3.97
J Oberoi Soc Dem	64	0.14	

corporate responsibility. Shadow minister: Home Office 2017-; digital economy 2016-17; cabinet office 2015-16. Ed: Sheffield HS; University of Nottingham (BA politics).

CHALLENGERS
Gordon Gregory (C) NHS doctor. Worked at Royal Hallamshire and Northern General Hospitals. Cllr, Boston BC 2015-. **Joe Otten** (LD) Software business owner. Cllr,

Sheffield CC 2011-. Contested Sheffield Central 2015. **Howard Denby** (Ukip) Electrical engineer. Widower: blames the NHS for her suicide. **Declan Walsh** (Green) Works for local co-operative businesses.

CONSTITUENCY PROFILE
Wide ranging seat in the south of the city, running from middle-class suburbs to postwar inner city estates. 30 per cent of people have no qualifications and an almost identical number live in social housing. Higher than average benefit claimants. In 2010 the BNP achieved more than the five per cent deposit threshold here. Safe Labour seat.

EU REFERENDUM RESULT

57.2% Leave   Remain 42.8%

Sheffield South East

LABOUR HOLD MAJORITY 11,798 (27.1%)

CLIVE BETTS
BORN Jan 13, 1950
MP 1992-

Former economist with a wide range of cttees under his belt. Economist: TUC, Derbyshire CC, S Yorks CC, Rotherham BC. Chairman, S Yorks Pension Authority. Cllr, Sheffield CC 1976-92; leader 1987-92. Contested: Louth 1979; Sheffield Hallam 1974. Backed Remain; voted for Article 50 bill. Listed as neutral to Jeremy Corbyn by leaked party papers 2016. Was banned from parliament for seven days after employing Brazilian former male escort as parly researcher 2003; came out as gay during the scandal. Called for return of shadow cab elections 2016. Opp whip 1997-

	Electorate	Turnout %	from 2010 Change %
	68,945	63.23	
*C Betts Lab	25,520	58.54	+7.11
L Cawrey C	13,722	31.48	+14.10
D Dawson Ukip	2,820	6.47	-15.43
C Ross LD	1,432	3.28	-2.06
I Oberoi Soc Dem	102	0.23	

2001; asst whip 1997-98. Lord commissioner to Treasury 1998-2001. Chairman: communities and local govt select cttee 2010-; APPG football. In a civil partnership. Ed: King Edward VII Sch, Sheffield; Pembroke Coll, Cambridge (BA economics and politics).

CHALLENGERS
Lindsey Cawrey (C) Self-employed in publishing and marketing. Cllr: Lincolnshire CC 2017-; North Kesteven DC

2011-. Deputy chairman, Lincoln Conservative Association 2013-14. **Dennise Dawson** (Ukip) Contested Sheffield CC 2016. **Colin Ross** (LD) Cllr, Sheffield CC 1994-.

CONSTITUENCY PROFILE
Formerly industrial area of the city incorporating former mining villages and the suburbs up to Rotherham. The Meadowhall Shopping centre is part of this seat. Key industries are wholesale and retail, health and social work, and manufacturing. Just under a tenth of residents are Asian. 10 per cent of the population are Muslim. Strong Labour seat created in 2010.

EU REFERENDUM RESULT

66.3% Leave | Remain 33.7%

Sherwood

CONSERVATIVE HOLD MAJORITY 5,198 (9.7%)

MARK SPENCER
BORN Jan 20, 1970
MP 2010-

Local farmer and former businessman. Trustee, CORE Centre Calverton adult education centre. Former chairman, National Federation of Young Farmers' Club. Campaigned for Remain. Controversially defended sanctioning of jobseeker four minutes late for Jobcentre appointment saying he should learn 'timekeeping' 2015. Cllr: Nottinghamshire CC 2005-13, 2001-03; Gedling BC 2003-11. Whip 2017-; asst govt whip 2016-17. Member, environmental audit select cttee 2010-15. Works with coalfield communities APPG to restore former coalfield

	Electorate	Turnout %	from 2010 Change %
	76,196	70.04	
*M Spencer C	27,492	51.52	+6.48
M Pringle Lab	22,294	41.78	+5.91
S Bestwick Ukip	1,801	3.37	-11.22
B Thomas LD	1,113	2.09	-0.07
M Findley Green	664	1.24	-0.94

area's economies. Ed: Colonel Frank Seely Sch; Shuttleworth Agricultural Coll.

CHALLENGERS
Mike Pringle (Lab) Business owner, security systems manufacturer and installer. Cllr, Nottinghamshire CC 2014-. Backed Jeremy Corbyn's leadership in 2015. **Stuart Bestwick** (Ukip) Small business owner. Former consultant in charity sector. Chairman, Ukip Gedling. **Becky Thomas** (LD)

Learning technologist helping international students access UK universities.

CONSTITUENCY PROFILE
A residential area in north Nottingham including Robin Hood's Sherwood Forest. Strong mining tradition due to the Dukeries coalfield. The last mine here closed in 2015. Very ethnically homogeneous with a 97.5 per cent white population. Low unemployment. Major industries include retail, manufacturing, and health and social work. Gained by the Conservatives in 2010, preceded by Labour MP Paddy Tipping for 18 years.

EU REFERENDUM RESULT

63.7% Leave | Remain 36.3%

Shipley

CONSERVATIVE HOLD MAJORITY 4,681 (8.8%)

PHILIP DAVIES
BORN Jan 5, 1972
MP 2005-

	Electorate	Turnout %	from 2010 % Change
	73,133	73.01	
*P Davies C	27,417	51.35	+1.35
S Clapcote Lab	22,736	42.58	+11.63
C Jones LD	2,202	4.12	+0.27
S Walker Women	1,040	1.95	

Former senior marketing manager for ASDA. First MP to publicly call for Britain to Leave the EU. Controversially called for women and equalities cttee to drop reference to women from its name; hit out at feminist zealots at men's rights conference; accused of regularly filibustering in an attempt to undermine bills including those relating to animal rights and domestic violence. Contested Colne Valley 2001. Parliamentary spokesman, Campaign Against Political Correctness. Select cttees: panel of chairs 2017-; women and equalities 2016-17; justice 2015-17; CMS 2006-15.

Executive, 1922 cttee 2006-12. Ed: University of Huddersfield (history and political studies).

CHALLENGERS
Steve Clapcote (Lab) Medical scientist and lecturer, University of Leeds. Member, Scientists for Labour. **Caroline Jones** (LD) Works in primary school. Cllr: Burley PC 2006-13; Ilkley PC 1995-2006. **Sophie Walker** (Women) Former journalist, *Reuters*. Leader, Women's Equality Party 2015-. Stood to oust Philip Davies who she said

was a "sexist misogynist who puts his own ego ahead of his constituents".

CONSTITUENCY PROFILE
Northwest of Bradford, the top of this west Yorkshire seat borders the Yorkshire Dales. It is largely residential, combining the towns of Bingley and Shipley and incorporating a number of small villages. Contains the World Heritage site of Saltaire, a village and former textile mill. Low levels of unemployment. Education and retail are the main industries. Considered a safe Conservative seat despite being held by Labour from 1997 to 2005.

EU REFERENDUM RESULT

52.2% Leave   Remain 47.8%

Shrewsbury & Atcham

CONSERVATIVE HOLD MAJORITY 6,627 (11.4%)

DANIEL KAWCZYNSKI
BORN Jan 24, 1972
MP 2005-

	Electorate	Turnout %	from 2010 % Change
	79,043	73.63	
*D Kawczynski C	29,073	49.95	+4.43
L Davies Lab	22,446	38.57	+10.72
H Fraser LD	4,254	7.31	-0.58
E Higginbottom Ukip	1,363	2.34	-12.10
E Bullard Green	1,067	1.83	-2.32

Former international account manager in telecommunications. Polish-born. Campaigned for Leave. First MP to come out as bisexual. Allegedly told a disabled beggar outside parliament to get a job. Chairman, APPG for Saudi Arabia and Libya. Set up dairy farming APPG and first past the post APPG. Select cttees: foreign affairs sub 2016-17; foreign affairs 2015-17; int dev 2008-10; justice 2007-09; environment, food and rural affairs 2005-07. Contested Ealing Southall 2001. Ed: University of Stirling (BA business studies with French and Spanish).

CHALLENGERS
Laura Davies (Lab) Neurosurgery trainee. Former armed forces medical officer. Key priorities: against cuts to NHS, social care, education, child protection and youth workers; retaining access to the single market. **Hannah Fraser** (LD) Hydrogeologist. Business owner. Cllr, Shropshire 2012-. **Edward Higginbottom** (Ukip) Previously worked at National Provincial Bank. Born in Iran. Former cllr: Shrewsbury and

Atcham BC; Great Hanwood PC. Key priorities: cutting foreign aid; points-based immigration system. **Emma Bullard** (Green) Shropshire Council worker.

CONSTITUENCY PROFILE
Bordering Wales, this seat is centred around Shrewsbury and the surrounding rural area. A historic market town, its main industries are now retail and health and social work. Despite lower than average unemployment rates, some areas remain very deprived. Conservative-held since 1924, although it was lost to New Labour in 1997 then regained in 2005.

EU REFERENDUM RESULT

52.9% Leave   Remain 47.1%

Shropshire North

CONSERVATIVE HOLD MAJORITY 16,355 (29.4%)

OWEN PATERSON
BORN Jun 24, 1956
MP 1997-

Traditionalist, outspoken and conservative Eurosceptic with a history of anti-EU rebellions. Countryside businessman who spent 20 years working in the leather industry; former MD, British Leather. Founder and chairman of thinktank UK2020. Contested Wrexham 1992. Environmental conservationist who once had a pet badger. Known as a climate change sceptic. Believer in small government. Called "a complete tube" by Sinn Fein's Gerry Adams. Heckled by locals on visit to flooded Somerset Levels 2014. PA to John Biffen, GE 1987. Opp whip 2000-01. Shadow min:

	Electorate	Turnout %	from 2010 % Change
	80,535	69.04	
*O Paterson C	33,642	60.51	+9.07
G Currie Lab	17,287	31.09	+11.03
T Thornhill LD	2,948	5.30	-0.69
D Kerr Green	1,722	3.10	-1.80

transport 2006-07; environment 2005-06. SoS: environment 2012-14; Northern Ireland 2007-10. Married, three children. Ed: Radley Coll; Corpus Christi Coll, Cambridge (BA history); National Leathersellers College, Northampton.

CHALLENGERS
Graeme Currie (Lab) Qualified social worker, runs independent social work business across West Midlands. Sec, Oswestry Labour Party. Contested Shropshire North 2015. **Duncan Kerr**
(Green) Children's social worker and former local govt employee. Converted a redundant chapel into community arts centre. Cllr, Oswestry TC 2013-. Contested Shropshire North 2015.

CONSTITUENCY PROFILE
Rural seat on the Welsh border made up of small market towns and villages. Over 98 per cent of the population is white and 70 per cent Christian. One tenth of residents were born in Wales. Levels of social housing and unemployment are lower than average. Very safe Conservative seat, historically considered the safest in the country, according to the Electoral Reform Society.

EU REFERENDUM RESULT
59.8% Leave   Remain 40.2%

Sittingbourne & Sheppey

CONSERVATIVE HOLD MAJORITY 15,211 (29.6%)

GORDON HENDERSON
BORN Jan 27, 1948
MP 2010-

Working-class Eurosceptic. Grew up on a council estate. Mixed employment history: dir, Swale Community Action Project; self-employed management consultant; operations manager, Beams UK; dir, Unwins Wine Group; manager, Woolworths. Children's book and short story author. Ran restaurant in South Africa. Former constituency agent to Roger Gale. Contested: Sittingbourne 2010, 2005; Luton South 2001. Pro-Brexit. Fond of Facebook rants: called those who defaced his campaign posters scum; he was criticised the day after the London Bridge attack for saying that terrorists find

	Electorate	Turnout %	from 2010 % Change
	81,715	62.89	
*G Henderson C	30,911	60.15	+10.69
M Rolfe Lab	15,700	30.55	+10.96
M Baldock Ind	2,133	4.15	
K Nevols LD	1,392	2.71	-0.46
M Lindop Green	558	1.09	-1.31
M Young Loony	403	0.78	+0.23
L McCall Ind	292	0.57	

sanctuary in the midst of British Muslims. Former cllr for Swale BC and Kent CC. Married, three children. Ed: Fort Luton HS, Chatham.

CHALLENGERS
Mike Rolfe (Lab) Former national chairman, Prison Officer's Association and prison officer, HMP Elmey. Outspoken in media coverage of prisons. **Mike Baldock** (Ind) Ukip cllr for
Swale BC. Former cllr for Kent CC. Could not take part in Kent CC debate as he had not paid his council tax.

CONSTITUENCY PROFILE
North Kent seat covering the Isle of Sheppey, separated from the mainland by the Swale and Sittingbourne. The island is largely marshland and features nature reserves, caravan parks and three prisons. Industry includes retail, manufacturing and construction. Local employers include Kent Science Park and Kemsley Paper Mill. Initially created in 1997, the seat was claimed by Labour but taken by the Conservatives in 2010.

EU REFERENDUM RESULT
65.4% Leave   Remain 34.6%

Skipton & Ripon

CONSERVATIVE HOLD MAJORITY 19,985 (34.4%)

JULIAN SMITH
BORN Aug 30, 1971
MP 2010-

Former junior international squash player turned entrepreneur. Founder, executive recruitment business Arq International. Was advisory board member at think tank Reform. Helped to bring the Tour de France to the UK. Campaigned for Remain; claimed abuse he got doing this left him feeling threatened. Pushed for EU reform; was a member of the Fresh Start Group and has been co-chairman, APPG European Reform. Voted for Article 50 bill. PPS to: Justine Greening 2012-15; Alan Duncan 2010-12. Dep chief whip 2017-; whip 2016-17; asst whip Treasury 2015-16. Select

Electorate	Turnout %	from 2010 %	Change
78,108	74.43		
*J Smith C	36,425	62.65	+7.21
A Woodhead Lab	16,440	28.28	+10.89
A Brown Green	3,734	6.42	+0.71
J Render Yorkshire	1,539	2.65	

cttees: selection 2015-17; Scottish affairs 2010. Married. Ed: Balfron High Sch, Stirling; Millfield School, Somerset; University of Birmingham (BA English and history).

CHALLENGERS
Alan Woodhead (Lab) Former NHS administrator and health worker. Public sector IT project manager. Treasurer, Labour Ripon. **Andy Brown** (Green) Retired former teacher. Contested Skipton and Ripon 2015. Cllr, Craven DC 2017-. **Jack**

Render (Yorkshire) 19-year-old apprentice.

CONSTITUENCY PROFILE
Large rural Yorkshire constituency covering swathes of the Yorkshire Dales and two of the Yorkshire Three Peaks. The main settlements are former mill town Skipton and the cathedral city of Ripon; although the seat also encompasses numerous market towns and hundreds of small villages. Agriculture, particularly sheep farming, and tourism to the local abbeys and castles drive the economy. Unemployment is low and 16 per cent of people are self-employed. Safe Conservative seat.

EU REFERENDUM RESULT
53.2% Leave   Remain 46.8%

Sleaford & North Hykeham

CONSERVATIVE HOLD MAJORITY 25,237 (38.4%)

CAROLINE JOHNSON
BORN 1978
MP 2016-

Consultant paediatrician who qualified as a doctor in 2001 and continutes work at Peterborough City Hospital alongside being an MP. Campaigned for Leave. Contested Scunthrope 2010. Member, 1922 cttee. Yet to rebel against party whip. Chairwoman, APPG on rural crime. Married, two daughters, one son. Ed: Gordonstoun Sch, Moray; Newcastle University (MBBS medicine).

CHALLENGERS
Jim Clarke (Lab) Council bin lorry driver and former postman. Member, GMB. Contested Sleaford and North

Electorate	Turnout %	from 2010 %	Change
90,925	72.36		
*C Johnson C	42,245	64.21	+8.02
J Clarke Lab	17,008	25.85	+8.59
R Pepper LD	2,722	4.14	-1.51
S Chadd Ukip	1,954	2.97	-12.72
F McKenna Green	968	1.47	
P Coyne Ind	900	1.37	

Hykeham by-election 2016. **Ross Pepper** (LD) Optical assistant, Specsavers. Cllr, Skellingthorpe PC 2015-. Chairman, LD Lincolnshire Federation. Contested Sleaford and North Hykeham by-election 2016. **Sally Chadd** (Ukip) Formerly worked at London Stock Exchange. Previously head of continuing education, University of London. Contested: Sherwood 2015 for Ukip; Rushcliffe 1997 for Referendum Party.

CONSTITUENCY PROFILE
To the south of Lincoln, this mostly rural seat in west Lincolnshire covers the towns of Sleaford and North Hykeham. Large retired population with about half of residents aged over 45. The defence industry is an important employer as several RAF bases are located here. Low levels of unemployment. Very safe Conservative seat: held by Douglas Hogg who stood down in 2010 due to controversy over expense claims, preceded by Stephen Phillips who resigned due to irreconcilable differences with the government causing a by-election in 2016 won by Caroline Johnson.

EU REFERENDUM RESULT
61.6% Leave   Remain 38.4%

Slough

LABOUR HOLD MAJORITY 16,998 (31.3%)

TAN DHESI
BORN Aug 17, 1978
MP 2017-

Businessman. President, Gatka Federation UK (a Sikh martial art). Controversial candidate after Labour advertised the post as female-only. Cllr, Gravesham BC 2007-; mayor 2011. Chairman, Gravesham Labour Party. Grew up in India and UK. Sikh. Married, two children. Ed: UCL (BSc mathematics with management studies); Keble Coll, Oxford (MSc applied statistics); Fitzwilliam Coll, Cambridge (MPhil history and politics of South Asia).

CHALLENGERS
Mark Vivis (C) Lawyer. Board member, Chiltern Chamber.

	Electorate	Turnout %	Change from 2010 %
	83,272	65.20	
T Dhesi Lab	34,170	62.93	+14.42
M Vivis C	17,172	31.63	-1.69
T McCann LD	1,308	2.41	-0.23
K Perez Ukip	1,228	2.26	-10.73
P Janik Ind	417	0.77	

Former school governor. Contested Chesterfield 2015. Cllr, Amersham TC 2011-15; mayor 2016-17. **Tom McCann** (LD) Health charity worker. Campaigning for referendum on terms of Brexit deal. Key priorities: housing crisis; reversing local traffic schemes; management of local children's services. Cllr: Wokingham BC 2012-16, 1999-2002, 1990-94. **Karen Perez** (Ukip) Primary school teacher. Volunteer tennis coach. Key priorities: education;

the NHS; housing shortages; immediate withdrawal from EU.

CONSTITUENCY PROFILE
Large commuter town and major business hub situated to the west of London. Mars Inc and Lego still have head offices in Slough, and it was home to Blackberry and Nintendo for years. Ethnically diverse, with a declining white population of just 45 per cent. Large Sikh community and almost a quarter of residents are Muslim. Retail and transport and storage are its main sources of industry. Held comfortably by Labour since 1997, with a 14.4 per cent increased majority in 2017.

EU REFERENDUM RESULT

54.1% Leave	Remain 45.9%

Solihull

CONSERVATIVE HOLD MAJORITY 20,571 (36.2%)

JULIAN KNIGHT
BORN Jan 5, 1972
MP 2015-

Former journalist: personal finance and community affairs reporter, BBC News 2002-07; money and property editor, *The Independent on Sunday*, 2007-14. Author, including: *British Politics for Dummies* 2015; *Cricket for Dummies* 2013; *Wills, Probate & Inheritance Tax for Dummies* 2008, criticised for containing tax avoidance advice. Campaigned for Remain. Select cttees: communities and local govt 2015-17; culture, media and sport 2016-17. Married. Ed: University of Hull (BA history).

CHALLENGERS
Nigel Knowles (Lab) Author

	Electorate	Turnout %	Change from 2010 %
	77,784	72.96	
*J Knight C	32,985	58.13	+8.92
N Knowles Lab	12,414	21.88	+11.48
A Adeyemo LD	8,901	15.69	-9.97
A Garcarz Ukip	1,291	2.27	-9.34
M McLoughlin Green	1,157	2.04	-0.94

and playwright, including *Baldwin – the Abdication*. Former: carpet weaver; education officer, General Federation of Trade Unions. Contested Wyre Forest 2010. Cllr: Wyre Forest DC; Worcestershire CC; mayor of Kidderminster 2000-01. Married, two children. **Ade Adeyemo** (LD) Chartered civil engineer and risk management professional, insurance sector. Chairman, Solihull and Meriden Lib Dems. Former rugby player. Cllr, Solihull BC 2016-.

CONSTITUENCY PROFILE
Quaint and affluent commuter town for Birmingham's middle class within a stone's throw of Birmingham Airport. Surrounded by green belt land, it boasts one of the country's highest proportions of home ownership, with low levels of social housing and unemployment. Home to Jaguar Land Rover. Long history of returning Conservative MPs, but the Liberal Democrats surprisingly won a majority in 2005 after gaining traction on the city council. It was reclaimed by the Conservatives in the Liberal Democrat wipeout of 2015.

EU REFERENDUM RESULT

53.3% Leave	Remain 46.7%

Somerset North

CONSERVATIVE HOLD MAJORITY 17,103 (27.6%)

LIAM FOX
BORN Sep 22, 1961
MP 1992-

	Electorate	Turnout %	from 2010 % Change
	80,538	76.97	
*L Fox C	33,605	54.21	+0.70
G Chambers Lab	16,502	26.62	+12.30
R Foord LD	5,982	9.65	-3.05
D Davies Ind	3,929	6.34	
C Pattison Green	1,976	3.19	-3.27

Scottish former GP and army doctor once exiled to backbenches in disgrace. Surprising career comeback in the May premiership. Resigned as SoS for defence (2010-11) after revelations he had given a friend inappropriate access to MoD and taken him on official overseas trips. Two failed leadership bids in 2005 and 2016. Supported wars in Iraq and Afghanistan. Pro-Brexit. MP for Woodspring 1992-2010. Contested Roxburgh and Berwickshire 1987. Appointed first SoS for int trade 2016-. Shad SoS: defence 2005-10; foreign 2005; health 1999-2003. PPS to Michael Howard 1993-94; ran Howard's 2003 leadership campaign. Co-chairman, Con Party 2003-05. Parly under-sec, FCO 1996-97. Patron, Mencap. Founded charity Give Us Times. Married: two children. Ed: St Bride's HS; University of Glasgow (MB; ChB medicine).

CHALLENGERS
Greg Chambers (Lab) Junior doctor. Has worked in IT and insurance. Contested Somerset North 2015. **Richard Foord** (LD)

Former army education officer and civil servant. Deputy head of international partnerships, University of Exeter.

CONSTITUENCY PROFILE
Commuter seat nestled between the urban hubs of Bristol and Weston-Super-Mare. Sandwiched by the rivers Avon and Congresbury Yeo as well as the Severn Estuary. Bristol airport and the redeveloped Portishead port provide key commercial links. The Victorian seaside town of Clevedon and the inland Nailsea are the area's major towns. Has one of the highest number of home owners. Comfortable Conservative seat.

EU REFERENDUM RESULT
47.6% Leave   Remain 52.4%

Somerset North East

CONSERVATIVE HOLD MAJORITY 10,235 (18.9%)

JACOB REES-MOGG
BORN May 24, 1969
MP 2010-

	Electorate	Turnout %	from 2010 % Change
	71,350	75.74	
*J Rees-Mogg C	28,992	53.65	+3.87
R Moss Lab	18,757	34.71	+9.88
M Rigby LD	4,461	8.25	+0.37
S Calverley Green	1,245	2.30	-3.18
S Hughes Ind	588	1.09	

Former stockbroker and businessman: investment analyst for Rothschild; founder, Somerset Capital Management. Eccentric Brexiteer and unlikely social media star (#moggmentum) who enjoyed a spell of media attention after his anachronistic personality spawned meme pages during election campaign. Famed for campaigning with nanny and for children's elaborate names. Son of late editor of *The Times* Lord (William) Rees-Mogg. Noted for his RP accent, humorous speeches and filibustering abilities. Rebelled 107 times during coalition years. Compared the EU to the mafia in 2016 LBC interview. Contested: The Wrekin 2001; Fife Central 1997. Contested Treasury select cttee chairmanship but lost to Nicky Morgan 2017. Practising Catholic. Married, five sons, one daughter. Ed: Eton Coll; Trinity Coll, Oxford (BA history).

CHALLENGERS
Robin Moss (Lab) Manager of charity for young people. Formerly owned antiques business. Cllr: Bath and North East Somerset 2011-; Westfield PC 2011-. **Manda Rigby** (LD) Former journalist turned IT sector marketer. Cllr, Bath and North East Somerset 2011-15.

CONSTITUENCY PROFILE
Bizarrely shaped seat that surrounds Bath and is made up of diverse areas. To the north, an affluent commuter area to both Bath and Bristol featuring the southern-most tip of the Cotswolds, whilst the southeast dips into the Mendip Hills. The bulk of the seat is rural. Manufacturing and construction are now important industries. A traditionally Tory seat lost to Labour in 1997, regained in 2010.

EU REFERENDUM RESULT
51.6% Leave   Remain 48.4%

Somerton & Frome

CONSERVATIVE HOLD MAJORITY 22,906 (35.9%)

DAVID WARBURTON
BORN Oct 28, 1965
MP 2015-

	Electorate	Turnout %	from 2010 %	Change
	84,435	75.31		
*D Warburton C	36,231	56.97	+3.98	
M Blackburn LD	13,325	20.95	+1.57	
S Dromgoole Lab	10,998	17.29	+9.97	
T Simon Green	2,047	3.22	-5.79	
R Hadwin Ind	991	1.56	+0.95	

Outspoken and enterprising. Sparked controversy when he described SNP members as "massively vocal whinge-and-resentment experts" in local newspaper article. Entrepreneur: managing partner and founder, Oflang Partners LLP property restoration company; co-founder and director, MyHigh online retailer; founder and chairman, The Pulse youth orchestra; founder and CEO, Pitch Entertainment Group mobile entertainment software firm. Former music teacher. Select cttee, European scrutiny 2016-17. Deputy chairman, Wells Conservative Association.

Volunteer advocate, Age UK Somerset. Fellow, RSA. Member, Mensa. Married, one son, one daughter. Ed: Reading Sch; Waingels College; Royal Coll of Music (Dip RCM; M Mus); King's College London (PhD music composition).

CHALLENGERS
Mark Blackburn (LD) Treasurer and dir, Social Liberal Forum. Contested Westminster North 2010. Chairman, Cities of London and Westminster Liberal

Democrats 2007-09. **Sean Dromgoole** (Lab) Works in market research. Vice-chairman, Somerton & Frome Labour 2013-. Was a member of the ACTT and BECTU trade unions.

CONSTITUENCY PROFILE
Located in Somerset and reaching from the suburbs of Bath to the market towns of Frome, Somerton and Langport. It's largely rural with scattered woodland and the fringes of Cranborne Chase tickling the east of the seat. The area has lower than average unemployment and social housing. The Liberal Democrats held the seat from 1997-2015.

EU REFERENDUM RESULT
50.3% Leave   Remain 49.7%

South Holland & The Deepings

CONSERVATIVE HOLD MAJORITY 24,897 (49.5%)

JOHN HAYES
BORN Jun 23, 1958
MP 1997-

	Electorate	Turnout %	from 2010 %	Change
	76,381	65.87		
*J Hayes C	35,179	69.92	+10.37	
V Kowalewski Lab	10,282	20.44	+7.99	
N Smith Ukip	2,185	4.34	-17.48	
J Cambridge LD	1,433	2.85	-0.13	
D Wilshire Green	894	1.78	-1.43	
R Stringer Ind	342	0.68		

Traditional and socially conservative Eurosceptic. Grew up on ca ouncil estate. Former sales director for an IT company. Accelerated frontbench career under Iain Duncan Smith. Elaborate and eloquent speaker. Awarded CBE in David Cameron's resignation honours 2016. Sustained serious head injury in car crash when younger; suffers slight disabilities from this. Strong supporter of brain injury Hedway Charity. Brexiteer; claimed Britain would be better at combatting terrorism outside the EU. Contested North East Derbyshire 1992, 1987. Held a number of ministerial and

shadow ministerial positions 2000-, including transport min 2016-. Vice-chairman, Con party 1999-2000. Co-founder and chairman, Cornerstone. Cllr, Nottinghamshire CC 1985-97. Pro-life Christian. Married: two sons. Ed: Colfe's GS; University of Nottingham (BA politics; PGCE history and english).

CHALLENGERS
Viyteck Kowalewski (Lab) Polish-born auditor and

consultant who moved to UK in 1982. Has engineering degree. **Nicola Smith** (Ukip) Cllr, Lincolnshire CC 2013-17.

CONSTITUENCY PROFILE
Situated in East Midlands in the heart of the Lincolnshire Fen covering the towns of Spalding and Market Deeping. Bordering one side of The Wash, reclaimed fenland is incredibly fertile meaning that agriculture, farming and bulb growing are the backbone of the local economy, although the area also has one of the highest numbers of people working in wholesale and retail. A safe Conservative seat.

EU REFERENDUM RESULT
71.1% Leave   Remain 28.9%

South Ribble

CONSERVATIVE HOLD MAJORITY 7,421 (13.5%)

SEEMA KENNEDY
BORN Oct 6, 1974
MP 2015-

Property lawyer: board dir, Tustin Developments; solicitor, Slaughter and May; Bevan Brittan. Moved to Iran as infant, forced to flee during Islamic revolution. First MP of Iranian descent. Part of the cross-parliamentary commission on loneliness began with colleague Jo Cox. Campaigned to Remain in the EU. Resigned as constituency chairwoman for St Albans in 2009 after unsuccessful deselection campaign against Anne Main after expenses questioned. Controversially selected for a constituency 200 miles away from her home in St Albans, 40

	Electorate	Turnout %	from 2010 %	Change
	75,752	72.39		
*S Kennedy C	28,980	52.85	+6.42	
J Gibson Lab	21,559	39.32	+4.24	
J Wright LD	2,073	3.78	-0.63	
M Smith Ukip	1,387	2.53	-11.56	
A Wight Green	494	0.90		
M Jarnell NHAP	341	0.62		

days after she became local cllr in St Albans 2014-15. Contested Ashton-under-Lyne 2010. Speaks French and Persian. Married, three sons. Ed: Westholme School, Blackburn; Pembroke Coll, Cambridge (MA Oriental studies); Coll of Law.

CHALLENGERS
Julie Gibson (Lab) Postal worker for Royal Mail. Cllr, West Lancashire BC. Member: Unite; CWU. **John Wright** (LD)

Founder and dir of IT services company. Cllr, Norwich CC 2010-; leader of LD group.

CONSTITUENCY PROFILE
Located in fairly rural West Lancashire with limited access to the Irish Sea through the River Ribble. Major towns are Leyland and the Preston suburb of Penwortham. The number of Christians and home owners is incredibly high while unemployment is lower than average. Industry includes manufacturing, public administration and defence. The seat was held by Labour from 1997-2010, but was Conservative both before and after that.

EU REFERENDUM RESULT

56.6% Leave   Remain 43.4%

South Shields

LABOUR HOLD MAJORITY 14,508 (35.6%)

EMMA LEWELL-BUCK
BORN Nov 8, 1978
MP 2013-

Replaced David Miliband as South Shields' first female MP. Child protection social worker. Resigned from frontbench in 2016, saying she was heartbroken at the state of the party but abstained in no confidence vote. Was then banned from walking with local mining heritage group at Durham Miner's Gala 2016. PPS to Ivan Lewis 2013. Shadow min: children and families 2016-; communities and local govt 2016. Select cttees: work and pensions 2015-16; environment, food, rural affairs 2013-15. Cllr: South Tyneside BC 2004-13. Member, Co-op party. From family of shipyard workers. Married. Ed:

	Electorate	Turnout %	from 2010 %	Change
	63,449	64.26		
*E Lewell-Buck Lab	25,078	61.51	+10.25	
F Buchan C	10,570	25.92	+9.32	
R Elvin Ukip	3,006	7.37	-14.62	
S Ford Green	1,437	3.52	-0.93	
G Gordon LD	681	1.67	-0.09	

Northumbria University (BA politics and media studies); Durham University (MA social work).

CHALLENGERS
Felicity Buchan (C) Contested South Down 2015. Brexit campaigner. **Richard Elvin** (Ukip) Runs own travel business, former teacher. Bag of excrement posted through his campaign office door 2015. Contested: Houghton and Sunderland South 2015; South

Shields 2013; Middlesbrough 2012.

CONSTITUENCY PROFILE
Seaside south Tyneside town that has not quite recovered from the closing of the mines and decline of the shipyards. Despite emergence of retail and manufacturing there is still a high level of unemployment. One third of residents are in social housing and have no qualifications. Largely white but also contains a small and integrated Muslim community. Home to the first purpose-built mosque in Britain. Only seat since 1832 to have never elected a Conservative MP.

EU REFERENDUM RESULT

62.1% Leave   Remain 37.9%

Southampton Itchen

CONSERVATIVE HOLD MAJORITY 31 (0.1%)

ROYSTON SMITH
BORN May 13, 1964
MP 2015-

	Electorate	Turnout %	from 2010 %	Change
	71,716	65.23		
*R Smith C		21,773	46.54	+4.81
S Letts Lab		21,742	46.47	+9.93
E Bell LD		1,421	3.04	-0.53
K Rose Ukip		1,122	2.40	-11.04
R Pearce Green		725	1.55	-2.65

Engineer who spent 10 years in the RAF and 16 years as an aeronautical engineer for British Airways. Cllr, Southampton CC 2000-16; leader 2010-12. Gained the seat for Conservatives in 2010 with a majority of 2,316 after losing out to Labour's Jon Denham in 2010 by 192 votes. Won in 2017 by 31 votes, the smallest Conservative majority in the country. Dubbed the "least active" new MP by *The Independent* 2016. Pro-Brexit. Chairman, Hampshire Fire and Rescue. Awarded George Medal for bravery after he tackled murderer seaman Ryan Donocan on board HMS Astere in 2011.

Grew up on a council estate in Southampton.Ed: Bitterne Park School.

CHALLENGERS
Simon Letts (Lab) Science teacher. Former business owner. Cllr, Southampton CC 2006-; leader 2013-. **Eleanor Bell** (LD) Career in further and higher education. Contested Southampton Itchen 2015. **Kim Rose** (Ukip) Questioned by police in 2015 for bribing voters with sausage rolls. Controversy

after quoting from Mein Kampf at hustings. **Rosie Pearce** (Green) Communications asst, The Forest Trust.

CONSTITUENCY PROFILE
Covers Southampton city centre and a number of postwar council and private housing estates in the east of the city. The busiest marinas of this port and one of the city's two universities, Southampton Solent, fall within the constituency. Nearly a quarter of residents live in social housing, and the area has low levels of home ownership although unemployment matches the national average. Labour held from 1992-2015.

EU REFERENDUM RESULT
60.3% Leave   Remain 39.7%

Southampton Test

LABOUR HOLD MAJORITY 11,503 (24.5%)

ALAN WHITEHEAD
BORN Sep 15, 1950
MP 1997-

	Electorate	Turnout %	from 2010 %	Change
	70,194	66.82		
*A Whitehead Lab		27,509	58.65	+17.38
P Holmes C		16,006	34.13	+1.58
T Gravatt LD		1,892	4.03	-0.83
A Pope Southampton		816	1.74	
K Morrell Ind		680	1.45	-0.31

Charity director and former professor of public policy at Southampton Institute. Cllr, Southampton CC 1980-92; leader 1984-92. Contested: Southampton Test 1992, 1987, 1983; New Forest 1979. Won Southampton Test in 1997 after it had been held by the Conservatives for 18 years. Campaigned for Remain; voted against triggering Article 50. Expert in energy policy and local government. Sells electricity produced from solar panels on his home back to the national grid. Shad min for energy and climate change 2015-. Married, two children. Ed: Isleworth GS;

University of Southampton (BA politics and philosophy; PhD political science).

CHALLENGERS
Paul Holmes (C) Special adviser to Sir Patrick McLoughlin 2016-. Former sales manager and parly adviser to Stephen Hammond MP. Cllr, Southampton CC 2008-12. Contested Mitcham and Morden 2015. **Thomas Gravatt** (LD) Modern history and politics student at University of Southampton. Interested in

addressing the root causes of inequality, advocates electoral reform, and is a campaigner against a hard Brexit.

CONSTITUENCY PROFILE
The larger of the two Southampton seats, Test includes the University of Southampton (although student halls fall in other constituencies), as well as the more affluent suburbs of the city. Despite this wealth, home ownership levels are well below average and just less than a quarter of residents live in social housing. A bellwether seat until 2010, Alan Whitehead has kept hold of Southampton Test for the last two decades.

EU REFERENDUM RESULT
49.4% Leave   Remain 50.6%

Southend West

CONSERVATIVE HOLD MAJORITY 10,000 (21.2%)

SIR DAVID AMESS
BORN Mar 26, 1952
MP 1983-

Socially conservative staunch patriot and monarchist. Famously tricked into condemning fake drug "cake" in 1997 Brass Eye sting. One of four male MPs to back 2005 prohibition of abortion bill. Supports capital punishment. Anti-fox hunting. MP for: Southend West 1997-; Basildon 1983-97. Contested Newham North West 1979. Pro-Brexit. Sparked security alert on health cttee trip 2007; told officials his bag had been packed by Osama Bin Laden. PPS to: Michael Portillo 1988-97; Lord Skelmersdale 1988; Edwina Currie 1987-88. Select cttees:

	Electorate	Turnout %	from 2010 %	Change
	67,677	69.73		
*D Amess C	26,046	55.19	+5.37	
J Ware-Lane Lab	16,046	34.00	+15.68	
L Salek LD	2,110	4.47	-4.81	
J Stansfield Ukip	1,666	3.53	-14.00	
D Ellis Green	831	1.76	-2.92	
T Callaghan Southend	305	0.65		
J Pilley Ind	187	0.40		

admin 2015-17; panel of chairs 2001-17. Former junior school teacher turned underwriter. Knighted in 2015 for public service. Cllr, Redbridge BC 1982-86. Married, five children, including actress Katie Amess. Ed: Bournemouth Coll of Technology (BSc economics).

CHALLENGERS
Julian Ware-Lane (Lab) IT software testing consultant,

Cognitran. Former civil servant. Cllr Southend BC 2012-. Contested: Southen West 2015; Castle Point 2010; Rayleigh 2005.

CONSTITUENCY PROFILE
Western part of seaside resort Southend-on-Sea. A pocket borough that serves as a dormitory town for London. It boasts one of the highest proportions of people employed in finance and insurance in the country, largely due to the nearby HMRC VAT office. Mainly residential although it is infringed by London Southend Airport to the north. Tory safe seat that has been held by four members of the Guinness family.

EU REFERENDUM RESULT

55.1% Leave	Remain 44.9%

Southport

CONSERVATIVE GAIN MAJORITY 2,914 (6.1%)

DAMIEN MOORE
BORN Apr 26, 1980
MP 2017-

Formerly retail manager at Asda. Cllr, Preston CC 2012-; deputy leader of the Conservative group. Former chairman, Preston Conservative Assoc. Office, Lancashire Area exec. Contested Southport 2015, narrowly missed out on winning the seat. Key priorities: improving Southport's rail links; boosting local businesses. Gay. Ed: University of Central Lancashire (BA history).

CHALLENGERS
Liz Savage (Lab) Teacher. Cllr, West Lancashire BC 2010-. Gave speech on education at 2014 Labour conference. Contested Southport 2015.

	Electorate	Turnout %	from 2010 %	Change
	69,400	69.10		
D Moore C	18,541	38.66	+10.70	
L Savage Lab	15,627	32.59	+13.38	
S McGuire LD	12,661	26.40	-4.55	
T Durrance Ukip	1,127	2.35	-14.50	

Ed: University of Bradford (BA international relations). **Sue McGuire** (LD) Works at a digital start-up company. Cllr, Sefton BC 2003-; leader of LD group. Contested South Ribble 2015. School governor. Ed: Newcastle University (BSc biology). **Terry Durrance** (Ukip) Retired ambulance control superintendent. Chairman, Ukip Southport. Trustee, Ainsdale Community Care charity.

CONSTITUENCY PROFILE
A semi-coastal seat containing

the seaside town of Southport, which is a popular home for those commuting to Liverpool and Preston. A considerable retired population, with half of residents aged over 45. The population is predominantly white and Christian. High levels of home ownership and one of the lowest levels of social housing in the country. Unemployment is lower than the national and regional averages. A Liberal Democrat/ Conservative marginal, it has changed hands between the two parties three times since 1992. It was a Tory-Liberal marginal pre-1992. The Liberal Democrats held the seat from 1997 to 2017.

EU REFERENDUM RESULT

46.3% Leave	Remain 53.7%

Spelthorne

CONSERVATIVE HOLD MAJORITY 13,425 (26.8%)

KWASI KWARTENG
BORN May 26, 1975
MP 2010-

Calm and confident demeanour. One of 11 Conservative MPs involved in the 2016 Saudi Arabia fact-finding mission controversy. Contested: London Assembly list 2008; Brent East 2005. Select cttees: public accounts 2016-17; finance 2015-17; DWP 2013-15; transport 2010-13. Chairman, Bow Group 2005-06. Financial analyst: WestLB; JP Morgan Cazenove; Odey Asset Management. Journalist and author. Born in UK to Ghanaian parents. Ed: Eton Coll (King's scholar; Newcastle scholar); Trinity Coll, Cambridge (BA classics and history, MA; PhD economic history; on winning

Electorate	Turnout %	from 2010 %	Change
72,641	68.99		
*K Kwarteng C	28,692	57.25	+7.57
R Geach Lab	15,267	30.46	+11.89
R Shimell LD	2,755	5.50	-0.95
R Cunningham Ukip	2,296	4.58	-16.27
P Jacobs Green	1,105	2.20	-1.31

University Challenge team 1995); Harvard (Kennedy Scholar).

CHALLENGERS
Rebecca Geach (Lab) Media planner, Sky. Contested Spelthorne 2015. **Rosamund Shimell** (LD) Lib Dem parly adviser on health and education. Associate, FCA. Cllr, Southwark BC 2010-. Senior account exec, Portcullis Public Affairs 2010-12. Contested Spelthorne 2015. **Redvers Cunningham** (Ukip) Barrister. Chief exec of several

insurance businesses. Contested Spelthorne 2015. **Paul Jacobs** (Green) Health worker, former project manager.

CONSTITUENCY PROFILE
Commuter-heavy Surrey seat bordered by Heathrow to the north and the Thames on the south. Geographically small – around 20 square miles. A campaign for the constituency's principal town Staines to become part of London was spearheaded by local business owners. 20 per cent of it is underwater and 65 per cent is green belt land. Very dependent upon London and Heathrow for employment. Held by the Conservatives since 1950.

EU REFERENDUM RESULT

60.3% Leave	Remain 39.7%

Stafford

CONSERVATIVE HOLD MAJORITY 7,729 (14.9%)

JEREMY LEFROY
BORN May 30, 1959
MP 2010-

Former coffee and cocoa trader. Extensive business and charitable experience in Tanzania, worked there for 11 years with Schluter Group. MD, African Speciality Products. Co-founder, Equity for Africa charity. Chartered accountant, Arthur Andersen. Grad trainee, Ford Motor Co. Cllr, Newcastle-under-Lyme BC 2003-07. Contested: Newcastle-under-Lyme 2005; European parliament 2004. Self-described "One-Nation Conservative". Occasional rebel during coalition years. Member, 1922 exec cttee 2017-. Member: Amnesty International; Countryside

Electorate	Turnout %	from 2010 %	Change
68,445	75.86		
*J Lefroy C	28,424	54.74	+6.34
D Williams Lab	20,695	39.86	+10.27
C Tinker LD	1,540	2.97	+0.20
T Pearce Green	1,265	2.44	-0.41

Alliance. Christian. Married, two children. Ed: Highgate Sch; King's Coll, Cambridge (BA classics).

CHALLENGERS
David Williams (Lab) Barrister. Appointed Queen's Counsel 2013. Chairman, Society of Labour Lawyers 1990-. Nominated for International Family Lawyer of the Year. Contested Wycombe 2015. **Christine Tinker** (LD) Tennis coach and former executive dir, British Tennis Coaches' Association.

Former army officer. Contested Shrewsbury and Atcham 2015.

CONSTITUENCY PROFILE
Made up of the traditional shoe-making town of Stafford and its rural surroundings. A considerable commuter town for Stoke and Birmingham, the decline of shoe-making has led the way for electrical engineering to dominate the town's industry. The M6 bisects the constituency which is likely to become a HS2 hub. A traditionally Conservative seat, it was lost to Labour in two landslides in 1945 and 1997, with David Cameron unsuccessfully contesting the seat in the latter year.

EU REFERENDUM RESULT

57.5% Leave	Remain 42.5%

Staffordshire Moorlands

CONSERVATIVE HOLD MAJORITY 10,830 (24.3%)

KAREN BRADLEY
BORN Mar 12, 1970
MP 2010-

	Electorate	Turnout %	from 2010 %	Change
	66,009	67.65		
*K Bradley C	25,963	58.14	+7.02	
D Jones Lab	15,133	33.89	+6.66	
N Sheldon Ind	1,524	3.41		
H Jebb LD	1,494	3.35	-0.78	
M Shone Green	541	1.21	-1.67	

Sure-footed chartered accountant who came to politics when seconded to Michael Howard's shadow treasury team by KPMG. Policy exchange. Deloitte. Associate member, Institute of Chartered Accounts in England and Wales, ACA, and Chartered Institute of Taxation CTA. Contested: Richmond BC 2006; Manchester Withington 2005. SoS for CMS 2016-. Parly under-sec, Home Office 2014-16. Whip 2013-14; asst whip 2012-13. Select cttees: administration 2012-14; procedure 2011-12; work and pensions 2010-12. Special interest in beer and pub issues having grown up with her family running The Queen's Head, Buxton. Married, two sons. Church of England. Ed: Buxton Girls' Sch; Imperial Coll, London (BSc mathematics).

CHALLENGERS
Dave Jones (Lab) Lecturer in neuroscience at Keele University. Cllr, Newcastle-under-Lyme BC. **Nicholas Sheldon** (Ind) Works in IT for Leek United Building Society. Campaigner fighting to save Leek Moorlands Hospital from possible closure. **Henry**

Jebb (LD) Cllr, Staffordshire Moorlands DC 1991-.

CONSTITUENCY PROFILE
Staffordshire Moorlands combines several commuter villages just east of Stoke, the town of Leek and the south western chunk of the Peak District. It is home to multiple nature reserves, while Alton Towers in the south provides jobs and a boost for the tourism industry. One of the whitest areas in the country and boasts one of England's highest proportion of home owners. Traditionally Conservative, it fell to Labour in 1997 before being reclaimed in 2010.

EU REFERENDUM RESULT
64.7% Leave   Remain 35.3%

Staffordshire South

CONSERVATIVE HOLD MAJORITY 22,733 (44.5%)

GAVIN WILLIAMSON
BORN Jun 25, 1976
MP 2010-

	Electorate	Turnout %	from 2010 %	Change
	73,453	69.58		
*G Williamson C	35,656	69.76	+10.33	
A Freeman Lab	12,923	25.29	+6.92	
H Myers LD	1,348	2.64	-0.28	
C McIlvenna Green	1,182	2.31	-0.30	

Baby-faced bruiser who has rapidly ascended through the ranks. Appointed as chief whip in 2016. PPS to: David Cameron 2013-2015; Patrick McLoughlin 2012-13; Owen Paterson 2012; Hugo Swire 2012. Select cttee, NI affairs 2010-11. Chairman, motor neurone disease APPG. Contested Blackpool North and Fleetwood 2005. Cllr, North Yorks CC 2001-05. Formerly managing director of an architectural design practice. Interested in manufacturing and Staffordshire pottery industry. Former: chairman, Stoke on Trent Conservative Association; trustee, local CAB. Married, two daughters. Ed: Raincliffe Sch; Scarborough Sixth Form Coll; University of Bradford (BA social sciences).

CHALLENGERS
Adam Freeman (Lab) Secretary and campaign coordinator, South Staffordshire Labour. Contested South Staffordshire CC 2017. **Hilary Myers** (LD) Services manager for Onside Advocacy, a charity that supports disabled and mentally ill people in Worcestershire and Herefordshire. Formerly:

development manager, Rochdale Boroughwide User Forum; development worker, Rochdale & District Mind. **Claire McIlvenna** (Green) Background in nursing and therapeutic counselling.

CONSTITUENCY PROFILE
Bizarrely shaped constituency on the western flank of the West Midlands. It is made up of rural and commuter villages that loop around the west of Dudley up to the west and north of Wolverhampton. Industry is fairly dependent on retail, manufacturing and construction. Jaguar Land Rover has recently built a large engine plant in the area. Safe Conservative seat.

EU REFERENDUM RESULT
65.2% Leave   Remain 34.8%

Stalybridge & Hyde

LAB CO-OP HOLD MAJORITY 8,084 (19.0%)

JONATHAN REYNOLDS

BORN Aug 28, 1980
MP 2010-

Solicitor. An extremely rare rebel but defied whip to vote in favour of a more proportional electoral system December 2016. Backed Remain, but after referendum believed that Labour had to end support for free movement to become electorally credible again. Shadow cabinet: economic secretary 2016-; transport min 2015-16; energy and climate change min 2013-15; opp asst whip 2010-11. Member: Co-operative party; Unite. Christian. Married, four children, had first son aged 22 with a previous partner. Ed: Houghton Kepier Comp; Sunderland City Coll; Manchester University (BA

	Electorate	Turnout %	from 2010 %	Change
	71,409	59.46		
*J Reynolds Lab Co-op	24,277	57.18	+12.22	
T Dowse C	16,193	38.14	+9.48	
P Ankers LD	996	2.35	-0.71	
J Wood Green	991	2.33	-2.17	

politics and modern history); BPP (GDL; LPC).

CHALLENGERS
Tom Dowse (C) Works for a local engineering firm. Cllr, Stockport BC 2016-. Leave campaigner. Governor of the Pendlebury Centre for children and young adults with special needs. **Pauk Ankers** (LD) Data analyst for Co-op Insurance, previously British Gas. Cllr, Manchester CC 2005-11. Three children. **Julie Wood** (Green) Teaches English as another

language to adults. Food bank volunteer.

CONSTITUENCY PROFILE
Stalybridge and Hyde is on the eastern edge of Greater Manchester, with the Pennines situated to its east. The area has seen a rise in unemployment and the proportion of workless claimants is above average. Incomes are below the UK average. The retail and manufacturing industries are key employers. It has elected a Labour MP at every election since 1945, and the previous MP was James Purnell, who resigned from Gordon Brown's government in 2009.

EU REFERENDUM RESULT

59.3% Leave   Remain 40.7%

Stevenage

CONSERVATIVE HOLD MAJORITY 3,384 (6.9%)

STEPHEN MCPARTLAND

BORN Aug 9, 1976
MP 2010-

Former membership dir, British American Business, a transatlantic business organisation. Worked as a campaign manager for local, parliamentary and European elections. Busy backbencher who has chaired several APPGs focusing on healthcare, education and technology. Came under fire in 2015 for having a number of second jobs, despite telling voters in 2010 that Stevenage needed an MP who "treats it as a full-time job". Brexit supporter. PPS to Lord Livingston 2014-15. Trustee of local charity, The Living Room, which offers free

	Electorate	Turnout %	from 2010 %	Change
	70,765	69.71		
*S McPartland C	24,798	50.27	+5.73	
S Taylor Lab Co-op	21,414	43.41	+9.23	
B Gibson LD	2,032	4.12	+0.81	
V Snelling Green	1,085	2.20	-0.66	

addiction treatment. Married. Ed: Liverpool Coll; University of Liverpool (BA history); Liverpool John Moores University (MSc technology management).

CHALLENGERS
Sharon Taylor (Lab Co-op) Senior civilian management postholder at Hertfordshire constabulary. Worked for British Aerospace and John Lewis. Cllr: Hertfordshire CC 2006-; Stevenage BC 1997-, leader 2006-. Member, Labour National Policy Forum.

Contested Stevenage 2015, 2010. **Barbara Gibson** (LD) Business communication professional and former chairwoman, Int Assoc of Business Communicators. Lecturer at Birkbeck University. Cllr, Hertfordshire CC 2017-.

CONSTITUENCY PROFILE
Consists of the town of Stevenage and the rural area to its southwest. Relatively diverse for the region, since about one in six residents is neither white nor British. Social renting is well above average at a quarter of households and incomes are slightly below the East England average. A bellwether seat since its creation in 1983.

EU REFERENDUM RESULT

57.0% Leave   Remain 43.0%

Stirling

CONSERVATIVE GAIN MAJORITY 148 (0.3%)

STEPHEN KERR
BORN Sep 26, 1960
MP 2017-

Businessman specialising
in sales and marketing.
Sales operations leader for
Kimberley-Clark. Formerly
owned a sales management
consultancy and sales dir, Unico.
Contested Stirling 2015, 2005.
Chairman, Stirling Conservative
Association. Member of The
Church of Jesus Christ of Latter-
Day Saints (LDS), served as an
Area Seventy and president of
the first LDS pageant in Britain.
Married, four children. Ed:
Forfar Academy; University of
Stirling (BA business).

CHALLENGERS
Steven Paterson (SNP) MP

	Electorate	Turnout %	from 2010 Change %
	66,415	74.31	
S Kerr C	18,291	37.06	+13.94
*S Paterson SNP	18,143	36.76	-8.86
C Kane Lab	10,902	22.09	-3.43
W Chamberlain LD	1,683	3.41	+0.74
K Rummery Women	337	0.68	

for Stirling 2015-17. Previously
worked as a parly asst to Bruce
Crawford MSP and as press
officer for national tourist board
Visit Scotland. Author and guide.
Cllr, Stirling DC 2007-15; deputy
SNP group leader 2013-15.
Gained local media attention
for claiming expenses for dog
care in 2016. **Chris Kane** (Lab)
Journalist, marketing consultant
and former radio presenter.
Runs media protection company.
Community fundraiser and
campaigner. Cllr, Stirling DC

2015-. Trustee of Stirling Smith
Art Gallery and museum.
Wendy Chamberlain (LD)
Former police officer, now works
for global drinks manufacturer.

CONSTITUENCY PROFILE
Much of this large, rural seat
is in the Scottish Highlands.
The city of Stirling is home to
the University of Stirling, and
to 9,000 students. It is a more
affluent constituency than most
in Scotland and was held by the
Conservatives from its creation
in 1983 until being gained by
Labour in 1997. Like all but three
Scottish seats, it was won by the
SNP in 2015, but was regained by
the Tories in 2017.

EU REFERENDUM RESULT

32.2% Leave   Remain 67.8%

Stockport

LABOUR HOLD MAJORITY 14,477 (34.8%)

ANN COFFEY
BORN Aug 31, 1946
MP 1992-

Low-key moderate figure in
the parliamentary party. One
of the 89 backbench MPs who
voted against the triggering of
Article 50. Select cttees: draft
HoL reform bill 2011-12; issue
of privilege (police searches on
parliamentary estate) 2009-10;
modernisation of the Commons
2000-10. Joint PPS to: Alistair
Darling 2007-09, 1998-2002; PM
Tony Blair 1997-98. Opp health
spokeswoman 1996-97. Opp whip
1995-96. Cllr, Stockport MBC
1984-92. USDAW. Divorced,
one daughter. Remarried. Ed:
Bodmin and Bushey GS; South
Bank Poly (BSc sociology);
Walsall College of Education

	Electorate	Turnout %	from 2010 Change %
	63,425	65.50	
*A Coffey Lab	26,282	63.26	+13.40
D Hamilton C	11,805	28.42	+3.93
D Hawthorne LD	1,778	4.28	-3.37
J Kelly Ukip	1,088	2.62	-10.51
G Lawson Green	591	1.42	-3.00

(PgCert education); University
of Manchester (MSc psychiatric
social work).

CHALLENGERS
Daniel Hamilton (C) Senior
director, FTI Consulting.
Formerly: partner, Bell Pottinger;
dir, Big Brother Watch. Cllr,
Runnymede BC 2007-11. Former
adviser to Nirj Deva MEP.
Freeman of the City of London.
Author. **Daniel Hawthorne**
(LD) Works for New Chartered
Housing Trust. Cllr, Stockport

MBC 2010-. **John Kelly** (Ukip)
Chairman, Ukip Stockport.

CONSTITUENCY PROFILE
A compact seat in the south
of Greater Manchester which
contains most of the town
of Stockport. Relatively high
unemployment but average
incomes are slightly above
the northwest average, if
significantly lower than in
neighbouring Hazel Grove and
Manchester Withington. Over
a fifth of residents live in social
housing. The constituency was
recreated in 1983 and held by
the Conservatives until 1992,
but Stockport has only elected
Labour MPs since then.

EU REFERENDUM RESULT

46.8% Leave   Remain 53.2%

Stockton North

LABOUR HOLD MAJORITY 8,715 (20.4%)

ALEX CUNNINGHAM
BORN May 1, 1955
MP 2010-

Background as a trained journalist, previously worked in newspapers and radio. Runs own PR/web design consultancy having worked in PR for the gas industry as head of communications, Transco. Cllr: Stockton-On-Tees BC 1999-2010; Cleveland CC 1984-97. Led campaign supporting a ban on smoking in cars. Member, Socialist Education Assoc. Nominated Andy Burnham for leader in 2015. Voted no confidence in Jeremy Corbyn in 2016. Shad min: pensions 2016-; environment, food and rural affairs 2015-16. Rarely rebels. Campaigned to Remain,

	Electorate	Turnout %	from 2010 % Change
	66,279	64.47	
*A Cunningham Lab	24,304	56.88	+7.76
M Fletcher C	15,589	36.48	+8.51
T Strike Ukip	1,834	4.29	-14.87
S Brown LD	646	1.51	-0.72
E Robson Green	358	0.84	

voted to trigger Article 50. Christian. Married, two sons. Ed: Branksome Comp; Queen Elizabeth Sixth Form Coll; Coll of Technology, Darlington.

CHALLENGERS
Mark Fletcher (C) Works for PM's trade envoy. Former school governor. **Ted Strike** (Ukip) Contested Stockon South 2015, criticised for suggesting online that wild storms were "God's reply" to gay marriage laws. **Sarah Brown** (LD) Works in

higher education. Health and social care campaigner.

CONSTITUENCY PROFILE
Located in the North East, the main population centres are the towns of Stockton and the former chemical manufacturing base of Billingham. Lower incomes and higher unemployment than the UK average, and that of its southern neighbour. Created in 1983, the sitting MP of the predecessor seat was Bill Rodgers, one of the four SDP founders. Rodgers contested Stockton North at its first election, but finished third. Since then it has been a safe Labour seat.

EU REFERENDUM RESULT

66.3% Leave   Remain 33.7%

Stockton South

LABOUR GAIN MAJORITY 888 (1.6%)

PAUL WILLIAMS
BORN Aug 23, 1972
MP 2017-

Practising GP and public health doctor. CEO, Hartlepool and Stockton Health. Led a hospital and community health programme in Uganda for five years, implemented health insurance scheme to 60,000 locals. Co-chairman, World Initiative for Science and Healthcare 2011-15. Patron, Stockton-based charity Justice First. Two daughters. Ed: Newcastle University (MBBS medicine; MSc public health); University of Liverpool (Dip tropical medicine and hygiene).

CHALLENGERS
James Wharton (C) MP

	Electorate	Turnout %	from 2010 % Change
	75,619	71.18	
P Williams Lab	26,102	48.50	+11.48
*J Wharton C	25,214	46.85	+0.08
D Outterside Ukip	1,186	2.20	-8.38
D Durning LD	951	1.77	-0.87
J Fitzgerald Green	371	0.69	-1.15

for Stockton South 2010-17. Qualified solicitor. Parly under-sec for: international development 2016-17; DCLG Northern powerhouse 2015-16. Select cttee, public accounts 2010-12. **David Outterside** (Ukip) Criminal barrister at Nottingham's No. 1 High Pavement Chambers, called 2004. **Drew Durning** (LD) Local business-owner, sells organic products. Former marketing director. Environmentalist. **Jo Fitzgerald** (Green) Urged

hustings audience to "Please, please vote Labour".

CONSTITUENCY PROFILE
This is the more affluent of the two Stockton-on-Tees constituencies, with higher average incomes and much lower unemployment. Home ownership is well above the national average, and far more work in managerial occupations than in its northern counterpart. Unlike Stockton North, this seat was won by an SDP MP when it was first created in 1983, but was held by the Conservatives between 1987 until 1997 and then by Labour until James Wharton narrowly gained the seat in 2010.

EU REFERENDUM RESULT

57.8% Leave   Remain 42.2%

Stoke-on-Trent Central

LAB CO-OP HOLD MAJORITY 3,897 (11.8%)

GARETH SNELL
BORN Jan 1, 1986
MP 2017-

Union official and community campaigner. Cllr, Newcastle-under-Lyme BC 2010-16; leader 2012-14; made council a living wage employer and part of cooperative council network. Says fighting for working people is in his blood: grandfather Ron Snell was mayor of Stowmarket in the 1990s. Tweeted that Jeremy Corbyn was an "IRA supporting friend of Hamas career politician" during leadership campaign 2016, but later said he fully backed him as leader 2017. Campaigned for Remain. Co-operative politician, came into office in high profile 2017 by-election after Labour

	Electorate	Turnout %	Change from 2010 %
	58,196	56.95	
*G Snell Lab Co-op	17,083	51.54	+12.23
D Jellyman C	13,186	39.78	+17.24
M Harold Ukip	1,608	4.85	-17.80
P Andras LD	680	2.05	-2.12
A Colclough Green	378	1.14	-2.47
B Fielding Ind	210	0.63	-6.19

MP Tristram Hunt resigned. Member, science and technology cttee 2017-. Married, one daughter. Ed: Stowmarket High School; Keele University (BA history and politics).

CHALLENGERS
Daniel Jellyman (C) Cllr, Hanford & Trentham CC 2015-. Small business owner, DiscoveryMarketing and a ceramics company. Voted for Brexit. **Mick Harold** (Ukip)

Self-employed businessman, property development manager. Chairman, Ukip Stoke-on-Trent.

CONSTITUENCY PROFILE
Stoke-on-Trent Central contains the campus of the University of Staffordshire, and over 8,000 students live here. Relatively ethnically diverse, as 1 in 10 residents are of Asian descent. The lowest home ownership of the three Stoke constituencies, with over a quarter of households in the social rented sector. Represented by Labour MPs since its creation in 1950, although 2017 is the first time their majority has been under 4,000 at a general election.

EU REFERENDUM RESULT

64.8% Leave   Remain 35.2%

Stoke-on-Trent North

LABOUR HOLD MAJORITY 2,359 (5.6%)

RUTH SMEETH
BORN Jun 29, 1979
MP 2015-

Lifelong Labour Party trade unionist and campaigner who claims she has leafleted for the party since the age of 8. Criticised Jeremy Corbyn for not cracking down on antisemitic abuse after receiving 25,000 abusive messages. Left an antisemitism event in tears after being accused of being part of a media conspiracy by an audience member. Contested Burton 2010. Select cttees: defence 2015-17; defence sub-cttee 2015-17; armed forces bill 2015. Name came to attention of press when mentioned as a source on US communiques about a potential 2009 snap election in UK with

	Electorate	Turnout %	Change from 2010 %
	72,368	57.74	
*R Smeeth Lab	21,272	50.91	+10.99
B Adams C	18,913	45.26	+17.86
R Whelan LD	916	2.19	-0.75
D Rouxel Green	685	1.64	-1.18

a recommendation to strictly protect her identity. Remainer; voted for Article 50. Former deputy dir, Hope not Hate. Parents were trade unionists. Born in Edinburgh. Married. Ed: University of Birmingham (BA politics and international relations).

CHALLENGERS
Ben Adams (C) IT consultant, runs own company, Request Systems. Cllr, Staffordshire CC 2009-; cabinet member for learning and skills. Contested

Stoke-on-Trent-North 2015. Believes Brexit will open up new ceramics markets. **Richard Whelan** (LD) Local party activist.

CONSTITUENCY PROFILE
Stoke-on-Trent North is the least affluent area in Stoke, with residents earning slightly less than those in Stoke Central and considerably less than those in Stoke South or Newcastle-under-Lyme. Residents are likelier than average to have jobs classed as routine. Held by Labour since it was created in 1950, but, as in Stoke Central, Labour's 2017 majority of 2,359 is the smallest it has ever been.

EU REFERENDUM RESULT

72.1% Leave   Remain 27.9%

Stoke-on-Trent South

CONSERVATIVE GAIN MAJORITY 663 (1.6%)

JACK BRERETON
BORN May 13, 1991
MP 2017-

	Electorate	Turnout %	from 2010	Change %
	66,046	63.12		
J Brereton C		20,451	49.05	+16.38
*R Flello Lab		19,788	47.46	+8.29
I Wilkes LD		808	1.94	-1.41
J Zablocki Green		643	1.54	-1.09

Youngest Tory MP in 2017 intake. First Conservative to win Stoke-on-Trent South. Wants the constituency to receive more funding. Cllr, Stoke-on-Trent CC 2011-; deputy leader of the Conservative group; cabinet member for regeneration, transport and heritage. Elected cllr at the age of 19. Contested Stoke-on-Trent by-election 2017. Governor, Hillside Primary Sch 2011-. Admires Winston Churchill. Enjoys watching *Game of Thrones* and listening to Coldplay. Born in Stoke-on-Trent. Married. Ed: Keele University (BA politics and international relations); UCL.

CHALLENGERS
Rob Flello (Lab) MP for Stoke-on-Trent South 2005-17. Labour activists proposed a motion of no confidence against him after he called on Jeremy Corbyn to resign. Shadow min, justice 2010-13. CEO, Malachi Community Trust 2003-04. Previously worked for Cadbury. Tax adviser: Arthur Andersen 1995-99; Price Waterhouse 1989-95. **Ian Wilkes** (LD) Voted to leave EU. Cllr, Newcastle-under-Lyme BC 2004-16. **Jan Zablocki** (Green) Contested Stoke-on-Trent Central 2015. Advocate of a £10 per hour minimum wage. Member, Communication Workers Union.

CONSTITUENCY PROFILE
Stoke-on-Trent South is the whitest of the three Stoke seats, with about 7,000 ethnic minority residents out of 90,000. Nearly two thirds of its residents own their own home. It is also the Stoke seat with the lowest level of unemployment. This area had been held by Labour since it was created in 1950, but was the most marginal in 2015 and it saw a dramatic swing to the Conservatives in the 2017 election.

EU REFERENDUM RESULT

71.1% Leave   Remain 28.9%

Stone

CONSERVATIVE HOLD MAJORITY 17,495 (35.0%)

SIR BILL CASH
BORN May 10, 1940
MP 1984-

	Electorate	Turnout %	from 2010	Change %
	67,824	73.77		
*B Cash C		31,614	63.19	+8.47
S Hale Lab Co-op		14,119	28.22	+8.06
M Lewis LD		2,222	4.44	-0.82
E Whitfield Ukip		1,370	2.74	-13.46
S Pancheri Green		707	1.41	-1.12

Solicitor with own practice. Ardent Eurosceptic. Chairman, European scrutiny select cttee 2010-15. Shadow SoS, constitutional affairs 2003. Shadow attorney-general 2001-03. Embattled after expenses scandal revealed that he claimed £15,000 to pay his daughter's rent. He later repaid the money. Wrote biography of Victorian liberal John Bright 2012. Has disassociated himself from his son William who unsuccessfully contested Warwickshire North for Ukip. Married, one daughter, two sons. Ed: Stoneyhurst Coll; Lincoln Coll, Oxford (BA history).

CHALLENGERS
Sam Hale (Lab Co-op) Treasury graduate scheme employee, The Cooperative Bank. Representative: National Members' Council; The Co-operative Group. Formerly, specialist complaints handler, CAPITA. Remediation Services trustee, British Youth Council 2010-12. **Martin Lewis** (LD) Retired civil servant for HMRC for 37 years. Member, PCS. **Samantha Pancheri** (Green) Green Party policy development coordinator. Formerly Green Party spokeswoman for schools 2015-16.

CONSTITUENCY PROFILE
Stone is a large and mostly rural Staffordshire seat predominantly to the south of Stoke-on-Trent. Over half of residents are aged 45 or above, and a fifth are 65 or over. Nearly four in five households in the constituency are owner-occupied, and average incomes are higher in the seat than in most constituencies in the West Midlands region. The seat, including its predecessor of Stafford and Stone, has been held by the Conservatives at every election since 1918.

EU REFERENDUM RESULT

57.5% Leave   Remain 42.5%

Stourbridge

CONSERVATIVE HOLD MAJORITY 7,654 (16.2%)

MARGOT JAMES
BORN Aug 28, 1957
MP 2010-

Businesswoman, co-founder of healthcare PR company Shire Health. Parly under-sec, BEIS 2016-. Assistant whip 2016. Select cttees: arms export controls 2010-12; BIS 2010-12. Remainer; voted for Article 50 bill. Cllr, Kensington and Chelsea BC 2006-08. Contested Holborn and St Pancras 2005. Joined the Conservatives aged 17. Daughter of a Midlands coalman turned haulage firm boss. Lives with her long-term female partner. Ed: Millfield School; LSE (economics and government).

CHALLENGERS
Pete Lowe (Lab) Former nurse.

	Electorate	Turnout %	from 2010 % Change
	70,215	67.13	
*M James C	25,706	54.54	+8.49
P Lowe Lab	18,052	38.30	+6.79
G Wilson Ukip	1,801	3.82	-13.07
C Bramall LD	1,083	2.30	-1.04
A Mohr Green	493	1.05	-1.17

Cllr, Dudley MBC 2006-; leader 2014-17. Leader of Labour group and its spokesman for policy. **Glen Wilson** (Ukip) RAF veteran. UKIP Stourbridge Chairman. Homes4Heroes Stourbridge fundraising manager 2012-13. Disabled after suffering a stroke in 2003. **Christopher Bramall** (LD) Qualified solicitor, former schoolteacher. Pro-HS2. **Andi Mohr** (Green) Green party media co-ordinator 2016-. Business performance team leader, data analysis at SCC

2013-. Appeared on BBC's *Sunday Politics* 2016. Won the Dudley College school debate 2017.

CONSTITUENCY PROFILE
An urban West Midlands seat to the south of Dudley, Stourbridge is characterised by relatively high levels of home ownership, mainly at the expense of private renting, and by higher incomes and lower unemployment than neighbouring seats such as Dudley South or Halesowen and Rowley Regis. Created in 1997, this seat was held by Labour between 1997 and 2010, but Margot James has increased her majority at every election since 2010.

EU REFERENDUM RESULT

63.7% Leave   Remain 36.3%

Strangford

DUP HOLD MAJORITY 18,343 (47.3%)

JIM SHANNON
BORN Apr 21, 1964
MP 2010-

Countryside enthusiast. Served in: Royal Artillery 1977-78; Ulster Defence Regiment 1974-77. Member: NI Assembly 1998-; form for Political Dialogue 1996-98. Select cttees: Northern Ireland affairs 2016-17; arms export controls 2016-17; defence sub-committee 2015-16; defence committee 2015-16. Married, three sons. Ed: Coleraine Academical Inst.

CHALLENGERS
Kellie Armstrong (Alliance) Former Northern Ireland director of Community Transport Association. Secured highest ever vote in Strangford

	Electorate	Turnout %	from 2010 % Change
	64,327	60.24	
*J Shannon DUP	24,036	62.03	+17.66
K Armstrong Alliance	5,693	14.69	+0.88
M Nesbitt UUP	4,419	11.40	-2.95
J Boyle SDLP	2,404	6.20	-0.68
C Murphy SF	1,083	2.79	+0.21
R Bamford Green	607	1.57	
C Hiscott C	507	1.31	-5.08

for an Alliance Westminster candidate in 2015. **Mike Nesbitt** (UUP) Former sports presenter, BBC NI. MLA 2011-. Leader, UUP 2012-17. Appointed a victims' commissioner to promote the interests of victims of the Troubles. **Joe Boyle** (SDLP) Cllr, Ards and North Down Borough 2005-. **Carole Murphy** (SF) Involved in Civil Rights movement in Belfast during internment. Playwright.

CONSTITUENCY PROFILE
Strangford is a large seat to the southwest of Belfast, named after the large body of water, the Strangford Lough. At the 2011 census, 17 per cent of Strangford's residents were listed as Catholic while 73 per cent were Protestant. Levels of home ownership are above average and unemployment, while high, has been falling rapidly in recent years. Originally held by the DUP, Strangford has never elected a nationalist MP since it was created in 1983, and the combined vote share of the unionist parties has always outstripped that of the nationalists.

EU REFERENDUM RESULT

55.5% Leave   Remain 44.5%

Stratford-on-Avon

CONSERVATIVE HOLD MAJORITY 20,958 (41.0%)

NADHIM ZAHAWI
BORN Jun 2, 1967
MP 2010-

Founder of YouGov. Fled Saddam Hussein's regime in Iraq with his family age nine. Won £200,000 in libel damages after false reports he bought crude oil from Islamic State, May 2017. Spoke out against President Trump's Muslim travel ban, January 2017. Campaigned to Leave the EU. First Iraqi Kurd MP. Co-authored book about 2008 banking crash, *Masters of Nothing* 2011. Member, Prime Minister's policy board with special responsibility for business 2013-17. Select cttee, foreign affairs 2012-. Married, three children. Ed: UCL (BSc chemical engineering).

Electorate	Turnout %	from 2010 % Change
72,609	72.35	
*N Zahawi C	32,657 62.17	+4.50
J Kenner Lab	11,699 22.27	+9.29
E Adams LD	6,357 12.10	+0.09
D Giles Green	1,345 2.56	-1.57
J Spurway Ind	255 0.49	
T Darwood Ind	219 0.42	

CHALLENGERS
Jeff Kenner (Lab) Law professor at Nottingham University and visiting professor at Columbia, New York City and Oxford. Specialises in employment and EU law. Contested Stratford-on-Avon 2015, came third. Cllr, Shipston DC 2012-15. **Elizabeth Adams** (LD) Training as a commercial barrister. Grew up on a council estate in North Solihull. **Dominic Giles** (Green) History and politics teacher.

Contested Stratford-on-Avon 2015.

CONSTITUENCY PROFILE
Stratford-on-Avon is a large rural seat in Warwickshire based around the historic town after which it is named. More than a fifth of residents are aged over 65. Residents are likely to be self-employed and there is a significant skew towards managerial professions. It is one of the most affluent constituencies in the West Midlands. The seat has elected a Conservative MP at every election since its 1950 recreation. Its MP from that election until 1963 was John Profumo.

EU REFERENDUM RESULT

51.0% Leave   Remain 49.0%

Streatham

LABOUR HOLD MAJORITY 26,285 (47.1%)

CHUKA UMUNNA
BORN Oct 17, 1978
MP 2010-

Employment law solicitor 2002-11. Son of a Nigerian immigrant and a solicitor. Ran for Labour leadership in 2015 but withdrew after three days, citing press intrusion into his family life. Streatham's first MP to have grown up in the area. SoS, BIS 2011-15. Remain campaigner, later voted to trigger Article 50. Has criticised Jeremy Corbyn supporters for behaving with "demand, through threat, through online thuggery". Chairman of Vote Leave Watch and Independent Inquiry into the Labour Party's Support Amongst Britain's Ethnic Minorities. Christian. Married.

Electorate	Turnout %	from 2010 % Change
78,532	71.05	
*C Umunna Lab	38,212 68.49	+15.47
K Caddy C	11,927 21.38	-3.74
A Davies LD	3,611 6.47	-2.52
N Griffiths Green	1,696 3.04	-5.81
R Stephenson Ukip	349 0.63	-2.58

Ed: St Dunstan's College; University of Manchester (Law); Nottingham Law School.

CHALLENGERS
Kim Caddy (C) Chartered accountant. School and hospital governor. Trustee, First Touch. Deputy Mayor of Wandsworth. Back Boris campaigner. **Alex Davies** (LD) Senior parly assist. Lambeth cllr. **Nicole Griffiths** (Green) Student of applied social science, community and youth work at Goldsmiths. Part-time

arts support officer at a north London school.

CONSTITUENCY PROFILE
Streatham is a dense, urban constituency in south London. It is a diverse seat, where two in five are BME, mostly black and mixed race, and one in eight is an EU national. Fewer than two in five households are owner-occupied and the seat suffers from high youth unemployment. Created in 1918, Streatham elected Conservative MPs until 1992, and has elected Labour MPs since. Although it is now a safe Labour seat, Umunna's first majority in 2010 was 3,259 votes over the Liberal Democrats.

EU REFERENDUM RESULT

20.5% Leave   Remain 79.5%

Stretford & Urmston

LABOUR HOLD MAJORITY 19,705 (39.3%)

KATE GREEN
BORN May 2, 1960
MP 2010-

Former magistrate 1993-2009 and chief executive of the Child Poverty Action Group 2004-09. Greater Manchester ambassador for LGBT homeless charity Albert Kennedy Trust 2013-. Member and former chairwoman of APPG group on poverty; justice; European scrutiny. Shadow ninister for women and equalities 2015-16. Edinburgh-born. Divorced. Ed: Edinburgh University (LLB).

CHALLENGERS
Lisa Cooke (C) HR consultant. Davyhulme East councillor. Community campaigner.
Andrew Beaumont (Ukip)

	Electorate	Turnout %	from 2010 %	Change
	71,840	69.86		
*K Green Lab	33,519	66.78	+13.75	
L Cooke C	13,814	27.52	-0.32	
A Beaumont Ukip	1,094	2.18	-8.75	
A Fryer LD	1,001	1.99	-0.94	
M Ingleson Green	641	1.28	-3.44	
R Doman CPA	122	0.24		

Born in Urmston, Davyhulme resident. Against green belt development. His partner is a mental health nurse. **Anna Fryer** (LD) Consultant liaison psychiatrist in the NHS. Volunteered with the Royal Coll of Psychiatrists. APPG, domestic violence. On the board of trustees at her local hospice. **Michael Ingleson** (Green) Research chemist and lecturer in Manchester. Born in Newport, South Wales. Won 2012 RSC Harrison-Meldola prize for his work in borocation chemistry.

CONSTITUENCY PROFILE
This seat stretches southwest from central Manchester through Trafford, Stretford and the more suburban Urmston. It is home to the Old Trafford football and cricket grounds. Social renting is higher than average at over a fifth of households. Stretford and Urmston is a safe Labour seat, the party has held it and its predecessor, Stretford, since 1983. Before that Labour had only won the seat in 1945 and 1966, elections when they won big majorities in the Commons.

EU REFERENDUM RESULT

48.9% Leave   Remain 51.1%

Stroud

LAB CO-OP GAIN MAJORITY 687 (1.1%)

DAVID DREW
BORN Apr 13, 1952
MP 2017-; 1997-2010

Worked as a teacher. NASUWT member, branch sec 1984-86. Became senior lecturer at UWE 1986-97. Cllr, Stevenage and Stroud 1981-95. On the left of the party. Has a reputation for being a serial rebel, against the Iraq war and terror legislation. Staunch Eurosceptic but did not vote for Brexit because of framing of Leave campaign. Shadow Defra min 2017-. Supported John McDonnell's leadership bid 2007. Friend and vocal supporter of Jeremy Corbyn. Married, two daughters, two sons. Ed: Kingsfield Sch, Kingswood; University of Nottingham (BA economics);

	Electorate	Turnout %	from 2010 %	Change
	82,849	77.03		
D Drew Lab Co-op	29,994	47.00	+9.27	
*N Carmichael C	29,307	45.92	+0.19	
M Wilkinson LD	2,053	3.22	-0.21	
S Lunnon Green	1,423	2.23	-2.34	
G Gogerly Ukip	1,039	1.63	-6.34	

University of Birmingham (PGCE); Bristol Polytechnic (MA historical studies).

CHALLENGERS
Neil Carmichael (C) MP for Stroud 2010-17. Former cow and sheep farmer turned PR consultant. Took the Antarctic Act 2013 through parliament. Campaigned to Remain in the EU; voted for Article 50 bill. Visiting lecturer in British political history and rural econ at Sunderland and De Montfort universities. **Max Wilkinson** (LD) Account manager for Camargue. Cllr, Cheltenham BC 2014-.

CONSTITUENCY PROFILE
Stroud is a mostly rural expanse in Gloucestershire. The town of Stroud itself is home to about 13,000 people in a constituency of 100,000. Home ownership is above average at nearly three quarters. Having won Stroud in 1945 and 1997, this is the first time Labour has won the seat when in opposition. David Drew and Neil Carmichael have been the Labour and Conservative candidates in Stroud at every general election since 2001.

EU REFERENDUM RESULT

45.9% Leave   Remain 54.1%

Suffolk Central & Ipswich North

CONSERVATIVE HOLD MAJORITY 17,185 (30.4%)

DANIEL POULTER
BORN Oct 30, 1978
MP 2010-

NHS hospital doctor who has worked in mental health services. Openly critical of Jeremy Hunt's junior doctor contracts 2015. Helped to secure a new heart unit at Ipswich Hospital. Help for Heroes fundraiser. Introduced new language checks for overseas health staff as parly under-sec in dept of health 2012-15. Backbencher 2015-. Select cttees, energy and climate change 2015-16. Chairman of APPGs on: global health; public admin and constitutional affairs. Ed: University of Bristol (LLB); King's College London (MBBS, AKC).

	Electorate	Turnout %	from 2010 %	Change
	78,116	72.36		
*D Poulter C	33,992	60.14	+4.09	
E Hughes Lab	16,807	29.73	+10.93	
A Van de Weyer LD	2,431	4.30	-1.83	
R Scott Green	1,659	2.94	-1.99	
S Searle Ukip	1,635	2.89	-10.90	

CHALLENGERS
Elizabeth Hughes (Lab) Technical management for Procter and Gamble. Hounslow cllr 2004-. Contested North Essex 2005. Supporter of Credit Union movement. **Aidan Van de Weyer** (LD) Business and IT consultant, previously commissioning editor in academic publishing. Leading campaigner on rural transport issues. Cllr, Orwell and Barrington DC 2013-. **Stephen Searle** (Ukip) Former Royal

Marines commando turned leisure centre manager.

CONSTITUENCY PROFILE
The seat contains residential suburbs to the north of Ipswich and large swathes of rural Suffolk up to the Norfolk border. The area is relatively affluent: levels of home ownership and earnings are above the national average. An overwhelming majority of the population are white British. It has a large number – about 12,000 – of retirees. An ultra-safe Conservative seat, Suffolk Central and Ipswich North has returned a Tory MP to Westminster since the 1950s.

EU REFERENDUM RESULT

54.9% Leave	Remain 45.1%

Suffolk Coastal

CONSERVATIVE HOLD MAJORITY 16,012 (27.6%)

THERESE COFFEY
BORN Nov 18, 1971
MP 2010-

Ex-BBC property finance manager, after working at Mars Drinks. Chartered management accountant. Was grilled by the Defra cttee over the government's air quality policy in 2016. Tabled a proposal to hide identities of MPs who had been arrested 2016. Remainer, voted for Article 50 bill. Parly under-sec, Defra 2016-. Parly sec and dep leader of House 2015-16. Asst whip 2014-15. Select cttees: environmental audit 2016-17; CMS 2010-12. Contested: European parliament SE England 2009, 2004; Wrexham 2005. Former PPS to Michael Fallon. Campaigned

	Electorate	Turnout %	from 2010 %	Change
	79,366	73.17		
*T Coffey C	33,713	58.05	+6.15	
C Matthews Lab	17,701	30.48	+12.47	
J Sandbach LD	4,048	6.97	-1.62	
E O'Nolan Green	1,802	3.10	-2.82	
P Young Ind	810	1.39		

to stop A14 toll. Ed: St Mary's Coll, Crosby; St Edward's Coll, Liverpool; Somerville Coll, Oxford (BSc chemistry); UCL (PhD chemistry).

CHALLENGERS
Cameron Matthews (Lab) Firefighter. Supports: abolition of tuition fees; free hospital parking; outlawing zero-hour contracts. **James Sandbach** (LD) Cllr, Saxmundham TC. Former social policy officer at CAB. Contested: Suffolk Coastal

2015; Putney 2010; Castlepoint 2005. **Eamonn O'Nolan** (Green) Volunteer ambulance first responder. Cllr, Woodbridge TC.

CONSTITUENCY PROFILE
Covering most of Suffolk's coastline, Suffolk Coastal includes Felixstowe, the UK's busiest container port which processes about a third of the container cargo going in and out of the country. There is a sizeable retired population, and high levels of home ownership. A safe Conservative seat, it has been blue since its creation in 1983, although the Conservative majority dipped below 5,000 in 1997 and 2001.

EU REFERENDUM RESULT

55.2% Leave	Remain 44.8%

Suffolk South

CONSERVATIVE HOLD MAJORITY 17,749 (32.7%)

JAMES CARTLIDGE
BORN Apr 30, 1974
MP 2015-

	Electorate	Turnout %	from 2010 % Change
	75,967	71.39	
*J Cartlidge C	32,829	60.53	+7.46
E Bishton Lab	15,080	27.80	+8.54
A Aalders-Dunthorne LD	3,154	5.82	-1.98
R Lindsay Green	1,723	3.18	-1.16
A Powlesland Ukip	1,449	2.67	-12.54

Entrepreneur, mortgage broker and founder of Share to Buy Ltd. Host of the *London Home Show*. Former volunteer business adviser for homeless charity St Mungo's Broadway. Cllr, Babergh DC 2013-15. Contested Lewisham Deptford 2005. Voted against the 2017 Queen's speech amendment to give emergency and public service workers a pay rise. Select cttees: work and pensions 2016-17; public accounts 2015-17. Chairman, APPG on housing and planning. Campaigned to Remain in the EU. Drummer in a local pub band. His father-in-law is the Conservative MP and former defence minister Gerald

Howarth. Married, four children. Ed: Manchester University (BSc economics).

CHALLENGERS
Emma Bishton (Lab) Works in health improvement for NHS. Qualified music therapist. Contested Suffolk South 2015, came second. **Andrew Aalders-Dunthorne** (LD) Chief executive, Consortium Multi-Academy Trust for rural primary schools. Scout Leader. Former exec headteacher, Waveney

Partnership Federation of Schools. **Robert Lindsay** (Green) Contested Suffolk South 2015. Cllr, Babergh DC 2014-17.

CONSTITUENCY PROFILE
Stretching from Suffolk's border with Essex to the peninsula south of Ipswich, the landscape is mostly rural, but also covers the market towns of Sudbury and Hadleigh and several suburbs of Ipswich. There is a considerable number of retired people and high levels of home ownership; nearly two fifths of residents own their homes outright. It is a safe Conservative seat, and has been held by the party since 1983.

EU REFERENDUM RESULT
54.0% Leave   Remain 46.0%

Suffolk West

CONSERVATIVE HOLD MAJORITY 17,063 (33.0%)

MATTHEW HANCOCK
BORN Oct 2, 1978
MP 2010-

	Electorate	Turnout %	from 2010 % Change
	76,984	67.22	
*M Hancock C	31,649	61.16	+8.99
M Jefferys Lab	14,586	28.19	+10.71
J Flood Ukip	2,396	4.63	-17.10
E Tealby-Watson LD	2,180	4.21	-0.79
D Allwright Green	935	1.81	-1.81

Worked as a Bank of England economist after graduating. Announced in 2016 a ban on charities from using public grants to lobby ministers soon after receiving a £4,000 donation from the IEA. Pledged in 2016 to make all employers find out in job interviews if candidates are privately educated. Chief of staff to shadow chancellor 2005-10. Paymaster general 2015-16; Min: digital policy at CMS 2016-; energy and climate change 2014-15; BIS 2014-15. Campaigned to Remain in the EU. Select cttees: public accounts 2010-12; standards and privileges 2010-12. Took paternity leave prior to

the birth of his third child 2013. Married, three children. Ed: Exeter Coll, Oxford (BSc PPE); University of Cambridge (MSc economics).

CHALLENGERS
Michael Jeffreys (Lab) Former Newmarket Coll assistant principal. Cllr, Newmarket TC. Fourth time running for parliament. **Julian Flood** (Ukip) Cllr, Suffolk CC 2013-17. Public transport campaigner. **Elfreda Tealby-Watson** (LD) Self-

employed property investor. Former carer to her mother who suffered from dementia.

CONSTITUENCY PROFILE
Although mainly rural, Suffolk West contains Haverhill, an industrial manufacturing town nestled between the Essex and Cambridgeshire borders. The constituency is also home to Newmarket, famous for horse racing and two large US Air Force bases. It has received higher than average levels of EU immigrants, particularly since 2001, and wages are below the national average. It is a safe Conservative seat, although Ukip made inroads in 2015.

EU REFERENDUM RESULT
63.2% Leave   Remain 36.8%

Sunderland Central

LABOUR HOLD MAJORITY 9,997 (22.2%)

JULIE ELLIOTT
BORN July 29, 1963
MP 2010-

Sunderland born and raised. Policy, media and research officer, GMB. Regional organiser, GMB and Labour Party. Spent one year on National Asthma Campaign. Remainer; concerned about effect Brexit will have on Nissan. Listed in 'core group negative' in leaked Jeremy Corbyn hostility list 2016. Nominated Liz Kendall for leadership 2015. PPS to Caroline Flint 2010-13. Shadow min ECC 2013-15. Select cttees: CMS 2015-17; BIS 2011-13; European Scrutiny 2010-15. Four children. Ed: Seaham Northlea Comp; Newcastle Poly (government and public policy).

	Electorate	Turnout %	from 2010 %	Change
	72,728	62.03		
*J Elliott Lab	25,056	55.54	+5.36	
R Oliver C	15,059	33.38	+9.96	
G Leighton Ukip	2,209	4.90	-14.25	
N Hodson LD	1,777	3.94	+1.29	
R Featherstone Green	705	1.56	-2.52	
S Cockburn Ind	305	0.68		

CHALLENGERS
Robert Oliver (C) Politics teacher; runs school debating society and law club. Has worked with charity Raleigh International on local govt project in Chile. Cllr, Sunderland CC 2004-. Contested: Houghton and Sunderland South 2010; Sunderland South 2005. **Niall Hodson** (LD) Art historian. Has worked with galleries and museums. Cllr, Sunderland CC 2016-.

CONSTITUENCY PROFILE
Encompassing several coastal villages and the city of Sunderland, this is a former shipbuilding and coalmining town. Both industries have all but disappeared and, despite some regeneration, wages are low and unemployment exceeds the national average, particularly for those aged 50 and over. Few people are homeowners and a significant proportion live in social housing. In addition, more than 26 per cent of children in the area live in poverty. It is a safe Labour seat, and although Ukip did well in 2015, Labour continues to reign supreme.

EU REFERENDUM RESULT

59.9% Leave   Remain 40.1%

Surrey East

CONSERVATIVE HOLD MAJORITY 23,914 (40.4%)

SAM GYIMAH
BORN Aug 10, 1976
MP 2010-

Born in UK but spent childhood in Ghana. Investment banker for Goldman Sachs, and directed series of businesses. Chairman of Bow Group 2006-07. Contested: Gisport 2009; Kilburn 2006. PPS to David Cameron 2012-13. Govt whip 2013-14. Parly sec at cabinet office 2014-15; parly under-sec: education 2015-16; prisons and probations 2016-. Remainer. Filibustered sexual offences pardon bill, accused of reinforcing stereotypes of gay men. Married, one son. Ed: Achimota Sch, Accra; Freman Coll, Herts; Somerville Coll, Oxford (BA PPE; pres Oxford Union).

	Electorate	Turnout %	from 2010 %	Change
	82,004	72.20		
*S Gyimah C	35,310	59.64	+2.23	
H Tailor Lab	11,396	19.25	+7.44	
D Lee LD	6,197	10.47	+1.22	
A Parr Ind	2,973	5.02	+4.37	
H Windsor Ukip	2,227	3.76	-13.27	
B Southworth Green	1,100	1.86	-1.99	

CHALLENGERS
Hitesh Tailor (Lab) Born in Kenya. Cllr, Ealing C 2010-; cabinet member for health and adults. MD of Private Investment Group in central London. **David Lee** (LD) Cllr: Surrey CC 2017-; Tandridge DC 2015-, 2010-12. Customer service trainer. Contested Surrey East 2015, 2010. **Andy Parr** (Ind) Community organiser, garnered support from a disenchanted East Surrey electorate.

CONSTITUENCY PROFILE
Bordering Croydon, Kent and West Sussex, this seat comprises extremely affluent commuter towns and villages in the London green belt, set amongst the North Downs countryside, just outside Gatwick Airport, a major employer. Impressively low levels of unemployment, relatively good health, high levels of education and a high proportion of property owners with very low levels of social renting. A very safe Conservative seat, no opposition party has achieved more than 34 per cent of the vote since 1974. Most notably represented by former chancellor and foreign secretary Geoffrey Howe.

EU REFERENDUM RESULT

54.2% Leave   Remain 45.8%

Surrey Heath

CONSERVATIVE HOLD MAJORITY 24,943 (43.1%)

MICHAEL GOVE
BORN Aug 26, 1967
MP 2005-

	Electorate	Turnout %	from 2010 %	Change
	80,537	71.80		
*M Gove C	37,118	64.19	+4.33	
L Atroshi Lab	12,175	21.06	+9.85	
A Barker LD	6,271	10.85	+1.78	
S Galliford Green	2,258	3.91	-0.50	

Vocal former journalist for *The Times*, BBC News and STV. A lead Brexiteer and co-convener of Vote Leave campaign cttee. Made a controversial leadership bid at expense of Boris Johnson. Subsequently returned to write a column for *The Times*, and secured first UK post-US election interview with Donald Trump. Returned to govt as environment sec after 2017 election, despite trying to remove climate change from geography curriculum in 2013 and opposition to elements of EU environmental legislation. Former chairman, Policy Exchange. Entered govt in 2010 with a turbulent turn as SoS for education, followed by demotion to chief whip 2014. Appointed lord chancellor and SoS for justice 2015, until he left govt in 2016. Married to *Daily Mail* columnist Sarah Vine, two children. Ed: Lady Margaret Hall, Oxford (BA English).

CHALLENGERS
Laween Atroshi (Lab) Labour's first Kurdish parly candidate. Clinical researcher. Vice-chairman of the Young Fabians. Contested Surrey Heath 2015.

Ann-Marie Barker (LD) Leads a business research team. Vice-chairwoman, Woking Lib Dems. Cllr, Goldsworth Park 2016-.

CONSTITUENCY PROFILE
A homogeneous region which is 91 per cent white, in keeping with the South East. Enjoys very good health, high levels of home ownership, education and one of the lowest rates of unemployment in the country. A large percentage of residents work in managerial roles. There are relatively few 16-24-year-olds. Safe Tory seat represented by Gove after his predecessor Nick Hawkins was deselected by the local association.

EU REFERENDUM RESULT

51.9% Leave   Remain 48.1%

Surrey South West

CONSERVATIVE HOLD MAJORITY 21,590 (35.7%)

JEREMY HUNT
BORN Nov 1, 1966
MP 2005-

	Electorate	Turnout %	from 2010 %	Change
	78,042	77.44		
*J Hunt C	33,683	55.74	-4.14	
L Irvine NHAP	12,093	20.01	+11.52	
D Black Lab	7,606	12.59	+3.11	
O Purkiss LD	5,967	9.87	+3.60	
M Webber Ukip	1,083	1.79	-8.09	

Long-serving health secretary and former management consultant. Co-founded £35m education publishing business, Hotcourses 1996; remains a 48 per cent shareholder. An EU Remainer and centre-right Conservative. Heavily criticised SoS for health 2012-: negotiations for a new junior doctors contract led to strikes 2016. Attacked for claiming the NHS had a "Monday to Friday culture" in 2016. As SoS for CMS 2010–12, he oversaw the 2012 London Olympics. Shadow: min, work and pensions 2005–07; dep PM 2007-10. Former pres, Oxford University Conservative Association. Spent two years in Japan teaching English. Married, three children. Ed: Charterhouse; Magdalen Coll, Oxford (BA PPE).

CHALLENGERS
Louise Irvine (NHAP) GP. Chaired Save Lewisham Hospital campaign, which took the government to court in 2012 and won. Formed prog alliance with Labour and Green. Member, BMA council. **David Black** (Lab) IT Manager. Contested Wokingham 2005. **Ollie Purkiss** (LD) Games designer.

CONSTITUENCY PROFILE
Affluent area which borders Sussex and Hampshire. Very homogeneous, even for the South East, at 96 per cent white. Enjoys excellent health and high levels of education. High number of managers, directors and senior officials live in the area. Surrey South West and its predecessors have been represented by the Tories since 1910 by three cabinet ministers in a row: former SoS for employment, Maurice McMillan; former SoS for health, Virginia Bottomley; and Jeremy Hunt.

EU REFERENDUM RESULT

40.7% Leave   Remain 59.3%

Sussex Mid

CONSERVATIVE HOLD MAJORITY 19,673 (31.9%)

SIR NICHOLAS SOAMES

BORN Feb 12, 1948
MP 1983-

	Electorate	Turnout %	from 2010	Change %
	83,747	73.59		
*N Soames C	35,082	56.92	+0.80	
G Mountain Lab	15,409	25.00	+11.12	
S Osborne LD	7,855	12.75	+1.26	
C Jerrey Green	1,571	2.55	-1.72	
T Brothers Ukip	1,251	2.03	-9.97	
B Thunderclap Loony	464	0.75	+0.18	

Witty and outspoken backbencher, more recently known for his inventive Twitter hashtags. Winston Churchill's grandson. Knighted in 1994. Served in 11th Hussars and was equerry to Prince of Wales 1970-72. Worked as a stockbroker, and PA to Sir James Goldsmith. Previously MP for Crawley 1983-97. Contested Central Dunbartonshire 1979. Controversially barked at a female SNP MP in 2017 as she spoke in the chamber, and has been accused of sexism. Remain campaigner, voted for Article 50. Strong interest in the military: SoS for defence 2003-05; min for armed services 1994-97. President, Conservative Middle East Council. Twice married, three children. Ed: Eton Coll; Mons Officer Cadet Sch.

CHALLENGERS
Greg Mountain (Lab) Benefits manager, HMRC. Former policy manager, DWP. Contested Sussex Mid 2015. **Sarah Osborne** (LD) Former City worker, now a psychotherapist and counsellor. Co-founder of Sussex alcohol counselling service. Cllr, Lewes DC 2011-.

CONSTITUENCY PROFILE
An affluent, homogeneous constituency comprised of small villages and situated in the northeast of West Sussex. Home ownership is high with some of the lowest rates of council renting, benefits claimants and unemployment in the country. Long held by the Conservatives, with Liberal Democrats presenting the primary opposition until 2015 when their support fell dramatically and Labour ate into the Conservative's comfortable majority.

EU REFERENDUM RESULT

46.4% Leave	Remain 53.6%

Sutton & Cheam

CONSERVATIVE HOLD MAJORITY 12,698 (24.4%)

PAUL SCULLY
BORN Apr 29, 1968
MP 2015-

	Electorate	Turnout %	from 2010	Change %
	70,404	73.82		
*P Scully C	26,567	51.12	+9.58	
A Ahmad LD	13,869	26.69	-7.00	
B Craven Lab	10,663	20.52	+9.40	
C Jackson-Prior Green	871	1.68	-0.43	

Backbencher of Burmese heritage. Founding partner, Nudge Factory consultancy. Parly asst to: Alok Sharma 2010-12; Shailesh Vara 2007-09. Cllr, Sutton BC 2006-10. Rarely rebels. Campaigned to Leave EU. Controversy after being one of 24 Tory MPs to use Conservative HQ's RoadTrip battle buses and not declare it in expenses. CPS took no action. Select cttees: petitions 2015-17; international development 2016-17. Participated in Conservative Party's Project Maja in Bangladesh 2011. Volunteer at St Helier Hospital. Married, two children. Ed: Bedford Sch; University of Reading (BSc chemistry and food science).

CHALLENGERS
Amna Ahmad (LD) Born in Pakistan, grew up in Lewisham. Communications consultant. Associate dir, Incisive Health 2015-16. Shadow sec for refugees. Contested: GLA for Sutton and Croydon 2016; Streatham 2015. **Bonnie Craven** (Lab) Trade union officer. Former City worker and primary school teacher. Jeremy Corbyn supporter, worked on both his leadership campaigns. Helped write Labour NHS policy 2016.

CONSTITUENCY PROFILE
A Tory/Lib Dem marginal in the southwestern edge of London. Held by the Lib Dems from 1997 until 2015 when it was taken by Paul Scully. In the last two general elections Lib Dems have lost support to Labour, who gained a 9.4 per cent swing in 2017. Less ethnically diverse than the rest of London but considerably more so than the rest of the UK: almost a quarter of its residents were born outside the UK. Low unemployment and above average levels of property ownership.

EU REFERENDUM RESULT

51.3% Leave	Remain 48.7%

Sutton Coldfield

CONSERVATIVE HOLD MAJORITY 15,339 (29.0%)

ANDREW MITCHELL
BORN Mar 23, 1956
MP 2001-; 1987-97

	Electorate	Turnout %	from 2010 % Change
	75,652	69.87	
*A Mitchell C	32,224	60.96	+6.33
R Pocock Lab	16,885	31.94	+9.60
J Wilkinson LD	2,302	4.36	-0.81
D Ratcliff Green	965	1.83	-0.98
H Sophia Ind	482	0.91	

Synonymous with Plebgate, losing his libel case against *The Sun*, and resignation as chief whip in 2012. Served in the army before a career in finance. Lost Gelding seat in 1997. Contested Sunderland South 1983. SoS for int dev 2010-12. Shadow: SoS, Home Office 2005-10; min, home affairs 2004-05; min, Treasury 2003-04. Parly under-sec, DDS 1995-99. Whip: govt 1994-95; asst govt 1992-93. Vice-chairman, Conservative Party 1992-93. Vocal on the importance of access to female contraception. Founder of Project Umubano, a Conservative project in central and West Africa. Son of Tory MP Sir David Mitchell. Married, two daughters. Ed: Rugby School; Jesus Coll, Cambridge (BA history; pres, Cambridge Union).

CHALLENGERS
Rob Pocock (Lab) Founder, MEL Research, social and behaviour change consultancy. Cllr, Birmingham CC 2012- . **Jennifer Wilkinson** (LD) Forensic accountant. Only joined Lib Dems in 2015. School governor. **David Ratcliff** (Green) Retired metal industry worker.

CONSTITUENCY PROFILE
An affluent, middle-class constituency situated to the north of Birmingham. There are high levels of home ownership in Sutton Coldfield, where unemployment is low and wages outstrip the regional average. Residents are typically educated to a high standard: nearly half have A Level qualifications or above. It is a safe Tory seat. Although Tony Blair's Labour nearly halved the Conservative majority in 1997, the Tory vote share has increased in each election since 2005.

EU REFERENDUM RESULT

51.7% Leave　　　Remain 48.3%

Swansea East

LABOUR HOLD MAJORITY 13,168 (37.5%)

CAROLYN HARRIS
BORN Sep 18, 1960
MP 2015-

	Electorate	Turnout %	from 2010 % Change
	58,521	60.08	
*C Harris Lab	22,307	63.45	+10.48
D Boucher C	9,139	25.99	+10.70
S Phillips PC	1,689	4.80	-5.60
C Johnson Ukip	1,040	2.96	-14.23
C Hasted LD	625	1.78	-2.36
C Evans Green	359	1.02	

Former barmaid, dinner lady and charity worker: regional manager for Children's Cancer Charity. Parly asst to Sian James MP 2005-15. Campaigned to Remain; voted for Article 50. Advocates scrapping of child burial fees. Shadow min: women and equalities 2017-; home affairs 2016-17. Rebelled to vote against renewing Trident. APPG chairwoman: children in Wales; fixed odds betting terminals; home electrical safety; state pension inequality for women. Ed: Llwyn y bryn GS; Brynhyfrd Junior (BSc primary education); Swansea University (BSc social history and social policy).

CHALLENGERS
Dan Boucher (C) Parliamentary affairs dir, CARE UK. Welsh AM candidate: South Wales West 2016; Swansea East 2011. MEP candidate Wales 2014. **Steffan Phillips** (PC) Freelance design consultant: dir, Totem Logic. Founder, Cwmbath Community Gardens Project. **Clifford Johnson** (Ukip) Trade union officer. Contested: Welsh Assembly, Swansea East 2016; Swansea East 2015.

CONSTITUENCY PROFILE
Covering the large council estates, docks and industrial estates along the river Tawe, Swansea East is more working class and less ethnically diverse than its western neighbour. Employment is dominated by the services sector, and over a quarter of the workforce are employed in administrative or sales occupations. Unemployment is above the UK average, and the number of benefit claimants has increased in recent years, especially among 18-24 year-olds. One of the highest proportion of residents with poor health in the country. A very safe Labour seat.

EU REFERENDUM RESULT

61.8% Leave　　　Remain 38.2%

Swansea West

LAB CO-OP HOLD MAJORITY 10,598 (28.4%)

GERAINT DAVIES
BORN May 3, 1960
MP 2010-; 1997-2005

MP for Croydon Central 1997-2005. Former group product manager for Unilever and marketing manager for Colgate-Palmolive. Businessman. Founder: Pure Crete; Equity Creative. Cllr, Croydon BC 1986-97. Appointed to Environment Agency Wales in 2005 to lead a team protecting Wales from flood risks. First newly elected MP in 2010-15 parliament to present a private bill - the credit card regulation (child pornography) bill 2010. Remain campaigner; submitted letter to parliament requesting second referendum, voted against triggering Article 50. Nominated

Electorate Turnout % from 2010 % Change			
	56,892	65.53	
*G Davies Lab Co-op	22,278	59.76	+17.18
C Lawton C	11,680	31.33	+8.77
R Fitter PC	1,529	4.10	-2.34
M O'Carroll LD	1,269	3.40	-5.64
M Whittall Green	434	1.16	-3.91
B Johnson SPGB	92	0.25	+0.11

Yvette Cooper for Labour leadership 2015. Occasional rebel. Member, parly assembly of the council of Europe 2010-17. Member, GMB; MSF. Married, three daughters. Ed: Llanishen CS, Cardiff; Jesus Coll, Oxford (BA PPE).

CHALLENGERS
Craig Lawton (C) Senior policy and comms adviser for Welsh Assembly. Cllr, Forest of Dean DC 2015-. Former legal aid

worker. **Richard Fitter** (PC) Caseworker, Welsh Assembly.

CONSTITUENCY PROFILE
Previously an industrial town, the economy is now heavily based around the services industry and is a retail hub for much of western Wales. It contains Swansea University and due to the large student population, the number of 16-24 year-olds living here is well above the national average. Income is much higher than its eastern neighbour. There is a large Asian and Arab population. Dominated by Labour since 1964, Alan Williams held the seat for 46 years until 2010.

EU REFERENDUM RESULT
43.4% Leave   Remain 56.6%

Swindon North

CONSERVATIVE HOLD MAJORITY 8,335 (15.2%)

JUSTIN TOMLINSON
BORN Nov 5, 1976
MP 2010-

Student politician who was national chairman of Conservative Future. Marketing executive and businessman: owned and ran TB Marketing, a major print supplier for local Conservative parties. Cllr, Swindon BC 2000-10. Reported Sadiq Kahn to police for allegedly using a phone while driving. Suspended and faced calls for resignation in 2015 when it was revealed that he leaked public accounts cttee information to Wonga. com. Brexit campaigner. Parly under-sec for disabled people 2015-16. PPS to Ed Vaizey 2014-15. Contested Swindon North

Electorate Turnout % from 2010 % Change			
	80,194	68.47	
*J Tomlinson C	29,431	53.60	+3.26
M Dempsey Lab	21,096	38.42	+10.65
L Webster LD	1,962	3.57	+0.31
S Halden Ukip	1,564	2.85	-12.49
A Bentley Green	858	1.56	-1.74

2005. Divorced wife and started a relationship with his junior researcher in 2016. Ed: Harry Cheshire HS, Kidderminster; Oxford Brookes University (BA business and marketing).

CHALLENGERS
Mark Dempsey (Lab) Environmental policy adviser, HP. Cllr, Swindon BC 2010-. Contested The Cotswolds 2010. School governor. **Liz Webster** (LD) Runs a nanny and household staff recruitment

agency, previously worked in advertising for Saatchi & Saatchi.

CONSTITUENCY PROFILE
Stretching northwards from Swindon town centre to the surrounding suburban area and the market town of Highworth. The majority of constituents live in the suburbs or close to the centre of Swindon. The manufacturing, retail, transport and financial services sectors are all key employers. Higher than average levels of property ownership. Unemployment is slightly lower than its southern counterpart. Conservative-leaning marginal and bellwether since its creation in 1997.

EU REFERENDUM RESULT
57.3% Leave   Remain 42.7%

Swindon South

CONSERVATIVE HOLD MAJORITY 2,464 (4.8%)

ROBERT BUCKLAND
BORN Sep 22, 1968
MP 2010-

Barrister (QC) interested in criminal justice policy and planning. Solicitor general 2014-. Centrist, warned against a Conservative Party shift to the right. Member: Conservative Group for Europe; Tory Reform Group. Keen pro-European. Voted for Article 50. Interested in disability and chaired APPG on autism. Won Grassroots Diplomat Policy Driver award for campaigning on SEN. Contested: South Swindon 2005; Preseli Pembrokeshire 1997; Islwyn 1995. Cllr, Dyfed CC 1993-96. Crown Court Recorder. Co-ordinator, Swindon SEN Network. Anglican. Married, two

	Electorate	Turnout %	from 2010 %	Change
	72,391	70.83		
*R Buckland C	24,809	48.39	+2.15	
S Church Lab Co-op	22,345	43.58	+9.09	
S Pajak LD	2,079	4.05	+0.37	
M Costello Ukip	1,291	2.52	-9.50	
T Kimberley-Fairbourn Green	747	1.46	-2.11	

children. Ed: St Michael's School, Bryn; Hatfield Coll, Durham (BA law).

CHALLENGERS
Sarah Church (Lab) Army veteran. Volunteers with Poppy Legion and Girlguiding. **Stan Pajak** (LD) Cllr, Swindon BC 1985-; mayor 2002-03. Turned down one per cent rise in cllr allowances. Contested Swindon South 1997. **Martin Costello** (Ukip) Former Wiltshire special constable.

CONSTITUENCY PROFILE
Covers the southern half of the town of Swindon and the rural areas surrounding it. Marginally more Labour than its northern neighbour with more social housing and ethnic diversity. The number of UK-born residents is much lower than the rest of the South West. Formerly a centre for railway manufacturing, it houses several industrial estates and large companies, including Nationwide HQ. 46.1 per cent of residents are in full-time employment, one of the highest rates in the country. Swing seat, held by Labour from 1997 until 2010, and has since seated Conservative Robert Buckland.

EU REFERENDUM RESULT
51.7% Leave | Remain 48.3%

Tamworth

CONSERVATIVE HOLD MAJORITY 12,347 (26.2%)

CHRISTOPHER PINCHER
BORN Sep 24, 1969
MP 2010-

Former IT management consultant. Drama-free and relatively quiet backbencher, noted for heckling Jeremy Corbyn in 2016. Campaigned for Iain Duncan Smith in 2001 leadership contest. Vehemently opposed to HS2. Campaigned to Leave the EU. Contested: Tamworth 2005; Warley 1997. Whip 2017-. Assistant whip 2016-17. PPS to Philip Hammond 2015-16. Select cttees: regulatory reform 2015-17; armed forces bill 2011; ECC 2010-15. Midlander, born and raised in Staffordshire. Has spent time working in Saudi Arabia and France. Worked in consultancy as a manager

	Electorate	Turnout %	from 2010 %	Change
	71,319	66.06		
*C Pincher C	28,748	61.02	+10.98	
A Hammond Lab	16,401	34.81	+8.73	
J Pinkett LD	1,961	4.16	+1.14	

at Accenture. Member: 1922 committee; Hodge Lane Nature Reserve; the Peel Society. Patron, Canwell Show. Ed: Ounsdale Sch, Wolverhampton; LSE (BA history).

CHALLENGERS
Andrew Hammond (Lab) Worked for the Labour govt after 2005. **Jenny Pinkett** (LD) Retired teacher at a local secondary school. Worked in a manufacturing and distributions company. Contested Tamworth 2015, 2010, 2001, 1997. Sec, Lichfield Lib Dems.

CONSTITUENCY PROFILE
This Staffordshire seat, which spreads from Tamworth market town to rural Lichfield, is dominated by family households. It has low unemployment with only 0.7 per cent of its population claiming benefits and wages are relatively high. Around a fifth of its workers are in the wholesale and retail trade, well above the UK average. Historically associated with Sir Robert Peel, whose 1834 manifesto was the foundation of the modern Conservative Party. Voted Labour from the seat's creation in 1997 until 2010 when it was won by the Conservatives and subsequently held.

EU REFERENDUM RESULT
66.0% Leave | Remain 34.0%

Tatton

CONSERVATIVE HOLD MAJORITY 14,787 (30.1%)

ESTHER MCVEY
BORN Oct 24, 1967
MP 2017-; 2010-15

Former TV presenter, journalist and businesswoman parachuted in to replace George Osborne after losing her Wirral West seat in 2015. Chairwoman, British Transport Police Authority 2015-17. Former senior adviser to communications company and honorary fellow of Liverpool University. Runs career encouragement charity based on book she wrote, *If Chloe Can*. First MP to employ an apprentice. John McDonnell once described her as "stain on humanity"; earned nickname McVile for her disability benefits cuts. Supports Thatcherite group Conservative Way Forward. MP

	Electorate	Turnout %	from 2010 %	Change
	67,874	72.36		
E McVey C	28,764	58.56	-0.05	
S Rushworth Lab	13,977	28.46	+10.11	
G Wilson LD	4,431	9.02	+0.52	
N Hennerley Green	1,024	2.08	-1.70	
Q Abel Ind	920	1.87		

Wirral West 2010-15. Contested Wirral West 2005. At the DWP as: MoS 2013-15; parly under-sec 2012-13. Ed: Queen Mary & Westfield University (LLB law); City University (MA radio journalism); Liverpool John Moores University (MSc corporate governance).

CHALLENGERS
Sam Rushworth (Lab) Runs small research and consultancy business. Former college lecturer and tutor at University of East

Anglia. Was senior manager in British Red Cross.

CONSTITUENCY PROFILE
Semi-rural Cheshire seat consisting largely of affluent villages and small towns with an above average proportion of homeowners, self-employed workers and those aged 45 and over. High Jewish and Christian populations. Traditionally Tory but won by independent candidate Martin Bell in 1997 after the incumbent Neil Hamilton was embroiled in a cash-for-questions scandal, when Labour and the Lib Dem stood aside. George Osborne won it in 2001 when Bell did not stand.

EU REFERENDUM RESULT
45.6% Leave   Remain 54.4%

Taunton Deane

CONSERVATIVE HOLD MAJORITY 15,887 (25.2%)

REBECCA POW
BORN Oct 10, 1960
MP 2015-

Career centred on agriculture and the environment and has championed these interests in parliament. Grew up on a farm and worked for the National Farmers Union. Former journalist on environment and farming issues for BBC, ITV and Channel 4. Ran the Taste of Somerset, an organisation supporting local food and drink producers. Set up communications and PR agency Pow Productions. Select cttees: environment, food and rural affairs 2015-17; environmental audit 2015-16. APPGs: chairwoman, animal welfare. Chairwoman, Defra backbench

	Electorate	Turnout %	from 2010 %	Change
	85,466	73.78		
*R Pow C	33,333	52.87	+4.76	
G Amos LD	17,446	27.67	+6.32	
M Jevon Lab	9,689	15.37	+6.13	
A Dimmick Ukip	1,434	2.27	-9.68	
C Martin Green	1,151	1.83	-2.72	

cttee. PPS to Gavin Barwell 2016-. Remain campaigner. Married, three children. Ed: La Sainte Union Convent, Bath; Wye Coll, London University (BSc rural environmental science).

CHALLENGERS
Gideon Amos (LD) Chartered architect. Chief executive for Town and Country Planning Assoc, awarded OBE for work reinventing the Garden City concept. Cllr, Oxford CC 1992-

96. **Martin Jevon** (Lab) Works for care organisation. Contested Taunton Deane 2010. **Alan Dimmick** (Ukip) Engineer. Cllr, Somerset CC 2013-. Contested Somerset and Frome 2015.

CONSTITUENCY PROFILE
Covers the Somerset county town Taunton, industrial town Wellington and surrounding villages. A high proportion of white residents at 97.2 per cent, with a fifth of residents aged 65 and over. A low unemployment rate and proportion of people claiming benefits. Traditionally Tory but won by the Lib Dems in 1997 and 2010, the Conservatives have tightened their hold since.

EU REFERENDUM RESULT
52.9% Leave   Remain 47.1%

Telford

CONSERVATIVE HOLD MAJORITY 720 (1.6%)

LUCY ALLAN
BORN Oct 2, 1964
MP 2015-

	Electorate	Turnout %	from 2010 %	Change
	68,164	65.56		
*L Allan C	21,777	48.73	+9.14	
K Sahota Lab	21,057	47.12	+9.32	
S King LD	954	2.13	-0.15	
L Shirley Green	898	2.01	-0.28	

Family rights campaigner who has been involved in a series of controversies: accused of faking an online death threat in 2015; accused of bullying staff 2015. Cllr, Wandsworth BC 2006-12, forced to stand down after council launched a child protection investigation, ultimately discontinued, into her son's wellbeing after Allan's visit to GP for depression. Founded Family First Group to improve child protection system. Started career as chartered accountant at PwC before moving on to investment management. Former dir: UBS Warburg; Gartmore Investment; First State Investments. Set up employment law consultancy, Workplace Law for Women, specialising in discrimination and maternity issues. Pro-Brexit. Select cttees: women and equalities 2017; education 2015-17. Married, one son. Ed: Durham University (anthropology); Kingston Law School (MA employment law).

CHALLENGERS
Kuldip Sahota (Lab) Indian-born businessman. Cllr, Telford and Wrekin C 2001-; leader 2011-16. **Susan King** (LD) Infamously claimed feminising hormones in tap water were affecting people's sexuality. Landscape specialist.

CONSTITUENCY PROFILE
A manufacturing seat consisting of several old industrial towns and rapidly growing new town developments. A large number of families with children, a high proportion of whom are aged 15 and under. Lower qualifications than the national average, with over a quarter holding none and just under a fifth holding Level 4 and above. A large Sikh population. Telford has been traditionally Labour since its creation in 1997, but it was gained by Lucy Allan in 2015.

EU REFERENDUM RESULT
66.2% Leave   Remain 33.8%

Tewkesbury

CONSERVATIVE HOLD MAJORITY 22,574 (38.2%)

LAURENCE ROBERTSON
BORN Mar 29, 1958
MP 1997-

	Electorate	Turnout %	from 2010 %	Change
	81,442	72.55		
*L Robertson C	35,448	60.00	+5.47	
M Kang Lab	12,874	21.79	+6.97	
C Clucas LD	7,981	13.51	-0.28	
C Cody Green	1,576	2.67	-1.32	
S Collins Ukip	1,205	2.04	-10.84	

Right-winger from a working-class Labour background. Career in industry, manufacturing and consultancy. Faced "cash for access" accusations when he gave a Commons pass to lobbyist after receiving funds. Was criticised for employing both his wife and new partner. Campaigned to Leave EU. Contested: Ashfield 1992; Makerfield 1987. Eurosceptic and pro-Brexit. Shadow min: Northern Ireland 2005-10; Treasury 2003-05; trade and industry 2003. Opposition whip 2001-03. Chairman, Northern Ireland select cttee 2010-15. Christian. Divorced, one daughter. Ed: St James' CofE Secondary Sch; Farnworth GS; Bolton Higher Education Inst (Dip management service).

CHALLENGERS
Manjinder Singh Kang (Lab) Solicitor. Dir, Kang Defence solicitors. Originally from Birmingham. Contested The Cotswolds 2015. Sikh. **Cait Clucas** (LD) HR specialist in social housing sector. Former cllr and group leader, Tewkesbury BC. Chair of governors, local primary school; parish councillor. **Cate Cody** (Green) Independent environmental consultant.

CONSTITUENCY PROFILE
A large rural constituency that includes the outskirts of Cheltenham and Gloucester. Population is skewed away from the young, with a fifth of residents aged 65 or over and almost a third aged 45 to 64. Fairly prosperous, with an above-average proportion of households owned outright and a low unemployment rate. A large white population at 97 per cent of residents. Reliably Conservative.

EU REFERENDUM RESULT
53.6% Leave   Remain 46.4%

Thanet North

CONSERVATIVE HOLD MAJORITY 10,738 (22.2%)

SIR ROGER GALE
BORN Aug 20, 1943
MP 1983-

	Electorate	Turnout %	from 2010	Change
	72,657	66.51		
*R Gale C	27,163	56.21	+7.23	
F Rehal Lab	16,425	33.99	+16.11	
C Egan Ukip	2,198	4.55	-21.16	
M Pennington LD	1,586	3.28	-0.21	
E Targett Green	825	1.71	-1.95	
I White CPA	128	0.26		

Former broadcaster and producer: Radio Caroline, Radio 270, Radio London, Radio 4, BBC director of children's television. Accused of sexism when referring to employed family members as "girls" on BBC Radio 4. Only former pirate radio disc-jockey to become a MP. Contested Birmingham Northfield 1982. Vice-chairman, Conservative Party 2001-03. Member, Parly Assembly of the Council of Europe 2012-15. Select cttees: ecclesiastical 2015-17; procedure 2007-15; panel of chairs 1997-2017; home affairs 1987-92. Remain campaigner. Divorced twice, remarried. Three children. Ed: Guildhall School of Music and Drama.

CHALLENGERS
Frances Rehal (Lab) Dir, Sure Start children's centre. Awarded MBE in 2009 for services to children and families. Studying for a PhD at Canterbury Christ Church University. Contested Thanet North 2015. **Clive Egan** (Ukip) Worked in financial services, journalism and consultancy. Former chairman, Ukip Westminster and City branch. **Martyn Pennington** (LD) Retired, previously worked for overseas aid organisations. Cllr, Thanet DC 2015-.

CONSTITUENCY PROFILE
Consists of the northeastern coast of Kent, made up of seaside towns and rural areas. Considerable retired population, almost half of residents are aged over 45-years-old. Higher unemployment rate than the South East average and slightly above the UK average. Safe Conservative seat, held by Sir Roger Gale since its creation in 1983, when Cherie Blair stood for Labour.

EU REFERENDUM RESULT
65.2% Leave   Remain 34.8%

Thanet South

CONSERVATIVE HOLD MAJORITY 6,387 (12.8%)

CRAIG MACKINLAY
BORN Oct 7, 1966
MP 2015-

	Electorate	Turnout %	from 2010	Change
	72,342	68.77		
*C Mackinlay C	25,262	50.77	+12.64	
R Ara Lab	18,875	37.94	+14.17	
S Piper Ukip	2,997	6.02	-26.42	
J Williams LD	1,514	3.04	+1.16	
T Roper Green	809	1.63	-0.55	
T Garbutt Ind	181	0.36	+0.24	
F Fisher CPA	115	0.23		

Firm right-winger, founder of Anti-Federalist League, which later became Ukip. Ukip founding treasurer and vice-chairman 1993-97; briefly Ukip leader 1997 but was demoted to deputy leader 1997-2000. Defected to Tories in 2005-. Chartered accountant and tax specialist. Cllr, Medway BC 2007.- Charged by CPS for overspending during 2015 election campaign. Contested: Gillingham 2005, 1997, 1992; Totnes 2001; European parliament 2004, 1999, 1994. Married. Ed: Rainham Mark GS; University of Birmingham (BSc zoology and comparative physiology); ICAEW (FCA); CIOT (CTA).

CHALLENGERS
Raushan Ara (Lab) Moved to area in 1988 to set up a family restaurant. Bangladeshi origin. **Stuart Piper** (Ukip) Harley Davidson riding reverend. Former helicopter technician. Ramsgate TC 2015-. Served at Pilgrims Hospice for seven years, but was dismissed when he was unsuccessfully charged for alleged gross misconduct. **Jordan WIlliams** (LD) Works for an international airline, formerly in retail management.

CONSTITUENCY PROFILE
Located in coastal Kent, tourism is an important industry. Residents are less qualified than the South East average, just over a fifth hold a Level 4 qualification or higher. High rates of unemployment and benefit claimants. Comedian Al Murray stood in 2015. Held by the Conservatives during the Thatcher years but fell to Labour in 1997, but recaptured by the Conservatives in 2010.

EU REFERENDUM RESULT
61.7% Leave   Remain 38.3%

Thirsk & Malton

CONSERVATIVE HOLD MAJORITY 19,001 (34.0%)

KEVIN HOLLINRAKE
BORN Sep 28, 1963
MP 2015-

	Electorate	Turnout %	from 2010 %	Change
	78,670	71.09		
*K Hollinrake C	33,572	60.03	+7.42	
A Avery Lab	14,571	26.05	+10.61	
D Keal LD	3,859	6.90	-2.08	
T Horton Ukip	1,532	2.74	-12.17	
M Brampton Green	1,100	1.97	-2.62	
J Clark Lib	753	1.35	-0.81	
P Tate Ind	542	0.97	-0.35	

Businessman, worked in property. MD and co-founder, Hunters Estate Agents. Pro-fracking, resigned as vice-chairman of unconventional oil and gas APPG in 2016 due to constituents' complaints over the group's funding. Remain supporter. PPS to David Lidington MP 2016-17. Select cttee, communities and local government 2015-17. Married, four children. Ed: Easingwold Sch; Sheffield Hallam University (BSc physics –uncompleted).

CHALLENGERS
Alan Avery (Lab) Retired army officer, runs Blackthorn Press

publishers. Anti-fracking in North Yorkshire. Cllr, Pickering TC. Contested Thirsk and Malton 2015. **Dinah Keal** (LD) Media and communications manager at Alzheimer's Society. Cllr, Rydale DC 2012-, 2003-11. Contested Thirsk and Malton 2015. **Toby Horton** (Ukip) Ex-broadcaster: former MD, Radio Tees; founding dir, Minster Sound Radio, York. William Hague's former aide, defected to

Ukip in 2006. Contested: Thirsk & Malton 2010 for Ukip; Rother Valley 1993 for Tories.

CONSTITUENCY PROFILE
An affluent rural area in north Yorkshire with a high rate of owner-occupiers. Thirsk and Malton's population is disproportionately made up of white residents aged 45 and over. The economy is largely based on tourism and agriculture, but many residents commute to York. The seat and its predecessors have returned Conservative MPs since the 19th century, apart from a one-year Liberal Democrat stint after a by-election in 1986.

EU REFERENDUM RESULT
56.4% Leave   Remain 43.6%

Thornbury & Yate

CONSERVATIVE HOLD MAJORITY 12,071 (23.8%)

LUKE HALL
BORN Jul 8, 1986
MP 2015-

	Electorate	Turnout %	from 2010 %	Change
	67,927	74.62		
*L Hall C	28,008	55.25	+14.23	
C Young LD	15,937	31.44	-6.50	
B Mead Lab	6,112	12.06	+4.29	
I Hamilton Green	633	1.25	-1.46	

Career in retail: former southwest regional manager for Farmfoods; became a sales assistant at Lidl aged 18. Remain campaigner, but voted to trigger Article 50. Campaigned to protect the green belt and improve transport services in South Gloucestershire. Select cttees: environmental audit 2015-17; work and pensions 2016-17; petitions 2016-17. Chairman, APPG on retail. Nominated for 2013 National Conservative Excellence awards. Married. Ed: John Cabot Academy.

CHALLENGERS
Claire Young (LD) Former

software engineer, who worked for IBM. Cllr, South Gloucestershire 2007-; deputy leader of Lib Dem group 2011-. **Brian Mead** (Lab) Works in security industry, formerly held local, regional and national positions in RMT union. Filton Town councillor for six years; vice-chairman of finance committee. Member, Unite. Local chairman of the Co-operative party. **Iain Hamilton** (Green) Scottish-born, career in the prison service. Community payback supervisor. Contested

Thornbury and Yate 2015. Married, two children.

CONSTITUENCY PROFILE
The seat Yale is made up of affluent commuter towns and villages to the north of Bristol. It has low levels of unemployment and almost a third of workers are in managerial, administrative or professional occupations. With little ethnic diversity, it contains a high proportion of white residents at 97.6 per cent. The seat's predecessor, Northavon, was narrowly won from the Conservatives by Liberal Democrat Steve Webb in 1997 but the Conservatives regained control in 2015.

EU REFERENDUM RESULT
52.2% Leave   Remain 47.8%

Thurrock

CONSERVATIVE HOLD MAJORITY 345 (0.7%)

JACKIE DOYLE-PRICE
BORN Aug 5, 1969
MP 2010-

Managed to hold this marginal seat again, after having to endure two recounts in 2010. Co-sponsored private members' EU referendum bill, but voted to Remain. Interest in finance, used to work for Financial Services Authority. Junior health minister 2017-. Assistant whip 2015-17. Select cttees: committee of selection 2015-17; public accounts 2010-14. Contested Sheffield Hillsborough 2005. Assistant private secretary, Lord Mayor of the City of London 2000-05. Roman Catholic. Ed: Notre Dame RC Sch, Sheffield; University of Durham (BA, economics and politics).

	Electorate	Turnout %	from 2010 %	Change
	78,153	64.39		
*J Doyle-Price C	19,880	39.50	+5.83	
J Kent Lab	19,535	38.82	+6.22	
T Aker Ukip	10,112	20.09	-11.62	
K McNamara LD	798	1.59	+0.29	

CHALLENGERS
John Kent (Lab) Lifelong Thurrock resident. Cllr, Thurrock 1997-. **Tim Aker** (Ukip) Conservative defector. MEP for East of England. Cllr, Thurrock BC 2014-. Contested Thurrock 2015. **Kevin McNamara** (LD) Seasoned Lib Dem campaigner. Contested: Essex PCC 2016; Ealing North 2015; Kent CC 2013; Thurrock BC 2012.

CONSTITUENCY PROFILE
Working class seat on the Thames Estuary, but also covers more affluent areas. The constituency is four fifths white, which is lower than the averages for the east of England and UK, and it has a large black African population. Historically industrial, work tends to be provided by the retail sector now. However, unemployment is high. The seat was held by Labour from 1992 to 2010. There was a fierce three-way battle between the Conservatives, Labour and Ukip in 2015 as they received 34, 33 and 32 per cent of the votes respectively. Thurrock is the only seat in which Ukip received over 10,000 votes in 2017.

EU REFERENDUM RESULT
70.3% Leave   Remain 29.7%

Tiverton & Honiton

CONSERVATIVE HOLD MAJORITY 19,801 (34.2%)

NEIL PARISH
BORN May 26, 1956
MP 2010-

Former Somerset farmer who still lives on family farm. MEP for SW England 1999-2009. Previously a local cllr. Contested Torfaen 2005. Chairman, Defra select cttee 2015-; led inquiries into flood prevention, air quality, the EU's common agricultural policy and treatment of domestic pets in 2015 parliament. Established three APPGs: beef and lamb; eggs, pigs and poultry; dairy. Helped set up foot and mouth inquiry. African politics expert: election monitor during 2000 presidential elections in Zimbabwe. Barred from entering Zimbabwe by Mugabe after campaigning for British

	Electorate	Turnout %	from 2010 %	Change
	80,731	71.61		
*N Parish C	35,471	61.35	+7.36	
C Kolek Lab	15,670	27.10	+14.39	
M Wilson LD	4,639	8.02	-2.44	
G Westcott Green	2,035	3.52	-2.83	

govt to reject legitimacy of the ZANU-PF govt in 2008; the ban still stands. Left school at 16 to run family farm. Married, two children. Ed: Brymore Sch.

CHALLENGERS
Caroline Kolek (Lab) Mayor and chairwoman, Honiton TC 2015-. Previously philosophy and RE teacher, head of dept, Taunton Academy 2000-16. Taught teacher training in Tripura, NE India. Contested Tiverton and Honiton 2015. **Matthew Wilson** (LD) Entrepreneur and teacher.

Gill Westcott (Green) Parish cllr. Helped start Exeter Community Energy and local currency the Exeter Pound.

CONSTITUENCY PROFILE
This East Devon seat has a large population of over 65s and is 98.5 per cent white. A significant proportion of residents are self-employed and much of the workforce is in the agriculture, forestry and fishing industries.Unemployment is low, while the number of benefits claimants is also small. Ultra-safe Conservative seat; neither it nor its predecessors, Tiverton or Honiton, have ever been held by any other current party.

EU REFERENDUM RESULT
57.8% Leave   Remain 42.2%

Tonbridge & Malling

CONSERVATIVE HOLD MAJORITY 23,508 (41.3%)

TOM TUGENDHAT
BORN Jun 27, 1973
MP 2015-

British Army 2003-13. Served in Iraq and Afghanistan. Worked as a journalist in Beirut. Established one of Lebanon's first PR companies. Later a management consultant and energy analyst in the City. Helped set up first non-warlord administration since the Soviet Invasion in Helmand Province, Afghanistan 2005-07. Remains a reserve officer. Chairman of foreign affairs select cttee 2017-. Select cttee, Speakers' advisory on works of art 2016-17. Campaigned to Remain in EU. Dementia and Alzheimer's campaigner. Son of Mr Justice Tugendhat. Married, two children. Ed: University of

	Electorate	Turnout %	from 2010 Change %
	77,234	73.68	
*T Tugendhat C	36,218	63.64	+4.23
D Jones Lab	12,710	22.33	+8.17
K Miller LD	3,787	6.65	-0.16
A Clark Green	2,335	4.10	-0.31
C Bullen Ukip	1,857	3.26	-11.93

Bristol (BA theology); Cambridge (MA Islamics).

CHALLENGERS
Dylan Jones (Lab) Operations manager for Royal Mail, ex-postman. Fundraising co-ordinator for learning disability charity. **Keith Miller** (LD) Cornwall-born son of RAF pilot. Contested Tonbridge and Malling 2015. Founding member of SDP. Worked as a pharmaceutical rep for 30 years. Mental health campaigner. **April**

Clark (Green) HR director. Joined party in Green surge of 2015. Former vice-chairwoman, disability charity Attitude is Everything.

CONSTITUENCY PROFILE
Rural seat which includes an affluent commuter belt. Large white population at 95.9 per cent, above average for the southeast. Low unemployment with an above average proportion working in finance, professional, scientific and technical activities, and real estate. Safe Conservative seat held by Sir John Stanley from its creation in 1974 until his retirement in 2015.

EU REFERENDUM RESULT

52.9% Leave	Remain 47.1%

Tooting

LABOUR HOLD MAJORITY 15,458 (26.6%)

ROSENA ALLIN-KHAN
BORN May 10, 1977
MP 2016-

Former junior A&E doctor, St George's Hospital, Tooting. Working-class background with mixed Polish and Pakistani heritage. Cllr, Wandsworth BC 2014-. Succeeded Sadiq Khan after he became Mayor of London. Nominated Owen Smith for Labour leadership 2016. Remainer; voted against triggering Article 50. Shadow min, CMS, 2016-. Amateur boxer. Married, two daughters; Welsh husband converted to Islam and raising children as Muslim. Ed: Trinity St Mary Sch; Brunel University (BSc medical biochemistry); Lucy Cavendish Coll, Cambridge (medicine).

	Electorate	Turnout %	from 2010 Change %
	77,960	74.62	
*R Allin-Khan Lab	34,694	59.64	+12.45
D Watkins C	19,236	33.07	-8.82
A Glassbrook LD	3,057	5.26	+1.32
E Obiri-Darko Green	845	1.45	-2.66
R Coshall Ukip	339	0.58	-2.29

CHALLENGERS
Dan Watkins (C) Founder, Contact Law legal tech company. Governor, Oak Lodge School for the Deaf. Volunteer, Shaw Trust unemployment charity. Founder, Tooting Voluntary Force. Member, RSPB. Contested Tooting by-election 2016, 2015. **Alex Glassbrook** (LD) Barrister, Temple Garden Chambers. Teacher, court skills and ethics. Author of *The Law of Driverless Cars: An Introduction*. Contested Tooting by-election 2016. **Esther**

Obiri-Darko (Green) Contested Tooting 2015, finishing third ahead of the Lib Dems and Ukip.

CONSTITUENCY PROFILE
Tooting is an urban, densely populated and traditionally working-class area. It is home to a large Asian population, mainly Indian and Pakistani residents, and a large black community, though both are slightly below the London average. There is a high number of middle-class professionals in the finance, information and communication, and real estate sectors. Almost half of residents are aged 25 to 44. Labour fought off a strong Conservative challenge in 2015.

EU REFERENDUM RESULT

25.6% Leave	Remain 74.4%

Torbay

CONSERVATIVE HOLD MAJORITY 14,283 (27.9%)

KEVIN FOSTER
BORN Dec 31, 1978
MP 2015-

Criminal defence paralegal; worked for Coventry City Council, including two years as deputy leader of the council 2011-13. Worked with MEP for the West Midlands on project opposing Labour government's plans to implement regional government. Member, Torquay Town Centre Community Partnership Steering Group. Contested Coventry South 2010. Select cttee, public accounts 2015-. Campaigned for fairer school funding and to regenerate town centres. Married. Ed: Hele's Sch; Warwick University (law LLB; international economic law LLM).

	Electorate	Turnout %	from 2010 % Change
	75,936	67.39	
*K Foster C	27,141	53.04	+12.37
D Brewer LD	12,858	25.13	-8.70
P Raybould Lab	9,310	18.19	+9.53
T McIntyre Ukip	1,213	2.37	-11.23
S Moss Green	652	1.27	-1.96

CHALLENGERS
Deborah Brewer (LD) Consultancy business owner. Former senior manager of a multinational travel, transport and tourism company. Choir member. **Paul Raybould** (Lab) Branch secretary, GMB Union Torbay. Former nurse, Torbay Hospital. Member: South West TUC; GMB Regional Council. **Tony McIntyre** (Ukip) Former English and history teacher. Chairman, Ukip Devon County Branch.

CONSTITUENCY PROFILE
Coastal seat where tourism, particularly food, accommodation and retail, are important employment sectors. High retired population at almost a fifth, while nearly a quarter of residents are aged 65 and over. High white population, well above average for the UK and just above average for the southwest. High rates of unemployment for region. Marginal between Liberal Democrats and Conservatives; former Liberal Democrat MP Adrian Sanders had a majority of only 12 when he was elected in 1997. Held by the Liberal Democrats until 2010.

EU REFERENDUM RESULT

62.5% Leave   Remain 37.5%

Torfaen

LABOUR HOLD MAJORITY 10,240 (26.6%)

NICK THOMAS-SYMONDS
BORN May 26, 1980
MP 2015-

Former politics tutor and lecturer, St. Edmund Hall, Oxford. Later practising barrister, civil and public law, Chambers Civitas Law. Author: *Attlee: A Life in Politics* 2012; *Nye: The Political Life of Aneurin Bevan* 2015. Former secretary, Blaenavon Labour branch, Torfaen CLP. Quit front bench protesting Jeremy Corbyn's leadership. Remainer; voted to trigger Article 50. Shadow: home affairs min 2017-; solicitor general 2016-17; work and pensions 2015-16. Married, two daughters. Ed: St Alban's RC HS, Pontypool; St. Edmund Hall, Oxford (BA PPE).

	Electorate	Turnout %	from 2010 % Change
	61,839	62.14	
*N Thomas-Symonds Lab	22,134	57.60	+12.95
G Smith C	11,894	30.95	+7.84
J Rees PC	2,059	5.36	-0.36
I Williams Ukip	1,490	3.88	-15.11
A Best LD	852	2.22	-1.13

CHALLENGERS
Graham Smith (C) Engineer, rail industry, formerly aerospace. Former Conservative Torfaen CBC group leader. Cllr, Torfaen 2008-16. **Jeff Rees** (PC) Businessman. Plaid Cymru Torfaen group leader and Cllr in Torfaen since 2008. **Ian Williams** (Ukip) Owner of a taxi business. Former: soldier; factory worker; electronics manager. Secretary, Ukip Wales. **Andrew Best** (LD) Has been a teacher at two schools in Worcestershire.

CONSTITUENCY PROFILE
Seat to the north of Newport with an above-average white population for both Wales and the UK. A high proportion of housing is socially rented, while a low proportion is privately rented. Once famed for its coal and iron industries, these have been replaced by manufacturing and retail. Leo Abse, the pioneer of gay rights legislation in the 1960s, was Torfaen's MP from 1951 to 1987. It is a safe Labour seat held, along with its predecessor, since 1918. Though the majority had been steadily declining from its 1997 peak, it increased from 8,169 in 2015 to 10,240 in 2017.

EU REFERENDUM RESULT

60.8% Leave   Remain 39.2%

Totnes

CONSERVATIVE HOLD MAJORITY 13,477 (26.8%)

SARAH WOLLASTON
BORN Feb 27, 1962
MP 2010-

	Electorate	Turnout %	from 2010	Change %
	68,913	72.95		
*S Wollaston C	26,972	53.65	+0.70	
G Messer Lab	13,495	26.85	+14.13	
J Brazil LD	6,466	12.86	+2.95	
J Hodgson Green	2,097	4.17	-6.12	
S Harvey Ukip	1,240	2.47	-11.67	

An NHS doctor for 24 years, including 11 spent as a GP. An independently minded backbencher: the first MP to have been selected as a parliamentary candidate for a major British party through a postal open primary. Voted against Syrian military intervention 2013. *Spectator* backbencher of the year 2014. Political Studies Association backbencher of the year 2015. Abandoned the Leave campaign in June 2016; voted Remain. Criticised Theresa May's government for NHS cuts 2017. Chairwoman, health select cttee 2010-. Keen runner and cyclist.

Married, three children. Ed: Guy's Hospital (medicine).

CHALLENGERS
Gerrie Messer (Lab) Tesco employee, community-based role. Equalities Officer, USDAW. Women and Equalities Officer, Totnes Labour Party. **Julian Brazil** (LD) Helps local businesses with accounts. Former science teacher. Former chairman, Green Liberal Dems. Cllr, Devon CC 2005-. **Jacqi Hodgson** (Green) Freelance environmental adviser. Cllr: South Hams DC 2011-; Totnes TC 2009-, Totnes's first Green mayor 2014-.

CONSTITUENCY PROFILE
Accommodation, food, farming and fishing are key industries. There are many service sector jobs and unemployment is low. Home ownership is high and the proportion of people aged 65 or over is among the highest in the UK at more than a quarter. An affluent and picturesque area that has been represented by the Conservatives since 1924, although until 2015 the Liberal Democrats were always contenders.

EU REFERENDUM RESULT

53.9% Leave	Remain 46.1%

Tottenham

LABOUR HOLD MAJORITY 34,584 (70.1%)

DAVID LAMMY
BORN Jul 19, 1972
MP 2000-

	Electorate	Turnout %	from 2010	Change %
	72,883	67.70		
*D Lammy Lab	40,249	81.58	+14.25	
M Stacey C	5,665	11.48	-0.48	
B Haley LD	1,687	3.42	-0.71	
J Francis Green	1,276	2.59	-6.65	
P Rumble Ukip	462	0.94	-2.62	

Born and raised in Tottenham. Admitted to the Bar of England and Wales in 1994. First black Briton to study Masters in law at Harvard. Minister of state: higher education 2008-10; CMS 2005-07. Active backbencher 2010-. Campaigned to Remain; strong advocate of free movement. Vote of no confidence in Jeremy Corbyn 2016, defended him on BBC *Sunday Politics* 2017. Came fourth in London Labour Party mayoral selection 2015. Married, three children. Ed: SOAS (law); Harvard (MA law).

CHALLENGERS
Myles Stacey (C) Outreach officer between community groups. School governor. Previously policy adviser UN and London 2012 Olympics & Paralympics government relations team. **Brian Haley** (LD) Stood as Lib Dem candidate for London Mayor in 2011. Former Haringey cllr. Defected from Labour in 2010. Affordable housing campaigner. **Jarelle Francis** (Green) Former small business owner, fashion industry. Tottenham-born, grew up in social housing.

CONSTITUENCY PROFILE
Densely populated inner city seat in North London with a multicultural population. Over a quarter of residents are black and there is a significant Asian ppopulation. There are also large Cypriot, Turkish, Irish, eastern European, Muslim and Jewish communities. Social and private renting is common, while home ownership is low. The region is blighted by crime and is notorious for its riots in 2011 and 1985. The latter took place after the death of Cynthia Jarrett and is remembered for the murder of PC Keith Blakelock. It is a safe Labour seat, returning Labour MPs since 1935.

EU REFERENDUM RESULT

23.8% Leave	Remain 76.2%

Truro & Falmouth

CONSERVATIVE HOLD MAJORITY 3,792 (6.7%)

SARAH NEWTON
BORN Jul 19, 1961
MP 2010-

	Electorate	Turnout %	from 2010 %	Change
	74,691	75.84		
*S Newton C	25,123	44.35	+0.35	
J Kirkham Lab	21,331	37.66	+22.50	
R Nolan LD	8,465	14.94	-1.90	
D Odgers Ukip	897	1.58	-9.99	
A Pennington Green	831	1.47	-7.23	

Former: marketing officer: IBIS; Citibank; American Express. Director of Age Concern England; founder and initial director, International Longevity Centre. Key priorities: Cornwall's public services; better transport links; health and social care. Remainer; voted for Article 50 bill. Parliamentary ambassador for carers 2013. Parliamentary under-secretary: vulnerability, safeguarding and countering extremism 2016-; assistant whip 2015-16. Select cttees: ecclesiastical 2014-15; science and technology 2012-15; administration 2010-12. Married, three children. Ed: Falmouth Comprehensive School; King's College London (BA history).

CHALLENGERS
Jayne Kirkham (Lab) Falmouth School employee. Former Falmouth Citizens Advice Bureau lawyer. Member, UNISON. **Rob Nolan** (LD) Runs B&B with wife. Cllr, Truro CC 2009-; mayor 2016-17, 2011-12. **Duncan Odgers** (Ukip) Water industry. Former apprentice electrician. Key priority: devolved power from Westminster. **Amanda Pennington (**Green) Refugee aid project organiser. Cllr, Wadebridge TC 2011-.

CONSTITUENCY PROFILE
A coastal seat which is popular with tourists, where accommodation, food and retail are large employers. The area has a large white population and the number of retired residents is above average. Low unemployment and benefit claimancy. Previously a strong Lib Dem seat, the Conservatives pipped the party in 2010 after boundary changes and clung onto the seat in 2017 despite a 22.5 per cent swing to Labour.

EU REFERENDUM RESULT

45.9% Leave   Remain 54.1%

Tunbridge Wells

CONSERVATIVE HOLD MAJORITY 16,465 (30.4%)

GREG CLARK
BORN Aug 28, 1967
MP 2005-

	Electorate	Turnout %	from 2010 %	Change
	75,138	72.15		
*G Clark C	30,856	56.92	-1.77	
C Woodgate Lab	14,391	26.55	+12.34	
R Sadler LD	5,355	9.88	+1.44	
C Hoare Ukip	1,464	2.70	-9.90	
T Bisdee Green	1,441	2.66	-2.51	
C Thomas Women	702	1.29		

Worked for the Boston Consulting Group, posted in USA, Mexico, South America and Iceland. Special adviser to secretary of state for trade and industry, Ian Lang 1996-97. BBC controller, commercial policy. Director of policy for the Conservative Party under William Hague, Iain Duncan Smith and Michael Howard 2001-05. Hails from the soft left of the Conservative Party. SoS for BEIS 2016-. Minister for universities, sciences and cities 2014-15. Previously: financial secretary to the Treasury 2012-13; minister of state in the Department for Communities and Local Government 2010-12. Remainer. Ed: Magdalene Coll, Cambridge (economics); LSE (PhD).

CHALLENGERS
Charles Woodgate (Lab) International Director at Santander UK 2014-. Previously Global Trade and Receivables Finance at HSBC 2012-14. Kent-born. **Rachel Sadler** (LD) AXA PPP healthcare personal adviser 2015-. Former adviser at fashion brand Hobbs. Contested Bexhill and Battle 2015. **Chris Hoare** (Ukip) Former cllr, Kent CC.

CONSTITUENCY PROFILE
The area consists of the affluent town of Royal Tunbridge Wells and swathes of rural Kent. Predominantly white, the percentage of black, Asian and Arab residents is well below the averages for the southeast and the rest of the UK. Its affluence is highlighted by its high levels of home ownership, private renting and wages. A safe Conservative seat, it was held by Sir Patrick Mayhew, the former secretary of state for Northern Ireland, from 1974 to 1997.

EU REFERENDUM RESULT

44.6% Leave   Remain 55.4%

Twickenham

LIBERAL DEMOCRAT GAIN MAJORITY 9,762 (14.7%)

SIR VINCE CABLE
BORN May 9, 1943
MP 2017-; 1997-2015

	Electorate	Turnout %	from 2010 Change %
	83,362	79.52	
V Cable LD	34,969	52.75	+14.75
*T Mathias C	25,207	38.03	-3.23
K Dunne Lab	6,114	9.22	-2.27

Incoming Liberal Democrat leader and one of the party's few recognisable MPs. Surprising loss to the party in 2015. Strong background in economics: SoS for BIS 2010-15; shadow chancellor 2003-10; appointed Shell's chief economist in 1995 after joining in 1990; special adviser on economic affairs for the Commonwealth secretary 1983-90; deputy director, Overseas Development Institute; Treasury finance office, Kenyan government 1966-68; former economics lecturer, Glasgow University. Labour cllr, Glasgow 1971-74. Contested: City of York 1987, 1983; Glasgow Hillhead

1970. Widowed, three children, two grandchilren. Remarried. Two grandchildren. Keen dancer, appeared on the 2010 *Strictly Come Dancing* Christmas show. Ed: Cambridge (natural sciences and economics); Glasgow University (PhD economics).

CHALLENGERS
Tania Mathias (C) MP for Twickenham 2015-17. Former: NHS eye doctor; refugee officer, United Nations Relief and Works Agency in the Gaza Strip and Africa. Remainer; voted for Article 50 bill. **Katherine**

Dunne (Lab) Overseas European research projects, National Physical Laboratory. Cllr, Hounslow 2014-; cabinet member, housing.

CONSTITUENCY PROFILE
Affluent area on the banks of the Thames with good rail links to London and low unemployment. Higher white population and proportion of homeowners than the London average. Highly qualified population with the highest voter turnout in the UK in 2017. Though unseated in 2015, Cable regained his majority in 2017 with the highest vote percentage for the Liberal Democrats in any constituency.

EU REFERENDUM RESULT
33.3% Leave   Remain 66.7%

Tynemouth

LABOUR HOLD MAJORITY 11,666 (20.5%)

ALAN CAMPBELL
BORN Jul 8, 1957
MP 1997-

	Electorate	Turnout %	from 2010 Change %
	77,434	73.43	
*A Campbell Lab	32,395	56.98	+8.76
N Varley C	20,729	36.46	+3.65
J Appleby LD	1,724	3.03	+0.05
S Houghton Ukip	1,257	2.21	-10.02
J Erskine Green	629	1.11	-2.66
A The Durham Cobbler ND	124	0.22	

Former history teacher, sixth form head and head of history department. Member of public accounts select cttee during first parliament. Campaigned to Remain in EU. Considered hostile towards Jeremy Corbyn's leadership; defied him and voted in favour of airstrikes in Syria. Rarely rebels against party whip. After 2001 election became PPS to Adam Ingram 2004-05. Assistant whip under Tony Blair 2005; whip 2006-08. Promoted to Home Office as parly under-sec 2008-10. Opposition deputy chief whip 2010-. Select cttees: cttee of selection 2010-17, 2006-08; armed forces bill

2005-06. Campaign coordinator, Tynemouth Labour. Married, one daughter, one son. Ed: Blackfyne SS, Consett; Lancaster (BA politics); Leeds (PGCE); Newcastle Poly (MA history).

CHALLENGERS
Nick Varley (C) Associate dir, Stonehaven. Cllr: Chiltern DC; Chesham TC. Head of Vote Leave ground campaign. **John Appleby** (LD) Head of mechanical engineering,

Newcastle University. Contested N Tyneside Mayor 2017. **Stuart Houghton** (Ukip) Psychology teacher. Contested N Tyneside Mayor 2017. **Julie Erskine** (Green) Dog-walker. Contested Tynemouth 2015, 2010.

CONSTITUENCY PROFILE
Large white population, in step with the rest of the North East. High proportion of homeowners and those with Level 4 qualifications or above. Regeneration projects are taking place in areas once dominated by coalmining and shipbuilding. The seat returned Conservative MPs 1950-97 but has been safely Labour ever since.

EU REFERENDUM RESULT
47.6% Leave   Remain 52.4%

Tyneside North

LABOUR HOLD MAJORITY 19,284 (37.2%)

MARY GLINDON
BORN Jan 13, 1957
MP 2010-

Electorate		78,914	65.76
	Turnout %	from 2010 %	Change
*M Glindon Lab	33,456	64.47	+8.53
H Newman C	14,172	27.31	+8.09
G Legg Ukip	2,101	4.05	-12.22
G Stone LD	1,494	2.88	-1.55
M Collins Green	669	1.29	-1.79

Former Civic Mayor. Practising Roman Catholic. Interested in health and older people. Pro-Remain. Resigned over Jeremy Corbyn's leadership despite being considered a supporter of him in the party; joined shadow cabinet after his re-election 2016. PPS to: shadow transport team 2014-16; Mary Creagh 2013-14. Shadow min farming and rural communities 2016-. Select cttees: transport 2015-16; CLG 2013-15; environment, food, rural affairs 2010-15. Cllr, North Tyneside 1995-2010; mayor 1999-2000. Former administrative officer at the Child Support Agency and DWP 2008-10. Voluntary sector worker, ran North Shield's People's Centre. GMB. Founder, Battle Hill Community Development Project. Married, one daughter, two stepchildren. Ed: Newcastly Poly (BSc Sociology).

CHALLENGERS
Henry Newman (C) Dir, Brexit think tank Open Europe. Former adviser to Michael Gove in Ministry of Justice. SOAS politics tutor. **Gary Legg** (Ukip) Rail industry worker. Former

RAF serviceman. Chairman, Ukip North Tyneside. **Greg Stone** (LD) Carer for his partner. Former account director. Cllr, Newcastle CC 1998-.

CONSTITUENCY PROFILE
Stretches along the Tyne through former mining communities. Mining and ship-building communities have seen decline over the last few decades. Public administration and defence now a major industry with service and administrative occupations proportionately high. High white population. Large amount of social housing and unemployment. Has been held by Labour for decades.

EU REFERENDUM RESULT

59.5% Leave	Remain 40.5%

Tyrone West

SINN FEIN HOLD MAJORITY 10,342 (23.8%)

BARRY MCELDUFF
BORN Aug 16, 1966
MP 2017-

Electorate		64,009	67.94
	Turnout %	from 2010 %	Change
B McElduff SF	22,060	50.73	+7.25
T Buchanan DUP	11,718	26.95	+9.49
D McCrossan SDLP	5,635	12.96	-3.71
A Clarke UUP	2,253	5.18	-10.71
S Donnelly Alliance	1,000	2.30	+0.05
C McClean Green	427	0.98	-1.04
B Brown Citizens	393	0.90	

Long-time republican activist. MLA, Tyrone West 1998-2017. Elected to NI Forum for Tyrone West 1996. Cllr, Omagh DC 2000. Contested Ulster Mid 1992. Member, Sinn Fein national officer board. Spoke out about perils of loss of EU peace funding in the region. Forced to repay £900 to Stormont after breaking rules over spending money on party political letters 2015. Played Gaelic football at senior level for Carrickmore and at a minor level for Tyrone. Married, three children. Ed: Christian Brothers GS, Omagh; Queen's University, Belfast (BA political science & Celtic studies).

CHALLENGERS
Thomas Buchanan (DUP) One of DUP's members of the NI policing board. Cllr, Omagh DC 1993-; vice-chairman 2004. Promotes teaching of creationism in schools and told children attending a public event that homosexuality is an "abomination". **Daniel McCrossan** (SDLP) Writing his PhD in law. SDLP constituency rep for Tyrone West 2011-16.

Contested Tyrone West 2015. **Alicia Clarke** (UUP) Public relations officer and freelance journalist.

CONSTITUENCY PROFILE
Large white population, in step with the rest of Northern Ireland. A third of the population has no qualifications. Omagh was the scene of the 1998 IRA car bomb that killed 29 people. Agriculture, mining and quarrying, construction and manufacturing are important employers. Above average unemployment. Has one of the largest Catholic populations in Northern Ireland and is overwhelmingly nationalist.

EU REFERENDUM RESULT

33.2% Leave	Remain 66.8%

Ulster Mid

SINN FEIN HOLD MAJORITY 12,890 (27.6%)

FRANCIE MOLLOY
BORN Dec 16, 1950
MP 2013-

Veteran republican who cut his teeth during 1960s civil rights campaign. MLA, Ulster Mid 1998-2013; principal speaker 2011-13. Elected to Northern Ireland Forum 1996, then Stormont 1998. Cllr, Dungannon C 1984-89. Contested European elections 1994. Dir of elections for Bobby Sands during the 1980s. Temporarily suspended from Sinn Fein after speaking out against party policy on BBC radio. Described British govt's decision to authorise airstrikes on Syria as "Brits back to what they do best, murder", and tweeted that David Cameron was "the real terrorist" 2015.

	Electorate	Turnout %	from 2010 %	Change
	68,485	68.18		
*F Molloy SF	25,455	54.51	+5.80	
K Buchanan DUP	12,565	26.91	+13.55	
M Quinn SDLP	4,563	9.77	-2.58	
M Glasgow UUP	3,017	6.46	-8.98	
F Watson Alliance	1,094	2.34	+0.44	

Defended abstentionism despite potential to block Theresa May's Queen's Speech 2017. Marched with Jeremy Corbyn in Bloody Sunday protest in the 1980s. Married, four children. Ed: St Patrick's Sch, Dungannon; Felden Govt Training Centre (engineering); Newry Further Education Coll (foundation studies humanities); University of Ulster.

CHALLENGERS
Keith Buchanan (DUP) MLA,

Ulster Mid 2016-. Involved with the Loyal Orders. Worked for food processing company. **Molachy Quinn** (SDLP) Health worker. Introduced living wage to Mid Ulster council, leading to a 12.5 per cent pay rise.

CONSTITUENCY PROFILE
A predominantly white population, the local economy is largely centred on agriculture, but also has one of the highest percentages of people working in the construction industry in the country. Ulster Mid has exceptionally low rates of recorded crime. A safe Sinn Fein seat that was held for 16 years by Martin McGuinness until 2013.

EU REFERENDUM RESULT

39.6% Leave   Remain 60.4%

Upper Bann

DUP HOLD MAJORITY 7,992 (15.6%)

DAVID SIMPSON
BORN Feb 16, 1959
MP 2005-

Previously worked in the food manufacturing industry for Universal Meat Company in Portadown. MLA for Upper Bann 2003-10. Former VP, DUP. DUP Westminster spokesman: Communities and Local Government 2010-15; EFRA 2015-; BIS 2009-. Accused Sinn Fein's Francie Molloy of the 1979 killing of his cousin in 2007. Spoke and voted against same-sex marriage bill. Against reducing capital gains tax. Cllr, Craigavon BC 2001-10; mayor 2004-05. Contested Upper Bann 2001. Proponent of creationism. Free Presbyterian Church. Married, two daughters, one son.

	Electorate	Turnout %	from 2010 %	Change
	80,168	63.94		
*D Simpson DUP	22,317	43.54	+10.86	
J O Dowd SF	14,325	27.95	+3.40	
D Beattie UUP	7,900	15.41	-12.47	
D McAlinden SDLP	4,397	8.58	-0.40	
T Doyle Alliance	2,319	4.52	+0.75	

Ed: Killicomaine HS, Portadown; Coll of Business Studies, Belfast.

CHALLENGERS
John O Dowd (SF) Trained as a chef before entering politics. Min for education in Sturmont Exec 2011-16. Member of NI Assembly for Upper Bann 2003-; deputy first minister 2011. Previously cllr and school governor. **Doug Beattie** (UUP) "Born in barracks" as father was a professional soldier. Followed his father, completed 28 years of

service in Bosnia, Kosovo, Iraq and Northern Ireland. Cllr 2014-. **Declan McAlinder** (SDLP) Plasterer. Chairman of his local Gaelic Athletic Club. Cllr.

CONSTITUENCY PROFILE
A largely urban seat which has the highest population of any NI constituency. Home to a strong manufacturing sector, but also contains some of the most deprived wards in Northern Ireland. Underwent some of the worst violence of the Troubles. This was the seat of David Trimble, then Ulster Unionist leader, who was defeated by the current MP in 2005 after a bitter contest.

EU REFERENDUM RESULT

52.6% Leave   Remain 47.4%

Uxbridge & Ruislip South

CONSERVATIVE HOLD MAJORITY 5,034 (10.8%)

BORIS JOHNSON
BORN Jun 19, 1964
MP 2015-; 2001-08

	Electorate	Turnout %	from 2010	Change
	69,938	66.76		
*B Johnson C	23,716	50.79	+0.55	
V Lo Lab	18,682	40.01	+13.64	
R Robson LD	1,835	3.93	-1.01	
E Kemp Ukip	1,577	3.38	-10.78	
M Keir Green	884	1.89	-1.26	

Bumbling sesquipedalian turned foreign secretary 2016-. A figurehead of Vote Leave, to the chagrin of David Cameron, after which Johnson's leadership campaign was fatally wounded by Leave ally Michael Gove. Mayor of London 2008-16, incurring regular press speculation about his relationship with Cameron and leadership ambitions. MP for Henley 2001-08. Sacked from front bench by Michael Howard in 2004 after lying about an affair. Previously fired from *The Times* for falsifying a quote. Editor, *The Spectator* 1999-2005. Author of books on ancient Rome, Churchill and London. Born in New York. Bullingdon Club alumnus. Divorced, remarried, five children. Ed: Balliol Coll, Oxford (BA classics; president, Oxford Union).

CHALLENGERS
Vincent Lo (Lab) Researcher in public policy, UCL. Treasurer, Chinese Labour. Member: Co-op Party; Unite. Parents migrated to the UK in the 1970s from Hong Kong. **Rosina Robson** (LD) Director of Nations and Children, Pact trade association. Led local campaigns to introduce 20mph speed limit.

CONSTITUENCY PROFILE
An ethnically diverse commuter-belt seat in west London. Relatively affluent, with a low percentage of people claiming benefits. Contains a large student population as both Buckinghamshire New University and Brunel University have a campus here. Close to Heathrow airport so a high proportion of residents are employed in the transport industry. Historically a safe Conservative seat, but saw a large swing to Labour in 2017.

EU REFERENDUM RESULT

57.2% Leave   Remain 42.8%

Vale of Clwyd

LABOUR GAIN MAJORITY 2,379 (6.1%)

CHRIS RUANE
BORN Jul 18, 1958
MP 2017-; 1997-2015

	Electorate	Turnout %	from 2010	Change
	56,890	68.00		
C Ruane Lab	19,423	50.21	+11.86	
*J Davies C	17,044	44.06	+5.04	
D Wyatt PC	1,551	4.01	-3.04	
G Williams LD	666	1.72	-0.87	

Veteran MP knocked out of his seat by the Conservatives in 2015. Contested Clwyd North West 1992. Former primary school teacher and deputy head teacher. Member, NUT. Cllr, Rhyl TC 1988-2000. Trustee, Oxford Mindfulness Centre. Founding member, Rhyl anti-apartheid, environmental association. PPS to: David Miliband 2009-10; Caroline Flint 2007-08; Peter Hain 2003-07, resigned in protest at decision to renew Trident. Remain supporter; has consistently voted for more EU integration. Shadow Wales min 2017-. Opposition whip 2011-13. Set up mindfulness APPG, produced Mindful Nation report 2015. Catholic. Married, two daughters. Ed: University of Wales Coll, Aberystwyth (BSc economics); University of Liverpool (PGCE).

CHALLENGERS
James Davies (C) MP for Vale of Clwyd 2015-17. NHS GP and dementia clinical champion. Known locally for holding surgeries in supermarkets and pubs. Select cttees: Welsh affairs 2015-17; health 2015-17. Cllr: Prestatyn TC 2008-; Denbighshire CC 2004-. **David Wyatt** (PC) Southampton-born Arriva bus driver.

CONSTITUENCY PROFILE
Positioned on the north coast of Wales, the Vale of Clwyd is sparsely populated and contains the seaside towns of Rhyl and Prestatyn. The former is one of the most deprived areas in Wales. Much of the employment along the coast is seasonal and a high proportion of households have no adults in employment. It was held by Labour from its creation in 1997 until 2015, when it was won by just 237 votes by the Conservative candidate James Davies.

EU REFERENDUM RESULT

56.6% Leave   Remain 43.4%

Vale of Glamorgan

CONSERVATIVE HOLD MAJORITY 2,190 (4.1%)

ALUN CAIRNS
BORN Jul 30, 1970
MP 2010-

Secretary of state for Wales, 2016-, after the mini-reshuffle prompted by Iain Duncan Smith's resignation. Junior Wales minister 2014-16. Select cttees: public administration 2011-14; Welsh affairs 2010-11. AM, South West Wales 1999-2011. Supported Remain during the EU referendum. Suspended from the Conservatives in 2008 for referring to Italians as "greasy wops" live on BBC radio, for which he apologised. Contested: Vale of Glamorgan 2005; Gower 1997. Career before politics working for Lloyds Banking Group as a consultant and a field manager. Fluent Welsh speaker.

	Electorate	Turnout %	from 2010	Change %
	73,958	72.63		
*A Cairns C	25,501	47.47	+1.45	
C Beaven Lab	23,311	43.40	+10.78	
I Johnson PC	2,295	4.27	-1.32	
J Geroni LD	1,020	1.90	-0.65	
M Hunter-Clarke Ukip	868	1.62	-9.09	
S Davis-Barker Green	419	0.78	-1.27	
S Lovell Women	177	0.33		
D Elston Pirate	127	0.24		

Married, one son. Ed: Ysgol Gyfun Ystalyfera; University of Wales, Newport (MBA).

CHALLENGERS
Camilla Beaven (Lab)
Caseworker for Jane Hutt AM. Previously worked in special education, developing an interest in autism. Contested local elections 2017. **Ian Johnson** (PC) Plaid Cymru's head of policy

and a councillor in Barry 2012-. **Jennifer Geroni** (LD) Scientific researcher.

CONSTITUENCY PROFILE
Vale of Glamorgan covers the countryside along the south Wales coast to the southwest of Cardiff. The main population centre is the large resort and industrial port of Barry. Cardiff airport is a major employer within the seat, but many residents also commute to Cardiff. It contains higher levels of household income and home ownership than the Welsh average. Historically a marginal seat but it has remained in Conservative hands since 2010.

EU REFERENDUM RESULT
52.6% Leave   Remain 47.4%

Vauxhall

LABOUR HOLD MAJORITY 20,250 (36.8%)

KATE HOEY
BORN Jun 21, 1946
MP 1989-

Prominent Labour campaigner for Brexit. Born in County Atrim and was Northern Ireland high jump champion 1965. Educational adviser for Arsenal, Tottenham Hotspur and Chelsea before being elected. First female sports minister 1999-2001. Voted against the Iraq war. Visited Zimbabwe undercover in 2003 and 2005 to investigate political/ humanitarian crisis. Select cttees: public administration and constitutional affairs 2015-; European scrutiny 2015-; Northern Ireland 2007-. Honorary VP, Surrey County Cricket Club. Daughter of farmers. Ed: Belfast Royal

	Electorate	Turnout %	from 2010	Change %
	81,907	67.20		
*K Hoey Lab	31,576	57.37	+3.60	
G Turner LD	11,326	20.58	+13.67	
D Theis C	10,277	18.67	-8.59	
G Hasnain Green	1,152	2.09	-5.54	
H Iyengar Women	539	0.98		
M Chapman Pirate	172	0.31	-0.11	

Academy; Ulster College of Physical Education; City of London College (economics).

CHALLENGERS
George Turner (LD)
Investigative journalist. Head of office for Simon Hughes MP for Bermondsey and Southwark 2009-13. Born in Croatia, raised in London. **Dolly Theis** (C) Policy researcher, Centre for Social Justice 2015-. Founder of the Cube Movement, a social

media campaiging network against modern slavery.

CONSTITUENCY PROFILE
An inner-city seat in Lambeth that faces Westminster across the River Thames. Vauxhall is very ethnically diverse with large Jamaican and Ghanaian communities. Contains vast inequality: home to many top professionals, but the area also has above average rates of unemployment and a high percentage of social housing. Densely populated with one of the lowest levels of home ownership in the country. Held by Labour MPs since its 1983 creation.

EU REFERENDUM RESULT
22.4% Leave   Remain 77.6%

Wakefield

LABOUR HOLD MAJORITY 2,176 (4.7%)

MARY CREAGH
BORN Dec 2, 1967
MP 2005-

	Electorate	Turnout %	from 2010 % Change
	70,340	65.80	
*M Creagh Lab	22,987	49.67	+9.40
A Calvert C	20,811	44.96	+10.78
L Brown Yorkshire	1,176	2.54	
D Cronin LD	943	2.04	-1.41
W Ali Ind	367	0.79	

Former lecturer in entrepreneurship at Cranfield School of Management and coached owner-managers. Pro-business. Shadow SoS: international devt 2014-15; transport 2013-14; Defra 2010-13. Opposition asst whip 2010. PPS to: Andy Burnham 2006-09; Lord Warner 2006. Announced she was running for labour leadership in 2015 but withdrew candidacy. Campaigned to Remain. Disappointed with Jeremy Corbyn's lacklustre performance in referendum campaign and signed vote of no confidence. Supported air strikes in Syria. Introduced children's food bill 2005. Cllr, Islington BC 1998-2005; leader Lab group 2000-04. Speaks French and Italian fluently. Married, one daughter, one son. Ed: Bishop Ullathorne RC CS; Pembroke Coll, Oxford (BA modern languages); LSE (MSC European studies).

CHALLENGERS
Anthony Calvert (C) PR consultant. Dir, HardHat communications consultancy. Cllr, Wakefield 2004-07. **Lucy**
Brown (Yorkshire) Freelance writer, author of lesbian fiction. Chairwoman, Yorkshire Party.
Denis Cronin (LD) Works in university student recruitment.

CONSTITUENCY PROFILE
With the River Calder flowing through it, this Yorkshire seat contains the city of Wakefield, the town of Horbury and a smattering of neighbouring villages. Predominantly white with a significant Pakistani community, the area is characterised by high unemployment and low levels of home ownership. The seat has returned a Labour MP in every election since 1932.

EU REFERENDUM RESULT
62.8% Leave   Remain 37.2%

Wallasey

LABOUR HOLD MAJORITY 23,320 (48.2%)

ANGELA EAGLE
BORN Feb 17, 1961
MP 1992-

	Electorate	Turnout %	from 2010 % Change
	67,454	71.68	
*A Eagle Lab	34,552	71.46	+11.10
A Livsey C	11,232	23.23	+0.57
D Caplin Ukip	1,160	2.40	-9.28
P Childs LD	772	1.60	-0.73
L Clough Green	637	1.32	-1.65

Former shadow cabinet member who launched an abortive leadership campaign in July 2016, withdrew after losing a vote among Labour MPs to Owen Smith. Accused Jeremy Corbyn of allowing a "permissive" environment to flourish in which MPs opposed to Corbyn faced abuse 2016. Shadow cabinet: SoS for BIS 2015-16; leader of the commons 2011-15; chief sec to the treasury 2010-11. Minister for pensions 2009-10. Select cttees: Palace of Westminster 2015; House of Commons commission 2015. Whip 1996-97. Told to "calm down, dear" by David Cameron at PMQs in 2011, sparking accusations of sexism. First female MP to have come out as gay while in office, 1997. Identical twin, Maria, is also an MP. Civil partnership. Ed: Formby Comp HS; St John's Coll, Oxford (BA, PPE).

CHALLENGERS
Andy Livsey (C) Self-employed builder and Vote Leave campaigner. Contestant on the television shows *Blind Date* 1988 and *The Crystal Maze* in 1990.
Debbie Caplin (Ukip) A small business and sales manager. Treasurer, Ukip Wirral. Former Labour voter.

CONSTITUENCY PROFILE
Wallasey is a diverse coastal seat which suffers from severe deprivation. Unemployment is high, particularly among young people, and a large number of residents are in bad health. A £60m regeneration project is under way in New Brighton and has introduced a new cinema, casino and hotel to the area. Angela Eagle won the seat from the Conservatives in 1992 and it has since become a Labour stronghold.

EU REFERENDUM RESULT
49.9% Leave   Remain 50.1%

Walsall North

CONSERVATIVE GAIN MAJORITY 2,601 (6.8%)

EDDIE HUGHES
BORN Oct 3, 1968
MP 2017-

Trustee, Walsall Wood Allotment Charity. Chairman, Walsall Housing Group. Deputy chief executive, YMCA Birmingham. Cllr, Walsall 1999-. Positions held on council: decision-making cabinet; chairman, children's services scrutiny committe; audit committee. Born in Birmingham. Married, two children. Ed: Handsworth Grammar School; University of Glamorgan (civil engineering).

CHALLENGERS
David Winnick (Lab) MP for: Walsall North 1979-2017; Croydon South 1966-70. Former: advertising manager;

	Electorate	Turnout %	from 2010 %	Change
	67,309	56.63		
E Hughes C	18,919	49.63	+15.86	
*D Winnick Lab	16,318	42.81	+3.79	
L Hazell Ukip	2,295	6.02	-16.00	
I Parasram LD	586	1.54	-0.74	

branch chairman, Clerical and Administrative Workers Union. West Midlands's longest serving MP. Strong voice in House of Commons for human rights: against the Taliban and Sadam Hussein; for 2003 invasion of Iraq. Contested: Croydon Central 1974; Croydon South 1970; Harwich 1964. Select cttees: home affairs 1997-2017, 1983-87; treasury and civil service sub 1989-92; procedure 1989-97; treasury and civil service 1987-89; home affairs 1983-87; environment 1979-83. One son.

Liz Hazell (Ukip) Cllr, Walsall 2014-; leader of the Ukip group.

CONSTITUENCY PROFILE
The West Midlands seat is littered with areas of severe deprivation. Wages are low and, as a result, the number of people who own their own home is significantly smaller than regional and national levels. In addition, a considerable number of residents are unemployed and more than 34 per cent of the children living in the area are in poverty – 14 per cent higher than the national average. The seat was represented by the longstanding Labour MP David Winnick from 1979 to 2017.

EU REFERENDUM RESULT

74.2% Leave   Remain 25.8%

Walsall South

LABOUR HOLD MAJORITY 8,892 (20.2%)

VALERIE VAZ
BORN Dec 7, 1954
MP 2010-

Solicitor, local govt lawyer; set up community law firm Townsend Vaz. Deputy district judge; joined government legal service 2001. Presenter, BBC TV Network East 1987. Cllr, Ealing 1986-90. Contested Twickenham 1987. Shadow leader of the House of Commons 2016-. Vice-chairwoman, PLP. Select cttees: environment, food and rural affairs 2016; science and technology 2015-16; regulatory reform 2010-15; health 2010-15. Married, one daughter. Sister of Keith Vaz MP. Ed: Twickenham County Grammar Sch; Bedford Coll, University of London (BSc biochemistry).

	Electorate	Turnout %	from 2010 %	Change
	67,417	65.37		
*V Vaz Lab	25,286	57.37	+10.19	
J Bird C	16,394	37.20	+4.37	
D Bennett Ukip	1,805	4.10	-11.54	
A Wellings Purvis LD	587	1.33	-0.28	

CHALLENGERS
James Bird (C) Dir at communications consultancy, Remarkable Group. Former: associate dir, Quatro Public Relations; consultant, Curtin & Co; freelance broadcast journalist, BBC. Cllr, Birmingham CC 2010-14. Contested Birmingham Hall Green 2015. **Derek Bennett** (Ukip) Former West Midlands regional organiser, Ukip. Has been Ukip's candidate in Walsall South at every election since 2001, his vote peaking in 2015.

CONSTITUENCY PROFILE
The seat covers Walsall town centre and several suburbs, including the towns of Darlaston and Bentley. The area is diverse: nearly a third of the population is Asian/Asian British and there are about 3,500 black residents. As with many former industrial towns, the local economy is relatively dependent on the retail and services sector and has experienced a considerable level of difficulty since the recession. The constituency has high levels of unemployment. Walsall South has elected Labour MPs since 1974, although the Conservatives were within 2,000 votes of gaining it in 2010.

EU REFERENDUM RESULT

61.6% Leave   Remain 38.4%

Walthamstow

LAB CO-OP HOLD MAJORITY 32,017 (66.5%)

STELLA CREASY
BORN Apr 5, 1977
MP 2010-

Energetic campaigner, perhaps best known for her crusade against unregulated payday lending. Lobbied to allow children at Calais jungle camp to come to UK, and tabled amendment to 2017 Queen's Speech to allow NI women to get free NHS abortions in England and Wales, resulting in policy's adoption by the government. Former lobbyist consultant, researcher and speechwriter to Labour MPs. Cllr, Waltham Forest BC 2002-06; mayor 2003. Came second in Labour deputy leadership contest 2015. Jeremy Corbyn critic. Remainer; voted against triggering Article

	Electorate	Turnout %	from 2010 %	Change
	68,144	70.65		
*S Creasy Lab Co-op	38,793	80.58	+11.72	
M Samuel C	6,776	14.07	+0.71	
U Obasi LD	1,384	2.87	-1.10	
A Johns Green	1,190	2.47	-3.89	

50. Shadow min: business 2013-15; Home Office 2011-13. Ed: Colchester HS; Magdalene Coll, Oxford (BA psychology); LSE (PhD psychology, winner Richard Titmuss prize).

CHALLENGERS
Molly Samuel (C) Former World and European karate champion. 1989 **Sunday Times** international sportswoman of the year. IT skills tutor, Crisis homeless charity. MBE 2015. Contested Walthamstow 2015. Married, two daughters.

CONSTITUENCY PROFILE
This east London seat is densely populated, diverse and in parts deprived. Nearly a quarter of residents are Asian/ Asian British and other ethnic minorities represent nearly 30 per cent of the population. There is also a large number of EU immigrants. Income and earnings are much lower than the London-wide average and there are low levels of home ownership; many residents live in social housing. Having last elected a Conservative in 1987, Walthamstow is a safe Labour seat, and Stella Creasy has increased her majority in every election she has won.

EU REFERENDUM RESULT
33.5% Leave   Remain 66.5%

Wansbeck

LABOUR HOLD MAJORITY 10,435 (24.6%)

IAN LAVERY
BORN Jan 6, 1963
MP 2010-

Worked at Lynemouth and Ellington collieries. General secretary, National Union of Mineworkers (Northumberland Area) 1992-2010. President, NUM 2002-10. Cleared of wrongdoing after allegations that £75,000 from the union's benevolent fund went on his mortgage. Apologised to the Commons after failing to declare the union's share in his home 2013. Labour chairman, and campaign co-ordinator 2017-; shadow cabinet office min 2016-17. Select cttees: DECC 2010-15; NI affairs 2010-11. Married, two children. Ed: Youth Training Scheme (construction industry).

	Electorate	Turnout %	from 2010 %	Change
	62,099	68.37		
*I Lavery Lab	24,338	57.33	+7.32	
C Galley C	13,903	32.75	+10.98	
J Tebbutt LD	2,015	4.75	-1.50	
M Hurst Ukip	1,483	3.49	-14.71	
S Leyland Green	715	1.68	-2.09	

CHALLENGERS
Chris Galley (C) Global distribution scheduling manager, Shell. Farmer. Member: NFU; National Sheep Association; Zwartbles Sheep Association; Chatham House (Royal Institute for International Affairs). Quaker background, worships at Anglican church. **Joan Tebbutt** (LD) Qualified teacher and social worker. Student welfare service, Newcastle University. Cllr, Morpeth TC 2005-; mayor 2013-14.

CONSTITUENCY PROFILE
North of Newcastle, the constituency covers the towns of Ashington, Morpeth and the coastal town of Newbiggin. A former mining area (the final deep coalmine ceased operations in 2005), Wansbeck faces significant economic challenges. There is high unemployment and wages are low. The closure in 2012 of the aluminium plant at Lynemouth, which was Northumberland's largest private sector employer exacerbated these problems. The seat is safe Labour and the three MPs elected since the creation of the constituency in 1983 have been former miners.

EU REFERENDUM RESULT
56.3% Leave   Remain 43.7%

Wantage

CONSERVATIVE HOLD MAJORITY 17,380 (27.3%)

ED VAIZEY
BORN Jun 5, 1968
MP 2005-

Helped to introduce 4G as min for culture and the digital economy 2014-16. Junior culture min 2010-14. Remain voter. Former barrister and director of a PR company. President of Didcot Town Football Club and SUDEP Action, a local epilepsy charity. Trustee of the National Youth Theatre and Britdoc. Honorary fellow of Royal Institute of British Architects and the Radio Academy. Road safety campaigner. Married, one child. Son of Lord John Vaizey, who was a Labour peer. Ed: St Paul's Sch; Merton Coll, Oxford (BA history, vice-president Oxford Union).

	Electorate	Turnout %	from 2010 %	Change
	87,735	72.49		
*E Vaizey C	34,459	54.18	+0.87	
R Eden Lab Co-op	17,079	26.85	+10.83	
C Carrigan LD	9,234	14.52	+1.47	
S Ap-Roberts Green	1,546	2.43	-2.69	
D McLeod Ukip	1,284	2.02	-10.48	

CHALLENGERS
Rachel Eden (Lab) Co-ordinating director of a small consultancy company. Chartered management accountant. Cllr, Reading BC 2010-; lead cllr for adult social care 2013-. Former tutor at BPP 2007-13. **Chris Carrigan** (LD) Scientist, Wantage-born. Head of strategy and transformation at Maersk. Head of application architecture at Marks & Spencer 2013-17; global transformation, Oxfam 2009-12.

CONSTITUENCY PROFILE
This rural Oxfordshire seat encompasses Didcot, called "the most normal town in England" by statisticians, and the market towns of Faringdon and Wantage. It is affluent: wages exceed the regional average, there are high levels of home ownership and unemployment is very low. The local economy is centred on high-tech industry. The constituency is home to the Diamond Light Source synchrotron facility and the Williams F1 team. Wantage has been Conservative since its 1983 creation, apart from a brief spell when former MP Robert Jackson defected to Labour in 2005.

EU REFERENDUM RESULT

46.5% Leave   Remain 53.5%

Warley

LABOUR HOLD MAJORITY 16,483 (41.0%)

JON SPELLAR
BORN Aug 5, 1947
MP 1992-; 1982-83

An archetype of Labour's old trade union right. Political officer of EEPTU, the electricians' and plumbers' union, 1969-92 a role in which he helped to fight against Bennism in the 1980s. Shadow minister, FCO 2010-15. Assistant chief whip 2008-10. Minister: Northern Ireland 2003-05; transport 2001-03; armed forces 1999-2001. Select cttee, defence 2015-. MP for Birmingham Northfield 1982-83, winning a by-election but losing at the subsequent general election. Also contested: Birmingham Northfield 1987; Bromley 1970. Did not declare Brexit stance; voted for Article

	Electorate	Turnout %	from 2010 %	Change
	63,724	63.09		
*J Spellar Lab	27,004	67.16	+8.98	
A Mangnall C	10,521	26.17	+6.84	
D Magher Ukip	1,349	3.36	-13.13	
B Manley-Green LD	777	1.93	-0.20	
M Redding Green	555	1.38	-2.49	

50 bill. Ed: Dulwich Coll; St. Edmund Hall, Oxford (BA, PPE).

CHALLENGERS
Anthony Mangnall (C) Senior adviser to William Hague 2016-. Former parliamentary researcher to William Hague 2011-12. Former CPP broker 2012-16. Spent summer 2009 as shepherd/herdsman on the Isle of Mull. **Darryl Magher** (Ukip) Chairman: Ukip Sandwell branch; local community neighbourhood forum.

CONSTITUENCY PROFILE
Situated to Birmingham's west, Warley includes the town of Smethwick. The area is characterised by economic deprivation: earnings fall short of the regional average and the rate of unemployment is more than double the national figure. More than a quarter of residents are Asian/Asian British and there are large Muslim and Sikh communities. The Conservatives won the predecessor seat Smethwick in 1964 in a campaign remembered for its racism, otherwise the constituency has returned Labour members to Westminster since the Second World War.

EU REFERENDUM RESULT

61.6% Leave   Remain 38.4%

Warrington North

LABOUR HOLD MAJORITY 9,582 (19.7%)

HELEN JONES
BORN Dec 24, 1954
MP 1997-

Worked as an English teacher, solicitor and development officer for the mental health charity MIND. Various frontbench posts, including most recently shadow home office minister 2013-15. Left front bench to focus on community and to speak freely about topics such as fracking and HS2. One of 66 Labour MPs to vote for Syrian air strikes 2015. Supported Remain. Contested: Ellesmere Port and Neston 1987; North Shropshire 1983. Cllr, Chester CC 1984-91. Married, one son; husband employed as parly assistant. Ed: Ursuline Convent, Chester; University of Liverpool.

	Electorate	Turnout %	from 2010 %	Change
	72,015	67.37		
*H Jones Lab	27,356	56.38	+8.56	
V Allen C	17,774	36.63	+8.46	
J Ashington Ukip	1,561	3.22	-13.86	
S Krizanac LD	1,207	2.49	-1.65	
L McAteer Green	619	1.28	-1.51	

CHALLENGERS
Val Allen (C) Engineering business owner. Awarded an MBE for services to the community and businesses in Halton and Warrington 2015. Volunteer: Bolton and Bury Business Board, NSPCC 2011-15; Patron, Compassion in Action 2010-; vice-chairwoman, Halton Chamber of Commerce and Enterprise 2009-. Contested: Sefton 2015; St Helens South and Whitson 2010. Cllr, Culcheth and Glazebury.

CONSTITUENCY PROFILE
Warrington is a former industrial town situated between Manchester and Liverpool. It has a buoyant economy: wages are relatively high; more than two thirds of residents are homeowners and the unemployment rate is below the national average. The constituency includes the large village of Culcheth and the business parks in Birchwood, which employ about 5,000 people. United Utilites, the UK's largest water company, is based in Warrington. The seat is safe Labour; the area has been represented by Labour since 1945.

EU REFERENDUM RESULT

58.1% Leave   Remain 41.9%

Warrington South

LABOUR GAIN MAJORITY 2,549 (4.1%)

FAISAL RASHID
BORN Sep 15, 1972
MP 2017-

Relationship manager, Natwest 2006-17. Team manager, HBOS 1999-2005. Cllr, Warrington BC 2011-; mayor 2016-17. Member, finance committee, Warrington Borough Council's Labour group. Member, Unite. Trustee, St Rocco's Hospice. Ed: business administration, MBA.

CHALLENGERS
David Mowat (C) MP for Warrington South 2010-17. Chairman, young persons' charity, Fairbridge. Primary school governor. Qualified chartered accountant. Global managing partner, Accenture 2001-04. Supported Remain

	Electorate	Turnout %	from 2010 %	Change
	85,755	72.29		
F Rashid Lab	29,994	48.38	+9.33	
*D Mowat C	27,445	44.27	+0.59	
B Barr LD	3,339	5.39	-0.23	
J Boulton Ind	1,217	1.96		

in 2016 EU referendum. Cllr, Macclesfield BC 2007-08. Junior health minister 2016-17. Select cttees: public accounts 2015-16; Scottish affairs 2010-12. **Bob Barr** (LD) Urban geographer. Taught geography at Manchester University for 30 years. Awarded an OBE for services to geography 2008. Former governor, Cherry Tree School. Cllr, Warrington BC 2004-; deputy leader, Lib Dem group; executive board member for planning, regeneration, housing and property 2006-11.

CONSTITUENCY PROFILE
Covering most of Warrington and the large village of Lymm, it is a fairly homogeneous – 95 per cent of residents are white – and affluent constituency. More than three quarters of residents are homeowners, and earnings are well above the national average. Typically constituents are well educated. Although it is a marginal seat, it is not quite a bellwether: between 1992 and 2010 it was held by Labour, before being secured by David Cameron's party in two consecutive elections. In 2017 Warrington South was reclaimed by Labour with a decisive 4.4 per cent swing.

EU REFERENDUM RESULT

51.1% Leave   Remain 48.9%

Warwick & Leamington

LABOUR GAIN MAJORITY 1,206 (2.2%)

MATT WESTERN
BORN Nov 11, 1962
MP 2017-

Spent 24 years working in various management roles for Peugeot. Founded Oxygency, a branding, marketing and business development consultancy 2008. Volunteer careers mentor, Campion Sch. Cllr, Warwickshire CC 2013-. Member, Unison. Enjoys coffee and cycling. Arsenal FC fan. Lives with partner. Ed: St Albans Sch; University of Bristol (BSc geography).

CHALLENGERS
Chris White (C) MP for Warwick and Leamington 2010-17. Freelance PR consultant, formerly at

	Electorate	Turnout %	from 2010 % Change
	74,237	72.81	
M Western Lab	25,227	46.67	+11.79
*C White C	24,021	44.44	-3.50
N Solman LD	2,810	5.20	+0.23
J Chilvers Green	1,198	2.22	-1.73
B Dhillon Ukip	799	1.48	-6.79

Centric Public Relations. Previously engineer, MG Rover. Member, Warwickshire Coll Advisory Board. Patron, Cord international development charity. Remainer; voted to trigger Article 50. Contested: Warwick and Leamington 2005; Birmingham Hall Green 2001. **Nick Solman** (LD) Political theory student, University of Birmingham. Former career as property manager. **Jonathan Chilvers** (Green) Project leader, Salvation Army.

CONSTITUENCY PROFILE
The neighbouring towns of Warwick and Royal Leamington Spa account for more than four fifths of this seat's population. More than 9,000 students live in the area, which contains the University of Warwick. Residents tend to enjoy higher than average incomes and unemployment is very low. The seat has a significant Sikh population, numbering about 5,000. Having elected Conservatives for more than 90 years, this seat was won by Labour in 1997, holding it until 2010, so this is the first time Labour have held the seat despite being in opposition.

EU REFERENDUM RESULT

41.6% Leave   Remain 58.4%

Warwickshire North

CONSERVATIVE HOLD MAJORITY 8,510 (18.0%)

CRAIG TRACEY
BORN Aug 21, 1974
MP 2015-

Hard-headed former insurance broker. Senior partner, Dunelm Insurance Brokers 1996-2015. Former dir of Politically Correct, a political consultancy. Leave supporter. Select cttees: business and energy 2016-; education 2015-16; business and innovation 2015-16. Co-chairman, insurance and financial services APPG. Board member, Southern Staffordshire Employment and Skills Board. West Midlands co-ordinator, Conservative Voice 2012-15. Trustee, Lichfield Garrick Theatre 2012-16. Chairman, North Warwickshire Conservative Assoc 2012-14. Family comes from a mining

	Electorate	Turnout %	from 2010 % Change
	72,277	65.27	
*C Tracey C	26,860	56.93	+14.63
J Jackson Lab	18,350	38.90	+2.87
J Cox LD	1,028	2.18	+0.11
K Kondakor Green	940	1.99	+0.11

background near Durham. Married. Ed: Frawellgate Moor Comprehensive Sch.

CHALLENGERS
Julie Jackson (Lab) Cllr: Nuneaton and Bedworth BC 2004-, mayor 2006-07; Warwickshire CC 2009-17. Chairwoman, North Warwickshire and Bedworth Labour Party. Married, three daughters. **James Cox** (LD) English literature student at Birmingham. Co-chairman of Open Britain, UoB.

CONSTITUENCY PROFILE
Situated to the northeast of Birmingham, the seat encompasses the towns of Atherstone and Bedworth. Given its proximity to the second largest city in the UK, the constituency is a haven for commuters. There is relative affluence: nearly three quarters of dwellers are homeowners and comparatively few live in social housing. There is a considerable number – about 10,000 – of retired people. The seat is a Labour/Conservative marginal. It was won by Labour in 1992, but since 2010 has returned Conservative MPs to Westminster.

EU REFERENDUM RESULT

67.8% Leave   Remain 32.2%

Washington & Sunderland West

LABOUR HOLD MAJORITY 12,940 (31.9%)

SHARON HODGSON

BORN Apr 1, 1966
MP 2005-

Former accounting clerk and Northern Rock book-keeper turned Labour Party organiser. Passionate about women's issues and health; chairwoman APPG ovarian cancer. Inspired to enter politics after seeing Margaret Thatcher's effect on northeast. Formerly Union's Labour-link co-ordinator. Passed private members' bill SEN Act 2008 into law. Resigned from shadow cabinet over Jeremy Corbyn's leadership 2016. PPS to: Dawn Primarolo 2008-09; Bob Ainsworth 2007-08; Liam Byrne 2006-07. Shadow min: public health 2016-; education 2015-16, 2010-13; equalities

	Electorate	Turnout %	from 2010 %	Change
	67,280	60.31		
*S Hodgson Lab	24,639	60.73	+5.76	
J Gullis C	11,699	28.83	+9.96	
B Foster Ukip	2,761	6.80	-12.85	
T Appleby LD	961	2.37	-0.30	
M Chantkowski Green	514	1.27	-1.66	

2013-15. Opposition whip 2010; assistant whip 2009-10. Fabian society member 2004-. Women's officer, Tyne Bridge CLP 1998-2000. Married, two children. Ed: Heathfield Senior HS, Gateshead; Newcastle Coll (HEFC English); National Education Centre (TUC Dip Lab party organising).

CHALLENGERS
Jonathan Gullis (C) Citizenship teacher. Cllr, Stratford DC 2011-12. **Bryan Foster** (Ukip)

Contested Sunderland Central 2015. Chairman, Ukip Sunderland & Washington. **Tom Appleby** (LD) Quantity surveyor. Cllr: Tynedale DC 2006-09; Wylam PC.

CONSTITUENCY PROFILE
Comprising the 1960s new town of Washington and the western suburbs of Sunderland, this seat was known for its pits. Nissan is now a major employer in the area. A third of constituents live in social housing, and unemployment is above the national average; profiled in a locally criticised *New York Times* article about Brexit. A safe Labour seat.

EU REFERENDUM RESULT

61.9% Leave	Remain 38.1%

Watford

CONSERVATIVE HOLD MAJORITY 2,092 (3.6%)

RICHARD HARRINGTON

BORN Nov 4, 1957
MP 2010-

Wealthy businessman. Born in Leeds to a British Jewish family. Member: Tory Reform Group; Conservative Friends of Israel. Conservative Party treasurer 2008-. Parly under-sec: work and pensions 2016-17; Home Office 2015-16; communities and local government 2015-16; international development 2015-16. Select cttee, international development 2010-12. Governor, University College School, Hampstead. Chairman and trustee, Variety Club Children's Society 1998-2001. Shareholder and non-exec dir, Eden Financial. Founded Harvington Properties. Was responsible

	Electorate	Turnout %	from 2010 %	Change
	86,507	67.75		
*R Harrington C	26,731	45.61	+2.15	
C Ostrowski Lab	24,639	42.04	+16.03	
I Stotesbury LD	5,335	9.10	-8.98	
I Green Ukip	1,184	2.02	-7.74	
A Murray Green	721	1.23	-1.14	

for redevelopment of One Devonshire Gardens hotel in Glasgow. Married, two sons. Ed: Leeds GS; Keble Coll, Oxford (law).

CHALLENGERS
Chris Ostrowski (Lab) Runs an English-language training company. Polish father settled in England after the Second World War. **Ian Stotesbury** (LD) Consultant, Surrey Satellite Tech Ltd. Formerly consultant, ChaseFuture 2014-16.

CONSTITUENCY PROFILE
Part of the commuter belt, this constituency consists of Watford and several extra-urban villages. As with London, it is a diverse area. It has a large Asian/Asian British population and a considerable number of EU immigrants. Watford is home to several large business HQs, such as JD Wetherspoon and Mothercare, and the seat is affluent: wages exceed the regional average. It is a Conservative/Labour marginal: blue throughout the 1980s, Labour won the seat in Tony Blair's 1997 landslide, then Watford returned to the Conservatives in 2010.

EU REFERENDUM RESULT

51.2% Leave	Remain 48.8%

Waveney

CONSERVATIVE HOLD MAJORITY 9,215 (17.5%)

PETER ALDOUS
BORN Aug 26, 1961
MP 2010-

Suffolk born and raised, and from farming background. Work before entering parliament includes working on the family farm and being a chartered surveyor. Member of the environmental audit cttee from 2010. Member, Countryside Alliance. Contested Waveney 2005. Cllr: Waveney DC 1999-2002; Suffolk CC, deputy leader of the Conservative group 2002-05. Member: Royal Institue of Chartered Surveyors; Farmers' Club. Chartered surveyor. CofE. Sports enthusiast, season ticket holder Ipswich Town FC. Ed: Harrow; Reading (BSc land management).

	Electorate	Turnout %	from 2010 % Change
	80,784	65.20	
*P Aldous C	28,643	54.38	+12.03
S Barker Lab	19,428	36.88	-0.85
B Poole Ukip	1,933	3.67	-10.85
E Brambley-Crawshaw Green	1,332	2.53	-0.85
J Howe LD	1,012	1.92	-0.10
A Barron Ind	326	0.62	

CHALLENGERS
Sonia Barker (Lab) Former teacher and NHS worker. Cllr, Waveney DC, 2013-. Now leader of Labour oppposition group. Married, one daughter. **Bert Poole** (Ukip) Cllr, Norfolk CC 2013-17. Formerly chairman, Lound Parish Council.

CONSTITUENCY PROFILE
Situated in the northeast of Suffolk, Waveney includes the coastal town of Lowestoft.

Once a fishing port and home to Shell's southern operations, it is now the renewable energy capital of the UK. Still, the constituency has relatively high unemployment and lower wages than elsewhere in the region. There is a large retired population and more than two thirds of households are owner occupied. It is a marginal Conservative seat: Labour won in the landslide of 1997, but since 2010 the seat has been in the hands of the Conservatives. Ukip had some success here in 2015; in 2017, reaping the rewards of the Ukip collapse, the Conservative vote share increased from under 2,500 to nearly 10,000.

EU REFERENDUM RESULT

63.4% Leave   Remain 36.6%

Wealden

CONSERVATIVE HOLD MAJORITY 23,628 (39.1%)

NUSRAT (NUS) GHANI
BORN Sep 1, 1972
MP 2015-

One of 12 British Pakistanis in the new parliament. Attracted media attention when she proposed legislation to ban the term "honour killing". Select cttees: home affairs 2015-; armed forces bill 2015. Contested Birmingham Ladywood 2010. Prior to 2015 election, selected on open primary of 400 members of public. Worked as a health policy campaigner for Age Concern and Breakthrough Breast Cancer. Headed communications and fundraising for BBC World Service. Parents are Kashmiri immigrants. Married, one son. Ed: Bordesley Green Girls' Sch; University

	Electorate	Turnout %	from 2010 % Change
	81,425	74.26	
*N Ghani C	37,027	61.24	+4.22
A Smith Lab	13,399	22.16	+11.35
C Bowers LD	6,281	10.39	+1.30
C Stocks Green	1,959	3.24	-3.11
N Burton Ukip	1,798	2.97	-13.76

of Central England; Leeds University (MA international relations).

CHALLENGERS
Angela Smith (Lab) Works with victims of domestic violence. Trustee of local substance abuse charity. Married, two children. **Chris Bowers** (LD) Writer and tennis commentator. Cllr, Lewes DC 2007-15. Former Lib Dem Group leader. Contested Wealden 2015, 2010. Consultant, European Federation for

Transport & Environment. Wrote Nick Clegg's biography.

CONSTITUENCY PROFILE
Situated in East Sussex, the seat covers the towns of Uckfield, Crowborough and Hailsham. Although there is a sizeable retired community, these are commuter centres. By all accounts, the constituency is affluent: residents are typically well educated; there are high levels of home ownership; and earnings are considerably greater than elsewhere in the UK. The rate of unemployment is exceptionally low. Wealden is a safe Conservative seat, blue since its creation in 1983.

EU REFERENDUM RESULT

52.8% Leave   Remain 47.2%

Weaver Vale

LABOUR GAIN MAJORITY 3,928 (7.8%)

MIKE AMESBURY
BORN May 6, 1969
MP 2017-

	Electorate	Turnout %	from 2010 %	Change
	69,016	73.34		
M Amesbury Lab	26,066	51.50	+10.06	
*G Evans C	22,138	43.74	+0.58	
P Roberts LD	1,623	3.21	+0.23	
C Copeman Green	786	1.55	-0.97	

Adviser to Andy Burnham and Angela Rayner during last parliament. Director, City South Manchester Housing Trust 2010-17. Cllr, Manchester CC 2006-17. Labour National Policy Forum elected representative 2010-15. Former convenor for Unison, working for careers services in Manchester. Member of Unison and GMB. Married, one son. Ed: University of Bradford (BA sociology, psy, pol, econ); University of Central England (dip careers guidance).

CHALLENGERS
Graham Evans (C) MP for Weaver Vale 2010-17. PPS to:

Michael Fallon 2014-15; Greg Barker 2014-15. Select cttees: DWP 2012-15; administration 2011-13. Cllr, Macclesfield BC 2000-09. Contested Worsley 2005. Sales and marketing management, roles with Hewlett Packard and BAE Systems. Former special constable for the Cheshire Constabulary. Married, three children. Ed: Poynton County HS; Manchester Met (business, dip marketing management). **Paul Roberts** (LD) Retired accountant. Worked for Kimberley-Clark for nearly

20 years. Taught management at the Open University. Former cllr, Chester CC. Contested Crewe and Nantwich 2005.

CONSTITUENCY PROFILE
Cheshire seat made up of some of Runcorn as well as the towns of Frodsham and Northwich. The latter is an old industrial town known for its chemical and salt production. It was home to a large chemical plant owned by Tata until 2014. Dwellers are typically middle class: a considerable number of people work in professional occupations and earnings outstrip the UK average. It is a marginal, held by Labour from 1997 until 2010.

EU REFERENDUM RESULT
50.6% Leave   Remain 49.4%

Wellingborough

CONSERVATIVE HOLD MAJORITY 12,460 (23.4%)

PETER BONE
BORN Oct 19, 1952
MP 2010-

	Electorate	Turnout %	from 2010 %	Change
	79,258	67.17		
*P Bone C	30,579	57.44	+5.35	
A Watts Lab	18,119	34.03	+14.52	
A Shipham Ukip	1,804	3.39	-16.18	
C Nelson LD	1,782	3.35	-1.09	
J Hornett Green	956	1.80	-2.60	

Qualified chartered accountant. Select cttees: panel of chairs 2010-17; backbench business cttee 2015-16, 2010-12; health 2007-10; statutory instruments 2005-10; trade and industry 2005-07. Investigated by police for an alleged £100,000 benefit fraud concerning care home fees for his mother-in-law in February 2014. The case was dropped due to insufficient evidence in March 2014. Rebelled 56 times. Known for quoting the breakfast-table remarks of his wife to David Cameron at PMQs. Member of the Parochial Church Council. Cricketer and marathon runner.

Married, three children. Ed: Westcliff-on-Sea GS.

CHALLENGERS
Andrea Watts (Lab) Works for a major logistics company. Trade unionist. Cllr, Wellingborough BC 2011-. Born and raised in Wellingborough. Member of LGBT community and carer for her disabled brother. **Allan Shipham** (Ukip) Self-employed in construction industry. Chairman, Wellingborough Ukip branch.

CONSTITUENCY PROFILE
Situated in the east Midlands, the seat includes the towns of Wellingborough and Rushden. Traditionally the area was famous for its shoe-making; Dr Martens has a factory in Wollaston. The local economy is now retail centric and buoyant: earnings are higher than the UK average; unemployment is lower. The constituency has some diversity: about 10 per cent of residents belong to an ethnic minority and a number of EU migrants have settled here. The seat is marginal: although Labour gained at Blair's peak in 1997, the Conservatives regained the seat in 2005.

EU REFERENDUM RESULT
63.0% Leave   Remain 37.0%

Wells

CONSERVATIVE HOLD MAJORITY 6,582 (12.5%)

JAMES HEAPPEY
BORN Jan 30, 1981
MP 2010-

Former army major, served with The Rifles in Afghanistan, Northern Ireland and Kenya. Worked for chief of the defence staff, MoD, then became a self-employed management consultant. Former researcher to Liam Fox. Apologised for telling a schoolgirl to "f*** off" after she said she would vote for Scottish independence if there was another referendum. Reluctant Remainer; voted to trigger Article 50. Vice-president, Association for Decentralised Energy. Married, one son, one daughter. Ed: University of Birmingham (BA politics); RMA Sandhurst.

	Electorate	Turnout %	from 2010 %	Change
	82,449	73.79		
*J Heappey C	30,488	50.11	+3.98	
T Munt LD	22,906	37.65	+4.85	
A Merryfield Lab	7,129	11.72	+5.07	
L Corke CPA	320	0.53		

CHALLENGERS
Tessa Munt (LD) Wells MP, 2010-15. Formerly worked at Midland Bank, solicitors firm and hotel chain before entering politics. Contested: Wells 2005; Suffolk South 2001; Ipswich by-election 2001. Revealed in 2014 she was a survivor of child sexual abuse. CND member. PPS to Vince Cable 2012-15; quit to vote against fracking. **Andy Merryfield** (Lab) Retired teacher, community development worker. Contested Wells 2010, 2001. Member, Co-operative Party.

CONSTITUENCY PROFILE
A rural Somerset seat including England's smallest city: Wells, and the coastal resort of Burnham-on-Sea. The constituency is home to several landmarks, notably the cheddar gorge and Glastonbury Tor, and tourism is important to the economy. As with much of rural England, the population is largely white. The seat has a sizeable retired population and there are high levels of home ownership in the area. Wells was Conservative throughout the 20th century. Since the 1970s it has been a Conservative/Lib Dem marginal and was won by the Liberal Democrats in 2010.

EU REFERENDUM RESULT

53.6% Leave   Remain 46.4%

Welwyn Hatfield

CONSERVATIVE HOLD MAJORITY 7,369 (14.3%)

GRANT SHAPPS
BORN Sep 14, 1968
MP 2005-

Resigned as a minister in November 2015 over his appointment of Mark Clarke, who was at the centre of a Conservative Party bullying scandal. Founder of PrintHouse Corporation. Minister: international development 2015; without portfolio, Cabinet Office 2012-15; housing 2010-12. Shadow minister, housing and planning 2007-10. Campaigned to Remain; voted for Article 50. Select cttee, public administration 2005-07. Holds a pilot's licence. Married, three children. Ed: Cassio Coll, Watford; Manchester Polytechnic (HND business & finance).

	Electorate	Turnout %	from 2010 %	Change
	72,888	70.89		
*G Shapps C	26,374	51.04	+0.69	
A Miah Lab	19,005	36.78	+10.63	
N Quinton LD	3,836	7.42	+1.17	
D Milliken Ukip	1,441	2.79	-10.27	
C Sayers Green	835	1.62	-1.85	
M Jones Ind	178	0.34	-0.09	

CHALLENGERS
Anawar Miah (Lab) Public law specialist. Called to the Bar by Lincolns Inn in 1998. Listed in the Who's Who? Legal 500 directory. Born in Bangladesh, came to the UK in 1957. **Nigel Quinton** (LD) Works in underground oil exploration, QX Energy, 2005-. Contested Hitchin and Harpenden 2010.

CONSTITUENCY PROFILE
Located in Hertfordshire and bordering the London Borough of Enfield, Welwyn Hatfield is a large commuter seat with a significant student population. It includes Welwyn Garden City which is one of the only two garden cities in the country. Considered a Conservative/Labour marginal seat, although it has mostly been won by the Tories. Ethnically diverse, with an 8 per cent Asian and Asian British population. Low levels of home ownership, at 55 per cent, and extremely high levels of residents live in social housing. Health, education and job quality are above average for the region and unemployment is very low.

EU REFERENDUM RESULT

52.8% Leave   Remain 47.2%

Wentworth & Dearne

LABOUR HOLD MAJORITY 14,803 (33.7%)

JOHN HEALEY
BORN Feb 13, 1960
MP 1997-

Disability campaigner for three national charities. Edited *The House* magazine. TUC campaigns director before being elected. Contested Ryedale 1992. Champions large-scale public investment in housing and infrastructure. Member, GMB. Brownite, popular in the PLP. Leadership nominations: Owen Smith 2016; Yvette Cooper 2015. Shadow SoS, housing 2016-. Only rebels on procedure. Remainer; voted to trigger Article 50. Minister: housing 2009-10; local government 2007-09. Financial sec 2005-07; economic sec 2002-05. Shadow SoS, health

	Electorate	Turnout %	from 2010 % Change
	74,890	58.68	
*J Healey Lab	28,547	64.96	+8.07
S Jackson C	13,744	31.27	+16.36
J Middleton LD	1,656	3.77	+1.14

2010-11. PPS to Gordon Brown 1999-2001. Married, one son. Ed: Lady Lumley's CS, Pickering; Peter's Sch, York; Christ's Coll, Cambridge (BA social and political science).

CHALLENGERS
Steve Jackson (C) Engineer who works on regenerating brownfield sites. Cllr, Harrogate BC 2011-. Contested Penistone and Stocksbridge 2015. **Janice Middleton** (LD) Retired head teacher. Chairwoman, Rotherham & Barnsley LDs. Contested Rotherham 2015.

CONSTITUENCY PROFILE
The area around and including Wentworth and Dearne was a major coal mining region, but since the industry's decline in the 1980s niche manufacturing, processing and retail have become the dominant sectors for the local economy. A Labour stronghold, the seat has, in various forms, been held by Labour for nearly a century. The area is demographically homogeneous: 97 per cent of residents are white British and 70 per cent are Christian. Levels of education are low and unemployment high. Median income is significantly below the national average, at £20,000.

EU REFERENDUM RESULT

70.3% Leave   Remain 29.7%

West Bromwich East

LABOUR HOLD MAJORITY 7,713 (19.7%)

TOM WATSON
BORN Jan 8, 1967
MP 2001-

Big beast. Labour deputy leader 2015-; shadow SoS, CMS 2016-. Led "curry house plot" against Tony Blair, leading to Watson's resignation as defence minister in 2006. Resigned from Miliband shadow cabinet over Falkirk selection row 2013. Attempted to broker Jeremy Corbyn's resignation before Owen Smith's leadership bid 2016. Campaigned against Rupert Murdoch by leading investigations into phone hacking which resulted in the Leveson Inquiry. Alleged there was a Westminster VIP paedophile ring, leading to creation of Operation Midland; later closed without any charges

	Electorate	Turnout %	from 2010 % Change
	63,833	61.25	
*T Watson Lab	22,664	57.97	+7.78
E Crane C	14,951	38.24	+13.31
K Trench LD	625	1.60	-0.40
J Macefield Green	533	1.36	-0.31
C Rankine Ind	325	0.83	

being brought after a 16-month inquiry, Watson apologised for describing late Lord Brittan as "evil" after police found no case to answer. Former national political officer, AEEU. Separated, one daughter, one son. Ed: King Charles I Sch, Kidderminster; University of Hull (BA politics; president, students' union).

CHALLENGERS
Emma Crane (C) Runs a property management firm.

Adviser to Antoinette Sandbach MP. Anti-HS2 campaigner. Cllr, Rugby BC 2015-.

CONSTITUENCY PROFILE
An ultra-safe Labour seat, which has been held by Labour since the 1970s with relatively small majorities. Manufacturing is a significant industry in the area and unemployment is very high. A heterogeneous region which is one fifth Asian and Asian British and 6 per cent African, Caribbean and Black British. There are low levels of education, health, job quality and home ownership and almost 30 per cent of the population live in social rented accommodation.

EU REFERENDUM RESULT

68.2% Leave   Remain 31.8%

West Bromwich West

LAB CO-OP HOLD MAJORITY 4,460 (12.4%)

ADRIAN BAILEY
BORN Dec 11, 1945
MP 2000-

Former school librarian and study skills teacher. Later full-time political organiser, Co-operative Party. Cllr, Sandwell BC 1991-2000; deputy leader 1997-2000. Contested: Wirral by-election 1976; Nantwich February 1974, October 1974; South Worcestershire 1970. Voted for airstrikes in Syria 2015. Remainer; voted for Article 50. Chairman, business select cttee 2010-15. PPS to: Bob Ainsworth 2007-08; Adam Ingram 2006-07; Hilary Armstrong 2006; John Hutton 2005-06. Married, one stepson. Ed: Cheltenham GS; University of Exeter (BA economic

	Electorate	Turnout %	Change from 2010 %
	65,956	54.72	
*A Bailey Lab Co-op	18,789	52.06	+4.73
A Hardie C	14,329	39.70	+15.82
S Anderton Ukip	2,320	6.43	-18.80
F Clucas LD	333	0.92	-0.65
R Buckman Green	323	0.89	-1.10

history); Loughborough Coll of Librarianship (PgDip).

CHALLENGERS
Andrew Hardie (C) Retired NHS GP, currently locum. Volunteers in Uganda. Cllr, Birmingham CC 2014-. Contested West Bromwich West 2010. **Star Anderton** (Ukip) Cllr, Dudley MBC 2014-. Ukip spokeswoman, disabilities and welfare. Wheelchair user. Resigned from Conservatives after posting photos online

holding golliwog dolls. Separated from Ukip MEP Bill Etheridge.

CONSTITUENCY PROFILE
Made up of Tipton and Wednesbury, towns famed for coalmines, iron foundries and steel mills. Labour safe seat, although the BNP made some inroads and received 10 per cent of the vote in 2005. Very high unemployment which is at 4.8 per cent. About 15 per cent of residents are Asian/Asian British. Job quality, health and education are low in the seat. Home ownership is low, with more than 30 per cent of residents in social housing. It was Betty Boothroyd's seat from 1974 to 2000.

EU REFERENDUM RESULT
68.7% Leave   Remain 31.3%

West Ham

LABOUR HOLD MAJORITY 36,754 (60.5%)

LYN BROWN
BORN Apr 13, 1960
MP 2005-

Former social worker. Cllr, Newham BC 1988-2005. Later chairwoman, LGA cultural services cttee. Co-founder, London Libraries Development Agency. Contested Wanstead & Woodford 1992. Member: Co-operative Party; Fabian Society. Leadership nominations: Owen Smith 2016; Yvette Cooper 2015. Voted against Article 50 bill. Temporarily replaced Diane Abbott as shadow home secretary when Abbott stood aside due to ill health on eve of polling day. Shadow min: policing 2016-; fire 2015-16; communities 2013-15. Married in House of Commons chapel by

	Electorate	Turnout %	Change from 2010 %
	92,243	65.81	
*L Brown Lab	46,591	76.75	+8.31
P Spencer C	9,837	16.20	+0.77
P Reynolds LD	1,836	3.02	+0.32
R Beattie Ukip	1,134	1.87	-5.61
M Spracklin Green	957	1.58	-3.45
K Shedowo CPA	353	0.58	-0.12

fellow Labour MP Chris Bryant. Ed: Plashet CS; Whitelands Coll, Roehampton (BA English and religion; president, students' union).

CHALLENGERS
Patrick Spencer (C) Researcher, Centre for Social Justice. Former commodities trader and financial consultant. Son of Michael Spencer, former Conservative party treasurer and founder of interdealer broker Icap.

CONSTITUENCY PROFILE
This deprived seat, comprising a young electorate, returns very safe Labour majorities. Suffered from the East End decline, particularly of the dockers' industry in the 1950s and 1980s, although industry and employment levels have increased, in small part thanks to the London Olympic Village and Park. Unemployment is still high, at 2.9 per cent. One of the most diverse places in the country, where over a third are Asian and nearly a quarter are black. Very high levels of social renting. Has the second lowest average incomes in the region, after East Ham.

EU REFERENDUM RESULT
48.0% Leave   Remain 52.0%

Westminster North

LABOUR HOLD MAJORITY 11,512 (26.6%)

KAREN BUCK
BORN Aug 30, 1958
MP 1997-

Former research and development worker, Outset disabled charity. Disability and public health officer, Hackney BC. Later health directorate researcher and campaign strategy co-ordinator, Labour Party. Cllr, Westminster CC 1990-97. Named Child Poverty Action Group's MP of the year 2009. Nominated Owen Smith in 2016 and Yvette Cooper in 2015 for the Labour leadership. Voted against renewing Trident, 2007. Voted against Article 50 bill. PPS to Ed Miliband 2013-15. Shadow minister: DWP 2010-11; education 2011-13. Junior transport minister

	Electorate	Turnout %	from 2010 %	Change
	63,846	67.81		
*K Buck Lab	25,934	59.90	+13.07	
L Hall C	14,422	33.31	-8.51	
A Harding LD	2,253	5.20	+1.52	
E Tandy Green	595	1.37	-1.97	
A Dharamsey Ind	91	0.21		

2005-06. Chairwoman, London regional select cttee 2009-10. Catholic. Married, one son. Ed: Chelmsford County HS for girls; LSE (BSc economics).

CHALLENGERS
Lindsey Hall (C) Runs West End family art and antique business. Former TV reporter. Cllr, Westminster CC 2007-. Council's anti-housing benefit fraud tsar. Contested Westminster North 2015. **Alex Harding** (LD) Former chairman, Liberal

Youth. Volunteered on Macron's presidential campaign.

CONSTITUENCY PROFILE
Westminster North is home to some of the highest wages in London, boasting a median salary of more than £80,000. A marginal seat and regular source of hope for the Conservatives, but it has been stubbornly held by Labour since 1997. It is ethnically diverse and enjoys considerable levels of private renting. Unemployment is lower than the national average and residents tend to have highly skilled jobs, many of which are in the financial, insurance, scientific and technical sectors.

EU REFERENDUM RESULT
33.7% Leave   Remain 66.3%

Westmorland & Lonsdale

LIBERAL DEMOCRAT HOLD MAJORITY 777 (1.5%)

TIM FARRON
BORN May 27, 1970
MP 2005-

Leader of the Liberal Democrats, 2015-17. Critic of coalition, didn't hold ministerial brief. Rebelled to vote against tuition fee hike and bedroom tax. Dogged during election by questions about his faith and attitudes towards gay sex and abortion. Cited issue of reconciling his faith and leadership of the Liberal Democats in his resignation speech. Worked in higher education before entering politics. Contested: Westmorland & Lonsdale 2001; South Ribble 1997; Durham North West 1992. Lib Dem party president 2011-14. Remainer; voted against triggering Article 50. Brought

	Electorate	Turnout %	from 2010 %	Change
	66,391	77.85		
*T Farron LD	23,686	45.83	-5.67	
J Airey C	22,909	44.32	+11.12	
E Aldridge Lab	4,783	9.25	+3.82	
M Fishfinger Ind	309	0.60		

up by single mother. Married, two sons, two daughters. Ed: Lostock Hall HS; Runshaw Coll; Newcastle University (BA politics, first Lib Dem president of Union Society).

CHALLENGERS
James Airey (C) Prize-winning sheep farmer. Cllr: Cumbria CC 2009-; South Lakeland DC 2008-. Contested: Morecambe and Lunesdale 2005; Barrow and Furness 2001. Amateur clay pigeon shooter. **Eli Aldridge** (Lab) 18-year-old A-level student

at time of election. Youth officer, Westmorland & Lonsdale CLP.

CONSTITUENCY PROFILE
In the south of Cumbria, Westmorland and Lonsdale was a Conservative seat from its creation in 1983 until it fell to Tim Farron in 2005. It enjoys high levels of education and home ownership, low levels of social renting and one of the lowest unemployment rates in the country. Although a significant proportion of the population is retired, the seat has large accommodation and food service sectors, while 16 per cent of the workforce are in skilled trade occupations.

EU REFERENDUM RESULT
47.1% Leave   Remain 52.9%

Weston-Super-Mare

CONSERVATIVE HOLD MAJORITY 11,544 (20.5%)

JOHN PENROSE
BORN Jun 22, 1964
MP 2005-

Millionaire publisher. Former chairman, Logotron educational software company. Previously MD: Longman; Thompson. Risk manager, JP Morgan; consultant, McKinsey. Contested: Weston-super-Mare 2001; Ealing Southall 1997. Calls for a UK sovereign wealth fund. Outspoken advocate of energy price cap. Remainer; voted to trigger Article 50. Minister: constitutional reform 2015-16; CMS 2010-12. Government whip 2013-15. Anglican. Married, two daughters. Ed: Ipswich Sch; Downing Coll, Cambridge (BA law); Columbia University (MBA).

Electorate	Turnout %	from 2010 %	Change
82,160	68.66		
*J Penrose C	29,982	53.15	+5.19
T Taylor Lab	18,438	32.68	+14.43
M Bell LD	5,175	9.17	-1.27
H Hims Ukip	1,932	3.42	-14.40
S Basu Green	888	1.57	-3.36

CHALLENGERS
Tim Taylor (Lab) Human resources manager, performance and reward, Lloyds Banking Group. Cllr, Weston TC 2011-15, 2003-07; finance and personnel cttee. Contested Weston-super-Mare 2015. **Mike Bell** (LD) Policy and campaigns officer, RNIB. Previously editor, Bennett B2B publishing company. Cllr, North Somerset C 2011-; Lib Dem leader. Contested: Weston-super-Mare 2010; Somerset North 2005.

CONSTITUENCY PROFILE
The Somerset town of Weston-super-Mare has been a popular seaside resort since the early 19th century, although tourism severely declined in the second half of the 20th century. The town is now undergoing regeneration. A marginal seat which has been held alternately between Conservatives and Liberal Democrats since 1918. A fifth of the workforce are employed in retail and wholesale and unemployment is below 2 per cent, although the seat does contain pockets of deprivation. The population is 97 per cent white with low levels of health and education.

EU REFERENDUM RESULT

57.2% Leave   Remain 42.8%

Wigan

LABOUR HOLD MAJORITY 16,027 (33.7%)

LISA NANDY
BORN Aug 9, 1979
MP 2010-

Career in third sector before entering parliament: senior policy adviser, The Children's Society 2005-10; policy researcher, Centrepoint 2003-05. Parly researcher to Neil Gerrard MP. Cllr, Hammersmith & Fulham BC 2006-10. Nominated Andy Burnham for Labour leadership 2015; Owen Smith 2016. Remainer; voted to trigger Article 50. Shadow: SoS, ECC 2016; min, Cabinet Office 2013-15; min, education 2013. Indian father, English mother. Ed: Parrs Wood Comp, Manchester; Newcastle upon Tyne (BA politics); Birkbeck Coll, London (MSc politics & government).

Electorate	Turnout %	from 2010 %	Change
75,359	63.09		
*L Nandy Lab	29,575	62.21	+10.05
A Williams C	13,548	28.50	+7.77
N Ryding Ukip	2,750	5.78	-13.68
M Clayton LD	916	1.93	-0.84
W Patterson Green	753	1.58	-1.23

CHALLENGERS
Alexander Williams (C) Works for Ernst & Young. Cllr, Trafford MBC 2003-; deputy leader and exec member for investment. Married to Baroness (Susan) Williams of Trafford. **Nathan Ryding** (Ukip) Branch chairman of Wigan Ukip and, at 19, the youngest in the country. Enrolled in the army at 16 but left due to back injury. **Mark Clayton** (LD) Formerly MD of an IT company. Cllr, Manchester CC 1998-2014. Founder member,

Lib Dems. Contested Wigan 2015, 2010.

CONSTITUENCY PROFILE
Formerly an important mill town and coalmining district, but these industries declined in the latter part of the 20th century. Wigan is now a food manufacturing centre and it has some of Europe's largest food production sites. Residents are predominantly white and it has a relatively high number of Christians. Unemployment is high, while health, education and job prosperity are well below national and regional averages. A safe Labour seat that the party has held since 1918.

EU REFERENDUM RESULT

63.0% Leave   Remain 37.0%

Wiltshire North

CONSERVATIVE HOLD MAJORITY 22,877 (42.6%)

JAMES GRAY
BORN Nov 7, 1954
MP 1997-

	Electorate	Turnout %	from 2010 %	Change
	71,408	75.21		
*J Gray C	32,398	60.32	+3.09	
B Mathew LD	9,521	17.73	+2.12	
P Baldrey Lab	9,399	17.50	+7.75	
P Chamberlain Green	1,141	2.12	-2.52	
P Singh Ukip	871	1.62	-9.88	
L Tweedie Ind	376	0.70	-0.07	

Career in shipping and futures broking before entering politics: Anderson Hughes, GNI Freight Futures, The Baltic Futures Exchange. Spent seven years in Territorial Army. Former dir, Westminster Strategy public affairs consultancy. Special adviser to Michael Howard and John Gummer. Contested Ross, Cromarty and Skye 1992. Survived two deselection attempts after having an affair while his wife had cancer treatment. Said MPs should spend less time on constituency casework because it diverts from holding government to account. Expenses rows over second home redecoration. Brexiteer. Occasional rebel on Europe and HS2 high-speed rail project. Shadow Scotland secretary for 11 days, 2005. Divorced, remarried, two sons, one daughter. Ed: High Sch of Glasgow; University of Glasgow (MA history); Christ Church, Oxford (MA history).

CHALLENGERS
Biran Mathew (LD) Aid worker. Water, sanitation and hygiene adviser. Postings to Zimbabwe, Zambia and Sudan with WaterAid. Contested: Wiltshire North 2015; Somerset North 2010.

CONSTITUENCY PROFILE
Predominantly rural and very affluent, Wiltshire North is safe Conservative territory. The proportion of those renting social or privately owned housing is below average and 72.5 per cent of homes are owner occupied. More than half of households own two or more cars. The population is well-educated and a high number of residents are employed in managerial roles.

EU REFERENDUM RESULT
50.3% Leave   Remain 49.7%

Wiltshire South West

CONSERVATIVE HOLD MAJORITY 18,326 (33.5%)

ANDREW MURRISON
BORN Apr 24, 1961
MP 2001-

	Electorate	Turnout %	from 2010 %	Change
	76,898	71.20		
*A Murrison C	32,841	59.98	+7.32	
L Pictor Lab	14,515	26.51	+13.06	
T Carbin LD	5,360	9.79	-0.83	
C Walford Green	1,445	2.64	-3.14	
L Silcocks Ind	590	1.08		

Spent 18 years as Royal Navy medical officer and surgeon commander, recalled for six month tour in Iraq, 2003. Locum consultant and GP. Former research asst to Lord Freeman. Member, Bow Group. Brexiteer. Never rebelled. Supported Andrea Leadsom's 2016 leadership bid. Trade envoy to Morocco and Tunisia 2016-. Special representative for Great War centenary commemorations 2011-. Parly under-sec: NI 2014-15; defence 2012-14. PPS to Andrew Lansley 2010-12. Chairman, APPG on clinical leadership and management. Married, five daughters. Ed: Harwich HS; Britannia Royal Naval Coll, Dartmouth; University of Bristol (MD, MBChB); Hughes Hall, Cambridge (DPH).

CHALLENGERS
Laura Pictor (Lab) Manager in local charity with focus on community development and engagement. Freelance visual artist. Contested local elections 2017. **Trevor Carbin** (LD) Driving instructor and former archaeologist. Cllr, Wiltshire CC 2009-. Contested Wiltshire SW 2015, 2010. **Christopher Walford** (Green) Retired organic food entrepreneur. Previously plumber and heating engineer.

CONSTITUENCY PROFILE
Sparsely populated and rural, Wiltshire South West is home to a considerable retired community with 19.4 per cent of residents aged over 65. Social security is an overrepresented industry and the area houses several military facilities. Low unemployment but earnings are below the southwest average. Along with its predecessors, it has been Conservative since 1924.

EU REFERENDUM RESULT
56.9% Leave   Remain 43.1%

Wimbledon

CONSERVATIVE HOLD MAJORITY 5,622 (10.9%)

STEPHEN HAMMOND
BORN Feb 4, 1962
MP 2005-

Former investment banker: dir of equities, Dresdner Kleinwort Benson; dir, Pan European Research. Joined transport firm Inmarsat in £800-per-hour advisory role months after he was sacked as transport minister. Contested: Wimbledon 2001; North Warwickshire 1997. Shadow min for transport 2005-10. Parly under-sec for transport 2012-14. Select cttees: statutory instruments 2015-17; treasury 2015-17; public accounts 2014-15. Married, one daughter. Ed: King Edward VI Sch, Southampton; Richard Hale Sch, Hertford; Queen Mary Coll, London (BSc economics).

	Electorate	Turnout %	from 2010 %	Change
	66,771	77.17		
*S Hammond C	23,946	46.47	-5.62	
I Uddin Lab	18,324	35.56	+9.53	
C Quilliam LD	7,472	14.50	+1.84	
C Barraball Green	1,231	2.39	-1.71	
S McDonald Ukip	553	1.07	-4.04	

CHALLENGERS
Imran Uddin (Lab) Qualified solicitor, suspended in May 2017 due to investigation into "suspected dishonesty" in his practice. Cllr, Merton BC 2014-17. **Carl Quilliam** (LD) Former civil servant. Public affairs executive at London housing association, Metropolitan. Contested Leyton and Wanstead 2015. Candidates officer for Liberal Democrats 2012-13; policy adviser, economy and transport, Lib Dem group at LGA 2012.

CONSTITUENCY PROFILE
A wealthy borough in southwest London renowned for its annual tennis tournament. Generally safely held by the Conservatives and has only fallen to Labour twice during landslide years. A commuter-sustained urban economy, encompassing high-end areas such as Wimbledon Village and more deprived areas of social housing such as Merton Abbey. A much whiter demographic than the rest of London. Education and health standards are exceptionally high with an unrivalled proportion of the population in managerial and professional jobs and low levels of unemployment.

EU REFERENDUM RESULT
29.4% Leave   Remain 70.6%

Winchester

CONSERVATIVE HOLD MAJORITY 9,999 (17.5%)

STEVE BRINE
BORN Jan 28, 1974
MP 2010-

Former radio journalist for the BBC, Radio Five Live and WGN Radio in the USA. Businessman and consultant for The Azalea Group. Worked for Conservative Central Office during William Hague's leadership and in 2005-10 parliament. Remainer; voted to trigger Article 50. Opposed legalising gay marriage 2013. Parly under-sec, health 2017-. Assistant whip 2016-17. PPS to: Jeremy Hunt 2015-16; Mike Penning 2013-15. Handful of minor rebellions during coalition years. Married, two children. Ed: Bohunt Comp; Highbury College; Liverpool Hope University Coll (BA history).

	Electorate	Turnout %	from 2010 %	Change
	72,497	78.84		
*S Brine C	29,729	52.01	-2.99	
J Porter LD	19,730	34.52	+10.09	
M Chaloner Lab	6,007	10.51	+2.17	
A Wainwright Green	846	1.48	-3.30	
M Lyon Ukip	695	1.22	-6.24	
T Skelton JACP	149	0.26		

CHALLENGERS
Jackie Porter (LD) Trustee of youth charity Street Reach. Former primary school teacher and buyer for Marks & Spencer. Contested Winchester 2015. Cllr, Hampshire CC 2005-. Campaigner for child and health matters. **Mark Chaloner** (Lab) Self-employed family law barrister. Cllr, Southampton CC 2012-; cabinet member for finance. Contested Winchester 2015. GMN member. **Andrew**

Wainwright (Green) IT director. Choir member.

CONSTITUENCY PROFILE
This wealthy borough is home to 'Cathedral city', which is a key Hampshire tourist destination. Unemployment in the area is extremely low, at 0.8 per cent. The University of Winchester is located here and there is a sizable student population. Incomes are significantly higher than the southeast average. IBM has its headquarters in the area and is a large employer. A Tory/Lib Dem marginal, historically held by the Conservatives but it was taken by the Lib Dems from 1997 until 2005.

EU REFERENDUM RESULT
39.6% Leave   Remain 60.4%

Windsor

CONSERVATIVE HOLD MAJORITY 22,384 (41.5%)

ADAM AFRIYIE
BORN Aug 4, 1965
MP 2005-

Entrepreneur who founded
IT company Connect Support
Services. Wealth estimated
at £50m. London chairman of
Business for Sterling. Committed
to Brexit. Anti-immigration. The
first black Conservative MP. In
the shadow cabinet before 2010,
but on the backbenches since
then. Rarely rebels except on
Europe issues. Shad min for
science and innovation 2007-10.
Select cttee, members' expenses
2011-15. Born in Wimbledon
to Ghanaian father. Divorced,
remarried, one daughter,
two sons, one stepson. Ed:
Imperial Coll (BSc agricultural
economics).

	Electorate	Turnout %	from 2010 % Change
	73,595	73.27	
*A Afriyie C	34,718	64.39	+1.00
P Shearman Lab	12,334	22.87	+9.49
J Tisi LD	5,434	10.08	+1.46
F McKeown Green	1,435	2.66	-0.99

CHALLENGERS
Peter Shearman (Lab)
Technology developer for
Cisco. Previously worked
on government policy for
Broadband Stakeholder Group.
Helped to develop government
policy for superfast broadband.
Julian Tisi (LD) Chartered
accountant, previously
Pricewaterhouse Coopers
in Guernsey and Barbados.
Chairman, Lib Dems for
Electoral Reform. **Fintan
McKeown** (Green) Actor,
known for National Theatre

performances and role in *Game
of Thrones.*

CONSTITUENCY PROFILE
One of the most affluent seats
in the UK, with incomes among
the highest in the southeast.
Nestled among the villages
lining the River Thames are
emblems of British affluence,
such as Windsor Castle and Eton
College. A significant proportion
of residents boast managerial
and professional roles, with a
high number in the information
and communication sector. The
region has a relatively large
Sikh and Hindu community.
Windsor has been held by the
Conservatives for over a century.

EU REFERENDUM RESULT
46.7% Leave   Remain 53.3%

Wirral South

LABOUR HOLD MAJORITY 8,323 (18.4%)

**ALISON
MCGOVERN**
BORN Dec 30, 1980
MP 2010-

Former public affairs manager:
Network Rail; The Art Fund;
Creativity Culture & Education.
Mainstream Labour, locally-
raised. Gave emotional speech
during emergency debate on
Aleppo, urging Parliament
to intervene. Shadow min:
treasury 2015; education 2014-
15; international development
2013-14. Opposition whip
2013. Select cttees: speaker's
advisory on works of art 2010-
17; international development
2010-13. Cllr, Southwark BC
2006-10; deputy leader Labour
group. Researcher, HoC 2002-
06. Chairwoman of Progress
2015-. Member, Unite. Married,

	Electorate	Turnout %	from 2010 % Change
	57,670	78.37	
*A McGovern Lab	25,871	57.24	+9.04
A Sykes C	17,548	38.83	+1.62
C Carubia LD	1,322	2.93	-0.60
M Roberts Green	454	1.00	-1.13

one daughter. Ed: Wirral GS
for Girls; UCL (BA philosophy);
Birkbeck Coll (PgCert
economics).

CHALLENGERS
Adam Sykes (C) Managing
director, Livepoint Software
Solutions and formerly at
Quanano. Cllr, Wirral BC 2011-.
Chris Carubia (LD) Background
in electrical engineering and
IT technical management.
Business owner. Author. Cllr,
Wirral BC 2014-. **Mandi Roberts**
(Green) Conservation biologist

and freelance environmental
consultant.

CONSTITUENCY PROFILE
Situated on the Wirral peninsula,
this Merseyside constituency
includes the towns of Bebington
and Heswall. It is an affluent
area: unemployment is low;
earnings exceed the UK
average; over three quarters of
residents are homeowners and
constituents are typically well
qualified. A Labour stronghold,
held by the party continuously
since 1997. Although the Labour
majority narrowed to just 531
votes in 2010, the Conservatives
were beaten decisively in 2015
and 2017.

EU REFERENDUM RESULT
46.5% Leave   Remain 53.5%

Wirral West

LABOUR HOLD MAJORITY 5,365 (12.2%)

MARGARET GREENWOOD
BORN Mar 14, 1959
MP 2015-

Web consultant. Former English teacher in secondary schools, lecturer in further education and an adult education tutor. Also worked as travel writer and web editor. Committed campaigner for the NHS and environmental issues. Launched the Save Hilbre and Dee Estuary campaigns. Appointed shad min for work and pensions 2016-. PPS to: Debbie Abrahams; Owen Smith. Member, environment audit cttee 2015-16. Campaigned to Remain in EU. Backed Jeremy Corbyn in 2016 confidence vote. Founding member of Defend our NHS, a Merseyside-based campaign group.

	Electorate	Turnout %	from 2010 %	Change
	55,995	78.49		
*M Greenwood Lab	23,866	54.30	+9.15	
T Caldeira C	18,501	42.09	-2.06	
P Reisdorf LD	1,155	2.63	-0.80	
J Coyne Green	429	0.98		

CHALLENGERS
Tony Caldeira (C) Cushion magnate. Textile entrepreneur and founder of Knowlsey-based Caldeira Holdings Ltd, started on a market stall and now largest cushion company in Europe. President of City of Liverpool Conservatives. Contested Mayor of Liverpool 2016, 2012. **Peter Reisdorf** (LD) IT analyst at Crowder water industry consultancy. Former insurance worker. Cllr, Wirral BC 2000-11. Contested: Wallasey 2001, 1997; Wirral West 2015, 2010.

CONSTITUENCY PROFILE
Wirral West covers an affluent and prosperous part of the Wirral peninsula, encompassing West Kirby and the seaside town of Hoylake. It is a distinctly middle-class area: residents are typically well qualified and nearly a quarter work in professional occupations. Average earnings outperform those found elsewhere in the northwest and indeed across the UK. A former Conservative stronghold, the constituency was won by Labour in 1997. Although the Conservatives recaptured it in 2010, it returned a Labour MP to Westminster in 2015 and 2017 with an increased majority.

EU REFERENDUM RESULT
44.7% Leave   Remain 55.3%

Witham

CONSERVATIVE HOLD MAJORITY 18,646 (37.9%)

PRITI PATEL
BORN Mar 29, 1972
MP 2010-

First female Indian cabinet min and Conservative MP. Former consultant. Very pro-Leave; one of six rebel ministers who led the Out charge. Criticised by Emmeline Pankhurst's great-granddaughter for likening anti-EU Women for Britain with the suffragettes. Very right-wing; anti-gay marriage, pro-death penalty. Advocate of tobacco industries – once represented British American Tobacco. Believes traditional Conservative policies match Asian values. Criticised for employing husband part-time; he has two other jobs including at Nasdaq. Contested Nottingham North 2005. SoS

	Electorate	Turnout %	from 2010 %	Change
	69,137	71.22		
*P Patel C	31,670	64.32	+6.81	
P Barlow Lab	13,024	26.45	+10.62	
J Hayes LD	2,715	5.51	-0.62	
J Abbott Green	1,832	3.72	-0.60	

for intl devt 2016-; MoS, DWP 2015-16; exchequer sec, treasury 2014-15. Deputy press sec to Hague when he was opp leader. Hindu. First UK Indian diaspora champion 2013. Married, one son. Ed: Westfield Girls' Sch, Watford; Keele University (BA economics); Essex University (MSc British government).

CHALLENGERS
Phil Barlow (Lab) Cllr, Braintee DC 2016-. Retired gas worker. Married, two children. **Jo Hayes** (LD) Barrister. Cllr, Colchester BC 2012-15. Member, LD National Policy cttee.

CONSTITUENCY PROFILE
Located to the northeast of Chelmsford, stretching up to the southern fringes of Braintree and the outskirts of Colchester. The constituency includes Witham, a former spa and wool town; Stanley, a suburb, and the old market town of Coggeshall. It is an affluent area with a sizeable retired population, high earnings and a significant number of home owners. Demographically homogeneous: it has virtually no ethnic minority representation and EU immigration is limited. It is a very safe Conservative seat.

EU REFERENDUM RESULT
60.5% Leave   Remain 39.5%

Witney

CONSERVATIVE HOLD MAJORITY 21,241 (34.9%)

ROBERT COURTS
BORN Oct 21, 1978
MP 2016-

Replaced David Cameron in 2016 by-election following the ex-PM's decision to leave parliament, beating Natasha Witmill, a Cameron aide, to the nomination. Trading standards and personal injury barrister. Called to bar 2003, Lincoln's Inn. Worked for New Zealand govt's Crown Law Office, 2008. Campaigned for Brexit. Cllr, West Oxford DC 2014-17. Volunteer speaker, Thames Valley Air Ambulance. Member: Federation of Small Businesses, Maritime Conservation Society, Parochial Church Council, Bladon. Married, one son. Ed: University of Sheffield (LLB).

	Electorate	Turnout %	from 2010 %	Change
	82,727	73.65		
*R Courts C	33,839	55.54	-4.65	
L Carter Lab	12,598	20.68	+3.50	
L Leffman LD	12,457	20.45	+13.69	
C Lasko Green	1,053	1.73	-3.35	
A Craig Ukip	980	1.61	-7.54	

CHALLENGERS
Laetisia Carter (Lab) Community liaison officer, Thames Valley Police. Former NHS mental health project manager. Cllr, West Oxfordshire DC 2014-. **Liz Leffman** (LD) Runs own global textile and clothing business. Contested 2016 by-election. Cllr: Oxford CC 2017-; West Oxford DC 2012-. Chairwoman, English Lib Dems. **Claire Lasko** (Green) Bafta winner and Emmy nominated director and producer. Credits include *Grand Designs, Jamie's Dream School.*

CONSTITUENCY PROFILE
A large rural seat including part of the Cotswolds and the towns of Witney, Carterton and Chipping Norton. It is middle class and affluent, boasting high incomes, a significant number of home owners and well-educated residents. There is an RAF base at Brize Norton, and the economy benefits from tourists attracted to the idyllic Cotswolds and Blenheim Palace. It is a very safe Conservative seat, although the Liberal Democrats came within 6,000 votes at the 2016 by-election.

EU REFERENDUM RESULT

46.3% Leave   Remain 53.7%

Woking

CONSERVATIVE HOLD MAJORITY 16,724 (30.3%)

JONATHAN LORD
BORN Sep 17, 1962
MP 2010-

Relatively quiet backbencher who is yet to make a splash in parliament; has not gained a cttee seat or frontbench position. Pro-Brexit. Voted against gay marriage. Contested Oldham West and Royton 1997. Selected to run for Woking in an open primary, 2013. Chairman, Guildford Conservative Association 2013-17; Anne Milton's 2005 GE campaign manager. Marketing consultant. Former director, Saatchi & Saatchi. Campaigner, Save the Royal Surrey. Advocate of Foundation status for hospitals. Cllr, Surrey CC 2009-10. Married, one daughter, one

	Electorate	Turnout %	from 2010 %	Change
	76,167	72.53		
*J Lord C	29,903	54.13	-2.06	
F Colley Lab	13,179	23.86	+7.71	
W Forster LD	9,711	17.58	+5.94	
T De Leon Ukip	1,161	2.10	-9.20	
J Brierley Green	1,092	1.98	-2.08	
H Akberali Ind	200	0.36		

son. Ed: Shrewsbury Sch; Kent Sch, Connecticut; Merton Coll, Oxford (BA modern history, OUCA president).

CHALLENGERS
Fiona Colley (Lab) Former Barclays equity strategist turned Greater London Authority Labour researcher. Cllr, Southwark BC 2002-. **Will Forster** (LD) Works for Catherine Bearder MEP. Cllr: Woking BC 2011-; Surrey CC 2009-. **Troy De Leon** (Ukip) Business analyst: Invesco Perpetual, Credit Suisse, HSBC Asset Management, JP Morgan.

CONSTITUENCY PROFILE
An affluent, middle-class area that includes the largest town in Surrey. Home to many London commuters. Economically active, the constituency has high employment and over two thirds of residents are home owners. Predominantly white, but the seat has significant Pakistani and Muslim populations. It has the first purpose-built mosque in Britain, the Shah Jahan Mosque. Conservative since the seat was created in 1950.

EU REFERENDUM RESULT

44.3% Leave   Remain 55.7%

Wokingham

CONSERVATIVE HOLD MAJORITY 18,798 (31.5%)

JOHN REDWOOD
BORN Jun 15, 1951
MP 1987-

	Electorate	Turnout %	from 2010 % Change
	79,879	74.73	
*J Redwood C	33,806	56.64	-1.10
A Croy Lab	15,008	25.14	+10.62
C Jones LD	9,512	15.94	+2.41
R Seymour Green	1,364	2.29	-1.45

One of Major's "Bastards"; contested Tory leadership: 1997, 1995. Clear intellect, but unable to present an empathetic image to break the Vulcan jibe that stuck. Long-term eurosceptic. Backbencher since 2005, with no executive or select committee roles. Keeps busy with extensive work outside parliament: regular media performer; chairman of Investment Committee at CS Pan Asset Capital Management. Author including: *Superpower Struggles* about the EU, China and the USA; *Just Say No* on why the UK should reject further European integration; *Singing the Blues*, a personal history of the Conservative Party. Head, Number 10 Policy Unit for Margaret Thatcher 1983-85. Fellow, All Souls. Divorced, one daughter, one son. Ed: Kent Coll; Magdalen Coll, Oxford (MA modern history); St Antony's Coll (DPhil modern history).

CHALLENGERS
Andy Croy (Lab) Accountant and former teacher. Cllr, Wokingham BC 2016-. Contested Wokingham 2015. **Clive Jones** (LD) Toy businessman. Former pres and chairman, British Toy and Hobby Association. Cllr, Wokingham BC 2016-. Contested Wokingham 2015. **Russell Seymour** (Green) Sustainability manager.

CONSTITUENCY PROFILE
Situated in Berkshire, the seat contains the town of Wokingham itself and the Reading suburbs of Earley and Winnersh. The area is characterised by affluence and prosperity: wages are higher than elsewhere in the southeast; unemployment is low; a majority of residents are home owners and many are highly qualified. The constituency has returned Conservative MPs since its creation in 1950.

EU REFERENDUM RESULT
42.7% Leave   Remain 57.3%

Wolverhampton North East

LABOUR HOLD MAJORITY 4,587 (12.6%)

EMMA REYNOLDS
BORN Nov 2, 1977
MP 2010-

	Electorate	Turnout %	from 2010 % Change
	60,799	60.05	
*E Reynolds Lab	19,282	52.82	+6.73
S Macken C	14,695	40.25	+10.33
G Eardley Ukip	1,479	4.05	-15.14
I Jenkins LD	570	1.56	-1.19
C Wood Green	482	1.32	-0.74

Campaigned with newborn baby during snap election. Established the APPG on aerospace in Wolverhampton. Remain campaigner; voted to trigger Article 50. Shadow SoS, CLG 2015. Shadow min: FCO 2010-13; CLG, housing 2013-15. Select cttees: exiting the EU 2016-17; health 2015-16; foreign affairs 2010-13. Special adviser to Geoff Hoon MP as minister for Europe. Political adviser to Robin Cook as president of Party of European Socialists in Brussels. Sec, APPG for British Sikhs. GMB. Locally-raised, Wolverhampton Wanderers fan. Married, one son. Ed: Perton Middle Sch; Codsall HS; Wulfren Coll; Wadham Coll, Oxford (BA PPE).

CHALLENGERS
Sarah Macken (C) Head of UK public affairs, Airbus. Formerly: managing director, Absolute Strategies; policy adviser, British Chambers of Commerce. **Graham Eardley** (Ukip) Associate of the Chartered Institute of Credit Management. Events officer, Bruges Group. Deanery Synod representative.

CONSTITUENCY PROFILE
Covers the northeast corner of Wolverhampton; Wednesfield, a residential suburb, as well as the large Low-Hill housing estate. Although it is marginally less diverse than the other Wolverhampton constituencies, it is as deprived: around a third of residents live in social housing and more than a third of constituents have no qualifications. Ranks within the top ten constituencies in the UK for its long-term unemployment level. The seat is staunchly Labour, and with the exception of the 1987 election, has always returned a Labour MP to Westminster.

EU REFERENDUM RESULT
67.7% Leave   Remain 32.3%

Wolverhampton South East

LABOUR HOLD MAJORITY 8,514 (23.5%)

PAT MCFADDEN
BORN Mar 26, 1965
MP 2005-

Career politician and Labour moderniser. Speechwriter for John Smith, adviser to Tony Blair and researcher to Donald Dewar prior to being elected to Parliament. Chairman, Scottish Labour Students 1986-87. Nominated Owen Smith for Labour leadership 2016; Liz Kendall 2015. Shadow Europe min 2014-16, alleged he was sacked due to his comments following the Paris terrorist attacks that apparently undermined Jeremy Corbyn's leadership. Shadow SoS, BIS 2010. Min: BERR 2007-09; BIS 2009-10. Parly Sec, Cabinet Office 2006-07. TGWU.

	Electorate	Turnout %	from 2010 %	Change
	69,951	51.90		
*P McFadden Lab	21,137	58.22	+4.89	
K Mullan C	12,623	34.77	+12.45	
B Hodgson Ukip	1,675	4.61	-15.70	
B Mathis LD	448	1.23	-1.06	
A Bertaut Green	421	1.16	-0.58	

Member, Labour NEC 2007-10. Ed: Holyrood Secondary Sch, Glasgow; University of Edinburgh (MA politics).

CHALLENGERS
Kieran Mullan (C) A&E doctor. Was independent adviser on govt inquiry into NHS England complaints procedures, following Mid Staffs scandal. **Barry Hodgson** (Ukip) Management consultant. Founder, former chairman, Wolverhampton Ukip. Contested European elections

2009. **Ben Mathis** (LD) Arriva worker.

CONSTITUENCY PROFILE
Contains a part of Wolverhampton and Bilston, an old steel town to the city's southeast. The area is diverse: some 18,000 residents are of Asian descent and there is a large black community. It is one of the most deprived seats in the UK. A large proportion of residents have no qualifications; the unemployment rate is more than twice the national average; and almost a third of people live in social housing. The seat has been a Labour stronghold since its 1974 creation.

EU REFERENDUM RESULT
68.1% Leave   Remain 31.9%

Wolverhampton South West

LABOUR HOLD MAJORITY 2,185 (5.2%)

ELEANOR SMITH
BORN Jul 5, 1957
MP 2017-

First black MP in Enoch Powell's old seat. Spent more than 30 years as theatre nurse at Birmingham Women's hospital. First ever black woman president of Unison 2011-12; urged to contest the seat by the union, the backing of which was crucial for win. Member, TUC general council. Good relationship with Jeremy Corbyn. Her Barbadian parents came to Britain in the 1950s. Two daughters. Ed: Mount Pleasant CS, Birmingham; Bournville Coll (foundation nursing course).

CHALLENGERS
Paul Uppal (C) Self-employed

	Electorate	Turnout %	from 2010 %	Change
	60,003	70.57		
E Smith Lab	20,899	49.35	+6.14	
P Uppal C	18,714	44.19	+2.98	
R Jones Ukip	1,012	2.39	-8.33	
S Quarmby LD	784	1.85	-0.25	
A Cantrill Green	579	1.37	-1.26	
J Singh Ind	358	0.85	+0.72	

businessman and commercial property manager. Contested Birmingham Yardley 2005. MP for Wolverhampton South West 2010-15. PPS to David Willetts 2012-14. Sikh of east African descent, trustee of a Sikh temple. **Rob Jones** (Ukip) History and politics student, University of Birmingham. Chairman, Wolverhampton Ukip. **Sarah Quarmby** (LD) Background in engineering and the media. Previously fraud analyst, HSBC.

Regional chairwoman, Young Liberals.

CONSTITUENCY PROFILE
A densely populated seat in the northwest of the West Midlands. Its Sikh population is among the largest in England and Wales. The constituency includes the main Wolverhampton University campus and Molineux stadium. A Labour-Conservative marginal seat, once regarded as safe Tory territory and held by Enoch Powell from 1950-74. It turned red in Labour's 1997 landslide, was snatched by the Tories in 2010 only to return to Labour in 2015 and held in 2017 with a slim majority.

EU REFERENDUM RESULT
54.4% Leave   Remain 45.6%

Worcester

CONSERVATIVE HOLD MAJORITY 2,508 (4.9%)

ROBIN WALKER
BORN Apr 12, 1978
MP 2010-

Entrepreneur who set up his own internet business. Later became a partner at Finsbury Group. Long-time Conservative activist: Press officer to Oliver Letwin MP 2005; asst to Richard Adams, PPC for Worcester 2001; PA to and driver for Stephen Dorrell 1997. Member, Tory Reform Group. Campaigned to Remain in the EU, voted to trigger Article 50. Parly undersec, Dexeu 2016-. PPS to: Liz Truss 2014-15; Andrew Robathan 2013-14. Son of Peter Walker, who held this seat from 1961 to 1992. Married. Ed: St Paul's Sch; Balliol Coll, Oxford (BA ancient & modern history).

Electorate	Turnout %	from 2010 %	Change
72,815	70.62		
*R Walker C	24,731	48.09	+2.77
J Squires Lab	22,223	43.22	+9.25
S Kearney LD	1,757	3.42	+0.04
P Hickling Ukip	1,354	2.63	-10.19
L Stephen Green	1,211	2.35	-1.72
A Rugg Ind	109	0.21	+0.07
M Shuker Compass	38	0.07	

CHALLENGERS
Joy Squires (Lab) Consultant in regeneration. Politics and European studies lecturer, University of Wolverhampton. Cllr, Worcester CC 2012-; chairwoman, Worcester scrutiny cttee. **Stephen Kearney** (LD) CEO, Regenerate community charity. Visiting lecturer, University of Brighton. Founding dir, UK Youth Parliament. Contested Henley by-election

2008. **Paul Hickling** (Ukip) Serial local election candidate.

CONSTITUENCY PROFILE
Situated 31 miles southwest of Birmingham, the city of Worcester used to be an industrial centre with a flourishing glove industry. Porcelain was made in the city until 2009. The city remains prosperous: wages are above the regional average and constituents tend to be highly educated. A Lab/Con marginal: held by the Tories throughout the 20th century, it was gained by Labour in the landslide of 1997 and recaptured by Cameron's Conservatives in 2010.

EU REFERENDUM RESULT

53.7% Leave   Remain 46.3%

Worcestershire Mid

CONSERVATIVE HOLD MAJORITY 23,326 (42.3%)

NIGEL HUDDLESTON
BORN Oct 13, 1970
MP 2015-

Particular interest in tourism and tech: member, CMS select cttee 2015-17. Former management consultant for Arthur Andersen and Deloitte. Industry head of travel, Google 2011-15. Cllr, St Albans DC 2011-. Contested Luton South 2010. Backed Theresa May in Conservative leadership election, 2016. Member, Tory Reform Group. Freeman of the City of Lincoln. Married, one son, one daughter. Ed: Robert Pattinson Comp; Oxford (BA PPE); UCLA (MBA entertainment management).

CHALLENGERS
Fred Grindrod (Lab) Policy

Electorate	Turnout %	from 2010 %	Change
76,065	72.42		
*N Huddleston C	35,967	65.29	+8.30
F Grindrod Lab	12,641	22.95	+8.49
M Rowley LD	3,450	6.26	-0.92
D Greenwood Ukip	1,660	3.01	-14.66
F Whitfield Green	1,371	2.49	-1.21

and communications official, NASUWT. Formerly: programme manager, The Education and Training Foundation; policy and campaigns officer, TUC. **Margaret Rowley** (LD) Former senior manager in the NHS. Campaigned to save local post offices, reduce motorway noise and for adequate flood alleviation measures. Cllr, Wychavon DC 1995-. Author of canal guides. Fourth time contesting Worcestershire Mid.

CONSTITUENCY PROFILE
To the south of Birmingham, made up of the countryside and villages surrounding the city of Worcester. Worcestershire Mid has a mostly white UK-born population and contains a high proportion of retired residents. The local economy largely consists of fruit growing, farming, distribution and tourism. Annual earnings are above the West Midlands average and unemployment is low, with a benefit claimant rate of 1.2 per cent, half the national average. Relatively low levels of rented and social housing. Safe Conservative seat with majorities of over 20,000 in 2015 and 2017.

EU REFERENDUM RESULT

59.4% Leave   Remain 40.6%

Worcestershire West

CONSERVATIVE HOLD MAJORITY 21,328 (37.8%)

HARRIETT BALDWIN
BORN May 2, 1960
MP 2010-

	Electorate	Turnout %	from 2010 % Change
	74,385	75.92	
*H Baldwin C	34,703	61.45	+5.37
S Charles Lab	13,375	23.68	+10.29
E McMillan-Scott LD	5,307	9.40	-0.30
N McVey Green	1,605	2.84	-3.64
M Savage Ukip	1,481	2.62	-11.73

Background in finance, specialised in currency markets for pension funds. Formerly national council member, Business for Sterling. Contested Stockton North 2005. Campaigns for greater workplace flexibility to encourage more women in politics and financial services. Remainer, voted to trigger Article 50. Handful of minor rebellions during coalition years, including over plain cigarette packaging. Parly undersec, defence 2016-; Treasury economic sec 2015-16; govt whip 2014-15. PPS to Mark Hoban 2012-14. Russophile: David Cameron's trade envoy to Russia before joining govt; former chairwoman, APPG on Russia. Married, two daughters, one son. Ed: Lady Margaret Hall, Oxford (BA French & Russian); McGill University, Toronto (MBA).

CHALLENGERS
Samantha Charles (Lab) Freelance marketing and social media coach. Former community midwife. **Edward McMillan-Scott** (LD) Joined Lib Dems in 2010 after expulsion from Conservative party. MEP: Yorkshire & Humber 1999-2014; North Yorkshire 1994-99. Vice-president, European parliament 2004-14.

CONSTITUENCY PROFILE
North of Tewkesbury and with the Rivers Severn and Avon running through it, this rural seat has returned a Conservative MP in every election since its creation in 1997. With over 50 per cent of the population aged over 45, home ownership is very high. House prices also sit above the national average. The constituency contains a number of farms and, as a result, its economy relies heavily on agriculture.

EU REFERENDUM RESULT

52.5% Leave	Remain 47.5%

Workington

LABOUR HOLD MAJORITY 3,925 (9.4%)

SUE HAYMAN
BORN Jul 28, 1962
MP 2015-

	Electorate	Turnout %	from 2010 % Change
	60,256	69.16	
*S Hayman Lab	21,317	51.15	+8.82
C Vasey C	17,392	41.73	+11.58
G Kemp Ukip	1,556	3.73	-15.86
P Roberts LD	1,133	2.72	-1.72
R Ivinson Ind	278	0.67	

Former social services worker. Communications consultant, previously managed comms for Michael Foster MP. The first female MP to be elected in the Borders region. Cllr, Cumbria CC 2013-15; vice-chairwoman, children's scrutiny cttee. Contested: Halesowen and Rowley Regis 2010; Preseli Pembrokeshire 2005. Trustee, Asha Women's Centre 2008-2011. Member: Labour Women's Network, RSPB, GMB, Labour Animal Welfare Society. Shadow: environment sec 2017-; environment min 2016-17. Opposition whip 2015-16. Former chairwoman, APPG on nuclear energy. Keeps hens. Married, two children. Ed: St Bartholomew's Comp; Cambridge Coll of Arts & Technology (BA English literature).

CHALLENGERS
Clark Vasey (C) Works in corporate affairs at Fujitsu. Founder, Blue Collar Conservatism. Former special constable. Specialises in defence, security & public affairs. **George Kemp** (Ukip) Pub-owner. Formerly cllr, Allerdale BC.

CONSTITUENCY PROFILE
A sparsely populated seat that covers the northwest of Cumbria. It has one of the highest proportions of UK-born residents in the country and 99 per cent of constituents are white. Workington contains a large retired community and half the population is aged over 45. Over two fifths of workers are employed in the manufacturing, construction or retail sectors. Businesses specialising in footwear, plastics and cardboard emerged after the decline of the coal and steelworks industry. Average yearly earnings are below the rest of the northwest. A safe Labour seat.

EU REFERENDUM RESULT

61.0% Leave	Remain 39.0%

Worsley & Eccles South

LABOUR HOLD MAJORITY 8,379 (18.4%)

BARBARA KEELEY
BORN Mar 26, 1952
MP 2005-

	Electorate	Turnout %	from 2010 % Change
	73,692	61.94	
*B Keeley Lab	26,046	57.07	+12.83
I Lindley C	17,667	38.71	+8.61
K Clarkson LD	1,087	2.38	-0.23
T Dylan Green	842	1.84	-1.11

Former IBM systems programmer and manager. Consultant, Princess Royal Trust for Carers 2001-05. Cllr, Trafford BC 1995-2004. Member, GMB. Known in parliament for interest in supporting carers and Waspi work; chairwoman, APPG for women against state pension inequality. Campaigned to Remain, voted to trigger Article 50. Nominated Andy Burnham for Labour leadership 2015; Owen Smith 2016. Shadow min: mental health and social care 2016-; health 2010, 2016-17; Treasury 2015; CLG 2010-11. Shadow deputy Commons leader 2010; deputy leader HoC 2010.

Asst whip 2008-09. PPS to: Harriet Harman 2007-08; Jim Murphy 2006-07. Married. Ed: Mount St Mary's RC Coll, Leeds; Salford University (BA politics & contemporary history).

CHALLENGERS
Iain Lindley (C) Marketing and communications manager, Rochdale Borough Housing. Cllr, Salford CC 2004-. Contested Worsley and Eccles South 2015, 2010. **Kate Clarkson** (LD) Humanist nurse specialising in child safeguarding. Saved

a life by donating a kidney to a stranger in 2013. Contested Worsley and Eccles South 2015.

CONSTITUENCY PROFILE
To the west of Manchester city centre, the seat covers the affluent and residential area of Worsley, former mining towns and the green belt farmland to the southwest. A fairly young population, with over 20 per cent of residents younger than 15 years old. Income is lower than the regional and UK averages and over a quarter of constituents have no qualifications. The seat and its predecessors have returned Labour MPs since 1945.

EU REFERENDUM RESULT

59.8% Leave   Remain 40.2%

Worthing East & Shoreham

CONSERVATIVE HOLD MAJORITY 5,106 (9.6%)

TIM LOUGHTON
BORN May 30, 1962
MP 1997-

	Electorate	Turnout %	from 2010 % Change
	75,543	70.31	
*T Loughton C	25,988	48.93	-0.55
S Cook Lab	20,882	39.31	+19.80
O Henman LD	2,523	4.75	-1.98
M Glennon Ukip	1,444	2.72	-13.85
L Groves Williams Green	1,273	2.40	-2.82
C Walker NHAP	575	1.08	-1.41
A Lutwyche Ind	432	0.81	

City fund manager before entering politics, worked at Montagu Loebl Stanley. Later dir, Fleming Private Asset Management. Contested Sheffield Brightside 1992. Appeared in Channel 4 reality programme *Tower Block of Commons*. Used parliamentary email account to sign up as a registered Labour supporter to expose farce of 2015 leadership contest; was blocked during the vetting process. Recruited Andrea Leadsom to Conservative party at 1981 Warwick University freshers fair; ran her 2016 leadership campaign. Brexiteer. Parly under-sec for children

and families 2010-12. Married, one son, two daughters. Ed: University of Warwick (BA classical civilisation); Clare Coll, Cambridge (MA Mesopotamian archeology).

CHALLENGERS
Sophie Cook (Lab) RAF engineer turned presenter. Former photographer for AFC Bournemouth. Transgender. **Oli Henman** (LD) Former head of

EU and partnerships, National Council for Voluntary Orgs. **Mike Glennon** (Ukip) Contested Worthing East and Shoreham 2015. Cllr, West Sussex CC 2013-17.

CONSTITUENCY PROFILE
A coastal constituency in west Sussex. Contains a largely white and UK-born population, with very few ethnic minority residents. Unemployment is low and incomes are considerably less than the regional average. It is less affluent than its eastern neighbour Hove. It has been held by the Tories since its creation in 1997, but Labour gained a swing of 19.8 per cent in 2017.

EU REFERENDUM RESULT

53.7% Leave   Remain 46.3%

Worthing West

CONSERVATIVE HOLD MAJORITY 12,090 (22.2%)

SIR PETER BOTTOMLEY
BORN Jul 30, 1944
MP 1975-

Industrial economist and backbench stalwart. Previously worked as a lorry driver. President, Conservative Trade Unionists 1978-80. Contested Woolwich West Feb and Oct 1974. Socially liberal: vocal supporter of gay marriage; signed Queen's Speech amendment calling for legal abortions for Northern Irish women 2017, but also voted in 2008 for the limit to be reduced to 22 weeks. One of two Conservatives to support EDM calling for Palestinian membership of the UN 2011. PPS to: NI office 1989-90; transport 1986-89; employment 1984-86.

Electorate	Turnout %	from 2010 %	Change
77,777	70.08		
*P Bottomley C	30,181	55.37	+3.91
B Cooper Lab	18,091	33.19	+17.52
H Thorpe LD	2,982	5.47	-3.35
M Withers Ukip	1,635	3.00	-15.26
B Cornish Green	1,614	2.96	-2.83

Trustee: Christian Aid; Nacro. Former chairman, Church of England Children's Society. Knighted in 2011. Married to Baroness (Virginia) Bottomley, three children. Ed: Westminster Sch; Trinity Coll, Cambridge (BA economics).

CHALLENGERS
Beccy Cooper (Lab) Public health consultant, runs healthy active life programmes. Women's officer, Worthing Labour. **Hazel Thorpe** (LD) Former maths

teacher and head of SEN dept. Cllr, Worthing BC 2016-, 2000-15. Contested Worthing West 2015, 2010.

CONSTITUENCY PROFILE
Sandwiched between Shoreham and Littlehampton on the south coast, Worthing West has taken on the appearance of a retirement haven. The seat has a high number of over 65s, with nearly a fifth of its residents in retirement. Consequently, over 70 per cent of people own their homes and few rely on social rented accommodation. The constituency has returned a Conservative MP in every election since its 1997 creation.

EU REFERENDUM RESULT
56.0% Leave   Remain 44.0%

Wrekin, The

CONSERVATIVE HOLD MAJORITY 9,564 (19.3%)

MARK PRITCHARD
BORN Nov 22, 1966
MP 2005-

Backbencher interested in defence and foreign policy. Background in marketing and communications. Worked in Number 10 policy unit and at Conservative HQ during GE 1997. Cllr: Woking BC 2000-03; Harrow BC 1993-94. Contested Warley 2001. An investigation into a rape allegation against him was dropped in 2014; called for a review of anonymity laws afterwards. Has introduced three animal welfare bills during parly career. Eurosceptic but campaigned to Remain in the EU. Chairman, APPG on aviation. Handful of minor rebellions during coalition

Electorate	Turnout %	from 2010 %	Change
68,642	72.15		
*M Pritchard C	27,451	55.43	+5.74
D Harrison Lab	17,887	36.12	+10.07
D Allen Ukip	1,656	3.34	-13.43
R Keyes LD	1,345	2.72	-1.60
P McCarthy Green	804	1.62	-1.55
F Easton Ind	380	0.77	

years. Orphan. Divorced. Ed: University of Buckingham (MA international diplomacy); London Guildhall University (MA marketing & management).

CHALLENGERS
Dylan Harrison (Lab) Social worker. Former manager, Sure Start Lawley & Overdale. **Denis Allen** (Ukip) Contested Telford 2015, 2010. Cllr, Wellington TC 2013-. **Rod Keyes** (LD) Contested The Wrekin 2015.

CONSTITUENCY PROFILE
This semi-rural seat surrounds the town of Telford and contains a number of commuter villages. Agriculture and tourism are key to the local economy. Defence is an overrepresented industry, as the seat contains RAF and army military bases. Harpers Adams University, the only agricultural university in the UK, is located here. Income is above the average for the West Midlands and unemployment is lower than the national and regional average. A Labour/Conservative marginal, it was held by Labour from 1997 until 2005, when it was taken by incumbent Mark Pritchard.

EU REFERENDUM RESULT
59.3% Leave   Remain 40.7%

Wrexham

LABOUR HOLD MAJORITY 1,832 (5.2%)

IAN LUCAS
BORN Sep 18, 1960
MP 2001-

Gateshead-born solicitor who set up his own firm; represented Trevor Rees-Jones, bodyguard and sole survivor of the car crash that killed Princess Diana. Contested Shropshire North 1997. Resigned from Tony Blair's cabinet over his refusal to name Downing Street departure date in 2006. Pro-Remain and Sceptical of Jeremy Corbyn; called for him to resign and said he was completely out of touch following EU referendum result. Voted to trigger Article 50. Nominated Owen Smith for Labour leadership 2016, Andy Burnham 2015. Tends not to rebel. Shadow min: defence

Electorate	Turnout %	from 2010 % Change
50,422	69.60	
*I Lucas Lab	17,153	48.88 +11.65
A Atkinson C	15,321	43.66 +12.03
C Harper PC	1,753	5.00 -2.65
C O'Toole LD	865	2.46 -2.84

2014-15; FCO 2011-14; BIS 2010-11. Parly under-sec BIS 2009-10. Asst whip 2008-09. PPS to: Liam Byrne 2007-08; Bill Rammell 2005-06. Married, two children. Ed: Newcastle Royal GS; New Coll, Oxford (BA jurisprudence); Coll of Law, Christleton.

CHALLENGERS
Andrew Atkinson (C) Dir of leisure centre social enterprise. Former caseworker, Antoinette Sandbach 2015-17. Cllr: Herefordshire CC 2011-15; Ross-on-Wye TC 2011-15. Contested

Wrexham 2015. **Carrie Harper** (PC) Cllr, Wrexham County BC 2017-, 2008-12. Contested Wrexham 2015.

CONSTITUENCY PROFILE
In the northeast of Wales, perched on the border with England, lies the seat of Wrexham. Its low house prices are matched by a low level of home ownership, which is four per cent below the regional average. A major employer in the area, Wrexham Industrial Estate is home to around 300 companies. It has remained a Labour stronghold since 1983 and only changed hands once since 1935.

EU REFERENDUM RESULT
57.6% Leave   Remain 42.4%

Wycombe

CONSERVATIVE HOLD MAJORITY 6,578 (12.3%)

STEVE BAKER
BORN Jun 6, 1971
MP 2010-

Chartered aerospace engineer who spent a decade in the RAF, reaching flight lieutenant. Later associate consultant, Centre for Social Justice. Co-founder, The Cobden Centre. Campaigner for banking reform. Brexiteer. Conducted parliamentary guerrilla campaign as leader of Conservatives for Britain to shape referendum rules of engagement: forced changes in legislation ensuring there was no snap vote; lobbied for question to be Remain/Leave rather than Yes/No; compelled government to guarantee purdah in run-up to polling day. Former leader, European Research Group.

Electorate	Turnout %	from 2010 % Change
77,089	69.39	
*S Baker C	26,766	50.04 -1.37
R Raja Lab	20,188	37.74 +15.21
S Guy LD	4,147	7.75 -1.09
R Phoenix Ukip	1,210	2.26 -7.84
P Sims Green	1,182	2.21 -3.79

Made Brexit minister in 2017 post-election reshuffle. Married. Ed: St Austell Sixth Form Coll; Southampton University (BEng aerospace systems engineering); St Cross Coll, Oxford (MSc computation).

CHALLENGERS
Rafiq Raja (Lab) Tax practitioner, Hacker Young. Cllr, Wycombe DC 2015-, 2003-07; Labour leader 2015-. Moved to the UK from Pakistan in 1966. **Steve Guy** (LD) Cllr, Wycombe

DC 2009-11. Contested Wycombe 2015.

CONSTITUENCY PROFILE
An affluent area in southwest Buckinghamshire made up of High Wycombe and its surrounding villages. Much more ethnically diverse than the rest of the region, and contains large Caribbean and Pakistani communities. Unemployment is low with 1.5 per cent of workers claiming unemployment benefit, compared to the national average of 2.4 per cent. Average annual income is slightly above that of the rest of the southeast. Wycombe has been held by the Conservatives since 1951.

EU REFERENDUM RESULT
48.5% Leave   Remain 51.5%

Wyre & Preston North

CONSERVATIVE HOLD MAJORITY 12,246 (23.3%)

BEN WALLACE
BORN May 15, 1970
MP 2005-

Soldier who was commissioned into the Scots Guards aged 20; served in Germany, Cyprus and Northern Ireland. Later left to work in aerospace industry; became dir, QinetiQ. Qualified ski instructor. MSP, NE Scotland 1999-2003. Named *Spectator* campaigner of the year after pushing for MPs' expenses transparency, 2008. Ally of Boris Johnson and managed his aborted 2016 leadership bid. Remainer, voted to trigger Article 50; voted against holding EU referendum, Oct 2014. Occasionally rebelled before ministerial career. Security minister 2016-; parly under-sec,

	Electorate	Turnout %	from 2010 % Change
	72,319	72.80	
*B Wallace C	30,684	58.28	+5.11
M Heaton-Bentley Lab	18,438	35.02	+10.22
J Potter LD	2,551	4.85	-0.59
R Norbury Green	973	1.85	-1.56

NI office 2015-16; asst whip 2014-15. PPS to Ken Clarke 2010-14. Appointed to privy council in wake of March 2017 Westminster attack. Married, three children. Ed: Millfield Sch, Somerset; RMA Sandhurst.

CHALLENGERS
Michelle Heaton-Bentley (Lab) Former civil service administrator. History MA student at University of Central Lancashire. **John Potter** (LD) Cameraman and video editor. Cllr: Lancs CC 2017-; Preston CC

2012-. **Ruth Norbury** (Green) School teacher.

CONSTITUENCY PROFILE
The predominantly rural Wyre and Preston North engulfs much of the farmland north of Preston and east of Blackpool. The constituency is characterised by its wealth: it has one of the lowest child poverty rates in the UK, wages are above the regional average and house prices are relatively high. Home ownership is therefore very high and the proportion of residents in social housing is the lowest in the UK. It has returned a Conservative MP in every election since its 2010 creation.

EU REFERENDUM RESULT

54.2% Leave   Remain 45.8%

Wyre Forest

CONSERVATIVE HOLD MAJORITY 13,334 (26.1%)

MARK GARNIER
BORN Feb 26, 1963
MP 2010-

Hedge-fund manager and investment banker. MD, South China Securities 1989-95. Partner: Severn Capital LLP 2008-12; Augmentor 2008-11; CGR Capital LLP 2005-08. Contested Wyre Forest 2005. Secretly recorded in 2014 dismissing "dog-end voters" in the "outlying regions" of Britain. Warned in 2015 that pledging to hold the referendum was already costing Britain investment. Campaigned to Remain, voted to trigger Article 50. Voted against gay marriage 2013. Tends not to rebel. Cllr, Forest of Dean DC 2003-07. Vice-chairman, Conservative Friends

	Electorate	Turnout %	from 2010 % Change
	77,734	65.77	
*M Garnier C	29,859	58.40	+13.10
M Lamb Lab	16,525	32.32	+13.06
S Miah LD	1,943	3.80	+1.32
G Connolly Ukip	1,777	3.48	-12.64
B Caulfield Green	1,025	2.00	-0.25

of America. Freeman of the City of London. Has served on Court of Worshipful Company of Coachmakers. Cousin of former Conservative MP Edward Garnier. Married, two sons, one daughter. Ed: Charterhouse Sch, Surrey.

CHALLENGERS
Matthew Lamb (Lab) Assistant principal, Sandwell Coll, West Bromwich. Cllr, Worcester CC 2010-. Contested Wyre Forest 2015. **Shazu Miah** (LD) Solicitor

who runs and owns SM Lawson. Cllr, Wyre Forest DC 2016-. **George Connolly** (Ukip) Self-employed bricklayer.

CONSTITUENCY PROFILE
Wyre Forest is formed of Kidderminster, Bewdley, Stourport-on-Severn and a cluster of neighbouring villages. It is predominantly white, with few residents from BAME backgrounds. While house prices are below regional and national averages, home ownership is high. Prior to Mark Garnier's 2010 electoral victory, Wyre Forest was represented by Richard Taylor, an independent, from 2001 to 2010.

EU REFERENDUM RESULT

63.1% Leave   Remain 36.9%

Wythenshawe & Sale East

LABOUR HOLD MAJORITY 14,944 (32.6%)

MIKE KANE
BORN Jan 9, 1969
MP 2014-

	Electorate	Turnout %	from 2010 % Change
	76,361	60.04	
*M Kane Lab	28,525	62.22	+12.08
F Green C	13,581	29.62	+3.91
W Jones LD	1,504	3.28	-1.17
M Bayley-Sanderson Ukip	1,475	3.22	-11.47
D Jerrome Green	576	1.26	-2.58
L Francis-Augustine Ind	185	0.40	

Self-described Blairite. Former teacher, Springfield Primary Sch. Later chief exec, Movement for Change, running payday lending reform campaign. Cllr, Manchester CC 1991-2008. Former office manager, Jonathan Reynolds MP. Elected after death of Paul Goggins MP. Introduced a bill to help mesothelioma sufferers. Remainer, voted to trigger Article 50. Resigned from shadow cabinet in wake of EU referendum result. Nominated Liz Kendall for Labour leadership 2015; Owen Smith 2016. Shadow min: schools 2016-; international development 2015-2016. PPS to James Purnell 2008-11. Cared for MS-suffering mother as a youth. Married. Ed: Manchester Metropolitan University (BA social sciences); University of Manchester (PGCE).

CHALLENGERS
Fiona Green (C) Mediator, Green Doors Mediation. Solicitor. Runs a free legal clinic. Contested Wythenshawe and Sale East 2015. **William Jones** (LD) Lead architect, DXC Technology. Chairman, Trafford Liberal Democrats. Co-founder, Sale Wombles litter-picking group.

CONSTITUENCY PROFILE
A varied constituency to the south of Manchester. It contains the interwar council estate of Wythenshawe, one of the largest in the country, and the suburban, middle-class areas of Sale. It is home to Manchester airport, which is a major employer, and Wythenshawe hospital. A third of the population lives in social housing, nearly double the national average. Unemployment is higher than average, at 5.5 per cent, and wages are low. A safe Labour seat.

EU REFERENDUM RESULT
49.6% Leave   Remain 50.4%

Yeovil

CONSERVATIVE HOLD MAJORITY 14,723 (24.8%)

MARCUS FYSH
BORN Nov 8, 1970
MP 2015-

	Electorate	Turnout %	from 2010 % Change
	82,911	71.65	
*M Fysh C	32,369	54.49	+12.02
J Roundell Greene LD	17,646	29.71	-3.43
I Martin Lab	7,418	12.49	+5.37
R Wood Green	1,052	1.77	-2.08
K Pritchard Ind	919	1.55	

Australian-born businessman who ran agriculture and healthcare start-ups. Worked for Mercury Asset Management; dir, London Wessex. Loyal backbencher with no rebellions from his first stint as an MP. Cleared by the CPS over 2015 expenses rule breach. Brexiteer. Tweeted that 2016 Treasury report forecasting shock outcomes of Brexit was "specious bollocks and severe specious bollocks". Member, international trade select cttee 2016-17. Cllr: South Somerset DC 2011-15; Somerset CC 2013-15. Moved to UK aged three. Married, two children. Ed: Winchester Coll; Corpus Christi Coll, Oxford (BA English literature).

CHALLENGERS
Jo Roundell Greene (LD) Granddaughter of former Labour PM Clement Attlee. Has worked as a bricklayer, cleaner and in a chicken factory. Cllr, South Somerset DC 2007-. **Ian Martin** (Lab) Quaker chaplain: University of Exeter; HMP Exeter 2004-10. Cllr, Exeter CC 2004-14. **Rob Wood** (Green) Consultant software engineer, Indra. Previously worked for aerospace company. **Katy Pritchard** (Ind) NHS worker. Cllr, Crewkerne TC 2013; vice-chairwoman, policy & resources.

CONSTITUENCY PROFILE
Situated in the southwest and home to over 100,000 residents. With a large population of over-65s, home ownership is high. Average wages and house prices are both very low. Manufacturing businesses are disproportionately large employers, providing over 9,300 jobs to residents. Yeovil was in Lib Dem hands between 1983 and 2015, but the Tories gained a majority of 14,723 in 2017.

EU REFERENDUM RESULT
59.9% Leave   Remain 40.1%

Ynys Mon

LABOUR HOLD MAJORITY 5,259 (14.1%)

ALBERT OWEN
BORN Aug 10, 1959
MP 2001-

Welsh former member of the merchant navy. Left school aged 15 before colour blindness thwarted his mariner ambitions. Worked as welfare and employment adviser for Citizens Advice Bureau and Anglesey CC. Backbench stalwart. Nominated Andy Burnham for Labour leadership 2015; Owen Smith 2016. Campaigned to Remain, voted to trigger Article 50 but rebelled in order to vote for Chuka Umunna's Queen's Speech amendment for the UK to remain in single market, June 2017. Regular rebel during New Labour years, including over ID cards and Iraq war. Married,

	Electorate	Turnout %	from 2010 %	Change
	52,448	71.25		
*A Owen Lab	15,643	41.86	+10.74	
T Davies C	10,384	27.79	+6.62	
I Jones PC	10,237	27.40	-3.07	
J Turner Ukip	624	1.67	-12.99	
S Jackson LD	479	1.28	-0.87	

two daughters. Ed: Holyhead County CS; University of York (BA politics).

CHALLENGERS
Tomos Davies (C) Associate partner, Newgate Comms. Former special adviser to SoS for Wales and policy adviser in the Wales Office. Trustee, National Library of Wales. **Ieuan Wyn Jones** (PC) AM for Ynys Mon 1999-2013; deputy first minister, Welsh Assembly 2007-11. Leader, Plaid Cymru 2006-12. MP, Ynys

Mon 1987-2001; stood down to concentrate on Welsh Assembly. Former solicitor.

CONSTITUENCY PROFILE
An island seat located off the northwest of Wales. Home to the Four Mile Bridge, Holy Island, Newlands Park, Llangefni and a collection of villages. Two RAF stations are situated on the island. With a large population of over-65s, home ownership is high. Median house prices are above the regional average, but they are £57,000 below national levels. Between 1987 and 2001, Ynys Mon was held by the former Plaid Cymru leader Ieuan Wyn Jones.

EU REFERENDUM RESULT

50.9% Leave   Remain 49.1%

York Central

LAB CO-OP HOLD MAJORITY 18,575 (35.0%)

RACHAEL MASKELL
BORN Jul 5, 1972
MP 2015-

Former care worker and senior NHS physiotherapist turned Labour and Co-operative MP. Chartered Society of Physiotherapy hospital and regional rep. Head of health, Unite. Father was trade union rep, uncle was prison reformer Terence Morris. Backed Andy Burnham in 2015 leadership race. Resigned from shadow cabinet over Labour's three-line Article 50 whip; voted Remain in 2016 and against the triggering of Article 50 in February 2017. Shadow transport min 2017-; shadow SoS for environment, food and rural affairs 2016-17. Shadow defence min 2015-16.

	Electorate	Turnout %	from 2010 %	Change
	77,315	68.66		
*R Maskell Lab Co-op	34,594	65.16	+22.77	
E Young C	16,019	30.17	+1.87	
N Love LD	2,475	4.66	-3.32	

Select cttees: ecclesiastical 2015-17; health 2015. Member, Labour NEC 2011-15. Ed: University of East Anglia (BSc physiotherapy).

CHALLENGERS
Ed Young (C) Communications dir, Tesco and former Brunswick Group associate. Worked at Conservative Party as chief of staff to party chairmen and as a speechwriter. **Nick Love** (LD) CAMRA activist contesting local pub closures. Presents business programme on local radio station. Contested York Central 2015.

CONSTITUENCY PROFILE
A densely populated seat which comprises the centre of York. With the University of York located just to the south of the constituency, there is a very high student population. As a result, home ownership is very low and a high percentage of people live in private rented accommodation. House prices are almost £50,000 greater than the regional average, yet around £20,000 lower than national levels. Few residents observe a religion. Even though it is not particularly affluent, child poverty levels are very low. Has returned a Labour MP in each election since its 2010 creation.

EU REFERENDUM RESULT

38.8% Leave   Remain 61.2%

York Outer

CONSERVATIVE HOLD MAJORITY 8,289 (14.4%)

JULIAN STURDY
BORN Jun 3, 1971
MP 2010-

Farmer. Campaigned to Leave the EU. Local campaigner, has fought to protect Yorkshire greenbelt. Supported Stephen Crabb in 2016 Conservative leadership race. Contested Scunthorpe 2005. Select cttees: consolidation bills 2015-17; energy and climate change 2015-16; transport 2010-12. APPG chairman: antibiotics; rural business; science and technology in agriculture. Cllr, Harrogate BC 2002-07. Married, two children. Ed: Ashville Coll; Harper Adams Agricultural Coll.

CHALLENGERS
Luke Charters-Reid (Lab) Non

	Electorate	Turnout %	from 2010 %	Change
	75,856	75.71		
*J Sturdy C	29,356	51.12	+2.00	
L Charters-Reid Lab	21,067	36.68	+11.92	
J Blanchard LD	5,910	10.29	-1.34	
B Vincent Green	1,094	1.91	-2.84	

exec dir, Charters-Reid and Associates. Intern office assistant for Sir Hugh Bayley MP. 21-years-old. **James Blanchard** (LD) Communications adviser, NHS Trust. Cllr: Kirklees DC 2011-15; Islington BC 2002-06. Contested York Outer 2015. Former: head, Lib Dem youth and student office; Huddersfield campaign organiser 2009-14. Account manager, PPS Group 2014. **Bethan Vincent** (Green) Dir, Bright Ethics Company. Founder and managing dir, Vincent's Coffee. Founding

member, York Guild of Entrepreneurs.

CONSTITUENCY PROFILE
York Outer covers the city's suburbs, including the historic villages of Fulford, Osbaldwick and Skelton. It encompasses the University of York campus, and contains around 8,000 students. There is also a sizeable retired population. It is an affluent area: annual earnings are above average and a high proportion of residents - nearly 82 per cent - own their home. Held by the Conservatives since its creation in 2010, although Labour has increased their share in the two previous elections.

EU REFERENDUM RESULT

44.7% Leave   Remain 55.3%

Yorkshire East

CONSERVATIVE HOLD MAJORITY 15,006 (27.8%)

SIR GREG KNIGHT
BORN Apr 4, 1949
MP 2001-; 1983-97

Qualified solicitor. MP for Derby North 1983-97; one of the casualties of Tony Blair's 1997 landslide. Went viral during GE 2017 campaign for music video urging people to "get it right/vote for Greg Knight". Drummer and founding member of MP4, the world's only parliamentary rock group; released charity single alongside popular musicians to support launch of Jo Cox Foundation, 2016. Has written scripts for broadcast and six books. Eurosceptic, joined Vote Leave campaign. Vice chamberlain, HoC whip 2012-13. Shadow minister: transport 2005; EFRA 2003-05; CMS 2003.

	Electorate	Turnout %	from 2010 %	Change
	81,065	66.56		
*G Knight C	31,442	58.27	+7.71	
A Clark Lab	16,436	30.46	+9.77	
C Minns LD	2,134	3.96	-1.98	
A Dennis Ukip	1,986	3.68	-14.23	
T Norman Yorkshire	1,015	1.88		
M Jackson Green	943	1.75	-1.71	

Minister of state, industry 1996-97. Dep chief whip and treasurer 1993-96. Lord commissioner 1990-93. Appointed to privy council 1995. Knighted 2013. Ed: Alderman Newton's GS; Coll of Law, Guildford.

CHALLENGERS
Alan Clark (Lab) Lorry driver. Former dir of building, repair and maintenance contractor. Cllr, Hull CC 2010-. **Carl Minns** (LD) Self-employed consultant

and MEP researcher. Formerly leader, Hull CC 2006-11.

CONSTITUENCY PROFILE
Stretching from the eastern fringes of York to the coastal town of Bridlington, Yorkshire East includes the market town of Driffield and several small villages. The proportion of residents without any qualifications is above the national average. Nearly all of the constituency's residents are white, and almost a quarter are over 65. There are high levels of home ownership. Although Ukip did well in 2015, it is a safe Conservative seat and has been blue since its creation in 1997.

EU REFERENDUM RESULT

63.7% Leave   Remain 36.3%

Index to candidates